Luminos is the Open Access monograph publishing program
from UC Press. Luminos provides a framework for preserving and
reinvigorating monograph publishing for the future and increases
the reach and visibility of important scholarly work. Titles published
in the UC Press Luminos model are published with the same high
standards for selection, peer review, production, and marketing as
those in our traditional program. www.luminosoa.org

The publisher and the University of California Press Foundation
gratefully acknowledge the generous support of the Joan Palevsky
Imprint in Classical Literature.

Publication of this book has also been aided by a grant from
the von Bothmer Publication Fund of the Archaeological
Institute of America.

Societies in Transition
in Early Greece

Societies in Transition in Early Greece

An Archaeological History

Alex R. Knodell

UNIVERSITY OF CALIFORNIA PRESS

University of California Press
Oakland, California

Suggested citation: Knodell, A. R. *Societies in Transition in Early Greece: An Archaeological History*. Oakland: University of California Press, 2021. DOI: https://doi.org/10.1525/luminos.101

Cataloging-in-Publication Data is on file at the Library of Congress.
Names: Knodell, Alex R., author.
Title: Societies in transition in early Greece : an archaeological history / Alex R. Knodell.
Description: [Oakland, California] : [University of California Press], [2021] | Includes bibliographical references and index.
Identifiers: LCCN 2020041112 (print) | LCCN 2020041113 (ebook) | ISBN 9780520380530 (paperback) | ISBN 9780520380547 (ebook)
Subjects: LCSH: Social archaeology—Greece. | Bronze age—Greece. | Iron age—Greece. | Mediterranean Region—Civilization.
Classification: LCC CC72.4. K56 2021 (print) | LCC CC72.4 (ebook) | DDC 930.1/6—dc23

LC record available at https://lccn.loc.gov/2020041112
LC ebook record available at https://lccn.loc.gov/2020041113

28   27   26   25   24   23   22   21
10   9   8   7   6   5   4   3   2   1

For my parents

CONTENTS

ILLUSTRATIONS

FIGURES

MAPS

All maps created by the author. The maps in this book were created using ArcGIS® software by Esri. Basemaps are derived from Esri's Terrain: Multi-Directional Hillshade layer (Source: Airbus, USGS, NGA, NASA, CGIAR, NLS, OS, NMA, Geodatastyrelsen, GSA, GSI and the GIS User Community). ArcGIS® and ArcMap™ are the intellectual property of Esri and are used herein under license.

TABLES

I wrote this book for many reasons, several of which unfold at length in the pages that follow. A few personal notes seem warranted at the outset, however, along with some warm thanks and acknowledgements.

As I was preparing to write this book, I saw a need for synthesis in the ever-growing body of material associated with early Greece, by which I mean the Mycenaean Bronze Age and the Early Iron Age, a pre-/protohistoric span of time, in which linguistic and cultural traditions related to later Greek populations can be clearly identified, but before their widespread institutionalization in the Archaic and Classical periods. Writing a book on the whole Greek world seemed impossible, however, without losing the regional specificity that has emerged as an essential concern for the period at hand. I therefore chose to focus on central Greece: a critical macro-region for the time in question, which allows for the identification of both broad trends (as distinct from the Peloponnese, the Aegean islands, and Crete, for example) and regional specificity. A key goal has been to balance discussions of well-known sites and regions with underrepresented periods and places, in order to examine the diversity and undulation of early Greek societies. What is more, it seemed to me that it was during precisely this period that central Greece became central, both within the developing Greek world and in certain wider sets of Mediterranean affairs.

From a theoretical perspective, I wanted to combine my interests in archaeologies of landscape and interaction to develop a multi-scalar approach to the study of complex societies—especially one that accounts for both variety and nonlinear trajectories in the development of social organization. Many questions have come up along the way: How can we integrate and fill gaps in large, multiregional datasets? How did human societies live and interact across multiple scales, from the local to the Mediterranean? How can archaeological analysis cross these scales? How do the trajectories of early Greek societies relate to those of other human groups (or not)? These questions are necessarily broad, and in this book I have aimed to address them in a way that will resonate with archaeologists interested in other parts of the world as well. With this in mind, I set out to write an archaeological history relevant to people working in a variety of disciplinary traditions—archaeologists and historians of ancient Greece, as well as anthropological archaeologists concerned with the broader archaeology of complex societies.

The arguments in this book are built on the achievements of generations of previous scholars. I hope to do justice to their work in discussing it here, incorporating it into new analyses or visualizations, or reframing it in new interpretations. Even if I am in occasional disagreement with these scholars, I have tremendous respect for the efforts of fieldwork, interpretation, and publication that have allowed for the type of synthesis presented here. This book deals with a broad range of evidence and ideas, and it is inevitable that I have gotten some of it wrong. There are certainly sites, discoveries, or interpretations that I have overlooked, and the relevant dataset is ever evolving. Nevertheless, I hope to have provided some new insights concerning early Greece and the Mediterranean world, in ways that will be useful to other scholars as well.

My interests in early Greece and the archaeology of complex societies were fostered early on by teachers and mentors at the Joukowksy Institute for Archaeology and the Ancient World at Brown University and at the American School of Classical Studies at Athens—particularly by John Cherry, Sue Alcock, Steve Houston, John Papadopoulos, and Peter van Dommelen. Many of the ideas in this book were initially formulated in the doctoral dissertation supervised and examined by this group.

Since those days, this project has been supported and enriched by a postdoctoral fellowship from the Getty Research Institute's Visiting Scholars Program on *Connecting Seas* and funding of various types from Carleton College (especially from a Class of '49 Fellowship, a Hewlett Mellon Fellowship, the Dean of the College Office, and the Humanities Center). Much of this book was written while on sabbatical as a National Endowment for the Humanities Fellow at the American School of Classical Studies at Athens. All of these institutions, as well as the University of Cincinnati, the Norwegian Institute at Athens, and a number of conferences, have provided opportunities to present and discuss the research published here. I also wish to express my gratitude to the Archaeological Institute of America and to Dean Beverly Nagel and the Carleton College Dean of the College Office for providing the subventions that allowed for the open-access publication of this work with the Luminos program of University of California Press.

I am very grateful to the individuals who read and commented on drafts of this book or its various parts. Sue Alcock, Michelle Berenfeld, John Cherry, Sylvian Fachard, Ioannis Georganas, Rachel Heilbronner, Steve Houston, Carl Knappett, Barbara Leone, Bartek Lis, Sarah Murray, Dimitri Nakassis, Anthony Snodgrass,

Catie Steidl, Trevor Van Damme, and Peter van Dommelen all provided thoughtful and generous feedback at a variety of different stages. Sue Alcock, John Cherry, Sylvian Fachard, and John Papadopoulos deserve special thanks for the crucial role they played in helping me to get this project off the ground (more than once) and for their encouragement and advice at every stage. I especially appreciate the individuals who read and commented on the manuscript in its entirety as it neared completion: John Papadopoulos, Hüseyin Öztürk, Bill Parkinson, and David Small were instrumental in refining this project as a coherent whole, as were Eric Schmidt and the review process at University of California Press. I am also grateful to Gabriel Bartlett and Ayla Çevik for their keen attention to detail in the course of copyediting and index preparation.

I wish to thank several individuals for their contributions to the datasets and illustrations presented here, especially Sarah Murray and Robert Consoli for sharing and discussing databases; Sam Wege and MJ Fielder-Jellsey for their work on my own database; Wei-Hsin Fu and Tom Garrison for their generous expertise in GIS and spatial analysis; John Cherry, Sylvian Fachard, and Evan Levine for their keen eyes for cartography; Denitsa Nenova and Christina Kolb for their help conceptualizing and producing certain figures; and Ioanna Damanaki for her assistance with image permissions. I also thank the Hellenic Ministry of Culture and Sports and the Ephorates of Antiquities of Boeotia, Euboea, Phokis, and Karditsa for the permission to publish certain images.

Still others contributed through stimulating discussions that have inspirited me and in some cases remained with me for a very long time: Matt Buell, Brendan Burke, Bryan Burns, Alex Claman, Alex Clapp, Chris Cloke, Sarah Craft, Jan Paul Crielaard, Jack Davis, Liza Davis, Emily Egan, Mike Galaty, Thanasis Garonis, Tom Garrison, Walter Gauß, Johanna Hanink, Clara Hardy, Katerina Kanatselou, Jessica Keating, Mark Kenoyer, Lori Khatchadourian, Fotini Kondyli, Antonis Kotsonas, Irene Lemos, Tom Leppard, Evan Levine, Stella Makarona, Austin Mason, Maeve McHugh, Jeremy McInerney, Sarah Morris, Jake Morton, Elizabeth Murphy, Denitsa Nenova, Bill North, Daniel Pullen, Jeff Rop, Zarko Tankosic, Gert Jan van Wijngaarden, Chris Witmore, Jim Wright, and Chico Zimmerman.

I have had the great privilege of conducting fieldwork and visiting archaeological sites with a number of talented archaeologists over the years, especially in the contexts of the Brown University Petra Archaeological Project, the Mazi Archaeological Project, and the Small Cycladic Islands Project. At Carleton, my courses are regularly animated by keen and engaged students. Members of all these groups have continually led me to see archaeological landscapes in new ways and to think critically and carefully about what archaeology can and should do—both for archaeologists and in the wider world.

Finally, I thank my family and friends (who know who they are, and among whom I count many of those named above). Your constant support and care mean more to me than I can say, and I could not have written this book without you. Thank you.

Introduction

An Archaeology of Early Greece

In studies of early Greece, the standard narrative involves the rise of Mycenaean states, followed by their collapse, followed by a dark age. An eighth-century "renaissance" came next, with the rise of the polis, the emergence of Panhellenic ideas (and ideals), and the dispersal of Greek populations to various parts of the Mediterranean, leading to notions of an ethnocultural genesis in the early Archaic period. It is a sequence most archaeologists of Greece are fairly comfortable in accepting, even if they tend to debate the specifics—especially terms like collapse, dark age, renaissance, and so on. These debates are important, to be sure, but they do not always happen in ways relevant to wider dialogues in the archaeology of complex societies. What is more, the often divergent disciplinary priorities of Aegean prehistory, classical archaeology, and ancient history often stand in the way of more holistic understandings of the early Greek world. This book examines the development of early Greece in the comparative light of sociopolitical complexity. Are early Greek polities like other complex societies? How did they operate locally and globally, and across a variety of social and spatial scales? What can we say about cycles of emergence, collapse, and recovery? What can we gain by trying to step back from teleologies of *the state* or *the polis*? We might also ask how the small-scale Mediterranean societies of early Greece came to play such an outsized role in the modern cultural imagination. And why does that matter?

This book is about landscape, interaction, and social complexity in Late Bronze Age and Early Iron Age Greece (ca. 1400–700 BCE). It is about how societies change over time and about the ebbs and flows of power relationships through different types of communication and material networks. It is about the analysis and explication of how societies *work*—how they constitute and reconstitute themselves—on multiple scales, ranging from the local to the regional to the trans-Mediterranean, from the community to the polity to the interaction zone. An integrated approach to geography, connectivity, and material culture can be used to explain and interpret the sweeping changes that affected the societies of early Greece across the late second and early first millennia BCE—changes that would have long-lasting consequences for the history of the Mediterranean. The focus here is on central Greece—in Aegean prehistory often overlooked in favor of the Peloponnese or Crete—especially those regions defined by the maritime conduit of the Euboean Gulf and the land routes connecting Attica, Boeotia, Phokis, East Lokris, Malis, and Thessaly (map 1).

The study area is defined by (1) the geographical distribution of Mycenaean material culture outside of the Peloponnese and (2) our earliest geographical descriptions for how regions connect and cohere (Homer's Catalog of Ships: *Iliad* 2.494–759). Boundaries or gaps in the distribution of Mycenaean material culture to the north and west provide natural breakpoints between the contiguous regions discussed in this book (map 2), while Homer provides regional descriptions that bear a remarkable similarity to what is known from later periods. The total area therefore corresponds roughly with the modern administrative district of *Sterea Ellada*, plus Thessaly to the north and Attica to the south. In this way central Greece is set apart from the Peloponnese, the Aegean islands, and northern Greece.

Current research on early Greece is more prevalent and interesting than ever before. There remain several key gaps, however, not least as Greek archaeology relates to the broader archaeology of complex societies. Material studies and pottery chronologies have long been a strength, and the excavations and publications of certain key sites have dramatically changed our knowledge of this period in recent years. Regional syntheses are increasingly common as well. There are not, however, recent examples of integrated studies of settlement systems (as opposed to distribution maps), multiregional comparison, or studies that aim explicitly to address the multiscalar dynamics between local, regional, and long-distance interaction. Key disciplinary divides between the study of the Bronze Age world of the Mycenaeans and the Iron Age world of pre-Classical Greece also muddy the waters between history and archaeology, where at a certain point the former tends to overtake the latter as texts become the dominant source of evidence. Finally, there are relatively few examples of modeling and comparison in the archaeology of early Greece, a fact that limits its participation in dialogues with other world archaeologies.

A multiscalar, multiregional, comparative study presents an opportunity to put archaeological data from various parts of central Greece in dialogue with each other, with other parts of the Greek world, and with the wider Mediterranean. While the focus here is on the societies of early Greece, there is a general goal also to develop tools to better understand the behavior and trajectories of social groups in relation to their wider geographical and intercultural circumstances. In

MAP 1. General maps of the Mediterranean (top) and mainland Greece and the Aegean (bottom), showing major regions and places mentioned in the text.

this introduction, I summarize the arguments of this book in their historical and disciplinary contexts and provide a brief outline of the chapters that follow, which comprise an archaeological history from Mycenaean times to the emergence of the Archaic Greek world.

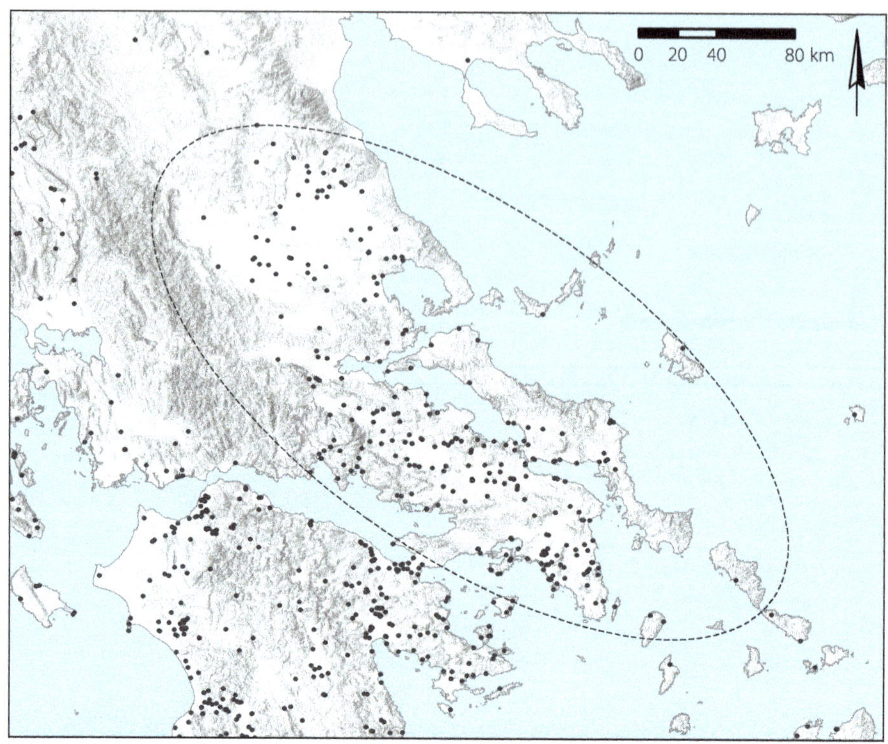

MAP 2. The distribution of Mycenaean material culture and limits of the study area (site data from the Mycenaean Atlas Project).

THE ARGUMENT

This book contains several interrelated arguments concerning the archaeology of Late Bronze Age and Early Iron Age Greece, archaeological approaches to landscape and interaction, and the study of complex societies. Throughout this book, I argue that previous approaches to early Greece have been stymied by the diffuse disciplinary priorities of the subfields with a stake in the relevant time periods. Aegean prehistory is especially concerned with state formation and eastern Mediterranean geopolitics; Early Iron Age archaeology with "Dark Age" monikers and notions of collapse and revolution on either end of it; ancient history with the rise of the polis, hoplite warfare, and tyrannies, aristocracies, and democracy. None of these allows for a unified view of the development of the early Greek world. This book builds on the achievements of these subfields by taking a step back from them, providing an archaeological history written from the perspective of the archaeology of complex societies. The integration of landscape, interaction, and complexity perspectives provides a multiregional study of settlement and society that goes beyond descriptive historical narratives and simple dots on a map. Such an outlook can shed much new light on this well-documented but still underappreciated period of world history.

I argue first that significant fluctuations characterize early Greek societies until the Classical period. These happen in fits and starts through the Late Bronze Age and Early Iron Age and exhibit a wide variety of regional patterns. The most significant variations happen in the oft-neglected span of time following the collapse of the Mycenaean palaces. I also demonstrate a need to recast our focus on the Mycenaean palatial world. Rather than seeing the palaces as the culmination of an evolutionary trajectory of state formation followed by a collapse, we might see them as historical anomalies and societal experiments, which were ultimately unsuccessful. The reconstituted societies that followed the palaces represent more a restoration of a previous mode of social organization than a fall from grace—one of simpler societies that were nonetheless engaged in complex regional and interregional networks and modes of polity. A tipping point was reached in the eighth century BCE when a media revolution (in words and images) and an intensification of settlement activity coincided to codify and disperse notions of "Greek" society in an unprecedented way—one fundamental to the emergence of the highly connected Archaic and Classical Mediterranean.

Second, I argue that vacillations in social complexity are historically contingent but have common traits that can be identified in a variety of places and times, often as a combination of mutually intensifying (or stagnating) processes. Complex societies are remarkably undertheorized outside the realm of primary state formation. We need better documented examples of secondary states, multipolity cultures, nonstate complex polities, village societies, small-scale or middle-range ranked societies, and other "in between" social formations in order to develop better understandings of modes of social organization that do not culminate in states. The prehistoric Aegean offers several case studies on this topic, and these need to be put into better dialogue with other world archaeologies. The case presented here—on the pre- and protohistory of Greece in its wider Mediterranean setting—exhibits a variety of challenges: nonlinear societal trajectories, regional variability, biased chronological representation, problematic textual and material datasets, and research traditions with conflicting priorities. Many of the same circumstances and challenges are faced by archaeologists working in other parts of the world. Maya city-states, Mississippian chiefdoms, Transcaucasian polities, and the "middle-range" societies of the American Southwest often seem to have more in common with early Greek societies—at least in terms of social organization—than the Near Eastern states and empires that were the contemporaries and neighbors of early Greeks. A comparative approach has much to offer, but in the past this approach has been used chiefly in the context of working backward from the Archaic/Classical period or in ill-fitting comparisons with contemporary neighbors, such as Hittites and Egyptians. I argue that most early Greek societies are best thought of as complex communities or village societies and should not be shoehorned into narratives concerning kingdoms or states. This does not mean that such political entities did not exist in the early Greek world—they did—but they should not be considered the norm. In particular, I argue that village societies describe the form and operation of communities across much of the ancient Greek landscape, most of the time. At the same time, complex communities offer a flexible and dynamic model for understanding variation in social organization across space and time. So, within societies characterized mostly by village life, some communities are more or less complex—a feature that can be charted through time and across the landscape as a whole.

Third, settlement, mobility, and things (both as participants in and media of interaction) are three interrelated themes through which societal dynamics can be approached. These themes converge in particular coastal and inland corridors throughout the study area. Like much of the Mediterranean world, central Greece is characterized by constellations of microregions, linked by particular paths over long and short distances. While recent studies of long-term social change in the Mediterranean have emphasized the role of the sea in interactive practices, we must also consider the role of terrestrial movement through the landscape, especially in the more mundane connections of daily life. Through the use of spatial analysis and interpretative approaches to things as media, there are great gains to be made by integrating the extensive datasets of regional archaeology with previous studies that have focused on the more conspicuous evidence of large settlements, elite burials, and exotic imports. Evidence of settlement, mobility, media, and technology can therefore become proxies for social landscapes and interaction between complex communities.

In this book I examine how ancient societies operate and interact across a variety of social and spatial scales. In studying change over time, we must also pay attention to disjuncture. Rather than seeing societies of the Late Bronze Age as uniformly Mycenaean or of the Iron Age as uniformly Greek, we need also to articulate local and regional specificity and difference. Making such distinctions requires stitching together multiscalar histories that are explanatory, interpretative, and contingent. While such an approach is culturally and temporally specific, it also lends itself to a comparative perspective concerning the development of particular types of human groups.

CONTEXTS: EARLY GREECE BETWEEN PREHISTORY AND HISTORY

The centuries spanning the second millennium and early first millennium BCE saw the rise and fall of markedly varied political systems, fundamental changes in material culture, and the expansion of long-distance networks, intensifying first in the eastern Mediterranean and eventually expanding to include nearly all shores of the Middle Sea. In Greece, this period is comprised of the Late Bronze Age, or

TABLE 1 Chronology and abbreviations for the Aegean in the Late Bronze Age (LBA) and Early Iron Age (EIA)[*]

Cultural period	Ceramic period	Dates BCE
Early Mycenaean period (ca. 1750–1400)	Middle Helladic III (MH III)	1750/20–1700/1675
	Late Helladic I (LH I)	1700/1675–1635/00
	Late Helladic II A (LH IIA)	1635/00–1480/70
	Late Helladic II B (LH IIB)	1480/70–1420/10
Palatial Bronze Age (ca. 1400–1200)	Late Helladic III A1 (LH IIIA1)	1420/10–1390/70
	Late Helladic III A2 (LH IIIA2)	1390/70–1330/15
	Late Helladic III B (LH IIIB)	1330/15–1210/1200
Postpalatial Bronze Age (ca. 1200–1050)	Late Helladic III C (LH IIIC)	1210/1200–1070/40
	Early	1210/1200–1170/60
	Middle	1170/60–1100
	Late	1100–1070/40
Prehistoric Iron Age (ca. 1050–800)	Early Protogeometric (EPG)	1070/40–1000
	Middle Protogeometric (MPG)	1000–950
	Late Protogeometric (LPG)	950–900
	Early Geometric (EG) / Subprotogeometric (SPG)	900–850
	Middle Geometric I (MG I) / Subprotogeometric (SPG)	850–800
Protohistoric Iron Age (ca. 800–700/650)	Middle Geometric II (MG II)	800–750
	Late Geometric (LG)	750–700 (or 650?)
Archaic period (ca. 700–480)	Proto-Attic; Proto-Corinthian; "Orientalizing;" Subgeometric (depending on region)	725–625
	Black-figure style	620–480
	Red-figure style	525–300s

[*] For dates up to LH III B, see Manning (2010, 23, table 3.2); from the end of LH III B to EPG, see Weniger and Jung (2009, 416, fig. 14), although I have amended this to conflate LH III C Developed and LH III C Advanced into LH III C Middle and I have included Submycenaean in LH III C Late (see Rutter 1978; Papadopoulos, Damiata, and Marston 2011 for problems with Submycenaean as an independent phase); for MPG to LG see Dickinson (2006, 23, fig. 1.1) and Coldstream (2003, 435, fig. 128); for an extension of the late Geometric period into the seventh century, see Papadopoulos (2003, 146; 2018). Note that both the black- and red-figure styles continue well after the Archaic period, albeit in different forms.

Mycenaean period, and the Early Iron Age, usually defined by the Protogeometric and Geometric ceramic periods (table 1).[1] These time periods fall within the

1. For topical and chronological overviews of the Bronze Age, see Cullen 2001; Shelmerdine 2008; Cline 2010. On the Postpalatial period specifically, see Deger-Jalkotzy 1998; Deger-Jalkotzy and

disciplinary purviews of at least five groups of specialists: Aegean prehistorians, archaeologists interested in the transitional period of the Postpalatial Bronze Age to the Early Iron Age, classical archaeologists, ancient historians, and scholars of early Greek language and poetry (see also Morris 2000, 40–41; Kotsonas 2020, 78–84). Archaeological scholarship has in general focused more on synchronic problems of characterization or classification—of artifact types or social structures, for example—than diachronic narratives of development. This is not a matter of fault, since the former is necessary in order to produce the latter, but it is a welcome trend in recent years that transitional periods have come increasingly to the fore and disciplinary boundaries are more frequently crossed (see, e.g., Foxhall 1995; Thomas and Conant 2003; Deger-Jalkotzy and Lemos 2006; Dickinson 2006; Knodell 2013; Mazarakis Ainian, Alexandridou, and Charalambidou 2017; Murray 2017; Sherratt and Bennet 2017; Lemos and Kotsonas 2020; Middleton 2020).

The different research priorities and the traditions of different disciplines further complicate the picture. Ancient historians, for example, might employ archaeological evidence in the absence of written sources, but when the documentary record becomes available it tends to take pride of place. By contrast, archaeological evidence is available across all periods. Archaeology is therefore the only way to compare the periods in question on even terms. The documentary record can and does provide useful data in different contexts, but any holistic study must start with material culture.

At the same time, the material culture priorities of archaeology are not always best suited to studies of social organization. Rather than follow the traditional division of chronological periods based on ceramic styles, I adopt a more descriptive periodization: the Palatial and Postpalatial Bronze Age, followed by the Prehistoric and Protohistoric Iron Age (see table 1).[2] While no periodization is perfect, one based on cultural characteristics beyond ceramic typology is certainly preferable in the context of societal history (and the correspondence with relevant ceramic chronologies is easy enough to follow). I refer to this period as a whole

---

Zavadil 2003, 2007; Deger-Jalkotzy and Bächle 2009. For recent approaches to maritime networks in Mycenaean times, see Tartaron 2013; Kramer-Hajos 2016. On the Early Iron Age, Snodgrass (1971) 2000 still provides the best overview of the period. Other key syntheses include Desborough 1952, 1964, 1972; Coldstream (1977) 2003, 1980; Morris 1987, 2000; Whitley 1991; Mazarakis Ainian 1997; Lemos 2002; Morgan 2003; Osborne 2009. See also the following recent edited volumes: Mazarakis Ainian 2011; Descoeudres and Paspalas 2015; Vlachou 2015; and Handberg and Gadolou 2017. Several recent books aim to deal with this transitional period of early Greece holistically. See, for example, Mazarakis Ainian, Alexandridou, and Charalambidou 2017; Murray 2017; Lemos and Kotsonas 2020; Middleton 2020. For longer-term views on social change in Greece, see Bintliff 2012; Small 2019.

2. Throughout the text I capitalize Palatial and Postpalatial when referring to the Palatial and Postpalatial Bronze Age as the specific period defined here; the same applies to the Prehistoric and Protohistoric Iron Age. When these words are used simply as descriptive adjectives, they are left lowercase. Knapp (2008) adopted a similar set of terms for Cyprus. There is also the example of Protopalatial and Neopalatial Crete (see, e.g., Åberg 1933; Platon 1968).

as early Greece, since it encompasses the first definable period on the mainland that ancient Greeks themselves demonstrably looked back to as part of their own past—a pre-/protohistorical time we call the Mycenaean period, but before the wide dispersal of the city-state culture that would define the historical world of Archaic Greece from the seventh century onward.

In the interest of making this book accessible to nonspecialists, I provide a brief summary of the period in question. Aegean prehistory can be viewed as a series of booms and busts revolving around three core areas—Crete, the Cyclades, and the Greek mainland. The Early Bronze Age witnessed the development of long-distance networks, voyaging, and technological discovery in ceramics and metals, culminating in an "international spirit" that touched all three of these core zones, as well as parts of Anatolia. By contrast, the Middle Bronze Age can be seen as a period of imbalance, with relative stagnation throughout much of the Greek mainland and Cyclades, even as the first state-level societies in the Aegean emerged in Minoan Crete during the Old and New Palace periods, probably through a mix of endogenous developments and contacts with more "advanced" states in the eastern Mediterranean. At the same time, the island of Aegina saw significant growth in its influence throughout the Aegean. Against this backdrop—and at least partially in response to these developments—the Greek mainland underwent its own period of intensifying complexity, beginning in the MH III period with the appearance of monumental graves and more complex architectural formations. The individuals buried in these graves (most notably the "shaft graves" at Mycenae) represent a swiftly emergent elite, at least some of whose status is tied to an exclusivity of access to exotica, particularly arriving from or via Crete. The Early Mycenaean period ends in LH IIIA with the appearance of the Mycenaean palaces, which have certain similarities to the earlier Minoan palaces—unsurprisingly, considering the material connections that had existed for some 300 years prior to the emergence of these institutions on the mainland.

The core area of Mycenaean civilization is generally considered to stretch from the Peloponnese to Thessaly on the mainland, and also to encompass the Cyclades and Crete, at least in terms of cultural influence. A Mycenaean takeover of Minoan Crete is often posited, based (among other things) on the change in administrative script on Crete from Linear A (used to record the Minoan language, which remains unknown) to Linear B (adapted from Linear A to record the Mycenaean Greek language). Mycenaean palaces are characterized by heavy fortifications (cyclopean masonry), a centralized layout focused on a megaron complex, the presence of craft specialists, an apparent monopoly over the consumption and distribution of exotica, and an administrative system that recorded tight control of certain aspects of craft and agricultural production in unfired clay tablets inscribed with Linear B. Palaces have been discovered in the Peloponnese at Mycenae, Tiryns, and Midea in the Argolid, at Aghios Vasileios in Laconia, and at Pylos in Messenia. While the palaces of central Greece are more difficult to define, archaeological sites with palatial attributes have been recorded at the following places: Athens in Attica; Thebes, Orchomenos, and Gla in Boeotia; and Dimini and Volos in Thessaly (see further in chapter 3). Kanakia, on Salamis, is also sometimes described as palatial. While we often apply the idea of the Mycenaean Palatial period throughout the Aegean, I argue here that many parts of the Mycenaean world—that is, the geographical remit of Mycenaean material culture—do not seem to have been dominated by a palace. These areas are often talked about as "provinces" or "peripheries," but I would suggest they are better thought of as simply nonpalatial.[3]

Truly palatial remains and activities are limited to the LH III period of about 200 years. After their emergence in LH IIIA2, there was a series of destructions at palatial sites throughout the LH IIIB period. These destructions are coincident with other "times of troubles" in the eastern Mediterranean that afflicted especially the Hittites and Egyptians, along with the city-states of the Levant. This is often referred to as the "Late Bronze Age Collapse" of around 1200 BCE—a series of events that continues to puzzle archaeologists and historians and to generate reams of scholarship (see, e.g., Middleton 2017a, 2020; Cline 2014; Knapp and Manning 2016; Murray 2017). This collapse is often seen as some kind of historical moment, though it is probably better seen as a process or series of events occurring over about 200 years (indeed, throughout much of the Mycenaean Palatial period).

The Postpalatial period is often dismissed as an aftermath to the collapse. Nevertheless, life went on in the twelfth to mid-eleventh centuries BCE (LH IIIC in ceramic terms). As a sort of microcosm of earlier cycles of ups and downs, LH IIIC material remains are highly variable, both regionally and chronologically. In some areas there is relative continuity at palatial and other significant sites into LH IIIC Early; in others, there is a significant break. A "revival" or "developed" stage is often highlighted in LH IIIC Middle; this is characterized by fortified sites and painted pottery depicting maritime and combative imagery, which likely signaled mobility and violence as central features of social life. In terms of cultural traits, this period has much in common with the subsequent Early Iron Age, which is distinguished by the advent and dispersal of iron technology.[4]

The Postpalatial Bronze Age and Early Iron Age are situated on the disciplinary boundaries of Aegean prehistory and classical archaeology.[5] Traditionally,

---

3. On the formation of Mycenaean civilization, see Wright 2006, 2008. On palaces, see Galaty and Parkinson 2007; Shelmerdine 2008; Maran and Wright 2020. On Linear B, see Ventris and Chadwick (1956) 1973; Chadwick 1958, 1976; Palaima 2010; Nakassis 2013a; Steele 2020. On provinces and peripheries, see Froussou 1999; Kramer-Hajos 2008, 2016; Feuer 2011.

4. On the Postpalatial period and LH IIIC, see Deger-Jalkotzy and Lemos 2006; Deger-Jalkotzy 1998; Deger-Jalkotzy and Zavadil 2003, 2007; Thomatos 2006; Deger-Jalkotzy and Bächle 2009.

5. For extended discussions of disciplinary contexts, see also Snodgrass 1987; Morris 1994; Knodell 2013, 16–64; Kotsonas 2020. For disciplinary discussions of Aegean prehistory and Bronze Age archaeology, see Cullen 2001; Cherry, Margomenou, and Talalay 2005; Shelmerdine 2008; Tartaron 2008; Cline 2010. On the archaeology of the Early Iron Age, see Papadopoulos 1993, 1996a, 2014; Morris 2000; Kotsonas 2016; Murray 2018b.

the interest of the former ends with the fall of the Mycenaean palaces, while the interest of the latter picks up with the "renaissance" of the eighth century BCE. For a variety of reasons, the periods in between have often been referred to as the "Dark Age" of early Greece, which is thought to represent a significant decline in terms of population, connections to the wider Mediterranean world, and overall quality of life (Snodgrass [1971] 2000, 1–21). The "Dark Age" was also meant to reflect our state of knowledge regarding the period in question. The disappearance of Linear B with the collapse of the Mycenaean palaces meant that writing would not return to the Aegean world until the development of the Greek alphabet, most likely sometime in the eighth century BCE. A measurable decline in the number of known sites, representational art, and overall amount of material evidence meant simply that there was much less to say about the centuries between Mycenaean times and the Archaic period. While the quantitative metrics of decline described above are often valid, the pejorative notions and interpretive bias that the term "Dark Age" introduces have led to the adoption of the more neutral "Early Iron Age" as the predominant referent.[6]

In the Early/Prehistoric Iron Age (c. 1050–800) BCE, communities are for the most part relatively small scale and show little sign of social differentiation or contact with the outside world, with few exceptions. Structural remains are mostly simple constructions in semidispersed villages. In ceramic terms these are the Protogeometric and Early Geometric periods, in which geometric designs on painted pottery are the defining quality.[7] While these trends apply to most Early Iron Age sites, there are also examples of precociousness. Sensational discoveries at Lefkandi in the 1980s revealed that some parts of Greece were much wealthier and more widely connected than traditionally thought. A monumental building and its adjacent cemetery showed connections to Cyprus, Egypt, and the Levant as markers of elite status and authority, much as they had been in previous periods. Since then the pendulum has swung in the other direction, with regular exclamations of "new light on a dark age" attending groundbreaking discoveries and landmark studies.[8]

The final period examined in this book is the Protohistoric Iron Age (the eighth to early seventh centuries BCE or the Middle to Late Geometric periods). The archaeological record signals a major boom in this period, which is represented by a dramatic increase in settlement numbers, first on the Greek mainland and eventually in the establishment of "colonies"—*apoikiai*—in southern Italy, Sicily, and the northern Aegean (a trend that continued through the Archaic period of

6. On "Dark Age" nomenclature, see Papadopoulos 1993, 1996a, 1999; Morris 1997b, 2000; Knodell 2013; Kotsonas 2016; Murray 2018b.

7. For overviews, see Snodgrass (1971) 2000[; Desborough 1972; Coldstream (1977) 2003. On trade and the economy, see Murray 2017. On pottery, see Desborough 1952; Coldstream (1968) 2008; Lemos 2002; Papadopoulos and Smithson 2017. On settlement and construction, see Mazarakis Ainian 1997.

8. Langdon 1997; see also Morris 1992, 140. For important monographs, see Morris 1987, 2000; Whitley 1991; Lemos 2002; Morgan 2003; Langdon 2008.

the seventh and sixth centuries). This is often referred to as the eighth-century "renaissance" or "revolution." The reappearance of writing in the Aegean in the form of an alphabet adapted from the Phoenician script occurred at the same time as a rapid proliferation of visual imagery and the development of regional styles in pottery production. These changes in media of communication and representation coincided with the emergence of Panhellenic sanctuaries, which quickly became hubs of interaction for people and things in a growing Greek world. This relatively short span of time, around the middle of the eighth century, is often seen as the spark that ignited the emergence of Greek city-states across the Mediterranean in the Archaic period.

The material or archaeological narratives outlined above are complemented (and often muddled) by the arrival of new datasets: texts in the form of early Greek writing and the mythohistorical narratives that come from Homer, Hesiod, and later authors referring to this period (e.g., Herodotus and Thucydides). In *Works and Days*, Hesiod explicitly discusses daily life in his own times (probably the later part of the eighth century BCE). Homer, whose poems were the product of a centuries-long oral tradition, contains a sort of conflative temporality, blending cultural elements of his own days with those extending backward at least to the Palatial period (and probably beyond), together with everything in between.[9] So, in addition to what we can detect archaeologically, we also have the task of parsing later myth or misconception from useful information about the societies under study—of detecting past realities and material trends amid mythohistorical glimpses of an imagined past (as in the cases, for example, of the Trojan Legend, the Seven Against Thebes, or the Lelantine War).[10] The problematic nature of the evidence means that it has most often either been overemphasized or dismissed entirely in archaeological discourse (see, e.g., Dickinson 2020). In this book, I aim for a contextual middle ground: I argue that some texts can be useful for telling us

9. The date and identity of Homer are the subject of an entire subfield of scholarship. See, for example, Wace and Stubbings 1962; Nagy 1996; Morris and Powell 1997; Snodgrass 2017. Dates typically range from the eighth to the sixth century BCE, with general agreement that a formative period of codification happened during this time, regardless of whether the works were yet in written form and well defined. I do not engage with questions of the date or historicity of a poet named Homer, though this book assumes that most elements of the Homeric poems were present by the end of the eighth century. The bibliography on "Homeric society"—the amalgamated society that Homer describes—is also huge. See, for example, Lorimer 1950; Finley 1954; Vermeule 1964; Carter and Morris 1995; Morris and Powell 1997; Snodgrass 1998; Latacz 2004; Gottschall 2008; Ulf 2009; Sherratt and Bennet 2017.

10. Works on early Greece with disciplinary roots in ancient history often begin with the Mycenaean period and protohistorical periods that follow, although archaeological evidence is often superceded in favor of the documentary record when the latter is available. Studies of Archaic Greek history are therefore much more rooted in sources derived from the later part of the period (the seventh and sixth centuries BCE), reflecting a very different set of priorities than those of the present book. On the historiography of Archaic Greece, see Davies 2009. For recent syntheses and companions, see Hall 2007; Lane Fox 2008; Osborne 2009; Raaflaub and van Wees 2009; Cartledge and Christesen, forthcoming. On dissonances between the interests of historians and archaeological data, and the interests of archaeologists and historical data, see Foxhall 2013.

TABLE 2 Term searches for chronological periods in the Nestor
bibliographic database (December 2020)

Term	Number of occurrences
Late Bronze Age	1195
Mycenaean	3133
Palatial	346
Postpalatial (+post-palatial)	80
Late Helladic	164
LH	156
IIIA	120
IIIB	97
IIIC	181
Early Iron Age	650
Dark Age	249
Protogeometric	79
Geometric	312

certain types of things and in some cases may reflect more or less specific aspects of social memory, even if they cannot be taken at face value.[11] In this way the societies of early Greece are neither entirely prehistoric nor entirely historic, but in most cases are more aptly termed protohistoric. That is, they themselves did not produce intentional histories, and the documentary record they did leave behind does not compare well with sources available to historians of the Archaic period (seventh to sixth centuries BCE) onward.

Of the periods covered by this book, the Mycenaean Palatial period and the eighth century BCE have received by far the most attention. This is reflected in the major discrepancies in the bibliography concerning the periods covered here (see table 2). One problem is that, because these "boom" periods are not regularly viewed alongside more than cursory treatments of the following and preceding periods, our understanding of how they came to be is hampered. While the amount of scholarship on the period between the fall of the Mycenaean palaces and the eighth century has increased dramatically in recent years, there is still a tendency to compartmentalize these in-between years as something separate from what comes before or after them. Much recent work forwards the goal of spanning the "iron curtain," a dark age mirage that separates the Bronze and Iron Ages in disciplinary terms (Papadopoulos 1993, 195; 2014, 181). Yet very few studies seek to assess the material systematically and to explain social change from the "Mycenaean" world of the Late Bronze Age *through* the emergent "Greek" world of the eighth century. It is still far more common for researchers to express interest in bridging such a gap while remaining for the most part on one or the other side of

11. See recent approaches by Mac Sweeney 2016, 2017; see also Wallace 2018.

it.[12] This book provides a diachronic history of early Greek society from the Palatial Bronze Age to the Protohistoric Iron Age with equal treatment for all periods. The focus on central Greece particularly highlights the importance of regionalism, comparing and contrasting the landscapes of central Greece not only with each other but also with other parts of the early Greek world.

SUMMARY: A GUIDE TO WHAT FOLLOWS

This introduction has outlined the basic arguments of this book and situated them in their wider historical and disciplinary contexts. In chapter 1, I present a theoretical framework that combines elements of landscape, interaction, and complexity in order to provide a new approach to synthesis in the archaeology of early Greece. A combined relational and spatial approach to modeling and interpreting sociopolitical geography is widely applicable, but it is particularly useful when focused on diachronic change. The multiscalar perspective developed here, taking as a starting point the mesoscale of a multiregional synthesis, offers the opportunity to focus on a specific case study with a view also to bigger-picture processes that involve the wider Mediterranean world.

Chapter 2 discusses the archaeological and landscape context of central Greece and the regions that comprise it. The analysis of land routes and potential interconnections between sites has been carried out in several individual areas previously, but it is only by articulating a wider whole that landscapes, coastscapes, and seascapes can be brought together to traverse regional boundaries that—while real concerns—are necessarily fluid and permeable. By combining archaeological data accumulated over several decades with geographical and environmental data that has not previously been considered in this context, fresh perspectives are offered on both microregional and larger-scale patterns of settlement.

The heart of this book (chapters 3, 4, 5 and 6) provides a diachronic explication of social dynamics across local, regional, and trans-Mediterranean scales. The chronological arrangement corresponds with the four principal periods under study: the Palatial Bronze Age (chapter 3), the Postpalatial Bronze Age (chapter 4), the Prehistoric Iron Age (chapter 5), and the Protohistoric Iron Age (chapter 6). These four chapters provide an integrative study of a variety of related, though seemingly divergent, social phenomena, including shifting and coexisting modes of polity (from palaces to village societies); the disappearance of Linear B and the adaptation of the Greek alphabet from the Phoenician script; the technological

---

12. There are important exceptions, to be sure, although these tend to be focused on thematic aspects of society or a particular issue. Dickinson (2006) divides his synthesis topically into sections on craft, trade, and settlement. Murray (2017) focuses on the economy—namely in terms of trade, economic and population decline, and eventual recovery. Zurbach (2017) offers a text-based approach to land and agricultural labor. Bintliff (2012) and Small (2019) examine settlement and social complexity across these periods, though as parts of studies with much wider chronological remits.

transition from bronze to iron as the dominant utilitarian metal; and major shifts in the nature of long-distance maritime interactions. The detailed study of these four periods is bracketed by discussions of state formation that occur on either side of it: the emergence of the Mycenaean palaces and the formation of Archaic Greek poleis.

Each historical chapter proceeds in three general parts: (1) The core of each chapter is a discussion of settlement evidence and what this can tell us about the political landscapes of various parts of central Greece. (2) Each chapter turns next to technologies and media of interaction, focusing on a particular sociotechnological process of special significance for the interstitial role it played. In the Palatial Bronze Age I focus on Linear B and exotica as centralizing features for political authority. In the Postpalatial period evidence of pottery production indicates new patterns of connectivity, especially in the Euboean Gulf. In the Prehistoric Iron Age new pyrotechnologies emerge as relevant to both pottery and metal production, which can be tracked especially through their rapid dispersal. In the Protohistoric Iron Age we see a media revolution in the proliferation of writing and figural imagery in an increasingly multicultural Mediterranean world. (3) The final part of each chapter comprises a discussion of the wider Mediterranean context with which early Greek societies were inextricably intertwined, albeit in very different ways throughout the periods in question. The reflexive approach taken here examines how interconnectivity affected the communities of central Greece in particular, as well as the impacts of Greek communities on the wider world stage.

This framework and the resulting interpretations offer several contributions relevant to the archaeology of Greece in the Late Bronze Age and Early Iron Age, as well as to the archaeology of complex societies: (1) an integrative approach to landscape, interaction, and social complexity; (2) a demonstration of the effectiveness of network and complexity thinking as explanatory and interpretative frameworks in writing an archaeological history; (3) an analysis of power relationships, the construction and legitimation of authority, and conceptions of landscape, seascape, and distance; (4) a dynamic model of social organization in a diachronic framework; (5) a synthesis of social change in Late Bronze Age and Early Iron Age central Greece that questions or nuances a variety of previous models. These contributions are drawn out in the conclusions of this book, which reflect first on Greece in transition—especially the diversity of the political landscape and how central Greece becomes central in wider Mediterranean spheres—and second on the comparative insights the case study of early Greece offers, especially to wider studies of nonlinear trajectories in complex societies and archaeologies of protohistory.

From the outset, it should be clear that this book deals with a long span of time (ca. 1400–700 BCE) in a large geographical area, ranging from the local landscapes of central Greece to the vast expanse of the entire Mediterranean basin. Such an approach fills a void in Mediterranean archaeology and history, which has become quite good at site-specific and microregional studies, as well as the grand syntheses in the style of Braudel (1972), Horden and Purcell (2000), and Broodbank (2013). There are fewer examples that aim explicitly to focus on a mesoscale and examine past interactions across both maritime and terrestrial environments. It is precisely the need to articulate interactions between the local and the global that drives the narratives here. To that end, I examine the development of early Greece as a contingent archaeological history. The central focus is on the changes and reformations of sociopolitical organization across a well-connected culture area (central Greece) that exhibits both regional distinctions and connection to a wider interaction zone (the Mediterranean). The development of regional trends, in dialogue with local and interregional processes, provides insights into notions of territoriality, regionalism, polity, and identity that are only evident when considered together.

1

Landscape, Interaction, Complexity

*The discipline emerges as a restless body of observations upon particular
classes of data, between a certain range of scales, held together by a network
of changing methodology and implicit theory.*

—DAVID CLARKE, "ARCHAEOLOGY: THE LOSS OF INNOCENCE"

This chapter outlines the theoretical framework of the present work: an integrative
approach that incorporates archaeologies of landscape, interaction, and complexity. From a landscape perspective, I examine the distribution of settlement evidence in central Greece and how this evidence changes through the Late Bronze
Age and Early Iron Age. As an archaeology of interaction, this book focuses on
the modeling and articulation of networks on multiple scales—local, regional,
and long-distance—and how these are manifest in the archaeological record.
These approaches to landscape and interaction combine in what is ultimately an
archaeology of social complexity, focused on the constitution and development of
societies in the late second and early first millennia BCE.

AN ARCHAEOLOGY OF LANDSCAPE:
COMMUNITIES IN CONTEXT

As an archaeology of landscape, the following chapters analyze archaeological evidence for settlement, burial, politics, and production, as distributed through the
regions of central Greece. This study of settlement patterns involves the quantification and comparison of settlement evidence, alongside spatial models of territory
and connectivity. More qualitative aspects of landscape archaeology are engaged
through the themes of space, place, and landscape—categories that are socially
constructed in ways informed by the physical environment, human experiences,
and collective memory. While physical spaces form the contexts in which humans
live, operate, and interact, place-making activities condense interactions in the
landscape by bringing together individuals participating in local and regional networks of particular practices, such as communal feasting or festivals at regional

sanctuaries. Iterative movements through the landscape traverse local, regional, and more distant spaces, habituating connections between individuals and groups. Like other types of interactions, practices of this sort are related to social complexity in the sense that they are both inclusive and exclusive, serving to create and reinforce social bonds, inequalities, and associations with place. In a similar way, technology and production deserve special attention. Agricultural activity and craft production bring together people and things across local and regional landscapes, as raw materials, products, and technological knowledge travel. Mobility and movement between places, spaces, and landscapes are the means by which social life is constituted and are necessarily multiscalar. In this section I focus first on the fundamental relationship between geography and society and then move on to define my approach to the region as the crucial scale of analysis. I discuss the regional datasets and methods of analysis in detail in chapter 2.

Connective Contexts in Mediterranean Geography

Maritime and terrestrial geography provide complementary sets of landscapes, coastscapes, and seascapes in which the movements and dynamics of human societies play out. On the largest scale, we are concerned with the Mediterranean writ large, the fractal geography of which has resulted in a particular form of connectivity (map 1) (Braudel 1972; Horden and Purcell 2000; Broodbank 2013). Microecologies of certain landscapes—coastal plains, mountain plateaus, river valleys, upland steppes—characterize a highly fragmented geographical area, where different zones are better suited to different modes of production. At the same time, these areas tend to be geographically distinct from one another, often with clear natural boundaries that easily allow the demarcation of territory or regional identity. Nevertheless, this fragmentation drives interaction between microregions, in order to diversify patterns of consumption (of agricultural and craft products) and socialization (through marriage relationships and alliances). As a response, communities develop practices of social storage and risk buffering that ensure that bad years or crop failure in certain regions can be ameliorated by exchange relationships with others (Halstead 1989; Broodbank 2000, 84). In practical terms, such interaction is most likely to be carried out along particular paths, again owing to the particular topographic fragmentation of Mediterranean microregions.

The Aegean Sea and the particularly varied geographies of mainland Greece are at a crossroads whose significance is paramount in the long-term history of the Mediterranean. As a bridge between Asia and Europe, the Aegean and the Greek mainland have been traversed time and again by migrants coming across both land and sea—from the earliest human populations of the area (crossing through northern Greece) to the first farmers in Europe (in Crete and in Thessaly) to present-day refugees fleeing various conflicts. When the eastern Mediterranean world expanded into one of states, empires, and traders in the Late Bronze Age and Early Iron Age, the Aegean's centrality was particularly significant, forming a bridge between the eastern and central Mediterranean.

As our focus narrows to the study region at the center of this book, so, too, can the demonstrable geographies of centrality and connectedness. From a maritime perspective, the Euboean Gulf is a conduit that runs between the central Greek mainland and the island of Euboea (map 1); it is a sheltered channel that also links the northern and southern Aegean Sea. This corridor is surrounded on all sides by a diverse set of landscapes that make up the regions of Attica, Boeotia, Malis, Thessaly, and Euboea (see further in chapter 2). It has been a critical nexus of human interaction in many phases of history, where geography, individuals, groups, and materials have come together in the course of day-to-day local practices, as well as in long-distance voyages that spanned the Aegean and in some cases the entire Mediterranean.[1] From a terrestrial perspective, the landscapes of central Greece are home to a diverse array of agricultural land, mountain pastures, and routes of movement. Parallel to the Euboean Gulf, the Great Isthmus Corridor (between, roughly, Delphi and Lamia) brings the region of Phokis and Mount Parnassos into the fold and provides the same type of northwest-southeast land route as the Euboean Gulf does on the eastern side of the study area.

A Regional Perspective: Multiple Scales, Hierarchies of Space

On a fundamental level, this book is a contribution to the archaeology of settlement in central Greece in the Late Bronze Age and Early Iron Age. From there it branches out to wider sets of relations. I use evidence from archaeological surveys and excavations to examine how landscapes were inhabited and traversed and how they changed over time. The regional perspective put forward here is multiscalar in that it seeks to integrate archaeological and landscape evidence across a variety of social and spatial scales that often overlap (figure 1). Regions themselves can be defined on multiple scales, which are nevertheless geographically coherent. Their boundaries—distinguishable, but permeable—can be identified by features in the landscape (mountains, streams, or the sea), and in size they range from microregions, such as a mountain plain or a river valley, to mesoscales comprised of several microregions, like Boeotia or Thessaly, to macroregions, like central Greece. These classifications exist alongside conceptions of social space, which come together in the context of landscapes.

In using the term "landscape," I refer mainly to the combination of the physical environment and lived activities and experiences within it. The archaeology of landscape presented here examines the distribution of evidence for these activities and experiences diachronically and regionally, as well as with the goal of understanding human experiences in their broader cultural and environmental contexts. In practical terms, this begins with mapping the distribution of

---

1. On sea routes in the Aegean and maritime connectivity, see Agouridis 1997; Arnaud 2005; Papageorgiou 2008; Sauvage 2012; Tartaron 2013 (especially on local connectivity and the particular importance of short-distance seafaring). On the physical geography of Greece and its relationship to human history, see Philippson 1951; Bintliff 1977b; Horden and Purcell 2000; Knodell 2017.

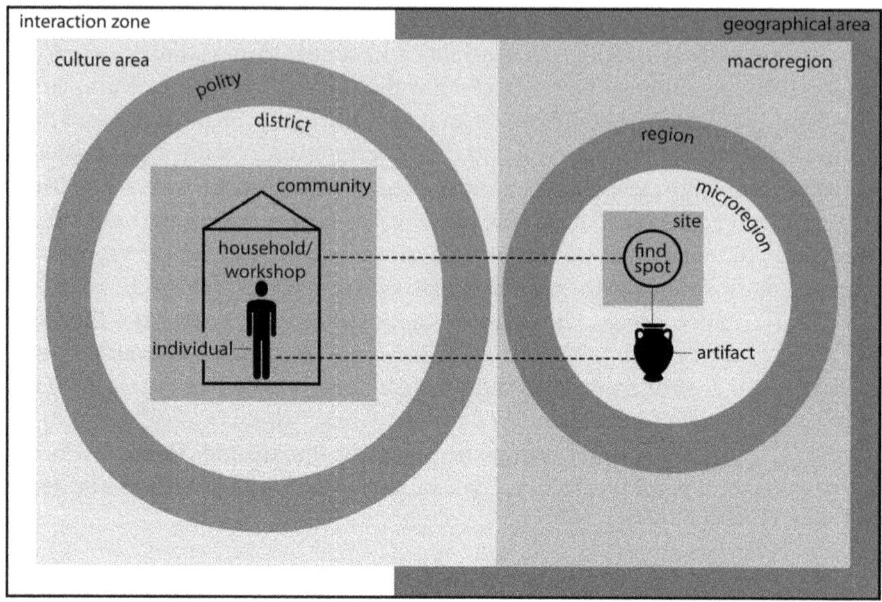

FIGURE 1. Nested (but often overlapping) scales of social and spatial units: spatial modes of organizing territory on the right, with socially defined entities on the left; these categories naturally overlap and coexist: e.g., multiple artifacts within one of several findspots at a site may provide information about individuals or a household within a community; a region may contain multiple polities, each comprised of a number of communities, which in some cases may be grouped into administrative districts (illustration by Denitsa Nenova).

archaeological remains, then analyzing and interpreting them in terms of their relationships to other places, both near and far (see further in chapter 2).

The archaeology of regions has been a major focus of research for some time in Greek archaeology, though issues of scale remain a challenge (Cherry 1983b; Bennet and Galaty 1997; Alcock and Cherry 2004; Tartaron 2008; Knodell and Leppard 2018). Large-scale regional studies—for example, of mainland Greece or the island of Crete—need to integrate a wide variety of datasets from surveys and excavations, usually to address particular historical problems. The most successful examples have examined topics such as different pathways to complexity in the north and south Aegean, the emergence of the polis, breakages in the Hellenistic world, and the landscapes of Roman Greece (Alcock 1993, 1994, 2002; Halstead 1994; Bintliff 1997). Further successful examples integrate data across smaller regions—for example, the northeast Peloponnese (Cherry and Davis 2001; Wright 2004b). It remains difficult, however, to integrate diverse datasets across large geographical areas with more than broad strokes between uncharacterized dots on a map.

Archaeologists have increasingly recognized the need to integrate regional data across multiple scales (e.g., Parkinson 2018). The vast majority of human activity occurs within local or regional extents. While many face-to-face interactions take place within the bounds of a household or a neighborhood, the spatial extent of daily life ranges far beyond the individual site or community, especially in agropastoral societies. Household production is highly localized at the level of an individual site, but it requires raw materials from farther afield. Agricultural production extends beyond dwelling locations and may involve cultivation in areas quite distant from a habitation location. Pastoral activities are by nature distributed across the landscape in the constant quest for fodder. At a broader scale, individuals move between communities in order to arrange suitable marriage partners and to ensure a diversification of products and subsistence strategies. *Findspots* or *sites* (both archaeological categories) may or may not represent an individual *community* (a social category) (see figure 1). At the same time, individuals move across and between regions as well, which can be conceived of in social terms as polities, culture areas, or interaction zones.

Interaction between different types of social groups requires us to consider notions of community identity, polity, and territory, all of which are embedded deeply in notions of place, space, and landscape. Studying how these spheres of spatial production and interaction are interwoven is a central feature of the landscape archaeology proposed in this book. An equally important focus concerns how the interconnectivity between places leads to the redefinition of regions in territorial and political terms (rather than, say, physical ones) (see, e.g., de Montmollin 1989; Smith 2003; Bevan 2010; Kosiba and Bauer 2013). The settlement evidence is therefore presented qualitatively, quantitatively, and relationally in the chapters that follow. Site types and hierarchies are defined for each period, then evaluated in terms of what type of activities and communities they most likely represent. Relationships between communities are modeled as well, in order to explore the interactive workings of early Greek societies.

AN ARCHAEOLOGY OF INTERACTION: NETWORKS AND TECHNOLOGIES

As an archaeology of interaction this book examines how sites, communities, and landscapes are woven together on multiple scales. On the one hand, this is integrated into the settlement pattern analysis. On the other, I look to two other proxies for interaction for each of the periods in question. First, technology and media offer evidence of and catalysts for mobility and knowledge-sharing. Second, more traditional forms of evidence for long-distance interaction—imports, exports, diplomatic texts, and historical or literary accounts—are also examined where available. In each case, I am concerned first with connectivity within and between the regions and microregions of central Greece and second with the place of central Greece in the wider Aegean and Mediterranean world.

In chapters 3, 4, 5 and 6 I model networks of interaction in geographical space in a Geographic Information Systems (GIS) framework. Models of local and regional interaction networks illustrate how and where people likely moved through and between the landscapes and communities of central Greece. I examine longer-distance interactions through an interpretative analysis of material culture, especially in relation to production and media technologies (involving questions of know-how, style, and regional identity). Aspects of network theory concerning centralization, small worlds, and the strength of weak ties are invoked at various points to explain the models and evidence presented here in relation to the Greek landscape and the societies inhabiting it.

This approach differs from many other studies of interaction in embracing both qualitative and quantitative approaches. Such a strategy is appropriate in considering the potpourri of interaction studies in archaeology and anthropology.[2] While much excellent work has been done, there remains no unified body of theory on the topic. This is probably because *interaction* could be used to describe nearly all aspects of human behavior—from face-to-face conversations (Goffman 1967) to long-distance trade (Renfrew 1975). An explicitly integrative, multiscalar approach is a productive way forward.

Multiscalar Networks and Diachronic Change

Over the last decades, networks have emerged as a powerful approach to the study of interaction, especially in archaeological contexts (Peeples 2019; Donnellan 2020). At their most fundamental level, networks are a way of abstracting entities (nodes) and relationships between them (links). Here, the graphic representation and analysis of these relationships form the basis of the network study. As with the term "interaction," however, "networks" can refer to a wide range of theoretical or methodological approaches (see, e.g., Knappett 2011, 37–58; Knodell 2013, 65–96; 2017; Brughmans 2013; Brughmans, Collar, and Coward. 2016; Mills 2017). Most archaeological and historical applications of networks fall into three general categories:

1. The term "network" is used metaphorically to describe interconnectivity among individuals or groups: the Late Bronze Age eastern Mediterranean was home to a complex network of interactions between various cultures and polities (e.g., Horden and Purcell 2000; Broodbank 2013).
2. Concepts from social network theory (especially centrality, small worlds, scale-free growth) are used to describe social relationships, primarily as an interpretative

2. Approaches include description-based catalogs of imports, diffusionist models (Childe 1925, 1936, 1958), interaction spheres (Caldwell 1964), trade studies (Renfrew 1969, 1975; Chang 1975), systems perspectives (Clarke 1968, 1972; Flannery 1968; Renfrew 1972), peer-polity interaction (Renfrew and Cherry 1986), world-systems theory (Wallerstein 1974; Kohl 1987; Blanton and Feinman 1984; Sherratt and Sherratt 1993; Kristiansen and Larsson 2005; Kardulias and Hall 2008; Parkinson and Galaty 2010), its critiques (Schneider 1977; Stein 2002), globalization (Hodos 2017, 2020), and various types of network theory (Knappett 2011, 2013; Blake 2014; Brughmans, Collar, and Coward 2016; Iacono 2019; Peeples 2019). On the persistent problem of the diffuse nature of the concept, see Schortman and Urban 1987, 1992; Schortman 1989; Iacono 2019, 8–13).

aid: Mycenaean palaces reorganized regional networks to make them highly centralized, putting a large amount of power (and vulnerability) in the central node (the palace) (e.g., Malkin 2011; Tartaron 2013; Kramer-Hajos 2016).
3. Formal or quantitative methods of network analysis are deployed in the generation and examination of models based on material evidence: analysis can show patterns of clustering across the study area, variable levels of centrality in different nodes in the network, or the convergence of different attributes of material culture (e.g., Broodbank 2000; Knappett 2011; Blake 2014; Brughmans, Collar, and Coward 2016; Iacono 2019).

This final category ranges widely, often incorporating approaches from social network analysis (SNA) or complexity studies and network science. The main uses of networks in this book are as a dual geographical and relational approach that combines elements of all three categories, though chiefly 2 and 3.

For the most part, the *nodes* discussed in this book are archaeological sites—in particular, the ones in the dataset that represent past communities. At times, nodes can refer more specifically to institutions or individuals or more broadly to regions in the wider Mediterranean context. This flexibility is necessary in attempting to reconstruct networks on multiple scales and of different types. *Links* must be defined with equal flexibility. The individuals, groups, things, and places that act as nodes are mediated by a variety of other individuals, groups, things, and places, which necessarily result in multiple types of interactions. The types of links represented here can be strictly material (e.g., a direct contact situation of trade or raw material procurement) or more ephemeral (shared technologies or aspects of material or visual culture).

Networks are used here to articulate multiple geographical scales, while maintaining a relatively unified theoretical framework.[3] In general, discussions in the following chapters refer to (1) local networks, which link individuals within or between nearby communities; (2) regional networks, which join communities, landscapes, and polities; and (3) interregional networks, which connect polities or cultural groups across the Aegean or even the Mediterranean. These should not be seen as stark divisions but rather as groupings with relatively fluid boundaries (see figure 1). It is the mesoscale—which is best understood through a study of the archaeological landscape—that bridges local and regional distances and that receives the most explicit treatment here in terms of modeling (see further in chapter 2).

---

3. Knappett (2011) has taken a different approach to networks on multiple scales (largely centered around ceramic production and distribution in the Minoan Aegean), analyzing microscale networks of proximate interactions, mesoscale networks concerned with communities of practice, and macroscale networks of regional interactions. More recently, Donnellan (2016) has examined funerary practices at the multicultural settlement of Pithekoussai from the perspective of multiscalar networks.

Certain general trends in network behavior can be drawn on as interpretative tools or principles. Four patterns feature here: scale-free growth, centrality, small worlds, and the strength of weak ties (see also Malkin 2011, 3–28; Knodell 2013, 346–47; Kramer-Hajos 2016, 20–21). Scale-free networks essentially describe "the rich get richer" phenomenon, whereby places that are well connected are likely to become better connected, often at an exponential rate (Barabási and Albert 1999). In terms of centrality, highly centralized networks have few hubs through which all interactions must go (Baran 1964). This puts much control over interaction in a single node, which can thus be very powerful and efficient. However, the entire system is left vulnerable to collapse since, if the hub is removed, the whole system breaks down. Decentralized networks, in which hubs emerge almost naturally in many different places, are much more common. Distributed networks have fewer or no hubs.

A small world is a type of network in which most nodes are connected to their nearest neighbors but certain links exist that connect other small worlds to each other (Milgrim 1967; Pool and Kochen 1978; Watts and Strogatz 1998). A concept that operates within small-world networks is the strength of weak ties (Granovetter 1973). While interactions between near neighbors are likely to be more frequent (or stronger), the less frequent, often longer-distance interactions between other small-world networks—that is, the weak ties—can be particularly significant. Such weak ties can introduce new ideas or materials to a small-world network.

While network theory is increasingly prevalent in archaeology and ancient history, the integration of geographical realities into such an approach is significantly rarer (but see Bevan 2010; Mills et al. 2015; Peeples 2019, 471–80; Brughmans and Peeples 2020). Moreover, most archaeological studies of networks seek to document or analyze interaction as recorded in things—for example, through shared elements of ceramic style or technology (Knappett 2011; Blake 2014). My goal is rather to model assumed interactions in space heuristically, based on the idea that communities would have interacted with neighboring communities. In particular, I use (1) nearest-neighbor networks based on habitual contact with a certain number of proximate sites and (2) a connectivity model of routes in the landscape (on methods, see further in chapter 2).

Texts, Technologies, and Things

Beyond network models, I examine several other proxies for interaction, which are chiefly regional and interregional in scope. These comprise words, images, and things. Texts that refer to interaction and population movement signal an eastern Mediterranean in transition, with mobility and migration as powerful forces (Demand 2011; Aslaksen 2016; Isayev 2017; Driessen 2018; Wallace 2018). At the same time, technologies—and their dispersal through different regions and culture areas—are important proxies for interactions (Feldman 2007, 2014; Brysbaert 2011; Ferrara 2015). One final relevant element of interaction studies highlights *things* as social actors at the core of the archaeological project (Witmore 2007; Hodder 2012; Olsen et al. 2012). Things are both media of interaction, through which messages move and meanings are transferred, and they themselves play important roles in social interactions, expressing meanings that can range from indeterminate exoticism to projecting particular political messages (A. Smith 2015; Khatchadourian 2016).

Images and texts have special significance, since they carry specific messages *by design*. In some cases, the meanings these media carried were deliberate and clear; in others, the meanings were unintentional and subtle. Changes in media and technology as mobile and lasting carriers of cultural information are therefore paramount to tracking and explaining social change alongside landscapes of settlement and models of interaction.

AN ARCHAEOLOGY OF COMPLEXITY: SOCIETIES IN TRANSITION

As an archaeology of complexity, this book examines the development of societal organization from the Late Bronze Age to the Early Iron Age. Archaeologies of landscape and interaction serve as the context and articulation of what is ultimately an archaeology of complex societies—that is, an approach to ancient communities that aims to understand their sociopolitical organization, variation, and change over time.

Complex societies have historically been viewed in contrast to simple societies, though these terms can each apply to a range of sociopolitical formations. Complex societies are generally defined as human groups in which levels of social hierarchy are present, along with a variety of roles and specializations represented among the individuals that comprise them. Social complexity has comparative value as a flexible concept applicable to a wide variety of cultural circumstances (see, e.g., Trigger 2003; A. Smith 2003; M. E. Smith 2011; Small 2019). Because of its relationship to variation and hierarchy, complexity is often a stand-in for levels of social inequality (Chapman 1990, 2003). This complexity usually refers to states and other social formations with clearly demarcated differentiation in social status and roles, though it can (and should) apply also to a range of modes of sociopolitical organization, both loosely and strictly defined.

Complex adaptive systems offer an inroad to the study of ancient societies where an understanding of the individual parts does not necessarily result in the understanding of the whole (Kauffman 1993; Martin and Sunley 2007; Mitchell 2009). Shifting networks of interactions result in change across the system in its entirety, which is comprised of various types of agents. In considering the system as a dynamic whole, patterns such as emergent behaviors, phase transitions, and collapse can be identified, a fact that has obvious implications for understanding complex societies as dynamic systems (Bentley and Maschner 2003; Kohring and Wynne-Jones 2007; Kohler 2012). Complexity thinking thus provides a useful framework within which to describe *and understand* the dynamic behaviors of past social groups.

The archaeology of social complexity examines how interconnectedness relates to the emergence of new properties in a social system (van der Leeuw 1981; Cherry 1983a, 1986; Chapman 1990, 2003; Halstead 1994; Bintliff 1997; Smith 2003; Ames 2008; Knodell and Leppard 2018). Archaeologists of complex societies are particularly concerned with how societies become comprised of larger, more internally diverse, and more complex (yet integrated) social structures, and how social inequality is present through the manipulation of these structures. Such processes are nonlinear and multidirectional. That is to say, simplification is as worthy an object of study as growth. Renfrew (1979) made a similar point concerning the collapse of ancient states and the aftermath, pointing particularly to patterns of "catastrophe and anastrophe." Similarly, in modeling the rise of the polis in early Greece, Snodgrass (1980a, 44–47) has emphasized the need to pay attention also to communities that did *not* become poleis, a call picked up more thoroughly by Morgan (2003). In general, then, complexity should be viewed on a nonlinear, variable scale. Complexity does not conform to strict definitions or sets of attributes but has to do with structure, interaction, and power—scales of settlement and territory, the integration of institutions, and levels of inequality.

Like other complex systems, social complexity is fluid and dynamic, and it develops in an ongoing way. Reorganization is therefore a major theme; scale also factors in the relationship between time and change (Lock and Molyneaux 2006). If we consider Braudel's (1972, 20–21) tripartite conception of timescales—the *longue durée, conjoncture,* and *histoire événementielle* (long-term, societal, and individual rhythms of time)—we might draw parallels between these and their social-historical correlates. In the long term, societies continuously reconstitute themselves—quite slowly, as their institutions become entrenched and reformulated through daily practices (Bourdieu 1977; Giddens 1984; Nakassis 2013b, 246). These processes of entrenchment and reconstitution occur on the resilient and rhythmic scales of the long and medium term. Such continuous processes are often not visible in the archaeological record and, when they are visible, they read as slow-moving, gradual development (e.g., long-lasting practices concerning agropastoral lifeways or household organization). More rapid, large-scale change is often observable archaeologically; it can be compared to patterns of punctuated equilibrium in evolutionary theory (Cherry 1983a; Gould 2007; Manning 2018). Such punctuated equilibria can be detected in the medium term or the rhythmic/ iterative timescale that we would associate with more distinct and recognizable social change (e.g., in political organization or material culture traditions). Finally, an archaeological perspective rooted in complexity must recognize the capacity for short-term, agentive, and events-based change to have dramatic impacts across a much wider system (e.g., political transitions, conflicts, and disasters). While specific events are rarely detectable archaeologically, their consequences often are, especially when they are viewed in combination with hints afforded by other sources of information, such as contemporary and later written records.

Social Complexity in Early Greece

Despite a long tradition of archaeological research, our understanding of early Greek sociopolitical organization is rather poor. We know more about some periods and places than others, and there is a wide range of evidence and of organizational scales represented across the Aegean world. In general, discussions of political organization tend to focus on palatial administration and kingship in the Mycenaean Palatial period, more localized forms of leadership in the Postpalatial period and Early Iron Age, and the development of the polis beginning in the eighth century (in which various forms of tyranny, oligarchy, aristocracy, and democracy would eventually appear). Many of these discussions, however, involve the projection or retrojection of political forms known from earlier or later textual sources across the early Greek world as a whole (*wanax, basileus,* etc.). In taking into account the diversity of *archaeological* evidence, I argue that *regionalism* should be the priority over any uniform view of early Greek society.

Most discussions of Mycenaean palatial systems focus overwhelmingly on (and extrapolate from) what we know about certain archetypes—Mycenae from the perspective of material culture and Pylos from the perspective of Linear B texts that tell us about the operation of the palace. These were relatively centralized polities with an administrative system whose activities were documented via the nonpermanent medium of unfired clay tablets (Ventris and Chadwick [1956] 1973; Shelmerdine 2008; Parkinson and Galaty 2007; Nakassis 2013a; Killen 2015). Social hierarchies can be distinguished in the archaeological record by elaborately constructed burials with wealthy grave goods, and family tombs suggest some degree of inherited status. The monumental fortifications of the period and other large-scale building projects suggest the ability to organize and control large labor forces for complex tasks. This general picture appears to be the case in most areas where we have Mycenaean palaces. However, we have little reason to believe that all Mycenaean palaces functioned in the exact same way and many reasons to believe they functioned quite differently from each other (see further in chapter 3).

Beyond the operation of the palaces themselves, secondary state formation is a significant topic of broader anthropological interest, to which the Mycenaean case can contribute (Parkinson and Galaty 2007). Explicit studies of Mycenaean state formation as such, however, are relatively rare, usually being limited to particular site-based or regional case studies, mostly in the Peloponnese (Laffineur and Niemeier 1995; Cherry and Davis 2001; Cosmopoulos 2005, 2006; Galaty and Parkinson 2007; Fitzsimons 2011; Pullen 2011b; Ruppenstein 2012; Kramer-Hajos 2016).

For the Postpalatial Bronze Age, debates revolve largely around notions of collapse and recovery, with a "revival" period somewhere in between. Other than among specialists, this period is often rendered indistinct from either the Palatial period (because it is still Mycenaean) or the Early Iron Age (because it is still part of the postcollapse "Dark Age"). Specialists who do make these distinctions have lamented that the reorganization that followed the end of the Palatial period has been a "lost opportunity" in studies of urbanism in the Aegean (Lemos et al. 2009).[4] Kramer-Hajos (2016) has recently pointed out that the sociopolitical organization of this period in fact looks quite similar to what immediately preceded the emergence of the palatial systems, at least in central Greece—complex communities in which local elites engaged in regional and interregional competition and trade. It seems to me that this world, much more than the Palatial age, is reflected in Homer's imagination of a heroic past—a time of violent conflict, loose political organization, and high levels of mobility (see also Crielaard 2006, 2011b).

A range of sociopolitical complexity also seems to have been present in the Early (Prehistoric) Iron Age. Well-connected centers with demonstrable social hierarchies, such Lefkandi, Athens, Argos, and Knossos, represent one end of the spectrum, while the vast majority of other sites seem to have operated on a much smaller scale.[5] These hierarchies are manifest more on local scales of the individual site rather than across entire regions. For example, politically coherent settlement hierarchies seem to be nonexistent. While a site hierarchy is employed in this book in order to differentiate between major settlements, minor sites, and isolated findspots representing a range of activities, there is less that we can say explicitly about, say, a single main site and subsidiaries within a particular locale. Previous treatments of sociopolitical organization tend to focus on hierarchy as manifest within an individual settlement and look also to later textual references to the *basileus* (as described by Homer and Hesiod) as a sort of "big man" or chief-like figure (Mazarakis Ainian 1997; Dickinson 2006; Crielaard 2011b; Kõiv 2016).

The picture changes considerably in the eighth century (Protohistoric Iron Age), when Greece began the transition from a world of villages to a world of towns. By 700 BCE there were probably dozens of towns with populations of over 1000 individuals, whereas in the previous period there were likely only three or four: Argos, Knossos, Athens, and Lefkandi (Morris and Knodell 2015, 348–51;

---

4. On urbanism in Aegean prehistory, see Branigan 2001; Owen and Preston 2009; Letesson and Knappett 2017. For comparative views, see Marcus and Sabloff 2008; Yoffee 2015. For a recent critique of urbanism in certain (Middle Bronze Age) contexts in the Aegean, see Cherry 2017.

5. The exemplary sites are also the best published. On Lefkandi, see Popham, Sackett, and Themelis 1980; Catling and Lemos 1990; Popham, Calligas, and Sackett 1993. On Athens, see Papadopoulos 2003; Papadopoulos and Smithson 2017. Nichoria is a well-published example of a much smaller-scale settlement: see McDonald, Coulson, and Rosser 1983. For a recent summary of archaeological and later textual evidence for political organization in the Early Iron Age, especially the question of leadership and *basileia*, or Homeric kingship, see Kõiv 2016.

see also Whitley 1991, 184–90; Mazarakis Ainian 1997). Such growth in the number and population of communities in central Greece necessitated restructuring political and settlement strategies, and it is at this point that we see the nascent development of (in some areas) early Greek poleis and (in others) regionally collective *ethne*, groups that exhibited a variety of modes of social organization (Morgan 2001, 2006; Sakellariou 2009; Papadopoulos 2016a). While standard narratives of the early polis lead us to believe that the eighth century was a sort of crucible for political development, other sources, such as the poetry of Hesiod and Homer, suggest that we are still dealing mostly with small-scale village societies, although we do see the emergence of clearer gradations in social class and wealth within some larger communities, such as Athens or Eretria. At the same time, an interregional political consciousness became more pronounced, as can be witnessed in the growth of Panhellenic and regional sanctuaries. It was not until the subsequent Archaic period, however—beginning in the seventh century rather than in the eighth—that we really see the growth of the kinds of communities and political institutions (tyranny, oligarchy, aristocracy, democracy) that have come to characterize our understandings of ancient Greek city-states (Snodgrass 1980a; Hansen and Nielsen 2004).

Early Greece in the Archaeology of Complex Societies

Greece plays a rather minor role in the comparative archaeology of complex societies. It makes occasional appearances in the archaeology of early cities and the archaeology of empire, along with approaches to interpolity relationships and state formation, but it is rarely at the forefront (though see, e.g., Renfrew and Cherry 1986; Hansen 2000; Alcock et al. 2001). Part of the reason for this is that early Greek political formations do not compare well with the "Archaic States" that are often the subject of comparative literature in anthropological archaeology (e.g., Trigger 2003; Feinman and Marcus 1998; Yoffee 2005; M. Smith 2011; Routledge 2014). Cross-cultural, anthropological discussions of state formation tend to focus on the "pristine" states of Mesopotamia, Egypt, the Indus Valley, China, Mesoamerica, and the Andes. These are large states with extensive territories that have very little in common with the polities of early Greece. Secondary state formation and the operation of nonstate complex societies are discussed much less frequently. Moreover, for all the attention that is given to state formation and collapse, there is remarkably little theoretical attention given to oscillations in sociopolitical complexity and to the question of how societies reconstitute themselves after periods of collapse or decline.[6] These themes are precisely where the Aegean is well poised to contribute to wider, comparative discussions.

---

6. There are, however, occasional examples of dynamic models, dual processual models, and evolutionary approaches in Aegean archaeology: see, e.g., Parkinson and Galaty 2007; Small 2009, 2019, drawing on Marcus 1998; Blanton et al. 1996.

This book provides a case study in the archaeology of political formations that are smaller in scale and complexity than (1) state-level societies that feature in most of the comparative literature and (2) many of the contemporary states with which Aegean societies were in contact. Indeed, it is worth questioning whether the term "state" is appropriate for any period under study, at least as compared to the other eastern Mediterranean "states" with which the Aegean world was in contact. But if these are not good analogues, what are?

Similar scales of societies and political trajectories (secondary state formation, collapse, decline, reconstitution) can be found in several other contexts across the globe, although in a variety of guises. The archaeology of "nonstate" social complexity can encompass everything from hunter-gatherers to highly complex chiefdoms (Price 1981; Earle 1997; Kirch 2010). The problems of the band-tribe-chiefdom-state models of social evolution have long been acknowledged, and I do not advocate for any kind of neoevolutionary conceptual framework here (Sahlins and Service 1960; Sahlins 1972; Fried 1975). Nevertheless, some of these terms can and do retain descriptive and explanatory utility when not viewed strictly in evolutionary terms (Earle 1987; Parkinson 2002; Fowles 2002). Other researchers have sought less loaded terminology. Ranked societies; middle-range, intermediate, or small-scale societies; transegalitarian groups; complex communities— all of these have been put forward as models and descriptors for situations in which social hierarchies, heterarchies, and complexity are present but not institutionalized or codified at a scale associated with states (Crumley 1995; Arnold 1996; Ames 2008; Porter 2013). In particular, emphasis on what societies do, rather than on what they are called, is useful in discussions of "tribal societies" or "village societies," which have existed from the Neolithic through the Modern period, often alongside more complex or urban political or settlement formations (Parkinson 2002; Bandy 2004; Bandy and Fox 2010). While the range of parlance presents certain challenges, such models can accommodate variability and dynamism in social organization. For example, the term "chiefdom" is often subject to critique because of the range of social formations it is deployed to describe (Yoffee 1993; Pauketat 2007).[7] This might be seen rather as a strength, since it can highlight the variety of strategies and material manifestations of social groups exhibiting similar behaviors, as in Earle's (1997) comparative study of Denmark, Hawaii, and Peru, or in Beck's (2003) analysis of chiefdom variability in the Mississippian communities of the southeastern United States. While I do not adopt the term "chiefdom" here in any technical sense, I do draw on several studies of societies that have been defined as chiefdoms by other scholars, precisely because of this variability.

7. Debates about the appropriateness of the term "chiefdom" and its evolutionary implications are as old as Service's original formulation and do not need to be rehearsed here (Service 1962; Sahlins 1963; Fried 1967). For more recent literature on the subject, see Earle 1987, 1997; Kirch 2010, along with critiques by Yoffee 1993; Pauketat 2007.

The archaeology of village societies is perhaps more salient for much of the early Greek landscape. Villages are typically defined as self-contained, relatively egalitarian social systems, which nevertheless have mechanisms for reaching beyond themselves. As is true of the neoevolutionary terms of band, tribe, and chiefdom, the definition is broad and can refer to a wide range of social formations (Fowles 2002; Gerstel 2020). In general, villages can be defined negatively as permanent communities that are not large enough to be urban. Territorial extents were probably not greater than they were required to be to meet local subsistence needs, and they were probably not clearly demarcated beyond the level of individual households, kin groups, and neighboring communities. In terms of sociopolitical complexity and regional integration, variation again is the rule, ranging from independent collections of a few households (the majority of cases) to more integrative modes of regional organization (in and around larger communities). Most significantly for this study, villages in the ancient Greek world are best understood through their rurality and their connections to the landscape and surrounding communities (Foxhall 2020).

Porter (2013) has proposed "complex communities" as a model for Early Iron Age societies in Jordan where complexity (1) is present, but variable across a culture area; (2) is dynamic; and (3) is not easily compared to contemporary or chronologically proximate political formations that are better known (e.g., Near Eastern states and empires). I have adopted this terminology throughout this book as a means of describing the range of societal formations witnessed in early Greece, which range across a sliding scale of being more or less hierarchical and politically complex. This terminology builds on the work of McGuire and Saitta (1996), who proposed "communal complexity" as a framework for understanding how communities oscillate between more hierarchical and more egalitarian. This terminology also acknowledges the capacity for entirely different modes of political organization to coexist simultaneously across the landscape. The appeal here is a flexible model for social complexity that can apply across a range of periods and social formations without prescribing certain sets of characteristics or teleological narratives.

Fowles (2002) has argued convincingly for a shift in comparative emphasis from types of entire societies to types of historical processes or societal trajectories. Trajectories similar to those witnessed in early Greek societies can be seen at different times in the fortress-building cultures of the Late Bronze Age Caucasus and the subsequent Urartian civilization (Smith 2003), in Mississippian chiefdoms (Blitz 2010), in maritime chiefdoms in Pacific and other contexts (Kirch 2010; Ling, Earle, and Kristiansen 2018), and in other modes of tribal organization (Parkinson 2002). Whether we call early Greek societies secondary states, chiefdoms, early complex polities, tribal societies, village societies, or complex communities is not especially important to the arguments in this book. Relative matters of scale, complexity, and development are important, however, and for this some use of analogy can be fruitful. Complex communities and village societies provide starting points, not so much as strict terminology but as a way of breaking free from restrictive narratives concerning states, palaces, or poleis. While critiques of this sort have a long history in other regions and are certainly part of scholarship on the Aegean, alternative models remain few. By thinking beyond state structures to landscape, interaction, and societal dynamics, there is an opportunity also for the Aegean to contribute to other world archaeologies, especially ones exhibiting nonlinear trajectories and a range of modes of social organization.

2

___

Articulating Landscapes
in Central Greece

*Archaeology in essence then is the discipline with the theory and practice
for the recovery of unobservable hominid behaviour patterns from indirect
traces in bad samples.*

—DAVID CLARKE, "ARCHAEOLOGY: THE LOSS OF INNOCENCE"

Archaeologists necessarily work with bad data derived from a variety of inconsistent sources. Moreover, these data are not always well suited to answering the social questions of greatest interest to our discipline. A certain amount of model building is therefore necessary to fill gaps and make connections between what we can know—the hard facts of archaeological materials—and what we can infer based on these facts. This chapter presents the baseline evidence and the models drawn on in the analysis of landscape, interaction, and complexity that forms the core of this book—that is, the archaeological remains of human activity, the question of how they are distributed across the Greek landscape, and the methods used to articulate relationships between places in geographical space. I begin with some overall characterization of the archaeological dataset compiled and parsed from a number of different types of fieldwork, reports, and publications. I next provide some contextual description of the geography and history of research for each of the regions under study. Finally, I outline the analytical framework of articulating relations between communities and within landscapes and regions—spatial approaches to modeling connectivity and territory.

THE BASELINE EVIDENCE: SITES, COMMUNITIES,
AND REGIONAL DATASETS

The dataset that forms the core of this analysis is comprised of about 400 archaeological sites, drawn from various types of archaeological survey and excavation data (map 3; see also appendix for a complete list and locations of all sites used in this study). These sites were cataloged in a database that recorded precise spatial

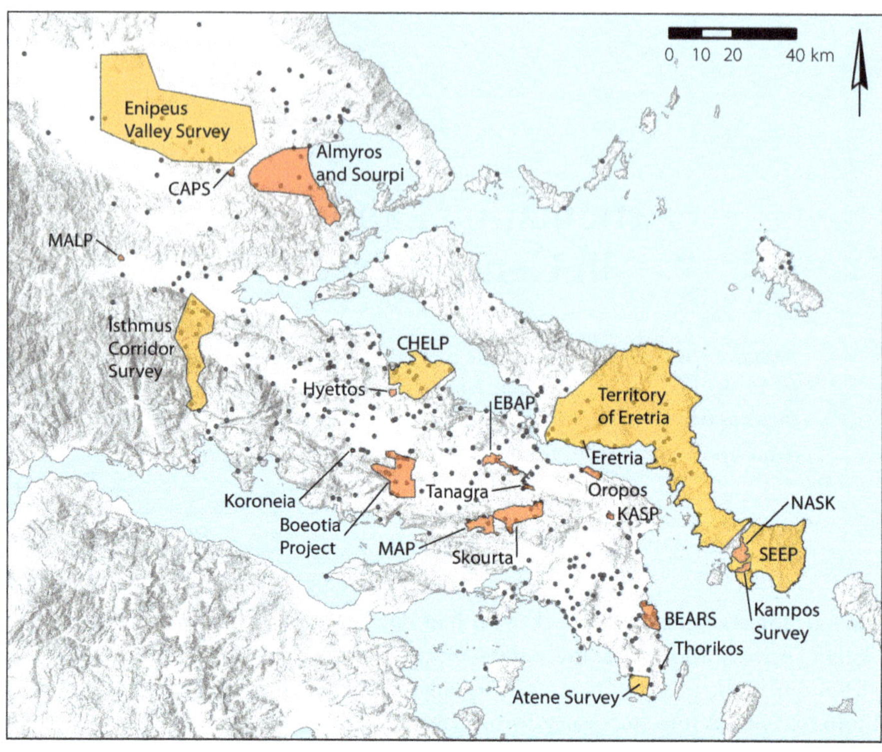

MAP 3. Archaeological surveys conducted in central Greece, with the location of archaeological sites used in the present study in the background (darker shading = intensive survey; lighter shading = extensive survey).

locations, type of site (artifact scatter, settlement, cemetery), fieldwork history, bibliography, and physical description, along with information concerning the ceramic chronology, periods represented, a site scale/hierarchy score for each period, the periods in which the site represents an independent community (a place of dwelling for a coherent social group, as opposed to a material findspot representing any other type of activity), and number of imports per period.

These sites were identified from a number of different data sources (table 3), and in any such study a certain amount of "source criticism" is necessary in order to evaluate and make compatible data collected in various different ways and for different purposes (see, e.g., Alcock 1993, 33–37; Pullen 2003; Alcock and Cherry 2004; Cunningham and Driessen 2004; Wright 2004b). As an example, Euboea illustrates the range of quality and type of archaeological data collected across a large area: Euboea is a clearly bounded island that can nonetheless be divided into multiple regions. Relevant datasets for the island include (1) gazetteers that cover all of Greece; (2) extensive surveys of the island as a whole; (3) large-scale surveys of parts of the island (for example, the territory of the polis of Eretria or the

TABLE 3 Archaeological surveys and gazetteers for the study area

Project[*]	Region	Methods	Representative publication(s)
Gazetteer of Aegean Civilization	Greece	Gazetteer/Catalog	Hope Simpson and Dickinson 1979
Mycenaean Greece	Greece	Gazetteer/Catalog	Hope Simpson 1981
The Transition Years (1200–700 BC)	Greece	Gazeteer/Catalog	Syriopoulos 1983
Prehistoric Habitation of Greece	Greece	Gazetteer/Catalog	Syriopoulos 1995
Atene Survey	Attica	Site survey/ Extensive	Lohman 1985, 1993
Thorikos Survey	Attica	Site survey	Docter and Webster, forthcoming
Bays of East Attica Regional Survey (BEARS)	Attica	Intensive	Murray et al., forthcoming
Kotroni Archaeological Survey Project (KASP)	Attica	Intensive	Andrikou et al. 2020
Skourta Plain Project	Attica/Boeotia	Intensive	Munn and Munn 1989, 1990
Oropos Survey Project	Attica/Boeotia	Intensive	Cosmopoulos 2001
Mazi Archaeological Project	Attica/Boeotia	Intensive	Knodell, Fachard, and Papangeli 2017
Topography and Population of Ancient Boeotia	Boeotia	Gazetteer/Catalog	Fossey 1988
Boeotian Landscapes	Boeotia	Gazeteer/Catalog	Farinetti 2011
Archaeological Reconnaissance of Uninvestigated Remains of Agriculture (AROURA)	Boeotia	Extensive/ Intensive	Lane et al. 2016, 2020
Cambridge/Bradford Boeotia Expedition (Boeotia Project)	Boeotia	Intensive	Bintliff and Snodgrass 1985; Bintliff, Howard, and Snodgrass 2007; Bintliff et al. 2017
Leiden Ancient Cities of Boeotia Project	Boeotia	Intensive	Bintliff et al. 2013
Eastern Boeotia Archaeological Project (EBAP)	Boeotia	Intensive	Burke, Burns, and Lupack 2009; Aravantinos et al. 2016a
Ancient Topography of Opountian Lokris	East Lokris	Gazetteer/Catalog	Fossey 1990

(Contd.)

TABLE 3 *(Continued)*

Project[*]	Region	Methods	Representative publication(s)
Mycenaean East Lokris	East Lokris	Gazeteer/Catalog	Kramer-Hajos 2008
Cornell Halai and East Lokris Project (CHELP)	East Lokris	Extensive/Intensive	Coleman et al. 1992; Kramer-Hajos and O'Neill 2008
Ancient Topography of Eastern Phokis	Phokis	Gazetteer/Catalog	Fossey 1986
Folds of Parnassos	Phokis	Gazetteer/Catalog	McInerney 1999
Great Isthmus Corridor Survey	Phokis/Phthiotis	Extensive	Kase et al. 1990
Makrakomi Archaeological Landscapes Project (MALP)	Malis/Phthiotis	Intensive	Papakonstantinou et al. 2013
Antiquities and public works in Fthiotida, 2004–2014	Malis/Phthiotis	Extensive/Rescue	Papakonstantinou 2015
Mycenaean Thessaly	Thessaly	Gazetteer/Catalog	Feuer 1983
Enipeus Valley	Thessaly	Extensive	Decourt 1990
Almiros and Sourpi Plains	Thessaly	Intensive	Reinders 2004; Stissi et al. 2015
Central Achaia Phthiotis Survey (CAPS)	Thessaly/Phthiotis	Intensive	Haagsma 2019
Euboea Survey	Euboea	Gazetteer/Catalog/Extensive	Sackett et al. 1966
Territory of Eretria	Euboea	Extensive	Fachard 2012
Eretria Survey	Euboea	Intensive	Simon 2002
Southern Euboea Exploration Project (SEEP)	Euboea	Extensive	Keller 1985; Keller and Hom 2010; Cullen et al. 2013; Wickens et al. 2018
Kampos Survey	Euboea	Intensive	Tankosic and Chidiroglou 2010
Norwegian Archaeological Survey of the Karystia	Euboea	Intensive	Tankosic et al., forthcoming

[*] In addition to the projects and gazetteers listed here I have made extensive use of the following databases: the Mycenaean Atlas Project (http://helladic.info); the Aristeia project's online database of Early Iron Age and Archaic sites (http://aristeia.ha.uth.gr/); and a database of LBA and EIA sites in Greece and Crete compiled by Murray (unpublished, but now integrated in the Mycenaean Atlas Project and discussed in detail in Murray 2013, 2017).

Karystia); (4) intensive surveys of particular microregions, such as the Kampos Plain within the Karystia; (5) large-scale foreign research excavations of major sites (for example, at Eretria, Lefkandi, or Plakari); and (6) a wide range of salvage excavations conducted by the Greek Archaeological Service.[1] Similar hodgepodges of data with a diversity of resolution, methods of collection, and level of publication can be observed for most regions in Greece.[2]

Taken as a whole, such a dataset is quite different from the carefully collected microregional datasets produced by modern intensive survey projects. The fact of the matter, however, is that the haphazard concatenation of evidence from travelers' accounts, extensive explorations, intensive surveys, rescue excavations, and research excavations is simply what we have for the vast majority of the archaeological landscape. If we are going to address research questions of relevance beyond the individual field project, we need to find ways to put often unwieldy bodies of evidence in dialogue with each other—and not just from large, well-excavated sites or systematic intensive surveys.

Sites

In this study I take the *site* as the common denominator across the archaeological landscape. While many modern surveys consider the individual artifact the basic unit of analysis, this approach is impractical if not impossible when conducting a comparative study over multiple regions, involving information from dozens of projects. Sites are defined here as findspots or groups of findspots at which a demonstrable presence from at least one of the periods in question has been identified. In combing through the datasets outlined above, each site was classified first as one of five types of archaeological assemblage: (1) artifacts (found as surface scatters or in excavations not associated with other remains); (2) isolated tombs; (3) cemeteries (more than one tomb or remains estimated to be from more than one tomb); (4) settlements (defined by the presence of architectural remains for habitation or other permanent activity); and (5) sites that combine many of the

1. For relevant gazetteers and surveys, see table 3. Synthetic studies have focused on particular periods or topics, such as prehistory (Sackett et al. 1966), medieval towers (Lock 1986, 1996), or the territory of Eretria (Fachard 2012). The longest running foreign excavations in Euboea are at Eretria, by the Swiss School of Archaeology in Greece (ESAG) (see annual reports in *Antike Kunst* and the 25-volume *Eretria* publication series) and by the British School of Archaeology in Greece (BSA) at Lefkandi (*Lefkandi* Vols. I–IV). A Dutch team has more recently started an excavation project at Plakari (Crielaard et al. 2015). A recent conference on the archaeology of the island as a whole has both filled gaps and revealed new ones, especially concerning the northern part of the island; see Tankosić, Mavridis, and Kosma 2017. The work of the Greek Archaeological Service is published almost exclusively in Greek in *Archaiologikon Deltion*, *Athens Annals of Archaeology*, and in various national and regional conference proceedings (e.g., Mazarakis Ainian 2006, 2009, 2012c, 2016, 2020).

2. Recent handbooks (Lemos and Kotsonas 2020; Middleton 2020) provide syntheses for several of the individual regions dealt with in this book: Athens and Attica (Alexandridou 2020; Osborne 2020); Boeotia (Aravantinos 2020; Maggidis 2020); Euboea (Lemos 2020); East Lokris and Phokis (Livieratou 2020); and Thessaly (Karouzou 2020). *An Inventory of Archaic and Classical Poleis* (Hansen and Nielsen 2004) is also an invaluable resource for the political geography of later periods.

TABLE 4 Types of sites by period

Type of site	Early Mycenaean	Palatial BA	Postpalatial BA	Prehistoric IA	Protohistoric IA	Total
Artifacts	24	78	26	34	63	132
Isolated tomb	2	15	8	6	2	20
Cemetery	21	63	39	39	46	106
Settlement	26	51	30	25	25	62
Multicomponent	41	69	49	48	67	81
Total Sites	114	276	152	152	203	401*

*Note that this number represents the sum of totals on the Y-axis but not the X-axis. On the X-axis a single site may date to multiple periods, but on the Y-axis each site is given only a single designation for the type of remains present. See the appendix for a list of sites, with type indicated and periods represented.

above components or have some other special function (such as a sanctuary or ritual site) (table 4).

There have been periodic efforts to integrate site information across all of Greece for all or parts of the period in question. For the Bronze Age, Hope Simpson and Dickinson's *Gazetteer* (1979) is particularly relevant, even if now quite dated (see also Hope Simpson 1981). For all of prehistory up to the Geometric period, Syriopoulos (1995) has mapped and characterized all archaeological sites in Greece, following an earlier catalogue on the "transition years" (1200–700 BCE) (Syriopoulos 1983). On central Greece in the Early Mycenaean period, Phialon (2011) is also an essential resource. Electronic databases are the more modern, accessible, and adaptable versions of gazetteers. For the Bronze Age, Consoli's Mycenaean Atlas Project is a crucial resource for sites in Greece and elsewhere in the Aegean (www.helladic.info). For the Early Iron Age, the Aristeia project has catalogued sites from all over the Greek world (Mazarakis Ainian, Alexandridou, and Charalambidou 2017; http://aristeia.ha.uth.gr). Another recent dataset relevant to this study was compiled by Murray, who mapped and tabulated site counts for all of mainland Greece and Crete (table 5; Murray 2013, 2017, 137–42).[3] Across all these databases, there are some significant differences in methods of site definition, quantification, and detail of coverage, which result in a different shape of the data overall. One important aspect of all of these datasets is the number of sites that come from rescue excavations in the large urban centers of Athens, Thebes, Lamia, and Volos. While these are typically counted as individual sites, I counted them as *findspots* within a single larger site that encompasses several findspots (see figure 1). For example, downtown Athens contains over 160 sites in the Aristeia database, while in my reckoning it is only counted as one, albeit

3. This database was shared with me and has now been integrated into the Mycenaean Atlas Project, accessed December 4, 2020, http://www.helladic.info. See Murray 2013 for an earlier list and a tabulation of sites.

TABLE 5 Numbers and types of sites recorded by Murray (2017, 141, table 3.12) for the Greek mainland and Crete

Type of site	LH IIIB	LH IIIC	Protogeometric	Geometric
Artifacts	610	318	260	450
Cemetery	450	205	245	332
Settlement	306	132	95	166
Total sites	1366	655	600	948

one of great significance. Whether this is the "right" approach to site definition is debatable, and one might also imagine a dataset with well over 1,000 sites for the large study area delimited here. One of these approaches is not more accurate than the other; they simply employ different methods of site definition, which result in different quantifications. The approach to site definition adopted here is meant to filter through a certain amount of noise and inflation that happens in highly populated areas that have received more attention from archaeologists (especially in the form of rescue excavations), in order to come up with a more balanced picture of settlement across the central Greek landscape. Scalar differences made apparent through extensive archaeological work in certain areas are nevertheless significant, and they are reflected in the way that a site scale or hierarchy score is ascribed to each site.

Settlement Patterns and Hierarchies

Settlement pattern analysis often includes some designation of hierarchy, or at least differentiation in scale (see, e.g., Willey 1953; Wright 1977; Bintliff 1997; Driessen 2001; Bevan and Conolly 2006; Bevan and Wilson 2013). While strict notions of hierarchy have become somewhat unfashionable, they remain useful designations in establishing a baseline pattern, especially with large datasets. It is important to recognize, however, the multiplicity of hierarchical relationships in the landscape, and to consider heterarchy, cooperation, and collective action alongside these relationships (Crumley 1995; DeMarrais and Earle 2017).

In this study of settlement patterns, all sites are classified based on *scale*—that is, where they fall in a relative hierarchy, which also recognizes the likely presence of heterarchical (or alternatively, simply nonhierarchical) relationships. Here, scale is determined by the type and extent of archaeological remains at a given site, with four general levels (table 6): (1) findspots of artifacts or isolated tombs that demonstrate little more than human presence dating to a particular period; (2) minor sites, which can be represented by evidence of any type, including substantial sherd scatters and limited architectural or cemetery remains; (3) major sites, which are distinguished from minor sites based on factors such as size, quantity of archaeological remains, evidence for social stratification, fortification and other major building projects, level of connectivity (as evidenced by regional or

TABLE 6 Numbers of sites and communities occupied during each period, with settlement hierarchy indicated

Level in Settlement Hierarchy	Characteristics of archaeological evidence	Palatial BA	Postpalatial BA	Prehistoric IA	Protohistoric IA
1	Findspot of a few artifacts or isolated tomb	58 (21%[*])	29 (19%)	38 (25%)	49 (24%)
2	Limited settlement or cemetery site	157 (57%)	95 (63%)	86 (57%)	113 (55%)
3	Extensive settlement and/or cemetery site, major buildings, evidence for social stratification, regional prominence	55 (20%)	26 (17%)	24 (16%)	35 (17%)
4	Site with monumental building, interregional preeminence in political, ritual, or economic activities	6 (2%)	3 (2%)	3 (2%)	6 (3%)
Total sites		276	152	152	203
Total communities (% of sites)		190 (69%)	114 (76%)	110 (72%)	136 (67%)

[*]Percentages indicate the percentage of the total number of sites for that period.

interregional imports, and location within the wider settlement network), or reference in the documentary record; (4) exceptional sites, such as palaces, major centers, or regional sanctuaries.

These distinctions are often arbitrary, especially since many similarly sized sizes have received different levels of archaeological attention. While both Psachna in Euboea and Eleon in Boeotia appear to be major sites during the Palatial Bronze Age based on the surface record, only the latter has been confirmed as such by systematic excavation (Burke et al. 2020). Many more sites are known only through surface survey or limited excavation, though it would be a mistake to exclude them from the wider analysis. It is therefore often necessary to offer a best estimate in determining a hierarchy score, especially when dealing with sites known only from surface remains.

This type of ranking is *not* intended to indicate a definite political hierarchy. For example, level 3 sites should not be understood to control or dominate level 2 sites, although in some cases such a relationship may be present. Site ranking is provided rather to signal differences in scale and intensity of occupation in the landscape. More specific political hierarchies can be elucidated in other ways, depending on the organization of the political landscape for the period in question.

Unlike some studies of settlement patterns, this one does not engage in systematic quantifications involving site size and population estimates, at least not across the dataset as a whole. This is simply because these things cannot be clearly documented or accurately modeled for the majority of the early Greek landscape, where sites have been defined and measured in a variety of ways that are rarely consistent.[4] Rather, I draw comparative data from the more consistently discernable (though admittedly loosely defined) scale of the archaeological record itself, as represented by sites. I see this as a preferable alternative to "guestimates" regarding site-size averages and population data that are largely impossible to define across much of the dataset.

By focusing on archaeological sites, I document and model scalar differences in archaeological remains in relative terms, and in a way that accounts for ambiguity and diversity across the dataset as a whole. By keeping this system consistent within this study, and examining change over time, we can go beyond simple dots on a map to describe a settlement pattern that includes both palatial constructions and nondescript activity zones, represented by archaeological remains ranging from monumental fortifications to small scatters of a few pot sherds. From there we can move to questions of social organization as represented by the (often uneven) material record of individual sites and across the landscape as a whole.

Communities

I have also evaluated sites based on their relationship to other nearby sites/findspots in order to assess whether and when a site represents an independent *community*. Community has proven a useful framework for discussing social groups in a variety of archaeological contexts, most notably in Mesoamerica (Canuto and Yaeger 2000), the Middle East (Porter 2013), and both sides of the Mediterranean (Steidl 2020). Here I define communities as coherent social groups whose members, by virtue of proximity, have had habitual interactions with one another in a

---

4. The archaeological record of early Greece as a whole is particularly ill-suited to systematic estimates of site size and population, since most sites are known only through fragmentary surface remains or limited excavations. Our ability to estimate the extent of a site also varies depending on the system of site definition and measurement employed by an individual researcher or project. There also is not a standard or reliable formula in Mediterranean archaeology to translate site size or living surface into number of households or individuals living at a site. Population estimates involve even more variables and are often dependent on even more inconsistent data (see, e.g., Chamberlain 2006; Bintliff 2020, 24). Estimates based on the burial record may return different results from those based on habitation zones, and the textual record (when it exists) may suggest something different entirely. Urban and rural areas will also have different population densities, and these, too, will vary over time. This does not mean that discussions of demography are not worth having; they certainly are, and there are several good examples, based on a number of factors: site numbers, modeled site sizes, regional carrying capacity, level of urbanization, aggregated radiocarbon dates, and so on (for early Greece, see, e.g., Bintliff 1977b, 2012, 2020; Murray 2017, 211–46; Weiberg et al. 2019; Vidal-Cordasco and Nuevo-López 2021).

way that makes them distinct from other social groups; these may or may not be part of a larger sociopolitical formation (see figure 1).

In archaeological terms, *community* refers to the material signature of a site where one or several kin groups were dwelling in physical proximity to one another and interacting with the surrounding landscape and other such places of dwelling. We can assume a shared identity based on habitual interactions within a particular zone of interconnected places. In this study, in the case of several findspots or sites whose relationship can be demonstrated or inferred by proximity or some other means, one is selected to be representative of the community as a whole. For example, let us consider Late Bronze Age Tanagra, a settlement with a number of cemeteries surrounding it. While there are numerous sites (a settlement site with architectural remains, some cemeteries, some isolated tombs, several clusters of artifacts), they most likely represent a single, relatively coherent community. A similar approach was used in Wright's (2004b, 119) study of the northeastern Peloponnese, which also integrated site information from multiple sources in order to avoid "double counting" settlements and their cemeteries. So, while all individual sites are mapped, only one in the group would be designated as representative of the collective community. This distinction takes an interpretative step beyond site distributions in order to make better sense of human social groups and relations between them, as interactions between communities are modeled using nearest-neighbor analyses (see further below). At the same time, connectivity models between sites signal pathways between the locations of archaeological remains (which still represent important loci of human activity). Sites and communities thus remain equally important—but qualitatively different—designations of physical archaeological remains (sites) representative of hubs of human social activity (communities).

Deciding what constitutes a community is naturally a subjective process given the unequal nature of the dataset. In the context of this study, this decision involved going through the dataset as a whole and looking at each site in context. Based on its scale, the type of remains present, and its location in relation to other sites, it was decided whether and in what periods a site represented a community. For example, Larymna is clearly a significant community in the Late Bronze Age owing to the architectural remains and the widespread artifactual finds dated to LH IIIB. The Postpalatial period, however, is represented only by a few sherds, which is enough to put it on the map as a site but probably does not justify calling it a community, by which I mean a discreet place of habitation for a coherent social group.

Diachronic Patterns and Regional Trends

Diachronic trends and patterns in the numbers and types of sites and communities are naturally telling, and some preliminary observations are worth highlighting here (see also table 4). The first is that the Mycenaean Palatial period is an anomaly in the history of the settlement of central Greece. With 276 sites of that period, it represents a massive expansion of material evidence from the preceding Early Mycenaean period, with 108 sites, or 154 if one also counts sites that are ambiguously reported as "Mycenaean." (The reasoning here is that LH III Palatial period pottery is often easier to distinguish, so Mycenaean pottery of uncertain date is likely to be earlier.) This latter number is generally consistent with the number of sites in the Postpalatial period (152) and in the Prehistoric Iron Age (152). A significant period of growth is observed in the Protohistoric Iron Age (203 sites), but this is still a far cry from the Mycenaean Palatial boom. Second, the numbers of sites that represent individual communities are lower in the Palatial Bronze Age and Protohistoric Iron Age than in the Postpalatial Bronze Age and Prehistoric Iron Age (see table 6). This difference is attributable to the number of sites represented only by artifacts or cemetery remains that are found in close proximity to one another, usually in the course of rescue excavations. This may also have something to do with the greater recognizability of Mycenaean Palatial and Late Geometric pottery.

The basic pattern outlined above for central Greece follows a general trend that is similar to the rest of Greece in terms of the rise and fall in site numbers, but it does so on a significantly less dramatic scale. That is to say, the percentage increases and decreases are much higher for Greece as a whole than for central Greece. In tabulations for Greece as a whole (see table 5), the number of sites is cut in half, from the Palatial to the Postpalatial Bronze Age. This is followed by a modest drop in the Early Iron Age and a roughly 50 percent increase in the Geometric period. While these variations follow the general trend seen in central Greece, the *degree* of change is quite different. This discrepancy indicates a need to break from global discussions of the Greek world during this transitional period. Significant variation can be detected, for example, between central Greece, the Peloponnese, Crete, and the Aegean islands. Moreover, regional patterns within central Greece also reveal major departures from the overall trends (figure 2). While Attica and Boeotia show dramatic variation over the periods in question, Euboea, Phokis, Malis, and East Lokris remain fairly steady in their site numbers; Thessaly is somewhere in between. The pattern for Greece as a whole is most closely approximated by the case of Boeotia, but this overall trend simply does not obtain when the dataset is broken down by region.

THE ARCHAEOLOGICAL LANDSCAPES
OF CENTRAL GREECE

Central Greece has been defined in a variety of ways. On the one hand, there is the modern administrative district of Sterea Ellada, including the subregions of Boeotia, Euboea, Phokis, Phthiotis, and Evritania. When defined geographically, it includes the regions above, as well as Attica and Aetolia-Acarnania in western Greece; in this way central Greece is set apart from the Peloponnese, the Aegean

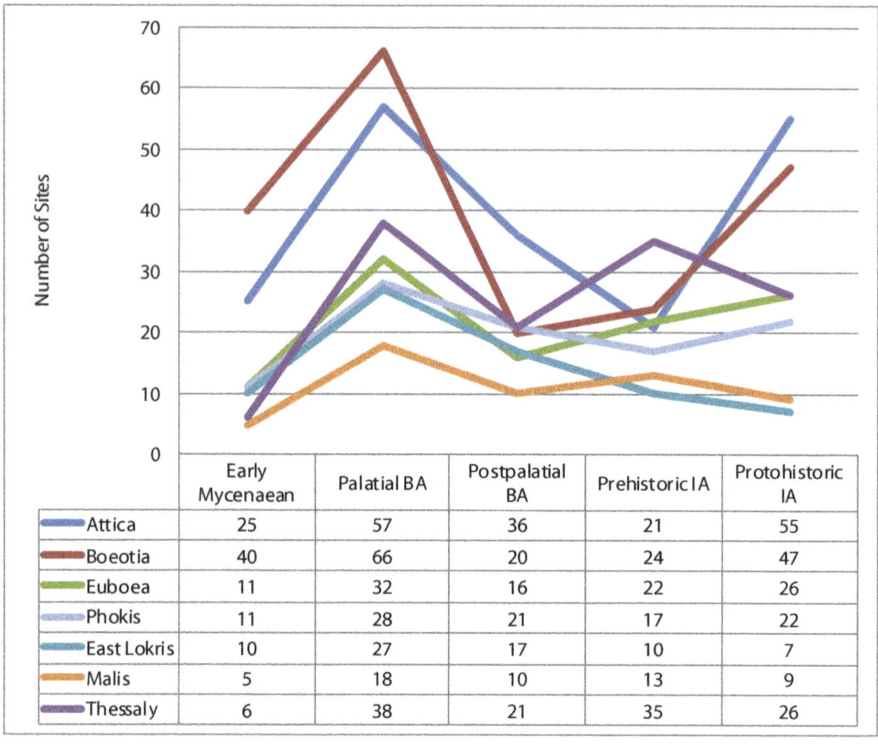

	Early Mycenaean	Palatial BA	Postpalatial BA	Prehistoric IA	Protohistoric IA
Attica	25	57	36	21	55
Boeotia	40	66	20	24	47
Euboea	11	32	16	22	26
Phokis	11	28	21	17	22
East Lokris	10	27	17	10	7
Malis	5	18	10	13	9
Thessaly	6	38	21	35	26

FIGURE 2. Line graph and table of number of sites by period, by region, in central Greece (see also appendix for site names, regions, and periods).

islands, and northern Greece. These zones are further connected by two key conduits that facilitate connectivity across the macroregion as a whole. On the eastern side of the study area, the Euboean Gulf provides a maritime axis through which every region in this study is connected except for Phokis (Knodell 2013, 2017). On the western side of the study area the Great Isthmus Corridor Route plays a similar role, connecting the Euboean and Corinthian Gulfs, along with southern, central, and northern Greece (Kase et al. 1991).

In the textual record, central Greece first appears in Homer's Catalog of Ships (*Iliad* 2.303), where Aulis is named as the mustering point for the Greek army bound for Troy. Homer proceeds to make his way roughly clockwise through the regions considered in this book (Jasnow, Evans, and Clay 2018). He starts with the towns of eastern Boeotia, then moves on to western Boeotia and Phokis, before returning to East Lokris on the coast. Shifting to Euboea, whose inhabitants are the Abantes, Homer describes the entire island as a coherent geographical unit, with settlements listed from north to south (*Iliad* 2.536–45). From Karystos, Homer crosses over into Attica and records the Athenian contribution, mentioning no other places in Attica except Salamis (2.546–58). Only after mentioning

Athens does Homer move to the contingents from the Peloponnese that played the leading role in his narrative. After these he comes to Malis/Phthiotis and Thessaly (2.681–715).

The catalogue thus provides information about regional designations and the polities within them that would be maintained in similar form throughout the Classical period and, in some cases, until the present day (see also Hope Simpson and Lazenby 1970; Visser 1997; on polities of Archaic and Classical times, see Hansen and Nielsen 2004). So, while political territories changed over time, the geographical regions in which they were embedded were considered coherent landscapes—in this case Boeotia (divided into east and west), Phokis, Lokris, Euboea, and Attica, with Malis and Thessaly being somewhat apart. Given this resilience and the basis of these groupings in physical geography and relational space, it seems likely that these groupings would have obtained in earlier periods as well, at least in some form. The regions included here also correspond with the distribution of Mycenaean material culture on the mainland north of the Peloponnese and on Euboea (see map 2). In this way, the material and textual reasons for lumping these regions together also bracket the two ends of the chronological spectrum treated in this book. Following Homer, I begin with Boeotia and move roughly clockwise around the study area to summarize the geographical features, the connective routes, and (briefly) the history of research for each region.

Boeotia

The borders of Boeotia are clearly defined by Mounts Kithairon and Parnes to the south and Mount Chlomon (the southeastern end of the Kallidromon range) in the north (map 4). The area between contains a valley system with plains much larger than those found elsewhere in central Greece, with the exception of Thessaly. The principal geographical features of Boeotia are the two large, fertile, agricultural plains within and around which archaeological evidence for settlement is concentrated. These plains are dominated by the sites of Thebes and Orchomenos, although several other, independent communities flourished in various periods (Farinetti 2011).

From the west, one can enter Boeotia from the Corinthian Gulf just north of Mount Kithairon, at Livadostro Bay and the site of Kreusis. Heurtley (1925) observed remains of a road along this route, which he thought were from a Mycenaean road toward Thebes. A land route then runs east-northeast along the north edge of Kithairon, past Eutresis, to Thebes, located roughly equidistant from the Euboean and Corinthian Gulfs. From Thebes, there are two principal paths one can take east to the Euboean Gulf, both of which begin in the direction of Eleon, before splitting there to go northeast toward Aulis and east-southeast toward Tanagra and the coastal sites of Plaka Dilesi and Skala Oropou (Oropos). Another path from Thebes to the Euboean Gulf leads north, then northeast and is funneled into the gulf at the location of Anthedon.

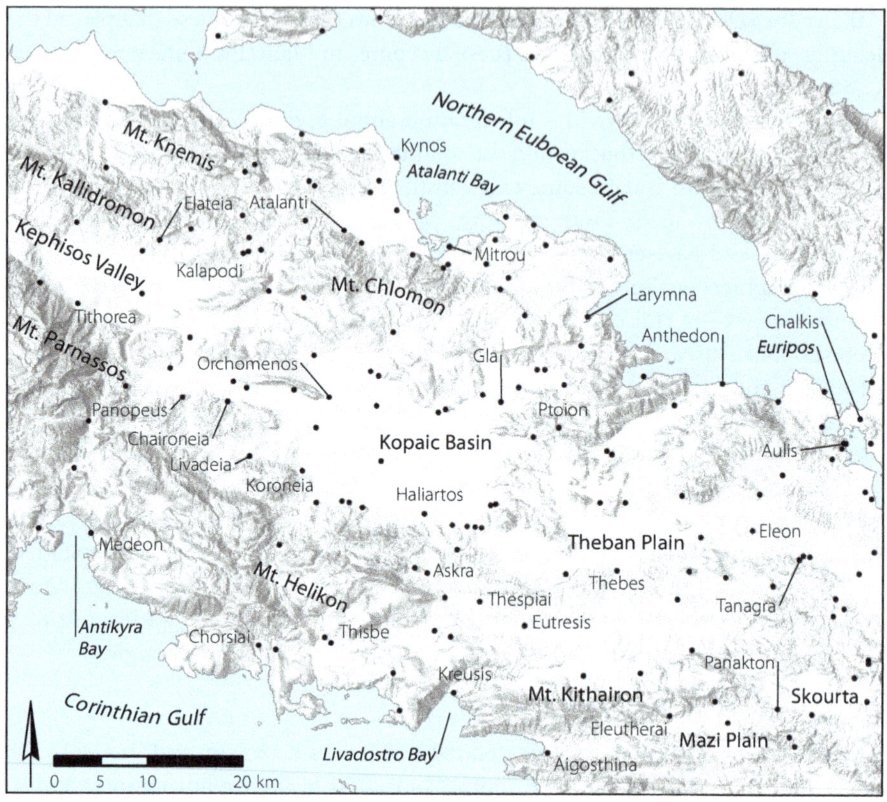

MAP 4. Topography and sites of Boeotia and East Lokris, with major sites and features labeled.

In the northern part of Boeotia, in the domain of Orchomenos, the Kopaic Basin is the major feature, the nature of which changed drastically in the span of time dealt with in this study. While this is naturally an area that fluctuates between lacustrine and marshy conditions, it was drained in the Mycenaean Palatial period (LH III A2/B1, ca. 1300 BCE), reclaiming an area of approximately 300 square kilometers for agricultural purposes through a system of dikes and canals (Knauss, Heinrich, and Kalcyck 1984; Knauss 1987; Iakovidis 2001; Lane et al. 2020). The implications of these massive landscape interventions are several but the interventions themselves were short lived, disappearing with the end of the Palatial era (see further in chapter 3). Like Thebes, Orchomenos is approximately equidistant from the Euboean and Corinthian Gulfs. To reach the Corinthian Gulf, the most direct route is to go either west toward Delphi, or south to Chorsiai. For the Euboean Gulf, one can either (1) follow the north side of the Kopaic Basin to Gla and then Larymna, (2) head east-northeast toward the eastern end of the plain of Atalanti, or (3) go north, past Kalapodi, to enter the plain of Atalanti on its western edge and arrive at the gulf from there. The final major route from Orchomenos leads northwest, following the course of the Kephisos River, along the southern edge of Mount Kallidromon, through Phokis and beyond. A western track through Phokis takes one to Delphi via Livadeia and eventually to the harbor at Itea, which is on the Corinthian Gulf.

Until now, Boeotia has been the subject of more rigorous study than other areas in central Greece. A long history of regional research has involved topographic study (Fossey 1988), as well as a long line of intensive survey projects, including the longest running regional survey in Greece, the Boeotia Project, which has existed in several iterations since the 1970s (Bintliff and Snodgrass 1985; Bintliff, Howard, and Snodgrass 2007; Bintliff et al. 2017). Other modern surveys include the Eastern Boeotia Archaeological Project (Burke, Burns, and Lupack 2009; Aravantinos et al. 2016a) and several projects along the southern border with Attica on the Skourta Plain, the Mazi Plain, and in the vicinity of Oropos (Munn and Munn 1989, 1990; Cosmopoulos 2001; Fachard, Knodell, and Banou 2015; Knodell, Fachard, and Papangeli 2016, 2017; Papangeli, Fachard, and Knodell 2018). In addition to the studies of settlement, there is a long tradition of research on land routes and archaeological evidence for roads in Boeotia (Heurtly 1925; Fossey 1988, 157–63; Hope Simpson and Hagel 2006, 163–64). A recent synthetic regional study (Farinetti 2011) has brought together diachronic evidence of settlement from the entire region and mapped the archaeologically testified or topographically likely routes that traverse Boeotia through a combination of GIS analysis and the evaluation of archaeological data across the region as a whole.

Phokis

Phokis is defined by two mountain ranges (map 5). The Kallidromon range forms the northeast border of Phokis and eventually runs into Boeotia. The second is the southern end of the Pindos range. Mount Parnassos dominates the landscape of the region and separates it into two parts. The northern part, which runs northwest-southeast, is defined by the Kephisos valley, with the river flowing into Boeotia near Chaironeia. The valley provided fertile agricultural land for several ancient polities and was one of the two principal land routes that connected Phokis and Boeotia to East Lokris and, beyond that, to Malis and Thessaly. The northern boundaries of the region therefore occupy a crucial dividing point between northern and southern Greece, most notably at the celebrated pass at Thermopylai. The southern part of the region is characterized by mountainous terrain that gives way abruptly to the Corinthian Gulf. From the bay of Itea to Amphissa, however, there is a well-watered plain of long-term significance. The bay of Itea, the port of Delphi, marked an important outlet to the sea on the west side of the region, with Antikyra Bay and the important site of Medeon on the east.

Historically, Phokis has played a vital role in the sociopolitical dynamics of the study region as a whole, having been linked to the affairs of Boeotia, East Lokris, and beyond (McInerney 1999). In addition to the Kephisos valley, which provided

MAP 5. Topography and sites of Phokis and Malis, with major sites and features labeled.

a natural extension north from Boeotia, the two bays of Itea and Antikyra provided outlets to the Corinthian Gulf, opening up to the west. For the periods under study here in particular, these zones were both locations of important Mycenaean coastal sites, and in the Early Iron Age Delphi was already becoming a major interregional sanctuary. On the northeast side of Phokis, Tithorea and Elateia were important settlements in the upper Kephisos valley. Kalapodi was a regional sanctuary of equal (and in some periods greater) significance to Delphi during the Late Bronze Age and Early Iron Age, occupying a confluence of east-west routes between East Lokris and Phokis (and the Euboean and Corinthian Gulfs) and north-south routes between Malis and Boeotia (Felsch 1996, 2007; Niemeier 2016). The town of Exarchos (associated with ancient Hyampolis) is located in a small valley connecting Kalapodi and Orchomenos, providing a further point of linkage between landscapes.

The centrality of Phokis—both geographically and historically—as a hub for ritual and commercial activity has long made it of interest to topographers and archaeologists (Oldfather 1916; Fossey 1986; Kase et al. 1991; McInerney 1999; Livieratou 2020). Regional survey in the area has been more limited. An extensive survey was carried out along the Great Isthmus Corridor Route; this also included a discussion of connections to the Spercheios River valley to the north (Kase et al. 1991). A variety of excavation work has also been carried out in the bay of Kirra, an outgrowth of the long-standing interests of the French School at Delphi (e.g., Dor et al. 1960; Zurbach et al. 2012–13). The bay of Antikyra, too, has seen important excavation work at Medeon (Vatin 1969; Pelon 1976, 238–39; Livieratou 2012, 2015; Sideris 2014); slightly inland from here, recent excavations at Kastrouli, near Desfina, suggest there is even more to the picture of settlement in this area than had been previously thought (Sideris and Liritzis 2018). In northern Phokis, work at the many significant sites in the upper Kephisos valley has been carried out by the Austrian Archaeological Institute at Athens, particularly at Elateia (e.g., Deger-Jalkotzy 2009) and in various other places by the Greek Archaeological Service (e.g., Dakoronia 2009).

East Lokris

East Lokris is a relatively narrow strip of land between the Kallidromon mountain range and the Euboean Gulf (see map 4). It is traditionally divided into two parts: Epiknemidian Lokris (the landscape of which is dominated by Mount Knemis) and Opountian Lokris (after the ancient city of Opous) (Dakoronia 1991). Both are located on the shores of the northwestern part of the Euboean Gulf and are often referred to together as East Lokris, a region geographically distinct from Ozalian Lokris, which is located on the Corinthian Gulf, on the opposite side of Phokis. The most central feature for settlement in East Lokris is the bay of Atalanti and the attached agricultural plain. Settlement evidence clusters in a triangle between the important sites of Atalanti (inland), Kynos (on the northwest side of the bay), and Mitrou (on the southeast side).

Topography has long been a concern in East Lokris (Fossey 1990; Pascual and Papakonstantinou 2013). In the late twentieth century, an archaeological survey of the region grew out of work at ancient Halai, with a more specific focus at Mitrou (Coleman et al. 1992; Kramer-Hajos and O'Niel 2008). This work was followed by long-term research excavations by the American School of Classical Studies at Mitrou, a site of particular importance for the transition from the Bronze Age to the Iron Age (van de Moortel and Zahou 2011, 2012; see also Tsokas et al. 2012; Vitale 2011; Lis 2017). The vast majority of the archaeological work in the wider area has been carried out in the form of research and rescue excavations by the Greek Archaeological Service, especially under the direction of Dakoronia (Dakoronia 2009; Papakonstantinou, Kritzas, and Touratsoglou 2018). For the region as a whole, Kramer-Hajos (2008, 18–34) provides a synthesis of evidence from the

Mycenaean period, as well as information about the geology, topography, climate, vegetation, and agriculture of the area (see also Livieratou 2020). Access to the Euboean Gulf is mediated through paths that work their way around and through the Kallidromon range, Mount Knemis, and Mount Chlomon. As is the case with Phokis, Kalapodi is a location of particular significance on the pass that connects the upper Kephisos valley running through Phokis and Boeotia to Lokris. This is the principal land route into Lokris from the south and west, whereas from the south or east one can skirt the slopes of Mount Chlomon to enter the plain of Atalanti on the east side, near Mitrou and Halai. To move northwest from Lokris, the easiest route is to follow the seaside edge of Mount Knemis up the coast to the Malian Gulf, passing Thermopylai to enter the coastal plain of the Malian Gulf. A recent, multidisciplinary study of the history and topography of Epiknemidian Lokris highlights the particular combination of mountains and sea that characterizes this microregion, as well as its clear relationships with the surrounding landscapes (Pascual 2009; Pascual and Papakonstantinou 2013).

Malis

Malis forms the heart of the modern prefecture of Phthiotis, which extends from southern Magnesia and the regional unit of Larissa in the north to Phokis and Boeotia in the south, and from the Malian Gulf in the east to Evritania in the west (see map 5). Phthiotis thus includes East Lokris and the upper Kephisos valley. The ancient region of Malis is the zone surrounding the Malian Gulf and Spercheios valley. The region demarcated in this study also includes (depending on fuzzy historical boundaries) areas associated with the names Doris, Ainianaia, Oitaia, Dolopia, and Phthia (see Decourt, Nielsen, and Helly 2004). For our purposes, the Spercheios valley is the central feature, and the region is bordered by Phokis and East Lokris to the south and Thessaly to the north. The natural features forming these boundaries are Mounts Oita and Kallidromon in the south and the Othrys range in the north.

The most comprehensive regional study of this area remains Béquignon's (1937) work on the Spercheios valley. Since then, survey work has been rather limited, although the Phokis-Doris expedition, focused on the Great Isthmus Corridor Route (Kase et al. 1991), included parts of this zone, most notably a summary of the Bronze Age and Early Iron Age evidence for settlement in the Spercheios valley (Dakoronia 1991). More recently, intensive survey work has been carried out in the western end of the valley by the Makrakomi Archaeological Landscapes Project (Papakonstantinou et al. 2013). The vast majority of our archaeological knowledge of the area comes from the numerous rescue excavations carried out by the Greek Archaeological Service (see, e.g., Dakoronia 1994, 1999; Karantzali 2013; Papakonstantinou 2009, 2015; Papakonstantinou et al. 2016).

The landscape of Malis and areas to the north are delimited quite starkly from regions farther south. The sheer northern face of Mount Oita forms an imposing

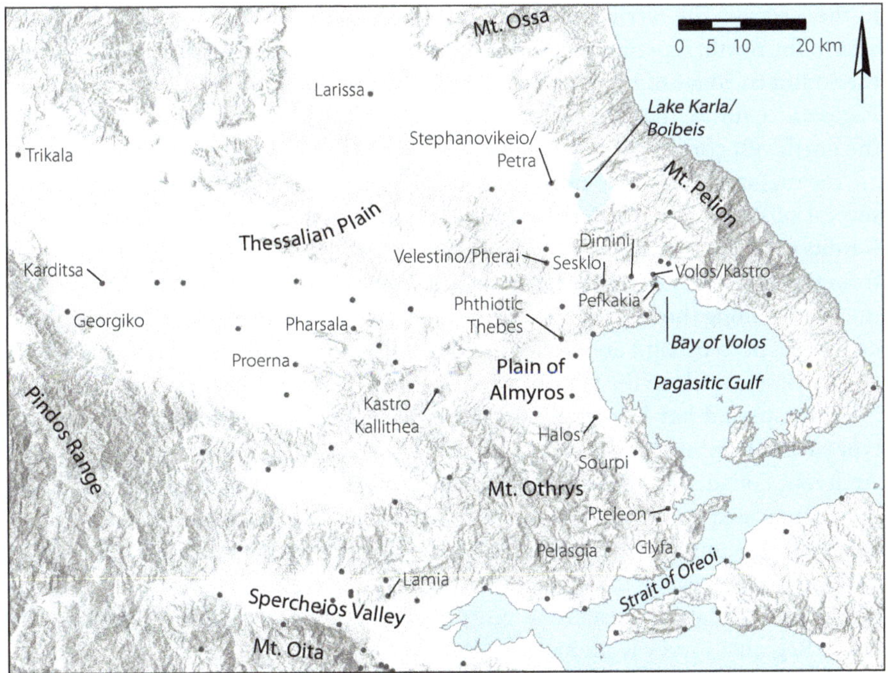

MAP 6. Topography and sites of Thessaly, with major sites and features labeled.

barrier when viewed from the Spercheios valley, and the difficulties of moving south from there by land are well documented in Herodotus's account of the Persian invasion of Xerxes and the strategic significance of Thermopylai, on the east side, and of the difficult-to-find Anopaia pass (see, e.g., Herodotus 7.215–17; Pritchett 1982; Rapp 2013; Rop 2019). Such narrow passes, of which there are few, were therefore of paramount importance and have had long-term influence in the history of settlement for the region. To the north, crossing Mount Othrys, there are more options to arrive in southern Thessaly and the historical region of Phthia.

Thessaly

The southern part of Thessaly (south of Larissa and southeast of Trikala) is the northern limit of the study area (map 6). North of the mountain passes connecting Thessaly to Malis, the expansive Thessalian Plain offers ample opportunity for agriculture and movement (Decourt 1990; Helly 1999). For access from the south, Mount Othrys is a major obstacle for travelers, generally forcing them west to the passes noted above to enter Thessaly near Proerna and Pharsala, or along the coast of the Euboean Gulf, between the mountain and the strait of Oreoi, to enter the plain of Almyros along the west side of the Pagasetic Gulf. The bay of Volos, at the northern end of the Pagasetic Gulf, provides the main point of connection to the Aegean. The territory to the east is dominated by Mount Peleon, as is the area to the north, separating the rich interior plain from the coast until one reaches the southern edges of the Thermaic Gulf. This means that—north of Lamia—the Pagasetic Gulf is the most favorable outlet to the Aegean until one reaches the northwest corner of the Aegean.

The major land route to northern Greece runs from Volos toward Larissa, with several offshoots into western Greece along the way, especially via Pharsala and Karditsa. People traveling south would have most likely entered the Euboean Gulf from the Pagasetic Gulf, passing along the length of this sea route and likely needing to stop along the way. The importance of Thessaly as a connection to the north of Greece, both by land and by sea, is paramount throughout the period of study.

The classic work on the prehistory of Thessaly is Wace and Thompson (1912). The Neolithic period has historically received pride of place, especially the Neolithic type sites of Dimini and Sesklo (see, e.g., Tsountas 1908; Theocharis 1973; Gallis 1992; Andreou, Fotiadis, and Kotsakis 2001). For historical times, scholarship highlights the complicated political geography of Thessaly and the surrounding areas (Morgan 2003; Decourt, Nielsen, and Helly 2004). Much recent work has focused on the Mycenaean period, most notably at the major centers of Dimini, Kastro Volos, and Pefkakia (Batziou-Efstathiou 2015; Skafida et al. 2016; Adrimi-Sismani 2017, 2018). Regional survey work has been limited to the catalog-type approaches of the gazetteers (Feuer 1983; Gallis 1992), and occasional extensive surveys (Decourt 1990). The only published intensive survey work in the region has focused on the Almyros and Sourpi Plains (Reinders 2004; Stissi et al. 2015), although the new Central Achaia Phthiotis Survey, building on a long-term project at Kastro Kallithea, has much potential (Haagsma 2019). Perhaps the most significant trend in the archaeology of Thessaly is recent conferences that have published a wealth of new information about a variety of periods and sites (Mazarakis Ainian 2006, 2009, 2012c, 2016, 2020). Synthetic studies of the region in the Late Bronze Age (Adrimi-Sismani 2007; Pantou 2010; Feuer 2011, 2016b) and the Early Iron Age (Georganas 2003, 2011; Karouzou 2017, 2020) provide a more comprehensive picture.

Euboea

Euboea has a varied natural environment, characterized by mountains and valleys, small agricultural plains, and wooded highlands. Routes of communication are largely determined by the contours of the landscape and the necessity to find favorable passes through often mountainous terrain (map 7). In general, however, this terrain is much more difficult to cross than that of Boeotia or Attica, which has in part led to historical territorial divisions between different parts of the island, also observed by archaeologists, historians, and geographers (Sackett et al. 1966; Fachard 2012; Tankosić, Mavridis, and Kosma 2017; see above, pp. 34–37, n. 1, for more on the history of research for the island).

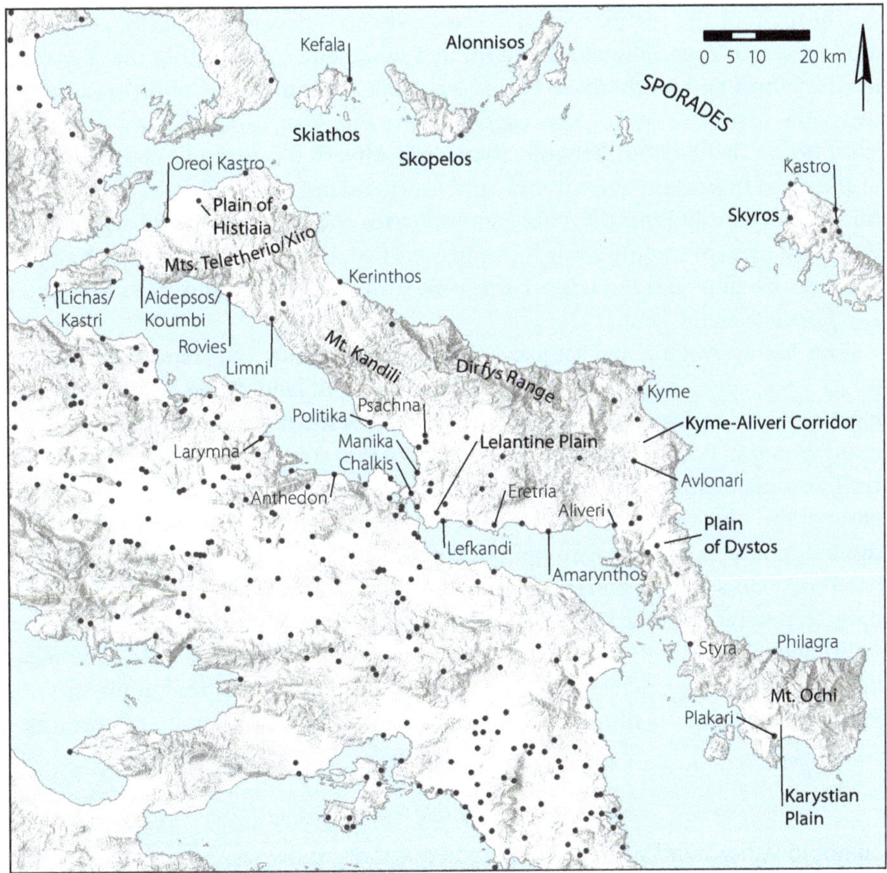

MAP 7. Topography and sites of Euboea and the Sporades, with major sites and features labeled.

A major feature of Euboea is the strait of the Euripos, where the Euboean Gulf narrows to a width of ca. 50 meters. This is also the location of Chalkis, the principal settlement of Euboea for much of its history. In later times this channel has been spanned by a variety of bridges. In the periods covered here, however, the famed unpredictability of the water currents would have made smaller vessels dependent on the tide to cross, and so would have forced them to wait in the northern or southern harbors (or at least their vicinity) until the appropriate time, further highlighting the geographical and historical importance of Chalkis (Bury 1887; Bakhuizen 1976, 1985; Kontogiannis 2012; Kosma 2015; Kalamara et al. 2015; Mastrogiannopoulou and Sampson 2017). This situation also would have increased the appeal of nearby harbors, for example at Lefkandi, Eretria, and Aulis to the south, and at Larymna and Anthedon (on the Boeotian coast) to the north.

Throughout the island, mountainous landscapes necessitate taking paths that are not direct, especially along the limited land routes connecting the disparate north, central, and southern parts. These geographic limitations are also a feature of the paths between the Aegean coasts and the Euboean Gulf, with a few notable exceptions. The corridor between Kyme and Aliveri, for example, contains some of the most important agricultural land on the island, with valleys branching off this main route linking the Euboean Gulf with the Aegean coast. Large coastal plains are present in only a few locations: at Histiaia in the north; at Psachna and between Chalkis and Eretria in the center of the island; and around Dystos and Karystos in the south.

The highly fragmented landscape of Euboea signals the importance of sea travel, especially along the Euboean Gulf. The use of land routes would certainly have been widespread, but these should be seen as small-scale and occurring only rarely over great distances. The implications of this are important for the Euboean Gulf as a major maritime corridor, since (1) contacts between polities in distant parts of the island are likely to have been primarily maritime in nature; (2) long-distance contacts coming through ports give such locations prominence in land-based networks as well; and (3) the gulf coast of the island is more connected from both terrestrial and maritime perspectives than is the Aegean coast, which has prominent sites only in the areas of Kyme and Kerinthos, both points of connection to the Sporades, which also have significant material cultural affinities with Euboea, especially in the Early Iron Age (Lemos and Hatcher 1986; Mazarakis Ainian 2012b).

Attica

Home to Athens and its well-documented system of demes, Attica is one of the most important parts of the Greek world for understanding the organization of ancient landscapes and territories (Traill 1975; Whitehead 1986; Fachard 2016). The Attic peninsula is delimited in the north by the Kithairon-Parnes range, which separates it from Boeotia, and on the west by the isthmus separating it from the Peloponnese (or, more specifically, Mount Pateras, which separates western Attica from the Megarid) (map 8). Attica itself can be divided into three parts: western Attica, extending from the Megarid to Mount Aigaleo and including the bay of Eleusis; the basin of Athens, between Mounts Aigaleo and Hymettos; and eastern Attica, which is bounded on the west by Mount Hymettos and on the east by the Euboean Gulf.

Passage through Attica is fairly straightforward and the landscape is generally less challenging than other places. On a regional scale, routes mainly involve negotiating Mounts Hymettos, Pentele, and Parnes, as well as the smaller mountains in southern Attica (Vanderpool 1978; Lohmann 2002; Korres 2010; Fachard and Pirisino 2015; Fachard and Knodell 2020). The importance of eastern Attica for the period in question (and later periods as well) is paramount. The rich silver and

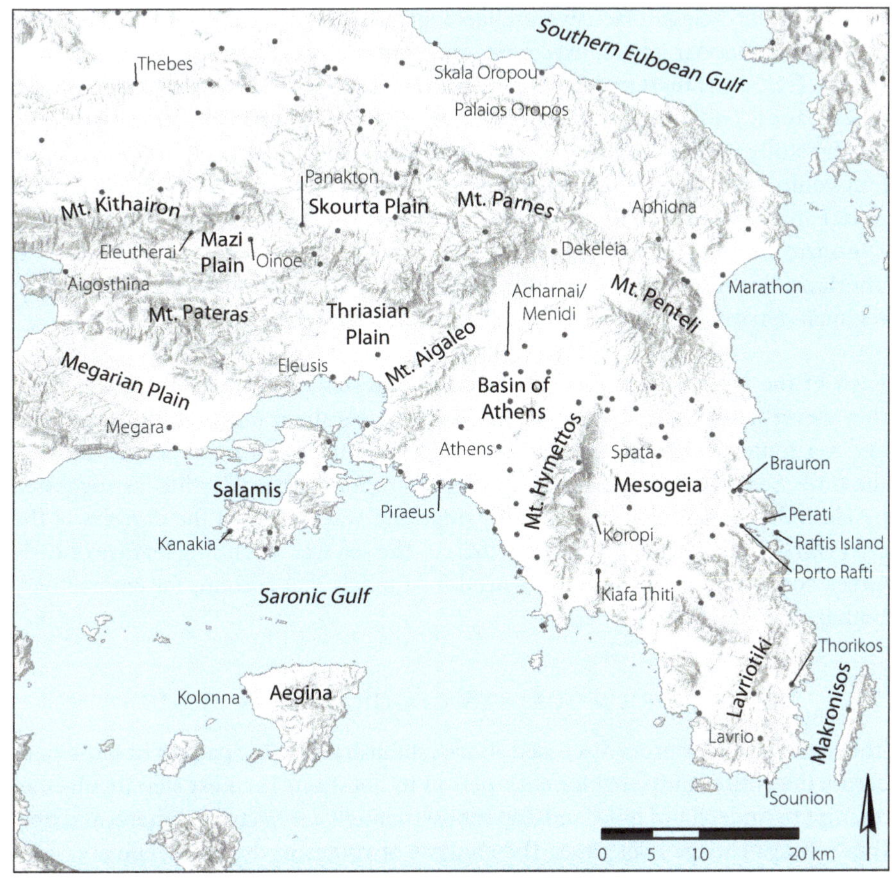

MAP 8. Topography and sites of Attica and the Saronic Gulf, with major sites and features labeled.

copper deposits of the Lavriotiki were major commodities, and the relative ease with which they could be accessed by sea was also significant (Lohmann 2005; Domergue 2008; Papadimitriou 2017; Kayafa 2020).

Finally, the routes coming into and out of Attica are more clearly circumscribed than movement is within Attica itself. Mounts Parnes and Kithairon present fairly substantial borderlands, forcing people traveling overland to take either a western or an eastern course. The former leads toward Boeotia and the Corinthian Gulf, which passes through the Mazi Plain and later border settlements and forts at Panakton, Eleutherai, and Oinoe (Fachard and Knodell 2020). The latter leads in the direction of the Euboean Gulf, skirting the east side of Parnes to enter Boeotia near Oropos, territory that was hotly contested in historical times (Cosmopoulos 2001).

Unfortunately, systematic survey on a regional scale is simply not possible in the vast majority of the region, dominated as it is by the sprawl of the modern capital. Nevertheless, extensive archaeological work has been carried out over centuries by topographers, explorers, and (especially) the Greek Archaeological Service (see, e.g., Stuart and Revett 1762–1816; Leake 1821; Traill 1975; Osborne 1985; Goette 2001; Lohmann and Mattern 2010). Now is an especially important time for the study of early Attica, marked by the recent publication of several important volumes on the prehistory and early history of Athens and Attica (Privitera 2013; Papadopoulos and Smithson 2017; Doronzio 2018; Dimitriadou 2019; Graml, Doronzio, and Capozzoli 2019; Papadimitriou et al. 2020). New survey projects at Thorikos, Porto Rafti, and Aphidna also promise to shed much new light on the regional dynamics of eastern Attica in the Late Bronze Age (see table 3).

Each of the regions described above varies internally in considerable ways, but they nevertheless have certain coherences that tie them together, not least land and sea routes. Overland travel was certainly the norm for most people, most of the time. Sea travel should be seen as less common in everyday life, as suggested by Hesiod, who traveled by boat only once and warns against the dangers of the sea (*Works and Days* 641–77). Nevertheless, the sea was a defining feature of early Greek society. There is therefore a need for models that account for connectivity both by land and by sea.

NETWORK MODELS IN GEOGRAPHICAL SPACE

The regional data sources discussed above establish a baseline pattern of settlement across the entire study area for each period in question. The next step involves an attempt to understand how landscapes of settlement connect and cohere, and how these things change over time. The analysis of routes in the landscape and connections between places is essential to understanding the organization of political landscapes. There is a nearly direct correlation between investment in communication infrastructure—including roads, paths, way stations, and guard posts—and level of social complexity. For example, in a comparative study of cases from North America, Central America, South America, and northern Mesopotamia, Earle (2010) has shown that only highly complex chiefdoms and states are typically engaged in road-building activities. This model generally fits our knowledge of early Greek infrastructure, which is rather limited, dating only to the Mycenaean and Classical periods, with a large gap in between (Kase 1972; Pritchett 1980; Goette 2002; Jansen 2002; Hope Simpson and Hagel 2006; Fachard and Pirisino 2015; Fachard and Knodell 2020). Direct archaeological evidence for movement in early Greece is therefore fleeting. It is limited to roads and road remains dated to certain times when centralized polities were investing in regional infrastructure (the Mycenaean Palatial period)—and even then the material evidence is by no means ubiquitous. In spite of this lack of evidence for infrastructure, we know that people were on the move almost constantly. *Routes* of potential movement or *paths* of habituated movement are other ways of conceptualizing such mobility (Earle 2010). Using the landscape to generate potential routes based on GIS modeling, considering also later maps and travelers' accounts, is one important way forward.

Network modeling provides a powerful means of approaching connectivity, and in multiple ways. As noted in chapter 1, network analysis in archaeology often aims to *document* or *analyze* interaction through perceived similarities in ceramic styles or production and exchange practices (see, e.g., Knappett 2011; Blake 2014). My aim is rather to *model* archaeologically ephemeral interactions on local and regional levels. Nearest-neighbor analysis is employed to provide a baseline for interaction, based on the assumption that any given site will interact with at least three of its nearest neighbors. This assumption stems from the fact that communities need to interact with one another in order to diversify agricultural and craft production, to participate in intercommunal social storage practices, and to make suitable marriages between what are generally small agricultural communities (Halstead 1989; Borck et al. 2015). Such issues are of fundamental importance in the Mediterranean microecologies of central Greece, with their varied and seasonally unstable resource bases.

The type of nearest-neighbor model employed here is similar to the proximal point analysis used by Broodbank (2000, 180–86) for the Early Bronze Age Cyclades, though it differs in that it includes only known sites, involves a larger area, and puts equal emphasis on both land- and sea-based interaction. The model connects each *community* (see above on the distinction from *site*) with a minimum of three nearest neighboring communities, establishing a baseline that is uniform throughout the study area.[5] This is not to suggest that these were the only interactions that took place, or even that these were the most important interactions for a particular community, but this model serves (1) to provide an architecture of interaction that is simply not possible to know in its entirety from material evidence alone, and (2) to show how likely interactions between settlements change over time, in the face of shifting settlement patterns. Rendering such connections graphically for each period in the chapters that follow allows us to see also how local or regional groupings emerge.

In addition to generating conceptual models of interaction between neighboring communities, I also map likely routes through which individuals and groups would have moved to make such connections. While general routes traversing and connecting the regions of central Greece are described above, smaller-scale paths between specific places also would have been important to early Greek communities. Least-cost paths are therefore used to create a connectivity model of sites in

---

5. Three is a conventional number of connections drawn in Proximal Point Analyses (see Broodbank 2000: 180–81; see also Terrell 1977). Models using four or five would not yield substantially different results, since the objective is to model relative connectivity rather than to suggest an absolute pattern. For a variety of models derived from a much larger dataset with different numbers of connections, see Brughmans and Peeples 2020.

the landscape for each of the relevant periods.[6] This connectivity model works in two ways. In the first place, it finds a single optimal route through which all *sites* in the model can be connected. In the second, it articulates the optimal paths through the landscape to connect each site to its nearest neighbors. What emerges is a two-tier model of main axes (displayed in the maps that follow as bold lines) and other routes (displayed as lighter lines) for each of the four periods discussed in the following chapters (see maps 10, 15, 19, 25). These least-cost paths therefore link all sites as activity zones represented in the archaeological record, even if they do not represent an independent community.

Research in Attica has demonstrated the particular utility of least-cost path models, especially because they tend to map well on to (1) material remains of road construction dated to the Mycenaean and Classical periods as well as (2) several other sites and findspots (Fachard and Pirisino 2015; Fachard and Knodell 2020). The application across several regions allows for the identification of much larger trends and regional specificity. Taken together, then, nearest-neighbor networks and connectivity models provide a layered approach to modeling networks of interaction across multiple geographical scales.

TERRITORIAL MODELS IN DYNAMIC LANDSCAPES

The contemporary world is comprised of states with relatively static borders that delimit contiguous territories. Political boundaries are demarcated by lines on maps, while strict national laws and international agreements denote what can and cannot be done within and between these zones. Political space would have been conceived quite differently in early Greece, along with much of the rest of the premodern world (see also Cherry 2010). Boundaries existed, to be sure, and we know from later historical sources that territories were present and contested, won and lost; but these must have been more fluid and relative than we tend to render them on maps. It may be more useful to think of territories as agglomerations of sites, networks, and routes—conceptions of territory and distance based on links that actively create relationships between places rather than boundaries that contain such places. In this way we might see territories as clusters of relationships whose character can sometimes be deduced through the material or documentary record but must also depend on a regional proxemics of frequented places and

6. Such methods are now well established in archaeological research as ways of modeling likely paths of interaction in the landscape (see, e.g., Howey 2007; McCoy and Ladefoged 2009; Gillings, Hacıgüzeller, and Lock 2020). The least-cost paths used in this study were generated using ESRI ArcGIS software to create a cost surface that models the relative effort of traversing the landscape. This model was based on a combination of slope, derived from a 30-meter resolution ASTER Digital Elevation Model and a study of the physiological energy cost of humans walking uphill (Minetti et al. 2002). Paths of least resistance were then modeled as likely routes by which people would move through the landscape.

the natural environment. We must also consider that conceptions of territory are necessarily fluid, and that they change over time and even vary within a particular society. For example, a polity's understanding of territory may be fundamentally different from that of an individual farmer or a shepherd. Nevertheless, geographical methods of modeling territory provide an important backdrop to these linkages and can offer suggestions for identifying potential border zones or landscapes of convergence.

The territorial interests of communities and polities vary throughout the periods discussed in this book. Based on the Linear B texts, we can say that Mycenaean palaces were concerned with land; they may also have had notional territorial limits. In early Greece, these polities are the closest we come to territorial states with definable boundaries until we arrive at the historically documented territorial disputes of Archaic Greek poleis. An implicit interest in boundaries is more difficult to detect in periods in between, where we might turn to more impressionistic analyses of networks, geography, and the amount of land required to sustain a community of a certain size.

I use two specific methods here to examine past interests in exploiting or controlling land: cost-based territorial allocations (for the Palatial period—see chapter 3) and site catchment analysis (where notions of political extent are less clear—see chapter 6). More impressionistic analyses of potential territory based on the distribution of archaeological sites, modeled paths, and the natural environment are also employed throughout this book (and indeed seem our best option in chapters 4 and 5). I describe the methods briefly here, though the models themselves appear in the period-specific chapters in which they are employed.

A long-popular way to render the territory of ancient polities is through the use of Thiessen polygons, which generate borders that are equidistant between each palatial center in the analysis (for Mycenaean palaces, see Renfrew 1975; Bintliff 1977a; Cherry 1977; Galaty and Parkinson 2007). The principle is similar to that of the territorial allocation employed here, except that Thiessen polygons are based on Euclidean distance and all land in the analysis is assigned to a center. This means that the territory of those palaces on the edges will go on indefinitely while those in the center are restricted. Cost allocations do something similar, but they use a cost surface model that integrates topographical information to take into account the relative effort of crossing the landscape (Bevan 2010). More complex models incorporate network centrality and routes (Bevan and Wilson 2013) or historical contingency and diachronic change (Whitelaw 2018; Ek 2020). This study does something similar in the context of Mycenaean palatial territories, although it abandons such centralized territorial modeling in later periods in favor of less prescriptive analysis (when regional centralization and hierarchy cannot be clearly demarcated across the study area).

In a cost-based model of territorial allocation, territory is assigned to sites designated as peer communities, based on whatever peer community in the designated set is closest in cost distance terms. The model for cost-based territorial allocation is employed here with a certain restriction—a maximum extent based on the outermost places mentioned in the Linear B tablets from Thebes that clearly fall within the political territory of the center. Significantly, all of the places mentioned in the Thebes tablets with clear territorial relationships to the palace fall neatly within this territorial model, while there is a line of major sites that are not mentioned, which fall just inside territory that would be ascribed to Orchomenos. At first glance, these boundaries are quite similar to those produced by Thiessen polygons, yet there are subtle differences that correspond with what we know about regional networks. The most meaningful distinction is the boundary between Thebes and Orchomenos that puts Larymna, which would have been an important outlet to the Euboean Gulf for Gla and Orchomenos, in Orchomenian territory in a cost-based allocation and in Theban territory in the Thiessen polygons (see further in chapter 3, pp. 73–84, maps 11 and 12).

Site catchment analysis has an equally venerable history in archaeological thought. Site catchments, or resource acquisition zones, can be modeled as the landscapes with which communities would be most familiar and within which members of communities would conduct most of their day-to-day activities, such as agriculture, animal husbandry, and social interactions. Early approaches to modeling site catchments (Vita-Finzi and Higgs 1970) suggested radii of five and 10 kilometers for sedentary and nomadic communities, respectively, based on analogies from animal subsistence territories. Of course, agropastoral societies exhibit a variety of ranges themselves, since shepherds may venture much more widely than farmers. Archaeological applications based on ethnographic analogies of rural villages proposed catchment radii of 2.5 kilometers (Flannery 1976). This settlement radius seems to apply to Boeotia, Attica, and Euboea in the Classical period (Bintliff 1999, 17–18; Fachard 2012, 76; Fachard 2016). While these do not necessarily prescribe political territories, and habitual activities may indeed have been more extended or curtailed, such notional models do provide a baseline that can be compared to the development of human settlement in the landscape over time, especially when these models are considered alongside the distribution of arable land and other resources. Site catchments are used here specifically to examine settlement expansion between the Early Iron Age and the eighth century BCE (see further in chapter 6, pp. 197–8, map 26).

CONCLUSIONS: CONNECTING THE DOTS

In this chapter I have described the geographical and archaeological contexts for what follows. A vast array of archaeological data relevant to the 700 years treated in this book has been compiled over the last two centuries. Much has been written, too, about the Greek landscape and its relation to the history of human settlement. In outlining these contexts I have aimed also to explain the specific methods and models—of settlement patterns, networks, and territories—with which we can fill some of the gaps in our knowledge. Such modeling (implicit or explicit) is the only way to articulate the dots of archaeological sites and blocks of individual regions in a multiregional study of societal development.

Archaeological sites come in a variety of forms, as do the evidence and research from which we are able to evaluate them. Even within sites characterized the same way in terms of type or place in a settlement hierarchy, we may have vastly different levels of knowledge. Returning to the example of Eleon in Boeotia and Psachna in Euboea, we might consider them both second-tier centers in the relative hierarchy of settlement for the Palatial Bronze Age. Eleon is the subject of systematic excavations with the Eastern Boeotia Archaeological Project (Burke et al. 2020), while Psachna is known only from surface remains documented in the middle of the twentieth century (Sackett et al. 1966, 54). Nevertheless, what we can infer about Psachna, based on the fragmentary evidence that does exist, suggests that it was probably similar to Eleon in size and local importance, or at least that it was more similar to Eleon than to Thebes or a minor village or hamlet. While we may not always be able to provide a clear picture of what a site looked like, how many people lived there, or how it was organized in sociopolitical terms, we can make inferences about its relative significance based on our knowledge of sites that *appear* to be similar. On the level of individual sites and communities, therefore, a certain amount of modeling or projection is required in order to move forward with any analysis that is truly regional or multiregional in scope.

A second level of modeling comes in the form of social and spatial networks, heuristic devices intended to show how local and regional landscapes cohere. Few would disagree that such interactions were necessary or took place, even if the details of specific routes or connections between places are debatable. A dual approach to modeling connections through nearest-neighbor analysis and physical routes by which connections may have been realized reveals much about potential modes of organizing and conceptualizing regional space. As loci of habitation change from period to period, so too did the overall network that knit the landscape together.

Finally, territorial models provide an opportunity to analyze how communities and polities may have conceptualized and partitioned the lands in which they lived. In this case, texts provide an uneven level of detail across the periods under study in this book, making a territorial model for Bronze Age palaces applicable to one period but not necessarily to others. In all periods, however, access to resources—most significantly agricultural resources—is a concern for all communities. Fluctuation in settlement density and distribution therefore need to be taken into consideration across all parts of the study area.

Overall, the combination of archaeological evidence, its qualitative evaluation, and its quantitative and spatial analysis provide the baseline for the archaeological history that follows. While certain individual points in this analysis may be subject to critique, model building remains the only way to articulate a detailed study of a large dataset derived from a variety of sources. To return to David Clarke (1973), archaeologists necessarily deal with a sample of a sample of a sample. If our goal is to study past human behavior, we are left only with evidence that takes a material form, that has been preserved, and that has been discovered (and published). The state of the evidence, moreover, varies considerably over a variety of social and spatial scales. Making sense of this mélange across the landscapes of central Greece and in reference to the wider Mediterranean context requires a layered approach to modeling and inference—one that allows us to go from compiling archaeological data in physical space to articulating meaningful societal histories.

3

Confronting Hegemony in Mycenaean Central Greece

Iron that's forged the hardest
Snaps the quickest.
—SEAMUS HEANEY, *THE BURIAL AT THEBES: A VERSION OF SOPHOKLES'*
ANTIGONE

The central Greek mainland looms large in the cultural imagination of ancient Greece—in some ways more so than the regions sporting the better-known palatial sites of Mycenae, Tiryns, or Pylos. Only Mycenae rivals the mythological significance of Thebes, which appears to have been the preeminent palatial authority in central Greece. A second locus of Boeotian palatial power was at Orchomenos, and a third at Gla. The settlement history of Late Bronze Age Boeotia as a whole is demonstrably tied to these central places. To the north and south, Thessaly and Attica also appear to have been home to Mycenaean palaces, yet these continue to raise more questions than answers in terms of political organization, territorial scope, and even the basic composition of their archaeological remains. Of one thing we can be relatively sure, however: that these are not our canonical Mycenaean palaces, at least as understood from the type sites of the Argolid and Messenia. Nevertheless, these places appear to have been the foremost centers in the Bronze Age political landscape, and they certainly featured in later Greek imaginings of the past. Mythological resonances aside, it also seems that a good portion of central Greece had very little to do with any palace or palatial authority, which suggests that a range of sociopolitical formations were present (an observation that may be equally valid for the Peloponnese).

A fundamental problem in the archaeology of Late Bronze Age Greece is the tendency to base assumptions concerning Mycenaean polities on what we can see at Mycenae—the pomp and circumstance of elite cemeteries, monumental architecture, mysterious religious activity—and what we can read at Pylos—in Linear B tablets that have been used to describe the organization of territory, political administration, and various types of production. There is an implicit expectation, then, for palaces to look like Mycenae and behave like Pylos. Researchers have long urged us to avoid the assumption that all palaces look and act the same (e.g., Galaty and Parkinson 2007), but we seem nevertheless stuck in the proverbial rut of trying to fit lesser-known centers into frameworks to which they are often not well suited.[1]

This chapter examines the rise and fall of sociopolitical complexity in Mycenaean central Greece across local, regional, and interregional scales. The topic of state formation is well rehearsed for the Mycenaean world (see, e.g., Wright 2006; Parkinson and Galaty 2007; Nakassis, Parkinson, and Galaty 2011; Maran and Wright 2020). Most such studies, however, generalize the development of complexity across Greece, based especially on Peloponnesian paradigms and focused almost exclusively on palatial centers. Even studies concerned specifically with central Greece (Phialon 2011; Kramer-Hajos 2016) draw heavily on Peloponnesian comparanda, at times eliding the particularity of the region(s) in question.

This chapter begins with a discussion of nascent social complexity in central Greece. The bulk of this chapter presents a region-by-region synthesis of the political landscapes of central Greece during the Palatial period. I provide an explication of social change and organization based on the spatial analysis of settlement patterns, focusing particularly on issues of territory and regional connectivity. I argue especially that substantial variety can be seen in modes of regional sociopolitical organization, ranging from territorial palatial states to nonstate complex communities and more modest village societies.

Next, I turn to the ways in which Mycenaean polities—palaces in particular—were organized between regional and interregional scales, mainly through their interests in particular modes of production and consumption. I argue that the centralized interests (if not control) of Mycenaean palaces in various aspects of rural production represented a rapid social transformation, departing from previous ways of life, and served to set the palaces apart from other political entities. In particular, palatial interests in recording technologies (writing), large-scale agricultural projects, and the centralized production and consumption of exotica signal a desire to integrate territory and workshops in ways that had previously been much more widely distributed. We therefore see marked divergences between palatial and nonpalatial modes of social organization.

Finally, I look outward to reevaluate relationships between the Aegean and other eastern Mediterranean polities. Aegean "states" in fact do not compare well with other old-world complex societies typically ascribed that appellation. Chiefdoms or other "nonstate" sociopolitical formations may well provide better cases for comparison, though these are perhaps better characterized as a varied range of

---

1. Nonpalatial modes of political organization and diversity across regional systems are increasingly recognized, however, especially for the Corinthia, the Saronic Gulf, Thessaly, Achaia, and Euboea (Pullen and Tartaron 2007; Tartaron 2010; Pantou 2010; Arena 2015; Knodell, forthcoming).

complex communities (Porter 2013). On an eastern Mediterranean stage of "great kings" and empires the Mycenaeans were probably rather poor players who have been given an outsized role, owing to the historical significance often ascribed to them (along with the Minoans) as "Europe's first states."[2]

PRELUDE: EMERGENT COMPLEXITY IN CENTRAL GREECE

Discussions of Mycenaean state formation focus on a number of related factors: burial evidence for growing social inequality, growth in the scale and number of monumental building projects, and an increase in the consumption of "elite" material culture—all in an increasingly centralized and exclusive manner. Processes begun in the Peloponnese in MH III culminate in the appearance of palace-centered states in LH IIIA2, in several parts of central Greece and the Peloponnese (see table 1; Dickinson 1977, 1994; Voutsaki 2001; Fitzsimons 2006, 18–22; Parkinson and Galaty 2007; Wright 2006, 2008). The role of Crete lingers somewhat uncomfortably in the background, ranging from influence or inspiration to adversity. Mycenaean leaders sought to establish and maintain social inequality through personal self-aggrandizement based on the exploitation of material and social networks rather than on the more integrative, distributed expressions of state authority practiced by the Minoan elite (Parkinson and Galaty 2007; see also Voutsaki 1998, 2001; Knappett and Schoep 2000).[3] This took the form of (1) a monopoly on the consumption and distribution of prestige goods, such as imports and high-status craft products; (2) the control of human resources necessary for constructing monumental architecture associated with palatial authority—elite tombs and the palaces themselves; and (3) full or partial control of aspects of production (agricultural and craft) used to support the palace administration.

In transitions to statehood in early Greece the fundamental shifts concern relationships between polity and territory (the importance of land in order to produce agricultural surplus) and the institutionalization of power (the transfer of political authority from the individual to an institution—the palace). In a process of secondary state formation, increasingly complex communities of the Early Mycenaean world would have learned how to do this partly by observation, especially from their Minoan neighbors and closest contacts, but perhaps

2. These notions go back to Evans (1921) and Schliemann (1874) and have deep roots in both European and Greek notions of cultural identity, which, through the late nineteenth and twentieth centuries, became increasingly rooted in prehistory (Childe 1925; Hamilakis 2002; Papadopoulos 2005b; Hanink 2017; Voutsaki 2017).

3. A similar pattern may be observed in comparing the impact of Greek and Roman influence with the tribes of Gaul in later times (Arnold 1995). For a more minimalist, estate-based model of Mycenaean political authority based on data from Pylos, see Small 2007.

also with influences from Ugarit and Cyprus.[4] Endogenous developments played an important role as well, but the trappings of statehood—writing, administration, palatial architecture—seem to have been imported from other systems quite directly. These processes essentially describe a stimulus diffusion model, though they might benefit from more relational thinking as well. Bennet (2017, 173) has suggested that these relationships are better described in terms of historical links rather than typological similarities or genetic descent. At any rate, such links provided the opportunity and inspiration for the active pursuit of the stately goals of integrating territory and political authority—first in the Peloponnese and later in central Greece. In the terminology of complexity theory, we might see this as a phase transition in which new palatial institutions developed out of ones previously based on households, and aggrandizers in certain places found new ways to integrate political and economic systems, fundamentally altering the structures of early Greek society (see also Small 2019, 98).

Most reviews of the development of Mycenaean civilization leading up to the Palatial Bronze Age focus on elaboration in elite burials, particularly the development of tholoi in Messenia and the Argolid, as well as increased differentiation in the wealth of grave goods and the attendant implications for social stratification (e.g., Rutter 1993; Wright 2008). These explanations are drawn almost exclusively from Peloponnesian datasets. More recently, several scholars have sought to remedy this imbalance for central Greece (Phialon 2011; Tartaron 2013, Knodell 2013, 2017; Kramer-Hajos 2016).

Monumental tholoi in central Greece appear in only a few locations (map 9). In Attica, there are two at Thorikos (plus three further monumental tombs), one at Marathon, and one at Menidi (Acharnai). In Boeotia the only example of a tholos is the Treasury of Minyas at Orchomenos. In Thessaly there is a concentration of tholoi around the bay of Volos, with two each at Dimini (Lamiospito and Toumba) and at Volos (at Kazanaki and Kapakli). The most remote tholos is located at Georgiko. In Phokis two tholoi have been recorded in association with the site of Medeon, and another one has been found recently at Amphissa. Smaller-scale tholoi are also found in Euboea in the corridor linking the Euboean Gulf and the Aegean coasts between Aliveri and Oxylithos, at Katakalou and Velousia. The miniature tholos tombs of Thessaly are much more widely distributed—about 60 of these are known from about 30 sites—although the vast majority seem to date to the Protogeometric and Geometric periods.[5] Of the tombs listed above, only

---

4. On the development of secondary states, in contrast to "pristine" states, see Parkinson and Galaty 2007. On the organization of Mycenaean and Minoan palatial polities, see Shelmerdine and Palaima 1984; Voutsaki and Killen 2001; Galaty and Parkinson 2007; Shelmerdine 2006, 2008; Nakassis, Parkinson, and Galaty 2011; Killen 2015.

5. See the following works, with further references, on the tholos tombs of central Greece. For Attica, see Privitera 2013. Immerwahr (1971, 150) speculates that there must have been one at Athens as well, although this is purely conjectural. For Boeotia, see Aravantinos et al. 2016b on Orchomenos; a possible tholos was also found at Vouliagma in Boeotia, in a chamber tomb cemetery, although

two seem to appear in central Greece before LH IIIA-B, at Thorikos and Kapakli (Cavanagh and Mee 1998, 44–46, 63–64). By contrast, tholos construction in the Peloponnese began as early as the end of MH III in Messenia, had spread throughout the Argolid by LH IIA. By LH IIIA–B, tholos construction became restricted to a small number of monumental tombs at major sites. At least 130 Bronze Age tholos tombs are known on the Greek mainland. Some 95 of these come from the Peloponnese, mostly from Messenia and the Argolid; of these, only about 30 have been assigned a date of construction in LH III or later (Pelon 1976; Kontorli-Papadopoulou 1995; Fitzsimons 2006; Banou 2008). Central Greek tholoi are therefore a rather late, secondary adoption, based on Peloponnesian influence.

Central Greek elaboration in funerary architecture can be seen in the form of funerary enclosures going as far back as the Middle Helladic period and in chamber tombs. Prominently sited enclosures, or periboloi, encircling elite cemeteries of the Middle Bronze Age and Early Mycenaean period are now known at several sites in central Greece, including Volos, Mitrou, Paralimni, Orchomenos, Eleon, Eleusis, and Vrana (at Marathon) (Spyropoulos 1971, 327–28; 1974, 322–23; Mylonas 1975; Cavanagh and Mee 1998, 29–39; Burke et al. 2020). The proliferation of wealthy chamber tomb cemeteries, especially at Thebes, Chalkis, and Athens, indicates other pathways toward social differentiation in the funerary record (Papadimitriou 2001).

Imports speak to the developing status of central Greece in wider Aegean networks. In LH II, Mycenaean palatial-type and pseudo-Minoan pottery are found at Athens, Kiafa Thiti, and Aegina, produced at both Kolonna and Athens; marine style pottery is also found at Kolonna, Athens, Thorikos, and Eleusis (Mountjoy 1999, 492; Tartaron 2013, 234). Based on the large number of imported, especially Cretan, finds at Thorikos (Laffineur 2010), it is clear that the Lavriotiki was important to Aegean traders, almost certainly as a source of copper and silver (Kayafa 1999, 311–13). The Euboean Gulf, too, may have already been seen as a route to the gold and silver sources of Macedonia. Aegina was another long-dominant player in the circulation of trade goods, with a long-distance pottery trade stretching from the Saronic Gulf to the Pagasetic Gulf in the Early Mycenaean period. At some point, Mycenae became dominant in the Saronic Gulf, while the decline of Kolonna's pottery exports was coincident with Mycenae's first verifiable palace in LH IIIA, after which Mycenaean fine wares began to appear in areas formerly under Aeginetan influence.[6] The relative decline on Aegina may have opened up opportunities farther north, in central Greece, via the Eubocan Gulf.

------

this was identified based on a thoroughly robbed-out depression in the ground (Farinetti 2011, 368). For Euboea, see Sackett et al. 1966, 73–74. For Thessaly, see Georganas 2000, 2002; Pantou 2010. For Medeon, see Livieratou 2012. For Amphissa, see Livieratou 2015, 97.

6. This picture is admittedly more complicated, however, since it also involves production sites in Attica (at Alimos), with exports of cooking vessels from Kolonna continuing throughout LH IIIB and LH IIIC (Tartaron 2013, 234–35; Gauß and Kiriatzi 2011, 245–47; Gilstrap, Day, and Kilikoglou 2016; Gauß and Knodell 2020).

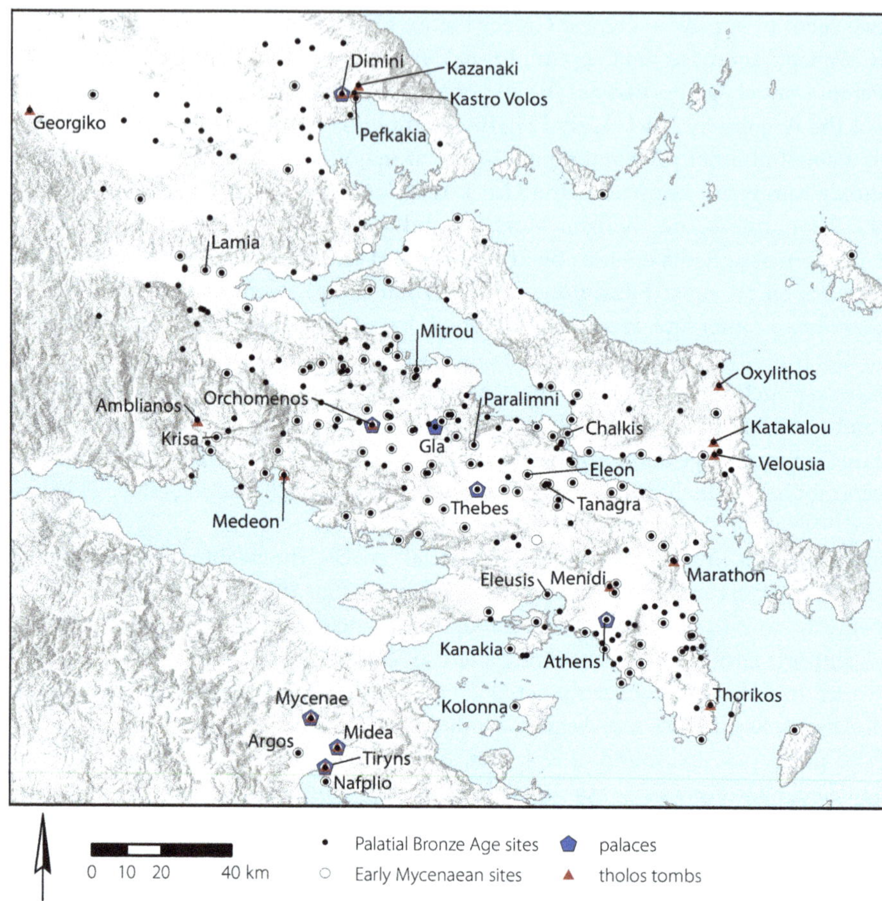

MAP 9. Early Mycenaean and Palatial Bronze Age sites in central Greece, indicating also the locations of tholos tombs and palaces (major sites in the Argolid indicated as well).

Our best evidence for state formation in central Greece is from Boeotia, namely from Thebes. The fundamental change came with the implementation of the institutionalizing framework of a palace system, which altered systems of leadership based solely on powerful individuals, as was likely the case in earlier (and later) periods, and in areas where palaces never appeared. Authority and power remained linked to individuals and households, but the office of the *wanax* lent greater legitimation to individual authority and allowed centralization to be perceived as occurring in the name of the state, rather than a particular person.[7] Moreover, the

7. On the sociopolitical role of the *wanax* (*wa-na-ka* in Linear B), see Palaima 1995, 2006; Nakassis 2012. There is little doubt that the *wanax* is the central figure in the Mycenaean sociopolitical hierarchy (Shelmerdine 2006), having a capacity to command comparable to other versions of kingship in early complex societies (Wright 1995). The etymology of the term is somewhat opaque, though its meaning

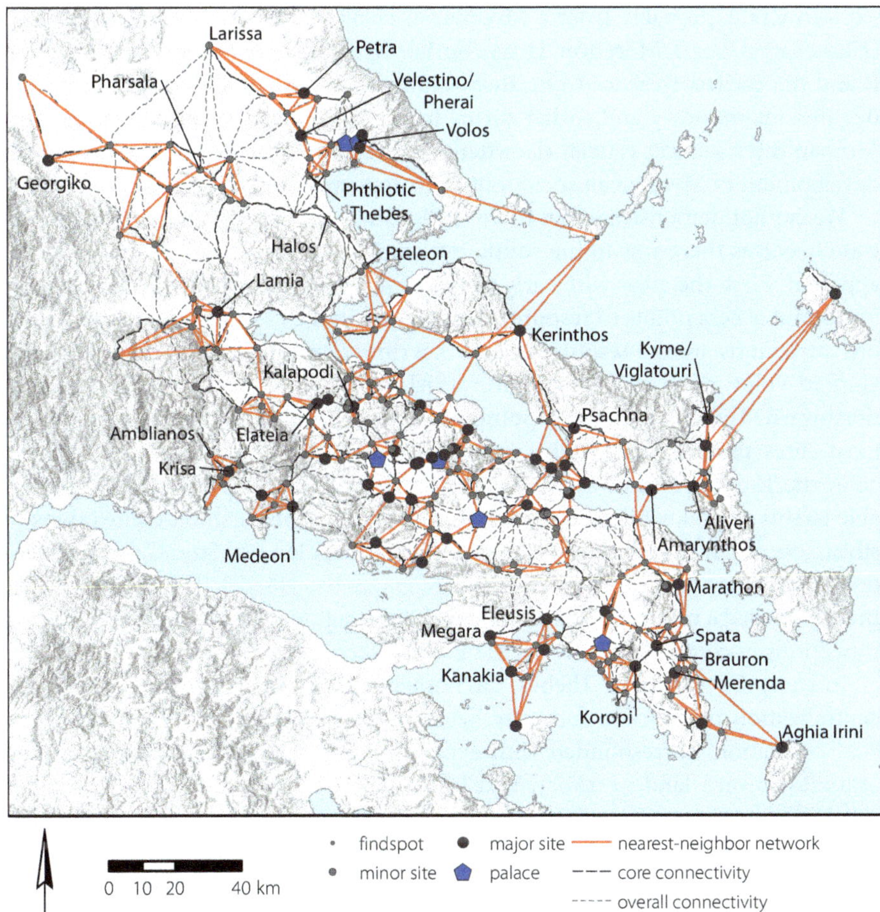

MAP 10. Palatial Bronze Age sites, joined by a connectivity model, with a nearest-neighbor network of communities (see also maps 9, 12, and appendix for additional place names).

control of agricultural resources—land—was expanded and systematized in new ways, eventually involving detailed record-keeping.

There was a strong Cretan connection at Thebes, evidenced by some 70 fragments of inscribed stirrup jars, nearly all of which are thought to come from

---

may be related to the Hittite word *hassu-* (king), which has to do with birth, fertility, and lineage—that is, the basis for kingship is linkage to ancestral (and divine) power and the capacity to produce for his people (Palaima 2006, 57). It is also noteworthy that the *wanax* and the second-in-command *lawagetas* (*ra-wa-ke-ta*) were the only individuals to possess a *temenos* (*te-me-no*), which is often interpreted as meaning landed estate but is clearly related to the later Greek word for sacred space (Palaima 2006, 62; Nikoloudis 2008b, 590). This linkage has implications for a relationship between kingship and religious authority, or at least suggests that the spaces inhabited by these individuals were important places of group religious practice.

western Crete, probably from a Mycenaean palace at Kydonia (modern Chania) (Haskell et al. 2011). Moreover, larnax burials from Tanagra dating to LH IIIA and B and the earliest frescoes from Thebes both show formal and stylistic similarities to contemporary and earlier forms in Crete (Brysbaert 2008a, 2008b). This Minoan interface was crucial elsewhere—especially in the Peloponnese—for the development of Mycenaean sociopolitical complexity.

We cannot demonstrate that there was as strong a Minoan connection in central Greece as there was in the south, but some general patterns are nevertheless apparent. First, the areas with early tholos tombs are mainly coastal and represent important access points to resources and routes: in the case of Thorikos, the obvious attractions are the resources of the Lavriotiki and the access to the Euboean Gulf; in Volos, there are the agricultural riches of Thessaly, along with land routes northward. These form anchor points on either end of the Euboean Gulf, where local elites profited from and were influenced by long-standing, long-distance contacts. The Lavriotiki was the source for much of the silver in the Aegean datable to this period, while the shaft graves at Mycenae also exhibit connections to silver sources in northern Greece (Stos-Gale and Gale 1982; Stos-Gale and Macdonald 1991, 273–79; Papadopoulos 1996b, 173; 2005, 588–91). The Euboean Gulf, then, provided a maritime axis along which interregional connections engendered transitions in complexity between the Early Mycenaean and Palatial periods.

In sum, the growth of Thebes, Orchomenos, Volos, and Athens suggests the centralization of political authority, which can be seen as a type of secondary state formation, corresponded with expanding regional networks and changing attitudes toward land, territory, and leadership. Each of these centers had the potential to command major agricultural resources in a way not shared by other significant Mycenaean sites. The control of land was a particularly important means of consolidating power. Agricultural expansion and surplus also created opportunities for specialization, as we see in episodes of state formation across the globe. Coastal areas were not in such a good position to intensify agricultural production, at least not on the same scale, and they may not have faced the same pressures to do so with easier access to the sea. The influx of imports in the Palatial period also suggests an expansion of interregional networks. This rapid intensification of interactions on multiple scales, then, can explain the apparent speed with which the palaces emerged in central Greece as a major transition in social organization.

THE POLITICAL LANDSCAPES OF MYCENAEAN
CENTRAL GREECE

The Palatial period coincides with a major boom in the number of settlements across the Greek mainland. In the first place, the number of Palatial versus Early

Mycenaean sites more than doubles, going from 114 to 276 (see map 9, table 4).[8] There are a few possible ways to explain this boom and its relationship to social change. Population increase could have led to more settlements and competition over territory, out of which leaders emerged to form administrative structures that had been adopted from other states. Alternatively, changing administrative structures could have led to the formation of new, more productive agricultural strategies and population growth as a result of state protection and without the threat of raiding from neighbors. Or there could be a question of archaeological visibility, with Palatial Mycenaean pottery being more prevalent and diagnostic than that of earlier periods; therefore, sites are much more recognizable as belonging to this period. A complexity perspective would suggest that the properties described in the first two scenarios—population growth, increasing social complexity, intensification of production—emerged together, in mutual dependence. The visibility issue probably applies as well, but it is difficult to accept as a sole explanation given the scale of change and number of well investigated sites that do not have Early Mycenaean remains.

A combined map of the settlement hierarchy and connections between communities shows clear clusters forming (map 10). While there is sometimes a pattern of second order sites relating clearly to palatial sites (as in Boeotia), most clusters in the model have no demonstrable relationship to palaces (e.g., in Phokis, Malis, Thessaly, Euboea, and the Saronic Gulf).

As for the palaces themselves, there are only six sites in all of central Greece that can be considered palatial in character, and there is a wide amount of variability between them. Boeotia offers the most straightforward cases, with palatial centers at Thebes, Orchomenos, and Gla. Athens seems also to have been home to a palace, although later building on the Acropolis has obliterated much of the evidence for it, so our understanding is sketchy at best. Thessaly offers another curious case with the palatial character of at least two sites, Dimini and Kastro Volos. The latter is subject to the same problems as Athens but has some Linear B tablets. Kanakia, on Salamis, is sometimes described as a palace as well, though this is less likely.

The architectural remains at these sites have some attributes in common. In relative terms they are simply much larger than other sites and building complexes in their respective regions. There is evidence for elite burials in the form of wealthy cemeteries, of a hierarchy of space indicated by defensive walls and restricted access to central buildings, and of preferential consumption of "elite" aspects of material culture at an institutional level—wall paintings, monumental architecture, painted pottery, feasting equipment, and exotica. Evidence for sponsored activities like feasting and administrative action is also apparent.

8. Some sites are designated simply "Mycenaean," based on ambiguous information in reports or databases meaning they could either be Early Mycenaean or Palatial. See appendix for the period designations of individual sites.

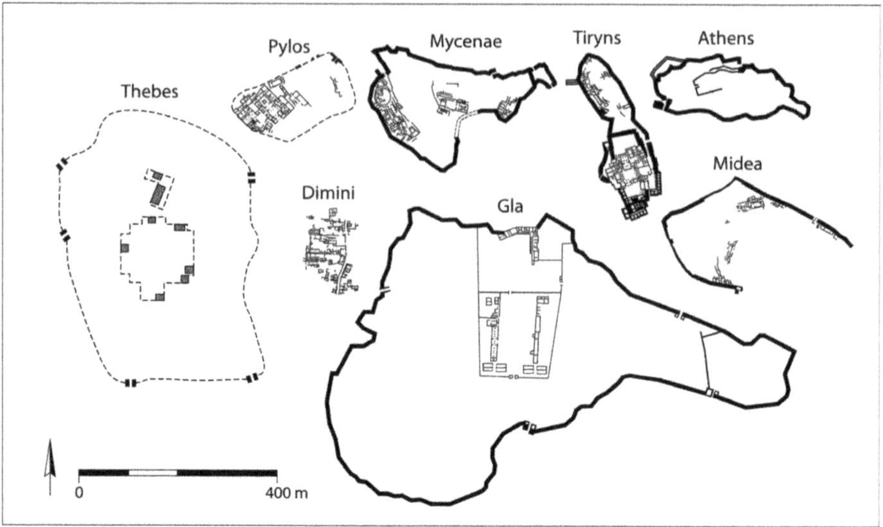

FIGURE 3. Comparative sizes of Mycenaean palaces, showing the form and extent of architectural remains where known and putative extents as dotted lines—that is, the putative extent of the citadel and palatial area at Thebes, which is largely obscured by the modern city (illustration by Denitsa Nenova, after Blegen and Lang 1961, fig. 1; Symeonoglou 1985, 33; Hope Simpson and Hagel 2006, fig. 2; Adrimi-Sismani 2007, 162).

All these characteristics are shared with palatial sites in the Peloponnese. But on closer scrutiny the palatial buildings of central Greece bear little resemblance to their southern counterparts. For one thing, we simply know much less about their architectural layout. While the central palatial buildings of Mycenae, Tiryns, and Pylos have all been excavated extensively, the same cannot be said for any of the palatial complexes of central Greece. Thebes, Orchomenos, and Kastro Volos are mostly buried by millennia of subsequent occupation and remain at the centers of modern towns. Palatial materials on the Acropolis of Athens are fragmentary, mostly obliterated by later constructions. Only Gla and Dimini are reasonably accessible, though the history of excavation at these sites pales in comparison to the Peloponnesian centers (Iakovidis 1989, 1998, 2001; Adrimi-Sismani 2017, 2018).

One thing we do know about the architecture is that there is a tremendous amount of variation in size (figure 3; see also Whitelaw 2017). Thebes and Gla are far larger than anything else in the Mycenaean world, their circuits (estimated in the case of Thebes) being several times larger than Mycenae, even at its greatest extent. None of the central Greek palaces has an obvious central megaron, a hallmark of palatial arrangements in the Peloponnese. On the contrary, Gla and Dimini both have double megaron structures that are often considered anomalous (see, e.g., Iakovidis 2001; Adrimi-Sismani 2018). No such structure has been found at Thebes or Orchomenos, and the closest proxy in Athens is a column base thought to come from a palace (Iakovidis 2006).

Taking a step back from the palaces themselves, we may ask the question: what did palatial territories and political organization look like? A fundamental shift in the relationship between land and polity and rulers and subjects happened in the Mycenaean Palatial period, when states aimed to centralize significant aspects of the subsistence-based agricultural systems that had been the norm in rural communities for the previous several millennia. This is clear in the siting of palatial sites in large agricultural plains, with immediate access to land capable of producing a significant surplus through intense cultivation.

The palaces also provide the only textual evidence we have for understanding the organization of society in the prehistoric Aegean. We do not have a good understanding of how agrarian systems looked before or after the palaces owing to the absence of documentary sources, but this very lack of administrative apparatus also means that the complex hierarchies present in the palaces could not have been maintained in the same way before or after. Such territories previously would have been under the control of powerful families and households, and they would have been much more fragmented. Palatial practices of centralization, fortification, and resource accumulation brought their products under one political roof.

Most of what we know about these territorial systems comes from the study of Linear B tablets—specifically, the two largest corpora from Pylos and Knossos.[9] While the Pylian system cannot be projected wholesale onto other Mycenaean palaces, it nevertheless provides the most complete example.[10] Territorial organization is best revealed through the administrative offices recorded in the tablets, which at Pylos demarcate three levels of territorial hierarchy: (1) the polity as a whole, controlled by the palace and its personnel—the *wanax* and his second in command, the *lawagetas*, and certain enforcers and administrators working directly for the palatial authority; (2) the regional units, or provinces, into which the polity was divided, which had administrative overseers; and (3) the local district, or *damos*, which seems to have had both administrators connected directly to the palatial system and local leadership institutions that appear to have existed before the advent of palatial administration—for example, the *basileus* or

9. Aravantinos (2010, 58) gives the following numbers for Linear B texts. Knossos: ca. 3,500 texts and many fragments; Pylos: ca. 1,200 texts and many fragments; Thebes: ca. 350 texts on tablets, 70 inscribed stirrup jars, many fragments, plus ca. 250 new texts from the Pelopidou street excavations; Mycenae: 70 or more texts and some fragments; Tiryns: 25 texts on tablets and a few on stirrup jars; Midea: 4 inscribed sealings; Dimini: 2 texts, a stone object and an inscribed pottery sherd; Aghios Vasileios: 3 fragmentary tablets; Chania: 4 fragmentary texts on tablets and several inscribed stirrup jars.

10. The Knossos tablets also shed light on territorial and administrative organization, and indeed may be significantly earlier than the Pylos tablets; however, the Pylos archive provides the most detailed snapshot from a particular time and place—around 1200 BCE (Bennet 2011, 2017; Godart and Sacconi 2020; Nakassis, Pluta, and Hruby 2021). Nakassis (personal communication) notes that the organization of Thebes resembles Knossos more closely than Pylos, based on the limited evidence available. This may suggest that Pylos was the anomaly, or that administrative systems developed in slightly different ways out of a common ancestor at Knossos.

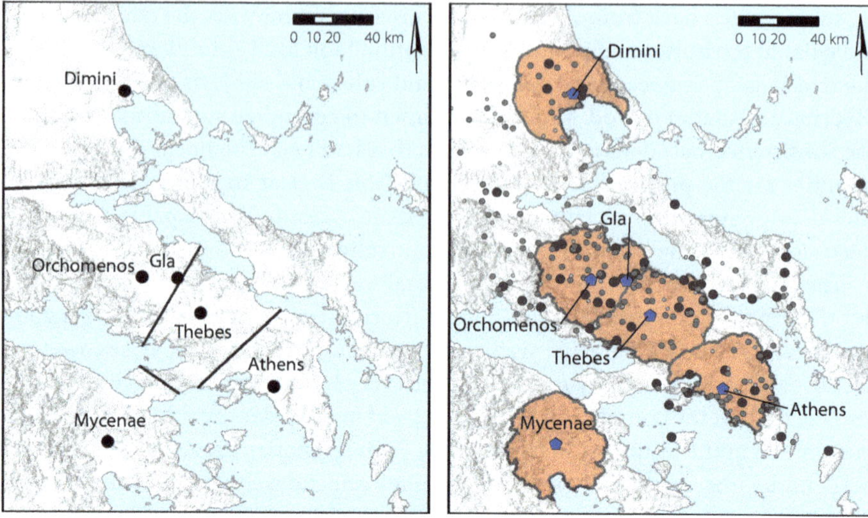

MAP 11. Comparative territories for Mycenaean palaces using Thiessen polygons (left) and a limited cost allocation method (right, showing also the settlement hierarchy for the Palatial Bronze Age).

chief and a single priest or priestess (Morpurgo-Davies 1979; Nakassis 2013a, 5–14). The terms for these latter two institutions both continue after the collapse of the palaces, along with *wanax* (as a less specific term for leader), while other terms do not, suggesting that the other terms were specific to this palatial system. The extent to which such a system applied to other palaces is subject to debate, but the evidence from Knossos and Thebes suggests similar general offices and structures: administrative offices at three levels; the division of space into subregional units; and some (but not all) communities that coincide with later place names.

Finally—and significantly—there is a large amount of settlement activity in the landscape that is quite far removed from any palatial center, in both spatial and network terms. Based on what we know of the remit of Mycenaean palaces, it seems highly unlikely that these other regions fell under any form of palatial control, although they could and probably would have been part of the same wider interaction spheres and cultural milieu.

The territorial and network models described in chapter 2 (pp. 56–60) offer new insights into regional connectivity, territoriality, and landscape diversity in central Greece during the Palatial period. A model of palatial territory based on Linear B texts in Boeotia, for example, can be applied to other palatial regions as a heuristic device (map 11). We can also use such a model to suggest which areas are better defined as simply "nonpalatial"—that is, outside the likely territorial remit of any known palace (see also Knodell, forthcoming). From there we can begin to reconstruct the political landscapes of central Greece on a region-by-region basis.

Some comparison between these modeled territories provides a convenient starting point. Most Mycenaean palaces are located somewhat inland, all at locations well positioned to control vast swaths of agricultural land. Access to the sea was also important, given the cultural significance of exotica, the dependence on bronze trade, and the more general participation in long-distance networks (see further below). Modeled territories are roughly similar in size; they are between 1,500 and 2,000 square kilometers, and so in general are larger than Renfrew's (1975, 14) estimate of 1,500 square kilometers in his Early State Module, even though these are all smaller than the territorial allocations that would result from Thiessen polygons. Estimates of Pylian territory based on various studies of Linear B documents also project a territory of about 2,000 square kilometers (Bennet 1995, 587; Whitelaw 2001, 64; Nakassis 2013, 236; see also Hope Simpson 2014). Notable clusters of sites occur within modeled territories; in the cases of Attica and Thessaly the resulting networks are distinct from areas outside of the territory. Clusters are also apparent around major sites outside the palatial territories—for example, in central Euboea, the island of Salamis, western Phokis, Doris, and Thessaly. In terms of site hierarchy, there is a significantly higher percentage of major sites within palatial areas, suggesting centralized investment or interest in sites within a particular territory, although larger-scale sites are also found outside areas that fall within the modeled remits of known palaces. Taken together, these patterns suggest a range of sociopolitical complexity in the networks of communities that can be identified throughout central Greece.

Contest and Confrontation in the Plains of Boeotia

Boeotia boasts a long tradition of archaeological research, especially in terms of regional survey (see table 3). This factor may contribute to the high number of known sites in the region, although the number of secondary and tertiary sites (with more obvious, long-known remains) is also quite high, suggesting that the large number of sites is not simply attributable to the history of research. In addition to the archaeological record of settlement, we also have textual attestations of the political landscape in the form of Linear B documents from Thebes (Chadwick 1970; Spyropoulos and Chadwick 1975; Olivier, Melena, and Piteros 1990; Aravantinos, Godart, and Sacconi 2001, 2002; Deger-Jalkotzy and Panagl 2006; Del Freo 2009; Palaima 2011).

Linear B tablets, nodules, and inscribed stirrup jars from Thebes (the latter found in other locations as well) offer evidence for conceptions of territory in the Mycenaean world in the form of toponyms, ethnics, and ethnic anthroponyms, though their meanings are often ambiguous (Del Freo 2009; Haskell et al. 2011) (table 7). As economic administrative documents, Linear B tablets record quantities of items going to or coming from particular locations. Sometimes place names are recognizable owing to their appearance in later periods, but there are only rarely clear indications of territorial control (contra Aravantinos, Godart,

TABLE 7 Connections with Thebes based on Linear B documents (see also map 12)

Linear B	Location	Interpretation
te-qa	Thebes	Palace
e-re-o-ni	Eleon (modern Arma)	Second-order center
e-u-te-re-u	Eutresis	Second-order center
ku-te-we-so	Unknown—likely close to Thebes?	Second-order center; suggested that it is close to Thebes based on location of other second order centers
ke-re-u-so	Kreusis	Port site on the Corinthian Gulf; possible second-order center; also possibly a personal name
a₃-ki-a₂-ri-ja	Unknown—likely a coastal site on the Euboean Gulf	Related to later Greek term used to refer to sandy shores; perhaps Glypha/Aulis?
po-ti-ni-ja wo-ko	Potniai (modern Tachi)	House/shrine of the potnia; unit of wool sent here
po-to-a₂-ja	Mount Ptoon	Group of men sent here
ra-mo	River "Lamos" flowing from Helikon (modern Archontitsa)	Unknown quantity of wool sent here
a-ma-ru-to	Amarynthos	One pig sent to Thebes (nodule Wu 58); shipment of wool to Amarynthos (tablet Of 25)
ka-ru-to	Karystos (?)	One pig sent to Thebes (nodule Wu 55)
[? ki-ta-]ro-na	Kithairon (?)	Something toward Mount Kithairon
wa-to	Western Crete	On inscribed stirrup jar; attested in Knossos tablets as near Chania
o-du-ru-wi-jo	Western Crete	On inscribed stirrup jar; attested in Knossos tablets as near Chania
i-si-wi-jo-i (anthroponym)	Isos (Pyrgos, near Anthedon)	Men from Isos as recipients of wine
mi-ra-ti-jo (anthroponym)	Miletos	Several tablets record allotments of barley
ra-ke-da-mi-ni-jo (anthroponym)	Lakedaimon	Records quantities of wheat coming in (?) and wine being sent there

and Sacconi 2001, 2002; Bennet 2017). For example, the names Amarynthos and Karystos, both of which are towns in Euboea, appear in the Linear B tablets from Thebes as *a-ma-ru-to* and *ka-ru-to* (Piteros, Olivier, and Melena 1990, 153–54; Del Freo 2009, 42, 47; Palaima 2011). Yet there is nothing that specifies a tributary relationship between the palace and these places on Euboea—they are listed only in the context of goods going to or coming from them. One pig is delivered from *a-ma-ru-to* to Thebes and some allotments of wool go to *a-ma-ru-to* from Thebes, while one pig is delivered to Thebes from *ka-ru-to*. The former seems to be a

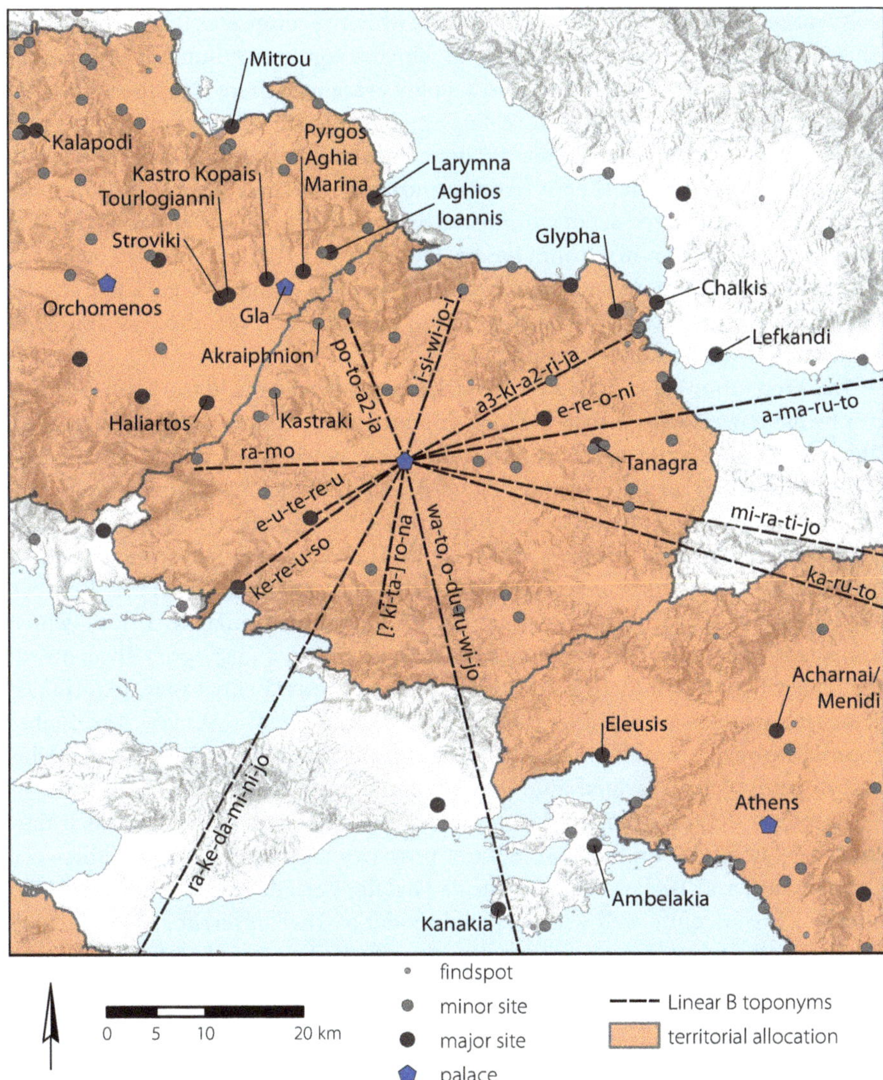

MAP 12. Network of sites mentioned in the Linear B tablets from Thebes and the modeled extent of Theban territory, with settlement hierarchy and significant sites indicated (see also table 7).

simple exchange and the latter hardly suggests some kind of hegemony. Following Palaima (2011), I would disagree with arguments that make Euboea part of the territory of Thebes (Aravantinos, Godart, and Sacconi 2002; Del Freo 2009, 66; see also Knodell, forthcoming).

The Linear B tablets from Thebes provide more information about the political geography of Boeotia. First, there is no question that Thebes is the dominant political center in at least its immediate area, which encompasses the Theban plain. This is the only site in central Greece at which a significant number of Linear B texts have been found, and the record keeping evidenced there is in line with other Mycenaean central authorities, revealing agricultural and other goods coming into and going out of the palace. Linear B documents have been found at no fewer than six separate locations in Thebes (Aravantinos 2015, 36); this suggests a somewhat more widely distributed set of administrative activities than, say, at Pylos (the only site where a proper archive room has been found). LH III Thebes is also by far the largest site in the region, with an enceinte comparable to that at Gla, which dwarfs the Mycenaean centers of the Peloponnese (see figure 3; see also Symeonoglou 1973, 1985, 31–32; Aravantinos 2010).

Del Freo (2009) argues that only four of the 25 toponyms in the Thebes tablets can be associated with a clear political hierarchy. The first is Thebes itself: *te-qa*. Three other sites appear as sort of second-order centers, which is argued based on the described size of their crops: *e-re-o-ni* (classical Eleon, near modern Arma), *e-u-te-re-u* (ancient Eutresis, now called Arkopodi), and *ku-te-we-so*, the location of which is unknown but probably close to Thebes.[11] Other sites that are mentioned do not seem to be involved in administrative activities. From this Del Freo (2009, 67) argues for a three-tier settlement hierarchy, similar to Pylos—which also has two second-order centers—and Knossos (Bennet 1985, 1995). By contrast, the Linear B tablets of Pylos record some 240 toponyms (Bennet 1995, 594; Nakassis 2013a), while those at Knossos record about 100 (Bennet 1985, 233). The Thebes records, however, come from only piecemeal excavations of the site, whereas Pylos and Knossos were excavated much more comprehensively.

Based on the texts that are known and the archaeological sites to which they can be related, Del Freo (2009, 66–67) proposes a territorial division between Orchomenos and Thebes, which is attested in later periods (see also Dakouri-Hild 2010a). This fits quite well with a spatial model of Theban territory, in which all the sites with recorded economic relationships to Thebes seem to fall into territory close to Thebes, or to the south or east (map 12).

Beyond the secondary centers of Eleon and Eutresis, two other major sites within the Theban polity are located along the projected border with Orchomenos: Potniai and Ptoon. Other major sites are located at the main access points to the sea. There is a fortified site in the protected bay of Livadostro/Kreusis (appearing in the Thebes tablets as *ke-re-u-so*) on the Corinthian Gulf, and there are three important sites on the Euboean Gulf near the Euripos, all of which are positioned at prominent topographical locations and seem to have been fortified. Drosia/Lithosoros is located in a small, sheltered bay on the north side of the Euripos.

11. Eleon has been the subject of recent excavations by the Eastern Boeotia Archaeological Project, which also conducted three seasons of intensive survey in the area. See Aravantinos et al. 2016a; Burke et al. 2020. On Eutresis, see Goldman 1931; Mountjoy 1983, 93–95; Farinetti 2011, 342; Van Damme 2017b, 96–99.

Glypha is across the Euripos from Chalkis. Dramesi/Paralia Avlidos is just to the south. Aulis, which also has Mycenaean remains, is located in between the latter two (Ghilardi et al. 2013). Together, these would have formed a set of strategic access points to the sea, surrounding an important choke point (the Euripos) that could only be passed at certain times of the day. In the southwest, Plataia was located near the Kaza Pass on the Boeotian side of Mount Kithairon (another liminal area mentioned in the Thebes tablets), which was the main route of access to Attica and the Peloponnese via the Mazi Plain. This area was apparently already a crossroads in Mycenaean times (Knodell, Fachard, and Papangeli 2017, 160; Fachard and Knodell 2020). In the southeast, Tanagra was sited over an important agricultural valley along another main route of access to the Theban Plain. Significantly, there are no locations mentioned in the Thebes tablets that fall within the modeled territory of Orchomenos.[12]

A final group of geographical referents is made up of anthroponyms: two are Cretan, three are Anatolian, and one is Laconian. The occurrence of such anthroponyms is not unusual, and these personal names do not necessarily mean a person was from the place in question; they do, however, illustrate some aspects of the wider world of which Thebes was a part. With the possible exception of Troy and Sminthos, the only other sites mentioned have significant Mycenaean components (see table 7). So, while the Linear B texts provide locations and goods coming or going, a geographical reading indicates that Thebes is mostly concerned with its significance as a regional power in Boeotia, with occasional indications of places and people farther afield. There is nothing in the Linear B texts about diplomatic relationships or long-distance trade (Murray 2017, 32–34).

The territorial models resulting from an analysis of the Thebes tablets provide a convenient starting point for understanding the extent and operations of other Mycenaean palaces, even if we should be cautious about considering such analogies absolute. While we have more to say about the specifics of the Theban case, the same factors may be kept in mind when considering the political landscapes of other palatial entities, most notably Orchomenos, from an archaeological perspective.

Orchomenos was a developing center in the Early Mycenaean period (and an important MH center well before), with cemetery remains spanning MH III–LH IIIA (Sarri 2010). Prehistoric material has been reported on the lower slopes of the Classical acropolis but this has only been scantily published (Schliemann 1881; de Ridder 1895; Bulle 1907). Most Mycenaean material comes from below—in the vicinity of the modern town and monastery of Panaghia Skripou. Orchomenos boasts several vestiges of a Mycenaean palace, including wall paintings, "palatial"

12. It has been occasionally suggested that *a-re-o* may represent Halai, which appears to be on the other side of Orchomenian territory. This appears to be a personal name, so it does not indicate a particular place; nor does it imply some sort of territorial relationship, even if it is an ethnic (Kramer-Hajos 2006).

buildings, and the only tholos tomb in Boeotia—the so-called Treasury of Minyas—which Pausanias (*Description of Greece* 9.36.4–5) compared to the walls of Tiryns and the pyramids of Egypt in its magnificence (Alcock and Cherry 2006; Aravantinos et al. 2016b). Near the monastery, Spyropoulos (1974) found architectural remains and fresco fragments, including scenes of an organized military and an armada.[13] This subject matter, together with the substantial buildings, the elite cemeteries, and the literary tradition, suggests that there was a palatial authority present, comparable to other Mycenaean centers.

The wider pattern of settlement for northwestern Boeotia is not as clear-cut as for Thebes. The cost-based territorial model employed here would put the northern boundary of Orchomenian territory well into East Lokris. We might also suggest a more modest territorial extent, bounded in the north by the natural geographical barrier of Mount Chlomon. This would imply a territory extending to the west and northwest of Orchomenos to Chaironeia and Panopeus; indeed, it seems likely that Orchomenian interests would have extended south to the outlet of the Corinthian Gulf at Medeon and Antikyra (see further below, on southern Phokis). To the north, the territory of Orchomenos may have extended farther up the Kephisos valley as far as Elateia and Kalapodi, although the latter would have involved entering the geographically distinct valley between Kallidromon and Chlomon. Eder (2007, 90–98) has demonstrated links between Medeon and Elateia (among other parts of the Mycenaean world) in the form of identical seals and sealings, which she associates with Orchomenos. Van de Moortel and colleagues (2019) have suggested that the expanding polity of Orchomenos may have been responsible for a widespread LH IIIA2 destruction at Mitrou. It seems, then, that the northern extents of Orchomenian territory were likely dynamic and contested. The most important territorial extent of Orchomenos was to the east, where a network of sites stretches to Larymna as a point of access to the Euboean Gulf and establishes a border with Thebes to protect this and the Kopaic Basin.

The drainage of Lake Kopais and construction of the fortifications at Gla represent a building and engineering effort greater than anything known in the Mycenaean world at the time. The drainage alone diverted four rivers through the construction of polders, embankments, and canals, many of which had cyclopean revetments. Building the dykes on either side of the canals involved moving an estimated 2 million cubic meters of earth and 250,000 cubic meters of stone. The total amount of land reclaimed was approximately 1,500 hectares (Knauss, Heinrich, and Kalcyk 1984; Knauss 1987; Iakovidis 2001; Kountouri et al. 2012; Lane et al. 2016, 2020). Recent work by the AROURA and MYNEKO projects has suggested that the drainage works in the Kopais are 300 to 400 years older than the fortification works at Gla, which are traditionally dated to LH IIIB1 (Lane et al. 2016). This date is surprisingly early and should be approached with some caution. This type and this scale of land amelioration is nearly impossible to imagine

13. These wall paintings can be viewed in the Thebes museum. See Tournavitou 2017 for comparable scenes from the West House at Mycenae.

without the aegis of some form of state-level authority, of which there is no other evidence in the Early Mycenaean period. Comparative research on complex societies in Mesoamerica has demonstrated that such large-scale systems of dykes and canals require massive collective action, are rare, and, when they do occur, appear well after the rise of hierarchical polities; smaller-scale networks of canals and dams, by contrast, can emerge much earlier (Carballo, Roscoe, and Feinman 2014, 116–17). It may be the case, therefore, that small-scale canal networks were created during the Early Mycenaean period but expanded substantially in Palatial times.

A regional program of fortification was undertaken in LH IIIB, with new sites or forts established at Pyrgos, Stroviki, Kastro Kopais, Aghia Marina Pyrgos, Aghios Ioannis, and Larymna (see map 12). Haliartos, on the southern border, was fortified as well. I argue that the purpose of this fortification system was threefold: (1) to protect the agricultural investment in the Kopaic Basin; (2) to secure the route between Orchomenos, Gla, and the Euboean Gulf; and (3) to monitor the nearby border with Thebes.

Gla was at the center of this program of agricultural innovation and fortification. The earliest pottery at Gla can be dated to LH IIIA2/B1. LH IIIA2 forms have parallels in LH IIIB1 and in any case are found in contexts dominated by LH IIIB1 forms. Iakovidis (2001, 142–45) thus dates the construction to the LH IIIB1 period, or around 1300 BCE. Occupation lasted until the citadel's destruction in LH IIIB2, shortly before 1200 BCE (Iakovidis 2001, 145). Gla has the largest complete circuit of any Mycenaean site, as well as numerous interior buildings.[14]

Gla has traditionally been interpreted as a military or agricultural redistributive center (Iakovidis 2001). Kramer-Hajos (2016, 115–25) has recently argued that the construction of Gla was a joint venture between Orchomenos and Thebes, noting that the wider system of fortifications was to the north of the Kopais rather than being oriented toward Thebes. This is true, but it does not account for the geographical division between the two territories. Moreover, there are significant fortified sites at entry points on the "Theban" side at Kastraki and Akraiphnion, and on the "Orchomenian" side near Haliartos. The northern fortifications were intended to protect and monitor this northern extent of territory, to be sure, but also to secure the important land route between Orchomenos, Gla, and the port of Larymna. The connection between these places in the landscape—all falling within a panoramic view from Orchomenos—lends further credence to an association specifically with this site and not with Thebes.

Contrary to arguments that Gla was an agricultural facility or some kind of joint venture, I suggest that Gla was built as a relocation of Orchomenian palatial authority in the center of a new agricultural and defense network (see also Knodell 2013, 165–66; forthcoming; Maggidis 2020). The palatial characteristics of the site itself are several. The monumental circuit wall is far larger than that of any other

14. Recent site clearance and geophysical survey at Gla have revealed that building remains were much more extensive than previously thought (Maggidis 2020, 114–15). A new program of survey and excavation, directed by Kountouri, is currently underway (2018–22).

Mycenaean site, containing gates on the west, north, southeast, and south sides. These gates open toward Orchomenos, Anthedon, Mount Ptoios, and Thebes, respectively. It is noteworthy that the gates facing Theban territory directly are the most heavily fortified. This was the largest single building project undertaken in Boeotia in the entire Bronze Age, its magnitude highlighted even further by the drainage project and the wider program of regional fortification.

The northernmost part of the site, the *melathron*, appears the most palatial in character, with two megara, whose presumed use was for the top officials at the site (Iakovidis 2001, 40). Iakovidis writes that the *melathron* complex at Gla was not designed for a *wanax* and his retinue, arguing that its size, its accessibility, and the two megara do not match other known examples from Mycenaean palaces, specifically Mycenae, Tiryns, and Pylos. But why should we expect it to be the same? Similarities in palace plans and the singular notion of a *megaron* as a defining characteristic apply to only a few cases, all of which are in the Peloponnese (Younger 2005). No megaron has been revealed in the limited excavations of palatial buildings at Thebes (Aravantinos 2015, 21–22), and there are also double megara at Dimini in Thessaly (Adrimi-Sismani 2007) and at Kanakia in Salamis (Lolos 2012). We also know very little about Orchomenos and what a palace there might have looked like. Moreover, access to the *melathron* at Gla was in fact much more restricted than Iakovidis argues. Visitors would have had to come first through the "agora" area and then enter another set of gates before approaching and gaining access to the terrace on which the *melathron* was built. From the perspective of architectonic exclusivity (Smith 1999), access was more restricted than at the more canonical palaces of Pylos, Mycenae, and Tiryns (Thaler 2015; see also figure 3). Numerous frescoes add to the palatial character of the site (Boulotis 2015), and fragments of Linear B-inscribed stirrup jars suggest further importance at a regional and interregional scale (Iakovidis 1989, 1998, 2001).

The evidence from Gla and the Kopais therefore suggests a dramatic reorientation of the political landscape in LH IIIB. The most obvious aspect of this reorientation is a shift eastward, toward the Euboean Gulf and the especially fertile eastern part of the drained basin, culminating with a relocation of palatial authority at Gla. This is not to suggest a replacement for Orchomenos, which, as the ancestral center of the polity, no doubt remained important. Indeed, such political practices are well known in other settings—as, for example, in the movement of the ancient Macedonian capital from Aigai to Pella, with Aigai remaining the royal burial ground (Miller 2016, 291; Aelianus, *Varia Historia* 14.17). Such lasting significance may be reflected in the Treasury of Minyas, for example. But the level of investment in the layout of Gla and in the landscape around it suggests that this was conceived of and functioned as the primary administrative center of the polity of which it was a part. The well-fortified site at the center of a wider defense network provided a base that was at once closer to sea routes and to the agricultural production that was the central focus of Mycenaean palatial polities. This move is coincident with similar developments in Thebes, which renovated its own fortifications in LH IIIB (Aravantinos 2010, 54), perhaps in response to the appearance of the citadel at Gla so close to its border.

Such territorial tensions may help to explain the numerous destruction levels at Orchomenos, Gla, and Thebes at the end of LH IIIB. Gla was destroyed in LH IIIB2, along with the drainage works in the Kopaic Basin and the system of fortifications protecting it.[15] This wiped out both the palatial authority at Gla and the agricultural resources of the Kopais. Spyropoulos (1974) notes that the palatial structure (an isolated megaron-like building) at Orchomenos was also destroyed at this time. Thebes seems to have suffered numerous destructions throughout the Palatial period; these have been variously dated to LH IIIA2-B1, LH IIIB1, and LH IIIB2 (Dakouri-Hild 2010b, 698; Aravantinos 2015).

Thebes and Orchomenos are much closer to each other than any other palatial centers in central Greece. Between them they have some of the richest agricultural land in the entire region. This proximity would have been a source of tension between these two polities, both of which seem to have pursued similar pathways to regional integration. Later literary traditions of conflict between the two polities may also be telling. From a spatial perspective, the drainage of Lake Kopais and the construction of the citadel at Gla would have changed the relationship between the Orchomenian and Theban polities significantly.

The wider context of these destructions and fortifications can be observed throughout the Mycenaean world. Palaces in the Argolid, too, seem to have pursued major fortification programs in LH IIIB. The scale of these projects and the large amount of time they would have taken to complete invite several potential explanations. In general, the walls and the blocks used to create them are far larger than would be needed to repel an invader or create a stable structure. In seeking to explain this architectural hyperbole, some have seen cyclopean fortifications (especially the Lion Gate at Mycenae) as imitations of Hittite citadels, geared toward a symbolic display of palatial power and an implicit control over human and natural resources (e.g., Maner 2012). Along the same lines, we might look to the Egyptian model of conscripted labor as a mode of state control during the nonagricultural season (Lehner 2015). Peer-polity interaction contributes a useful perspective as well, whereby rivalry and competition engender a set of shared symbolic practices (Renfrew and Cherry 1986). We might suggest more specifically that these monumental fortifications were built as a response to mounting tensions within or between Mycenaean polities. This may be viewed as a sort of symbolic "arms race" in interpolity relations, which can also be seen in patterns of fortification in the Maya world (Webster 2000) and in Classical Greek borderlands (Knodell, Fachard, and Papangeli 2017, 161).

---

15. This destruction date for the drainage works is problematic and is generally assumed, based on destructions and disuse at Gla and the surrounding sites.

The destructions in Boeotia at the end of LH IIIB represent the culmination of a variety of conflicts within and between Mycenaean polities. Based on the archaeological evidence and territorial models presented here, it seems that a series of confrontations occurred between Thebes, Orchomenos, and Gla resulting in the overthrow of palatial structures and institutions at all three sites. It is possible (though by nature speculative and tangential to the arguments above) that some of these events may have entered the mythological record as stories of Herakles (a Theban) flooding the Orchomenian Plain by diverting the Kephisos and destroying the citadel of the Minyans (Orchomenos) (Salowey 1994).

This end, of course, should not be seen as absolute, and several abandoned sites were later reoccupied. What is important, however, is that this marks the final end of the palaces per se. While later occupation and building occur, palatial architecture, art, and burial are not revived, nor are any traces of central administration (Linear B). This suggests that these events should not be attributed solely to interpolity conflict. In addition to any destruction by external forces, these events also represent an internal rejection of the palatial system in Boeotia, most likely as a collective response to dissatisfaction with state authority.

Euboea Between Two Worlds

Euboea offers a complement and a contrast to Palatial Boeotia, especially in terms of its apparent diversity in modes of sociopolitical organization. While relationships between the two regions are evident in the settlement, material, and textual record, the island nevertheless seems quite apart from the world of the palaces. Euboea has significant remains from the Palatial Bronze Age at a number of locations, with different regional patterns observable in the northern and central parts of the island and the south remaining devoid of Late Bronze Age settlement (see map 9). I argue that the settlement patterns of Euboea represent various nonpalatial modes of sociopolitical organization that are contemporary with the mainland palaces (see also Knodell, forthcoming).

The north is home to several widely interspersed small-scale sites, mostly along the Euboean Gulf, with two further coastal jumping-off points to the bay of Volos at Oreoi (ancient Histiaia) and to the Sporades or wider Aegean at Kerinthos. Based on the small-scale, thinly dispersed evidence, we can guess that these were simple, agropastoral communities that were nevertheless in contact with each other and with some communities on neighboring coasts. Nevertheless, cyclopean-style walls at Kerinthos, extensive pottery remains at Lichas, and an impressive chamber tomb at Limni (the only one north of the central plain) suggest that there is more to be revealed about Mycenaean northern Euboea (Sackett et al. 1966, 108–9; Sapouna-Sakelleraki 1995, 1996; Loader 1998, 36–37; Nikolopoulos 2015; Lemos 2020).

The bulk of settlement evidence comes from central Euboea, which is clearly in dialogue with palatial spheres of the mainland (see map 10). Based on the current evidence, we can approximate perhaps seven or eight peer communities in central Euboea, at Psachna, Chalkis, Lefkandi, Amarynthos, Aliveri, Avlonari, and Viglatouri/Oxylithos. These can be broadly described as complex communities, with limited evidence for social stratification in the form of funerary architecture and a small-scale settlement hierarchy in which the aforementioned sites are locally distinct in scale. These sites were probably controlled by powerful family groups that expressed their status through elaborate tombs and exclusive material culture—similar to what is present on the mainland in the Early Mycenaean period.

The Psachna Plain was home to several Mycenaean sites, most notably at Aghios Ilias—a prominent hill that dominates the plain and two points of access to it from the north and east. No systematic excavation has been conducted, but Sackett and colleagues (1966, 54) considered it to have been a major site throughout the Mycenaean period, based on dense pottery scatters at and around the site and terracing on the southwest slopes. The prominent location, evidence of large-scale terracing, and higher density and extent of finds than at other sites in the area suggests that this was an important center at the top of a settlement hierarchy local to the Psachna Plain. Mycenaean sherd scatters are reported in fields through much of the broader area, from Politika in the north to Manika in the south (Sackett et al. 1966, 54–57).

Chalkis is more difficult to understand. As is the case for most periods, settlement remains are likely buried under the modern city, the largest on the island (Kalamara et al. 2015). Nevertheless, the extent of the community can be inferred from the dispersed remains, which include several chamber tomb cemeteries, the considerable wealth of which is on display in the Chalkis museum (Hankey 1952). Sackett and others (1966, 57–60) record no fewer than nine sites with prehistoric remains, and Pei (also called Dokos), located to the north, may have been the location of a tumulus or tholos (Sapouna-Sakellaraki 1996).[16] The overall spread of remains across several parts of the modern city suggests a community of substantial size (Nikolopoulos 2015).

Lefkandi is less than 10 kilometers from Chalkis, in the southeast corner of the Lelantine Plain, near the outlet of the Lelas River. This was renowned agricultural land in antiquity, and the supposed cause of the mythohistorical Lelantine War between Chalkis and Eretria (see further in chapter 6). Already in the Bronze Age two major communities were located on opposite sides of the plain, in contrast to the palatial strategy in Boeotia of placing a dominant community in the center. This may suggest a more maritime orientation for Palatial period sites in Euboea, which was certainly the case in the Postpalatial period on the Euboean Gulf (see further in chapters 4 and 5). LH IIIC and PG building activity at Lefkandi has limited our knowledge of Palatial times, though the site was almost certainly

16. This interpretation is speculative at best, with no demonstrable tholos architecture and no documented Mycenaean finds that can be associated with the site. This badly degraded circular construction could also be a lime kiln.

occupied. Sherratt (1980) suggests that LH IIIC pottery traditions started earlier in Euboea than elsewhere, which may in part explain the relatively small amount of clear Palatial material from Lefkandi and Amarynthos in comparison to the amount of material from the Postpalatial phases. This argument is supported by the fact that Lefkandi seems to have been *the* preeminent center for the export of LH IIIC pottery in the Euboean Gulf (see chapter 4, pp. 137–41).

Amarynthos is the only site in Euboea that can be plausibly identified in the Linear B tablets from Thebes, as later inscriptional evidence identifies the site as the sanctuary of Artemis Amarysia (Sapouna-Sakelleraki 1989; Krapf 2011; Fachard et al. 2017). This community was located at a crucial node in a central Euboean network of Mycenaean sites that stretches from the Psachna Plain north of Chalkis to the Kyme-Aliveri corridor (see map 10). Its position on the east side of the Eretrian Plain leaves it well positioned to exploit this important agricultural surface, and at this point in the Bronze Age it is clearly the dominant site in this area (Sackett et al. 1966, 64–66; Parlama 1979; Sapouna-Sakellaraki 1989). By contrast, only fragmentary Mycenaean remains have been found at Eretria and Magoula (Müller-Çelka, Krapf, and Verdan 2013). The location of Amarynthos gives it close access to both the maritime route of the Euboean Gulf and the land route from Aliveri to Kyme.

The Aliveri-Kyme corridor passes through several small valleys that contain the most impressive evidence of Mycenaean funerary activity on the island: a series of small tholos tombs at the sites of Velousia, Katakalou, and Evrimia and Paralia, both located at Oxylithos (see map 9; figure 4a and 4b; see also Sackett et al. 1966, 68–77). This natural route is marked by the course of a modern road; it was undoubtedly a significant passage in the Mycenaean period as well, connecting the Aegean coast with the Euboean Gulf.

Aliveri (Magoula) was almost certainly the principal settlement on the southern end of this corridor, where it could access agricultural land to the northwest (toward modern Aliveri) and to the east toward Velousia, Lepoura, and Katakalou. Recent work by the Ephorate of Antiquities of Euboea has revealed further Mycenaean chamber tombs of LH IIIB–C date in the vicinity.[17] The tholoi of Velousia and Katakalou are both robbed, but their presence signals proximity to an important settlement (Sackett et al 1966, 68–71). These tombs may represent territorial claims of local elite families, but it is impossible to know if they belonged to the same community or polity. Farther south, near Dystos, Cyclopean walls have been documented at Loupaka, comprising the farthest south settlement remains documented in Euboea (Fachard 2009).

At Avlonari, located to the north, another substantial community seems to have occupied two hills (Palaiokastro and Antires) just west of the modern town. Wealthy tombs with gold objects, including a mask, were reported here, along with

17. See the press release here: https://www.culture.gr/el/Information/SitePages/view.aspx?nID = 2348.

FIGURE 4. Some lesser-known tholoi of central Greece: Katakalou tholos on Euboea (a: exterior, looking northeast, and interior, from the chamber, looking southwest, and b: interior, showing relieving triangle and lintel); Tholos A at Medeon (c: from the chamber, looking west); tholos tomb found at Amblianos, near Amphissa (d: from above, looking northwest); tholos tomb at Georgiko (e: exterior, looking north, and f: interior, from the dromos, looking north) (image permissions courtesy of the Ephorates of Antiquities of Euboea [a and b], Boeotia [c], Phokis [d], and Karditsa [e and f], ©Hellenic Ministry of Culture and Sports-Archaeological Receipts Fund).

an LH chamber tomb cemetery, though the tombs themselves were never located and finds are unconfirmed (Sackett et al 1966, 71–73).

Near the modern town of Oxylithos, an acropolis site (Viglatouri/Kyme) overlooks a river outlet with a rich set of cemeteries—the two previously mentioned tholoi, one of which contained a Mycenaean dagger, and a chamber tomb cemetery at Moni Mantzari (Sackett et al 1966, 73–76). The wealth of remains at Oxylithos and its location on the bay of Kyme suggest that this was the intended destination of some 17 pillow-type oxhide ingots that were found just off the coast near Enoria in 1906, south of Kyme's modern harbor (Sackett et al. 1966, 75–76, n125; Lolos 2001b; Paschalidis 2007, 436). Notably, the wealthy funerary remains only date to the Palatial period, indicating that this site may have declined in significance for long-distance trade in Postpalatial times, as sites on the Euboean Gulf began to thrive. At Viglatouri, however, there is substantial continuity with a series of buildings from Middle Geometric and Protogeometric times (sometimes referred to as a heroön) above a Mycenaean megaron-like building (Sapouna-Sakellaraki 1998, 61–63; Kourou 2015, 96; Charalambidou 2017, 93).

The absence of Mycenaean material in southern Euboea remains somewhat troublesome. *A-ma-ru-to* and *ka-ru-to* are associated with Euboea based on later place names, but this is complicated by uncertainties about their nature and exact location. While there is evidence of a substantial Mycenaean site at Amarynthos (see above), no more than a few sherds of Mycenaean material have been found in the entire region of Classical and later Karystos (Tankosić 2011; Cullen et al. 2013). This near complete absence is surprising for any part of central Greece, especially one that appears to feature in Linear B tablets. The location at the southern end of the Euboean Gulf, with the important Mycenaean centers of Thorikos, Brauron, and Marathon on the opposite coast, makes this all the more puzzling. It is possible that Mycenaean Karystos simply has not been found but this seems unlikely since the region has been subject to numerous campaigns of intensive and extensive archaeological survey since the 1980s (Keller 1985; Tankosić and Chidiroglou 2010; Cullen et al. 2013; Tankosić et al., forthcoming). Even if such a site exists but has not been found, it would need to be part of a wider regional system, of which we have no trace.

Overall, the pattern of settlement and social organization in Euboea varies dramatically across the island and also contrasts significantly with Boeotia. Small coastal settlements were found in the northern part of the island, with access to small agricultural plains and outlets across the Euboean Gulf or to the Sporades. The evidence does not provide much detail about sociopolitical organization, but these communities seem to have been less hierarchical and complex than those found in the central part of the island and do not seem to have been associated with any larger state apparatus. The communities of central Euboea seem to have been more complex, perhaps because of their stronger connections to the palatial mainland, and we might suggest several small, independent polities—small-scale complex communities that participated in Mycenaean modes of expressing hierarchy in terms of both central places and elite funerary architecture. Nevertheless, they seem to have been quite distinct from the polities of the mainland, and at any rate operated on a very different scale. An analogy might be found in the way some Early Mycenaean polities depended on relationships with Minoan palaces—participating in wider trade networks and exploiting the profits of them locally, without being integrated into their political systems.

Nonpalatial Worlds between Phokis and Thessaly

Between Boeotia and the bay of Volos there is nothing that can be reliably identified as a Mycenaean palace. The overall distribution and organization of settlement varies considerably. Across these areas (East Lokris, Malis, Phokis), there is an increase in the number of sites from the Palatial period, but there is no "top tier" occupied by identifiable palaces, and there is no landscape- or region-wide evidence for centralized organization. In general, these patterns of organization seem to have more in common with the nonpalatial world of Euboea than with either of the palatial polities in Boeotia. As is the case with Euboea, these regions are discussed together as blocks of contiguous areas, without suggesting a uniformity of political organization.

Two main axes define the regions grouped together here. The first is the Great Isthmus Corridor Route, running north-south and linking together the modern towns of Lamia and Itea, the ancient regions of Doris and Phokis, and the Corinthian and Malian Gulfs (Kase et al. 1991). The second runs east-west to join the northern Euboean Gulf and East Lokris to the upper Kephisos valley and the corridor route (see map 10). The connectivity model highlights three main pockets of communities that cluster around these routes. The first is in southern Phokis, in the vicinity of Delphi. The second is a rather long, east-to-west arc that extends from East Lokris on the Euboean Gulf into northern Phokis at the regional crossroads of Kalapodi and from there into the northern Kephisos valley. The third group of communities surrounds Lamia in the eastern Spercheios valley.

In southern Phokis there is a triangle of settlement framed by the bays of Itea and Antikyra and the pass between Livadeia and Delphi. I suggest that these groupings represent two different political entities (and indeed types of entities). As indicated above, the bay of Antikyra seems the most likely access to the Corinthian Gulf for Orchomenos. Numerous sites along the way create a clear route linking the western part of the Orchomenian Plain (occupied by the palatial site itself) to the bay. Moreover, Tholos A at Medeon (figure 4c) demonstrates a particular connection to Orchomenos in the form of a rare side chamber, examples of which are found only at Orchomenos, Mycenae (in the Peloponnese), and Fourni (on Crete). The aforementioned study by Eder (2007) links this site to Elateia, perhaps via Orchomenos. The acropolis sites at Medeon and across the bay at Kastro tou Stenou would have provided defensible lookouts from which to monitor traffic on either side of the bay. Unfortunately, little more can be said about the settlement sites (Vatin 1969; Sideris 2014). One aspect of the location of these sites in the bay of Antikyra is a relative lack of agricultural land, suggesting that the presence of large-scale settlement here was linked mostly to its role as a port.

By contrast, the bay of Itea boasts abundant and productive agricultural land (McInerney 1999). Krisa was a citadel-like fortified site with cyclopean walling, towering high above the Krisean Plain. Kase (1970, 1972) has argued that it was a major land power that controlled the plain of Itea, its bay, and the land route north, which had Mycenaean road remains (see also Kase et al. 1991; Livieratou 2020, 817–18). A fortified harbor site is located at Kirra (Orgeolet et al. 2017). A second fortified site at Itea Glas protected the western access of the plain. This settlement system, with smaller sites in the surrounding area, suggests that an independent polity dominated the valley and bay, with immediate access to agricultural resources, the Corinthian Gulf, and routes to the north. Krisa seems to be the most significant of these three fortified sites, suggesting it may have occupied the top place in a hierarchy between them (though this is difficult to say with any certainty). In this case, the influence of Krisa may have extended some distance north toward Amphissa, where a large tholos tomb was discovered at the site of Amblianos (figure 4d).[18]

Concerning the wider political landscape, it is possible that Orchomenos could have extended its influence this far, though Medeon seems a more likely point of access from Boeotia. While Medeon is on the very edge of a modeled maximum for Orchomenian territory, the bay of Itea is well outside of that maximum, making this an unnecessary stretch to reach the Corinthian Gulf (see map 11). An independent polity here with a powerful Boeotian neighbor not far away may in part explain the heavy fortifications. The corridor route northward conveniently bypasses Boeotia to come out in the upper Kephisos valley, and from there connects to Malis and eventually to Thessaly. Common attributes of matt-painted pottery from Delphi, Kirra, Pefkakia, and the Spercheios valley seem to indicate connections all the way from Itea to Volos from at least the Middle Bronze Age (Dakoronia 2010). This centrality within a wider network of land and sea routes is certainly part of what made Delphi such an important place later in the history of the region. Some of the same geographical forces were no doubt at work at Krisa.

The upper Kephisos valley was occupied by a handful of small-scale sites during the Mycenaean period, including a larger center at Elateia with abundant evidence of elites (Bächle 2007). Jewelry, seals, and weapons were found in an excavated chamber tomb cemetery of some 91 tombs, indicating significant levels of wealth (and inequality) within the community (Dakoronia 2009; Deger-Jalkotzy 2009). Identical seals from this site and Medeon may also indicate a common political

18. The discovery of the tholos tomb at Amblianos, near Amphissa, was announced in the newspaper *To Βήμα*. See "Ανακάλυψη Θολωτού τάφου μυκηναϊκών χρόνων," *To Βήμα*, July 29, 2014, https:// www.tovima.gr/2014/07/29/culture/anakalypsi-tholwtoy-tafoy-mykinaikwn-xronwn/.

link through Orchomenos (Eder 2007). Many of the tombs, however, date to the Postpalatial period and continue to be used into the Early Iron Age, demonstrating remarkable continuity not seen, for example, in neighboring Boeotia (see chapters 4 and 5). Wealthy grave goods from the Palatial period are seen elsewhere in the region only at Kalapodi and Zeli, which are both located to the east. From this evidence it seems likely that Elateia dominated the upper Kephisos valley, although we cannot rule out the presence of locally independent settlements elsewhere. The level of political integration across the landscape is largely unknowable based on the present evidence, and indeed Orchomenos may well have been influential or dominant in this area, too—as has been suggested by Eder (2007) and by the territorial model (see map 11).

Kalapodi occupies a critical crossroads between the upper Kephisos valley and East Lokris. Chamber tomb cemeteries in the surrounding area suggest that it was also an important region for settlement, with communities located at Kalapodi itself as well as at Zeli (to the west) and Golemi (to the east). It is noteworthy that both Delphi and Kalapodi—two early centers of regional cult activity—are located at major crossroads near the margins of modeled palatial territory. Cult activity at Kalapodi can now be traced back to the beginning of the Late Bronze Age, and at Delphi to LH III in the form of Phi and Psi figurines at the sanctuary of Athena Pronoia (Felsch 1981; Müller 1992; Niemeier 2016). Kalapodi, at least, seems to have functioned as a regional meeting place in much the same way such sites did in later periods. Other places probably functioned similarly as well, but within palatial territories these would have been rendered obsolete by the concentration of cultic and other social gatherings at the palaces themselves. In a way, then, such regional sanctuaries could have existed only outside the realm of the palaces, and they continued to function as loci for the agglomeration and dispersal of goods and ideas. The communities in the vicinity obviously benefited from this as well.

East Lokris seems to decline in the Mycenaean Palatial period, perhaps because it was overshadowed by the palaces of Boeotia. Kramer-Hajos (2016, 100) has referred to this process as the "domestication of the warrior," in which the warrior classes represented in the elite burials of the Early Mycenaean period were made largely obscure. Yet burials represent only certain aspects of sociopolitical affairs. It seems likely that the palaces of Boeotia were indeed creating imbalances in the consumption and distribution of prestige items, but the continuity of cultural practice between Early Mycenaean times and the Postpalatial period suggests that life in East Lokris went on with relatively little change. While Lokrian society was no doubt impacted by the palaces, it need not have been through political domination.

There are two east-west axes of communication that run from the Euboean Gulf to the Corinthian Gulf (see map 10). I suggest that one of these—the one running between the bay of Antikyra and Larymna—was largely controlled by the palatial polity of Orchomenos. The northern axis is more difficult to understand, since it represents a settlement network made up of communities with considerably less visible variety in size and hierarchy. To be sure, differentiation is still present, but here we might imagine a situation more like that found in central Euboea, with relatively small communities and territories organized on a local scale, and with limited evidence for social differentiation. Certain major sites are located along this axis, at Krisa, Kalapodi, Elateia, and Mitrou, which probably attracted palatial attention and were variously influenced by or perhaps in some cases incorporated into the palatial world.

Finally, the Spercheios valley and the region of Lamia (ancient Malis) comprise another distinct hub of settlement. There is little evidence for settlement between the upper Kephisos valley and Malis, there being only a few sites located along the principal land routes. A handful of sites dot the landscape on the southern end of the plain of Lamia, in the foothills of Mounts Kallidromon and Oita, occupying the major points of access to the plain and controlling passage into and out of it. Lamia itself seems to have been the dominant site in the region, as through much of its history, with additional, apparently wealthy, communities populating the Spercheios valley, especially at Kompotades, Vikiorema, Tymbanos, and Platania (Dakoronia 1990, 2009; Papakonstantinou 2009). Positioned at a strategic entry point to the valley, Hypati represents a sort of western limit. The organization of settlement in the area is difficult to discern, not least due to a lack of full publication for most of the Mycenaean material thus far only briefly reported. The general impression follows that of other nonpalatial areas, with a few distinct communities perhaps dominated by elite families—a pattern consistent from the Early Mycenaean period through LH IIIC. There is no clear center, although Lamia is of course a likely candidate for a central place of some kind. Without evidence for regional integration, and with dispersed communities represented by wealthy cemeteries that seem more or less evenly distributed and on par with one another, this looks similar to the nonpalatial situations of East Lokris, northern Phokis, and Euboea. On the other hand, there is a significant clustering of chamber tomb cemeteries around Lamia, suggesting that there may have been a principal site located there (as in later periods), perhaps analogous to the situation with Krisa in the bay of Itea.

Mycenaean Thessaly

Often called the "periphery," Thessaly is on the margins of what is traditionally defined as the Mycenaean world (Feuer 1983, 2011, 2016a, 2016b; Adrimi-Sismani 2007). Feuer (2016b) characterizes the region as existing in three parts: (1) a core zone around the north and west sides of the Pagasetic Gulf, (2) a border zone extending up the Enipeus and Pineios river valleys to Trikala and Larisa, and (3) a frontier zone beyond that. The defining criteria are essentially geographical—proximity to the sea and the palatial centers in Volos afforded opportunities for interface with the wider Mycenaean world to the south. The inland plains of central, western, and northern Thessaly were more extensive and set apart. Feuer's assessment is largely reflected in the distribution of material culture, and this pattern was used also to define the northern limits of the study area investigated in this book (see map 2).

A dense concentration of activity is located around the bay of Volos, with three sites exhibiting palatial aspects of material culture: Dimini, Kastro Volos (Palaia), and Pefkakia. Pefkakia was a major site with evidence for habitation, various aspects of craft production, and long-distance trade. This was most likely the principal port of the region, situated at the entry point of the Pagasetic Gulf. The current excavator of the site has suggested that this is the port of Dimini, which she and others have identified with legendary Iolkos (Batziou-Efstathiou 2015; see also Adrimi-Sismani 2007, 2016).

Dimini is the most intensively excavated of the major Mycenaean sites in Thessaly (Tsountas 1908; Adrimi-Sismani 2017, 2018), and it has the most characteristics associated with Mycenaean palaces. A double megaron structure is present, with a possibly shared courtyard separating two parallel architectural complexes (see figure 3). This appears to be a palatial settlement with elite structures, workshops, and storage facilities. Linear B has been found at the site as well in the form of a stone weight inscribed with three signs (Adrimi-Sismani and Godart 2005). Two tholos tombs signal elite activity in the funerary realm. The Lamiospito tholos and an early megaron under Megaron A have been dated to the end of the fifteenth century, or LH IIIA. Subsequently the double-megaron complex was built, along with the second tholos. The palatial complex was destroyed in LH IIIB2/C. Curiously, no Mycenaean fortification has been discovered at Dimini.

The final palatial location is at Palaia, or Kastro Volos, in the heart of the modern city of Volos (Theocharis 1956, 1957, 1960, 1961; Skafida et al. 2016). As in the case of Thebes and Orchomenos, the Mycenaean site is covered completely by the modern city. Monumental buildings from the fifteenth century BCE have been excavated, as well as two tholos tombs, at Kapakli, immediately northwest of Kastro Volos, and at Kazanaki, on the Volos ring road some distance to the north (Pelon 1976, 243; Adrimi-Sismani and Alexandrou 2009; Papathanasiou 2009). While the architecture and layout of Mycenaean Volos are less well understood than at Dimini, the finds are in some ways more impressive, including exceptionally wealthy burials in the tholos tombs (the tholoi at Dimini were looted long ago) and Linear B tablets (Stamatopoulou 2011, 77–78; Skafida, Karnava, and Olivier 2012). The Kazanaki tholos, moreover, had seven Linear B signs inscribed on its lintel (Adrimi-Sismani and Alexandrou 2009). A final interesting feature of Kastro Volos is the continuity of occupation well into LH IIIC, which does not happen at Dimini and Pefkakia (both lasting only until LH IIIC Early).

The political landscape of the bay of Volos is tied to the history of these three sites, but their specific relationships are more difficult to discern. Pantou (2010) provides the most sophisticated analysis of the political organization of the region, proposing a heterarchical model in which power may have been shared between these three centers, the collective influence of which may have extended well beyond the bay. She points out, however, that the "palatial" remains at Dimini and Kastro Volos are on a somewhat lower order of magnitude than those found at other palatial centers. The size and sophistication of buildings is less than at other known palatial sites—there are no remnants of frescoes, no traces of fortifications, and the evidence for Linear B administration is extremely limited (Pantou 2010, 395–96). There are at least three possibilities, then, for the political organization of the landscape: (1) a distributed sense of political authority representing a single polity in the bay of Volos; (2) a model in which centralized authority shifts in different phases between competing independent centers; or (3) two or more independent polities coexisting for the most part independently.[19] The adoption of some aspects of Mycenaean palatial systems (Linear B at Volos and the architectural complex at Dimini) suggests that there would have been some interest in centralizing authority and integrating large agricultural landscapes in two different places. The relatively small plain of Volos would have provided limited opportunity for agriculture, but there are other, larger surfaces that fall easily within a modeled territorial extent (see map 11). These tracts of land are located chiefly to the northwest, in the vicinity of Lake Karla (ancient Boibeis), and to the south, toward Almyros. These areas also fit neatly within the "core" zone of Mycenaean material culture as modeled by Feuer (2016b).

The rich agricultural landscape of Lake Karla may well have served as a sort of breadbasket for the palatial entity (or entities) of the bay of Volos, with Velestino (ancient Pherai) occupying an important crossroads in between, where another major plain opens up southward to Aerino. In the network model (see map 10) this group of sites fits together reasonably well. The massive fortifications at Petra, if their estimated extent of about four kilometers is accurate, are the largest Mycenaean fortifications in all of Greece (Hope Simpson 1981, 165), though this site is largely uninvestigated.

To the south, it is possible that palatial influence extended to the plain of Almyros as far as Halos, but the scale of known Mycenaean remains in this area pales in comparison to what is found to the north (see maps 6 and 10). The distribution of sites between Phthiotic Thebes and Halos suggests that the plain was being exploited in Mycenaean times but tells us little about its broader political relationships (Stissi 2004). South of here a few isolated settlements may have prospered as small-scale polities taking advantage of their dual location on land and sea routes. Pteleon sports an impressive cemetery comprised of five small tholos tombs, and it is well positioned in a sheltered bay at the entry point to the Pagasetic Gulf, on the one hand, and at the main land route to Lamia, on the other (Feuer 1983, 44).

19. A range of models has been suggested also for the crowded palatial landscape of the Argolid (see, e.g., Vermeule 1964; Kilian 1988; Cherry and Davis 2001; Demakopoulou 2007; Burns 2010). Mycenae and Tiryns are both clearly major palatial sites there, and they are accompanied by significant, if poorly preserved, remains at Argos and Nafplio, and another major palatial site (if not necessarily a proper palace) at Medea, which also has very wealthy cemeteries (see map 9).

To the west, another group of communities in the vicinity of Pharsala was distinct from those of the Pagasetic Gulf, both in network terms and in falling outside the modeled territorial extent for a polity centered in the bay of Volos. Pharsala itself boasted a significant Mycenaean settlement, one marked by continuous use through the Early Iron Age as well (Katakouta 2009). Scattered remains are documented at a variety of other sites on the eastern edge of the western Thessalian Plain, occupying and exploiting this agricultural land; from these one could also move south to the western end of the Spercheios valley. This is the first group of communities that Feuer (2016b, 190) identifies as falling within his border zone, which extends up to Karditsa and Larisa, both of which also have important Mycenaean sites—not least the impressive tholos tomb at Georgiko (figure 4e and 4f)— but fewer shared attributes with the "core" areas that connect most clearly to the rest of central Greece.

In the background of all of this we must consider the dearth of systematic surveys that have been carried out in Thessaly (see table 3). While a good number of sites have been documented, and most major sites are probably known, the lack of systematic study (1) across the landscape as a whole and (2) at sites of major significance leaves the picture somewhat unclear. For example, the scale of fortification architecture at Petra and the monumental tholos at Georgiko suggest that these "border" zones are far from peripheral and demand further, more detailed attention in order to elucidate issues of chronology, settlement patterns, and social organization.[20] What is clear, however, is that the political landscape of Mycenaean Thessaly is quite distinct from what we have seen elsewhere, although there are some elements there that are apparently similar to palace-oriented Boeotia and others that resemble the still poorly understood situation in the bay of Itea.

Integration vs. Fragmentation: The Question of Athens and Attica

I turn last to Athens and Attica. While it seems that more information should be available for the region in the Palatial period, the picture of sociopolitical organization we have here is in fact just as complicated as it is in Thessaly, and perhaps even more so (Osborne 2020). Traditionally, Athens has been considered a palatial center in the mold of Pylos, Mycenae, and Thebes. There is evidence of a Mycenaean fortification on the acropolis, a "secret spring" comparable to the one at Mycenae, and wealthy burials in various places, most notably in the area of the Classical agora (Mountjoy 1995a).[21] The acropolis is the natural choice for such a settlement at Athens and the fortifications and evidence of a double gate below the Nike bastion are strong indicators of a significant palatial site (Wright 1994).

20. The internal relationships of communities in southern Thessaly have been emphasized here, along with their relationships farther south, but there is also much to be said about the northern interfaces (see Feuer 2016a and 2016b).

21. For an overview, see Mountjoy 1995a; Privitera 2013. For the Acropolis, see Iakovidis 1962, 2006; Wright 1994; Mylonas Shear 1999. For the spring, see Broneer 1939, Gauß 2003, Van Damme, forthcoming. For the agora, see Immerwahr 1971.

Most other architectural evidence has been obliterated by later building, though it is telling that builders during the Classical period left parts of the Mycenaean walls deliberately exposed—a demonstrable connection to a legendary Bronze Age past, which was likely also connected to Athenian notions of autochthony (Hurwitt 1999, 82).

The evidence from the acropolis and the settlement and burial evidence around Athens suggest a major polity, likely something resembling other Mycenaean palatial sites. The form, organization, territory, and relationship to other sites in Attica are less clear, not least since several other sites in the region appear to have functioned as politically independent entities. These already muddy waters are sometimes disturbed even further by invocations of the mythical synoecism of Theseus. Thucydides (2.15) says that until the time of Theseus the inhabitants of Attica had independent communities and councils and were then unified under the legendary hero king. This should not, of course, be the basis of an archaeological history, and in recent years, archaeologists have increasingly questioned the idea of a unified Attica in the Bronze Age. They have done so based on distinct and impressive concentrations of finds at several other prominent sites, most notably Eleusis, Thorikos, and Marathon (see, e.g., Stubbings 1947; Papadopoulos and Kontorli-Papadopoulou 2014; Cosmopoulos 2014, 2015; Papadimitriou 2017; Papadimitriou and Cosmopoulos 2020).

In the network models employed here, distinct clusters of sites occur in several places, often with one community that clearly stands out in the settlement hierarchy (see map 10). The first- and second-order sites that likely represented independent political entities are Athens, Eleusis, Marathon, and Thorikos. The Mesogeia Plain of central eastern Attica is more complicated, with major sites at Brauron, Spata, and Koropi, which also may have represented independent polities. Finally, Salamis seems to have boasted at least two major sites on opposite sides of the island, at Kanakia and Ampelakia, one of which (Kanakia) is described by its excavator as a palace in its own right (Lolos 2007, 2012).

Continuity at most of these sites from the Early Mycenaean period suggests that their rise cannot be linked to a particular palatial center, as we saw in Boeotia. There is in fact some decline observed in certain communities in LH IIIB, which has led some scholars to suggest a centralization of regional resources at Athens, though this in itself does not constitute evidence for regional integration (Papadimitriou and Cosmopoulos 2020). Supposing Athens did expand its influence beyond the Athenian basin at some point in the Late Bronze Age, it is interesting that the same territorial model applied to Thebes would put Thorikos and Marathon outside its influence and Eleusis on its outskirts (see map 11). While Athens does seem to have been the largest, most powerful site in Attica, perhaps by an order of magnitude, there are numerous reasons to think its political territory was limited to the basin of Athens, with Mount Aigaleo providing a northwestern boundary, Mount Hymettos on the east, and the Parnes range to the north (see map 8). The Menidi tholos (at Acharnai) and its surrounding remains perhaps represent an extension of Athenian authority to the north, in order to control the agricultural zone they inhabit, though it is impossible to tell according to the presently available evidence. This is perhaps analogous to the situation between Orchomenos and Medeon, the latter of which provided access to the sea and was accompanied by monumental tombs as markers of territory and authority. At any rate, between the sizable agricultural extent of the basin of Athens and the access to the sea via Phaleron and Piraeus, a community at Athens would have occupied a strategic position similar to palatial centers elsewhere.

Thorikos boasts some of the most impressive Mycenaean remains in Attica. Between the wealth of funerary and settlement evidence at the site and its position to exploit the abundant metal resources of the Lavriotiki, its significance cannot be overstated (Laffineur 2010). Beyond the acropolis settlement of Velatouri, five monumental tombs, including two tholoi, signal a level of complexity and prosperity beyond any other community in eastern Attica. Pottery evidence from Mine 5 demonstrates mining activity at the site in LH IIIB2/C (Mountjoy 1995b). In the context of the spatial models presented here, Thorikos is also very much set apart from the rest of Attica (see maps 10, 11). It falls well outside even a sort of "maximum" territory for Athens, and it is also quite separate from the communities surrounding Brauron to the north and Kiafa Thiti to the northwest. The geographical orientation of Thorikos is seaward, toward Makronisos and Kea, providing convenient jumping off points elsewhere. It is also telling that Mycenae exhibits significant connections to Thorikos from the Shaft Grave period onward. Lead Isotope Analyses (LIA) of silver from several locations in the Mycenaean world (Mycenae, Vapheio, Athens, Menidi, Perati, and Thorikos) were used to argue that the Lavriotiki was almost the exclusive source for this metal during Mycenaean times (Stos-Gale and Gale 1982), though later analyses suggest that northern Greece, namely the Chalkidike, was a major source as well (Stos-Gale and Macdonald 1991, 272–79; see also Papadimitriou 2017). The large number of Cretan imports at Thorikos also suggests that this was an important destination for traders, both for metals and as an entry point to the Euboean Gulf. Control over the mines at Thorikos remains a key issue for the prehistory of eastern Attica.

The central Mesogeia Plain and coasts of eastern Attica were home to fairly dense occupation in the Bronze Age, which is well documented by the volume and quality of archaeological fieldwork conducted by the Ephorate of Antiquities in recent decades (see, e.g., Kakavogianni 2009; Vasilopoulou and Katsarou-Tzeveleki 2009; Andrikou 2015; Stefanis 2015; Papadimitriou et al. 2020). An important cluster of sites has been detected in the vicinity of Spata, located in the center of the plain. The influence of Spata may have extended as far west as Glyka Nera, although such an inference is based purely on proxemics (Grammenou 1996; Kakavogiannis 1999–2000; Kakavogianni 2003). Papadimitriou (2017) has argued that the significance of Spata might relate to its presence on a land route that links

Thorikos, Spata, Menidi, and eventually Boeotia (see also Fachard and Knodell 2020). This model may also explain a diachronic pattern according to which the Mesogeia Plain near Spata is the most densely occupied in the early Palatial period, and which coincides also with the construction of the Menidi tholos. The palatial trappings of Athens only appear at a relatively late stage (LH IIIB2).

Settlement connectivity models show clusters around prominent sites at Marathon, where settlement evidence at Plasi, MH–LH III tumuli at Vrana, and the tholos tomb (with horse burials) at Arnos signal a major occupation both in Early Mycenaean times and during the Palatial period (Polychronakou-Sgouritsa et al. 2016).[22] A significant long-term presence in the area is represented in the form of large-scale cemeteries from the Early Bronze Age onward (at Tsepi), and it is likely that this community remained consistently independent, situated as it was on an ample coastal plain, located on the important sea route of the Euboean Gulf. It was also the best positioned site in eastern Attica to connect to Boeotia by land, via Aphidna.

The wealthy graves of Brauron and the associated settlement indicate habitation from the MH period until LH IIIC, with a peak during the Palatial period of LH IIIA–B (Papadopoulos and Kontorli-Papadopoulou 2014). Again, continuous habitation and a flourishing community in the Palatial period suggests a consistent political trajectory rather than one in which an inland power came to dominate at some point.[23] In the LH IIIC period there is a shift in concentration of tombs, wealth, and imported goods to the next bay south (Porto Rafti) at Perati (Murray 2018a).

In the southern part of the Mesogeia, fortified communities at Koropi (Kastro tou Christou) and Kiafa Thiti may have represented still further independent sites, though gaps in the occupational history during the LH III period may suggest some sort of abandonment after the Early Mycenaean period (Maran 1992, 1993; Privitera 2013, 124). Lohmann (2010) has suggested that Athens may have integrated these centers into its own remit at this point.

Turning to western Attica, the central structure "Megaron B" at Eleusis seems to have been an important political/religious space within a much larger complex in use from the Early Mycenaean period to LH IIIB/C Early (Cosmopoulos 2014). The site itself occupied an important land route between Athens, Thebes, and the Peloponnese, as well as the protected port of the bay of Eleusis. The agricultural resources of the Thriasian Plain are also quite broad, which forms an interesting background to mythic associations with Demeter and Persephone, as well as to historical efforts by Athens to incorporate this space into its own territory, most

---

22. Current excavations at Plasi have been undertaken by a team from the University of Athens since 2014. See Marathon Excavations, accessed December 4, 2020, http://www.marathonexcavations.arch.uoa.gr/.

23. It should be noted, however, that most of the evidence from eastern Attica is in the form of tombs; settlement excavations have been extremely limited.

probably signaling earlier political independence.[24] Eleusis is also home to the only Linear B that has been found in Attica in the form of an inscribed stirrup jar with the sign *wa*. This has been interpreted as an abbreviation for *wa-na-ko-te-ro* (of the wanax), perhaps a leftover from a larger consignment destined for Thebes (Cosmopoulos 2014, 458; Papadimitriou 2017). Just as Thorikos or Marathon make natural points of entry from the sea to inland places in eastern Attica, so too does Eleusis for western Attica (Fachard and Knodell 2020).

Finally, Kanakia, on Salamis, clearly represents a major center (Lolos 2012), and it is unlikely to have been tied to another polity—for example, Athens or Eleusis. We know of no examples of mainland polities extending their influence to sites on islands (discounting such a relationship between Euboea and Thebes, as I argue above). Whether Kanakia should be considered a "palace" is another matter. It probably should not be, at least not when compared to larger centers. This site is much smaller in size and apparent territory than other palaces, and there is no evidence of Linear B, in spite of systematic excavations across the site. Building Γ is described as yet another "double megaron" building (compare to Dimini, Gla) that may have been the seat of a local ruler. There is also some evidence for specialized workshops and a small plaque stamped with the cartouche of Rameses II. The seaward orientation of the site suggests that this, rather than the agricultural inclinations of the mainland palaces, was its priority. In this way (and in terms of size and chronology) Kanakia had more in common with places like Pefkakia or later centers of the LH IIIC period—for example, at Lefkandi, Kynos, or Koukounaries. It is doubtful that this site exercised control over other large sites on the island (at Salamis Town and Ampelakia), considering the seaward orientation of Kanakia and the island topography, which set it quite apart from these other places. The cemetery of 204 chamber tombs on the other side of the island, at Ampelakia, suggests another major community there (Hope Simpson and Dickinson 1979, 204). While Salamis is located conveniently to form nearby connections to Eleusis, Megara, and Athens, we must also consider its position in the Saronic Gulf and its demonstrable connections to Aegina and the Argolid, especially the

24. There is considerable debate concerning the point at which Eleusis (and the rest of Attica in general) was incorporated into the territory of Athens (Padgug 1972; Diamant 1982; Mills 1997). While certainly part of a common cultural sphere from the Mycenaean period onward, clear signs of political incorporation are not present until the seventh century, possibly even the sixth; these are based on textual sources, which suggest that Eleusis was independent and allied with Megara before it came under Athenian control following a series of conflicts. The "synoecism of Theseus" may suggest an earlier date in the realm of mythohistory (Thucydides 2.15), which of course should not be accepted as fact. At any rate, even if we did follow the mythohistorical sequence, the period of conflicts between Athens and Eleusis would follow the supposed synoecism. Osborne (1994, 152–54) has argued that we should probably not see the synoecism of Attica as a singular event or series of events at all; rather, we should consider that Eleusis was part of Attica as long as Attica was an entity. This of course does not answer the question of when Attica became an entity.

sites of Kolonna, Aghios Konstantinos (Methana), and Korfos-Kalamianos (in the eastern Corinthia) (Tartaron 2013, 237–43).

The overall picture in Attica, then, seems to be one of fragmentation, though it is difficult to interpret the evidence with certainty. Athens is in the center—in all likelihood as a significant but not a hegemonic regional power. Its territory would have extended for some distance around it, but this territory was probably limited to central Attica. An equally important center was at Thorikos, which exploited the metal resources of the Lavriotiki from a very early date. The maritime orientation of Thorikos was probably also an important centralizing force for it to connect northward via the Euboean Gulf, southward into the Cyclades, and westward into the Saronic Gulf. Thorikos is also our most likely candidate as an early entry point for certain elements of elite Mycenaean culture (e.g., tholos architecture) coming first from Messenia or Crete, and perhaps later from the Argolid. Further major communities were located on Salamis and at Eleusis, at Marathon, and in the vicinity of Brauron. In general, the pattern of central sites is neatly dispersed across the landscape in natural habitation zones. Their geographic positions, the distribution of smaller sites around them, and their centrality in the network models presented above suggest political independence, at least in the absence of evidence for unification. While much of Attica was engaged with the palatial worlds in close proximity to it, Attica outside of Athens cannot really be described as palatial. And even Athens, in the absence of Linear B documents or a clearer set of architectural characteristics, is difficult to describe with any certainty. The pattern in Attica, as well as in the other regions of central Greece described above, suggests that palatial territories and organization must be considered the exception, rather than the rule, when it comes to the political landscapes of Mycenaean central Greece.

PRODUCING PALATIAL CULTURE: TECHNOLOGY AND POLITY

The foregoing discussion demonstrates the diversity of contemporary political landscapes in the Mycenaean world, chiefly through archaeological evidence concerning the scale, organization, and connectivity of regional settlement systems. Certain technologies also played a significant role in the perpetuation of political authority. The Palatial period—in palatial areas—witnessed an intensification and a centralization in modes of production, especially concerning agriculture and prestige goods. New technologies of writing were distinctly palatial, while aspects of craft production—for example, pottery—exhibit both continuity of tradition and expansion in scale.

Economies of production are revealed in some detail in the Linear B tablets from Pylos and Knossos, which describe regionally produced goods coming into the palaces, including leather, livestock, timber, grain, olives, and wool. This has allowed researchers to reconstruct aspects of palatial involvement in different types of agricultural and craft production.[25] While the Thebes tablets are less complete, they signal the same type of centralized authority, which took in enough agricultural produce for the palace to operate and also to impose itself across its territory.

It is no coincidence that Mycenaean centers are exclusively located on large fertile plains (Bintliff 1977b). Palaces were involved, both directly and indirectly, in the mobilization of resources through taxation, direct production, and a variety of unrecorded transactions (Halstead 2007, 67; Nakassis, Parkinson, and Galaty 2011; Nakassis, Galaty, and Parkinson 2016). Agricultural products included the predictable mix of grain, olives, and vines, as well as flax, honey, spices, and sheep. It is tempting to draw a direct association between the most prominent palatial centers in the Mycenaean period—Orchomenos, Gla, Thebes, Volos, and Athens—and the size of the plains they inhabit. Beyond the palaces, there is no doubt that substantial agricultural plains also coincide with Mycenaean sites of prominence; this is also the case for Oreoi, Psachna, Chalkis, Amarynthos, Krisa, Marathon, and Athens.

Networks of agricultural production that tie in to palaces are complex. Mycenaean economies were not redistributive in a strict sense but operated rather by systems of taxation that would support the palace. This system was still quite integrative, though, drawing in animal and agricultural products from throughout the hinterland and the surrounding territories. In some cases, the influx of products to the palace seems to represent a form of taxation, but in other cases it may represent an exchange-based relationship, as was likely the case for Amarynthos and Karystos, for which the volumes (one pig each) in transit are very small. The Thebes evidence suggests that the immediate surroundings of the palaces were the most integrated into this agricultural system, as is made clear by the relative proximity of second-order centers and the greater prominence of nearby places in the Linear B tablets. What we have, then, is a fairly integrated local network of agricultural production, partly overseen by the palace, partly controlled through taxation or exchange, and partly used to support the center and its related industries. Such accumulations were also used for state-sponsored public activities, such as feasting, itself an exercise in integration, group formation, and place-making (see also Small 2019, 89–91). Moreover, palatial architecture, especially the presence of storerooms in close proximity to the megaron, suggests that there was at least some symbolic aspect to certain types of agricultural storage—most likely involving oil and wine—as Hamilakis (1996) has argued for Bronze Age Crete. In sum, it is not necessary for Mycenaean agricultural systems to be fully

25. Halstead (1992, 2007) has been particularly active on this issue, and his interpretations are widely accepted. He emphasizes especially the complexity of production, networked across a regional landscape. See also Palmer 1992, 1994, 1998–99, 2001, 2008; Killen 1998, 2015; Nakassis 2013a; Palaima 2015.

redistributive in order for them to be highly integrated and crucial for the maintenance of symbolic and economic authority.

Certain aspects of craft production were tied closely to the palace as well. At Thebes, these included wall-painting, jewelry production, certain types of stoneworking, ivory and boar-tusk working, potting, and glass production (Dakouri-Hild 2005, 181–86). At Dimini there is also evidence of jewelry manufacture, ceramic production, and metal and ivory production (Adrimi-Sismani 2007, 164). The production and the use of seals in the integration of political networks seem also to have been key practices, especially in Boeotia, Phokis, and East Lokris (Eder 2007; Kramer-Hajos 2016, 84–100). Most of these technological processes are multiscalar by nature, involving materials and knowledge that coalesce in the palaces from a variety of locations. The influence of Minoan wall painting on Mycenaean industries is well known (Chapin 2010, 230) and Brysbaert (2008a, 2008b) has indicated similarities in production techniques between Thebes, Gla, and Orchomenos, raising the possibility of itinerant craftsmen operating regionally. Brysbaert (2008a, 2761) also notes a general decline in quality from LH IIIA to LH IIIB contexts, suggesting, perhaps, that Minoan craftsmen or influence may have been directly involved in the earliest Palatial wall paintings and not in the later ones. Moreover, the use of Minoan aspects of material and visual culture by the Mycenaean elite played an important role in state formation (and maintenance) processes, and the production of similar objects in palatial contexts seems to have been a major priority for the individuals controlling the palaces.

Of course, Minoan-Mycenaean connections are only one aspect of these technological networks (see, e.g., Brysbaert 2011). Raw materials, especially metals, had to be procured, often over long distances, as did other resources such as ivory and obsidian. Gold most likely came from Macedonia or Thasos, perhaps through a connection with the site of Thessaloniki Toumba, which exhibits evidence of gold melting and production (Vavelidis and Andreou 2008), or Methone, located on the Haliakmon delta and which also has ample evidence for early gold-working, as well as over 20 Mycenaean tombs.[26] It now seems clear that the Lavriotiki, the Cyclades, and the northern Aegean were all important sources for silver during the Bronze Age (Stos-Gale and Macdonald 1991, 272–79; Kayafa 1999). This has major implications for interactions between the Mycenaean "core" and the northern Aegean (Papadopoulos 1996b, 173–74; 2005, 589), implications that are reinforced by the presence of Early Mycenaean pottery at Torone (Cambitoglou and Papadopoulos 1993; Morris 2009/2010). Central Greece, significantly, has both land and sea routes through which communication between northern Greece and the Mycenaean heartland of the Peloponnese would have had to occur.

For copper, the Lavrio and Cycladic sources seem to have been used more in earlier periods than later ones (Bassiakos and Tselios 2012). The canonical

---

26. The ongoing work of the Ancient Methone Archaeological Project has shed much new light on the settlement history of the area (Morris et al. 2020).

representative of the Late Bronze Age copper trade is of course the oxhide ingot, examples of which are found across the Mediterranean and in several parts of Europe (Sabatini 2016). There is also a widely supported argument based on lead isotope analysis (LIA) that all oxhide ingots in the Mediterranean with a date of 1250 BCE or later likely came from Cyprus (Knapp 2012). Kayafa (1999, 405), on the other hand, shows that the Cyclades and especially Lavrio were important sources for many of the finished objects dating to the LH III period, even if most ingots came from Cyprus. While specifics are frequently debated, broad trends, such as a marked rise in Cypriot copper production in the Late Bronze Age and its impact on the Aegean, are clear.

Wood for fuel and construction were universal needs, but they were particularly important to the palaces for both construction and craft production. With the expansion of pyrotechnologies necessary for the manufacture of pottery and metals, fuel needs would have increased dramatically, especially at first and second order sites. While wood that could be used for fuel was fairly widely available, larger trees for monumental construction and shipbuilding had to be sought in the more thickly forested areas. Northern Euboea was known as an important source for timber and fuel in later times, as was the northern Aegean.

A diverse range of geographical connections was necessary for palatial production, though these are largely ephemeral, traceable only with certain types of well-preserved materials suitable for provenience study. We can, however, know something about the nature of these networks, based on what happens after the collapse of the palaces at the end of LH IIIB2. Contrary to conventional notions of decline in long-distance relationships after the collapse of the palaces, long-distance interactions are largely maintained, especially in the Euboean Gulf (Crielaard 2006; Parkinson 2010; Kramer-Hajos 2016). The aspects of palatial production that relied on imported goods would have been mediated by regional connections. This should be expected, given the inland location of nearly all the palatial centers. But it also gave the coastal settlements through which imports had to pass a stake in these networks, which they exploited following the LH IIIB destructions. So, while consumption and certain aspects of production would have redrawn the map of long-distance networks to focus on the palaces in the Palatial period, these polities would also have depended on their regional networks for raw material procurement. The distributed nature of craft production explains the continuation of some long-distance contacts following the collapse of the palaces, in contrast to the coincident loss of writing and other trappings of centralized palatial authority.

THE BIGGER PICTURE AT THE END
OF THE BRONZE AGE

The Late Bronze Age eastern Mediterranean was home to a variety of states, kingdoms, and empires, joined together by interactive systems of trade and diplomacy. The territorial empires of Egypt and Hatti were the most powerful of these, though

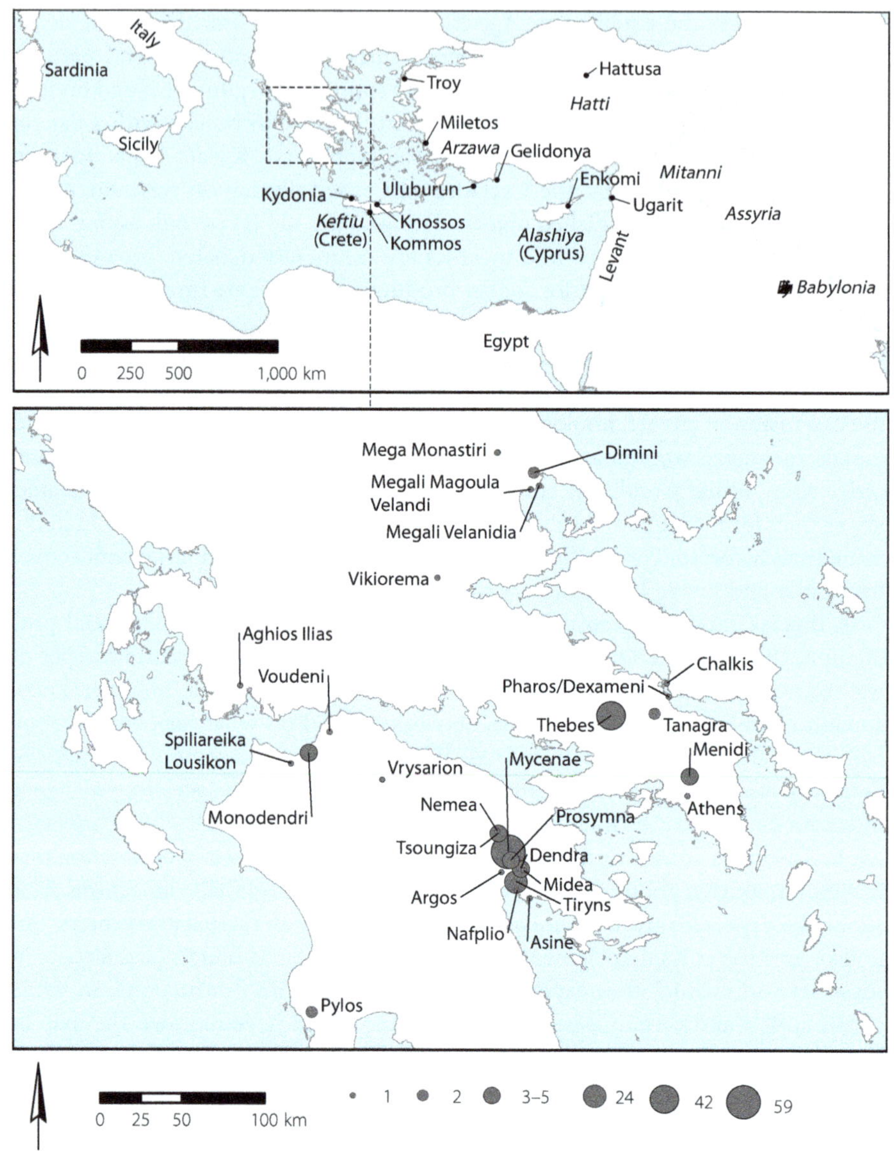

MAP 13. Sites and kingdoms of the Late Bronze Age eastern Mediterranean and Near East (top) and Imports to Greece of LH IIIB date (bottom) (import data from Murray 2017, 83–84, table 2.1).

major polities are also known from Cyprus (Alashiya), Anatolia (Arzawa, Troy/ Wilusa), Mesopotamia (Babylon, Assyria, Mitanni), the Levant (Ugarit), and Crete (Keftiu) (map 13). Mycenaean Greeks appear in Hittite records as Ahiyyawa, and they are mentioned in Egyptian texts as well. The presence of Aegean material culture throughout the eastern Mediterranean shows involvement in wider trade networks throughout the Bronze Age, as do imports, mainly in the form of luxury items or "exotica" at Aegean sites.

The archaeological and documentary records of Egypt, Hatti, and Mesopotamia show that these are territorial states with complex, hierarchical modes of sociopolitical organization. Political and religious institutions were well established, long-standing, and designed to enforce state control over multitiered systems of settlement. Less is known about political organizations elsewhere in Anatolia, in Cyprus, and in Crete, though these polities seem to have been smaller in scale—both physically and in terms of estimated territorial control or influence. Ugarit fits more of a city-state model and was an important precursor to the commercially oriented city-states known in the Levant in later times. A rich documentary record, primarily written in Akkadian cuneiform (the lingua franca of the eastern Mediterranean Late Bronze Age), highlights diplomatic and trade relationships as central modes of interpolity relationships. Rulers addressed each other as "my brother" or "great king" while negotiating trade agreements concerning copper, gold, silver, and timber; when exchanging gifts in the form of luxury items; and when negotiating alliances and diplomatic marriages. Territorial conflicts and war also feature in the documentary record, including extensive self-aggrandizement on the part of rulers and two different versions of who won the famous Battle of Kadesh (the Hittites and Egyptians each claim they did). The insights into elite life, a "globalizing" early economy, and multipolity statecraft are truly remarkable.

Two issues have long dominated discussion of the eastern Mediterranean Bronze Age: diplomacy and trade between "great kingdoms" and the "collapse" of civilizations around the year 1200 BCE (see, e.g., Bryce 2003; Cline 2014; Knapp and Manning 2016; Middleton 2017a; Murray 2017). These themes are often presented in a way that equates what was going on in Greece at the end of the Bronze Age with what was happening elsewhere in the eastern Mediterranean. Just as power relationships existed within complex societies, inequalities existed between them. The Mycenaean palatial states were not of the same order as their Near Eastern contemporaries, something that becomes clear from a comparative analysis of texts that indicate relationships between polities and scale of complexity as measured through administration, territory, and physical vestiges of stately authority. In the same way that all parts of the Mycenaean world were not palatial, not all parts of the eastern Mediterranean interaction zone were "great kingdoms." Here I highlight this disparity to reevaluate the place of early Greece in Late Bronze Age trade and geopolitics. I then turn to the ample evidence for Mycenaean involvement in the western Mediterranean, which is often left out of such discussions and may prove a useful case for comparison, especially in the long term. I leave the subject of collapse for the following chapter.

Commodities Trade in the Eastern Mediterranean

Archaeological evidence of materials on the move and textual correspondence concerning individuals and polities are our two main proxies for long-distance interaction in the Bronze Age eastern Mediterranean. Trade has played an important role in our understanding of Mycenaean society, as archaeological evidence of imported materials and finished products is paired with textual evidence for diplomatic relationships, resulting in a range of models (see, e.g., Renfrew 1975; Cline 1994; Knapp and Cherry 1994; Feldman 2006). Reciprocal gift giving between heads of state has received special attention as a way of explaining the relatively small amount of luxury "exotica" found in palatial contexts (Cline 1995). Such practices can only represent part of the picture, however, which also would have included subelite trading networks, independent merchants, raw material exchanges, tramping, and more, much of which is difficult to parse from the archaeological or textual record. Nevertheless, it is worth revisiting the archaeological evidence of long-distance trade and the textual evidence of diplomatic relationships in light of the local and regional political and production networks discussed above.

Data on all "international" imports to Mycenaean Greece were compiled long ago by Cline (1994), and this catalog has been put to a variety of uses since (see, e.g., Cline 2007, 2010a; Parkinson 2010; Burns 2010; Galaty 2018). Murray (2017) has updated and significantly expanded this dataset through a thorough reinvestigation of import records, taking into account excavations over the last 20 years, starting with the LH IIIB period (see map 13), and including LH IIIC, Protogeometric, and Geometric periods as well (discussed in subsequent chapters).

Cline's data has the advantage of including earlier Mycenaean periods (Cline 1994, 16–19, tables 6 and 7). The data show a clear shift in the amount of imports from the LH IIIA to LH IIIB periods, with the Cretan sites Knossos and Kommos having distinctly more imports than the mainland sites of Mycenae, Tiryns, and Thebes in periods before LH IIIB, followed by the opposite pattern in LH IIIB (Cline 1994, 89–90). This pattern could be the result of a Mycenaean takeover at Knossos (Cline 1997), and it at least seems to represent a reorientation of eastern Mediterranean trade networks toward the newly established Mycenaean palaces of the mainland and away from Crete. Significantly, Kommos, in southeastern Crete, seems to stay well-connected, suggesting that certain hubs remained important for long-distance trade, despite changes in political structures; this appears to be a long-term trend at Kommos, which has demonstrable Phoenician connections in the Early Iron Age as well (Shaw 1989, 2000; Callaghan et al. 2000).

For central Greece, Thebes has by far the most imports in the Palatial period. Cline (2007, 191) has pointed out that most of the 38 orientalia from Thebes come from a single context—a hoard of cylinder seals from the so-called "Treasury Room" (Porada 1981)—suggesting that they should be taken as anomalous. This is possible but, again, we must keep in mind that only small, fragmentary sections of Thebes have been excavated. If anything, we should expect much more such material from Thebes, given the wealth of imports found in only a few excavated contexts (Burns 2010, 135–39). The chronological scope and origins of excavated material from Thebes are also telling. There is no significant quantity of imports until LH IIIB, which is coincident with the expansion of the palace, the appearance of Linear B, massive expansion in the fortification of the site, and dramatic increase in settlement remains on a local and regional scale. The provenances of these imports are also significant, though they require thoughtful consideration. While their origins include different parts of the ancient Near East, including Egypt, Syro-Palestine, Cyprus, and Mesopotamia (Porada 1981, 46; Kopanias 2008), this does not mean that they came to Thebes directly from these original locations. Moreover, many of these seem to have been reworked in Theban workshops into more traditional Mycenaean motifs, such as the figure of eight shield, suggesting it was the exotic material rather than the particular message associated with foreign administration that bore symbolic significance (Burns 2010, 138; 2016).

The quantities and locations of import evidence are significant. In central Greece, they are limited to relatively few well-excavated sites, and they skew toward ones with Palatial remains. Overall, however, imports are much more abundant in the Argolid, though this may also have something to do with the history of research (see map 13).

There is extensive evidence that Mycenaeans exported pottery to various parts of the Mediterranean, especially to Cyprus and the Levantine coast (van Wijngaarden 2002; Jones et al. 2014; Murray 2017, 192–99). This wide distribution, which also includes western Anatolia and Italy, suggests that Mycenaeans were involved in trade networks during the Palatial period that included several other eastern Mediterranean states (Sauvage 2012). Trade is apparent through the broader circulation of pottery and the transfer of styles through different parts of the Mycenaean world, not least transport amphoras and inscribed stirrup jars (Haskell et al. 2011; Rutter 2014b; Demesticha and Knapp 2016; Knapp and Demisticha 2017). While this form of exchange appears to reach its height in the Palatial period, we should note that it also predates that period and lasts beyond it (van Wijngaarden 2016; Murray 2017, 194). This form of exchange cannot therefore be considered an exclusively palatial phenomenon; rather, it should be considered as one that was magnified by the palaces—probably through the increased demand they created for status-granting exotica and the desire to trade their own pottery, oil, textiles, and other products.[27]

The various ways in which we might view trade in the eastern Mediterranean Bronze Age should not be seen as mutually exclusive: centralized control, localized control, freelance trade, and gift exchange likely all operated simultaneously.

---

27. For an argument supporting palace-centric exchange of pottery between the Argolid and various Near Eastern states, see Jung 2015.

Such practices should be seen as co-constitutive types of long-distance interaction rather than as options from which we must select. For example, centralized control is dependent on localized control since, in the example of a Mycenaean palace, it is unlikely that a *wanax* made all trade-based decisions independently. Gift exchange can be seen as either an incidental, specific phenomenon or the terms in which the trade of particular goods are cast (Cline 1995). And the cargoes of shipwrecks, such as Cape Gelidonya (Bass 1967) and Uluburun (Bachhuber 2006; Pulak 2008), contained materials from multiple locations, which have been used to argue for a variety of the above-mentioned modes of exchange (see, e.g., Shelmerdine 2013, 451).

Although trade was probably mediated through both regional networks and freelance traders, consumption of exotic materials was certainly in the domain of the elite and was carefully controlled to project exclusivity and access (Burns 2010; Kramer-Hajos 2016). Tensions caused by this exclusivity, like conscripted labor and centralized elite consumption, among other things, may have contributed to the ultimate collapse and rejection of the Mycenaean palace system.

The Documentary Record and Geopolitics

While Linear B documents tell us nothing directly about interpolity relationships, toponymics and onomastics have slightly more to say. They suggest that a certain amount of multiculturalism was present in Mycenaean society in the form of resident foreigners as workers, settlers, or slaves with non-Greek names (Nikoloudis 2008a). The nature of interactions between Mycenaeans and "others" is far from clear, although the occurrence of them is certain. In central Greece the Thebes tablets indicate individuals with names related to Troy, Miletos, Sminthos in Anatolia, and Sparta. These names do not indicate that a particular individual is necessarily from this place, though that could be the case. They probably do signal an awareness of cultural geography beyond a particular community or region, which was likely highlighted at places like palaces that attracted greater amounts of long-distance exchange.

Hittite texts provide the most extensive and debated body of evidence for contact between the Aegean world and other polities. They make apparent reference to the Mycenaeans of mainland Greece with the term *Ahhiyawa*, which appears in some 29 documents from the Hittite capital of Hattusa. It is argued that this term is a form of "Achaia" and has led to much debate over whether (1) this linguistic connection is correct and (2) what type of entity it refers to (Güterbock 1983; Latacz 2004; Beckman, Bryce, and Cline 2011). This issue is generally referred to as the "Ahhiyawa question" or the "Ahhiyawa problem" (Fischer 2010) Most scholars now accept the identification of Ahhiyawa with some part of the Mycenaean world (Beckman, Bryce, and Cline 2011, 6). Whether this refers to a specific polity within the Mycenaean world or to the Mycenaean world collectively remains less certain (Bryce 2018). A relatively recent trend has been to suggest that these documents refer to a single polity ruled by a "great king" on par with others of the eastern Mediterranean (Latacz 2004; Kelder 2010; Eder and Jung 2015).

The "Tawagalawa Letter" (AhT 4) is from a king of Hatti to a king of Ahhiyawa and refers to him as "brother" and "Great King," a title used only for kings of Hatti, Egypt, Mttanni, Assyria, Babylon, and—in this one instance—Ahhiyawa.[28] Other comparisons between these polities and the Mycenaean world, however, fall short, both materially and in the documentary record. The corpus of Hittite texts contains around 1,000 total documents, of which only 29 make reference to Ahhiyawa. Egypt, Mitanni, Aleppo, Arzawa all appear much more frequently. The ways in which Ahhiyawa is referred to are also significant. Besides the document addressing an Ahhiyawan king as "Great King," there is one further document that gives this title (AhT 2), but the designation there appears to have been erased by the scribe, suggesting that it was a mistake (Beckman 1996, 101). One interpretation of this erasure is that the title was one that once applied but was no longer valid; it may also have been a simple mistake at the end of the list.

There is very little evidence of Mycenaean participation in anything that could be called statecraft. Only one letter from the Hittite corpus is meant to be from a king of Ahhiyawa to a Hittite king. It is written in Hittite, probably by an emissary or translator. This letter concerns a land dispute over some islands, presumably near the Anatolian coast, and it mentions a diplomatic marriage. Other letters concern trade restrictions to Assyria (AhT 2), Millawanda, which is typically associated with Miletos, and various conflicts or disputes either between Ahhiyawa and the Hittite empire or its allies. These include references to several places in the eastern Aegean, including—provocatively—Wilusa, which has been equated with Ilios/Troy. No texts in the Akkadian cuneiform lingua franca of the LBA eastern Mediterranean have been found in Mycenaean palatial contexts.

The maximalist interpretation of the Ahhiyawa texts is that they signal the presence of a single Mycenaean state that was a known participant in eastern Mediterranean relations, a state that occasionally caused problems for the Hittites by harrying their allies along the east Aegean coast. Most proponents of a single, unified Mycenaean polity would place the capital at Mycenae itself, based on the evidence for its long-distance connections (Kelder 2010, 93–99; Eder and Jung 2015). Others have suggested that such a capital would be at Thebes (Sergent 1994, 1997, 1999; Aravantinos, Godart, and Sacconi 2001; Latacz 2004), or that Ahhiyawa refers to Miletos specifically or the southeast Aegean/west Anatolian interface more generally (Mountjoy 1998, 2015; Niemeier 1999, 2005). An immediate problem with all of these arguments, however, is that the Linear B evidence contradicts any kind of argument for political integration across the Mycenaean world, since it refers only to individual regional systems centered on a particular palace.

28. Here I use the numbering system found in Beckman, Bryce, and Cline (2011) rather than the official tablet numbers of the Catalogue des Textes Hittites (CHT). For a comprehensive discussion of Hittite diplomatic texts, see also Beckman 1996.

Moreover, the very archaeological evidence often cited as a sign of unity (similar architectural layouts in palaces, administrative systems, pottery styles) is in fact quite varied from region to region, not least because much of the area grouped together as the Mycenaean world cannot be convincingly characterized as palatial.

As an alternative, Ahhiyawa could very well be a cultural designation, in much the same way that we think of the term "Mycenaean" as a cultural rather than a political designation (see also Bryce 2018). When references are made to the king of Ahhiyawa there should be no problem accepting this as a reference to *a* king-dom within the Mycenaean cultural sphere, even if it is a reference to a specific kingdom. Nor, as Beckman, Bryce, and Cline (2011) have pointed out, is there a problem with coalitions forming for various purposes, coalitions that the Hittites may have recorded as a singular entity. Most of what we know from later Greek textual sources, in fact, tells us that this practice was much more common than, say, a unified territorial state was. Homer, of course, refers to numerous leaders of the Achaians as kings, and Archaic and Classical political history is in many ways a history of alliances. Similar practices are seen in other early complex polities as well, such as the Classic Maya, who are characterized by shifting political histories of independence, conflict, alliances, and coalitions (Martin and Grube 2008; Garrison 2018; Ek 2020).

The Aegean also appears in documents from Egypt, the other great power of the Late Bronze Age, though evidence is limited. The most famous set of diplomatic texts from Egypt, the Amarna letters, do not discuss the Mycenaean world at all (although earlier Egyptian texts do seem to mention Crete as *Keftiu*). However, the more or less contemporary statue base of Amenhotep III, found at his funerary temple at Kom el-Hatan, contains an "Aegean List" in which several place names are given that can be tied to Crete and mainland Greece (Edel 1966; Cline and Stannish 2011), under the headings of Keftiu (*kftiw*) and "Tanaya" (*tny*, also read as Danaia, land of the Danaans). The order of the list is significant, as it seems to describe a geographical circuit beginning with Amnisos, Phaistos, Kydonia, Myce-nae, an unidentified *dqis* (possibly Thebes), Messenia (Pylos?), Nafplio, Kythera, Eleia, Knossos, Amnisos (for a second time), and Lyktos (possibly Siteia) (Cline and Stannish 2011, 7–9). The list goes from Crete to the mainland and back to Crete, apparently describing an itinerary. These place names are written on cren-elated ovals carved over bound captives—a standard practice in Egyptian depic-tions of foreigners. Egyptian-Mycenaean interaction is also represented in several faience plaques from Mycenae, bearing cartouches of Amenhotep III and Queen Tiye, and Knossos, Kydonia, and other sites have also revealed scarabs and seals (Cline and Stannish 2011, 10).

Much is made of Late Bronze Age trading systems and kingly gift exchange as a major part of both economic and diplomatic relations. Based on the Hittite and Egyptian texts described above, the Mycenaeans are seen to be participants in such a set of interactions. In only one, or perhaps two, of the Hittite documents there is reference to a "Great King" of Ahhiyawa. In the Egyptian text the reference to the Aegean is embedded in the iconography of subordination. The only other direct mention of the Aegean is in a single text from Ugarit—which is a letter from the king of Hatti (RS 94.2530). This letter indicates Ahhiyawan and Ugaritic participation in the trade of copper ingots.

From this fragmentary textual record, two observations can be drawn out. First, there is no definite evidence for a large territorial state—the size or nature of a Mycenaean kingdom is never described. More importantly, the Linear B evidence, where it exists, does not support this model, and the archaeological landscape, as described at length above, suggests an even larger degree of fragmentation, not unification. Second, there is no clear evidence for a Mycenaean "great kingdom" on par with other polities with that title. Assuming Ahhiyawa refers to Mycenaean Greece, it is only referred to by the Hittites; this would suggest that Hatti was the main broker of state-like dealings with a Mycenaean polity. The absence of other diplomatic correspondence is conspicuous, since other states, rulers, and institutions from all over the Near East are discussed at length. When considered together with the evidence of regional political organizations, we can say (1) that Mycenaean polities were comparatively small-scale in their territorial extent and (2) that their activities abroad were mostly focused on the eastern Aegean and western Anatolia.

Mycenaean palatial states were not proper peers of the older and much more territorially expansive states of Babylonia, Assyria, Egypt, Hatti, or Ugarit. This is evident in comparisons of territory, palatial plans, and overall urban character (see also Whitelaw 2004, 2017, 2018). However, Mycenaean polities were well aware of these more complex entities, interacted with them, and understood something of how they worked. Indeed, certain Mycenean centers even attempted to imitate other polities in their own political organization. The imposition of state-like modes of social organization in the Mycenaean world, however, happened in limited areas and for a relatively brief span of time, and it was ultimately not very successful.

Looking West

One of the most interesting features of the Mediterranean in the late second millennium BCE is the way in which the (mostly) small-scale societies of the western and central part of the basin were brought increasingly into contact with the more complex political formations of the east (see, e.g., Broodbank 2013, 431–44). Our evidence for these interactions is entirely archaeological and of a different character from that seen in the eastern Mediterranean. It comes mostly in the forms of Mycenaean and "Mycenaeanizing" pottery in southern Italy, with more modest quantities found in Sardinia, Sicily, and northern Italy (van Wijngaarden 2002, 2016; Eder and Jung 2005; Vianello 2005; Blake 2008; Cazzella and Recchia 2009; Jones et al. 2014; Iacono 2015, 2016a, 2016b). Iacono (2015) points out that the smaller communities in which cross-cultural encounters were happening in southern Italy makes them especially significant. That is, they would have been accessible to a larger amount of the population of a site, rather than restricted to an elite or merchant class. This seems borne out in the material record as well, as fine wares make up the vast majority of assemblages found at Levantine, Cypriot, and Egyptian sites, while Italian sites have more diverse assemblages with a range of types (Murray 2017, 196). It therefore seems to be the case that Mycenaeans were coming to southern Italy not just as incidental visitors and traders but as migrants with an interest in establishing a continuous presence.

Iacono (2016a) has made a compelling argument for the transfer of technological traits between "hegemonic" (Mycenaean) and "nonhegemonic" cultures (south Italian). We might also see this as a more equitable arrangement than we see in relations between the Aegean and the states of the Near East. Some Aegean societies were interested in adopting certain stately trappings of their Near Eastern neighbors and trading partners in the Late Bronze Age. By contrast, the societies of the central Mediterranean seem to have been more interested in material and technological practices, which had social value in their own right. What is viewed as the valuable contribution of one society—that is, cultural traits worth adopting—depends on the mode of encounter and the value systems of both social groups. It may well be that in this case the Aegean continued to play its long-standing role of geographical and cultural middleman, situated as it was between the stately societies of the eastern Mediterranean and the nonstate societies of the center and west, while Mycenaean Greece itself was comprised of polities occupying a range of sociopolitical formations. The Achaian connection to Italy is compelling in this sense. It is at a geographical crossroads to Italy and the Adriatic and it is also the likely source of much of the Mycenaean pottery found there (Papadopoulos 2001, 2003; Arena 2015; Jung, Mommsen, and Picciarelli 2015). This suggests that like may have been attracted to like in terms of trading relationships, with palatial sites directing the bulk of their attention toward the polities to which they aspired, while nonpalatial Mycenaean societies (e.g., in Achaia) looked elsewhere. Indeed, it may be the lesser-known orientations (westward) that were more meaningful in the long term, or at least more lasting than the short-lived palatial engagements with the east.

CONCLUSIONS: POLITY AND VARIETY IN THE MYCENAEAN WORLD

The political landscapes and interactions of Mycenaean central Greece involved a variety of regionally (and locally) distinct patterns of settlement and modes of social organization. This sheds new light on the particular polities of central Greece discussed here, on the wider Mycenaean world, and on the eastern Mediterranean in the Late Bronze Age. While settlement networks and landscape archaeology offer insights concerning particular relationships between places within central Greece, larger patterns of interaction can also elucidate some of the dynamic changes seen during the Palatial period. These are especially apparent in the regions where palaces existed, but these shifts had less exaggerated effects (and consequences) in areas devoid of palatial authority.

Mycenaean palaces came to thrive through the implementation of new sets of integrative and centralizing practices. After steady growth in sociopolitical complexity during the formative Mycenaean period, the palaces emerged very quickly as elites took advantage of long-distance trade relationships and new administrative technologies to consolidate and expand authority, reifying it both architecturally and practically through a new administrative system, partly borrowed from Crete. This rapid, deliberate growth in connections in effect kick-started a scale-free network, where communities attached preferentially to the most highly connected places—the palaces. This preferential attachment would have been based partly on the integrative actions of palatial authorities and partly on the restructuring of social relations that came with this new political form. But palatial influence did have limits.

Increased connectedness across the Mycenaean world as a whole, especially between palatial centers participating in peer-polity networks, also helps to explain the relative homogeneity that permeates much of Mycenaean material culture beginning slowly in LH IIIA and reaching an apex in LH IIIB. The links between palatial centers both within and outside the Aegean were felt regionally and locally as well, and were manifest in such things as monumental architecture, ceramic styles, bodily adornment, and burial forms (Mountjoy 1990, 245; Cavanagh and Mee 1998; Crowley 2008, 266; Nosch and Laffineur 2012; see also Kramer-Hajos 2016). So, while a great variety of political organization existed across the Mycenaean world, people—especially elites—were still participating in social networks that linked communities together. This is to be expected across a culture area with several independent political centers that operate at different scales in a variety of ways.

The Linear B tablets make it clear that the regional systems over which the palaces presided centralized several aspects of agricultural and craft production. This system allowed for the consolidation and, to some extent, the redistribution of such products, especially through state-sponsored feasts (Wright 2004a; Small 2019). These types of consolidation and consumption were opportunities to centralize social power and state authority through routinized practice. Such centralization, however, was built on weak institutions, was rapidly introduced, and left the whole system fairly vulnerable to collapse. This vulnerability explains the rapid disappearance of Linear B and the disappearance of palatial systems following the destruction of the palaces in LH IIIB2. It also suggests that a collapse of overseas trade networks was *not* a prime mover in bringing about the end of the palaces, though no doubt it could have been a contributing factor. I demonstrate in the next chapter that these long-distance connections do not in fact break down entirely, and that some of the material and settlement changes seen in LH IIIC are the direct result of efforts to reengage or maintain them. Moreover, the collapse of centralized systems at the end of the Palatial period resulted in even greater regional diversity as new centers emerged in new locations, with more focus on the sea and on practices of production and consumption that were less centralized.

The picture above follows the general consensus that Mycenaean palaces were independent, centralized regional polities. I depart from canonical views in suggesting that these polities were few, limited in territorial remit, and should be seen as historical anomalies that never had enough time to establish stable institutions (see also Sherratt 2001). Palaces certainly demand and deserve attention, with their monumental architecture, wealthy burials, and complex administration. But we must also keep in mind that these represent massive social inequalities that disrupted long-standing modes of social and political life. We should also remember that mainland palatial societies did not last very long. Whatever the circumstances of their demise—interpolity conflict, natural disaster, or peasant revolts—the palaces ended with a rejection of this system by those participating in it. From this perspective, we should not think that being outside the palatial world represents some kind of failure—quite the opposite, as we can see in the regions that come to thrive in the period that follows (chapter 4). Fragmentation and instability were the norm, and the palatial system imposed from above was ultimately rejected from below. Concerning views on the opposite end of the spectrum (e.g., Kelder 2010; Eder and Jung 2015), the evidence for centralized organization across the Mycenaean world seems to me entirely circumstantial. This desire to conceive of a Mycenaean empire on par with Hatti and Egypt is not well supported by comparative evidence, and it is better replaced with a model that allows for a range of sociopolitical complexity and organization both within early Greece and across the Mediterranean.

The Mycenaean palaces were peripheral participants in wider interaction spheres of the eastern Mediterranean, and nonpalatial entities likely participated as well in the capacity of raiders or traders, as they had in the Early Mycenaean period and would in the Postpalatial period (Hitchcock and Maeir 2016). Moreover, in comparison to other stately modes of political organization in the contemporary Near East, the Mycenaean palaces seem rather weak. For cases of comparison, for the palaces and especially for the other polities of Bronze Age Greece, we should turn away from models of pristine state formation, on the one hand, and the organization of contemporary polities in the Ancient Near East, on the other, not least because some of these other polities at this point were full-fledged empires. Rather, Mycenaean palaces developed as a type of secondary state on the Greek mainland, one that was heavily influenced by contacts with neighbors and trading partners, especially in Minoan Crete. As such, the palaces developed relatively quickly and without necessarily adapting other social structures to develop strong institutions and engender stability. The Mycenaean palaces, therefore, were never particularly strong states, and indeed the implementation of palatial systems was very much piecemeal across the Mycenaean world. From this perspective, it should be no surprise that these political formations collapsed. Nevertheless, the arrival and collapse of this new form of polity had dramatic effects on local and regional systems of settlement and subsistence. In nonpalatial areas, however, life went on, in dialogue with palatial zones, though well outside the limits of any palatial hegemony.

4

Reconstituting Polity in the Postpalatial Bronze Age

In ancient times, the Greeks and those of the barbarians living near the sea, on the mainland or in the islands, when they began to find their way to one another by sea, turned to piracy. The men leading them were not unpowerful, seeking profit for themselves and providing for their poorer followers.
—THUCYDIDES, *HISTORY OF THE PELOPONNESIAN WAR* 1.5.1

The disintegration of palatial civilizations in the Aegean, Anatolia, the Levant, and Egypt has inspired reams of scholarship and explanations that range from climate change to seafaring marauders to systems collapse. Generic characterizations of the past by later historians like Thucydides have often been taken as references to specific time periods or events, especially when it comes to major societal transitions. This is problematic at best, but may still reflect some general concerns or characteristics of past groups. In focusing principally on collapse, much scholarship has (1) elided the transformative character of other societal developments that took place in a variety of locations and (2) overlooked the substantial continuities that can be traced to the Palatial period and even before. For example, the "Sea Peoples," who are mentioned in an inscription of Rameses III at Medinet Habu, have generated a large literature that assigns them many different roles (e.g., Oren 2000; Cline 2014; Cline and O'Connor 2003; Hitchcock and Maeir 2016; Fischer and Bürge 2017). Such groups, which were never presented in ancient sources as unified or as having a common set of goals or behaviors, have too often been essentialized as either consequence of or cause for Late Bronze Age upheavals. Yet at the same time they cannot be dismissed entirely, since this period does show a general pattern of increased maritime mobility. Such large-scale developments in the eastern Mediterranean must be seen alongside local and regional shifts in settlement and production that took place in the Greek landscape.

In this chapter I first show how Mycenaean settlement networks were reorganized in the absence of palaces, both topologically and geographically. Some regions changed much more than others, depending especially on the mode of political organization present in the Palatial period. Diachronically, we can see that smaller-scale, regionally distributed societies, such as those in Attica, Thessaly, and the Euboean Gulf, were less susceptible to collapse than highly centralized palatial systems of Boeotia, which had also experienced the greatest growth in Palatial times. Second, I examine the changing pottery and metal production networks that articulate connections between communities and regions, especially in terms of their reorganization in the face of new modes of sociopolitical organization and an age of mobility. Finally, I argue that shifts in settlement in central Greece also reflect developments in the wider Mediterranean world at the end of the second millennium BCE—namely, an increasingly maritime orientation, a widespread decentralization of political organization, and a bourgeoning age of mobility.

PERSPECTIVES ON COLLAPSE

Monocausal notions of collapse are outdated and largely debunked (see, e.g., Dickinson 2010, 484; Knapp and Manning 2016; Middleton 2017a, 2020). Eisenstadt (1988, 242) notes that "ancient states and civilizations do not collapse at all, if by *collapse* is meant the complete end to those political systems and civilizational frameworks." Comparative perspectives on the collapse of complex societies largely follow Eisenstadt, demonstrating strong elements of continuity *and* change in case studies from post-collapse Teothihuacan, the Terminal Classic Maya, pre-Inka Peru, the Khmer Empire and its relationship to Angkor, and Rapa Nui (Easter Island), as well as from the Mycenaean palaces and their contemporaries in the Late Bronze Age Mediterranean (Middleton 2017a). Comparative perspectives reveal rather a need to focus on transformation, resilience, complexity, and historical context.[1]

The Mycenaean palaces came to an end somewhat suddenly and conclusively around the beginning of the twelfth century BCE. While this is often termed an abrupt collapse across a wide geographical area, it should rather be seen as a process that played out over at least several decades. In archaeological terms, however, this looks like a relatively rapid series of events. I suggest this series included: (1) an (over)extension of state authority as a result of palaces taking on monumental defensive building projects in the face of tension between Mycenaean polities; (2) the culmination of such tension in armed conflict; and (3) a rejection of palatial authority by those living under it, as evidenced through the total disappearance of Linear B, palatial architecture, and other accoutrements of centralized administrative hierarchy (see also Jung 2016 on class struggle, war, and "old" and "new" political orders). This palatial collapse occurred only in palatial areas but its effects were

1. For further perspectives on collapse, especially as a comparative phenomenon, see, for example, Tainter 1988; Yoffee and Cowgill 1988; Redman 2005; Schwartz and Nichols 2006; McAnany and Yoffee 2010; Butzer and Endfield 2012; Faulseit 2016; Knapp and Manning 2016; Cunningham and Driessen 2017; Middleton 2017a, 2017b, 2018; Knodell 2018.

felt throughout mainland Greece, restructuring the nature of polity, interaction, and social relations throughout the macroregion—albeit in widely disparate ways.

Palace destructions at Orchomenos, Gla, and Thebes may be the direct or partial result of conflicts between two polities represented by these three centers. The proximity of Thebes and Orchomenos would have been a source of tension between these two polities. This fits with the archaeological record of destructions at both sites, and it may be reflected in later literary traditions. The fortification of Gla drastically changed the relationship between the Orchomenian and Theban polities. Palaces in the Argolid also pursued major fortification programs in LH IIIB (Hope Simpson and Hagel 2006). We might term this an architecture of paranoia or an arms race in the face of mounting interpolity tensions. The subsequent destructions at the end of LH IIIB may have been the direct result of such tensions.

Not all palatial and palace-connected sites were destroyed at the end of LH IIIB, and several were reoccupied after a hiatus. Both Thebes and Eleon, for example, have significant occupation until LH IIIC Middle, when other centers in their vicinity start to thrive (Aravantinos et al. 2016a, 319; Van Damme 2017b, 349–50). It is important, however, that this marks the end of the palaces per se. While later occupation and building occur, specifically palatial architecture, art, and burial come to an end, along with any traces of central administration (Linear B). And while these events need not be attributed to interpolity conflict, they do represent a rejection of the palatial system, which we can interpret as a collective response to dissatisfaction with state authority in Boeotia.

Thessaly may reveal a less outright rejection of palatial systems. This may also suggest a less highly centralized nature of palatial authority. Dimini, Pefkakia, and Kastro Volos all continued to be occupied in LH IIIC Early, though only Volos endured after this period. Certain palatial aspects of material culture, most notably burial customs in the form of (diminutive) tholoi, persisted well into the Early Iron Age.

Athens, too, bears little evidence of destruction, and has a strong LH IIIC occupation. The archaeological record at Athens, however, is obscured by later building, so it does not demonstrate direct evidence of centralized authority. It is therefore impossible to tell whether it was purposefully destroyed and rejected. Broneer (1948, 1956) turned to historical sources describing a Dorian invasion that largely bypassed Athens to explain the combination of architectural elaboration (cyclopean fortifications, elaborate gates, secret springs) and lack of destruction. Dorians aside, such an idea may reflect some distant memory that Athens did not witness the same type of collapse that other polities did (though see also Van Damme, forthcoming, for another perspective).

The end of the Palatial period seems to have played out quite differently in different areas. Boeotia is perhaps the only region that fits a "standard" narrative of collapse, but even its situation must be viewed as complex, and understood as involving both interpolity conflict and a popular rejection of the palatial system. Otherwise one would expect that the distinctly palatial practices described above would have survived. This regionally specific overthrow, collapse, or however we wish to describe it, is reflected also in the fact that it is precisely the regions that did not host palaces that came to thrive in Postpalatial times.

While there is no denying that the Mycenaean palaces disappeared around 1200 BCE, this change should not be seen as the end of one society or culture and the beginning of another. The Mycenaean world endured, even if the palatial political system did not, with elements of continuity visible into the Early Iron Age and long after. As Murray (2017, 16) points out, scholars have long debated "whether we should see the transition from the Greek Bronze Age to the Iron Age as a story of disruption, stagnation, and reinvention or as a continuous and unified spectrum of development." This oft-invoked dualism of "continuity *or* change" is better replaced with a more inclusive framework. There are naturally elements of both.

RECONSTITUTING SOCIETIES IN THE POSTPALATIAL LANDSCAPE

The Postpalatial settlement pattern in the Aegean is typically seen in terms of contraction, decline, and population movement (Dickinson 2006, 58–67). Quantitative aspects of economic decline are documented as well, and they may be linked to demographic change (Murray 2017, 210–48). Hope Simpson and Dickinson (1979, maps 4 and 5) catalog only about 30 sites that date to this period in the regions surrounding the Euboean Gulf, in contrast to over 150 from the preceding LH IIIA2–B Palatial period. A more recent count (Crielaard 2006, 275) puts the number of LH IIIC sites much higher, at over 50, although there is still a significant drop from the preceding period. In an earlier study I included 64 LH IIIC sites in the Euboean Gulf area (Knodell 2013). If we look to the archaeological record of Greece as a whole (the mainland and Crete, excluding the islands); the number of total "sites" goes from 1366 to 655, a 52 percent decrease (Murray 2017, 141). For central Greece in the accounting of the present study we go from about 276 sites in the Palatial period to 152 in the Postpalatial period, which is a 44 percent decrease (map 14). The shift in number of communities is also a 44 percent decrease, going from 190 to 114 (see table 6; see discussion in chapter 2 for distinctions between sites, findspots, communities, etc.).

These numbers look quite different when parsed by region (see figure 2). In Boeotia there is a dramatic decrease in site numbers from 66 to 20 (70 percent), which is what we might expect with the collapse of a social system resulting in population drop or dispersal, or certain types of sites no longer being necessary. In Euboea, however, the drop is less, going from 32 to 16. In East Lokris, we go from 27 to 17. Attica is similar, going from 57 to 36. Thessaly goes from 38 to 21. Malis drops from 18 to 10. Phokis is the most resilient (a diachronic trend in this study), dropping from 28 to 21. From the simple metric of site numbers, then, it appears that Boeotia was much more dramatically affected by the palatial collapse than other parts of central Greece, which makes good sense since it seems to have been the most centralized and "palatial" part of the wider region. Thessaly and Attica were less affected, perhaps having had palatial systems of some kind, but more dispersed regional political landscapes. Nonpalatial regions (Euboea, East Lokris, Phokis, Malis) seem to have been affected least, especially considering that many of the Palatial Bronze Age sites that do not show signs of later occupation were mere findspots. An analogy for variable response to palatial collapse might be found in the Peloponnese, where Galaty and colleagues (2015) have attributed the depopulation of Messenia to the collapse of a single state at Pylos while noting substantial continuity in the Argolid, particularly at Tiryns after the fall of Mycenae. A case for further comparison can be found in Achaia, which had no palace and experienced a great deal of continuity into LH IIIC (Arena 2015). In addition to the change in numbers of sites, there is a dramatic shift in location as communities—prominent ones especially—move toward the sea. This can be seen in both the settlement hierarchy and in modeled networks of interaction (map 15).

If we examine the sites that flourish in the aftermath of the palatial decline, they are particularly the ones in the densest clusters of modeled interaction: Lefkandi in central Euboea, Kynos in East Lokris, Perati in Attica—all of which seem to have been located in zones outside of palatial control (see chapter 3). It should come as no surprise that places that never made the transition to palatial life experienced continuity—or even thrived—following the palatial collapse.

Four characteristics of the settlement pattern in central Greece during this transition stand out immediately (see maps 14 and 15):

1. There is a significant decline in the number of sites found on the fertile agricultural plains that formed the center of the settlement pattern and hierarchy in the Palatial period.
2. More sites (proportionately), including nearly all of the largest and best-connected centers, are located on or very near the coast.
3. LH IIIB pottery is found at nearly all sites where LH IIIC pottery is found, marking significant continuity.
4. The most significant sites and regions of the Postpalatial Bronze Age emerge in previously nonpalatial areas (i.e., in eastern Attica, Euboea, and East Lokris).

In this section I examine the reorganization of settlement patterns in Postpalatial times. I then turn to the archaeological evidence for the reconstitution of political authority that occurs at the end of the Late Bronze Age.

Settlement Reorganization

The palatial centers at Thebes, Orchomenos, and Gla left something of a vacuum when they abruptly came to an end. While Thebes and Orchomenos were occupied in the Postpalatial period, habitation there seems to have been on a smaller scale and there is no evidence for the sort of centralized administration seen before. This change is also borne out in the settlement pattern of the surrounding area. In the Palatial period, the exploitation of large agricultural plains was highly systematized. Palaces depended on extracting resources from the plains themselves, as well as the subsidiary centers, sites, and individuals within and around these plains. These smaller sites on the main plains (the Theban Plain and Kopaic Basin) were widely abandoned in the Postpalatial period (see map 14).

Eleon and Thebes maintained substantial populations throughout the Postpalatial period, although they look very different from the way they did in Palatial times. Continuity in occupation is demonstrated at Thebes by settlement evidence and through the continued use of tombs, signaling that at least some portion of the population stayed after the collapse of the palatial system (Tzavella-Evjen 2014, 63). Eleon exhibits strong influence from Thebes in LH IIIC Early, although it had already shifted its orientation toward the coast. Network changes in LH IIIC Middle, when interaction between coastal sites seems to intensify, began to exclude Eleon (Thomatos 2006; Van Damme 2017a). Nevertheless, Eleon demonstrates remarkable resilience throughout LH IIIC at the level of the household (Van Damme 2017b, 350; see also Small 1998).

Eutresis, on the other hand, is occupied only at the beginning of LH IIIC Early, suggesting that its population soon moved elsewhere, perhaps closer to the sea. Inland sites, when they do remain occupied, seem to have done so on account of their strategic locations and defensibility, rather than through the maintenance of relations with Thebes, which of course was preeminent in the previous period. This suggests (1) that the status of Thebes at the center of a regional settlement hierarchy was no longer relevant, and (2) that the agricultural and interregional connections facilitated by these sites did not remain important in their own right. In the Palatial period, settlements at Eutresis, Plataia, and Erythrai were strategically positioned on major land routes and in proximity to important agricultural areas. Kreusis was an important port on the Corinthian Gulf, which would have facilitated connections to the Peloponnese, western Greece, and perhaps the central Mediterranean. Mycenaean-built road remains on the mountain pass linking Kreusis and Eutresis demonstrate an infrastructural connection between these sites in the Palatial period (Heurtley 1925). Roads require substantial investment of organized labor, and in this case were almost certainly linked to a palatial authority. The shift in settlement pattern seems to signal the Postpalatial obsolescence of this connection between a secondary center of Thebes (Eutresis) and the sea (Kreusis).

The shift is even more dramatic in the former territory of Orchomenos. Gla, Chorsiai, and the network of fortifications around the Kopais was abandoned (see map 14). The cutoff in occupation at these strategic locations suggests that such places and the connections they offered were no longer seen as a priority for people in Postpalatial times. The overwhelming move in settlement toward the

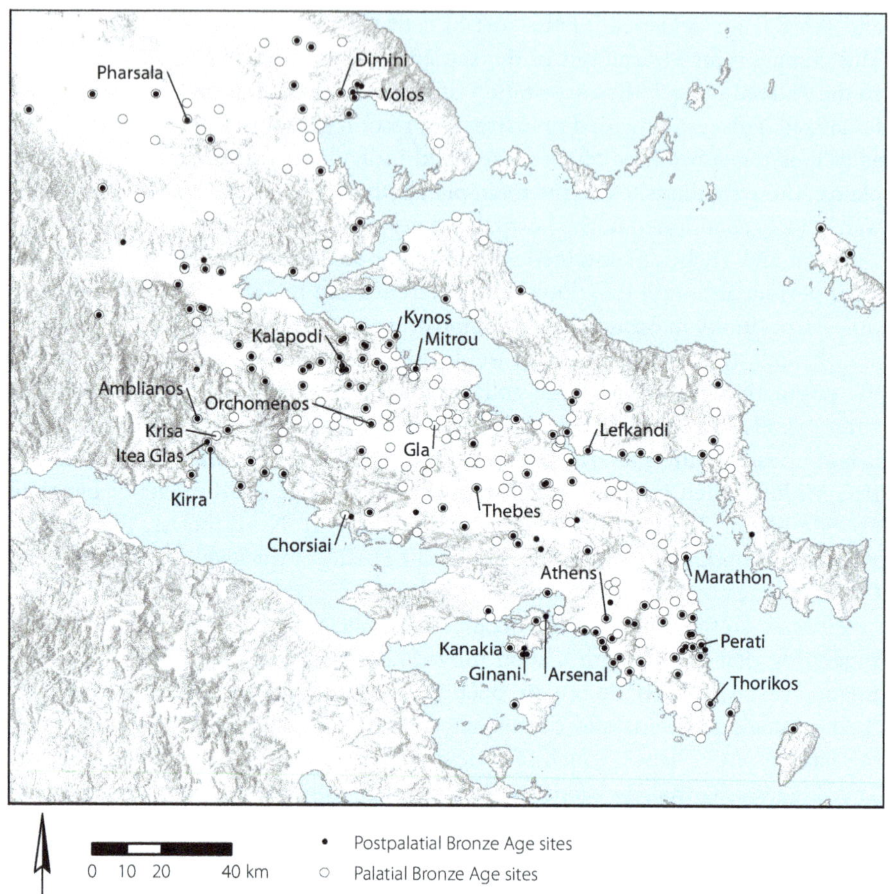

MAP 14. Postpalatial Bronze Age site locations compared to the Palatial Bronze Age.

sea, especially toward the Euboean Gulf but also in the direction of the Corinthian and Saronic Gulfs, suggests that connections and maritime resources were being actively sought between reconstituted communities. With palatial influence gone from maritime routes, these coastal zones provided new opportunities for enterprising individuals and communities to thrive. In this way, the coastscape reemerged as an important political space, after palatial interests had been oriented more inland toward agricultural plains.[2] Indeed, that very domination of inland plains in earlier times may have pushed certain people out into more marginal, coastal zones with poorer land, establishing communities that eventually would be well positioned to pursue new subsistence strategies following the palatial collapse.

2. See Tartaron (2013, 9–11) on coastscapes, specifically with respect to the Early Mycenaean period.

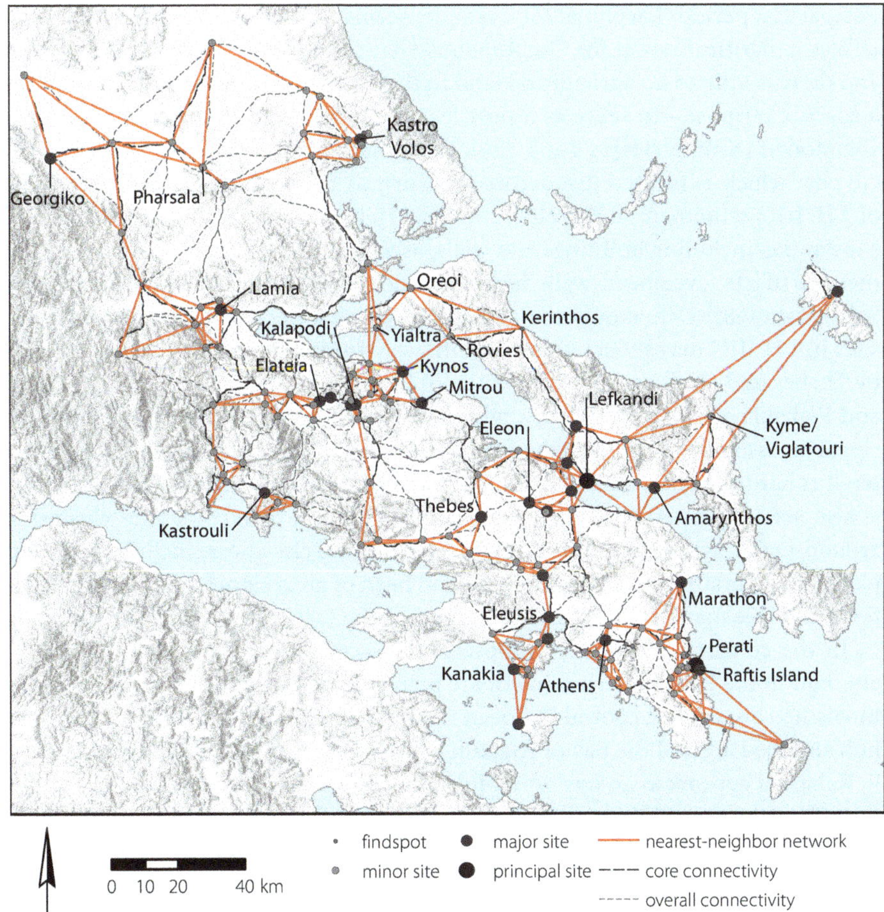

MAP 15. Postpalatial Bronze Age sites, joined by a connectivity model, with a nearest-neighbor network of communities (see also maps 14, 16, and appendix for additional place names).

There is a marked rise in the size and apparent importance of certain coastal sites on the Euboean Gulf. The sites that experienced the greatest growth are Kynos, Mitrou, and Lefkandi. While there are LH IIIB remains at all these sites, we see significant expansion in LH IIIC (Dakoronia 2003, 38; Sherratt 2006a: 304–5; van de Moortel 2009, 360–65). Kalapodi, while inland, is located on a major land route—connecting the sea and the upper Kephisos valley/Great Isthmus Corridor—and also grows in significance in Postpalatial times (Felsch 1996, 2007; Niemeier 2016). Many of these sites have been subject to recent programs of fieldwork, which have dramatically altered our knowledge of central Greece in the Postpalatial Bronze Age (Lemos 2012; Knodell 2013; Kramer-Hajos 2016).

In keeping with this pattern, there are also sites on the Euboean Gulf that seem to have been important in the Palatial period but that wane in significance in the

Postpalatial period. Larymna, for example, seems to have been established in LH IIIB as a maritime outlet for Orchomenos/Gla (see chapter 3, p. 81). It is fortified, and there is little to no agricultural land in the area, suggesting that it was built for a specific purpose—to serve as a port for a larger polity—and then more or less abandoned (Kramer-Hajos 2008, 129). Something similar may have happened at Glypha, which is located just across the Euripos from Chalkis. There are traces of LH IIIC settlement at Glypha, but the LH IIIA occupation was much more substantial, including buildings and walls, as well as numerous ceramic, glass, and metal artifacts; cyclopean walls have been documented there as well (Sapouna-Sakellaraki 1987; Demakopoulou 1988). The apparent decline in activity at certain sites in LH IIIC may reflect a power shift away from places previously controlled by Thebes and Orchomenos in Boeotia. In Thessaly, the abandonment of Dimini and Pefkakia after LH IIIC Early, while Kastro Volos continued to prosper, may signal an association between the former that was overcome eventually by the latter. It is hard to say much about Athens itself, but a change in locational emphasis is also seen in eastern Attica. In particular, there is a pattern of sites clustering around Perati, with the settlement pattern thinning elsewhere, including around places like Marathon and Thorikos that had been of great significance during Palatial times (see maps 14 and 15).

In the connectivity model proposed here, very different patterns are apparent than in the Palatial period (compare maps 10 and 15). In Boeotia, interactions intensified around the central Euboean Gulf, especially near the Euripos. Another hub emerged around the bay of Atalanti, with Kynos and Mitrou on either side of it. Kalapodi appears as an important inland node on the confluence of land routes from Boeotia, Elis, Phthiotis, and Lokris. The Malian and Pagasetic Gulfs seem to have been less well connected at this time, especially with sites farther inland, and the nearest-neighbor connections drawn from these sites are often much longer-distance than others. In general, Thessaly appears to have been quite isolated: it is only in the vicinity of the Pagasetic Gulf that a significant density of sites was maintained.[3] A natural interpretation of this pattern would be to suggest that it would lead to less frequent contacts between Thessaly and other regions, which seems to be borne out in the material culture of the period as well. While LH IIIC pottery styles are present at all of these sites, there is much greater regionalism visible than in the LH IIIB period, and, aside from these coastal locations, Thessaly diverges more than other regions from the LH IIIC regional style (often called a koine) that several authors identify around the Euboean Gulf (Desborough 1964, 146; Lemos 1998, 1999; Thomatos 2006; Van Damme 2017b, 411).

Euboea embarked on a new florescence of connectivity in LH IIIC, especially in the central part of the island, which would continue until the Archaic period. In

3. It is also interesting that in the Archaic and early Classical periods, Thessaly developed quite idiosyncratic political institutions, neither entirely aligned with the polis-states, nor with the tribal *ethne* (Morgan 2003; Decourt, Nielsen, and Helly 2004).

the north Euboea was connected to the mainland via just a few nodes—the small settlements at Oreoi, Yialtra, and Rovies (see map 15). Kerinthos stands almost alone on the Aegean coast of Euboea, at some distance from any other sites. While Kerinthos was apparently isolated, its status as one of the few good harbors on the Aegean coast of Euboea, with another located at modern Kyme, would have made it a valuable stopping point for sea traffic.

Central Euboea underwent significant change in the Postpalatial period, and it is quite similar to East Lokris in this respect. There was no Mycenaean palace, although important sites certainly existed at several locations in Palatial times (see chapter 3). Most of these sites remained occupied in the Postpalatial period and some seem to have grown, though at Lefkandi the pattern was accelerated and it quickly became the preeminent site in the region (Sherratt 2006a, 304–5). In addition to sites located on the Euboean Gulf, the Oxylithos/Kyme area was clearly a participant in these networks. Like Kerinthos, this area was a seemingly isolated locale on the Aegean coast of Euboea, but it is also at one end of several major land routes that connect the Aegean to the Euboean Gulf. If the Kyme area were an important place for maritime connectivity in the Palatial period, as evidenced by the ingot finds discussed in the previous chapter, it likely remained so afterward, not least in terms of its connections to Skyros, which also maintained a significant occupation in LH IIIC. At Viglatouri, which the excavator identifies as Mycenaean and Geometric Kyme, remains of a substantial settlement have been found that demonstrate continuous occupation from the Early Bronze Age to the Geometric period (Sapouna-Sakellaraki 1998, 61). The broader organization of settlement—mostly understood through little-known sites—seems largely to have been maintained in central and northern Euboea from Palatial to Postpalatial times, with a drop in the number of sites known from only a few finds.

Lefkandi itself seems to have risen quickly, perhaps on account of its location on the fertile Lelantine Plain, the nearby clay sources, and its shifting status within the political framework of central Euboea and eastern Boeotia. Its nonpalatial background and advantageous location near the Euripos allowed it to coopt long-distance trade networks while at the same time expanding local production to support a larger population. The site is also located on the principal land route that connects areas east of it to Chalkis. While a more northerly route is possible, it necessitates passing between Mounts Dirphys and Olympus, which would have been much more difficult (Fachard 2012, 103–5). By sea, Lefkandi had the advantage of a double bay, which could accommodate a great deal of maritime traffic. It was also an easy crossing to the mainland, making it an important go-between located just before the bottleneck of the Euripos. This position allowed Lefkandi to exert influence over the narrow strait without the risk of ships becoming trapped within Euripos itself.

On the other side of the Euboean Gulf, in Attica, a large division is apparent between eastern Boeotia and northeastern Attica, with the northernmost Attic site of any significance being Marathon. This absence results in the nearest-neighbor analysis effectively separating Attica from the rest of the study area (see map 15). While we should not interpret this to mean that Attica was a completely closed system, it may still reflect a relatively larger degree of isolation from the rest of central Greece. This is not to say that the region was isolated in the Postpalatial period. In fact, it seems to have prospered. Southeastern Attica has the highest density of sites of any area within the study region, and the cemetery at Perati reflects major connections with the outside world (Iakovidis 1980, 2003a, 2003b; Nightingale 2009). In a recent restudy of Perati, Murray (2018a) suggests that the exotica at Perati need not be interpreted simply as exotic status markers but should be understood rather as signifying specific aspects of mortuary ritual that reflect diverse origins. Drawing on evidence of foreign craftsmen remaining active at Tiryns in the Postpalatial period, Murray suggests that the evidence from Perati may reflect the establishment of a mixed community with members of various origins who dispersed from different parts of Greece in the wake of palatial collapse. This may also explain the lack of Palatial period evidence from the site, and it fits the wider pattern of movement toward the sea.[4]

The metal resources of the Lavriotiki were a continued draw for southeastern Attica, and indeed LH IIIC pottery has been found in a mineshaft in Thorikos (Mountjoy 1995b). It is possible that mineral resources became more widely available after the decline of a powerful center at Thorikos.[5] The overall impression in Attica is a Postpalatial settlement pattern similar to that observed elsewhere, with settlements moving toward the coast. Moreover, we should note that, unlike many of the regions described above, southern Attica enjoyed close access to the Saronic Gulf, another locus of Postpalatial activity. Kanakia on Salamis maintained its significance well into the Postpalatial period, while another acropolis site at Ginani and several Submycenaean cemeteries throughout the island, including the Salamis Arsenal site, seem to indicate significant growth (Lolos 2001a).

Some isolation of Attica from the rest of central Greece is also reflected in the regionalism seen in its ceramic styles (Mountjoy 1999), which have more in common with Rhodes and the Cyclades than with elsewhere on the mainland. This reflects different external interactions, where Attica was involved in long-distance trade networks and stylistic trends separate from its neighboring regions. Indeed, connections between southeastern Attica, southern Euboea, and the Cyclades

4. A major LH IIIC settlement was recently documented on Raftis Island, just opposite the chamber tomb cemetery at Perati. The work is carried out by the Bays of East Attica Regional Survey (Murray et al., forthcoming; Bays of East Attica Regional Survey, accessed December 5, 2020, http://bearsarchaeologicalproject.org/).

5. Ongoing work here, too, may prove enlightening, most notably with the Thorikos Archaeological Research Project of the Belgian School at Athens. See Thorikos Archaeological Research Project, accessed December 5, 2020, https://www.thorikos.be.

represent a long-term trend, going back to the Neolithic and Early Bronze Age (Tankosić 2011; Cullen et al. 2013; Nazou 2017).

Thessaly is somewhat similar to Attica in witnessing a partial, but not drastic, shift in settlement pattern. Most noticeable is the thinning out of the area around Pharsala. After the Palatial period, it seems that communities in this area dispersed as part of a wider set of movements toward the sea. This thinning out may also suggest greater regionalism and divergence between the groups of communities that clustered around Volos and Lamia in the Postpalatial period, since Pharsala is found on the main land route in between. Near Volos things changed as well. Most sites around the bay of Volos and in the plain of Lake Karla (Boibeis) demonstrate continuity of occupation into LH IIIC. However, of the three "palatial" sites at Dimini, Pefkakia, and Kastro Volos, only the last was occupied after LH IIIC Early. This may indicate some sort of conflict and consolidation of power in the region during the LH IIIC period. Unfortunately, our state of knowledge is not such that we can say much more with any degree of certainty, though this may actually indicate a sort of centralization of regional power, not unlike what is seen at the same time at Lefkandi.

Malis does not appear to have had major changes in its settlement patterns during Postpalatial times. There is a small decline in site numbers, though the Spercheios valley and Lamia demonstrate strong continuity of occupation from LH IIIB to LH IIIC. This is not surprising, considering that, of any region of central Greece with a dense concentration of Mycenaean sites, this appears to be the one most distant from any known palace, both geographically and in network terms. There was, however, some diminishment in the overall scale of sites, most of which are cemeteries with continuity of use between LH IIIB and LH IIIC.

A similar pattern can be seen in Phokis, with continued but diminished occupation at several sites. Notably, the major fortified center at Krisa is not occupied in the LH IIIC period whereas the more coastal sites of Kirra and Itea Glas are—as, indeed, are several sites in the neighboring bay of Antikyra. This nexus of settlement in this part of the Corinthian Gulf contrasts with the negligible distribution of sites farther east in Boeotia, and it suggests that relations with Achaia (on the other side of the Corinthian Gulf) may have been maintained across the period of the palatial collapse. This settlement pattern also suggests that this access to the main land route north (the Great Isthmus Corridor) remained significant. Nevertheless, the central place at Krisa seems to have experienced the same pattern of abandonment seen at other major centers of the Palatial period, perhaps lending credence to its inclusion in some models of Mycenaean settlement as the possible location of a palatial site (Renfrew 1975, 15; Galaty and Parkinson 2007, 2). The lack of LH IIIC occupation at Krisa would therefore fit the wider regional pattern of rejecting sites with trappings of palatial society and shifting settlement orientations toward the sea (although the fact remains that there is no definitive evidence that Krisa was a palace).

Given these shifts in the locations of settlements, as well as the reasons for growth and decline in particular areas, we can infer some significant lifestyle changes during the Postpalatial period. The first and most obvious is that populations were no longer living under the control, influence, or shadow of palatial regimes. Moreover, the end of the palaces was likely quite dramatic for people living at and around them, involving a certain amount of conflagration, death, and the abandonment of communities. In the absence of highly centralized authority, regional political organization was reconstituted more locally. This would have been felt most strongly in areas that had larger, more centralized palatial systems, most notably Boeotia, although even nonpalatial regions were in contact with and therefore influenced by their palatial neighbors. They responded to this disappearance, too. While this might be seen as a shift from authoritarianism to egalitarianism, the evidence suggests rather that new, different hierarchies emerged. The significant sites mentioned above still required organizational efforts for building projects, resource procurement, and, not least, maritime activities.

The connectivity model proposed here provides strong evidence for local and regional interaction in distinct patterns. Through the lens of peer-polity interaction we can see both characteristics of a shared symbolic culture and evidence for conflict in the form of relatively common destructions and upheavals at Postpalatial sites. Dakoronia (2003, 38) reports at least three destructions (two by earthquake and one by fire) at Kynos, and Lefkandi suffered similar misfortunes (Sherratt 2006a, 305–7). Earthquakes have been proposed in order to explain destructions at many other sites as well (Ambraseys 1996). This may make sense in a tectonically active area, yet sites along the Euboean Gulf especially must be regarded as highly connected, both by land and by sea, and earthquakes feature far too frequently as default explanations for destruction.[6] Other, sometimes violent, explanations for destructions must also be considered. Murray (2017, 256) has characterized this period as more "chaotic" or unrestful than the previous. On the contrary, I would argue that the imposition of palatial systems was a significant act of societal disruption far greater than their collapse. Nevertheless, this may well have been a violent time in which new contenders for dominance and prestige in the region were in regular conflict with each other, and this conflict was most likely responsible for the majority of destructions seen during this period. I think that we should ultimately imagine a culture that combined subsistence agriculture and raiding—things that were present in Early Mycenaean and Palatial times, too, but were perhaps rebuffed or suppressed in certain areas by palatial institutions.

6. There is a long tradition of using earthquakes as an explanation for site destruction and culture change, especially in the Aegean, going back all the way to Arthur Evans and his insistence that Minoan Crete was not overrun by Mycenaeans from "the continent." More recent studies, of course, are more scientific and systematic (e.g., Stiros and Jones 1996; Jusseret and Sintubin 2017). There has been a focus especially on the Argolid in relation to the destruction of Mycenaean palaces: see essays in Stiros and Jones 1996.

Interaction is manifest in other ways as well. Cooperation between communities must have existed alongside conflict and competition for resources. The drop in population and overall site numbers in the LH IIIC period would have in fact necessitated more connectivity between places than was seen in the previous Palatial period. Communities had to interact to remain viable—for the simple purposes of resource diversification between different microecologies, social storage, and intercommunity marriages. Modeled links are on the whole more coastal and involve greater distances (compare maps 10 and 15). In terms of how these connections happened, Dickinson (2006, 66) has highlighted the importance of movement on multiple scales, albeit in different terms, stating that "mobility might well be considered the most significant feature of the Postpalatial period, for it not only represents a continuing destabilizing factor, it underlines the limits on the coercive power of those trying to re-establish authority."

Maritime Reorientations

Ideological aspects of coastal settlement and increased amounts of maritime travel are apparent in other aspects of the material record as well. While palatial trade probably did not involve the ruling elite directly (that is, they do not seem to have gone on trading expeditions themselves), it was at least partly directed by them as exclusive consumers, and it likely involved agents of the palaces. With the settlement shift to the coast, however, and with aspects of maritime activity becoming less exclusively linked to palatial institutions, the sea must have loomed ever larger in the eyes of all people. In the sense of Tuan (1977), the sea represented an ever-present space of growing importance, through which people accessed places of special significance (other settlements, sanctuaries, and distant lands).

We also find evidence of anxiety and aggrandizement concerning the sea, as elite vessels (chiefly kraters used for drinking and serving at feasting events) bear depictions of ships with often violent imagery. Depictions of warriors and battle are not new in the LH IIIC period. Ship imagery appeared in the Mycenaean palaces of the mainland at Pylos and Orchomenos in the form of frescoes (Lang 1969; Brekoulaki et al. 2015; Spyropoulos 2015). There is, however, a new appearance of ship and siege imagery in LH IIIC on pottery (Petrakis 2011; Sauvage 2012), a portable medium designed for convivial contexts.

A dual maritime outlook—with the sea as a corridor and facilitator of movement but also as a dangerous place—may be reflected in figural representations found on painted pottery from Kynos and Lefkandi (Dakoronia 2006; Crouwel 2007, 2009; Lemos 2018). Sherds excavated from Kynos show a variety of maritime scenes (Dakoronia 1990, 1999, 2006). Figure 5a shows fragments of a krater with two boats, most likely engaged in combat; on a fragment from a lower part of the vessel a large fish attacks a fallen mariner, while other fish leap out at the people still on the boats. Figures 5b and 5c show less fine fragments, though they are similarly

FIGURE 5. LH IIIC seafaring images from Kynos (a and b) and Lefkandi (c); sherds from "siege kraters" from Thebes (d) and Kalapodi (e); a sherd from "feasting krater" at Lefkandi (f) (illustration by Christina Kolb, after Dakoronia 2006; Evely 2006, pl. 71; Niemeier 2013, 36, fig. 2; Petrakos 2014; Lemos 2018).

styled and display equally combative scenes. These images seem to reflect a culture for which maritime activity and conflict were in common thought, at least for the craftspeople producing these depictions—as well as for their consumers—which is a major departure from the previous Palatial period. Moreover, the sea is cast as a dangerous place, owing both to other people and to the nonhuman world. In addition to maritime imagery, "siege kraters" from Thebes and Kalapodi may preserve the memory of certain raids or other conflicts, or perhaps represent a generic theme of interest (figure 5d and 5e). Whether these are meant to represent real or imagined battles is impossible to know, but vessels bearing such images would have played an important role in social life, reflecting practices of communal drinking in which images served to express access to special products as well as to a particular type of imagery that was associated with status-building activities of seafaring and battle. Figural painting was still rare, and its distribution was quite uneven (Rutter 2014a). The owner of such a vessel would thus draw attention to such status activities while at the same time acting as host—another expression of social power. This is quite different from what we see in the Palatial period, when vase painting more often depicted symbols of elite power (individuals in chariots or powerful animals) than group activities like sailing or fighting.

While such imagery is not widespread, it is significant that it appears at some of the largest and best-connected sites on the Euboean Gulf, Kynos and Lefkandi, both of which seem to have suffered a series of destructions throughout the Postpalatial Bronze Age. While such a rivalry is not preserved in any particular mythohistorical accounts of the area, we might imagine competition between powerful rivals over control of this important maritime corridor (not unlike the territorial rivalry described in Boeotia, between Orchomenos and Thebes).

Political Authority and the Constitution of Society

Postpalatial societies formed new orders after the rejection of palatial systems. While occupation continued at some palatial sites, the physical and institutional structures of the previous polities—that is, the palaces themselves—were quite forcibly destroyed. Such patterns have been identified also in other complex polities that underwent dramatic social change or collapse, providing instructive examples of this type of rejection of institutions. Smith (2003, 168) describes a similar process in the Caucasus, whereby agents of the kingdom of Urartu destroyed structures associated with previous Late Bronze Age and Early Iron Age polities as an act of memory erasure and to displace the subjects of earlier regimes. Another relevant comparison might be the destruction of churches in France after the French Revolution (Clay 2003). Such acts of iconoclasm associated with political upheaval or overthrow occurred in many ancient polities—for example, in Mesopotamia and Mesoamerica—where symbolic destructions of material objects were deployed as enduring acts of violence against the collective memory of a place. Whatever the agency of the original destruction of the Mycenaean palaces (foreign invaders, interpolity conflict, popular uprising), the rejection of institutions that followed was lasting and reflects new interests in defining polity in opposition to them. In this way, the palatial destructions were an act of political production for some groups rather than simply the failure of others.

Large-scale resettlement is another mode of claiming authority in a landscape (Smith 2003, 168–69). In early Greece, such a deliberate strategy may be reflected in the depopulation of palatial territories and potential relocation to other areas—in central Greece or elsewhere. At the same time, there were also acts of reoccupation and rebuilding at previous locations of palatial authority, though in a different style. For example, the lower citadel of Tiryns was rebuilt extensively in the Postpalatial period on a different plan, while a new, smaller megaron was built over about half of the Palatial megaron (Maran 2001). Whatever the specific agency, we can see that new forms of political authority rose as societies were reconstituted—most likely in response to the rejected modes of palatial organization.

The degree of reorganization or change varied substantially by region, with the most dramatic shifts limited to previously palatial areas, as seen in the settlement data described above. Previously nonpalatial areas were affected too. Social integration took place both through the routines of everyday life, and in the dialectic construction of political authority (in the broad sense of Bourdieu 1977; Giddens 1984). Practices in the construction and legitimation of authority were smaller in scale than what was found in the palaces, and they were oriented more locally than regionally. Altogether, the constitution of political authority within the broader fabrics of society seems to have been an iterative, largely local process. Nevertheless, certain practices were shared throughout central Greece, even if there were apparent differences in scale. Certain of these, especially feasting, have direct antecedents in the Palatial period (and even earlier), though the practices were reconfigured as more local, less institutionalized negotiations of sociopolitical power.

Postpalatial society in general seems to have followed patterns established in the Early Mycenaean period. These were also maintained throughout the Palatial period in nonpalatial areas. As in the Palatial period, we should imagine a range of nonstate modes of social organization (see chapter 3). Nonpalatial societies in the Aegean might find parallels in middle-range ranked societies—which can also be characterized as transegalitarian—where social roles, status, and power relationships are somewhat informal and fluid (Ames 2008). The Postpalatial societies of central Greece are probably best characterized as occupying various positions along such a scale, represented by complex communities that exhibit a variety of modes of social organization. While centralized hierarchies no longer existed on a regional scale, local hierarchies became more apparent in certain areas, with more similarly sized centers, possibly controlled by nonhereditary leaders in regular contact and competition with one another (Whitley 1991, 184–86; Dickinson 2006, 110–11).

While it is difficult to know whether leadership was acquired or inherited, some combination of these characteristics seems most likely. Evidence for the continuous use of elite family chamber tombs in certain areas—Elateia, Medeon, and the Spercheios valley—suggests a maintenance of social status over generations, a trait that is also apparent in the chronologically amalgamated world of Homer. We might, then, imagine loose, sometimes hereditary systems that were not supported by formal institutions (such as a palace) and that also depended on the acquisition and maintenance of status on an individual basis. Systems of rank, status, and inequality were certainly present, but they were diverse and subject to rapid change on local or even individual levels.

Feasting played an important role in sociopolitical organization during this period (see, e.g., Dietler and Hayden 2001; Hitchcock, Laffineur, and Crowley 2008; Small 2019). Wright (2004a) notes that feasting can be traced from the Early Mycenaean period through the Postpalatial Bronze Age and Sherratt (2004) has linked aspects of ritual feasting seen in Homer to Mycenaean antecedents that were preserved through the Postpalatial period and into the Early Iron Age; these were associated especially with rulers' dwellings (Mazarakis Ainian 1997; Fox 2012; Alexandridou 2018; van den Eijnde 2018). In this way ritual feasting was a means of constituting and reinforcing asymmetrical power relationships within a society, as the host demonstrated the capacity to provide, entertain, and bring communities together. In the archaeological record of central Greece this is manifest in the forms of kraters, cups, and bowls as the most finely made and heavily decorated aspects of ceramic assemblages, suggesting that the practices with which they were associated (communal drinking and feasting activities) remained at the forefront of integrative social acts. In the Palatial period (in palatial areas), palaces coopted and institutionalized such practices, as evidenced in Linear B accounting concerning such events. In Postpalatial times, such practices were attached rather to individual agents who relied on the practice in the construction of personal (rather than institutional) authority. As in other cases, the palaces represent a scalar difference in a type of activity that elsewhere demonstrates a substantial continuity of practice. Van den Eijnde (2018, 10) looks to feasting as a "critical tool in building group identities, especially in the context of early states." Feasting is also a rather more general phenomenon, powerful outside of state contexts particularly for the implicit, noninstitutionalized power relationships it projects. The early Greek case is perhaps a cyclical one, where such social practices waver between the informal (Early Mycenaean, Postpalatial, Early Iron Age) and the institutional (Palatial, early polis) in political life. Nevertheless, more informal, perhaps "personal" contributions to feasting events likely persisted through palatial times as well, as Nakassis (2012) has argued in the case of Pylos based on Linear B texts that seem to record the generosity of the *wanax* (they use his personal name, *e-ke-ra2-wo*, in some places and call him the *wanax* in others). And as Small (2019) argues, feasting itself can serve also to create new social roles and institutions.

An even more significant change can be observed in the Postpalatial period, when feasting practices took on an interregional character in certain areas, chiefly in zones that did not witness centralized integration in palatial times, previewing certain characteristics of later interregional sanctuaries (de Polignac 1995). Ritual drinking and dining practices are evident at Kalapodi as modes of integrative and competitive social interaction, involving elites from the surrounding regions (Livieratou 2011, 150). Kramer-Hajos (2008, 141–43), drawing on faunal analyses by Stanzel (1991), argues that these practices were linked to the worship of Artemis, based on the presence of large numbers of deer bones, tortoise shells, and high-quality pottery of the aforementioned types. It is significant that Kalapodi is identified as the oracle of Apollo at Abai (Niemeier 2009) and it is probable that both deities were worshiped at the site—a frequent coincidence known also from later times.

Developments at Kalapodi may be part of a wider reorientation, in which regional, large-scale feasting events shifted toward ritual sites along important routes, both coastal and inland. In the LH IIIC period, for example, we see Amarynthos thrive, and in the area of the later sanctuary there is also Postpalatial and Early Iron Age material (Fachard et al. 2017; Reber et al. 2019). From later times, there are Artemis and Apollo sanctuaries at several other locations along the Euboean Gulf, including Plakari, Brauron, Eretria, Aulis, and Histiaia (see also Kowalzig 2018). While we do not have solid evidence of LH IIIC cult activity at these places, the existence of later sanctuaries at these locations may indicate a diachronic pattern of this type of practice starting at Kalapodi (and possibly at Amarynthos) in the Postpalatial period, and then spreading through central Greece in the Early Iron Age.

This trend continues at Kalapodi throughout the Early Iron Age and should be seen as a precursor to the regional sanctuaries in the eighth century and the early Archaic period.[7] McInerney (2011, 99–101) has recently shown that Kalapodi was the main regional sanctuary in central Greece until it was eclipsed by Delphi in the early Archaic period. In Postpalatial times, Kalapodi provided a venue for regional meetings between local elites and a place to engage in competitive aggrandizement, consumption, and display. It was in the Postpalatial Bronze Age, then, rather than in the Geometric period, that regional sanctuaries first became significant as decentralized loci of religious practice and began to play an important role in mediating the political landscape. Sealstones from Kalapodi indicate that ritual activity goes back to LH IIIA (Niemeier 2016), which suggests that such practices may have begun in nonpalatial or liminal areas even in the Palatial Bronze Age. This may have begun as a nonpalatial response to the political and administrative centralization of religious practice at the palaces, and then later came to thrive in Postpalatial times.

On a local level, smaller-scale feasting practices can be observed at Kynos, Lefkandi, and Mitrou. At Mitrou, such behaviors have definite antecedents in the

---

7. Snodgrass (1986) has discussed such centers in terms of peer-polity interaction, though, like de Polignac (1995), he is talking about polis formation in the early Archaic period.

LH IIIA2 period (Vitale 2008). At Lefkandi and Kynos, drinking vessels stand out with respect to quality and decoration (as in other places and times), which suggests that these are aspects of material culture deployed by a subset of society with special access to the "finer" things for a specific purpose—sharable marks of distinction in group eating and drinking events. For example, a pictorial krater from Lefkandi depicts feasting equipment (table, kylix, krater) and a seated figure (figure 5f). People came together to eat, drink, and socialize, and important individuals or groups acted as hosts. In this way, social bonds were reinforced and leadership was performed through everyday practices. Most importantly, such events served the purpose of bringing together people on a local scale in particular *places*, establishing new localizations of political authority, both at settlements and the interpolity contexts of regional sanctuaries. Such political acts were no doubt carried out on smaller scales throughout the landscape, too, as evidenced by the frequent occurrence of drinking sets in Postpalatial households and funerary contexts (Van Damme 2017b, 403–5; Small 2019, 102).

A further proxy for the emergence of leadership in new places can be found in evidence for storage. LH IIIC impressed pithoi from Kalapodi, Mitrou, Kynos, and Lefkandi suggest that storage practices were meant at least partly for display and that they carried sociopolitical messages as well (Lis and Rückl 2011). While there is again a scalar difference between the evidence at these sites and at previous palatial sites, there was nevertheless a focusing of resources in particular places, associated with the storage of staple products as wealth and perhaps its occasional redistribution in the form of communal events. LH IIIC assemblages of large cooking pots from Tiryns and Lefkandi also indicate that some houses had a much greater capacity to prepare and serve food than others (Lis 2015, 108). While there is no evidence for centralized or communal storage during the Postpalatial period, the storage capacities of Postpalatial households from several parts of Greece indicate that dry goods were being stored at a level above subsistence; there is also evidence for commensal dining in courtyards or large halls in households (Van Damme 2017b, 379–80). Together, this evidence suggests an individual- or household-oriented model for social display and the accumulation of prestige.

Rural populations comprised the wider world beyond the relatively few major sites serving as central places. In previously palatial areas these populations would have had to reorganize following the collapse of the palaces that seem to have, at least partly, centralized aspects of regional agricultural consumption. Risk-buffered farming has the opposite, decentralizing goal, necessitating greater connectivity on a regional scale between individuals and groups. This type of basic household- and community-based agriculture would have been the norm in non-palatial systems. The highly varied landscapes of central Greece were much better suited to this subsistence strategy than large-scale agriculture on sprawling plains. Halstead (2006, 26–31) discusses the dependence in Neolithic Greece of neighbors on one another in times of harvest for labor, and at all times for protection, exchange, and marriages. This shows up in later periods too, since risk-buffering strategies were often developed to adapt to new structural conditions in society—for example, in the Hellenistic period (Gallant 1989, 393). This mode of agricultural production contrasts sharply with the centralization of territorial resources seen in Palatial times. In the Postpalatial period, long-term strategies for risk buffering would have involved intercommunity connectivity, while short-term solutions to problems would have likely involved raiding for existing products rather than the acquisition of potentially productive territory. This is a fundamentally different relationship to land than can be seen in palatial systems, and also one that would have been antagonistic to them, which we can see especially if we extend such behaviors to nonpalatial areas during the Palatial period. This may offer yet another explanation for the palatial obsession with defensive architecture.

Conflicts between individuals and groups are characteristic of all societies, particularly in times of transition. As the political landscape of early Greece shifted, new opportunities and pathways to power opened on both local and regional scales. That conflict, especially maritime conflict, had become a significant feature of life in the Postpalatial period is evident in site destructions and in the figural representations discussed above (see figure 5), as well as in the increasing numbers of warrior depictions from a variety of LH IIIC sites (Crouwel 2007, 2009). This may represent a renewal of what Kramer-Hajos (2016) calls the "warrior ethos" of the Early Mycenaean period. Intercommunity conflicts can also be inferred from the choice of defensible site locations. While these are not the difficult-to-access refuge settlements of Crete or elsewhere in the Aegean (Nowicki 2000; Wallace 2010, 95–100; see also Haggis 2001), nearly all the major sites highlighted here (Mitrou, Kynos, Kastro Volos, Lefkandi, Amarynthos, Viglatouri, Athens) are either located on hilltops or are defensible promontories, which suggests that defensibility, along with access to the sea, remained a key concern.

The social changes at the end of the Palatial period, as well as the attendant shifts in settlement patterns, required new strategies of making connections between individuals and communities. Beyond these bare requirements for survival and sustainability, social practices would have developed to bring people together and certain individuals would have emerged "on top" in reformulated systems of social ranking, whether as a result of charisma, greater access to resources, or martial prowess. At any rate, the importance of certain integrative practices was not lost, and new local leaders emerged in all likelihood immediately after the palatial collapse if they were not already in place. Jung (2016) has argued that local leaders operating parallel to palatial systems may have played a role in the palatial collapse. This antagonism is a likely proposition that also helps to explain the lack of revival of palatial practices. Thus, hierarchy—as constituted and maintained through social integration and exclusion—was not new in this period; rather, it was reoriented. What is perhaps most novel is the emergence of regional ritual centers like Kalapodi (and possibly Amarynthos) as points of convergence and mediation for people from different communities, which anticipates later developments in Greek politics and religion.

CRAFTING IN NEW COMMUNITIES, RECONFIGURING PRODUCTION

Much of the settlement evidence discussed above comes in the form of pottery belonging to the LH IIIC style, which is related to—but distinct from—its Palatial precedents. While the LH IIIA and LH IIIB ceramics of the Palatial period demonstrate a higher degree of uniformity across regions, there is also a fair amount of regionalism present, especially in Euboea. LH IIIC ceramics show much greater regional variability (Sherratt 1980; Mountjoy 1999). The higher degree of uniformity in Palatial Mycenaean fine wares was the result of two related factors. First, this uniformity represented the emergence of regional production centers, some of which were located at palaces themselves—for example, at Thebes (Dakouri-Hild 2005, 185). The degree to which these were under the control of the palace is not well understood, and ceramic production is not widely represented in the Linear B tablets (Galaty 2007, 86). That being said, production and distribution on interregional and, especially, macroregional scales suggests some form of centralization, although this may well have more to do with consumption than production or with the fact that certain regions, such as the Argolid, exported large quantities. Moreover, it is clear that certain ceramics were being produced to suit elite tastes that were shared across the Mycenaean world. This can be seen as the result of regional integration and interregional interactions between polities, both palatial and nonpalatial. In some ways, the pattern of uniformity seen in the Palatial period represents integrated views of production and consumption, which had grown through the Middle Helladic and Early Mycenaean period. From this standpoint the LH IIIC stylistic divergence might be seen as a stylistic regression.

As an explanation for the above shifts, I suggest that the collapse of the palaces led to a dispersal of craft producers, who were formerly associated with palatial polities and who worked and trained apprentices in new social contexts in which ceramic production happened on local to regional scales. That is to say, pottery produced at local scales was then distributed through regional consumption networks, some of which were farther reaching than others. This explains regional divergences in style, on the one hand, and the surprisingly wide dispersal of sites exhibiting local styles of Mycenaean pottery during Postpalatial times, on the other.

Local patterns of LH IIIC ceramic styles fit the settlement pattern groupings created by the nearest-neighbor analysis fairly well, lending strength to the hypothetical connections generated in the network model (see map 15). Production itself seems to have occurred at the larger sites in the region, which suggests a degree of local-level centralization. Kilns have been excavated at Kynos and Pherai, and the clay sources at Phylla, near Lefkandi, seem to have been exploited for millennia on either side of the Postpalatial period (Dakoronia 1993, 125; Batziou-Efstathiou 1994; Kerschner and Lemos 2014). Lefkandi itself, then, was a likely production center as well.

LH IIIC pottery is also found dispersed somewhat more widely around the eastern Mediterranean. Population movement has long been used to explain this expanded distribution (Desborough 1972, 20–21; Dickinson 2006, 62–67; Murray 2017, 199–200). An additional (and likely) possibility is that craftspeople especially were on the move, along with goods and ideas, a phenomenon well documented for a variety of times and places in the Mediterranean (Blake 2008; Lis, Rückl, and Choleva 2015; Aslaksen 2016; Kiriatzi and Knappett 2016). By contrast, Yasur-Landau (2010), based on the magnitude of changes seen in material culture production in Cyprus and the Levant, has argued for the movement of whole populations. Whether we are talking about migration or travel, mobility is certainly present, and on a larger scale, affecting more members of society than in Palatial times. The most likely scenario is that mobility was expanding in the form of *both* travel *and* migration.

Pottery Networks in the Euboean Gulf

Stylistic groupings of pottery assemblages are often rendered through network models (Knappett 2013; Blake 2014). Sherratt (2006b, 218–20) notes a great deal of similarity between LH IIIC ceramics from Lefkandi and several other sites in central Greece, which can be illustrated as a simple stylistic network (map 16). We should note that no sites in Attica are included in this grouping, an exclusion also in the nearest-neighbor network of communities (see map 15). While these similarities should not be taken to mean that Lefkandi was the *only* production center for the whole region, they do indicate enough identical or shared elements of style to suggest frequent and consistent links through which other ideas could have flowed. These similarities are apparent in both stylistic features and (necessarily) sequences of production. Indeed, the presence of kilns at Kynos and Velestino-Pherai indicate local production, though clearly with a stylistic repertoire shared throughout a much larger region (Sherratt 2006b, 220).

The chronology of the extent of these similarities also has some explanatory power. What is significant here is the quantity of stylistic links for each period, as well as the question of when—in what period—new links are formed. The similarities of style during Phase 1 of the LH IIIC period at Lefkandi are telling, and they would seem to indicate a holdover from earlier modes of production. The similarities would have evolved out of the commonalities of the previous period and then spread via the dispersal of craftspeople to growing communities following the collapse of the palaces. This is indicative of already widespread styles coalescing in certain areas rather than a particularly Lefkandiot style dispersing. The chronology is especially important for Orchomenos and Eutresis, which only have LH IIIC Early pottery (Lefkandi Phase 1), indicating holdout at these places

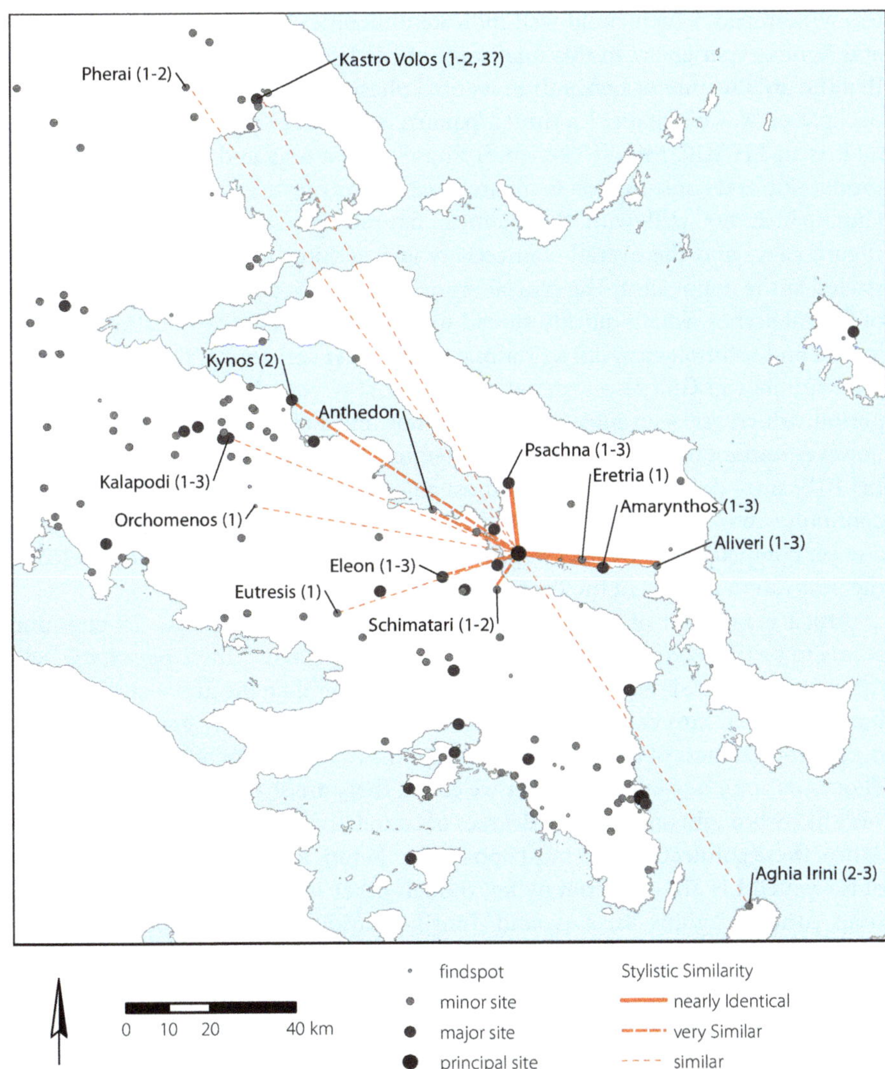

MAP 16. Lefkandi pottery network and settlement pattern in the Postpalatial Bronze Age, showing degree of similarity of pottery between Lefkandi and other major sites (connecting lines) and Lefkandi LH IIIC phases represented at the site (1–3, in parentheses) (data from pottery study by Sherratt 2006b, 218–19).

that had been significant during the Palatial period before they were eclipsed by new centers reaching their apogee in LH IIIC Middle. The distribution of Phase 2 ceramics is more reflective of the prosperity that sites on the Euboean Gulf enjoyed in this period generally, and it also shows the beginning and flourishing of stylistic links with more distant places like Kynos and Kea. Phase 3 is much less widespread, which could well indicate difficulties that sites such as Lefkandi and Kynos experienced in this final stage of LH IIIC: Sherratt (2006a, 307) notes that the architecture of Lefkandi in its final phase was heavily degraded although occupation was maintained; a similar pattern is found at Kynos (Dakoronia 2009).

It is in LH IIIC Middle (Lefkandi Phase 2) that a shared pattern of ceramic production and consumption is apparent across the northern and central Euboean Gulf, which fits well with the nautical figural representations of the period (figure 5a–c) and the overall connectivity and architectural elaboration demonstrated at the major sites. The crucial innovation in this phase was the florescence of figural scenes, which quickly spread to several locations, demonstrating ideological and technological links (Thomatos 2006, 141–42; 2007). The northern and central Euboean Gulf also experienced the most violent destructions during this period, which are seen most clearly at Kynos and Lefkandi. These destructions, however, cannot be compared to the systemic collapse of the palaces at the end of LH IIIB, since destructions are in almost all cases followed by quick recovery and continuity into the Protogeometric period. Indeed, it may have been the local and yet competing nature of craft production in the Postpalatial period that led to the innovations we see in the Protogeometric style.

Attica is not part of this stylistic network throughout LH IIIC. Its attention seems to be turned toward the Cyclades (especially Naxos), the Dodecanese, and the west coast of Asia Minor (not least Miletos) rather than the Euboean Gulf. Desborough (1964, 146) called this an Aegean koine, though there are doubts about the appropriateness of this term (Deger-Jalkotzy 1998, 115; Vlachopoulos 2003, 231; Thomatos 2006, 145–48). Whatever we call it, there are shared characteristics that were likely brought on by higher degrees of connectivity between certain places. In Attica, these connections are most apparent at Perati, which has the largest corpus of excavated LH IIIC material by far, though other important assemblages come from Athens, Aghios Kosmas, and Thorikos (Mountjoy 1999, 496–99). Other long-distance relations represented at Perati were to the east, although by LH IIIC Late Attic pottery begins to have more in common with that of the Euboean Gulf (Mountjoy 1999, 53). Much of this is so-called White Ware, which now appears to have been locally produced but also shows links between Attica, Euboea, and the islands to the east (Lis et al. 2020b). This may indeed have been crucial in establishing a network through which the Attic Protogeometric style spread so rapidly in the subsequent period. At the same time, the divergence of Attica from the rest of LH IIIC central Greece may help explain the rather isolated (and problematic) phenomenon of Submycenaean pottery.[8] Finally, it seems to be the case that potters themselves were on the move, at least in certain cases. A recent study of cooking pots from several locations along the Euboean and Pagasetic Gulfs indicate that a particularly Aeginetan *chaîne opératoire* was in use, and that this type of

---

8. On the problematic nature of the term Submycenaean as an independent phase, rather than a regionally specific style, see Rutter 1978; Papadopoulos et al. 2011.

technology transfer would have happened in the context of both itinerant activity and permanent relocation (Lis et al. 2020a). This is also quite likely to have been the case at other times and with other industries.

Metal Production and Consumption

In addition to pictorial pottery in LH IIIC Middle, metal artifacts, too, seem to indicate the proliferation of a warrior ethos, most clearly in so-called "warrior tombs" or "warrior burials" (Cavanagh and Mee 1998, 89–97; T. J. Papadopoulos 1999; Deger-Jalkotzy 2006; Steinmann 2012). Foremost among the various prestige goods that distinguished these graves were metal artifacts, including weapons, vessels, and toiletries such as combs, razors, tweezers, and mirrors (Deger-Jalkotzy 2006, 152). These types of graves are found widely in Achaia, although they are relatively rare outside of the northwest Peloponnese and Epiros (Deger-Jalkotzy 2006, 154; Douzougli and Papadopoulos 2011). The Argolid and Boeotia, in particular, stand out because they lack such burials. In the case of Boeotia, Deger-Jalkotzy (2006, 167–68) suggests that this is owing to the history of research and lack of discovery rather than to a lack of presence. Kramer-Hajos (2016, 164) points to the cemetery at Perati and two swords found in Euboea at Avlonari and Palioura—both from nonfunerary contexts—as evidence for "warrior tombs" in central Greece. On their own, these are not particularly strong arguments, but other categories of evidence (site destructions and iconography) suggest that the ideologies that produced warrior burials in Achaia may also be found in central Greece, again in areas that were not previously within the remit of palaces. Metal consumption would have been a key element of this ethos.

Linear B records from the Palatial period in Pylos provide us with a good example of the scale and location of metalworking in relation to the palatial economy. The Jn series of tablets mentions around 270 smiths, varying allotments of metal, and divisions of labor (Ventris and Chadwick [1956] 1973, 252–59; J. Smith 1993; Michailidou 2008, 534–35; Nakassis 2013a, 74–102). Whitelaw (2001, 9) places metal production somewhere between the palatial and nonpalatial sector, although Blackwell (2018) has recently associated metal hoards at several mainland sites from the Palatial period with allotments from and controlled by the palace. Like pottery production, metal production industries were specialized occupations before the time of the palaces, and they certainly were practiced outside palatial areas as well. Following the collapse of palatial systems, metalworkers from palatial areas—the most active in the Mycenaean world—would have needed to find new locations and reconfigure production in the absence of administrative structures. Self-organization, rather than central organization, had major consequences for connectivity. In the Postpalatial period, production remains from settlements are extremely scant, although coastal examples from Mitrou, Lefkandi, and Aigeira may indicate that maritime locations were also significant for this type of industry (Evely 2006, 288; Alram-Stern 2007, 17; Blackwell and O'Neill 2014).

Possible explanations for the lack of production remains at major sites include traveling smiths or smiths connecting to long-distance and regional networks of resource procurement and product distribution that did not leave substantial material traces; in fact, this lack of production probably stems from a mixture of both things. The crucial element here—one that is not present in the Palatial period and does not apply to ceramic production—is that smiths must have been much more active in their connection to long-distance networks. In the first place, metal sources are usually located at some distance from known production sites and, in the second, the centralized import of raw materials was not happening at palatial sites. Recycling must also be taken into consideration, and the presence of scrap found in bronze hoards suggests that this was an important activity at various times and places in the Bronze Age (Budd et al. 1995; Knapp 2000; Blackwell 2018; Sherratt 2000, 87–88). The Cape Gelidonya wreck (see map 17), which dates to the beginning of the Postpalatial period (ca. 1200 BCE or slightly later) and had LH IIIC pottery on board, provides evidence for traveling smiths and recycling in the form of metal scrap and bronze-working tools found in the cargo, along with more conventional ingots (Bass 1967). This evidence is in contrast to the earlier (Palatial period) Uluburun wreck, whose cargo of bulk goods (copper and tin ingots) and prestige items fits much better with the palatial model of consumption described above.

In central Greece, Lefkandi has the most significant metal production remains dating to the Postpalatial period. This is unsurprising, given its key location, demonstrable relations with Cyprus, and history of excavation. Finished products, production slag, crucibles, and molds were all found at the site (Evely 2006, 288). Recent excavations at Eleon have uncovered evidence for lead working, and there are also partial molds from Athens, including from the Mycenaean fountain (Van Damme, personal communication). Anthedon also has remains of bronze working (Rolfe 1890, 104–7; Catling 1964, 296–97; Schläger, Blackman, and Schäfer 1968). Finished products are fairly widely dispersed, but they are often difficult to date to LH IIIC specifically, since all but one of the Aegean sword types that appear in LH IIIC also appear in other periods (Molloy 2010, 405). Moreover, these are often decontextualized and are reported to come from tombs in generalized locations. Perati, unsurprisingly, provides the widest array of excavated metal artifacts from this period, which fits models either of conspicuous deposition of wealth in funerary contexts (Iakovidis 1980) or a community of displaced craft specialists (Murray 2018a). Either way, metal production and consumption remained an important social practice carried out within and across multiple regions.

AN AGE OF MOBILITY

The Mediterranean world witnessed dramatic shifts between ca. 1200 and 1050 BCE, especially in terms of expanding maritime activity (Broodbank 2013, 460–72). While political upheaval took place throughout much of the eastern

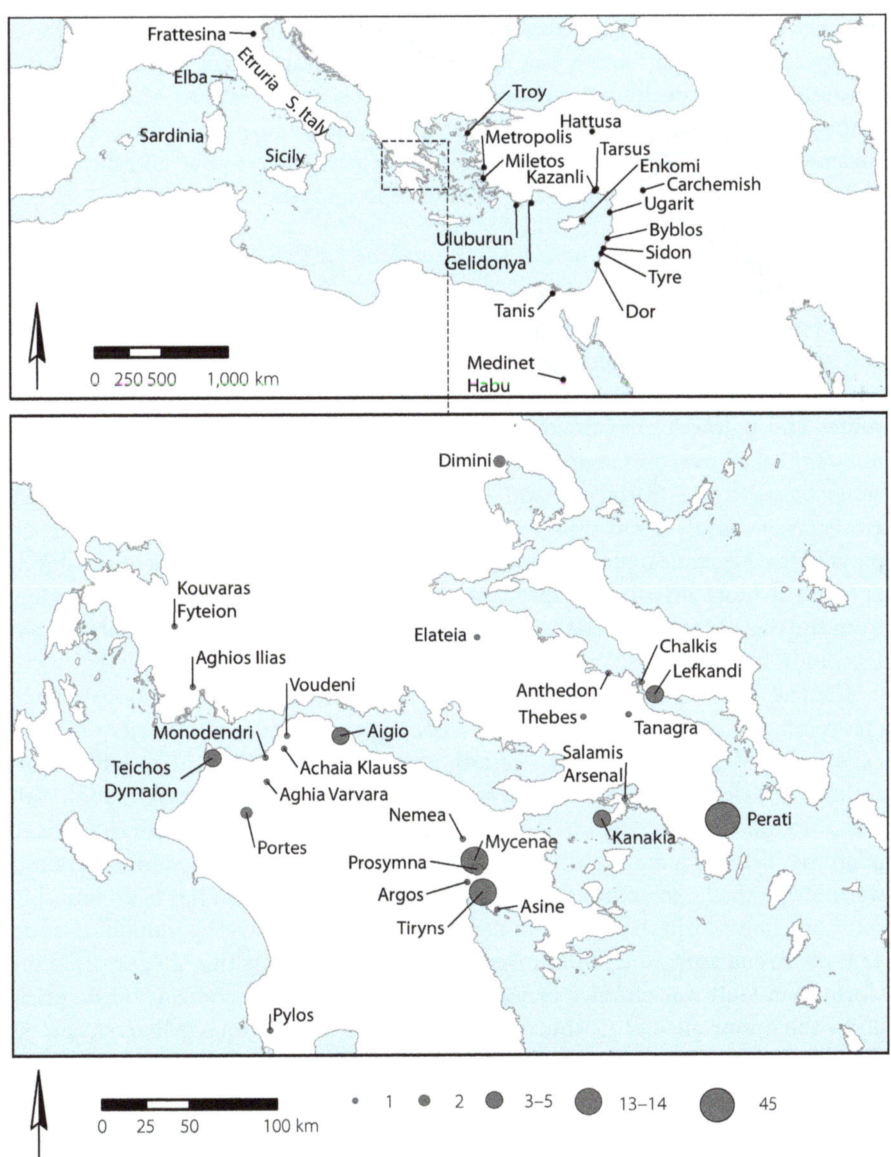

MAP 17. Mediterranean sites mentioned in the text (top) and imports to LH IIIC contexts in the Aegean (bottom) (import data from Murray 2017, 92–93, table 2.3).

Mediterranean during the thirteenth century BCE, the twelfth-century aftermath saw a robust Cypriot copper trade; the local production of Mycenaean or Mycenae-anizing (LH IIIC) pottery in Cyprus, the Levant, Italy, Sicily, and Sardinia; and the rise of Levantine (later lumped together by Herodotus as "Phoenician") city-states, out of which Tyre would eventually emerge as perhaps the greatest driver of long-distance ventures yet known (see map 17). The rearrangement of trade patterns that followed the decline of palace-centered states in the eastern Mediterranean at the same time spurred significant changes toward a more distributed economy. Meanwhile, changes in central Mediterranean societies led to the solidification of sustained and society-changing ties between east and west.

Societal Reorientations in Greece and the Eastern Mediterranean

Central Greece is by no means unique in the eastern Mediterranean in terms of its pattern of decentralization after 1200 BCE. The restructuring of settlement and social organization did not result in a collapse of interactions but rather in a reconfiguration of the networks through which they operated. Geographically, routes and pathways remained rather consistent, since favorable sea routes do not vary much over time and maritime technology did not experience any great shifts between the thirteenth and eleventh centuries BCE (Wachsmann 1998, 176; Sauvage 2012). It was rather a pattern of political decentralization in certain parts of the Aegean, Anatolia, Cyprus, the Levant, and Egypt that led to the development of more distributed, frequent, and varied types of interaction, ranging from the rise of merchant classes to population movements (Sherratt and Sherratt 1991, 1993; Iacovou 2005; Yasur-Landau 2010; Broodbank 2013).

Central Greece, especially in the regions surrounding the Euboean Gulf, enjoyed a sort of privileged status, as other regions, such as Crete, seem to have experienced depopulation and a certain attitude of fearfulness, with settlements shifting to defensible locations that were difficult to access (Nowicki 2000; Wallace 2010, 60–61; 2011, 59–60). Achaia in the northwest Peloponnese experienced relatively little settlement reorientation; it also seems to have been looking westward, given the large amount of LH IIIC Achaian pottery that has been found in southern Italy (Fisher 1988; Benzi and Graziadio 1996, 126; Papadopoulos 2001, 444–48; Arena 2015; Jung, Mommsen, and Picciarelli 2015). This suggests that the Corinthian Gulf was another major conduit, which should come as no surprise, given the importance of Corinth's later activity in the central Mediterranean. As discussed above, there was no palace in Achaia, and so no palatial collapse, leaving networks established earlier in the Mycenaean period to continue developing virtually uninterrupted. By contrast, Messenia seems to have experienced dramatic depopulation, while Laconia, Arcadia, and the Argolid experienced some continuity, though these areas did so in the context of political reorganization (Demakopoulou 2007; Galaty et al. 2015). The northern Aegean is more variable, clearly tied in to land routes to the wider Balkans and continental Europe, at least partly owing to its excellent metal resources (Morris 2009/2010).

The Cyclades and Dodecanese follow their own patterns in the Postpalatial period, with marked continuity from LH IIIB to LH IIIC, and in some cases even thriving in LH IIIC (Barnes 2016; Vlachopoulos and Charalambidou 2020).

Fortified settlements in the Cyclades at Koukounaries on Paros, Grotta on Naxos, and Xombourgo on Tinos suggest that the Mycenaean maritime worlds maintained vibrant and sometimes violent connections in this part of the Aegean well into the Postpalatial period (Kourou 2002; Lambrinoudakis and Philaniotou-Hadjianastasiou 2001; Schilardi 2016). These areas, like several parts of central Greece, are best considered nonpalatial zones in LH IIIB that seem actually to undergo an intensification of social complexity in the Postpalatial period, as do other areas connected to, but not part of, clearly palatial zones.

Looking beyond the Aegean to the archaeological record of imports and exports to and from Greece, there is a fair amount of consistency from LH IIIB to LH IIIC, though certain differences are telling (compare maps 13 and 17). Exports of Greek decorated pottery follow similar patterns in western Anatolia, southern Italy, Sardinia, and Cyprus, with a reduced presence in Syro-Palestine and an almost complete absence in Egypt (Murray 2017, 194). In many places, Mycenaean imports seem to be replaced eventually by local production. Imports to Greece maintain a wide distribution as well, although overall quantities decline (Murray 2017, 118). If the palaces are removed from the equation, however, the quantity and distribution of imports actually increase.

A series of political upheavals in the eastern Mediterranean also affected social and economic conditions in central Greece. The downfall of the Hittite kingdom caused a major restructuring of the political landscape in Anatolia. Several sites along the Aegean coast maintained connections with the broader Aegean area, as can be seen in the presence of mostly locally manufactured LH IIIC pottery from Troy, Bademgedeği Tepe and Yeniköy (both near Metropolis), Miletos, Tarsus, and Kazanli (see map 17) (Mountjoy 2006, 107). Locally produced LH IIIC pottery was widely dispersed at a variety of sites. This may suggest a decentralization of trading activities and perhaps more mobile craftspeople, and hence that local production was more common than imports. This interpretation of new networks forming, rather than a mass migration from the Greek mainland, is also consistent with the mortuary evidence from this area, which points to new modes of exchange and sociopolitical change rather than to mass migrations (Georgiadis 2009). Communities along the Aegean and Mediterranean coasts of Turkey were now relatively independent. Significantly, sites that experienced the greatest continuity from the preceding Hittite period seem to have experienced the least integration into the new networks forming in the eastern Mediterranean. This was particularly true of Carchemish, where a Hittite dynasty was maintained that developed into a trading center and the capital of a significant Neo-Hittite kingdom in the Iron Age (Aro 2013). The new orientations of western Anatolia may provide context for the much-debated formations of "Ionian" identity in the region (Mac Sweeney 2016; see further in chapter 5, pp. 187–89).

Cyprus is perhaps the most heavily researched example of Mycenaean activity abroad, which certainly affected aspects of social organization (Knapp and

Manning 2016, 132–34). The period covered in this chapter (ca. 1200–1050 BCE) straddles the Protohistoric Bronze Age and Earliest Iron Age in Cyprus (1250–950 BCE).[9] Major sociopolitical changes took place during this time, largely in relation to the wider eastern Mediterranean context. The question of Mycenaean colonization following the collapse of the palaces is highly controversial, although influence and contact is undeniable (Knapp 2008, 286–90). The larger issue is the role of metals and the general pattern of destabilization. The Late Bronze Age political landscape of Cyprus seems to involve elites at regional centers competing for power and control, while the Early Iron Age trends gradually toward ruling lines controlled by particular individuals or groups, which is also the case in later periods (Janes 2010, 135). That said, arguments have also been made for centralized control of the island, based at Enkomi, in the Protohistoric Bronze Age. Whatever the case may be, Late Bronze Age systems were disrupted significantly by (1) the destruction of Ugarit (ca. 1185 BCE), which destabilized Enkomi, and (2) a marked increase in Aegean presence. This destabilization paved the way for new groups and new practices of interaction to emerge, and it would have also led to the reconfiguration of off-island networks, which were reflected in the increased presence of Aegean and Levantine material and in the proliferation of Cypriot copper in the central Mediterranean (Lo Schiavo 2012).

The apparent growth of entrepreneurial trade at the end of the Bronze Age undermined palatial economies on the Levantine coast, most famously in the case of Ugarit, which was destroyed in 1185 BCE (Routledge and McGeough 2009, 29). Documents from merchants' houses in Ugarit suggest that a merchant class operated largely independently of the state and would have been able to continue with business more or less as usual in its absence, though with some necessary adjustments (Liverani 1987, 69–70; Snodgrass 1989, 25; Murray 2017, 257). In the aftermath, other areas of the Levantine coast rose to greater prominence and eventually came to dominate eastern Mediterranean trade by capitalizing on opportunities left in the wake of Ugarit, Hatti, and Egypt (Bell 2009). Mycenaean involvement in the Levant is evident in the form of painted pottery, although, as in Cyprus, the nature of the interactions evidenced by the presence of material culture is uncertain, with interpretations ranging from colonization to trade to stylistic influence (Yasur-Landau 2010).

Turning to Egypt, the Postpalatial Aegean overlaps chronologically with the end of the New Kingdom and Third Intermediate periods. The "Sea Peoples" as a distinct entity are principally an Egyptian conception, although as a construct they have taken on a sort of life of their own (see, e.g., Oren 2000; Cline and O'Connor 2003; Cline 2014; Fischer and Bürge 2017; Kopanias 2017). The reliefs on the mortuary

9. According to Knapp's (2008, 133) chronology, this period begins with the Protohistoric Bronze Age 3 period (1250–1100), which corresponds to the Late Cypriot IIC Late to Late Cypriot IIIA ceramic periods used in the conventional chronology. The Earliest Iron Age (1100–950) corresponds to the Late Cypriot IIIB period (ca. 1100–1050) and the Cypro-Geometric I period (ca. 1050–950) (Janes 2010, 129).

temple of Rameses III (r. 1186–1155 BCE) at Medinet Habu already suggest insecurity, which the ruler attempted to capitalize on through self-aggrandizement. These events are part of a wider pattern of destabilization in Egypt, which might be traced back as far as the end of the 66-year reign of Rameses II in 1213 BCE. Six different kings ruled in the span of the 29 years that separate Rameses II and Rameses III. Rameses III's rule was by no means a period of stability either. During this period, the Egyptian empire in western Asia was lost, internal problems were rampant, and foreign invasions were increasing concerns. Economic instability built until civil war erupted, resulting in the division of Egypt and the end of the New Kingdom and the beginning of the Third Intermediate period, which coincides roughly with the end of the Postpalatial Bronze Age in the Aegean. The twenty-first dynasty began with the reign of Smendes (1069–1043), who ruled from Tanis in the Delta (Bard 2008, 216, 265). By the time the *Tale of Wenamun* was recorded (likely during the reign of Smendes), Egypt's influence in the eastern Mediterranean had waned considerably. Wenamun, a messenger of the king, was robbed, waylaid, and made to wait months for an audience during the course of his mission to procure cedar. His recorded stops at Dor, Sidon, Tyre, Byblos, and Cyprus, illustrate the increasingly diffuse nature of connectivity in the eastern Mediterranean, as power relations had shifted between participants in exchanges.[10]

Shifting Networks in the Central Mediterranean

Engagement between the central and eastern Mediterranean is well documented through imported and imitated Mycenaean pottery in Italy, Sardinia, and Sicily from at least the LH I period (Vagnetti 1999; van Wijngaarden 2002, 2016; Jones et al. 2014), as are connections between Cyprus and Sardinia in the form of Cypriot oxhide ingots (Stos-Gale and Gale 1992; Lo Schiavo 2012). There is also an abundance of central Mediterranean (especially Adriatic) material found in the eastern Mediterranean dating to the thirteenth and twelfth centuries BCE—most notably in the form of impasto-style, handmade burnished ware (so-called barbarian ware), Sardinian pottery, urnfield bronzes, and Tiryns-type amber beads, which were also from the Adriatic (Broodbank 2013, 463). While some of these contacts seem to have been sustained over time (for example, Mycenaean connections to southern Italy) the frequency and the multicultural scale of interaction reach new heights at the end of the second millennium.

These interactions have been studied mainly in terms of the presence of Mycenaean or Mycenaeanizing pottery, the known quantity of which has been rising steadily over the last decades. Taylour (1958) recorded 17 sites and, with ever growing datasets, the number has risen to at least 78 (Vagnetti 1999, 156–61; see also Papadopoulos 2001, 440–41; Blake 2008). Smith (1987) has separated the LH IIIC material from the rest, which shows a pattern of wider dispersal than in

---

10. For a longer account of the *Tale of Wenamun* and its significance, see Broodbank 2013, 445–49.

previous periods. Besides imports, beginning around 1200 we see major changes in the societies of peninsular Italy, on both the Adriatic and Tyrrhenian coasts. On the Adriatic coast, a settlement on the Po appeared at Frattesina (Bietti Sestieri 2010, 186; see also Pearce 2007). In addition to imports of Aegean and Cypriot provenience, Frattesina was linked into more northerly networks supplying amber and metals, and to Etruria across the Apennines (Bietti Sestieri 1997; Vianello 2005, 91–93). In Etruria, too, metals seem to have been the main attractor, and exploitation of the region's ores (copper, silver, lead, antimony) intensified in the twelfth century (Bietti Sestieri 1997). The stretch of Etruria between the Arno and Ombrone rivers was remarkably well endowed, leading to the later regional referents Colline Metallifera and Etruria Mineraria. The region would become even more significant when the rich iron sources of the nearby island of Elba began to be exploited (see chapter 5, p. 174).

Southern Italy and Sicily exhibit by far the most Mycenaean interaction. While LH IIIC pottery found here probably comes from a variety of locations across the late Mycenaean world, the most common forms seem to be from Achaia, though relatively few provenience studies have been conducted (Fisher 1988; Vianello 2005, 9–10; Jones et al. 2014; Jung, Mommsen, and Picciarelli 2015). Nevertheless, this wide dispersal of LH IIIC material and styles speaks to an increasingly connected Mediterranean and belies any notions of Aegean isolationism or stagnation following the disappearance of the palaces.

Finally, Sardinia requires some additional attention as a rather more enigmatic entity at this time. There are marked rises in Cypriot activity on the island, as well as Aegean interventions, though the nature of these is not clear (Russell 2010, 114; Lo Schiavo 2012). Cypriot influence appears mainly in the form of metals and metalworking implements, not least in the preponderance of oxhide ingots. Aegean influence, as usual, is in ceramics. Sardinia was clearly valued for its copper resources, though the extent to which Sardinians were engaged in external trade before Cypriot involvement is difficult to say. It seems that, in this case, eastern interest sparked the formation of more local networks, which involved the wider Tyrrhenian Sea.

The ore deposits of Cyprus, Sardinia, and Italy attracted increasing attention from afar during the late second millennium BCE, which prefigured later, even more intensive exploitation. This trend is not necessarily new—earlier Mycenaeans certainly had a strong interest in Cyprus and Anatolia and at the very least dabbled in the central Mediterranean (van Wijngaarden 2002). Minimalist interpretations, however, have generally prevailed over ideas of "precolonization" (cf. Popham 1994; Blake 2008). As usual, the answer probably lies somewhere in between. There is a strong correlation between find locations of Mycenaean materials (especially from Achaia) and later Greek settlement in Italy and Sicily (Papadopoulos 2001, 441–48). The implication is that later Greeks were interested in these areas for the same reasons Mycenaeans were: metals. The quest for metals was nothing new in the Postpalatial period, and it has long been noted as a motivating factor for Mycenaean seafarers. Indeed, this is another arena in which the Early and Postpalatial Mycenaean world run parallel, while palatial emphasis on particularly eastern imports is more of an outlier. What is new is the *context* of this quest for metals. It is not until the LH IIIC period that Tyrrhenian, Adriatic, and eastern Mediterranean networks open up in such a way as to allow sustained interaction in multiple directions. The growth of regional networks in the central Mediterranean and the freeing of eastern Mediterranean networks from palatial constraints allowed new, decentralized systems to be formed, which is evident in the case of hybridizing Mycenaean and local production in Cyprus, the Levant, Italy, Sicily, and Sardinia. These patterns had already begun in LH IIIB, which suggests that interactions between crafting communities were already untethered from the palaces. In this way, the development of local networks made it easier for Mycenaeans and Cypriots to "plug in" to them, and it also created more diffuse distributions of material culture, perhaps through certain coastal entry points. This explains both how Greek-like material culture came to be produced in new locations and why in some cases it is found only as isolated examples. It also highlights the coastal nature of cross-cultural interaction during the period at hand, which is reflected as well in the regional settlement patterns of central Greece and elsewhere in the Mediterranean during this time of increasing maritime mobility.

CONCLUSIONS: CENTRAL GREECE ON CENTER STAGE

The patterns of settlement, production, and interactions in central Greece during the Postpalatial Bronze Age are part of a much larger process at work in the Late Bronze Age Mediterranean. Destabilization, mobility, and reorganization are key features, both for the Aegean and for the Mediterranean at large. The value of a multiscalar approach, however, lies in the capacity to move from the global to the local. In this way processes at work in the wider Mediterranean are also reflected in the local and regional networks of central Greece. New complex communities arose following the fall of the palaces, and new power relations developed, often through seaborne interactions. In these newly decentralized networks, political transformations occurred through particular individuals and groups that operated in relatively ill-defined, noninstitutionalized leadership systems. Societies of the Postpalatial period had less rigid but still politically significant systems of social hierarchy and regional organization. Manifestations of such reconstrued notions of society and polity are present at Kastro Volos, Kynos, Mitrou, Lefkandi, Perati, and Athens, among other places. At the same time, new regional interactions were negotiated, which resulted in the establishment of intercommunity ritual practices at Kalapodi. In stark contrast to the Palatial period, such regionally oriented group formation practices were disassociated with a single political power. Also divorced from palatial oversight, movement and interaction required new agency on the part of individuals; this translated into the emergence of community leaders who competed with rivals by land and by sea, probably taking part themselves in long-distance voyages. The movement of craftspeople (and probably also larger groups) also became widespread, as consumption of Mycenaean products in other parts of the Mediterranean continued, even in the face of stylistic regionalism.

The collapse of the palatial systems in parts of central Greece created new opportunities for the transformation of the political landscape, the reformulation of local and long-distance interactions, and the emergence of new forms of sociopolitical complexity. The northern and central Euboean Gulf went separate ways from the south, at least temporarily, and the Corinthian Gulf emerged as a significant conduit for connectivity to the west. This picture of fragmentation was part of a wider phenomenon of network shifts throughout the eastern Mediterranean, which eventually tapped expanding systems in the central Mediterranean. The result of this destabilization and reorganization was societies that were locally oriented in terms of territory but thrived on interaction at all scales—societies that were in regular conflict and collaboration with neighbors in their wider regional setting, yet had interests and influences that spanned significant distances. Despite the collapse of the palatial systems, the picture is far from one of *societal* collapse. In this chapter I have presented models and explanations for the *transitions* that characterized communities and networks in central Greece in the Postpalatial Bronze Age as certain communities reconstituted local and regional interactions and coopted overseas connections. The result was a more intricately intertwined Mediterranean world, which can be seen through a more variegated archaeology of Late Bronze Age societies.

5

Transforming Village Societies in the Prehistoric Iron Age

Fifth, far-seeing Zeus made yet another race of men, who have come to be on the fertile earth. I wish I were not among these fifth men but had died before or been born after. For now this is the race of iron.

—HESIOD, WORKS AND DAYS 173–76

Hesiod had already sketched a sharp contrast between the Bronze Age and Iron Age by the eighth century BCE, when he looked back to an "age of heroes," in contrast to the ceaseless toil that characterized his own time. In spite of Hesiod's denigrations, iron brought with it profound material and technological consequences for the ways in which societies would operate, not least owing to the utilitarian value and the general ubiquity of the material. The Early Iron Age in Greece is defined by transitions in settlement, pottery styles, and technologies, from the Mycenaean forms of the Bronze Age to the Protogeometric and Geometric styles of the Early Iron Age. But such changes did not happen overnight. Nor were they isolated phenomena. The Early Iron Age was a time of experimentation, and the exchange of ideas (more than great technological revolutions) that took place then must be viewed in terms of a transition from, rather than a break with, the preceding Bronze Age. New craft traditions and the reorganization of Mediterranean commerce provide an essential backdrop for wider sociopolitical developments in central Greece, especially as they are related to a (further) reorganization of settlement. Like other prehistoric periods, the lack of contemporary writing leaves us to depend most heavily on the material record to interpret social change.

In this chapter I argue that the major social and technological changes of the eleventh to ninth centuries BCE mark a crucial phase in the early Greek world. While village-based, complex communities continue to characterize the settlement pattern of central Greece, new technologies and production networks set in motion macroregional and trans-Mediterranean processes, which would come into full bloom with the revolutionary developments of the eighth century BCE (see chapter 6). Local leaders and regional practices are well evidenced and demonstrate major elements of continuity from the preceding Postpalatial Bronze Age. Indeed, in several places, processes of political recentralization begun in Postpalatial times seem to have intensified in the Early Iron Age. There is a noticeable redistribution of settlement that reflects changing attitudes toward the landscape while nonetheless maintaining several attributes of the previous transition to life after the palaces. Moreover, interactions were maintained in the wider Mediterranean, which saw some of its most meaningful shifts at this time, as the connections explored at the end of chapter 4 became more persistent and Levantine traders became more involved with both Greece and parts of the Mediterranean farther west.

I begin this chapter with the landscapes and regional developments of central Greece in the Prehistoric Iron Age (ca. 1050–800 BCE).[1] I show that significant social changes accompanied settlement pattern shifts and that the character of social complexity developed along multiple tracks. Eccentric network and settlement growth is apparent at Lefkandi and at Athens, while other regions demonstrate varied continuities or breaks with the preceding Bronze Age. I then discuss the major changes in metal and ceramic technologies in this period, and I demonstrate how production systems comprise proxies for interaction on multiple scales. Finally, I address the wider Mediterranean context of central Greece in the Early Iron Age, and I explore how the story told here by the archaeological record relates (or does not relate) to later historical accounts of mobility and migration.

HIERARCHY AND HETERARCHY IN THE EARLY IRON AGE LANDSCAPE

As in previous chapters, networks and spatial analysis are used here to model and discuss the settlement pattern of central Greece in terms of territory, connectivity, and social organization. I supplement these models with site- and region-specific discussions of networking practices by individuals and groups in Attica, central Euboea, and elsewhere in central Greece. This complex web of connections, and the range of entities involved—sites, individuals, regions—reveal multiple hierarchies within the social and political landscape. These are perhaps better termed heterarchies—that is, relationships between components that are either unranked or that could be ranked in multiple ways (Crumley 1995, 3). The Early Iron Age witnesses substantial variability in regional organization and in the expression

---

1. The Prehistoric Iron Age includes the Protogeometric, Subprotogeometric, and Early and Middle Geometric ceramic periods, depending on the regional chronologies (see table 1). This is an unconventional grouping, since Protogeometric usually is treated separately from, say, the Attic Early and Middle Geometric periods. These distinctions, of course, are based on ceramic chronologies rather than on societal developments. In considering the complexity, scale, and spatial distribution of Aegean societies during this period, I argue that this grouping fits well together and is distinct from both the Postpalatial Mycenaean period that precedes it and the Late Geometric period that follows it.

of inequality on individual levels, both within and between sites. In general, the settlement and the social organization of this period find their best parallels with village societies, operating mostly locally, with certain links farther afield that are particularly meaningful in the expression of social difference (Bandy and Fox 2010). Such difference is realized on an individual scale rather than institutionally. Again, we might characterize certain groups as complex communities, characterized by shifts between more hierarchical and more egalitarian modes of social organization (Porter 2013, 5).

In the Prehistoric Iron Age, new patterns emerged in the distribution of settlement throughout central Greece, though important elements of continuity also remained. The Euboean Gulf continued to act as a conduit for the individuals and groups living around it, despite the changing social structures that appear in the archaeological record. The main transitions from the preceding Postpalatial Bronze Age were shifts in settlement locations, a general (though not universal) decline in architectural scale and settlement size, and changes in burial practices.

Settlement Patterns in the Early Iron Age

The settlement pattern of the Prehistoric Iron Age does not depart dramatically from the preceding Postpalatial Bronze Age. Nevertheless, there are several significant developments (map 18). There is, again, regional variation in site numbers rather than a strict pattern of continuity from the previous period (see figure 2). There is a drop in the total number of sites in Attica, although there is an increased concentration of settlement in the vicinity of Athens itself. Boeotia experiences a small increase in the number of sites, but there is not major growth after the reduction that occurred in the Postpalatial Bronze Age. One interesting trend is the drop in site numbers in eastern Boeotia, especially around the Euripos, which suggests that the Boeotian interests in the region during the Bronze Age may have been eclipsed by the waxing community at Lefkandi in Euboea. Meanwhile, western Boeotia seems to have prospered, filling in the landscape toward East Lokris and Phokis, where the northwest-southeast axes on either side of Mount Parnassos form an arc of significant sites reaching from the Corinthian Gulf deep into central Greece. Moving north, East Lokris continued to prosper, especially in the bay of Atalanti and around Kalapodi. In Malis, in particular in the Spercheios valley and its surroundings, there is a general continuity of settlement locations, and there is even growth in the number of sites.

Thessaly, too, experienced growth in this period, nearly doubling in the number of sites from 21 to 35. It has 11 more sites than the next most heavily occupied region, which highlights the unique character and significance of an area once seen as peripheral (Georganas 2011; Karouzou 2017). Also noteworthy is the appearance of Kefala on Skiathos, just outside the northern outlet of the Euboean Gulf. This may have been an important stepping-stone on the sea route to the northern Aegean (Mazarakis Ainian 2012b).

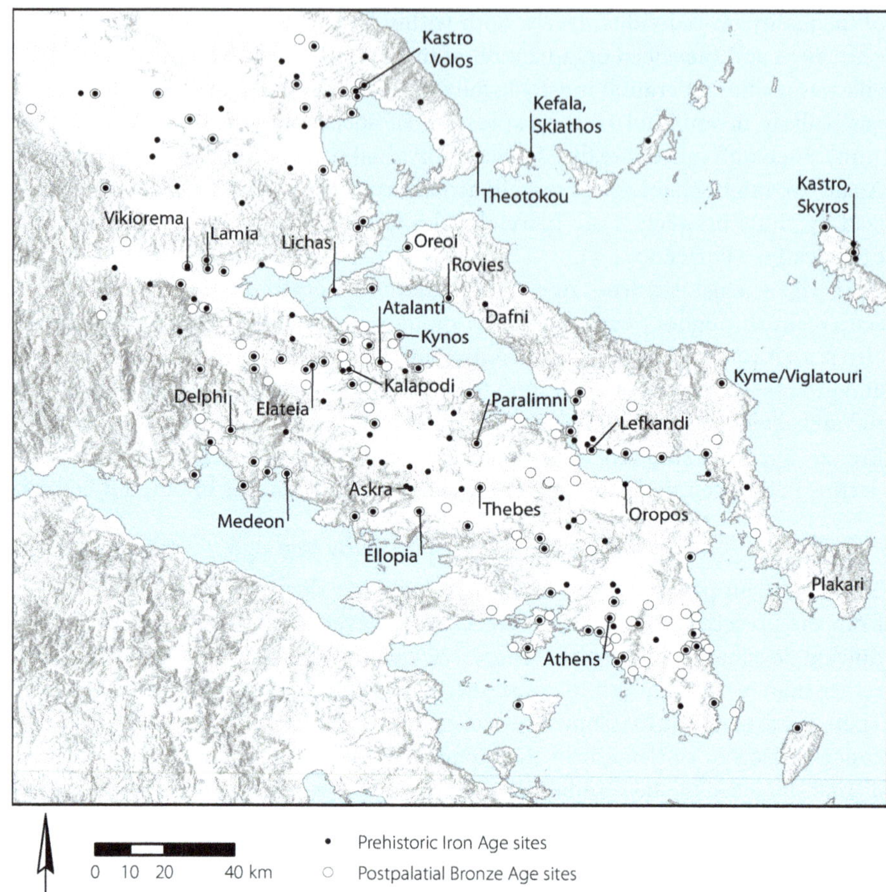

MAP 18. Prehistoric Iron Age site locations compared to the Postpalatial Bronze Age.

Central Euboea seems to swell in importance in the Early Iron Age, indicating a trend that began in the Postpalatial Bronze Age, most notably at Lefkandi. The location of sites elsewhere on the island is also significant. Rovies and Dafni are located across from prominent places in the bay of Atalanti. The cluster of sites on the Euboean side of the Euripos also grows in number. This growth is accompanied by the disappearance of settlement locations on the Boeotian coast. Finally, we should note the appearance of Plakari (ancient Karystos) in southern Euboea (Crielaard and Songou 2017). According to our present data, this is (surprisingly) the first new site established in southern Euboea since the Middle Bronze Age.

Sites vary greatly in terms of the quantity of material, the level of study, and whether or not they represent a settlement, a cemetery, or a handful of sherds. Owing to the relatively small size of all sites in this period, there was a need for these communities to interact with one another for basic subsistence and survival.

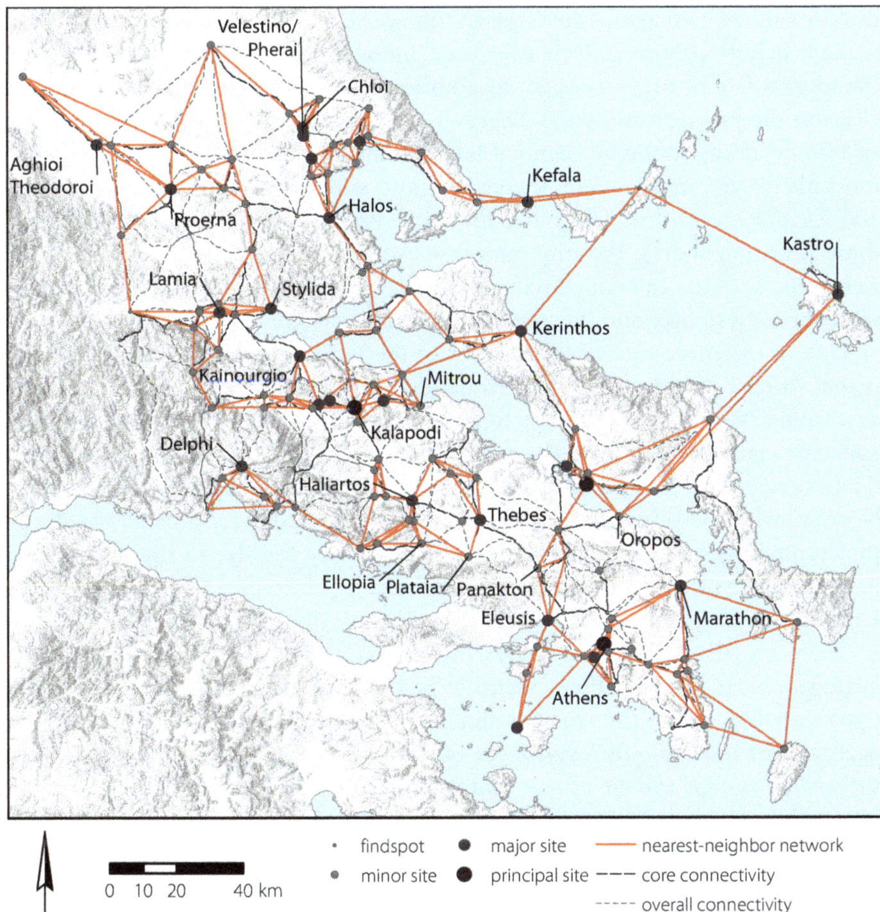

MAP 19. Prehistoric Iron Age sites, joined by a connectivity model, with a nearest-neighbor network of communities (see also map 18 and appendix for additional place names).

In the absence of a regionally centralized authority, these interactions would have been subject to change and improvisation, much as they were in the Postpalatial Bronze Age (and in other periods of Greek prehistory). The general pattern of modeled interactions in the Early Iron Age (map 19) is similar to that seen in the previous period (see map 15), though it is most noteworthy in the intensification of interaction in a few particular zones—namely, Athens/Attica, central Euboea, East Lokris/Phokis, and Thessaly.

In the Postpalatial Bronze Age, there was a clear separation between southern Attica and the rest of the Euboean Gulf, as Attica was more in touch with the Saronic Gulf and the Cyclades. This pattern was maintained in the Early Iron Age. Throughout this period, settlement patterns in Attica became more dispersed, and the size and influence of Athens grew: this was likely on account of demand for its high-quality pottery and its role as an innovator in the Protogeometric style (Snodgrass [1971] 2000, 43–44).[2] In addition to the ceramic evidence, which is clear on the primacy and wide dispersal of Attic pottery, the settlement pattern and the resulting model of regional interactions open up to link with Boeotia—most likely via Panakton and Thebes, but also with Euboea, Aghia Irini on Kea, and Zagora on Andros (although the Attic Protogeometric travels far beyond these near neighbors). Wealthy burials at Athens, on the Areopagus and at the Kerameikos, testify to connectivity—through trade in metals and luxury items—with northern Greece and the eastern Mediterranean.

One of the more significant features of the Early Iron Age in central Greece is that Athens emerges as the preeminent center of settlement across the region as a whole. No other site appears to be as large or influential in this period. The apparent extent of the town, the number of burials, the influential pottery production, and the connections to the rest of the Greek world all exceed what can be documented at other sites. With its remains scattered over some 200 hectares, the community at Athens appears to be about twice the size of the next largest in the Greek world, at Knossos (ca. 100 hectares) (Morris and Knodell 2015, 347; Dimitriadou 2019).

There are also diachronic trends that make Athens stand out. In the Early Protogeometric period, Athens seems to be the only occupied site in all of Attica (Alexandridou 2017), though it is difficult to know what to make of this. The apparent presence of only a single site of this date may ultimately say more about the evolution and spread of the Protogeometric style than about continuity of occupation. Nevertheless, Attica appears to have experienced marked growth in the Late Protogeometric and Early Geometric periods as Eleusis, Marathon, Brauron, and Thorikos emerged as significant centers. While the interregional orientations of Attica were mostly to the south and east during this period, long-distance links between Attica and northern Greece—most likely via the Euboean Gulf—are increasingly apparent and were part of a legacy that ran from much earlier in the Bronze Age well into the Classical period (Kotsonas 2015; Leone 2015).

Settlement in central Euboea also saw poignant intensification in this period, both locally and regionally. The network growth that is the result of more sites coming into the model seems to follow the behavior of scale-free networks, where new nodes attach preferentially to those that are already well-connected. There is no question that Lefkandi was a hub of exceptional importance, reaching far beyond the nearest neighbors modeled in map 19. This was anticipated in the influence of its ceramic workshops in the LH IIIC period (see map 16), and it is highlighted by the far-reaching connections to Cyprus, Egypt, and the Levant that

2. See Desborough 1952 for Athens as the origin of the Protogeometric style. See also Snodgrass (1971) 2000, 43–44; Dickinson 2006, 131–32.

made it exceptional in the Early Iron Age (Coldstream 2007; Nijboer 2008; Kosma 2012; Papadopoulos 2015). New sites, not occupied during the Postpalatial period, appear at Phylla, Nea Lampsakos, Kamari, and Magoula (see map 18; see appendix for particular locations), while others grow considerably at the end of this period and in the next (e.g., Eretria) (Coulton 2002; Verdan, Kenzelmann Pfyffer, and Léderrey 2009).

Elsewhere in central Greece, new settlement networks appeared—for example, in western Boeotia and central Thessaly—while others were largely maintained, even if in a thinning settlement pattern—for example, in southern Boeotia and northern Attica. The Skourta Plain, where four small sites are known, provides an interesting case (Munn and Munn 1989, 1990; Farinetti 2011, 394–96). In this model the sites appear to be maintained as important points of contact between Eleusis and Thebes, and indeed Panakton is one of the few sites to have a stratified sequence of LH IIIC to Protogeometric pottery (Munn 1996).

Settlement in eastern Boeotia also drops off considerably. The one site on the mainland coast of the Euboean Gulf between Marathon and Mitrou is Oropos (Skala Oropou), which seems to have more in common with Euboea in this period. Indeed, this site may have functioned as an extraterritorial outpost for Eretria in the Middle and Late Geometric periods and possibly before these periods as well (Mazarakis Ainian 2002; Charalambidou 2017). In Protogeometric times, Oropos was certainly closer to the Euboean network than to other sites in Boeotia. Beyond Oropos and the route through the Skourta Plain, Prehistoric Iron Age activity in Boeotia seems to be oriented to the west of Thebes, with Haliartos and Askra as other significant sites (see maps 4, 18, and 19).

Farther west, there is a significant concentration of sites between the bays of Itea and Antikyra, highlighting the significance of these locations as access points from the Corinthian Gulf through the Great Isthmus Corridor (Vatin 1969; Kase et al. 1991; Sideris 2014). A line of sites from Delphi to Lamia indicates that this was still an important route (Dakoronia 1991). Curiously, however, there is no Iron Age material documented at Amphissa until the eighth century. In the Kephisos valley, too, there is a decline in the overall number of sites, although this is another area of substantial continuity of occupation, especially at Elateia.

Kalapodi acted as a bridge between Phokis, East Lokris, Malis, and Boeotia and also shows marked continuity in cult activity (Kaiser, Rizzoto, and Strack 2011; Niemeier 2016). Several new sites appeared in its general vicinity as well, indicating growth in the significance of this inter-regional shrine.[3] While cult activity at Kalapodi can be traced back to at least LH IIIA, a change toward the "votive habits" that would characterize Geometric and Archaic sanctuaries happened as early as the 9th century BCE (Felsch 2007; Niemeier 2016).

3. The case of Kalapodi, even though it is an inland site, in fact highlights the importance of the Euboean Gulf, since its role as a regional sanctuary was eclipsed by Delphi after the Geometric period on account of network shifts (McInerney 2011).

East Lokris experienced a similar pattern of growth. Extensive burial evidence has been documented at Atalanti, and continuous occupation is also known at Agnanti (Papadopoulou 2017). Significant clustering in the network model occurs especially around the bay of Atalanti, where centers like Kynos and Mitrou also exhibit direct continuity from the Late Bronze Age to the Early Iron Age (Dakoronia 2003; Dakoronia and Kounouklas 2009; van de Moortel 2009).

Finally, the network that develops around the Pagasetic and northern Euboean Gulfs is particularly important. Several sites emerge as competing centers on this crossroads between the northern and southern Aegean. The bay of Volos is at the outlet to the sea for the major land route from the north, which we know was important for metals and other commodities, and there is a clear growth in settlement in this area at many locations that are better known for their prominence in later periods. A growing body of evidence from the Malian Gulf, Lamia, and the Spercheios valley shows that Malis, too, must be considered a significant player during the Early Iron Age (Papadopoulou 2017, 317, fig. 5). On Euboea, Lichas and Oreoi are important nodes along the strait that exits the Euboean Gulf for the Aegean; farther afield, Kefala (on Skiathos) and Theotokou (in Magnesia) are well positioned to catch traffic from both the gulf and the Aegean route to the north.

Overall, there is a gradual reordering of the settlement pattern in particular parts of central Greece, with new clusters forming and loosely interspersed sites in between. The broader dispersal of settlement that was characteristic of the Postpalatial Bronze Age (and was the direct result of decentralization) gave way to greater concentration in areas of growing importance. The areas that seem to be the focus of this settlement intensification had already come to the fore in LH IIIC, and in the Early Iron Age they remained significant as other areas dropped off and people moved closer to areas of greater interest. At certain sites—especially Lefkandi, Athens, and various places in Thessaly—new strategies of social differentiation were pursued that made use of both local efforts toward group integration, such as feasting and funerary practices, and exotica brought from long distances (see further below).

Finally, some comment must be made on the nature of the evidence. Most of the patterns discussed above are based on funerary evidence rather than on extensive evidence of settlement, which is relatively rare in the Prehistoric Iron Age (see table 4). This pattern may indicate the use of ephemeral materials for the construction of buildings and habitation areas. People were obviously living somewhere, but these locations may be less visible archaeologically than in other periods. Papadopoulou (2017) has suggested that the settlement and funerary evidence we do have from central Greece probably indicates social organization based on small family units for most communities. This is something that must be inferred for the vast majority of cases, since, of 152 sites in the study area, only a handful have Early Iron Age components that have undergone extensive excavations. The burial record, by contrast, offers some of the most widespread and significant evidence for the Early Iron Age (Morris 1987; Whitley 1991).

The Creation of Inequality through Individual Networks

Topologies of relationships between people operate most intensely on a local scale, though they make crucial use of regional and long-distance connections. In the Prehistoric Iron Age, we can see a variety of ways in which particular individuals used such networks in the expression of social and political inequality. Patterns do not occur uniformly across regions and even vary on a site-to-site basis. Yet in many places we do see an intensification of sociopolitical complexity, population growth, and overseas trade. These trends run contrary to notions of universal decline in the Protogeometric period, though we must also keep in mind that much of the Greek world does seem to experience a drop in population and material production (see, e.g., Snodgrass [1971] 2000, xxiv; Murray 2017). Early Iron Age burials, especially elite burials and the grave goods that accompany them, allow us to reconstruct certain networking practices of elites (the deceased and those who interred them).

Athens.   Funerary remains constitute our principal evidence for the size, extent, and population of the community of Athens during the Early Iron Age. Groups of wealthy graves of PG, EG, and MG I date are scattered throughout the present-day city (Dimitriadou 2019, 142–46; for abbreviations, see table 1). These indicate an overall settlement size of ca. 200 hectares, which was probably organized in semidistinct groups of households that nonetheless comprised a single large community, at least in terms of regularized social interaction. The main clusters of evidence all fall within the central area of the modern city, complicating our understanding of the period. Nevertheless, we can tell that the remains of early Athens are roughly bounded by the Eridanos and Ilissos rivers, and that they extend over most of the area of the later Classical city, demarcated by the Themistoklean walls. The spatial extent and complexity of the community indicate a different level of local (and perhaps regional) integration than seen elsewhere in the Greek world at the time. This seems to signal, along with the wide dispersal of Attic pottery, that Athens's star was already on the rise. Pockets of funerary evidence that likely correspond to semidispersed habitation clusters can be observed as early as LH IIIC (and include Submycenaean). Many of these zones continued to be used or expanded in the Protogeometric and Early–Middle Geometric periods. By the Late Geometric period, enough infilling had occurred to suggest more or less contiguous loci of habitation.

The large cemeteries, especially the Kerameikos, have received the most scholarly attention of any in Early Iron Age Greece, especially in terms of mortuary practice.[4] Beyond the Kerameikos, significant Early Iron Age funerary remains

---

4. Excavations at the Kerameikos site have been conducted by the German Archaeological Institute in Athens since 1913, following excavations by the Archaeological Society of Athens in the nineteenth century (Knigge 1991). Relevant publications include several volumes on graves that date from the twelfth to the eighth centuries (Kraiker 1939; Kübler 1943, 1954; Ruppenstein 2007). On synthetic studies of mortuary practice, see Krause 1975; Morris 1987; Whitley 1991; Papadopoulos 1993.

have been found at the location of Plato's Academy, where ritualized drinking assemblages have come to light from EG I (Mazarakis Ainian and Livieratou 2010; Mazarakis Ainian and Alexandridou 2011), and in the Agora, where ceramic production remains have been found alongside burials and possible signs of habitation (Papadopoulos 1996c, 2003; Mazarakis Ainian 2012a; Papadopoulos and Smithson 2017).

In general, the number of burials stays relatively consistent from PG to MG I, before an increase in MG II and a dramatic rise in LG I and LG II. Morris (1987, 93–96) uses these shifts as a starting point to argue not for a substantial population boom in LG but rather for formal burial as an indicator of social rank in the periods in which it is scarcer (PG–MG). The general picture of wealth found in some of the PG–MG graves, along with their relative rarity overall, suggests that burial itself (or at least archaeologically visible burial) was a privilege accessible to only the upper class of society and a strong indicator of social inequality and the presence of an aristocracy. In the eighth century, a shift occurs, which is argued to be coincident with the emergence of the polis. Burial came to be accepted for all citizens in an egalitarian effort that at the same time aimed to legitimate other social inequalities (for example, between Greeks and others, as well as between citizens and noncitizens). These points are well articulated by Morris (1987) and they are generally accepted by others (e.g., Papadopoulos 1993; Bintliff 2012, 226). Some factors complicate this picture, however. For one, graves of the eighth century were not ostentatiously marked but would nevertheless have still been sited among earlier, marked graves, and as deliberate expressions of social status (Small 2015, 80–82). Such practices would have been accompanied by drinking activities, oriented around monumental kraters and using utilitarian ones, which had continued relevance to expressions of political authority (Bohen 2017). Dimitriadou (2019), integrating data that has been gathered over the last 30 years, has shown that settlement evidence probably does correspond with actual population growth, as Athens evolved from dispersed clusters of habitation areas into a more coherent community (see also Papadopoulos 2003, 299, fig. 6.15). So, while Morris's shift in expression of burial is valid, real growth was likely occurring as well, alongside the long-standing, exclusionary and inclusionary practices surrounding death and burial in particular places.

The most famous of the Early Iron Age burials of Athens is the tomb of the "Rich Athenian Lady" (Smithson 1968; Coldstream 1995; Liston and Papadopoulos 2004; Stampolidis and Giannopoulou 2012). The grave goods indicate the wealth or status of the deceased, or at least of those aiming to associate themselves with her—presumably family members. Pottery items found with the burial were of extremely high quality and date to the EG II period; these include a belly-handled amphora used as a funerary urn, a small neck amphora, and several pyxides and model granaries—most notably, a chest with five model granaries on top (probably a jewelry box). A variety of other types of finely made pots were also present

(Smithson 1968, 83–109; Langdon 2008, 64). In addition to the pottery finds, metal pins, bronze fibulae, gold rings, gold earrings, a necklace, faience discs, glass beads, two ivory stamp seals, and one ivory disk were found (Smithson 1968, 109–16; Papadopoulos and Smithson 2017, 124–76). The overt wealth expressed in the deposition of such objects was complemented by their diverse origins. Coldstream (1995) noted the similarity to other wealthy burials from Athens, as well as from Lefkandi and Knossos; but before we draw special connections between these three sites, we should acknowledge that these are simply the wealthiest, best preserved, and best published Early Iron Age cemeteries in Greece. Feasting evidence is also apparent, with animal bones associated with the burial representing over 70 kilograms of meat that would have been consumed at the funerary event (Liston and Papadopoulos 2004, 29; Ruscillo 2017, 566–67). The spectacle of the funerary event must also be considered paramount to the assemblage, as we see in other places, such as Lefkandi.

The grave goods in this and other wealthy burials from Athens demonstrate connections to a variety of distant locations. Faience and ivory likely had Egyptian origins, although these materials probably would have come to Athens via Cyprus or the Levant, which are also possible points of origin for the bronze. Other metals—namely gold—were also imported, possibly from the northern Aegean, the Cyclades, or Egypt. These items were valuable in this local context precisely because they were distinctively nonlocal, making reference to a wider, exclusive network of connections in which the Rich Athenian Lady and those burying her were entangled. Indeed, such burials are part of a wider pattern of expression of Early Iron Age elite identity, which can be seen in the "princely" burials of both men and women in several parts of the Mediterranean world (Stampolidis 2012). This exclusivity was made even more explicit by two factors. The first and most obvious (if we accept Morris's 1987 thesis) is that many members of the population did not receive any type of burial whatsoever at this time. The second is that feasting practices were focused on the burial of a particular individual; they happened in open space, yet were a type of place-making activity that highlighted social inequalities by emphasizing (conspicuously) various types of consumption at a burial event (Hayden 2009; LeCount and Blitz 2010). This stands in contrast to the feasting practices of the Postpalatial Bronze Age, which seem to have occurred more frequently in nonfunerary social contexts. Funeral feasting at Athens, then, indicates a concentration of this particular type of social practice around elite individuals and their postmortem celebrations, rather than the living dispersal of resources seen in aspects of Bronze Age feasting. Nevertheless, Early Iron Age rulers' dwellings in Athens and elsewhere in Attica (the Academy, Eleusis, Thorikos) signal that the world of the living was important in the performance of status and inequality as well (Alexandridou 2018; van den Eijnde 2018).

Early Iron Age societies, including at Athens, find their best comparanda with "intermediate" or "transegalitarian" complex communities. The mortuary record signals that individuals within these societies were far from equal ("egalitarian" society is in most cases probably a misnomer), but there is little evidence for social inequality or political organization supported by strong, lasting institutions. Morris's (1987) model for dynamic patterns in the consumption of grave goods fits quite well with the idea of community complexity advanced by Porter (2013), which allows for looser modes of social organizations and fluctuations across space and time.

Lefkandi.   Snodgrass (1994, 87) called the Euboeans the "great discovery of early Greek archaeology since World War II." This was in no small part attributable to the spectacular finds at Lefkandi from the 1960s onward, although it was also related to increasing evidence for Euboean activity in the eastern and central Mediterranean throughout the Early Iron Age.[5] The discovery of the Toumba building at Lefkandi, and the wealthy burials within it, turned on its head the assumption that the Early Iron Age was exclusively a time of isolation and egalitarianism (Catling and Lemos 1990; Popham, Calligas, and Sackett 1993).[6] Lefkandi was a significant site throughout the Bronze Age, especially in the Postpalatial period (see chapter 4). Nevertheless, it is best known for its Early Iron Age cemeteries and the associated settlement at Xeropolis. The most important discoveries for the Early Iron Age are the elite burials located in the Toumba building, a monumental apsidal dwelling or funerary monument, and in the Toumba cemetery immediately east of it (figure 6). Together these burials reflect sustained practices of social differentiation, rooted in places of particular significance. Such significance was derived from the memory and repetitive performance of events that took place in the landscape and the social and material associations they bore.

The Toumba building is a long, apsidal structure on an east-west orientation, with verandas on the north and south sides and a porch on the east. Fill from the destruction of the building dates to the Middle Protogeometric period, or

5. For the Euboean "discovery," see Boardman 1957, 1959, 1980, 1990; Popham 1983, 1994; Lemos 1998, 2002. For repudiations of Euboean preeminence, see Papadopoulos 1997, 2011.

6. Archaeological investigations at Lefkandi have occurred in several phases. The site was included in the survey of Euboea conducted by the British School at Athens in the 1950s and 1960s (Sackett et al. 1966, 60–61, with earlier references), and excavations at Xeropolis began in 1964 (Popham and Sackett 1968). Beginning in 1968 and running throughout the 1970s, excavations took place at five cemeteries west of Xeropolis. The results of these excavations were published in *Lefkandi I* (Popham, Sackett, and Themelis 1980). The Toumba building was discovered in 1980, when it was illegally bulldozed by a farmer intending to use the land for a new outbuilding, and excavations resumed at this location and at the Toumba cemetery, immediately to the east. The Toumba building is published in two installments as *Lefkandi II* (Catling and Lemos 1990; Popham, Calligas, and Sackett 1993). The Toumba cemetery is the subject of *Lefkandi III*, though only the plates have been published since the excavation in the 1980s (Popham and Lemos 1996; for preliminary observations, see Lemos and Mitchell 2011). Excavations at Xeropolis resumed in 2003, under the direction of Lemos; annual fieldwork summaries have appeared in *Archaeological Reports* (see, e.g., Lemos 2010a; 2012, 22–24).

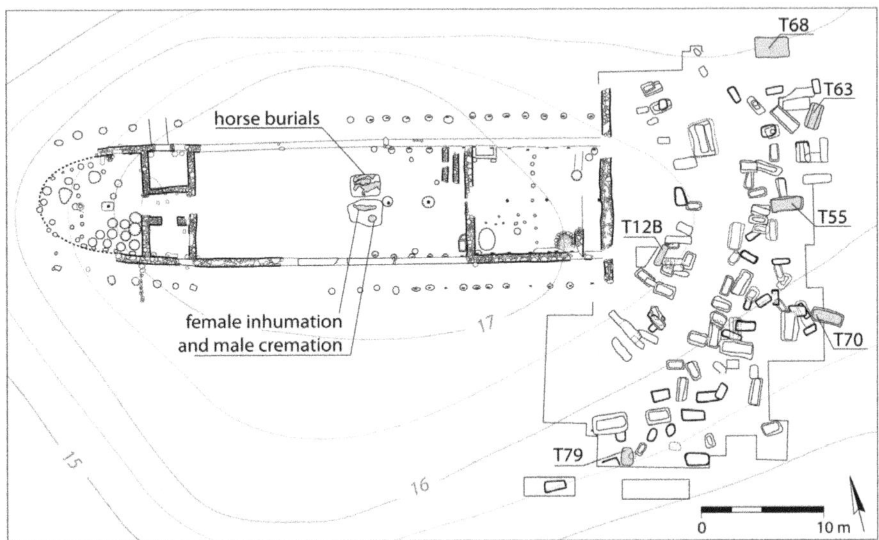

FIGURE 6. Toumba building and cemetery at Lefkandi (illustration by Denitsa Nenova, after Popham, Calligas, and Sackett 1993, plate 5; Popham and Lemos 1996, plate 3).

1000–950 BCE, and all evidence suggests that it was built in the same period, then quickly and deliberately destroyed and turned into a monumental mound that would have dominated the surrounding landscape (Catling and Lemos 1990, 92; Popham 1993, 98).[7] At about 50 by 14 meters, the building is monumental in scale, with an area over twice that of any contemporary building; indeed, no building of comparable size is known in the Greek world for the next 300 years (Mazarakis Ainian 1997, 48–49). Following the construction of the building, turning the site into a mound was itself a large-scale undertaking, and the excavators estimate that between 500 and 2,000 person-days of labor went into its construction (Coulton 1993, 55–56). Whatever the intention and agency behind the creation of this monument, it signals the mobilization of a large amount of human and material resources. The ultimate function of the building—as essentially a funerary marker—further highlights its association with particular individuals. Large-scale

7. The exact sequence of events for the construction of the Toumba building, the burials, and the mound remains contested. It is known that everything happened fairly close together (nearly all ceramics are MPG), but the archaeological record cannot reveal for certain whether the building was made as a rulers' dwelling and then demolished to turn it into a tomb, or whether it was built specifically to be a tomb (Popham 1993, 97; Antonaccio 1995, 236–41; Mazarakis Ainian 1997, 54–57; Morris 2000, 221). Moreover, its resemblance to early temple forms (which do not appear until the eighth century) has also led to discussions of the possibility of a religious function, though the rulers' dwelling/ funerary architecture interpretation is by far the most common and probably best (see also de Waele 1998; Pakkanen and Pakkanen 2000).

building projects in the Postpalatial Bronze Age, while present, were almost exclusively community-oriented, such as the settlement walls or other structures of more ambiguous function (e.g., at Kynos, Lefkandi, and Mitrou).

Despite its size, the Toumba building still had much in common with other structures of this period. It is comparable to "rulers' dwellings" or large houses at Emborio on Chios and Nichoria in Messenia (Mazarakis Ainian 1997, tables III and X), both in its apsidal form and internal features. A further parallel exists at Thermon, where the apsidal building, Megaron A, which was originally built in Mycenaean times, seems to have been standing and still in use for burials in the Early Iron Age (Mazarakis Ainian 1997, 44–45; Morris 2000, 222–28), which was when Megaron B was built (Papapostolou 2011). While these parallels exist, the short use-life and function of the Toumba building—seemingly built to be destroyed and turned into a funerary mound—make it one of a kind.

In the center of the Toumba building, two human burials and four horse burials were found below the floor (see figure 6). The human burials are of a cremated male, often referred to as the "Hero of Lefkandi" (Popham, Touloupa, and Sackett 1982; Morris 2000, 195; Antonaccio 2002), and of an inhumed female, who has sometimes been viewed as a suttee (Popham 1993, 21) but has more recently been thought of as a "princess" (Stampolidis and Giannopoulou 2012). Through these burials and their associated grave goods, as well as those in the adjacent Toumba cemetery, certain networking practices, whereby elite groups at Lefkandi engaged with both past and present material remains in an effort to construct power relationships and social inequalities, become apparent.

The "hero" of the male cremation burial was likely between 30 and 45 years old at the time of his death. The cremated remains were placed inside a large bronze amphora, most likely of Cypriot origin, dating to the thirteenth or twelfth century BCE, though vessels of this type have also been found in eleventh-century contexts on Cyprus (Catling 1993, 86–87). The bronze was thus at least 50 years old at the time of deposition, and more likely between 100 and 300 years old. The amphora is decorated on its rim and handles, which contain, respectively, a single register of lions, bulls, and archers, and double registers of lions and bulls. This iconography is also most likely derived from Cyprus, although there are hybridizing elements that blend together Aegean, Cypriot, and Levantine styles (Catling 1993, 86–92). As an heirloom, this object may signal meaningful continuities from the Postpalatial Bronze Age in terms of overseas contacts. In the amphora were found a linen robe or shroud and cremated human remains, all of which were covered by a bronze bowl. An iron sword, a razor, a whetstone, and a spearhead were found around the amphora (Popham, Touloupa, and Sackett 1982; Antonaccio 2002).

The female inhumation was found in the same shaft as the cremation, immediately to the north. She was laid out with arms and feet crossed, and she was adorned with grave goods at least as significant as those found with the male. These include an electrum ring, bronze and iron pins, a gold brassiere consisting of two gold discs over the breasts, and a lunate piece of gold between them (Popham, Touloupa, and Sackett 1982, 171–73; Popham 1993, 20). There was also a necklace of gold beads, faience, crystal, and a central gold pendant that has been identified as an Old Babylonian gorget, which would mean that the artifact was between 600 and 1,000 years old at the time of the burial (Popham 1994, 15; Morris 2000, 219; Lemos 2010b, 58). An ivory-handled iron knife was found next to her right shoulder; this led to the speculation that this person had been a human sacrifice (Popham 1993, 21). With no other evidence for such a practice, though, this speculation seems largely unfounded.

Turning to the context of these burials, we see that there are further meaningful markers. The first involves the presence of four horse burials in a shaft dug at the same time as the one for the human burials, but immediately to the north. These were almost certainly sacrifices that were part of the funerary event that took place at the site. There are many examples of horse burials associated with elite funerary remains from the Mycenaean period, some of which come from elsewhere along the Euboean Gulf—for example, from the Mycenaean tholos tomb at Marathon (Marinatos 1972, 190; Cavanagh and Mee 1998, 115). Horse burials were also common on Cyprus, with which Lefkandi was in demonstrable contact (Carstens 2005). The burials at Lefkandi also bear similarities to later ones, which recall Homeric practices, at Salamis, on Cyprus (*Iliad* 23.163–257; Blackwell 2010, 144–45).[8] While the horse burials at Lefkandi are unique in the Protogeometric period, horse sacrifices (like many Homeric features) had important antecedents in Mycenaean times, which could very well have been referenced deliberately. Regardless of these foreign and cross-temporal associations, the status that horses afforded in early Greece is well known, and horseback riding was an aristocratic practice in Greece and the wider eastern Mediterranean as early as the thirteenth century BCE (Kelekna 2009, 175–80; Kelder 2012). The sacrifice of four of these animals underscores social inequalities at Lefkandi, as well as the wider spatial and temporal distribution of such practices.

An enormous ceramic krater was placed over the burial shaft in the Toumba building (Catling and Lemos 1990, 25–26). This practice, too, has important Mycenaean roots and also anticipates later funerary ritual, since burial events were important occasions for feasting, drinking, offering libations, and sacrifice. Like other aspects of material culture at Toumba, this krater was monumental in scale; at 80 centimeters in height and 88 centimeters in rim diameter, it would not be surpassed in size until the Dipylon krater (from Athens) in the eighth century BCE. In addition to its exceptional size, the Toumba krater also invites visual

---

8. Homeric practices recalled in Cypriot burials include horse sacrifice, placing honey and oil in amphorae beside the dead, human sacrifice(?), cremation and pyres, putting out the funeral pyre with wine (asserted from unburned vessels found above the urn used for cremation), wrapping cremated remains and placing them in a container, construction of a funerary mound, coating furniture in ivory and silver (Blackwell 2010, 145, table 1).

associations with the east through the use of certain motifs—most notably the centrally displayed tree of life (Morris 2000, 228).

All these elements point to a funerary event on a grand scale. Clearly the persons buried in the Toumba building were important, and the people responsible for their burial sought to link themselves to these persons through a monumental building project, the deposition of prestige goods, and funerary practices involving feasting and drinking that were performed at the location of the burial. In addition to the evidence of the monumental krater placed above the burial, most of the vessels that can be associated with the use of the building (rather than the fill used to create the tumulus mound) have applications in feasting and funerary practices (Catling and Lemos 1990, 4).

The material associations with Toumba as a gathering place of collective memory survived long after the original burial event. References to the burials in the Toumba building can be seen in several of the 83 tombs and 34 pyres that were excavated in the Toumba cemetery, by far the wealthiest of the six known burial grounds at Lefkandi (see figure 6).[9] Among the most explicit references to the burials within the building are the horse burials contained in Tomb 68. Other such explicit references involve urn cremations and weapons burials in Tomb 79; Near Eastern heirlooms in Tomb 12B; an engraved, Near Eastern bronze bowl from Tomb 70 (probably from Cyprus); a double burial with an urn cremation and inhumation in Tomb 55; gold discs and necklace in Tomb 63; and several other burials containing weapons (Popham, Calligas, and Sackett 1989; Popham 1995; Popham and Lemos 1996). While warrior burials are not exclusive to the Toumba cemetery, their placement suggests that these and other tombs were deliberate references, rather than simply coincidental. Tomb 79 is also significant for its links to eastern Mediterranean trading systems, leading to the characterization of its inhabitant as "a Euboean warrior-trader" (Popham and Lemos 1995). This tomb contained 16 balance weights and fragments that have nearly identical parallels in Late Bronze Age Cyprus and the Levant, which highlights the importance of tying the deceased to long-distance interactions and their continuity over time (Kroll 2008). The associations between grave goods and sociopolitical status are complex, however. It is not sufficient to point to distance and quantity alone as markers of status. The context and particularity of objects must be examined as well. In the case of Lefkandi, several of the exotica found in Early Iron Age tombs are best described as trinkets, talismans, or amulets, which Arrington (2016) has argued represent multiple eschatological belief systems within a mixed community of locals and foreigners, tracing some particularities to Cypro-Phoenician traditions; Murray (2018a) has made a similar argument concerning the LH IIIC cemetery at Perati. Various modes of signification were therefore present in the Toumba

9. The list of parallels presented here is incomplete and must await the full publication of *Lefkandi III*; the plates of this volume were published in the 1990s and provided the basis for this analysis (Popham and Lemos 1996).

cemetery, setting the individuals buried there apart from the wider community in terms of both status and connections to the wider world.

The Toumba complex at Lefkandi attests to a degree of social inequality unprecedented in the Postpalatial Bronze Age or Early Iron Age. The practices exhibited here have more in common with the grave circles, tholoi, and wealthy chamber tombs of the Mycenaean period than with the warrior burials of the Postpalatial period, though there are of course some shared elements here as well. These commonalities are significant, as they indicate that the Lefkandi phenomenon is an exaggeration of preexisting practices rather than something completely new. The growth of Lefkandi—as a settlement and in its significance in wider networks in the Euboean Gulf, the Aegean, and the eastern Mediterranean—began in the Postpalatial Bronze Age, and then reached an apex in the Prehistoric Iron Age, far beyond any other site in the Aegean world, with the possible exception of Athens. The persons buried in the Toumba building, along with those who strove to make ancestral links with them, represent access to and consumption of foreign exotica and items of particular material value or technological novelty. The links Lefkandi forged with the east clearly served to make the central Euboean Gulf an important hub of activity throughout the Early Iron Age.

Continuity and Change in Early Iron Age Burial Customs.   Early Iron Age burial customs in the rest of central Greece were markedly varied, both within and between the landscapes under study in this book. Some sites demonstrate direct continuity from the Postpalatial Bronze Age, including deliberate engagements with the cemeteries of previous generations as well as evidence for transformation over time. In most areas, single burials became more common while multiple burials in conspicuous funerary structures are less so, unlike the examples discussed above (Papadopoulou 2017, 301; see also Mee and Cavanagh 1984, 58–62; Lemos 2002, 185–86; Dickinson 2006, 183–95). Medeon and Paralimni both exhibit direct spatial continuity, though with more "disorganized" burial forms (Papadopoulou 2017, 301–2). At the same time, Elateia saw continuous use of a Mycenaean chamber tomb cemetery, including the tombs themselves, until the ninth century BCE. The same happens in the Spercheios valley, where Mycenaean chamber tomb cemeteries at Vikiorema and Kompotades are also reused for multiple burials in the Early Iron Age, while other sites, such as Lamia and Stylida, change to single burial customs.

Southern Thessaly provides the clearest example of Early Iron Age regionalism, most notably through apparent population growth and its unique burial record, which features small Protogeometric-Geometric tholos tombs. As discussed in the previous chapters, there is not a clear "collapse" scenario in Thessaly in the Postpalatial Bronze Age, although there is a decline in overall site numbers (see figure 2). In the Prehistoric Iron Age, site numbers return nearly to the same level as in the time of the palaces—a pattern of growth also seen in Malis, though not quite on the same scale.

In Thessaly, the mortuary record shows that the use of certain burial grounds is maintained from LH IIIB to the Geometric period. Unlike elsewhere, tholos tomb construction expanded and even became widespread, and Mycenaean tholoi continued to be reused (Georganas 2011, 627). Over 60 examples of Protogeometric tholoi are known from some 35 sites (Georganas 2011, 628; Karouzou 2017, 364, fig. 2; see also Arachoviti 1994, 135, fig. 13; Georganas 2000). Most of these date to the Late Protogeometric period (950–900 BCE), though specific dating is often impossible. These tholoi are usually small (two to four meters in diameter) and built on or near topographic features of some prominence. They were family tombs; some were in use for well over a century; and finds—including ceramic and metal vases, rings, fibulae, and beads, as well as swords, knives, arrowheads in iron and bronze, and whetstones—are quite similar to those found in elite burials elsewhere in Greece (Georganas 2000, 51–52).

Thessalian tholos tombs demonstrate direct continuity from the Mycenaean period, and not only as loose imitations. Several small tholoi, along with the larger examples from Georgiko, Kapakli (at Volos), Kazanaki, and Dimini, were constructed in the Mycenaean period. The Mycenaean construction of smaller tholos tombs, measuring between 1.9 and 5.2 meters in diameter, was a clear precedent for the PG tholoi that followed. This tradition seems to have been strongest around the Pagasetic Gulf, perhaps initially as a result of its ties with other parts of the Mycenaean world via the Euboean Gulf. But once this tradition reached Thessaly (probably in LH IIIA, after the heyday of tholos construction in the Peloponnese), it stuck, and in the Protogeometric period it expanded.

The mortuary landscape across central Greece signals that there was not a clear, universal break with the Mycenaean world. Funerary practices changed in many places, to be sure, but there was strong continuity in tradition scattered throughout the landscape, especially in Phokis, Malis, and Thessaly. A sort of western/ northern group of communities with distinct funerary traditions might be seen in contrast to developments at Athens and Lefkandi, though we must also keep in mind that these latter two sites are exceptional and hardly representative of broader patterns. Boeotia, northern and southern Euboea, and elsewhere in Attica (at least until the Middle Geometric) seem to follow the intimations of decline so often made for this period.

Social Organization and Village Politics

What, then, can we say about the overall picture of social organization in Early Iron Age central Greece? The central question, as in other periods, is how to articulate the political organization and dynamics of nonstate entities, especially when they vary widely over space and time. This question is indeed relevant for all of Aegean prehistory, from the Neolithic period onward, where we are dealing with societies that are clearly complex but are not at a level of social or territorial integration where they would be classified as states. These are community-based social entities, which exhibit hierarchies, inequalities, and political economy, but have little central organization, interregional uniformity, or clear definitions of territory (with the exception of the short-lived Mycenaean palaces). The vast majority of individuals living in Greece from the Neolithic period to the Prehistoric Iron Age lived in what are probably best described as small-scale village societies, made of communities comprised of several households and kin groups.

One significant transformation that happened in the Prehistoric Iron Age was that differences between certain communities became more pronounced than they had been in the Postpalatial Bronze Age. Precocious centers like Lefkandi and Athens grew much larger than their contemporaries and exhibited much greater influence, both locally and regionally. At this point, these were the two largest sites in central Greece by an order of magnitude, enough to classify them above the level of other sites that might nevertheless be deemed "major" hubs during this period (see map 19). Thebes, too, seems to have been a major center, though later building and the history of excavation and publication make it difficult to define the nature of the Early Iron Age settlement there in clear terms. One difference between the better understood settlements of Lefkandi and Athens is that Lefkandi was clearly *the* principal draw in central Greece in terms of external imports in the Protogeometric period, while Athens does not demonstrate a similar level of attraction until later (Kourou 2015). Such centralized consumption is not unlike patterns in the Late Bronze Age. A similar pattern can be seen at Athens with respect to settlement size. While Athens, and perhaps Lefkandi, might have been on the cusp of developing into urban centers during this period, the rest of Early Iron Age central Greece remains a world of villages.

Most of the sites in the Early Iron Age settlement pattern are small-scale, comprised of fragmentary evidence that demonstrates the presence of a community but little else. Architecture, where it has been documented, is generally simpler than in the Mycenaean period. There is nothing in the Early Iron Age world that can be considered state-like or palatial, although the large houses sometimes called ruler's dwellings likely served political purposes at the level of the community (Mazarakis Ainian 1997). Papadopoulou (2017, 299–301) has argued that most of central Greece witnessed a shift from "complex" to "loose" patterns of organization during this period, though some communities—namely, Delphi, Medeon, and Elateia—retained elements of complex organization. To this list of sites we should add, of course, those discussed above, as well as Atalanti and certain other sites where social differentiation has been revealed by wealthy burials (such as Ellopia and Stylida). While these pockets of complexity are distributed in various regions throughout central Greece—and rather evenly—this probably should not be taken as evidence for regional centralization. It rather represents incidental concentrations of activities, people, and things in a regional landscape that did not experience political integration beyond the local level.

Signs of leadership are occasionally manifest in the central structures or elite burials mentioned above, though these are relatively few. Part of the problem, of course, is the preponderance of funerary over settlement evidence, which is why archaeologists have traditionally looked to the mortuary record for evidence of sociopolitical hierarchy and organization (Morris 1987; Whitley 1991). Others have looked to the textual records from other periods. One question is whether or not we can detect Hesiod's *basileis* or Linear B's *qa-si-re-u* in Early Iron Age society. If we can distinguish comparable roles in the Bronze Age and in the eighth centuries, it is a reasonable assumption that they existed in this period as well (see, e.g., Finley 1954, 142; Crielaard 2011b). The archaeological record suggests that elite individuals certainly existed, but it yields little definitive information about rulership or political organization. In well-documented cases, like Lefkandi from an archaeological perspective and Argos from later texts, there seem to have been oscillations in the nature of leadership in early Greece, sometimes more focused on an individual, at other times involving a number competing factions (Kõiv 2016). Without projecting forward or backward and while considering the variety in the settlement pattern across different regions, it seems risky to put much faith in evidence from Linear B or early Greek poetry. Looser notions of heterarchy and fluidity of power, within and between the communities of Early Iron Age Greece, seem much more likely.

As in other periods treated in this book, variation is the rule in the Prehistoric Iron Age. Major sites and centers vary considerably among themselves, but there is likely more baseline similarity among smaller groups with less complex organization. A typical Early Iron Age community probably consisted of several family units living in structures built of ephemeral materials (wood posts, waddle and daub, mudbrick). Political organization was loosely integrated and probably had multiple bases of power, including status within a family unit or kin group and personal prestige as perceived by the community as a whole—based on wealth, family, biography, and access to interpersonal and intercommunity networks. Papadopoulou (2017, 306) notes that patterns in burial offering might support status being tied to personal prestige rather than to family status, with the exception being a few groups with higher status or authority. Overall, then, things look quite similar to the Postpalatial Bronze Age, though we do see a pattern of certain sites, already powerful in the Postpalatial Bronze Age, consolidating and expanding in terms of political complexity, social inequality, and regional interest. The majority of people, however, were probably living in more loosely integrated, agropastoral communities.

TECHNOLOGY TRANSFER
AND PRODUCTION NETWORKS

Major innovations in metal and ceramic production technologies occurred in the Prehistoric Iron Age. These are, for metals, the inception and development of iron technology and, for ceramics, the spread of the Protogeometric style, which came with innovations in firing, decoration, and vessel forms. Processes from raw material procurement to the distribution of finished products (the full *chaîne opératoire*) must be accounted for if we hope to understand production systems as coherent social practices distributed across various spatial scales (Mauss 1935; Leroi-Gourhan 1964; Lemonnier 1993; Dobres 2000). A network approach emphasizes the links and nodes that make up production processes as wholes rather than privileging (1) particular points in those processes, (2) the finished products that are often better studied from the perspective of consumption (as seen in the burial contexts above), and (3) studies of imports and exports (on which see further below). Such an approach has the particular value of articulating interactions across local, regional, and (at times) interregional scales, even in the absence of direct evidence for particular connections. As in the Postpalatial Bronze Age, we should imagine that the mobility of traveling craftspeople played a key role in technological dispersals within and beyond central Greece.

The Coming of the Age of Iron

The transition from bronze to iron as the predominant utilitarian metal brought sweeping changes to Mediterranean life. New networks of production formed to accommodate this new material—often on a more regional basis than in the Bronze Age—on account of the wider obtainability of iron ores. This accessibility led Childe (1942, 183) to refer to iron as the material that "democratized" warfare, industry, and, perhaps most importantly, agriculture (with the advent of the iron ploughshare, which replaced wooden antecedents). Childe's ideas in this regard were largely prefigured in the writings of Engels ([1884] 1972, 220), who called iron "the last and most important of all the raw materials that played a historically revolutionary role." The specifics of the bronze-iron transition in Greece (and the wider Mediterranean) became a topic of major interest in the 1970s and 1980s (Waldbaum 1978; Wertime and Muhly 1980). Periodic reviews of new evidence have appeared since then (Sherratt 1994; Waldbaum 1999), although there is no up-to-date, comprehensive overview of the technology and archaeology of early iron metallurgy in the Mediterranean.[10]

The technology of early iron production is fundamentally different from other metallurgical practices (see, e.g., Rehder 2000). First, iron smelting (the conversion from ore to metal) is more complicated than copper smelting. Copper is smelted in a liquid state and melts at about 1083 degrees Celsius. The melting point of iron is 1530 degrees Celsius, but it is extracted from ores in a solid state at around 1100 to 1250 degrees. After the initial smelt, the product (the bloom) must be worked to squeeze out excess slag, hence the name "wrought iron." There are three processes, or heat treatments, used in the hardening of iron: carburization, quenching, and tempering. Carburization is essentially a diffusion process by which iron becomes

---

10. Snodgrass (1980b) wrote the closest thing to such a synthesis over forty years ago. Summaries for Greece specifically can be found in Snodgrass ([1971] 2000, 213–95) and Dickinson (2006, 146–50).

alloyed with carbon. Unfortunately, problems of preservation, especially on the edges of objects, make hardening processes difficult to detect in materials dating to the Early Iron Age. The data we do have, however, suggest that deliberate heat treatment and carburization developed as hardening techniques as early as the twelfth century BCE on Cyprus and are important markers for the spread of specialized ironworking to Greece (Tholander 1971; Snodgrass 1980).

The technological complexity of this process demonstrates that transfer must have happened in the context of relatively intense interaction between craftspeople from different societies. So, by what mechanisms did early iron technology develop and come to the Aegean specifically? Snodgrass ([1971] 2000, 237–39) attributed the adoption of iron technology in Greece to a bronze shortage, which was caused by political upheaval throughout the eastern Mediterranean and the disruption of the tin trade, which made the more widely available iron a natural commodity to turn to. This is the so-called *circulation model*. And yet, there have been several aspects of the material record uncovered since the 1970s that do not suggest a bronze shortage; in fact, they show most notably that bronze remains quite common in burials of the Early Iron Age (Waldbaum 1999, 29; Papadopoulos 2014, 181–86; Murray 2017, 174–77, 261–63, with further references on the debate). Bronze votives are also present in early sanctuaries across the Greek world, and even more so than iron, which was also a prestige good before it was a practical one (Voyatzis 1990).

The overwhelming majority of excavated iron objects come from mortuary contexts. This fact led Morris (1989) to suggest a *deposition model* for the increase in iron objects at this time. He argued that the increase in iron in mortuary contexts had to do with its status as a prestige rather than a utilitarian material. While it is no doubt true that many of the buried objects, such as weapons, had symbolic significance, Snodgrass (1989, 29) makes the important point that the evidence for carburization and heat treatment reinforces the argument that they were also made for utilitarian purposes—as, for example, in Cyprus—from a very early date. A middle ground incorporating elements of both deposition and circulation models, where both prestige and the economics of raw material availability can contribute to our understanding of early iron metallurgy, therefore seems most appropriate (Papadopoulos 2014, 182–83). A historical perspective is also useful. While there may not have been a particular shortage of bronze, the wider availability of iron only became relevant after its consumption and the technological knowledge of its production became more widespread, which in Greece took place over the course of the eleventh to the eighth centuries BCE.

Technological knowledge of iron production seems to have been carried to the Aegean in the eleventh century, not long after its innovation on Cyprus, which had long been a point of interface for Aegean traders and craft producers. Rather than there having been a tin shortage that caused a breakdown in the bronze trade, it seems that technological innovation spread through networks that were

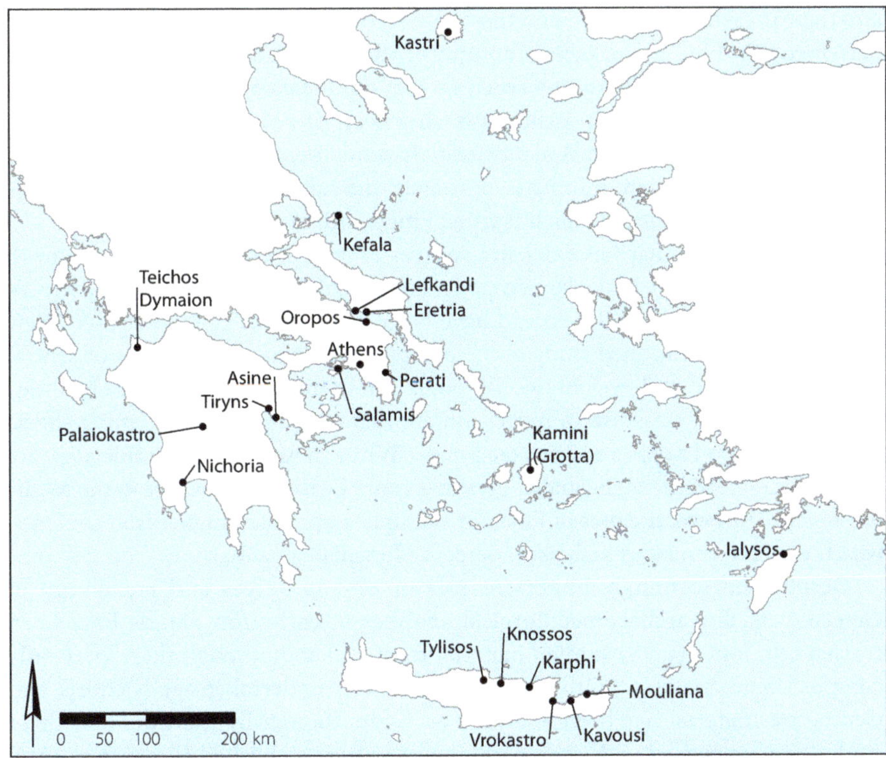

MAP 20. Location of early iron finds in Greece (after Dickinson 2006, 148, with additions).

reconstituted following the collapse of the Mycenaean palatial systems. This is probably better considered a context than a cause for the spread of early iron-working. Technological knowledge was transmitted first through long-distance interaction, probably at places like Lefkandi, and later dispersed through regional networks, which resulted in the rather rapid spread of iron metallurgy in Greece. It is noteworthy that the earliest evidence of iron metallurgy in Greece comes from sites that are demonstrably well connected to the eastern Mediterranean in earlier periods (map 20).

Greece is rich in iron ores. Morris (1992, 131–32) argued that rich metal deposits, including the iron orcs of Laconia, Euboea, Thasos, and western Crete, drew Phoenician interest and stimulated economic activity on a pan-Mediterranean scale. Greece also boasts types of ores that are not present on Cyprus.[11] Nevertheless, there is a fundamental difference between the occurrence of metal deposits

11. Muhly (2008, 71) writes that Cyprus has no iron resources, but he surely means no iron ores (even so, a complete absence seems unlikely). Iron resources are actually relatively abundant on Cyprus in the form of gossans, ochres, and umbers.

and their present workability, and the question of whether or not they would have been recognizable and workable in antiquity (Muhly 2008, 67–68). While we should not leap to conclusions in interpreting the significance of ore deposits, they should not be dismissed so easily as having been of poor quality and therefore insignificant for Early Iron Age smelters. A fundamental problem, of course, is that evidence for ancient mining is extremely difficult to detect in areas that have seen modern exploitation, which is true of many mineral resources in Greece.

Euboea in particular has extensive sources of iron ore (Bakhuizen 1976, 1977). These are easily visible in the landscape on account of their purple color and metalliferous appearance, and they could have been identified as soon as people knew what to look for. A limited study of the composition of the lateritic ores of central Euboea suggests that they contained enough iron to make them workable in antiquity, and that they possessed a nickel content that may have had hardening effects (map 21; see also Photos and Tylecote 1988).[12] While these ores are useable, they are not comparable to the high-quality ores that could be found elsewhere in the Mediterranean. The hematite ores of Elba, for example, have much higher iron contents, which vary but can be as high as 70 percent (Tanelli et al. 2001).

Despite the seemingly important role of iron resources and metallurgy in Greece, very few archaeometallurgical analyses of early iron objects have been carried out. Jones (1980) studied material from Lefkandi, though these were only compositional analyses.[13] Other studies have been undertaken for Nichoria and Geometric material has been analyzed at Asine, though by the time that these studies are concerned with, ironworking was better established (Rapp et al. 1978; Waldbaum 1999; Backe-Forsberg and Risberg 2002). The earliest remains of actual iron smelting in the Aegean come from Oropos, where slags and other evidence for metalworking have been excavated in contexts dated to the eighth and seventh centuries BCE (prior to this, finished objects are our only evidence of iron in Greece) (Doonan and Mazarakis Ainian 2007). Microstructural analysis has revealed that the slags were a product of iron smithing and at times contained inclusions of copper, suggesting side-by-side metalworking industries, which also occurred at Eretria (Doonan and Mazarakis Ainian 2007, 364–65; Verdan 2007). Oropos is therefore important for the social implications of metalworking as well as for its location on the Euboean Gulf and the interactions across it. Slags have also been found at the Early Iron Age site of Kefala on Skiathos (Mazarakis Ainian 2012b, 61). Other sites with iron production remains that have been metallurgically studied date to later periods (see, e.g., Kostoglou 2008). The amount of material studied from a technological perspective for all periods is quite low, and for the Early Iron Age it is almost nonexistent.

---

12. With a permit from the Institute for Geology and Mineral Exploration (IGME), I sampled ore sources throughout central Euboea to determine their chemical composition as a way of assessing usability and general quality.

13. Additional material from Lefkandi has been studied by other specialists, though this work has not yet been published.

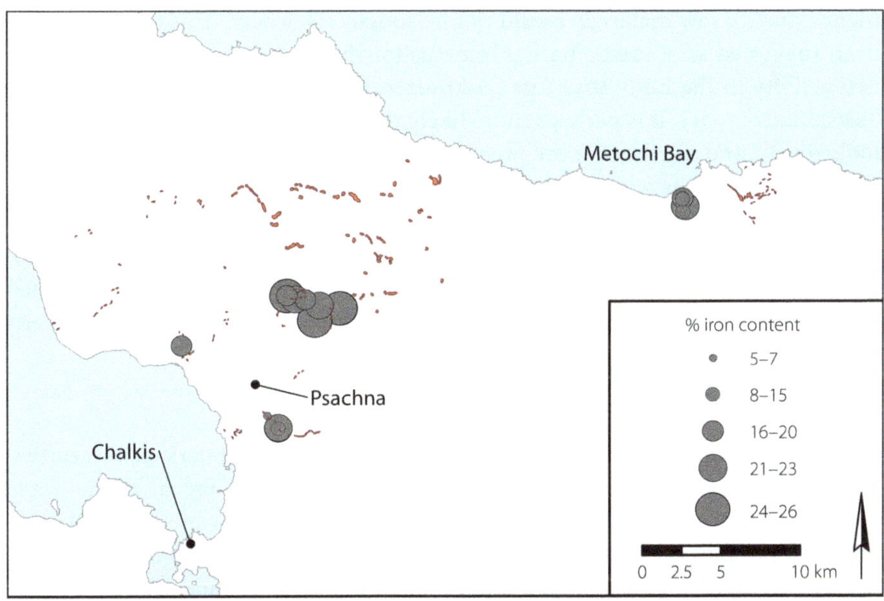

MAP 21. Map of iron ore sources in central Euboea (in red), with results of portable XRF analysis showing percent iron content of collected samples (top); photo of an iron ore source near Psachna (bottom).

In light of the distribution and the character of early iron remains in Greece, three points should be emphasized: (1) parts of Greece were quite rich in iron ores; (2) iron ore is like any other rock without the technical knowledge to smelt and smith it; and (3) even if there were locally available ores, this does not mean that higher-quality raw materials would not be sought elsewhere. This third point has been suggested as at least a partial impetus for the intensification of Greek colonial activity in the Early Iron Age (Bakhuizen 1976; Markoe 1992; Ridgway 1992; Tsetskhladze 1995). It is perhaps more likely that Greeks and Phoenicians initially looked west and north for more precious metals and located new sources of iron in the course of this wider search. Regardless of later endeavors in metals industries, the Prehistoric Iron Age witnessed the emergence of this new technology in the Greek world out of a milieu initially involving Greeks, Cypriots, and Phoenicians: it seems to have arrived first in the regions surrounding the Euboean Gulf, from which it then spread rather rapidly, not unlike other technologies of the Early Iron Age, like writing (see further in chapter 6).

Ceramic Production

The Protogeometric style of painted pottery is another hallmark of the earliest Iron Age in Greece. Its origins in Athens, its adoption in Euboea, and its rapid spread through much of the Aegean have led to discussions of various stylistic koinai, especially associated with Attica and Euboea (Murray 1975; Lemos 2002; Seroglou 2009; Donnellan 2017). Studies of Protogeometric and Geometric pottery have traditionally focused on typologies and sequences based on vessel form and decoration, generally following approaches applied to later black- and red-figure Greek vases of the Classical period (Whitley 2002, 23–25). In Protogeometric and Geometric contexts, these approaches attempt to identify and analyze distinctive styles, and to associate them with certain regions or individual painters. This is perhaps more difficult when dealing with designs that are abstract rather than figural. Nonetheless, variation in vessel form and decoration, as well as in fabric, can be used to discern regional traditions and in some cases to identify individual painters or potters. Scientific provenance studies have been relatively rarer for this period than for other prehistoric epochs, though they have recently shed considerable new light on Early Iron Age pottery from Euboea (Kerschner and Lemos 2014).

Discussion here focuses mainly on the Attic Protogeometric and its related styles, which are influential throughout the Euboean Gulf and much of the southern Aegean. At the same time, there are several areas of the Greek world where the ceramic styles of this period developed independently or have no relation to what is elsewhere considered Protogeometric. These areas include the western and northwestern Peloponnese, inland Thessaly, and parts of Macedonia (Snodgrass [1971] 2000, 84–89; Papadopoulos 2004).

The Protogeometric style is marked by the first use of the multiple brush, used to create the mechanically drawn concentric circles or semicircles that are characteristic of this period (Papadopoulos, Vedder, and Schreiber 1998). General elements of decoration involve dark paint applied to a lighter surface, whereon carefully placed bands emphasize the shape of the pot. In the Geometric period we see the further development of these tendencies. Geometric decoration became more complex and new diagnostic features, such as the meander pattern, began to appear. We also see the gradual introduction and elaboration of figural scenes, which often depict funerary narratives on large vessels deposited in burial contexts or used as grave markers.

Detailed stylistic analysis can be found in regional overviews of Protogeometric and Geometric pottery, which have also traced the circulation of ceramics in wider Aegean and Mediterranean contexts (see, e.g., Coldstream [1977] 2003, [1968] 2008; Lemos 2002). The areas that appear to have been most influential in this period are Athens and Euboea, the former recognized as a stylistic innovator and driver, the latter seen as the developer of a widespread koine and trading network (Lemos 2002). Some places within this sphere of influence have even been characterized as Euboean "outposts"—namely, Skyros, Oropos, and possibly Kefala on Skiathos (Lemos and Hatcher 1986; Charalambidou 2017, 93–94). On the contrary, other recent work has questioned whether koine is an appropriate term to describe stylistic similarities in pottery found in a northwest to southeast arc from Torone to Naxos. Donnellan (2017) has examined patterns of consumption in funerary contexts to suggest that there was in fact a significant amount of stylistic variation in assemblages from Torone, Marmariani, Volos, Lefkandi, and Skyros—all frequently mentioned as participants in such a koine. She suggests rather that consumption patterns were selective and variable across regions, and that the shared elements exhibited are perhaps better understood in theoretical frameworks of networks or interaction spheres (Donnellan 2017, 61). A network perspective has the advantage of highlighting such shared attributes while also signaling the specificity of their application. In the context of funerary practice, the consumption of particular goods with connotations of connectivity, either imported from or influenced by neighboring regions, shows the social importance of maintaining regional connections, especially for the aspiring elites discussed above.

While more nuanced and decentralized interpretations of consumption are welcome, recent provenience studies have confirmed the pivotal role of central Euboea. Thanks to an extensive program of sampling and neutron activation analysis, we now know that clay deposits at Phylla and Vasiliko were used extensively in a widely exported clay and pottery production industry from the Bronze Age to the present (Mommsen 2014). The clay source is located in the Lelantine Plain only about two kilometers north of Lefkandi, and it has been used in recent times for brick and tile production (map 22). Actual production remains in the form of kilns and workshops are scarce, although there is a relatively sparse record of landscape survey in central Euboea (see chapter 2).

Mommsen (2014) has identified a distinct grouping of chemical signatures shared among pottery coming from central Euboea and other nearby sites: the "Euripos Group." This signature is seen in both pottery found in Euboea and in

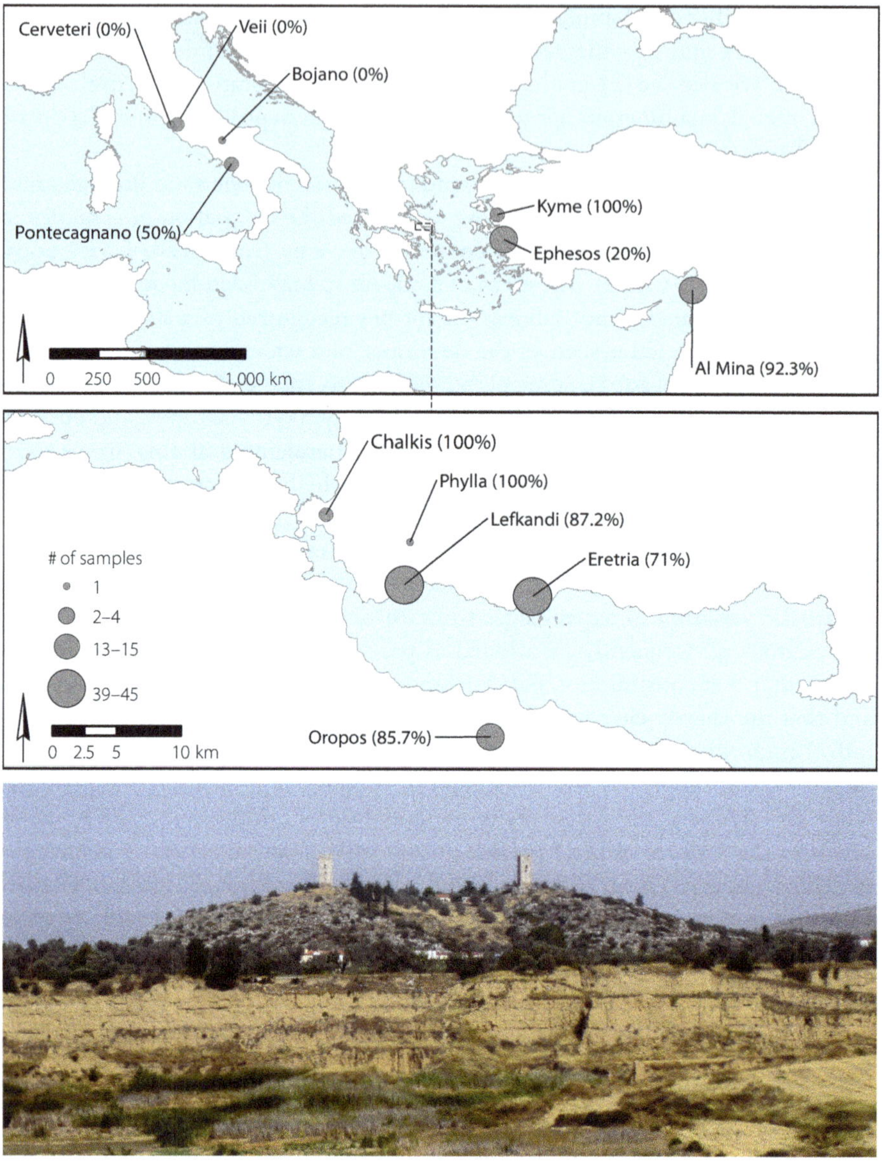

MAP 22. Clay source at Phylla (bottom) and combined map of sites analyzed by Mommsen (2014), showing the number of samples analyzed from each site and percentage of samples that match the "Euripos Group."

pottery in the Euboean style found elsewhere. Moreover, experimental analysis of the clay source itself has shown that all vessels in the Euripos Group were made of clay mined there. Of the 101 Late Bronze Age to Early Iron Age samples tested from the Euripos area, 76 belong to this group (Mommsen 2014, 17) (see map 22). Several previously analyzed vessels also belong to this group and source, including Late Helladic vessels from Thebes, Grey Minyan wares found on Aegina, three sherds from Troy, and pottery from various other sites along the Euboean Gulf. This group was also represented by 12 of 13 pendant semicircle skyphoi (a form associated particularly with Euboea) from Al Mina and certain sites in Italy (Pontecagnano) and western Anatolia (Ephesos, Kyme) (Mommsen 2014, 17–18). Based on these data, it seems that the Phylla clay source was one of the most important in central Greece, certainly for the Postpalatial Bronze Age and the Prehistoric Iron Age, and quite possibly for earlier periods as well. Resource procurement could have been closely observed by Lefkandi during this period, which also raises questions pertaining to its status in other periods. What was happening with this source in the Palatial Bronze Age? Is Lefkandi the production center for the bulk of the pottery in the LH IIIC koine discussed in chapter 4? What is the long-term history of this source, including the medieval and modern periods, when Chalkis was known as an important center for ceramic production?

Production remains for pottery, like those for metals, are relatively rare. Nevertheless, kiln fragments were excavated in the fill layers of the Toumba building at Lefkandi, along with a large amount of ceramics (Sackett 1993, 75–76). This lends further support to the idea that Lefkandi was a major manufacturing and distributive center in the Protogeometric period (and probably earlier). Further remains of ceramic production from the Early Iron Age have been excavated at Athens and Torone (Papadopoulos 1989, 2003, 2005). Analysis of production waste from pit and well deposits from the Early Iron Age potters' field in the Athenian Agora is unique in revealing aspects of experimentation in production. Here, test pieces were used to assess the behavior of paints and clays under firing (Papadopoulos 2003, 7–9). These were typically made from failed vessels (prefiring) and were removed with a hook or rod at different times in the firing session through a hole in the kiln. From these and other remains Papadopoulos (2003, 210) was able to reconstruct a three-stage firing process that included (1) firing under oxidizing conditions, (2) firing under reducing conditions, and (3) reoxidization with a subsequent gradual decrease in kiln temperature. This three-stage process had been available, more or less, since the beginnings of the Late Bronze Age, although it was applied to much different effect to create a black gloss in the Protogeometric period. Stylistic innovations, using the pivoted multiple brush to create concentric circles, spread quickly as well, first appearing in the Aegean and eventually also appearing on Cypriot and Phoenician wares (Eiteljorg 1980; Papadopoulos, Vedder, and Schreiber 1998). This evidence, which we observe first in Athens and then see spreading elsewhere, indicates the complexity of the technological process, which could have been transferred across regions only by people with technological knowledge on the move, often over significant distances.

MOBILITY, MIGRATION,
AND MEDITERRANEAN (PRE)HISTORY

While new technologies played interstitial roles in social interactions within and between Early Iron Age groups, these practices are difficult to trace in detail. Other aspects of long-distance interaction, such as trade in commodities and large-scale mobility, can be equally challenging. One might compare the complexity and the Mediterranean scope of such processes to the "international spirit" Renfrew (1972, 34) described for the Early Bronze Age. The Early Iron Age, however, is further complicated by a mythohistorical record that records migration events of Dorians, Ionians, and Aeolians, all of which have little or no material signature but which nevertheless factored significantly into later Greek practices of identity formation. They must therefore be examined alongside real proxies for long-distance interaction and mobility both within the Aegean and in the wider Mediterranean, which, during this period, becomes a coherent entity for the very first time. That is to say, this is the first time in the history of the Mediterranean basin that some of its inhabitants—namely Tyrian "Phoenicians" reaching Gibraltar—had a panoptic, itinerant conception of the sea as a whole in addition to connections between particular places that were sustained over generations. Even if archaeological and historical sources seem not to agree on what happened or how, one thing is clear: the more we learn about this period, the more we see people on the move, not only in Greece but also all around it (see, e.g., Molloy 2016; Kotsonas and Mokrišová 2020).

Sherratt and Sherratt (1993, 361–63) list a number of major developments that differentiate the first millennium from the second in the eastern Mediterranean: mercantile city-states replaced palace-states; iron production undercut centralized economies that flourished previously by controlling bronze making; new forms of political power came from economic shifts; tensions grew between agrarian and commercial interests; trading stations arose outside the "urban" world of the eastern Mediterranean; notions of political boundaries changed in response to the growth of sea trade; the spread of literacy highlighted ethnic differences; slave trade grew in volume and extent; demand for precious metals as economic currency increased. All these factors had major impacts on the Mediterranean interaction zone, of which the regions of central Greece were a part. Two specific cases deserve further explication: the Phoenician westward expansion and Euboean activities in the eastern Mediterranean. The Euboean Gulf served variously as a destination, a conduit, and a base for both. We should also consider why other parts of Greece seem to have been left out of this picture. I focus first on the tangible evidence of growing overseas interests between Phoenicians and Greeks, especially Euboeans. I then turn to a problematic literary record that may provide some vague context—but no clear answers—concerning larger developments in Greece and the Mediterranean world.

Phoenicians Sailing West

Sailors from Levantine city-states (collectively termed "Phoenicians") were the most active drivers in the nascent process of Mediterraneanization, though they are often overlooked in discussions of later "Greek" colonization.[14] An expansion westward began in the late second millennium BCE; the most important developments occurred in the early first millennium, initially preceding Greek expansions, and then took place later in both cooperation and competition. Metals were almost certainly a prime mover. Nearly all areas of early Phoenician interest (in Iberia, Sardinia, Etruria, the northern Aegean, and Cyprus) are rich in metals. The Phoenicians appear to have pursued a strategy of using key places to plug into developing networks that were already heavily involved in metal production and trade (map 23). So, while the Phoenician involvement in these regions had important antecedents in the Bronze Age, and while the Phoenicians made use of preexisting trade routes (Niemeyer 2006, 148), their ability to access local networks brought the pursuit of these commodities to a new level. This quest for metals—and the quest's arrival in Iberia—are recorded in the Greenland ice cores in the form of a noticeable spike in atmospheric lead pollution, which is linked to silver production dated to around 800 BCE (McConnell et al. 2018, 5729, fig. 3). This marker was preceded by the establishment of permanent settlements and mining operations in the western Mediterranean.

While metals may be considered a prime mover in a broad sense, there are, of course, other relevant factors, not least in the Phoenician homeland. The city-states of the Levantine coast arose in the wake of the troubled palace-states at the end of the Bronze Age (Ugarit, Alalakh, Hatti, and Egypt). Byblos and Sidon seem to emerge as the top contenders in the middle of the eleventh century, since they appear in the *Tale of Wenamun*, where Byblos is described as the primary exporter of cedar and Sidon is another destination of interest.[15] The city of Tyre seems to experience a meteoric rise in the early tenth century, initially as a dependent and then as a partner of Sidon, over which it would eventually assert hegemonic status (Aubet 2001, 31).

While Phoenician interest in the wider Mediterranean predates Tyrian preeminence, the floruit of westward expansion began in the tenth century. This outgrowth was possibly related to the establishment of Tyrian control over the large

---

14. "Phoenicians" (Φοίνικες) is a general term applied by various Greek authors to the peoples living along the northern Levantine coast, although this is not what they called themselves. Their name for themselves seems to have been closer to the biblical Canaanites, although their identity seems much more tied to particular city-states than any broader regional notion of ethnicity. See Aubet (2001, 6–13) for a discussion of terminology and etymology, and Papadopoulos (1997, 2011) for the Phoenicians' underrepresentation in discussions of Greek colonization. For more recent bibliography on the Phoenicians, see Bondì et al. 2009; Pappa 2013; Elayi 2018; Quinn 2018; López-Ruiz and Doak 2019.

15. But see Sass (2002) for other possible dates for the *Tale of Wenamun* (1075–925 BCE).

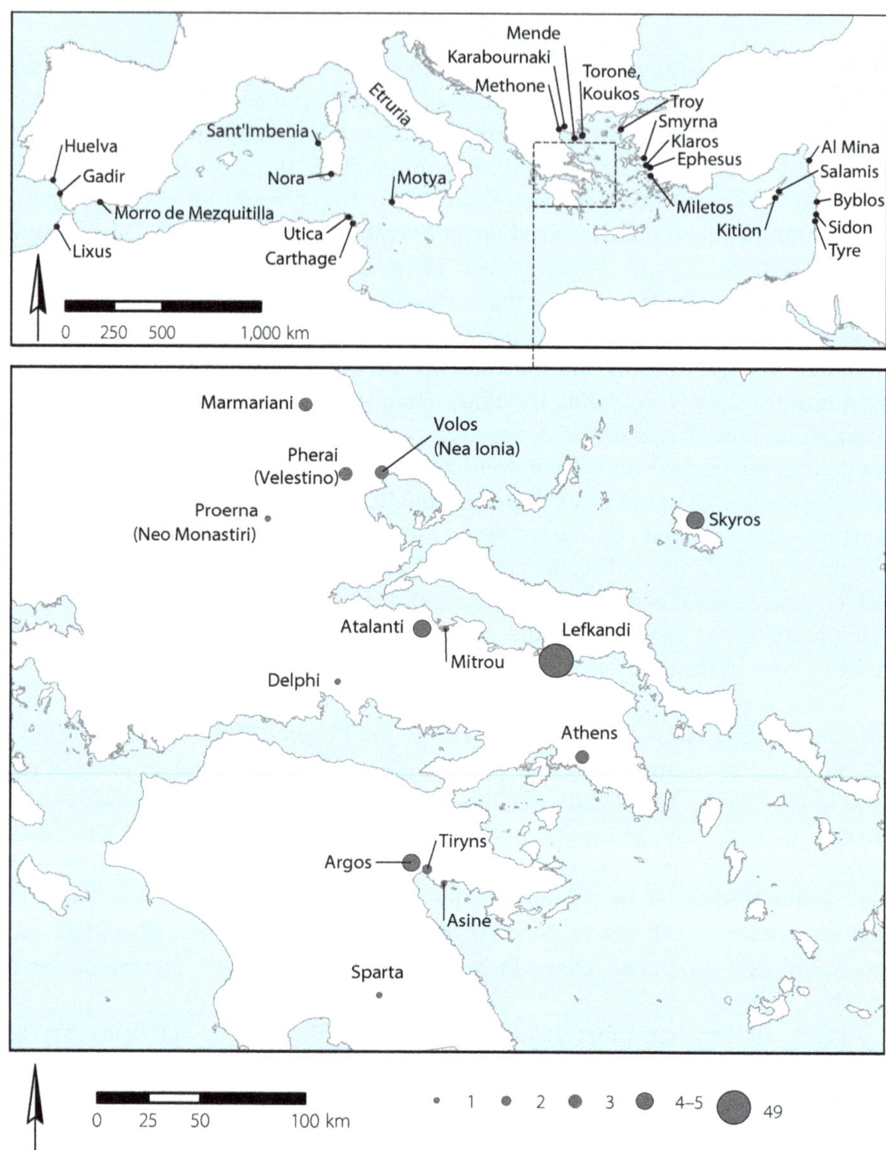

MAP 23. Sites mentioned in the text with evidence for long-distance interaction (top) and PG–MG imports in the Aegean (bottom) (import data from Murray 2013, 434–35; 2017, 102–11, table 2.5).

amounts of land that once belonged to other cities, such as Sidon. The presence of a nearby—but distributed—hinterland perhaps would have led the state to turn its attention elsewhere—in all likelihood to places that had long gripped the attention of enterprising merchants. Moreover, a general feature of increasing social complexity—one also seen in the Mycenaean Palatial period—seems to be an increased demand for commodities, whether in the form of raw materials (in this case metals) or foreign exotica. In the Tyrian case, where the economy seems to have been more commercially oriented than palace-driven, metals were pursued as the most flexible and valuable commodities available until their later (seventh century BCE) adaptation as coinage. From the tenth century BCE onward, we can see a Tyrian commercial expansion into the western Mediterranean, as well as at Kition and Salamis on Cyprus and in the Aegean—most notably at the precocious communities of Lefkandi and Athens (Negbi 1992). The so-called warrior-trader from Tomb 79 of the Toumba cemetery at Lefkandi was a contemporary of this expansion and may himself have been a Phoenician trader (Popham and Lemos 1995; Papadopoulos 2009, 115).

The earliest Phoenician settlements in the western Mediterranean are dated by historical sources to the twelfth century BCE (Aubet 2001, 161–63). These are Gadir, Lixus, and Utica (see map 23). However, the earliest archaeological evidence is not until much later. Until recently, there was no solid archaeological evidence for Phoenicians in the western Mediterranean before the eighth century (van Dommelen 1998, 70; 2005, 118). Recent work at Huelva, however, has revealed Phoenician material in southwestern Iberia dating to the ninth century; this has been interpreted as indicating "precolonial" activities (González de Canales, Serrano, and Llompart 2006; Nijboer and van der Plicht 2006). It is very likely that Phoenician traders were involved in other locations in the west as well; if so, this involvement would predate the foundations of permanent settlements at places like Morro de Mezquitilla, which may also go back to the ninth century BCE (Arnold and Marzoli 2009). In the central Mediterranean, the earliest dates come from Carthage—which has settlement remains from the late ninth and early eighth centuries—where there is also Euboean material, especially from the tophet (Docter et al. 2008).

In Sardinia, the Nora Stone has long been cited as the earliest Phoenician inscription on the island. It is dated to the ninth century BCE based on letter forms, though its lack of context makes this date somewhat problematic (van Dommelen 1998, 72). More interesting and reliable are the finds from Sant'Imbenia, which has Phoenician and Greek pottery, including a Euboean skyphos, from the late ninth century (Oggiano 2000). On the other hand, sites from which we would expect a similar date, such as Motya in Sicily, do not have clear evidence of Phoenician occupation until the end of the eighth century BCE. This Phoenician expansion coincides with the onset of the MG period in Greece, and it is noteworthy that when Greek material appears in the western Mediterranean contexts mentioned above, it seems to have arrived alongside Phoenician goods, and most likely through Phoenician agency (Kourou 2017). Only later did Greek sailors take a more active role in such enterprises.

So what drove these early Levantine interests in the west? In the ninth century BCE, trading expeditions clearly intensified, probably because of changing relations within the Levant. During the reign of the Assyrian king, Assurnasirpal

II (883–859 BCE), tribute payments were recorded as coming from Phoenician city-states; this may have fueled Tyrian interests in metals even further (Niemeyer 2000, 103; Aubet 2001, 88–95). Such demands for tribute became even more frequent in the eighth and seventh centuries, by which time permanent settlements had been established throughout the Mediterranean.

The Phoenician expansion westward was a complex process (Aubet 2001; van Dommelen 2005; Bondì et al. 2009). Long before permanent settlements were founded, Phoenician traders had inserted themselves in local and regional networks throughout the Mediterranean world, from Huelva and Gadir, west of Gibraltar, to Mesopotamia. This is also apparent in the fact that nearly all the sites with early archaeological evidence for Phoenician occupation are very much "mixed" in terms of the origins of material culture present. In the west, Huelva contains not only Phoenician but also Nuragic material from Sardinia. On Sardinia, Sant'Imbenia represents an indigenous Nuragic context, into which Phoenician and Greek material was introduced. There is a similar mingling of cultural elements in the earliest levels at Carthage.

The northern Aegean, too, was of interest from an early date, probably based on the rich metal sources of the Chalkidike and Pangaion. Later (eighth century) evidence in the form of Phoenician pottery comes from Methone (Kotsonas 2012, 238; Papadopoulos 2016b, 1246, fig. 7; Kasseri 2012), as well as Karabournaki (Tiverios 2004, 297), and Torone (Fletcher 2008). The delta of the Haliakmon River seems to have been a crucial node for multiple goods, since this part of Pieria is notably rich in both metals and timber, and the river itself is navigable for a great distance inland. Indeed, the more we learn about Methone, an Eretrian colony, the more significant it appears to have been in a network involving Euboea, Athens, various parts of western Anatolia, and Phoenicia (see most recently Morris et al. 2020).

Central Greece, the Northern Aegean, and the Eastern Mediterranean

From the evidence of imports, settlements in central Greece, especially those on or around the Euboean Gulf, seem to have been the largest draws of long-distance interaction in the Early Iron Age—most notably at Lefkandi and later Eretria (see map 23). Kourou (2015) describes four stages in the development of contacts between the Greek world and the eastern Mediterranean in the Early Iron Age:

1. There is a Protogeometric prelude in which a few objects may indicate limited or incidental contact, either with Cyprus or the Levant, limited to the EPG period.
2. There follows a first stage of regular contacts, characterized by LPG–EG imports at Lefkandi (Kourou also includes the MPG Toumba building burials in this phase). Atalanti, Marmariani, Volos (Nea Ionia), Velestino (Pherai), and Skyros have modest numbers of finds, while several other sites in central Greece have some as well (Neo Monastiri/Proerna, Mitrou, Delphi). Finds elsewhere are

limited to Tiryns, Argos, and Asine in the Argolid. There is a notable paucity of material from Athens and Attica. Crete, on the other hand, has a wealth of imports throughout these periods.

3. A second stage of regular contacts is characterized by proto-orientalizing metalwork in Attica. There is still an abundance of finds from Lefkandi, but this is now complemented by an influx of metalwork, especially filigree, granulation, and cloisonné in Athens and on the east coast of Attica. This phase begins in the Prehistoric Iron Age that is the subject of this chapter and blends into the Protohistoric Iron Age that follows.

4. A third stage of regular contacts is distinguished by the wealth of LG offerings (*athyrmata*) in sanctuaries (see chapter 6).

Several sites in the northern Aegean indicate connections with central Greece (especially Euboea) from a very early date (Tiverios 2008, 1–17). Views of Euboean prominence in colonization movements, both in the northern Aegean and in the central Mediterranean, have been challenged by Papadopoulos (1996b, 1997, 2011), who urges caution and points out the literary bias of arguments concerning the historicity of early Euboean activity abroad. Nevertheless, this should not be taken as a complete rejection of Euboeans playing a significant role outside their island, and increasing evidence, not least the archaeometric studies of Euboean ceramics discussed above, allows a more accurate reconstruction of the context and character of Euboean activities (Tiverios 2008, 12; Mommsen 2014; Charalambidou 2017).

In Euboea itself, Lefkandi is clearly the dominant site in long-distance trade networks. It was not simply the biggest consumer of foreign goods in the Aegean; it was clearly a *destination* for trade networks involving Cyprus, the Levant, and the northern Aegean. This trade network involved (at least in part) Euboean ceramics and metals from the Chalkidike. Certain individuals from Lefkandi seem to have been central to this trade, since nearly all tombs with Near Eastern imports also contained northern Aegean grave goods (Lemos 2001, 217; Leone 2015, 229; Charalambidou 2017, 87).

Numerous sites in the Chalkidike have significant quantities of Euboean pottery present. At Torone, an Early Iron Age cemetery has been excavated, revealing high numbers of imported Attic and Euboean PG pottery, in addition to apparently local imitations (Papadopoulos 2005a). Mende and Koukos extend this picture, as do recent finds at Methone, though the most significant of these are Late Geometric, corresponding with its establishment as a colony of Eretria (Kotsonas 2015; Morris et al. 2020). In this earlier period, the overall picture of people from Attica and Euboea in the north is not suggestive of colonization, but it certainly is of trade. In the earlier Prehistoric Iron Age, Attic ceramics appear in greater numbers, although eventually these give way to Euboean Subprotogeometric types, reflecting an intensification of Euboean (at this stage Lefkandiot) interests (Papadopoulos 2005a, 579–80).

The breadth of Euboean interests and activities is also reflected in the wide (if not dense) dispersal of Euboean pottery in Cypriot and Levantine contexts (Kourou 2017, 27–30; Murray 2017, 194–208, map 4.1). This has led to discussions of "precolonization" (Popham 1994), particularly involving pottery from Al Mina (Boardman 1959, 1990; Popham 1983). While several Al Mina vessels are now demonstrably of Euboean origin (Mommsen 2014), the quantification of pottery from Al Mina and other Levantine sites where Greek pottery has been found does not suggest that there was a permanent Greek population in these areas (Papadopoulos 1997, 196, table 1). It does, however, reflect participation in a network of exchange that links the production centers of the pottery to its find spot. At the very least, Al Mina was a port of trade and hub of interaction between the Aegean and the Levant (Luke 2003).

The larger distribution of Protogeometric pottery outside the central Greek heartland is somewhat problematic. Most recently, Murray (2017, 191, table 4.4) has quantified the distribution of Greek pottery in the central and eastern Mediterranean: there is a peak in LH IIIB (248 sites, ca. 9600 sherds), followed by a decline in LH IIIC (108 sites, ca. 3700 sherds), a very sharp drop in the Protogeometric period (9 sites, ca. 100 sherds), and some recovery in the Geometric period (96 sites, ca. 2350 sherds). These numbers do not, however, account for the large amount of Protogeometric pottery from western Anatolia, where some 25 additional sites (at least) have pottery from this date (Lemos 2002, 210–12; Vaessen 2015). Particularly significant were Miletos, Smyrna, Ephesos, and Klaros in Ionia, as well as Troy and several sites in the east Aegean islands. Lemos (2007) argued that quantities were quite small, though in years since it has been revealed that PG pottery dominates the total assemblage of several of these sites, in contrast to lower numbers in the Mycenaean period (Vaessen 2014). It is now clear that a Protogeometric nadir was not as extreme as previously thought. An actual quantification of Protogeometric pottery in western Anatolia would make the picture of Early Iron Age trade and production networks in the eastern Mediterranean look quite different.

At some point, at the beginning of the Middle Geometric period, Athens entered the scene, as evidenced in the growing presence of imports in wealthy tombs. There was also a change in emphasis from Cypriot imports to Phoenician. In PG and EG times, the rare imports found in Attic tombs were usually Cypriot bronze bowls (Blegen 1952; Korou 2015, 220). Cypriot artifacts diminished in the MG period, superseded by various Near Eastern objects such as faience and glass scarabs and beads—for example, in the tomb of the Rich Athenian Lady, in Kerameikos 42, and in Dipylon 13; Marathon, Anavysos, and Merenda also appear to have been major centers with ties to the Levant but not to Cyprus (Korou 2015, 220).

The overall pattern seems to be that Lefkandi was the dominant hub for long-distance trade in the Aegean during the earliest period of the Iron Age, probably building on its prosperity in the Postpalatial Bronze Age and its status as a booming center for pottery production. Its geographic centrality was also significant, connected as it was throughout the Euboean Gulf—the best route connecting the northern and southern Aegean. These historical and geographical circumstances made it a destination for traders from both the eastern Mediterranean and the north. At the same time, Athens was a flourishing settlement, active also in wider maritime spheres, initially through its innovations in ceramic production. Eventually it attracted the attention of Phoenician traders, perhaps through its assumption of control over the metal resources of the Lavriotiki, signaling another articulation of local, regional, and interregional modes of interaction. The onset of the MG period may represent the first time Athens itself assumes control of this part of eastern Attica, which may also be reflected in the metallurgical innovations that take place in Athens at this time, when new, Near Eastern techniques arrived in goldwork, along with metalworkers interested in the silver resources of Lavrio.

Literary Phantoms or Historical Migrations?

Migration plays a major role in both ancient and modern narratives concerning early Greece. Herodotus, Thucydides, and other ancient authors put certain migratory events—the Dorian, Aeolian, and Ionian migrations in modern parlance—between the "age of heroes" and the beginning of history with the first Olympiad (776 BCE) (Vanschoonwinkel 2006; Osborne 2009, 47–51). These population movements were used by ancient authors to explain the distribution of the three principal dialect groups of the ancient Greek language—Dorian, Ionic, and Aeolic—and are therefore usually in the domain of historians or historical linguists. Such themes are only rarely treated by archaeologists, not least because there is little archaeological evidence to support claims of large-scale migration, leading some to describe these and other migratory groups as "literary phantoms" (Papadopoulos 1997; see also Hall 1997; Mac Sweeney 2017; Kotsonas and Mokrišová 2020). Nonetheless, mobility and migration clearly form a part of Greek historical consciousness, which may also have extended back into pre- and protohistory.

The concept of the Dorian invasion can be traced to Herodotus (1.56–58), who discusses a group of people "coming down" into the Peloponnese as responsible for the Dorian dialect. Historians of the nineteenth and early twentieth century called this the Dorian invasion, suggesting that linguistic change followed a violent influx of new people who were also responsible for the collapse of Mycenaean civilization (e.g., Müller 1824; Casson 1921). One of the problems with this argument is that it is based on a text that does not actually describe what modern historians have often debated. Herodotus talks about the movement of people and dialects, but he says nothing about population replacement, violent conflict, or sociopolitical change. He discusses the "coming down of the Heraklidai" (the descendants of Herakles), which has been interpreted to mean the migration from the north of new groups of people who brought with them a new type of material culture. As Hall argues

(1997, 4–16), this narrative tells us more about nineteenth-century conceptions of culture change, positivist history, and ethnicity than about historical realities. Archaeological evidence demonstrates traceable continuities throughout the Late Bronze Age to Early Iron Age transition. No changes in material culture suggest population replacement. While some migratory events may well have taken place in what was certainly a highly mobile world, they can hardly be characterized as a singular or uniform process. On the linguistic side of things, the fact that Linear B records Mycenaean Greek clearly demonstrates continuity from the Late Bronze Age to the Early Iron Age. There cannot, therefore, have been a Dorian "coming of the Greeks." It is noteworthy also that most arguments concerning a Dorian invasion were developed before the decipherment of Linear B in 1952.

The tradition of the Aeolian migration holds that colonists traveled from Thessaly, Boeotia, Achaia, or some combination of these to the northeast Aegean, where they established settlements beginning some 60 years after the Trojan War and four generations earlier than the Ionian migration (see Rose 2008, who refers especially to Strabo 9.2, 13.1–3). This is linked, as are the other migration narratives, to the regions in which one of the three main dialects appears in later times—in this case, a northeast Aegean homeland. Bronze Age interactions between Aegean and Anatolian populations are evident both archaeologically, in the form of trade goods, and in Hittite diplomatic texts describing the kingdom of Arzawa (of which Troy/Wilusa was a vassal). By the tenth century, a trading network was in place involving Troy, Thessaly, and Lokris, which is linked to Troy in the tradition of the Lokrian maidens, women who were sent annually from Lokris to Troy as compensation for Ajax's rape of Kassandra. Rose (2008, 420–21) argues that there would have been centuries of interaction in the northeast Aegean, with a changing cultural blend of Luwian, Phrygian, Lydian, and Greek, but there is no one region or agent responsible for a single migration event.

The Ionian migration has been the subject of much recent scholarship, not least owing to an interest in explaining the origins of some of the more significant cities of the ancient Greek world in western Anatolia (Papadopoulos 2005a, 580–88; Vaessen 2015; Mac Sweeney 2016, 2017). The traditional narrative is that the Dorians destroyed the Mycenaean palaces; then refugees fled to Attica and, after some 60 years, to Ionia in an event called the Ionian migration:

> The most powerful victims of war or faction from the rest of Hellas took refuge with the Athenians as a safe retreat; and at an early period, becoming naturalized, swelled the already large population of the city to such a height that Attica became at last too small to hold them, and they had to send out colonies to Ionia. (Thucydides 1.2.6; see also Cook 1962).

Historians and archaeologists have tried to place this event chronologically in either the Postpalatial Bronze Age or the Prehistoric Iron Age, based mostly on literary sources. This chronology also depends on how one wants to date a mytho-historical Trojan War. Archaeological evidence for such a population movement is controversial, however. Protogeometric ceramics are found at some 25 sites scattered throughout western Anatolia. This led Lemos (2007) to suggest an earlier migration in the wake of the Mycenaean palatial destructions. We now know that the evidence for Greek pottery in Anatolia is in fact much more abundant in the PG period (Vaessen 2014). In turn, the archaeological evidence of Attica is more widespread in the Postpalatial Bronze Age, although this is followed by apparent growth and expansion at Athens in the Prehistoric Iron Age. Essentially, either period might be shoehorned into this migration hypothesis based on the archaeological evidence, which signals more activity in western Anatolia and less in Attica during the PG period than in the previous LH IIIC. Others (e.g., Crielaard 2009) reject the idea of an Ionian migration altogether, pointing to evidence of Mycenaean involvement in the region as early as the Palatial period (see also Vaessen 2015, 814–18). A recent assessment of archaeological and literary evidence as a whole concludes (1) that there is evidence for long-term Greek involvement in the region from Mycenaean times onward (perhaps even earlier, given the clear Minoan material at Miletos); (2) that the Early Iron Age evidence is not consistent with a sudden influx of people; and (3) that migration stories in antiquity came out of political needs to construct a shared identity, linked to Ionian and Athenian political interests (Mac Sweeney 2017, 412–15).

One feature of all these migration events is an emphasis on ancestry and founder heroes as a means to establish shared identity within a regional landscape. Several scholars have demonstrated that these are tied to the deliberate construction of ethnic identities that can be linked to various political agendas, and that they developed over time (Hall 1997; Malkin 1998, 2011; Rose 2008; Mac Sweeney 2017). The archaeological evidence in each case does not support a sudden influx or replacement of population, but it does support a large amount of long-distance interaction, probably involving multiple ethnic groups, that was sustained over a long period of time. While there is no specific "kernel" in any of these migration narratives, they probably do reflect general attitudes toward the mobility of people, both at the times in which the narratives were developing and in earlier periods as well. Linguistic evidence suggests that by the appearance of the alphabet in the eighth century, these dialect zones were already developed, and may even be traceable to the Mycenaean period (Janko 2018). However this may be, any distinct dialects that appear in the textual-historical record must have evolved in the linguistically murky waters of the preceding centuries, with roots in long-standing interaction processes going back at least to the Mycenaean period.

CONCLUSIONS: PATTERN AND VARIATION,
DEVELOPMENT VERSUS DECLINE

Variability appears to be the rule during the Early Iron Age. This obtains in regional settlement patterns, in the mortuary record, in social organization, and in terms of relationships with the wider world. While I have highlighted the main centers of dynamic activity, it must be kept in mind that places like Athens and Lefkandi represent exceptional—though certainly influential—cases, not unlike the palaces of the Palatial Bronze Age. The vast majority of sites dating to the Protogeometric and earlier Geometric periods lack evidence for overseas contact, long-distance exchange, or high levels of social complexity.

Such circumstances need not be seen in a negative light. Indeed, "lower" levels of social complexity generally signal lower levels of inequality, which is probably better viewed as a positive aspect of society. At the same time, certain technologies and innovations were nonetheless on the move, along with other cultural elements that are not detectable in the archaeological record—a developing oral tradition, religious practices dispersed across regional scales, and cycles of agricultural production and consumption. This, indeed, resembles the Iron Age of Hesiod, in which most people lived as subsistence farmers and shepherds: "mere bellies" (*Theogony*, 26). While Hesiod had a negative view of his own time, this must be seen as literary nostalgia rather than as some guide to work back from in terms of social or archaeological history. In spite of the mostly local and small-scale operations of Early Iron Age society, there were certain people and groups—craftspeople, traders, pirates, innovators—who traveled far and frequently. We see traces of them in the pottery styles and metal technologies that they dispersed across central Greece and the wider Mediterranean. So, while there are some aspects of the archaeological record that can be characterized in terms of decline, there is much more to the story, especially elements that are traceable through technology and other ephemeral evidence for interconnection. These processes in the Early Iron Age are not unlike what Renfrew (1972) described for the Early Bronze Age in his *Emergence of Civilisation*. Just as the Early Bronze Age Cyclades were part of a much wider eastern Mediterranean interaction sphere, so too was central Greece part of a much wider set of social, technological, and material networks in the Early Iron Age.

In spite of its (now dated) "Dark Age" moniker in Greece, the Early Iron Age is in fact the first period in which the entire Mediterranean comes together, in the sense that certain groups (Phoenicians) are involved in interactions across its entire extent. This is not to say that there were sudden transformations of notions of identity across the entire basin, but this was the first time that some individuals plying its shores could have reasonably conceived of it as a geographical whole, one spanning the Levantine coast to the Strait of Gibraltar.

The Prehistoric Iron Age is one of the more challenging periods to deal with in this book. For one thing, it is the longest, lasting some 250 years (see table 1). For another, it is the most variable, both among the regions of central Greece and in the wider Mediterranean world. What is more, it is difficult to distinguish clear *societal* transitions from the previous Postpalatial Bronze Age, even though the *material-technological* distinctions are quite obvious.

The sum of the evidence reveals a richly varied landscape across the early Greek world. Central Greece is crucial as certain hubs emerge at Athens and Lefkandi, dialogues with the past evolve in Thessaly, Malis, and Phokis, and a reorganization of settlement takes place in Boeotia. The Euboean Gulf shows how a route-based conception of connective geography supersedes a proximal one when we consider the means by which connections were made within the Aegean between north and south. Phoenician, Euboean, and Athenian traders were involved in networks that spanned distances far beyond the Aegean interaction spheres that transmitted stylistic preferences and technological knowledge. As in other periods, access to these networks was restricted to certain members of society and used very deliberately in the creation of difference and to make and maintain social inequality on a local level. In this way, networks were consolidated conceptually, even as they were expanding geographically. These multiscalar dynamics ushered in significant social change in the village communities of central Greece, as some grew in size and complexity, while others became retracted, small-scale, and localized. Such developments laid the foundations for the even greater social changes that would follow in the eighth century and after, when the few hubs of Mediterranean interaction in central Greece would expand into much more intense and widespread networks that would characterize the rest of early Greek history.

6

Expanding Horizons in the Protohistoric Iron Age

Then the gleaming-eyed goddess Athena said to him: "I will tell you these things truly: I am Mentes, son of wise Anchialos, and I rule over the oar-loving Taphians. I just now came down with ship and crew, sailing on the wine-dark sea to strange-talking men, to Temesa for copper. And I bring shining iron. My ship is put up in a field away from the city, in the harbor Rheithron, under woody Neion."

—HOMER, *ODYSSEY* 1.179–85

In Homer, space and time come together to create imaginary places, many of which are nevertheless rooted in real locations, experiences, and cultural memory. By referring to far-flung peoples and locales, and by stitching them together in the course of a narrative, Homer illustrates a highly connected Mediterranean world—or at least one that is acutely aware of its own diversity. In the passage above, Athena, speaking to Telemachos on Ithaca, poses as Mentes, who hails from the nearby island of Taphos. She also refers to Temesa, which scholars usually locate in southwestern Italy, as a destination both familiar and foreign, and of interest for the metals trade (Papadopoulos 2001, 447).[1] We are presented with information about the local topography, which "Mentes" knows. We are made aware of commodities, of strange languages, of short anchorages in unfamiliar places. Homer (especially in the *Odyssey*) is full of passages like this, which collapse geographical scales, multimaterial transactions, and intercultural relations into a single narrative moment that is meant to awe the listener with the vastness of the world and the capacity of characters to act within it. While this scene is part of an epic narrative, it has roots in a complex reality of increasingly contracted

---

1. An alternative location is sometimes given as Tamassos in Cyprus (Strabo, *Geography* 6.1.5). Either way, notions of significant distance obtain, though the westward orientation of much of the *Odyssey* (and indeed Ithaca itself) makes an Italian location more likely. On the geographic imagination in the *Odyssey*, see also Purves 2010, 16.

geographical and cultural distances, along with dramatic social intensification across the Mediterranean.

Snodgrass ([1971] 2000, 416) pointed out long ago that "the changes which came over the Aegean in the eighth century are so profuse that it is hard to enumerate them in any logical order." This is reinforced by the relatively tight span of time in which many of the major developments seem to have happened. Beginning in the eighth century—in ceramic terms, in the Middle Geometric II period (see table 1)—the pace of social change in the Aegean rose dramatically, escalating especially around 750 BCE in the transition to the Late Geometric (LG) period. Some of the most profound changes were technological, which can be seen in the form of a media revolution of images and text that spread rapidly through the Mediterranean. With the presence of contemporary texts in Greece, we reenter a period of protohistory—that is, one containing an indigenous textual and literary record, but without the specific goal of constructing a narrative of past events for informational purposes.[2]

The rapidity of development has led to characterizations of an eighth-century "renaissance" or "revolution" (Hägg 1983; Snodgrass [1971] 2000, 1980; Coldstream [1977] 2003; Morris 2009). Neither term, however, actually tells us much about the developments that took place among the communities of early Greece or about how those developments relate to their wider Mediterranean context. These designations also miss the crucial point that the biggest sociopolitical changes do not seem to have come until the seventh century, when we see a transition from early Greek villages representing a variety of more and less complex communities to widespread Archaic and Classical city-states (poleis).

Teleological views of the *state*, the *polis*, and *urbanism* have so dominated our narratives of social complexity that considerable effort is required to look at state formation as an iterative social process. When we consider the time periods under study in this book, what happened during the Geometric period in Greece had perhaps the most lasting effect of any of these eras but it is nevertheless rarely discussed in comparative terms. Moreover, rather than seeing the singular emergence of civilization or a state as an identifiable moment or process, we should broaden our perspective to allow for multiple emergences of complex social forms. This is borne out in the variety of modes of social organization seen in Archaic and Classical poleis, which we cannot really justify identifying until at least ca. 650 BCE (Hansen and Nielsen 2004). Other forms of social organization, such as *ethne*, were present alongside poleis, although they have received far less scholarly attention (but see, e.g., McInerney 1999; Morgan 2001, 2003, 2006; Papadopoulos 2016a).

This chapter begins by examining settlement shifts and regional networks in central Greece, which had extensive implications for territory, mobility, and social

---

2. This terminological distinction between "prehistory" and "protohistory" broadly follows the model of Knapp (2008). See further in the conclusions of this book, pp. 252–56.

reorganization. Next, I turn to more revolutionary subjects: the invention of the Greek alphabet and a resurgence of figural art. I argue that these shifts in media—or modes of signification and of encountering the world—served to condense networks conceptually, even as they expanded geographically. I argue also that these developments can be viewed in terms of technology transfer, as can the modes of craft production analyzed in previous chapters. Turning to the wider Mediterranean context, we see that this is the first period in which Greek permanent settlements emerge as "frogs around a pond" (Plato, *Phaedo* 109b). The various regions of central Greece played a crucial role in this emergence. Central Euboea was especially outward looking, continuing in the outsized role it played through the Postpalatial Bronze Age and the Early Iron Age. Nevertheless, the relative preeminence of the Euboeans soon waned, in many ways obviated by the very networks they themselves had managed to create. With the emergence of identifiably "Greek" notions of identity, the centrality of the Euboean Gulf in Mediterranean networks was diminished not long after reaching its apex in the eighth century.[3] Finally, I look ahead to the seventh- and sixth-century period of state/polis formation, bookending the examination of Mycenaean state formation at the beginning of chapter 3.

CROWDING THE LANDSCAPE: SETTLEMENT INTENSIFICATION AND REGIONAL DYNAMICS

Three crucial developments took place in the central Greek landscape during the eighth century BCE. First, even though it continued to exhibit marked regional variability, the settlement pattern changed significantly. Second, settlement shifts in certain areas, specifically in central Euboea, shed light on wider Mediterranean dynamics (founding settlements overseas) as well as local events (a semilegendary Lelantine war). Third, the sacred landscape was reconstituted, affecting local, regional, and eventually panhellenic ritual practices and notions of identity (de Polignac 1995).

Several interrelated trends in the settlement pattern set the eighth century apart from the preceding Prehistoric Iron Age. First, there is a sharp increase in the number of sites starting in MG II, which is followed by a dramatic surge in

3. See Malkin (2011) for a discussion of the role of networks and colonization in identity formation. As an exercise, any description of "Greek" identity will be somewhat fraught. Identity must be understood as a plural, mutable, and multiscalar concept (see also the discussion of nested scales of political and spatial units in chapter 1, figure 1). In this way, people can have local identities based on common daily practices or encounters with the landscape, or regional identities based on shared language, practices, etc. In referring to "Greek" identity, I mean that communities spread over very long distances shared aspects of culture, including language, religious practices, and mythohistorical traditions. This is not to obscure major differences between different groups but rather to say that notions of a "Greek" identity formed in the early first millennium BCE as interactions across the Mediterranean created a greater awareness of cultural differences. Around the same time, similarities were reinforced through the participation in common practices, such as regional and Panhellenic political and religious festivals, which were self-ascribed as exclusively Greek. See also Hall 1997, 2002; Jones 1997.

the Late Geometric period (map 24). The total number of sites in the study area rises from 152 in the Prehistoric Iron Age to 203 in the eighth century, representing a 33 percent increase. In parallel, the number of communities changes from 110 to 136, which is a 23 percent increase. The overall number of sites in the Greek mainland and Crete increases from 600 in the Protogeometric period to 948 in the Geometric period (a 58 percent increase), signaling a significant difference between central Greece and elsewhere in the earlier Iron Age and attributable, at least in part, to much lower site numbers in the Peloponnese during Protogeometric times (see table 5; see also Murray 2017, 141, table 3.12).[4]

While the pattern for central Greece (and the wider Greek world) is certainly one of growth, there is again considerable regional variation. Indeed, there is more regional discrepancy in this period than in any other (see figure 2). While Euboea and Phokis experienced marginal growth, East Lokris and Malis experienced a decline in the number of sites, and Thessaly had a significant drop—from 35 to 26. Meanwhile, Attica and Boeotia saw a veritable explosion of settlement. In Boeotia, the number of sites nearly doubled—from 24 to 47. In Attica, a similar trend can be observed, as site numbers increased from 21 to 55. Such a rapid expansion of settlement warrants explanation. Bintliff (1999) has discussed this trend in terms of competition for agricultural land and steady expansion, beginning in the Geometric period and culminating in the Classical period. He also notes the similarity between Attica and Boeotia and the ways in which Renfrew's (1975, 12–21) Early State Module can explain the rise of centers at Athens and Thebes: the growth of powerful centers within a region and the interaction between centers and the surrounding communities eventually led to increased integration (Bintliff 1999, 24–25). This also invokes peer-polity interaction, where connections between places intensify through a variety of forms of competition—as Snodgrass (1986) has shown in the case of early Greece.

In the nearest-neighbor model presented here, the expanding number of sites would have involved increased interaction between them, simply on account of their closer proximity (map 25). There seems to have been significant population growth as well; this observation is based on the numbers of sites and is supported by models of demographic growth leading up to the Classical period, from which we can ascertain better information (Murray 2017, 234).

On a regional level, the more frequent interfaces between more communities may have strengthened regional notions of common identity, on the one hand, and, on the other, made interaction over greater distances less necessary in order to make suitable marriages and exchange necessary goods. These factors would also have engendered the creation of hubs as central places where representatives from

---

4. A further note relevant to site numbers is that the Protogeometric period lasts only about 150 years, while the Geometric is at least 200 years—probably closer to 250 if it extends into the seventh century BCE. This difference in timescale may skew the data one way, which may be skewed the other way by considering—as here—a Prehistoric Iron Age of 250 years and a Protohistoric Iron Age of 150 to 200 years. More important, however, is the issue of regional and diachronic variation.

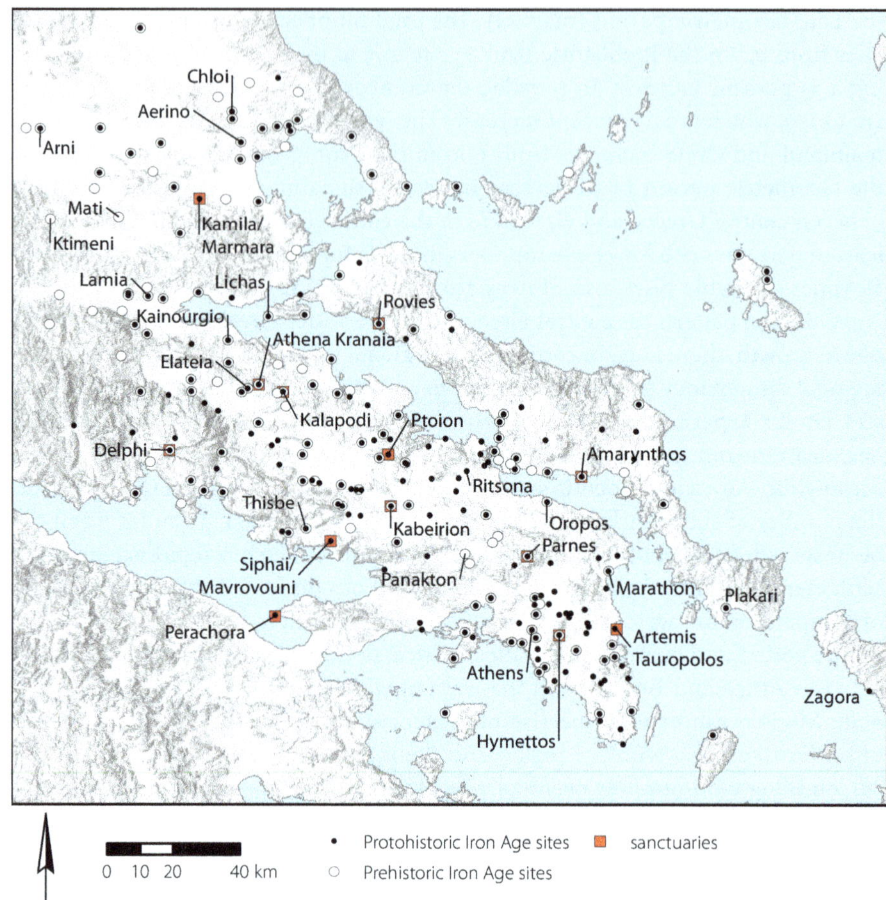

MAP 24. Protohistoric Iron Age site locations compared to the Prehistoric Iron Age, also show-ing select extra-urban sanctuary sites.

different communities could bring together goods and ideas. While centralization around major settlements, such as Thebes and Athens, was no doubt happening, this was very different from the type of political and economic centralization that occurred in palatial areas during Mycenaean times. It seems rather that different political formations were at play here, in a manner that is perhaps in line with Morris's (1987) "middling" effect, which caused a fissioning of the small-scale but still complex communities of the Postpalatial Bronze Age and Prehistoric Iron Age.[5] Small (2019, 126–29) also invokes fissioning in arguing that social differences on an individual scale (especially wealth differences) that are not recognized insti-tutionally would have created problems in Early Iron Age societies, and that, by the eighth century, these differences would have been driving certain communities

5. For a useful critique of Morris's "middling ideology," see Duplouy 2006.

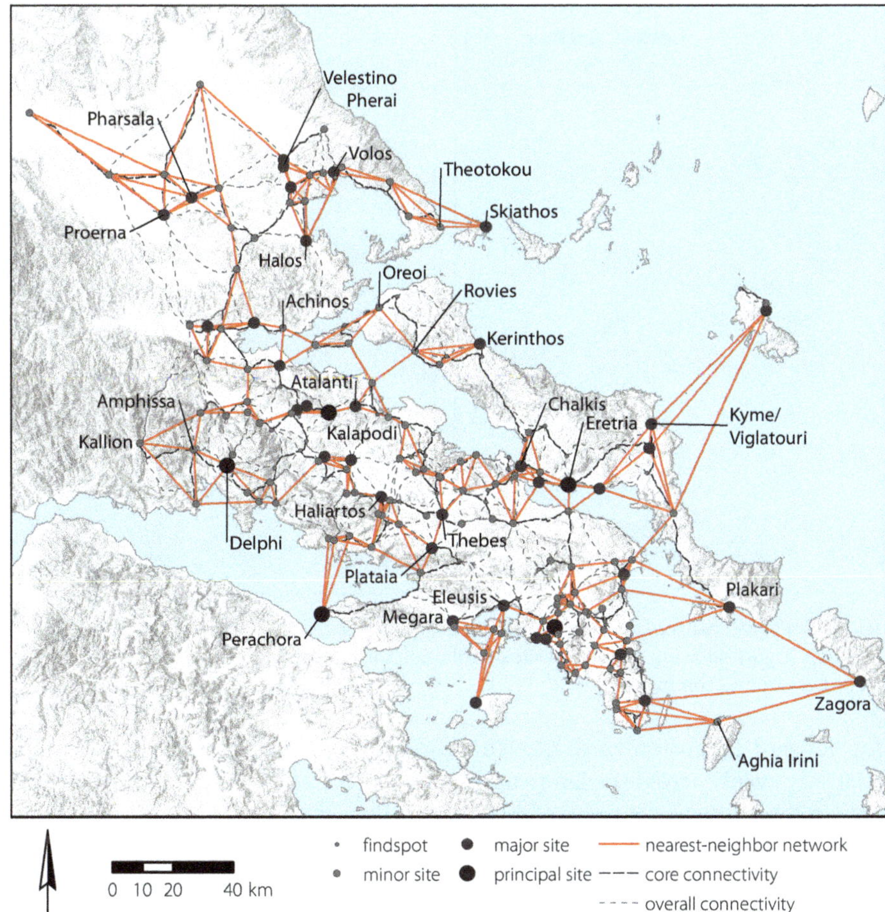

MAP 25. Protohistoric Iron Age sites, joined by a connectivity model, with a nearest-neighbor network of communities (see also map 24 and appendix for additional place names).

to break up. Such fission-fusion patterns of oscillation are documented also in the Pueblo societies of the pre-Hispanic American Southwest, in Mississippian chiefdoms, and in the formative period of the Titicaca basin, especially in response to scalar stress (McGuire and Saitta 1996; Blitz 1999; Bandy 2004). In the early Greek case, stressors such as population growth, a tightening of the settlement pattern, and growing inequality seem to have obtained in various parts of the landscape.

The close proximity of sites also would have influenced the ways in which territory was conceived. Taking notional site catchments of 2.5 kilometers around individual communities as a starting point (see chapter 2, p. 60), we can see that in the Prehistoric Iron Age there would have been little overlap of community territories in Boeotia and Attica, which suggests less competition for resources or stimulus

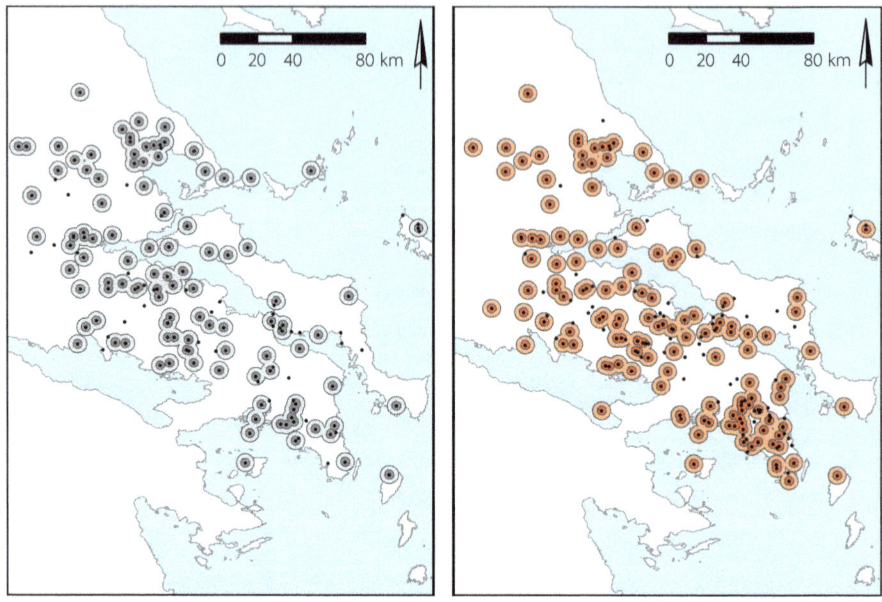

MAP 26. Parallel maps of site catchments in the Prehistoric Iron Age (left) and Protohistoric Iron Age (right), showing the overall site distribution for each period with 2.5- and five-kilometer buffers around communities.

for outward expansion (map 26, left). An influx of new settlement, distributed relatively evenly across the landscape, would have created much more overlap in potential catchments (map 26, right).

In reality, catchment territories would have varied based on site size, population, and the agricultural viability of the surrounding landscape, but a rough model across the study region as a whole nevertheless suggests that the communities of Boeotia and Attica would have interacted much more intensively in this period than in the previous one. It is also significant that central Euboea was already facing settlement pressure in the Prehistoric Iron Age, as were parts of Attica and the plain of Atalanti, which may help to explain their growth and outward-looking character in the Protohistoric Iron Age. Such proximity to each other and such potential for dispute over resource areas may also have historical implications, specifically in the case of a mythohistorical Lelantine war (see further below).

Convergence and Divergence in Settlement Networks

An immediate effect of the increased number of sites is that the average distance between sites and their nearest neighbors shrinks considerably (see map 25). While certain sites in the network model still have to cross long distances to reach their neighbors (e.g., Zagora, Kefala, Plakari), most—especially in Attica and Boeotia—have many more neighbors close by than they did in previous periods (compare maps 15, 19, and 25). The overall change in settlement networks would have had three principal effects:

1. Human interactions intensified across the entire landscape; this was in part responsible for the rapid social change at this time, as communities, craftspeople, and traders came into more intense competition and ideas became increasingly mobile.
2. The nexuses of interaction that formed in different parts of central Greece can be characterized as *small worlds*, insofar as their most frequent interactions occurred over short distances, but the network distances were quickly reduced through the introduction of only a few new links to join different small worlds. The settlement networks modeled here show interactions between neighbors, which must be viewed as frequent and habitual. In addition, *weak ties* linked together emergent centers, and regional and interregional land routes stitched together different landscapes
3. The regional networks that emerged within central Greece led to social intensification in new areas, which in some cases led to disengagement from others. This reorganization of interactions led to the reformulation of local and regional notions of identity, which was expressed through aspects of visual and material culture.

More particular patterns are apparent on a regional basis. Attica continued to flourish, as it had done in the Prehistoric Iron Age. The aforementioned increase in the number of sites led to a shift in the nearest-neighbor model, which now suggests some division between eastern Attica and the area of Athens, with Mount Hymettos acting as a divider. That said, the increasing importance of Athens as a hub and production center for Geometric pottery, along with the silver sources of the Lavriotiki, suggests that these areas were quite closely connected. The quadripartite regional interaction between southern Attica, Kea, Andros, and southern Euboea also continues to be significant, evidenced by the presence of Attic (and central Euboean) pottery at Aghia Irini, Zagora, and Plakari (Coldstream 2003, 209–11; Crielaard 2011a, 5; Crielaard and Songou 2017). Connectivity across this zone has important antecedents going back as far as the Neolithic and Early Bronze Age (Tankosić 2011; Cullen et al. 2013). The growth of Athens itself is known from the increased amount of Late Geometric pottery (nearly all unpublished) from the slopes of the acropolis and the number of Late Geometric tombs throughout the city (Papadopoulos 2003, 298–99; Papadopoulos and Smithson 2017; Dimitriadou 2019). Based on the rise in number of graves, Coldstream ([1977] 2003, 109) estimated that the population of Athens increased threefold in the eighth century. Morris (1987, 156–58), however, would attribute at least some of this change to burial practices becoming more democratic and less of a privilege of upper segments of society. The appearance of new sites in the vicinity of Athens should not come as a surprise either, and might be viewed in terms of the early development of demes.[6]

The relationship between Athens and the rest of Attica remains difficult to understand in this period, and it continues to be muddled by mythohistorical accounts of synoecism, territorial ambitions, and wars with Eleusis. These typify protohistory in that they have been dated variously to the "age of heroes" (Erechtheus and Theseus), usually associated with the Bronze Age in "real" time, or to the eighth century (Thucydides 2.15.2–3; van Gelder 1991; Morris 1992, 338–39; Lohmann 2010; Bohen 2017). While Athens was certainly the largest and most powerful settlement in Attica at this time, there is not yet any clear archaeological or historical indication of it exercising direct political control over the region. Nevertheless, this period may indeed have been when Athens finally achieved political dominance across Attica, since political integration is one possible response to settlement expansion and population growth—as seems to have been the case in Mycenaean Boeotia, for example. One thing that remains fairly clear in the material record is that Athens and western Attica—including Eleusis and Salamis—were in closer contact than Athens and eastern Attica.

The northern limits of Attica remain poorly understood in the Protohistoric Iron Age, with only a few sites documented: the cave of Pan and the sanctuary of Zeus on Mount Parnes and a few fragmentary finds at Dekeleia (Arvanitopoulou 1959; Mazarakis Ainian 1997, 315; Munn 1989, 240–42; Palaiokrassa-Kopitsa and Vivliodetis 2015). We should note also the sanctuary of Zeus on Mount Hymettos that occupies a liminal space between Athens and eastern Attica (Langdon 1976). This pattern may be the result of people desiring to be closer to emergent centers (such as Athens), rather than located in the relative isolation of a mountainous borderland. This trend is observed especially at Panakton, which boasts substantial remains from the early Mycenaean period, the Postpalatial period, and Protogeometric times, but has nothing from the Geometric period (Munn 1996). Recent intensive survey work in the Mazi Plain has revealed no evidence from any period of the Early Iron Age (Fachard, Knodell, and Banou 2015; Knodell, Fachard, and Papangeli 2016, 2017).

The settlement network of Boeotia changes substantially in the Protohistoric Iron Age (see map 25). Boeotia and Attica are hardly linked at all in the model generated here. They are entirely separated in the nearest-neighbor analysis. In the west, the connectivity model still signals important paths between Eleusis and Plataia. In the east, the connectivity model links Dekeleia and Oropos, although the true orientations of these sites seem to be elsewhere.

The site of Oropos, while sometimes included in Boeotia (Fossey 1988), was considered disputed territory in antiquity (Strabo 9.1.22), and it was often lumped

6. On the historical demes of Attica, see Traill 1975; Whitehead 1986. On their locations and potential territories, see Fachard 2016.

in with Attica by ancient geographers such as Pseudo-Skylax (Shipley 2010); some archaeological studies have done this as well (see, e.g., Cosmopoulos 2001). In this period, however, as in the previous one, Oropos demonstrates much closer connections to Euboea, as its nearest neighbors are Eretria and Amarynthos; this model is borne out by several aspects of the material record, including settlement organization, cult practices, and craft production (Mazarakis Ainian 2007a, 28; Mazarakis Ainian and Vlachou 2014; see also other essays in Mazarakis Ainian 2007b).

Northeastern Boeotia experienced a significant infilling of the settlement pattern after an apparent gap in the Prehistoric Iron Age. Drosia (Aghios Minas), Glypha, Vathy (Aghios Nikolaos), and Anthedon—all minor sites across the Euripos from Chalkis—were occupied in the eighth century (see map 24). Ritsona appears to have been a hub at the center of these, with some 10 graves dating to the Late Geometric period (Burrows and Ure 1907–8; Ure 1934). This site is considered to be ancient Mykalessos, which, alongside Graia and the other towns of Boeotia, appears in Homer (*Iliad* 2.494).

In central Boeotia, Thebes experienced significant growth in the eighth century. While archaeological remains, as in other periods, are piecemeal, the Late Geometric shows reoccupation of the Kadmeia and the establishment of organized cemeteries at Aghioi Theodoroi and Pyri, as well as at Aghia Elousa and Tachi. Kountouri (2014) has recently summarized the evidence of Geometric Thebes and argued that scattered habitation in the Protogeometric period had given way to the urbanization of Thebes in the Late Geometric period, complete with sanctuaries at the (later) Temple of Apollo Ismenios and a shrine to Herakles at the Electra Gate. An infilling of the rural landscape occurred at the same time in a pattern not unlike that seen in Athens, although it has been much less intensively researched.

North of Thebes, a string of sites reaches the Euboean Gulf at Anthedon, while another follows land routes to the border zone of the sanctuary of Apollo Ptoios (Ptoion) and Lake Paralimni, where the community at Paralimni Oungra is represented by Protogeometric and Geometric buildings and a rich LG tumulus at Mouriki Kamelovrisi (Farinetti 2011, 371). LG finds in the form of animal figurines at the Kabeirion and Ptoion also speak to wider religious activity in the regional landscape, which, based on proximity, connectivity, and later history, should at this point already be linked to Thebes. It is noteworthy that, with the inundation of the Kopaic Basin after the Mycenaean Palatial period, the area north and northwest of Thebes, previously in the domain of Orchomenos, is now much more closely tied to Thebes.

The densest clustering of sites in Boeotia in this period occurs along a northwest-southeast axis, roughly between Orchomenos and Thespiai, though this pattern may be partly attributed to the relative intensity with which this area, especially the southern portion, has been surveyed (see maps 3 and 4; see also Bintliff, Howard, and Snodgrass 2007; Bintliff et al. 2017; Farinetti 2011). The diachronic pattern and settlement hierarchy also reflect intense activity in this area throughout the Early Iron Age, with several significant sites present in the settlement hierarchy: Haliartos and Askra to the east of Mount Helikon; Thisbe and Chorsiai in some degree of isolation on the Corinthian Gulf; and a further cluster around Orchomenos. There are two important points that arise from this patterning. First, the Boeotian communities on the Corinthian Gulf were for the first time self-sufficient in that there were enough nearby communities with which to interact on a regular basis. While this does not mean that they should be viewed in isolation (they should not), it does mean that they did not *need* to look toward inland Boeotia to the extent that they would have had to do without these local networks. Second, they were well positioned on the increasingly important Corinthian Gulf. Boeotia, with its growing population and its rich land, and with less of a need to look beyond itself, may have become somewhat more self-contained in this period. The network model here suggests a greater amount of internal connectivity with fewer interregional connections; the apparent gaps without significant communities to the northwest and southeast suggest the same. Such a pattern may also be supported by Coldstream's ([1977] 2003, 201) characterization of Late Geometric Boeotian ceramics as the products of a cultural backwater, which displayed Attic, Corinthian, and Euboean influences but did so in a delayed and idiosyncratic way.

Northwest Boeotia, particularly Orchomenos, was a gateway to two major sanctuary areas in this period—Kalapodi to the north, and Delphi to the west. These were without question two of the most important destinations of the eighth century, though they also developed in quite different ways. Kalapodi had long been a significant regional center, while Delphi seems to have grown quite rapidly. Partly in response to these developing sacred landscapes, a number of significant communities were located around these sites, although they were more thinly dispersed than in Attica or Boeotia.

While the number of sites in Phokis grew slightly in the Protohistoric Iron Age, East Lokris and Malis witnessed some marginal decline. While such a drop may not be substantial in and of itself, it is significant in light of the rapid rise in settlements in neighboring Boeotia. The distribution is also significant, following a land route connecting the bay of Atalanti with Kalapodi and, from there, the upper Kephisos valley to the plain of Lamia and the Malian Gulf. The number and proximity of these sites to one another, and their aggregate separation from sites in northern Boeotia, would have led to the intensification of local interaction and may have led also to a decline in habitual interaction with the surrounding areas. Kalapodi continues in its capacity as an important regional sanctuary, although there is a significant shift in the character of ritual assemblages. While intercommunal feasting practices are evident at the site in LH IIIB, LH IIIC, and in the Protogeometric and EG–MG I periods, by MG II and LG, cooking wares nearly disappear, even as the number of cups, kraters, and other drinking vessels grow. These developments are accompanied by an increase in the number of metal votive objects, and they are paralleled by contemporary sanctuary sites in Greece (Kaiser, Rizzoto, and Strack 2011, 35–36). This pattern reflects a change in ritual behavior at Kalapodi, where drinking continued to be important but competitive display took on a new character, emphasizing the dedication of high-status goods—namely metals. While Kalapodi does not go on to become the type of panhellenic sanctuary seen at Delphi or Olympia, it nonetheless was an important locus of interpolity convergence in central Greece in the Protohistoric Iron Age, involving especially Phokians and Lokrians, and probably also others from farther afield. So, while East Lokris and Phokis may appear as a somewhat circumscribed network in map 25, Kalapodi and Delphi functioned as major hubs through which significant "weak ties" were maintained to the surrounding regions. A northern Euboean connection is also significant, both in the network model and in a neat axis of oracles to Apollo that run in a straight line from Orobiai (Rovies) to Kalapodi to Delphi, with Orobiai and Kalapodi in clear visual connection with Mount Parnassos (on the little-known sanctuary at Rovies, see Mariolakos et al. 2010).

Turning to the Malian Gulf, the pattern does not differ greatly from the Prehistoric Iron Age (see map 24), although there is significantly greater separation between the area of Lamia and Thessaly, as sites like Ktimeni and Magoula Mati, which may have represented in-between points on land routes linking the two regions, are no longer occupied (compare maps 19 and 25). Settlement sites from the Malian Gulf are almost entirely unknown from this period and must be inferred from the fragmentary cemetery remains mapped here. This can probably be attributed to three factors: (1) the presence of the modern city of Lamia over what is likely to have been the principal site in the region; (2) the lack of widespread systematic exploration; and (3) the heavy alluviation in the plains that would have been ideal for settlement. The sites mapped in the vicinity of Lamia are cemeteries, but the presence of settlements within reasonable walking distance can safely be assumed.

The concentration of sites located on the Malian Gulf and the strait of Oreoi (see map 25) reinforce the strategic location of this area. The linear arrangement of sites also makes interactions across water likely. Kainourgio, Achinos, and Lichas Kastri form a neat triangle on the western end of the strait of Oreoi, where they could have controlled access between the northern Euboean Gulf and the Pagasetic Gulf and the wider Aegean. The relative isolation of Theotokou in southern Magnesia and the new settlement at Skiathos (a transplant of the Prehistoric Iron Age site of Kefala) also suggest connections to Oreoi or Kerinthos (see map 25).

As the northernmost frontier of the Euboean Gulf interaction zone, the sites around the Pagasetic Gulf remain an important interface between northern and southern Greece both by land and by sea. In terms of habitual interactions, they can be viewed as relatively self-contained, although important connections to other small worlds would have been maintained by significant nodes at Theotokou and Halos.

The modeled connections of the northern Euboean Gulf do not differ markedly from those exhibited in the previous period (compare maps 19 and 25). Of course, this is because this model is dependent on the settlement pattern, which also does not vary widely between the Prehistoric Iron Age and the Protohistoric Iron Age. However, wider sets of interactions are certainly visible in the material culture of Thessaly, especially around the bay of Volos: Attic and Euboean influences are evident in the painted pottery; Thessalian sanctuaries exhibit Macedonian ornaments in bronze; and there are commonalities between handmade pottery found in Thessaly and Macedonia (Coldstream [1977] 2003, 206–9). Thus, the material culture largely suits the geographical position of Thessaly as an important interface between central and northern Greece. And in this period, Thessaly, more than other regions, was looking increasingly to the north.

Some consideration must be given to the question of why this rapid change in settlement pattern occurred at the same time as what must be considered a settlement shift on a much wider scale—the foundation of settlements overseas (*apoikiai*). Trade interests and population pressure are the most common explanations for the establishment of colonies overseas (see, e.g., Boardman 1980; Tsetskhladze 2006, 2008). Trade interest is an obvious prime mover, and the Phoenician expansion (see chapter 5, pp. 180–84) is followed closely by the Greek case. Moreover, the far-searching quest for metals was nothing new in the Greek world, having roots in the Mycenaean period (chapters 3 and 4). Nevertheless, the scale of overseas settlement in the eighth century was something new. The expanding site numbers may suggest population pressure, but the regions of central Greece whose site numbers expand most (Attica and Boeotia) were not involved in colonization at this stage. Moreover, even these regions are not likely to have had populations that put serious pressure on the landscape until the Classical period (Bintliff 1997, 3). Expanding site numbers in Attica and Boeotia may therefore reflect an intensification of land use at home, while other polities looked to expand their resource base through *apoikiai*.

The specter of climate change has long loomed in the background of the major shifts in settlement of the eighth century. Camp (1979) argued that several wells in Athens, which were either redug or went out of use during the eighth century, may indicate a period of drought and a lower water table. Accordingly, he suggested a revision of the land-hunger hypothesis for colonization, arguing for lower agricultural production rather than simple population growth as an impetus for settlement overseas. Recent paleoclimatic studies have indicated a drying trend in both Italy and the Aegean beginning in the eighth century (Finné et al. 2011, 3158). This trend coincides roughly with a rapid decline in total solar irradiance on a global scale (Steinhilber, Beer, and Fröhlich 2009, 3), which would have affected plant growth and therefore agricultural output. The degree to which these factors would have influenced ancient agricultural practices is debatable, and the Mediterranean climate is notoriously variable, so these factors need not indicate that a drought in Athens or elsewhere in central Greece took place. But recent studies do force us to consider the possibility. At the very least, climatic *instability* is a destabilizing factor, especially in the already vulnerable microecologies that characterize the Mediterranean (Kenett and Marwan 2015). In this case, climatic instability may have provided an impetus for change in agricultural regimes and the pursuit of new settlement strategies, which varied by region.[7]

Politics may also shed light on shifts in the settlement pattern. Small (2019, 126–29) suggests that "community fissioning" was a prime mover in the establishment of *apoikiai*, wherein competing elite factions (families) from Greek communities split off to establish settlements overseas, sometimes involving cooperating groups from other communities. According to this scenario, elite access to political power in new arenas was the principal motivation for new settlement; this is supported by the detailed descriptions of kin-relationships that appear in early accounts of colonization (see also Osborne 1998).

A mixed explanation, then, may be considered whereby individuals and groups living in certain parts of Greece already involved in long-distance endeavors sought to solidify footholds abroad as a sort of insurance in response to climatic variability. At the same time, other regions (especially fertile ones such Boeotia) expanded settlement in the agriculturally rich areas around them or pursued agendas of political integration (this may also be the case in Attica). Thessaly, with its vast tracts of agricultural land and its slightly different microclimate, may not have been threatened at all by climatic shifts, and the decline in settlement numbers there may in fact represent an unrelated consolidation of population. Whatever the underlying environmental or demographic factors, the landscape shifts in the eighth century have a distinctly political character to them, and they involved a complex set of human decisions to pursue new settlement strategies and modes of social organization.

Political Landscapes at Home and Abroad

Throughout the eighth century, a series of events took place in central Euboea that had far-reaching effects. The destructions at and the eventual abandonment of Lefkandi, along with the foundation and growth of Eretria, suggest disturbance, and later literary testimony tells of a large-scale conflict between the Chalkidians and Eretrians, which involved allies from all over the Greek world and which changed political relationships in various places in the Aegean, Sicily, and Italy (Thucydides 1.15). While many uncertainties surround the specific events on the Lelantine Plain in the eighth century, especially with regard to the literary tradition, they are worth revisiting in light of the archaeological, historical, and geographical context. Moreover, the Lelantine Plain provides a case study in how

---

7. A series of recent studies have focused on human responses to climate change through the use of multivariable models incorporating climate data with proxies for settlement, population, and societal stability (see, e.g., Weiberg et al. 2019; Vidal-Cordasco and Nuevo-López 2021).

multiple lines of evidence converge in the landscapes of the Protohistoric Iron Age to offer new perspectives on archaeological and historical questions.

The density of settlement in central Euboea, specifically around the Lelantine Plain, was greater in the Pre- and Protohistoric Iron Age than anywhere else in the regions surrounding the Euboean Gulf, with the exception of the immediate vicinity of Athens. This can be explained rather simply by historical and geographical factors: the area had been a hub at least since the Postpalatial Bronze Age, partly on account of its location, which afforded control of access between the northern and southern Euboean Gulf, and partly on account of its proximity to the fertile Lelantine Plain. The territorial catchments and nearest-neighbor network model also suggest rather intense interactions between these communities (see maps 25 and 26). With such intense interactions sustained over long periods of time, cycles of cooperation and conflict should come as no surprise.

Historians have long grappled over a mythohistorical event (or series of events) called the Lelantine War.[8] The most comprehensive account comes from Thucydides (1.15), who records a conflict between Chalkis and Eretria over the Lelantine Plain, noting that each of these cities had allies from various parts of the Greek world (see also Herodotus 5.99.1). Hall (2007, 3–8) has been skeptical regarding the question of what these references can tell us about a historical conflict, wondering even if such a conflict ever actually took place, and he has argued that there is little to suggest that the tradition of the Lelantine War was based on actual events. Other authors have been more optimistic about both the utility of the historical record and its usefulness in reconstructing interactions between early Greek polities (Coldstream [1977] 2003, 200–201; Walker 2004, 162; Lane Fox 2008). Despite such long-standing (and divergent) viewpoints, the question of the Lelantine War is worth reconsidering here from a landscape perspective.

The literary tradition concerning this conflict did not emerge ex nihilo. Moreover, the archaeological record, while not capable of "proving" the validity of historical records, is not in disagreement with them. The physical geography lends further insight into historical accounts and the interpretation of archaeological remains. All these factors should be viewed together in interpreting this storied landscape.

I make three interrelated arguments here: (1) that the inhabitants of Lefkandi moved to the location of Eretria gradually between 850 and 700 BCE; (2) that this move was the result of building tensions derived from shared circumstances on local, regional, and trans-Mediterranean scales that culminated in a conflict between Chalkis and Eretria; and (3) that a reorganization of the local landscapes and long-distance activities alleviated this strain and led to divergent trajectories for these two Euboean city-states.

8. Modern scholarship on the Lelantine War has not been intensive, but interest has cropped up at numerous points over the last century (e.g., Burn 1929; Bradeen 1947; Donlan 1970; Bakhuizen 1976, 34–36; Lambert 1982; Parker 1997; Knoepfler 1997; Walker 2004, 162–71; Hall 2007, 1–8, 20–21; Christodoulou 2015; Fachard and Verdan, forthcoming).

Strabo (10.1.10) presents the idea of an Old Eretria, the interpretation of which has troubled archaeologists and historians of Euboea for some time now. One common interpretation of this reference, in combination with the occupational history of Lefkandi, is to suggest that this site was Old Eretria and that its abandonment may be linked to a territorial conflict with Chalkis (see, e.g., Popham 1980; Walker 2004, 73–89).[9] In fact, it seems that Strabo never went to Euboea himself, so he may not be the most reliable source. If we remove the notion of "Old Eretria," the occupational and political history of central Euboea in the eighth century BCE are much clearer.

The local topography can help shed some light on this matter (map 27). The Lelantine Plain is clearly visible in the modern topography as some 30 square kilometers of agricultural fields, which are well watered by the Lelas River. The riverbed runs through the center of the plain, with Chalkis and Lefkandi nearly equidistant on either side (Lefkandi, on the east side, is slightly closer). Other sites of strategic importance are positioned at its corners at Nea Lampsakos, Dhokos, and Phylla. The southwestern foothills of Mount Olympos form its eastern border, and a narrow (less than one kilometer) strip of the Eretrian Plain runs along the coast until it opens up to a fuller agricultural plain east of Eretria, situated some ten kilometers to the east of Lefkandi. Eretria is about eight kilometers away from the eastern edge of the Lelantine Plain, putting it well outside the putative territorial catchment for agriculture (see map 26). Anything to the east of Eretria would be even further removed from the capacity to exploit and control such a territory (a point that leads to the rejection of Amarynthos or Magoula as potential candidates for an Old Eretria in such discussions). Of course, distance alone does not preclude territorial interest or control, but proximity matters, especially when a potential competitor (Chalkis) is located much closer to the land in which there was a mutual interest. Another argument for the importance of proximity can be found in the Bronze Age, when the highly centralized Mycenaean palaces, which sought to maintain hegemony over significant amounts agricultural land, often at some distance, were careful to station secondary centers in prime agricultural areas, as well as at other points of strategic importance (see chapter 3). The crucial point here is that control over agricultural territory is not

9. This question also relates to the identity of Lefkandi, the ancient name of which remains unknown. Strabo's account seems to place Old Eretria at the site of Eretria itself, though some have argued that Old Eretria should be Lefkandi (Popham 1980). Bakhuizen (1976, 7–13) argues that Lefkandi should be considered Old Chalkis. Powell (1991, 15–16) suggests that Lefkandi may have been Euboean Kyme, citing an unpublished talk by E. Touloupa. Others would place Old Eretria to the east, with Amarynthos or Magoula as possible locations (Boardman 1957, 22–24). One attractive argument for the ancient identity of Lefkandi is Argoussa or Argoura, from the root αργ- meaning "white" or "bright"— a possible reference to the white cliffs that characterize the site (Knoepfler 1981, 309–12; Fachard and Verdan, forthcoming). This is also the root of the eighteenth-century toponym: Lefkandi, from λευκό, meaning "white." Eretria, by contrast, is the "place of the rowers," from ερέτης.

feasible in the face of direct competition without maintaining close proximity or presence through a proxy.

The occupational histories of Lefkandi and Eretria lend the most credence to the argument that Eretria was a foundation of Lefkandi. It actually matters little for this argument whether the "Old Eretria" referred to by Strabo was a specific allusion to an older part of Eretria, Lefkandi, or somewhere else. Based on the archaeological evidence of settlement, the following narrative applies: Lefkandi flourished throughout the LH IIIC, Protogeometric, and Subprotogeometric periods, albeit with intermittent destructions (see, e.g., Sherratt 2006a; Popham and Sackett 1980). Beginning around 825 BCE there seems to have been a general decline in population at Lefkandi, based on numbers of burials and fewer settlement remains (though admittedly only a small section of the settlement has been excavated). The first traces of settlement found at Eretria date to the same period, in the form of burials with ceramics that suggest influences from both Lefkandi and Athens (Mazarakis Ainian 1987, 3; Verdan, Kenzelmann Pfyffer, and Léderrey 2009). Walker (2004, 92) follows Popham and Sackett (1980) in suggesting that the evidence from Lefkandi and Eretria indicates an attack on the former, followed by decline and a population movement to the latter, as Lefkandi remained an outpost positioned to exploit the Lelantine Plain. Occupation at Lefkandi seems to cease around 700 BCE, although a handful of Archaic and Classical sherds have been found at the site (Sackett et al. 1966, 61).

This sequence of events could be interpreted differently, but in this case the archaeological record seems fairly clear. More nuance might be gained by viewing this evidence in its broader temporal context. A number of destructions at Lefkandi from the LH IIIC period through the Early Iron Age indicates a long history of conflict at the site, which could have built up to a larger-scale conflict that eventually entered historical memory as the Lelantine War. This possible scenario is not unlike the one at Troy, where multiple destructions have been documented archaeologically, and may have coalesced into an eighth-century tradition of *the* Trojan War (see, e.g., Mac Sweeney 2018, 32–36).

There are several potential reasons that people from Lefkandi began moving to Eretria as a satellite settlement: population growth, decreased agricultural yield, or increasing competition over the Lelantine Plain. Eretria was well positioned on the west side of the Eretrian Plain, was close to Lefkandi, and at the same time afforded access to the coastal strip between the two sites. Moreover, Eretria offered intrinsic advantages, with a high acropolis and deep harbor. The cessation of settlement at Lefkandi in the Late Geometric period and the rapid expansion of settlement at Eretria combine to make about as direct a suggestion for population movement from one proximal site to another as one can hope to see. It is also possible that a closer connection between Amarynthos and Eretria was developing at this time, since in historical periods the sanctuary of Artemis Amarysia—on the east side of the Eretrian Plain—is known to have been under Eretrian control. This spanning of the Eretrian Plain reflects a clear shift in agricultural interests and priorities to

MAP 27. The landscape and topography of central Euboea, with modern agricultural fields showing the limits of the Lelantine and Eretrian Plains (background image: Esri's Imagery layer from ArcGIS online).

the east, away from the Lelantine Plain and toward other areas that would eventually comprise the territory of Eretria.

There are further similarities between Lefkandi and Eretria that support this settlement history. The warrior burials in the West Quarter of Eretria are suggestive and at times have been pointed to as the heroized dead of the Lelantine War (Bérard 1970; Walker 2004; Christodoulou 2015). The triangular heroön is considered the culmination of this tradition, and it has been dated to the late eighth or early seventh century (Bérard 1970; Blandin 2007). The burials are similar in content to those of the Toumba cemetery at Lefkandi, and they occupy a similar topographic position in relation to the main settlement. Both are on the western edge of the settlement, have conspicuous funerary markers, and face the rival polity of Chalkis. This may suggest the deliberate introduction of place-making practices at Eretria, where the customs of elite warrior burials were preserved in the Geometric cemeteries in the West Quarter, representing efforts to memorialize and heroize elites and to define the boundaries of the community. At the same time, a building of particular importance, the Geometric Temple of Apollo Daphnephoros, recalls the long, apsidal plan of the Toumba building, and it exhibits—in the Late Geometric period—significant evidence for feasting activity rather than an assemblage characteristic of later temples (although note that this apsidal form is not unusual for the period in and of itself: see Mazarakis Ainian 1997; Verdan 2013, 208–11). Unfortunately, we lack comparative evidence from Chalkis, because of the highly fragmentary nature of the archaeological record, which was largely destroyed and obscured by centuries of later occupation.

Between the settlement evidence and the historical tradition of a war between Chalkis and Eretria, it is not difficult to imagine some sort of conflict that forced the change in settlement location. Yet complications with the historical record remain. Strabo in fact seems to give the location of Old Eretria at Eretria, claiming that the site was destroyed by the Persians. This makes sense, but the distance he gives from Athens would put Old Eretria to the east, near the location of Amarynthos. We know well that Eretria had been in its current location at the time of the Persian Wars, so Strabo is already off the mark and internally inconsistent, which should come as no surprise. Confusion, internal inconsistency, and outright error in ancient sources must be allowed for, especially when historical context, archaeological evidence, and geographic realities support different stories, as is the case here. Yet at the same time these stories may have roots in reality, even if certain details are better rejected. Ultimately, the questions of whether something called Old Eretria existed and where it was located are much less relevant than what the archaeological record tells us: that occupation at Lefkandi ceases after a long history of conflict at the same time settlement at Eretria intensifies.

Such a case presents an opportunity for a combined historical and archaeological analysis of political relationships on multiple scales—within a local agricultural landscape and spanning the Mediterranean. Pithekoussai, on the island of Ischia

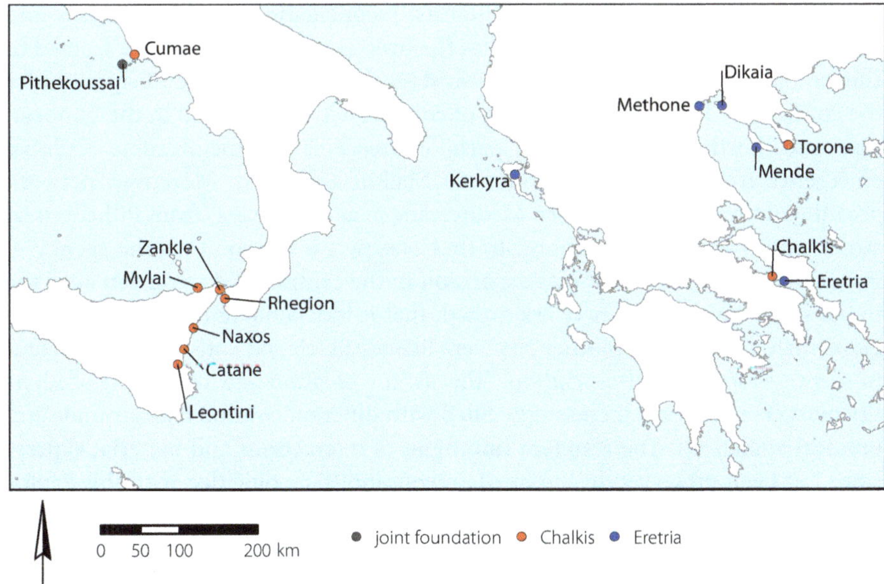

MAP 28. Euboean colonies, showing affiliations with Chalkis or Eretria, based on historical sources (note that some are joint foundations with other cities as well; for further details and historical sources, see Osborne 2009, 114–15; Knodell 2013, 298).

just off the west coast of southern Italy, is the earliest evidence we have for permanent Greek settlement overseas (Buchner and Ridgway 1993). Livy (*Ab urbe condita* 8.22.5–6) relates that the settlement at Pithekoussai was a joint foundation between Chalkidians and Eretrians. Not long after this, the Chalkidians are said to have founded Kyme (Cumae) on the adjacent mainland, and a long string of Euboean colonial foundations followed (map 28). Walker (2004, 142) argues that Pithekoussai was a joint foundation between Chalkis and Eretria, then war broke out on the Lelantine Plain, causing the Eretrians to expel the Chalkidians from Pithekoussai; the Chalkidians then founded Kyme on the Italian mainland. This site had no clear relation to a Euboean Kyme, which may not have existed until the modern period (Brodersen 2001). After the earliest foundation at Pithekoussai, the long-distance interests of Chalkidians and Eretrians declined and diverged considerably, though both groups later remained interested in some of the same general areas, such as the northern Aegean, although never the same precise locations (Tiverios 2008).

Thorough accounts of Euboean colonial activities can be found elsewhere (see, e.g., Crielaard 1996; Tsetskhladze 2006, 2008). The important point here is the pattern—the split that can be observed between Chalkidian and Eretrian interests that parallels local developments on the Lelantine Plain, reflecting a reorganization of networks across significant distance, based on a local breakdown of relations.

Despite this conflict and split in interests, reconciliation between Chalkis and Eretria may soon have been reached, as the overseas interests of Eretria seemed to shift to the north Aegean, which was most accessible through the Euripos, under the control of Chalkis. The explosion of colonial activities abroad in the Euboean case, and shortly after from other parts of Greece, is a prime example of global emergence from local interactions (see Malkin 2011, 210). Moreover, network growth continued in the western Mediterranean as "Euboeans" from Pithekoussai struck out to settle new locations. In these cases, it is not so much the agency of Euboeans in Euboea that affects expansion in the central Mediterranean after the initial settlement but the network growth that is independent of any mother city. Nevertheless, ties to the mother city were likely still felt and considered important in identity-forming self-ascription—that is, the creation and reification of identity markers in a world increasingly filled with different cultural backgrounds and political affiliations. The resultant imbroglio of interactions and material expressions has been preserved in the media revolution that coincided with this explosion of activity in both the Euboean Gulf and farther afield (see further below, pp. 215–25). The reorganization of the religious landscape across central Greece played an important role in mediating these shifting political relationships.

Sacred Landscapes as Hubs of Mediation

The growth of regional, and eventually panhellenic, sanctuaries in the eighth century forms another piece of network architecture in the revolutionary developments of the eighth century. Like colonization, this phenomenon is well known, especially through the seminal work of de Polignac (1994, 1995; see also Malkin 1987, 2011; Antonaccio 1995; Morgan 1993; Osborne 2009; McInerney 2011). The impact of religious practices on political and territorial developments can be seen clearly in the material record from local, regional, and panhellenic sanctuaries. Like other aspects of the early Greek landscape, such forms have roots in earlier periods but proliferate in this one.

On the level of individual communities, feasting events at "sacred houses" seem to have been important exercises in group formation, evolving out of similar practices in the Prehistoric Iron Age and Postpalatial Bronze Age (Whitley 1991, 62–64). In Attica, these were probably associated with elite kinship groups in different parts of the region—namely, Athens, Eleusis, and Thorikos—and were sometimes associated with local heroes (Alexandridou 2018; van den Eijnde 2018). In Athens alone several such buildings have been identified, some more confidently than others—at Plato's Academy, on the Areopagus, in the vicinity of the Classical Tholos at the Agora, and at Herakleidon Street, close to the Piraeus gate (Alexandridou 2018). The mortuary record offers a window into another type of sacred landscape, although this is extremely uneven across regions. In Attica, we can see the emergence of elite kinship groups in necropoleis, which may reflect competition between factions within a community (Alexandridou 2017). Mazarakis Ainian (1997, 384–85) argues that places of power would eventually evolve from rulers' dwellings into institutionalized religious structures such as temples, where the community as a whole would come together. Again, however, variation is probably the rule. While there are shared attributes between rulers' houses and early temples, this probably has more to do with the conception of temples as monumental houses (of gods). At any rate, one trend of the eighth century is to see sacred spaces increasingly develop as places of mediation within communities, a trend that is paralleled by sanctuaries between communities and even between regions.

On a local level, tomb cult was a defining practice in the Early Iron Age. While ancestor veneration, and perhaps even worship, may have had Prehistoric Iron Age precedents at places like Lefkandi, the tholoi of Thessaly, and the chamber tomb cemeteries of Phokis, the practice seems to become widespread in the Late Geometric period (Antonaccio 1995). In Attica and Boeotia, this seems to come out of a renewed interest in the Bronze Age landscape (Antonaccio 1994). This interest in the past and the creation of places of memory and ancestral significance in the landscape should be seen in relation to the increasingly close proximity of archaeological sites to one another and the need to establish territorial claims. I do not, however, wish to reduce this aspect of Greek religion to an economic argument. Bronze Age and Prehistoric Iron Age remains indicate that there had long been an interest in the past—people built on the same places and in some cases reused tombs, whether they belonged to relatives or not. Memories, of real or imagined connections, would have been tied to these places, which would have been habitually encountered in the course of daily life. What we see intensifying in this period is not necessarily interest in the past but *material engagement* with it. With the rapid infilling of the settlement pattern, it became increasingly important to leave material marks on places of collective memory and significance. This interest in the past (and in *creating* pasts) coincides with, but does not necessarily result from, literary concerns in the same vein: oral traditions and epic poetry having to do with an "age of heroes."

This period also saw shifts in the character of regional sanctuaries (see also Eder 2019). From the Palatial period onward, sites such as Kalapodi had functioned as regional mediators of interaction between various peer communities. While political relationships were clearly present, they were embedded in religious practice. Traces of cult activity have been found at numerous other sites but rarely to a degree that makes them stand out. This changed dramatically in the eighth century, as sanctuary dedications increased dramatically, even as the presence of luxury items (chiefly metals) in graves declined (Snodgrass 1980a, 53; Morris 1987, 141). This trend is best interpreted as the result of increasing interaction between individuals and polities on a regional scale, which occurred at sanctuary sites as competitive practices of dedication. These practices accompanied the athletic competitions for which these places were now the preeminent sites.[10]

---

10. While athletic competitions can be observed in the Bronze Age, a distinct association with regional sanctuaries is documented beginning in the eighth century.

In the Prehistoric Iron Age conspicuous consumption was largely tied to individuals, and operated on a local scale, which can be seen in wealthy burials at places such as Athens and Lefkandi. The eighth century witnessed a marked shift in this behavior, mainly in the dedication of large bronze tripods—symbolically charged items made of a valuable commodity—that were set up in highly visible locations of ritual and political significance that did not belong to any individual or polity but were places of mediation and competition between them. Papalexandrou (2005) has written extensively on the tripod as symbolic capital and its role in the visual poetics of power that played out in early sanctuaries, especially at Olympia and Delphi. Tripods also functioned as both symbolic and economic stores of value (Papadopoulos 2012). Moreover, a shift in the deposition of arms from local graves to regional sanctuaries has been taken to mean that military force shifted from the domain of the individual to the community and its political apparatus: this was an important marker also in the development of early poleis (Snodgrass 1980a, 52–53, 99–100; Morgan 1993, 27).

Extensive discussion of the role of regional sanctuaries in polis formation and the origins of Panhellenism can be found in the references above. Their importance here is as major nodes in a network architecture that spanned various spatial and social scales. Local sanctuaries and tomb cults served to reinforce boundaries and demarcate territory through ancestral links to the landscape. Regional shrines served as places of common ritual practice, mediation, and competition between local authorities. At the same time, regional cults were both codified and dispersed throughout the Mediterranean—for example, via the worship of Artemis along the Euboean Gulf or the dispersal of elements of Euboean cults across the Mediterranean (Cole 2000; Boffa and Leone 2017; Kowalzig 2018). During the eighth century, the networks of Olympia and Delphi grew especially quickly, and they emerged as the first Panhellenic shrines, whose importance and roles as mediators were highlighted through the introduction of formal competitions (both artistic and athletic) and oracular functions. Perhaps most importantly, they brought people together from across great distances, based on shared aspects of religious and linguistic identity. This is another example of scale-free network growth, where nodes (Greek polities) preferentially attached to two of many possible regional centers (Delphi and Olympia), causing accelerated network growth over a relatively short period of time. It is also an example of multidirectionality and pulsation in small-worlds scenarios, as habitual meetings in certain hubs brought people and images into contact with one another and then flung them back out again. That is, the network contracted on a single place, and then was released outward again after participants came into contact any number of people, things, and ideas that they normally would not have encountered.

That this network pulsation occurred at the same time as the first large-scale colonization movements is significant, although it is difficult to discern a simple causal relationship between them. The most likely explanation is that regional sanctuaries, such as Kalapodi, had been in use since the Bronze Age, although activities at them intensified and formalized in an increasingly mobile eighth-century world. Habitual encounters with difference created a need to reinforce commonalities, and the venues for this engendered competitions through which independent polities, represented by individuals, strove to "outdo" each other through acts of direct competition and conspicuous consumption. A clear example of how this took place in the Geometric period can be found in the dedicatory tripods with figural attachments in the form of horses, birds, and humans (Papalexandrou 2005); these fueled the quest for metals and at the same time promulgated an iconography that was eventually adapted to other forms of figural art. Sanctuaries thus provided the hubs that greatly reduced the physical and conceptual distance that images, motifs, and innovations needed to travel to reach anywhere else in the growing Greek world. In the context of this competitive and highly charged network, which was capable of spreading ideas over great distances very quickly, we can describe a media revolution that changed the face of material, visual, and oral culture.

A MEDIA REVOLUTION:
WORDS AND IMAGES ON THINGS

The invention of the Greek alphabet and the reemergence of figural art on pottery were among the most significant developments of the eighth century. The spread of these innovations was particularly rapid, and they had the added effect of carrying messages with them that were independent of utility, style, and technological knowledge. Much has been written about whether one of these innovations preceded the other—especially about figural art as a response to Homer (e.g., Carter 1972; Langdon 1993; Powell 1997; Snodgrass 1998). Langdon (2008) in particular has shown that figural art probably should not be seen as a direct response to Homer. I argue that writing and figural art emerge in the eighth century as part of the same phenomenon, representing new concerns with display and self-presentation, as well as with establishing permanence through recording on things the thoughts and expressions of a heretofore predominantly oral culture. This new materialization of social relations had important implications in an increasingly interactive world.

Technology Transfer from Potters to Poets:
The Invention of the Greek Alphabet

The innovation of Greek writing in the eighth-century Mediterranean was distinct from other writing systems in the circumstances of its creation, its rapid diffusion, and its far-reaching effects.[11] In this section I examine what the earliest writing

11. The literature on the introduction of alphabetic writing to Greece is extensive. See, most recently, Janko 2015; Papadopoulos 2016b; Clay, Malkin, and Tzifopoulos 2017; Whitley 2017; Pappa 2019;

in the Greek world *does* rather than what it *says* or what its linguistic roots are, though these concerns are certainly related. Whitley (2017) provides a recent and a compelling case for *archaeological* approaches to the history of early Greek script, focusing on its materiality and regional variability rather than on its relationship to literacy or universality across the Greek world. From a geographical perspective, the Euboean Gulf was an important conduit for this innovation, with the Euboeans themselves probably playing a central role. More specifically, the rapid proliferation of early Greek writing allows us to work backward to say something about the societies and circumstances under which it was introduced.[12]

The loosely organized village societies of the Prehistoric Iron Age did not use writing as an administrative technology. Writing systems of the Bronze Age were adapted specifically in the centralized political context of the palace, with an interest in controlling access to and the use of writing. By contrast, our evidence for the earliest use of writing in the eighth century BCE comes from three social contexts: pottery workshops, trade goods, and communal drinking events (on the latter, see especially Węcowski 2017).

The invention or adoption of a writing system constitutes a media revolution in nearly any cultural context in which it occurs. In this case, when widely visible and accessible, writing fundamentally changed the way people interacted with each other and the world around them: it gave permanence and portability to speech through the introduction of a new medium to interpersonal and intersocietal relations—words inscribed or painted on things. This can also be seen as a technological innovation, making use of various tools, materials, and specialized knowledge (Ong 1982, 81–82). Writing must therefore be learned and taught, adding a significant interactive element to the process. At the same time, however, describing writing as technology has its drawbacks, as to do so distances script

---

Bourogiannis 2020; Steele 2020. Classic studies of early Greek dialects and alphabets are by Kirchhoff (1887) and Jeffrey, the latter of which has been recently updated with a supplement by Johnston ([1961] 1990). There are several recent overviews as well (Woodard 1997, 2010; Wachter 2006; Voutiras 2007; Horrocks 2010; Węcowski 2017). Powell (1991, 2002, 2009) has dealt with script invention extensively, especially its relation to Homer and oral poetry. Recent work by Sass (2005) puts the invention of the Greek alphabet in its wider West Semitic context and argues for a much earlier adoption, which is an increasingly common feature of linguistic arguments (e.g., Waal 2018). A good deal of important, recent work has looked at early scripts from a comparative perspective, both for alphabetic scripts (Boyes and Steele 2020) and in earlier periods in the Aegean (Steele 2017). Beyond script invention, serious consideration has also been given to the impact of literacy on a heretofore oral culture (Ong 1982; Havelock 1986; Thomas 1992).

12. The Phrygian writing system was invented around the same time, and it has many shared characteristics with the Greek alphabet, including vowel use (Brixhe and Lejeune 1984). Recent chronological developments at Gordion (Rose and Darbyshire 2011), however, call into question the standard argument that Phrygian is derived from Greek, and may suggest a Phrygian precedence of the alphabet, yet this is far from definitive (Brixhe 2002; Sass 2005, 146–49). For the significance of the northern Aegean as a potential crossroads of the Greek and Phrygian alphabetic traditions, see Papadopoulos (2016b), who also notes the close similarities between Phrygian and Eretrian scripts.

from other ways of transferring meaning (Houston and Stuart 1992, 590). While writing involves the technical acts of other technological practices, it is ultimately a communicative, semiotic system that varies based on form, context, production, and response (Houston 1994, 28). Thus, writing cannot be viewed in strictly technological terms, although technological metaphors remain useful in considering the skill, craft, and transfer of knowledge required for its spread and deployment.

Communications technologies have dramatic impacts on the pace of social change in human societies (see, e.g., Robinson 2007; Powell 2009; Gnanadesikan 2009). The first writing appeared in the second half of the fourth millennium BCE in Sumer, which saw the emergence of the first state-level societies not long after. In the roughly 5,500 years since then the scale and complexity of human societies have increased in a way that would have been inconceivable to ancient Sumerians. In the 5,500 years before the invention of writing relatively little had changed, at least when compared to what came after. The long-term consequences of this revolution in human interactions are well worth considering in their particular cultural and historical circumstances, especially after a sustained period of the disappearance of writing (see also Baines, Bennet, and Houston 2008).

Greek alphabetic writing appears to be the first writing system that was not invented for the purpose of state or religious administration. It is also one of the first writing systems to give vowels separate phonetic designations, in order to encode human speech in words comprised of individual letter sounds rather than through syllables or consonants alone (Powell 1991, 115–18). In West Semitic alphabets, for example, words were written as a series of consonants, and it was left to the reader to fill in the vowels. This is not a problem if the reader knows the language, but it makes it more difficult for others to use and to adapt such a system. Powell (1991) has argued that this innovation was made by a single man from Euboea (the "adapter") specifically for the purpose of recording hexametric poetry.[13] While the motives and processes of adaptation are likely more complicated than this, the desire to write in this way does not seem to have had administrative roots.

The introduction of vowels was a practical matter in adapting the Phoenician script to record Greek, and it had great consequences later on. For example, the adaptability of the system, which encodes consonantal and vowel sounds separately, makes it highly flexible and accounts for its diffusion and further adaptation to record a variety of other languages. The addition of vowels made it possible to write sound and speech directly, resulting in a rapid diffusion around the Mediterranean. The Greek alphabet, in particular the Euboic alphabet, formed the basis for the Etruscan alphabet, various other Old Italic scripts, and eventually Latin. At the same time, the rapid development of epichoric alphabets, which were in place

---

13. This idea goes back to Wade-Gery (1952, 9–14). For a recent summary and critique, see Whitley (2017, 76–82).

by the seventh century BCE, show the regional creation and concentration of specific script communities within central Greece (see Jeffery 1990).

From an experiential perspective, the Greek alphabet also created a closer link between speech, song, and writing than had ever existed before; this likely influenced the rapidity of its spread in a predominantly oral culture. Yet literacy, as well as the awareness of and access to this new semiotic system, did not happen instantly. Writing must also be understood in the context of contemporary and previous symbolic vocabularies, beginning in the Prehistoric Iron Age. As signs on clay, the most significant of these are potters' marks.

Potters' marks are painted, impressed, stamped, or incised marks put on the surface of a pot before firing, and are attributed to the potter him- or herself (Papadopoulos 1994, 439; 2017b). Signs painted or incised after firing are typically not considered potters' marks, because their makers could have been anyone. Yet, as visual and symbolic referents, such marks may do similar things. The most common interpretation is that these were makers' marks, or that they were intended to play some role in production or distribution, or both (Papadopoulos 1994, 473). Cross-culturally, potters' marks are simple identity tokens, though on a very basic level they correspond to a person or entity; ultimately, the system of communication is quite limited, there being only a relatively small group of individuals to which they are relevant (Houston 2004, 227). Most importantly, they are non-linguistic. So, while the medium of expression is the same as that of the earliest (known) Greek writing—pottery—these notational systems (potters' marks and writing) are quite distinct. The only possible (though not insignificant) link to writing is that Early Iron Age potters' marks may demonstrate the desire of potters to inscribe meaningful signs on clay.

Powell (1989, 349) lists some 20 locations that should be included in the "first generation" of Greek alphabetic writing, the most significant being Pithekoussai, Eretria, Athens, and Kommos. To these can be added Methone and probably other places as well, as new evidence comes to light (map 29).[14] While Powell's "first generation" includes everything with a plausible date before 650 BCE, a more refined chronology is illuminating. The very first generation of certain alphabetic inscriptions comes in the eighth century, which is documented at the sites listed above. Predecessors in the form of single letters or Phoenician script appear slightly before (chiefly in Crete), and other very early inscriptions in Phyrgian are known from Gordion. Greek inscriptions dated to the seventh century are more widespread, including sites in Sicily, Asia Minor, and the Aegean islands. The pattern is clear: sites in or closely linked to central Euboea exhibit the earliest examples of alphabetic script, although writing spread quickly from there (see also Bourogiannis 2020, 158–63). The recent evidence from Eretria, Lefkandi, and Methone (an

14. For more on early inscriptions and data in map 29, see Wade-Gery 1940; Langdon 1976; Jeffery 1980, 1990; Boardman 1990; Sass 1990; Buchner and Ridgway 1993; Palme-Koufa 1996; Csapo, Johnston, and Geagan 2000; Coldstream 2003; Kenzelmann Pfyffer, Theurillat, and Verdan 2005; Theurillat 2007; Besios, Tzifopoulos, and Kotsonas 2012; Clay, Malkin, and Tzifopoulos 2017.

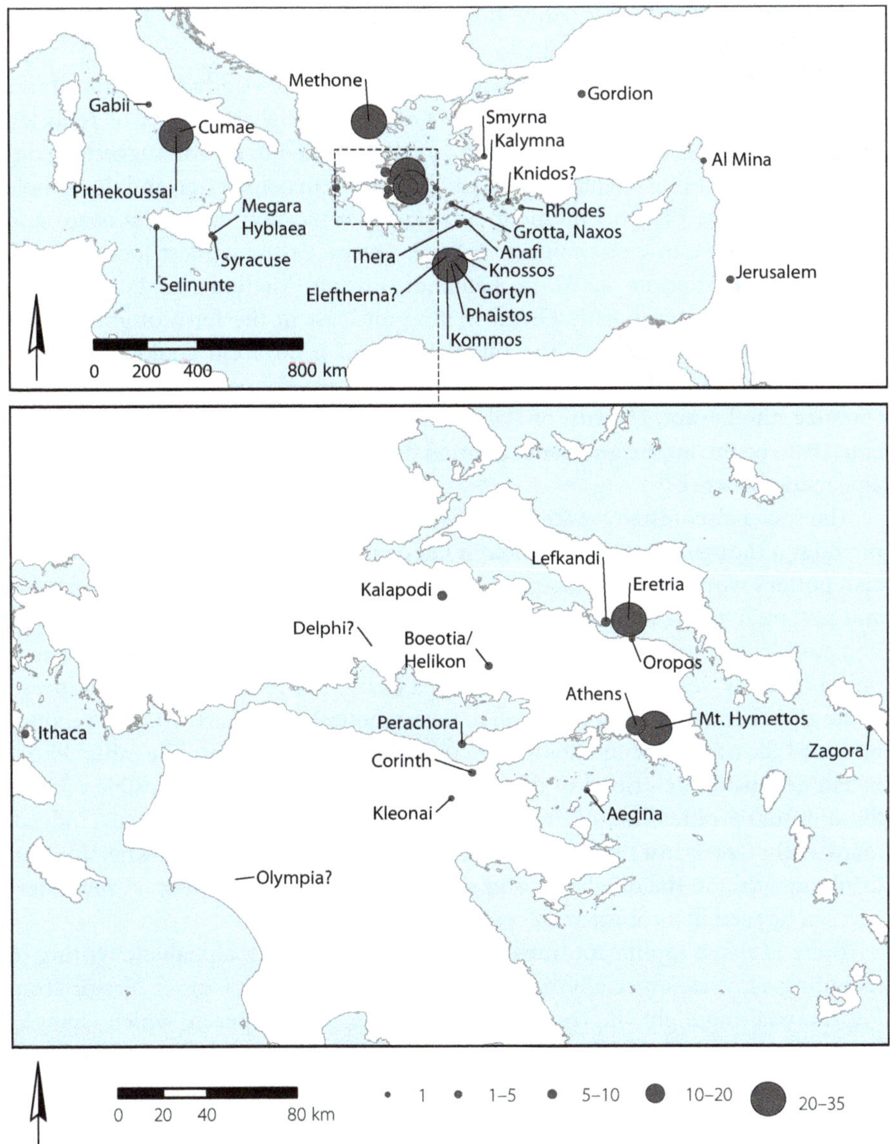

MAP 29. Early Greek inscriptions in the Mediterranean, showing location and quantity.

Eretrian colony) highlights this trend, adding to already significant quantities of evidence associated with Euboea. A look at the wider Euboean Gulf can also be instructive, as the earliest alphabets in Boeotia, Thessaly, Lokris, and Attica exhibit commonalities as links between these small worlds. The current evidence suggests that ideas may have traveled more quickly and more completely—for example, between Euboea and Pithekoussai—than they did between Euboea and Boeotia, or Euboea and East Lokris, since Boeotia and East Lokris adapted, rather than simply adopted, new innovations.

This distribution of the earliest writing overlaps quite clearly with other traces of Euboeans in the Aegean and Mediterranean—namely, in terms of reported colonial activity (compare maps 28 and 29). This has led to several suggested contexts for some kind of adaptive moment. The Euboean connection and the Euboic alphabet indicate that this moment occurred in a location where Euboeans and Phoenicians were in close contact. Indeed, several of the earliest loci of Greek script fit this criterion: Al Mina, Lefkandi, Eretria, Methone, or Pithekoussai, since both Semitic and early Greek writing (at least in the form of graffiti) has been found at these places. The initial stages of innovation could have taken place anywhere in the course of interactions between Euboeans and Phoenicians (Euboea, the Levant, Cyprus, or Italy), but the fact remains that central Euboea appears to be the most significant common denominator or central hub of an early alphabetic network.[15]

The social circumstances are of further interest. Gnanadesikan (2009, 208–14) provides a thought experiment about a Greek learning the alphabet in a Phoenician potter's workshop. She imagines a Greek potter being instructed in the value and potential of the alphabet for recording information. Such a situation is not implausible for the initial phases of the appearance of the alphabet, when we have only a name, a word, or a few letters. Pappa (2019) has recently linked the spread of the alphabet in the Mediterranean to the monetization of Early Iron Age economies and the use of documentation in credit-based transactions. The initial Phoenician expansion described in the previous chapter provides a plausible context for an initial proliferation of Phoenician writing on perishable materials. Indeed, many early Greek inscriptions and other marks seem to indicate ownership (on drinking cups, on the one hand, and storage and transport vessels, on the other) and can be seen in a commercial context.

There is also a significant transition in the use of Greek alphabetic writing to recording phrases, especially hexameters. Objects like the Cup of Nestor from Pithekoussai highlight the true innovation of recording speech, which changed the way material culture could *actively* participate in social contexts, such as sympotic situations involving communal dining, drinking, and the recitation of poetry (see figure 7a). Węcowski (2017) has argued that this combination of commercial and convivial interests indicate elite trade and symposia as the most frequent contexts for early Greek writing. We should also note that these contexts are

15. Papadopoulos (2016b) notes that Phrygians must be added to this mix too, since the similarity in Greek and Phrygian vowels suggests that they must have been developed together. This observation leads him to suggest Methone, in northern Greece, as the possible location of the invention. Indeed, the north Aegean, in general, and Methone, in particular, do have a significant confluence of Greek, Phoenician, and Phrygian elements. On the other hand, central Euboea has a much greater time depth of contacts with the Phoenicians.

I am the good-drinking cup of Nestor. Whoever drinks from this cup, immediately desire of beautiful-crowned Aphrodite will seize him.

a

b

c

FIGURE 7. Examples of Geometric pottery with early writing and figural scenes: "Nestor's cup" from Pithekoussai, with inscription and translation (a: photo by Marcus Cyron, CC BY-SA 4.0); the "Dipylon Krater," showing a funeral scene with mourners (b: photo made publicly available by the Metropolitan Museum of Art, CC O); the "London Abduction Krater" (c: © The Trustees of the British Museum, shared under CC BY-NC-SA 4.0 license).

almost exclusively in significant ports of trade, with evidence for both Greeks and non-Greeks (in the first place Phoenicians, but later others as well) operating in the same socioeconomic environments. Most importantly, these situations represent a change in what writing *does* and who uses it—it is no longer a part of state apparatuses; instead, it is used in small-scale, local practices of group formation and exchange in places of convergence between members of different cultural groups.

Figures, Narratives, and Visual Culture

The iconography of geometric vase painting can be divided into two broad and overlapping categories: scenes of life and scenes of myth (though the latter should be considered the exception rather than the rule).[16] Both involve narrative and play important roles in the construction of the social world of the observer. These scenes must also be viewed as the products of the social world of the maker. Scholarship on Homeric poetry has long focused on the dialectic between the subject matter of a distant past and the contemporary context of production, which results in the sort of conflative temporality described above. Visual art is more ambiguous, which may partly explain why less attention has been paid to similar such conflations in early Greek art (i.e., of a mythical world and a real world). Nevertheless, part of the reason for the rapid spread of early Greek writing was certainly the specificity of meaning that it carried. We might see a parallel case in the rapid proliferation of figural art in the Late Geometric period. As with writing, we have a few earlier examples in MG and even EG vase painting, especially from Athens (Coldstream [1968] 2008). Whitley (1991, 47–48) notes that there is also a considerable amount of Protogeometric figural material from other sites—namely, Knossos and Lefkandi. And figurines, while rarer in the Prehistoric Iron Age, were always present in the Greek artistic repertoire. The proliferation of images after 750 BCE, however, is coincident with other processes of intensification discussed above, and should therefore be viewed as part of the same broad set of social developments.

I argue that figural scenes of Geometric art prioritize contemporary life over myth, and that they are focused especially on circumstances with which their observers were likely to have been familiar. Morris (1987, 194) suggests that interest in an age of heroes was the likely cause for the resurgence of figural art in the mid-eighth century. This is in partial agreement with Snodgrass's (1980a, 65–78) view that the heroic and contemporary both play a role in Geometric figural art.

16. The classic studies of Geometric pottery are by Coldstream ([1977] 2003; [1968] 2008). Iconographic discussion has long dominated attempts to identify relationships between images in early Greek art and Homer and myth, as scholars have sought to find particular Homeric or mythological episodes in art that are presumably contemporary with the earliest literature (see, e.g., Carter 1972; Ahlberg-Cornell 1992). Thematic studies, including the relationship of art to citizenship, the Near East, Homer, and cult, can be found in Langdon (1997). Snodgrass (1998) provides a counter to earlier, Homer-focused scholarship; he lends Geometric artists more agency in creating particular episodes without needing to strictly adhere to, or even have knowledge of, Homer. Most recently, Langdon (2008) has shown how more commonplace topics of childhood, maturation, gender, and ritual feature in Geometric art; her particular emphasis is on rites of passage.

I would go beyond this to suggest that even scenes that can be interpreted as mythological are meaningful for their relationship to experiences familiar from the real world. This is similar to Langdon's (2008) view that narrative scenes in the Geometric period were meant to illustrate rites of passage, social inequality, and gender relationships. While a concern with the heroic world had long been present, its coincident expression in art and literature suggest that these things were part of a common interest in materiality.

Among the many narrative scenes, there is a preponderance of certain types. Funerals, battles, dances, and processions abound, and images associated with travel, both maritime and terrestrial, also stand out. Well-known examples, such as the massive Dipylon funerary krater and amphora, are self-referential rather than mythological in focus, in that they depict the type of event they are meant to commemorate (see figure 7b). It is doubtful that battle scenes referred only to epic and not to some violent realities to which the proliferation of weapons found in male burials would attest. Ritual scenes, such as collective dances, record group-formation practices well known in the later Greek world and for early agricultural communities in general (Garfinkel 2003, 85–97; Langdon 2008, 158). Such dances may have been part of the same sympotic events to which early inscriptions on drinking vessels refer (see figure 7a).

Numerous scenes involve travel by land or sea, with many of them placing a special emphasis on horses or chariots, on the one hand, and ships, on the other (Kirk 1949; Greenhalgh 1973; Crouwel 1992). The London Louterion shows a man leading a woman onto a ship with many rowers on one side, and a group of two chariots and a rider on the other (see figure 7c; Langdon 2008, 19–21). This composition has been interpreted variously as a depiction of a funerary scene culminating in a ship race; a specific mythological scene, such as the abduction of Helen (by Paris, or her return with Menelaos) or Ariadne or Medea; and a more general scene of abduction as a metaphor for marriage (Langdon 2008, 32). Taking a step back from these specific interpretations to look at the contextual details can also be instructive. At its most basic level, the pot shows a preoccupation with locomotion, regardless of the presence of reference, allusion, or metaphor. Movement—both by land and sea, and in chariots and ships respectively—is consistently linked to marriage, one of the types of necessary interactions presented in the nearest-neighbor model of intercommunity relations described above.

The specific and general themes of Greek Geometric imagery were created as an expression of collective, cultural identity in the face of a rapidly expanding world. That is, as people came into increasing contact with "others," an interest in expressing aspects of one's own cultural practices grew. This involved religious beliefs and funerary customs; depictions of especially significant events, such as the dangers of sea travel and battle; and aspects of elite life, such as hunting or horse taming. At the same time as this symbolic vocabulary was being established both in central Greece and elsewhere, regional styles became increasingly divergent, as craftspeople and regional cultures evolved material expressions in a world of increasingly apparent difference (Coldstream 1983). The role of images in identity formation thus worked on multiple levels, from the trans-Mediterranean to the local. Local identities were expressed through the depiction of particular regional styles and cultural practices, though these were often common across a wider region. Such a mode of expression served to reinforce what it meant to be "us" in a world increasingly encountering "them." Moreover, images served to communicate such messages over long distances and in ways that did not depend on a shared spoken or written language.

Creative Dialogues between Writing and Painting

At the core of the media revolution in the eighth century is the increased capacity to transfer words, symbols, images, and meaning through space and time. Visual culture and the written word are rarely treated together, despite the fact that *to write* and *to paint* are the same word in ancient Greek: γράφειν (Papadopoulos 2017b, 38). There is a long tradition of ascribing Homeric inspiration to various works of Geometric art, though this tradition obscures and precludes the creative and expressive capacity of artists, poets, and craftspeople other than Homer (Snodgrass 1998; Langdon 2008). Expressions of myth in writing and painting were part of the same phenomenon, rather than one following from the other. Discrepancies between depictions reflect a plurality of versions and a world in which inscription was a creative act, and not simply a means of recording. Writing and painting were therefore aesthetic and material practices, in which words and images on things became active participants in social life (see also Pappas 2011, 2017).

An archaeological perspective shows how writing and imagery developed together in the Protohistoric Iron Age as part of communal activities comprised of eating, drinking, poetry recitations, and competitive display. While such practices have a long history and, as we have seen, are rooted in feasting practices going back at least to the Mycenaean period, new and distinct material engagements appear in the Protohistoric Iron Age. At the same time, local practices took inspiration from stories brought from far-off locations, cross-cultural encounters, hazardous journeys, and encounters with other people, cultural practices, and expressions.

The subject matter of early poetry and images is also multiscalar, ranging from epic, long-distance journeys to the exigencies of daily life. Just as Homer and Hesiod stretch from the heroic to the mundane, early painting includes varied themes from shipwrecks to horse taming to marriages and funerals. The implications of the active practices and underlying structures evident in this media revolution are many, and they relate to aspects of Greek life—from politics to poetry. While the discussion in this section has been of the "Greek world" writ large, central Greece played a particularly significant role during this stage. With Boeotia as the homeland of Hesiod, the earliest personality in Greek literature, and with Euboea as a possible homeland of Homer, there is a significant literary presence.[17] More-over, the Euboean and especially the Attic styles of painting, especially figural painting, continued to be influential in other spheres. Finally, central Euboea in particular was a demonstrably significant hub in both early colonization move-ments and the rapid dispersal of the Greek alphabet. This confluence of develop-ment in central Greece is not coincidental but is rather the result of accumulative growth on a regional scale. Ultimately, however, written and visual culture reflect a world that is both more local and more "global" than anything we have seen up to this point in the Mediterranean.

THE MEDITERRANEAN CORRUPTED

"Progress is movement toward movement, movement toward increased movement, movement toward an increased mobility" (Sloterdijk 2006, 37). While Sloterdijk presents a formula for modernizing processes, this also applies to the revolution-ary self-intensification seen across the Mediterranean in the eighth century BCE.

The Protohistoric Iron Age saw the intensification, through permanent settle-ment and habitual use, of the first truly Mediterranean-scale networks across the "corrupting sea" of Horden and Purcell (2000). This was anticipated in the Pre-historic Iron Age with the beginnings of the Phoenician expansion (see map 23, pp. 181–84). By using the term "intensification" in this case, I point to two things: first, the sheer number of new settlements established from distant points of ori-gin; second, their permanence and the regular flows of people, materials, and information that followed.

Imports, Exports, and Depositional Patterns

There is a significant shift in spatial patterns of material consumption in the eighth century, patterns that represent an expansion of Greek activities throughout the Mediterranean. This is reflected both in the record of imports for foreign materials and products to Greece and in the dispersal of elements of Greek material culture (chiefly painted pottery) to other parts of the Mediterranean—from Iberia to the Levant (for the most recent summary, see Murray 2017, 103–12, 203–8).

There are more imports in Greece during the Protohistoric Iron Age than in any other period studied in this book (map 30). Murray (2017, 113) records some 543 objects from Geometric contexts in Greece, as opposed to 152 Protogeometric, 136 LH IIIC, and 228 LH IIIB objects.[18] The change in distribution and depositional

17. Hesiod identifies himself as a man from Askra (*Works and Days* 640). The identity of Homer is widely debated, including whether "Homer" even represents an individual. With no reliable bio-graphical information for such a semilegendary figure, several homelands have been posited. These include Chios, Ionia, and Euboea (Powell 1991; Morris and Powell 1997; Lane Fox 2008).

18. It should be noted that Murray's (2013, 2017) use of standard pottery chronologies for the division of periods is different from the periodization used in this book. The result in this study is

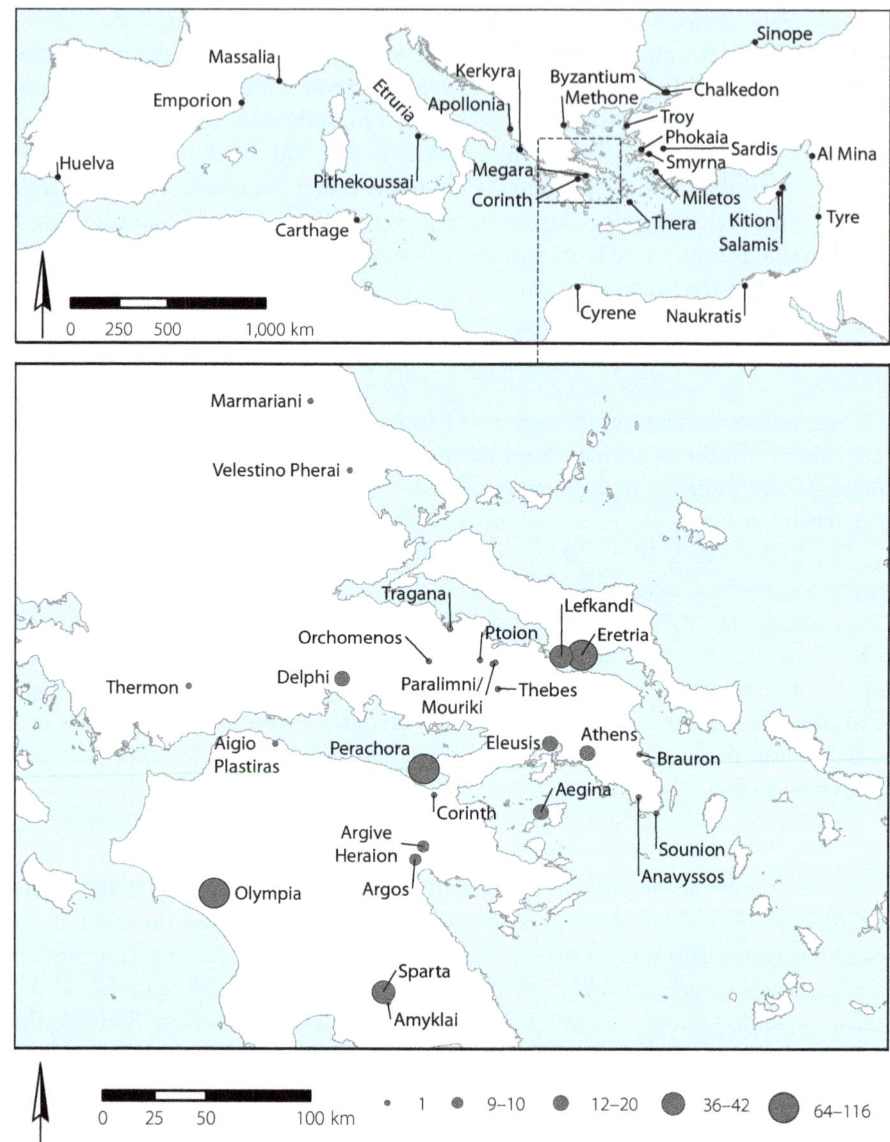

MAP 30. Sites mentioned in the text with evidence for long-distance interaction, especially colonies and mother cities (top) and Geometric period imports to Greece (bottom) (import data from Kourou 2015; Murray 2017, 102–11, table 2.6).

some evening between the Prehistoric Iron Age and the Protohistoric Iron Age, but since most of the Geometric imports described by Murray are either Middle or Late Geometric, the general pattern still holds. The biggest difference is that Murray would count many Subprotogeometric finds from patterns is also significant. Imports dated to the Protogeometric period show a clear spatial distribution along and around the Euboean Gulf, with a handful of examples coming from other locations (see map 23). This distribution reflects a pattern of long-distance interactions that began to intensify in this zone in the Postpalatial Bronze Age, and then became even more acute in the Prehistoric Iron Age. In the Geometric period, however, and really from the Middle Geometric (eighth century) onward, we see an influx of imported products across the Greek landscape. Most notably, there is a sudden infilling in the Peloponnese, which had been nearly empty of imports in Protogeometric times (compare maps 23 and 30; see also Kourou 2015; Murray 2017, 102–3).

The majority of these imports were deposited in sanctuaries, reflecting their growing significance as venues for interpolity competition and display, as discussed above. This stands in contrast to the tomb/individual-based consumption of imports noted in the Postpalatial Bronze Age and Prehistoric Iron Age. There are two possible reasons for this sudden influx of imported objects into sanctuaries. On the one hand, their exotic nature makes them valuable symbols of wealth, connectivity, and prestige for the individual or group dedicating them in this highly visible setting. On the other hand, this may already signal foreign interests (well known in later times) in particular Greek sanctuaries—most notably the ones that would become Panhellenic shrines later on.

Even as more foreign goods were coming into Greece than ever before, more were going out—at least in terms of the Greek pottery that has been documented in foreign contexts (Saltz 1978; Coldstream 2003; Fletcher 2008). The most significant concentrations of these materials are in the Levant, Cyprus, and western Italy, though finds in smaller quantities have at this point been discovered as far away as at Huelva, in Spain (Gonzáles de Canales, Serrano, and Llompart 2006). Most of the Italian finds from the beginning of the eighth century are Euboean, and they are limited in distribution to places that are associated with Euboean colonies. By the end of the eighth century, Corinthian wares could be found throughout much of the Italian peninsula. While a wide variety of contexts are present, many drinking and dining sets from elite tombs in Italy, Cyprus, and the Levant suggest that the people in these areas were especially interested in high-quality Greek pottery, particularly in contexts that were related to the convivial occasions so important for social display and cross-cultural interaction. For example, at the elite cemeteries of Salamis, on Cyprus, a wide range of Greek practices and materials is present; these probably represent a conflation and hybridizing of Greek and Cypriot traditions from the Bronze and Early Iron Age (Blackwell 2010). A wider range of pottery shapes is present in Anatolia and Italy than in Cyprus and the Levant, which is probably related to the foundation of permanent settlements in these locations.

---

the Toumba cemetery of Lefkandi as Geometric (since they are contemporary with Attic Geometric), while I include them in the Prehistoric Iron Age.

From Colonial Stories to Mediterranean Histories

Lane Fox (2008), drawing primarily on the evidence of myth, has highlighted "travelling heroes" from Euboea as key agents in the eighth-century Mediterranean. Later textual references to Greek settlements overseas also provide glimpses of early Greece in its Mediterranean context, although all these sources are written from temporally and culturally specific perspectives that result in a somewhat distorted view. While the case of Euboean *apoikiai* was discussed above, we must note that this was part of a larger set of movements involving both Greeks and their less textually visible counterparts throughout the Mediterranean.[19] The timing and distribution of these *apoikiai* is significant, not only for our understating of the period but also for our understanding of regionalism as variable and multiscalar. There are three elements that are relevant here:

1. Colonization movements as coherent entities are largely text-based phenomena—tied up in many of the same identity politics that plague notions of the Ionian or Dorian migrations (see, e.g., Malkin 1998; Hall 2008; Mac Sweeney 2017; see also chapter 5, pp. 187–89).
2. As we have seen in previous chapters, the intensification of Greek activities overseas in the eighth century is both part of a long tradition going back to the Mycenaean period and part of wider, multicultural processes in the Mediterranean (Papadopoulos 2001, 2014).
3. The reification of Greek colonization in modern scholarship has served to simplify a complex set of social phenomena in ways that have obscured both the variety of *apoikiai* and the significance of non-Greek actors (and indeed notions of "Greekness" as well) (Hurst and Owen 2005; Hodos 2006, 2020).

The main factor that makes the eighth century different in terms of Greek activities overseas is that during this period an intensification of activity resulted in permanent settlements that are preserved in the archaeological record, mentioned in historical sources, and last a significant amount of time. The timing and distribution of these settlements is significant. While the eighth century certainly saw revolutionary developments on this front, the bulk of Greek settlements outside of the Aegean were not founded until the seventh and sixth centuries.

Several explanations have been put forward concerning the timing of widespread colonization movements (Descoeudres 2008, 293–96). The two most common are (1) population growth and pressure on agricultural resources in the face of expanding settlement and (2) the quest for metals. Both fit well enough with

---

19. The bibliography on Greek colonization is vast. For overviews, see Boardman 1980; Ridgway 1992; Tsetskhladze 2006, 2008. The term "colonization" is still commonly used to describe these movements, even though it has long been argued that this is an unsatisfactory and misleading term (Purcell 1990, 56; Osborne 1998). Much recent work has rightly focused on the non-Greek contexts and counterparts of Greek *apoikiai* (e.g., van Dommelen 1998, 2005; Hurst and Owen 2005; Hodos 2006, 2009, 2020; Pappa 2013; Donnellan, Nizzo, and Burgers 2016; Lucas, Murray, and Owen 2019).

the combined evidence of diachronic settlement patterns and Greek activities in Italy going back to the Mycenaean period, but neither explanation is very satisfying by itself. Not all regions founded colonies or seemed to respond to settlement growth in the same way. We must therefore look to historical, contingent explanations for settlement expansion, as discussed above in the case of Chalkis and Eretria. Whether the specific interpretation of a relationship with the Lelantine War is correct, the practice of establishing *apoikia*, first in Italy and then elsewhere, does seem to have originated in Euboea, with other areas following suit quickly after. The rapidity of this development—as with others in the eighth century—must be linked to increased local and regional interconnectivity across mainland Greece as well as to other developments in intercommunity engagement (with regional sanctuaries) and media (writing and figural art). The overall pattern of regional variation in both timing and intensity of sending out colonies signals that different regions or polities were pursuing different routes toward their interactions abroad but also learning quickly from one another. Interaction at sanctuaries and competitive emulation must have played a major part in this phenomenon, along with fissioning groups within particular communities, from which individuals and families struck out to seek greater political fortunes in new landscapes.

The geography of the earliest *apoikiai* in the eighth century also sheds light on initial strategies on the part of Euboeans, which were probably learned from Phoenicians and then applied in other contexts. The initial positioning of new Greek settlements just outside areas of Etruscan influence and, in the Phoenician case, at places like Carthage is highly strategic and worth considering in light of other comparative contexts (see Gailledrat, Dietler, and Plana-Mallard 2018). Somewhat neutral locations, outside the interested parties' main spheres of influence, and with easy access to the sea or other corridors for movement, are typical of emporia and other places of initial settlement. These characteristics are highlighted in the location of Pithekoussai, just outside the bay of Naples, which would remain a long-term nexus of maritime activity. Methone, too, at the mouth of the Haliakmon River, offers the opportunity for inland navigation and lateral movement across the northern Aegean.

Cultures in Contact Across the Middle Sea

Toward the end of the eighth century, the city-states of Phoenicia, with the exception of Tyre, were overrun by the expanding Assyrian Empire, and even Tyre was forced to pay excessive tribute (Aubet 2001, 54–58). Part of this expansion may be attributed to the power vacuum in the Levant left by Egypt, which became increasingly fragmented during the Third Intermediate period (1069–664 BCE) and in the mid-eighth century was facing a Kushite incursion from the south (Bard 2008, 267). The tribute demands on Tyre magnified interest abroad in the metalliferous regions of the central and western Mediterranean, with which it had already established connections.

In Cyprus, both Phoenicians and Greeks maintained major interests and contacts, ethnically Greek and Levantine people having lived on the island since the Bronze Age (Iacovou 2005). The hybridity of the eighth century was by this point the result of a long, ongoing process, and the inhabitants of the island itself should be viewed as distinctively Cypriot, though with traceable Greek and Levantine backgrounds. Kition is typically seen as a Phoenician colony by this time, while the royal tombs at Salamis are suggestive of common ties to Greece, as noted above (Smith 2009, 6–13; Blackwell 2010). This mix of cultural elements and connections is hardly a surprise, since Cyprus lies geographically between the Phoenician Levant and Geometric Greek world of the eastern Aegean and western Anatolia.

By the time Greek and Phoenician settlers arrived in the central Mediterranean, Etruscans were already involved in a thriving central Mediterranean network that included Sardinia, trans-Alpine and trans-Apennine Europe, and the Baltic, as well as the entirety of the Italian peninsula and the Adriatic (Haynes 2005). This network had already been tapped by Phoenicians and (probably) some Greeks in the Prehistoric Iron Age and was tied together permanently in the eighth century. In Sicily, the reaction to new arrivals was quite different, as the centralized, hierarchical settlements of the Late Bronze Age and Early Iron Age seemed to retreat inland and become less socially stratified (Hodos 2006, 92).

North Africa saw the founding of Carthage under the agency of Tyre, which itself became a powerful colonizing force in the central and western Mediterranean, although the height of this activity did not occur until after the eighth century. The key point here is the position of Carthage as it relates to a wider central Mediterranean network, rather than a particular set of resources.

The foundation of permanent settlements created hubs that keyed into, but were outside of, the most active indigenous interaction zones. Thus Greek and Phoenician settlement overseas was by no means an attempt to cover or "colonize" the Mediterranean. While my focus here has largely been on Greeks and Phoenicians, there is still a need for a better understanding of local processes and responses to these Mediterranean expansions, as well as interactions between these two groups (see, most recently, Hodos 2020). Central Euboea, Pithekoussai, Methone, Al Mina, and Kition provide examples of such interactions. For the first time, these places created habitual engagements—material, personal, and conceptual—across the Mediterranean. And, from these locations, notions and material expressions of "others" were introduced into their own local and regional networks.

The multicultural settlement at Pithekoussai represents both a beginning and an end. Located almost in the exact center of the Mediterranean, it represents the lynchpin by which the entire basin for the first time becomes integrated through permanent settlements. By the time Euboeans settled here, Phoenicians had already established a presence in the bay of Cadiz, on the other side of the strait of Gibraltar (the Pillars of Herakles). The Phoenician, Greek, and Italic populations that lived together at Pithekoussai were thus connected by only a few links to all shores of the Mediterranean, were involved in established maritime networks on all sides, and shared new sets of social and economic material practices at a local level (Donnellan 2016). But certain separations also started to happen at this time as well. After Pithekoussai there do not seem to be any more "joint" settlements, and the colonial histories of Phoenicians and Greeks take decidedly different paths. In the central and western Mediterranean there is a fairly clear divide between the northeast for Greek and Etruscan activity and southwest for Phoenicians. This is not to say that interaction did not occur—it certainly did, and it is clear enough in both imports and exports, as well as in shared elements of "elite" material culture (Stampolidis and Giannopoulou 2012). In some ways, these interactions seem to have been more culturally significant during earlier periods, even though evidence for them is much more abundant from the "orientalizing" period of the seventh and sixth centuries BCE. Perhaps the divergence between Greek and Phoenician interests is simply a matter of who established lasting presences in these places first and how such presences were received by local communities. The Phoenician route, for example, was to go directly to the rich metal sources of southeast Spain and the Guadalquivir river valley, stopping at important points, including the metal-rich island of Sardinia, along the way. Pithekoussai was an outpost to access the metal-rich landscapes of Etruria, but it was perhaps eventually seen as too far out of the way of already established interests farther west. Maintaining networks requires considerable effort and cannot be sustained on all fronts at once. It should not be surprising, then, that different groups sought different interfaces after an initial period of growing together.

This geographical divergence is also manifest in aspects of material culture in the long term. While a sort of elite, international style did develop during this period, the media of decorated pottery are where we see the greatest divergence between the places of Greek and Phoenician interface. Etruria and southern Italy very quickly became consumers of Greek material and visual culture, though both developed their own distinct forms. Such blending seems to happen less in Phoenician colonies, but this impression is at least partly attributable to huge gaps in our knowledge concerning North Africa and considerable disciplinary separation between Iberian and other Mediterranean archaeologies. A final point of divergence is that concern with the sea and seafaring is not always directly manifest in aspects of Phoenician visual culture. This does not, of course, mean that it was not present in the visual experience and popular imagination, since it certainly was in places like Pithekoussai. One of the more noteworthy things to come out of this comparison is the rather stark difference between a Greek interest in seafaring in popular media and an apparent lack of such an interest in the Phoenician case (at least in terms of what is visible to us today).

Network distances shrank in the eighth century BCE. With the addition of just a few permanent (or at least habitual) links between central Greece and the central Mediterranean, it became possible to reach nearly any point in the Greek world from most places in the Mediterranean, passing through increasingly multicultural hubs. At any given time, then, individuals living in central Greece were just a few links away from inhabitants (both native and immigrant) in Italy or the northern Aegean. Moreover, through multiethnic places like Pithekoussai or Al Mina, they were only another link or two from Sardinia, Iberia, North Africa, the Levant, and the wider Phoenician world. It is not the novelty of making such connections that was significant but their intensification through the establishment of permanent communities, which were deliberately engaged in the more widely connected webs of their new locations.

CODA: FROM VILLAGES TO POLEIS

In concluding this chapter, I look to the Archaic period, pointing in particular toward the scalar differences that characterize it, and contrasting it with the periods to which the bulk of this book has been devoted. It is only in the seventh century (rather late, in fact, and continuing into the sixth) that the *transitional* period of early Greece concludes, arriving firmly in the Archaic Greek world.

Processes begun in the eighth century do not really become widespread until the seventh and sixth centuries, when we see a transition from a world of complex village communities to the world of Archaic and Classical Greek city-states. That this happened rather suddenly should come as no surprise, given the speed with which state formation tends to happen. The Aegean alone has several instructive examples, including the rapid development of Mycenaean palatial systems discussed in chapter 3 and models of revolution over evolution for Minoan Crete (Cherry 1983a; 2010, 138; Manning 2018). This is not to say that gradual changes do not happen, but rather that major changes tend to happen quickly, as punctuated equilibria that affect multiple subsets of society at once. Renfrew (1972, 36–44) described this as the "multiplier effect" in characterizing the Bronze Age emergence of civilization in the Aegean. This idea was revisited by Snodgrass (1980a, 54) in the case of eighth-century Greece, though the final result seems most applicable to the seventh.

The seventh century BCE—the early Archaic period—has long been problematic for archaeologists and historians. Étienne (2017, 9), for example, begins a recent summary with the heading: "Did the seventh century exist?" This is a reference to the difficulty in distinguishing this century materially and textually from the eighth, on one side of the chronological spectrum, and from the sixth, on the other. Athens and Attica have received by far the most attention in terms of both the archaeological and literary record. Studies of burial, settlement, and pottery decoration are neatly summarized by Osborne (1989), who highlights that these aspects of the material record are largely ignored by historians, up until history "begins" with the Kylonian affair of about 630 BCE (a coup which the recently discovered mass grave at Phaleron may—or may not—illuminate [Ingvarsson and Bäckström 2019]). There are also several problems in the archaeological record of the seventh century. The most fundamental of these concerns pottery chronologies and the fact that they most certainly overlap, with the Geometric period likely extending well into the seventh century, even as Orientalizing-period styles were developing simultaneously. A welcome influx of recent scholarship has focused on the seventh century specifically. This scholarship has begun to illuminate parts of Greece outside of Athens, and it has brought this crucial, if confusing, time period into sharper focus (Étienne 2010; Brisart 2011; Charalambidou and Morgan 2017; Lemos and Tsingarida 2019; Whitley 2020).

If the eighth century contains the revolutionary spark of the early Greek world, the seventh is where it truly kindled. While the eighth-century settlement pattern represents significant expansion, most of this dates to after 750 BCE, and even at that point the evidence is thin in comparison to the seventh and sixth centuries (Foxhall 2013, 215). The developments begun in the eighth century in terms of settlements overseas, polity formation, and early Greek script come fully to fruition in the seventh century, representing the most significant phase transition since the formation of Mycenaean palaces (van der Vliet 2011; Haggis 2013; Small 2019). What is different, however, is that the transition into the world of poleis was both more widespread and more lasting than the regionally specific false starts of the Mycenaean palaces. While problematic ceramic chronologies and settlement studies still have some catching up to do, this scalar difference is borne out through (1) the material signatures of settlement overseas, (2) the growth of central places (major settlements and sanctuaries), (3) the proliferation writing, and (4) the introduction of coinage.

The first wave of colonization movements discussed above seems largely to have been led by Euboeans. By the end of the eighth century, several other city-states were involved, and by the end of the seventh century, communities across the Greek world were establishing *apoikiai*. A recent count puts the number of *apoikiai* established in the eighth century at about 30 and the number established in in the seventh at about 60 (see Osborne 2009, 110–21, table 5). Geographical diversification occurred in the location of new settlements as well, as settlements were established in the Black Sea, North Africa, and the western Mediterranean (modern France and Spain), beginning in the seventh century and continuing into the sixth. Indeed, some of the most important and long-lasting examples of Greek settlements abroad were established during this era, reflecting also a much wider range of mother cities: Byzantium and Chalkedon (Megara is the mother city), Sinope (Miletos), Cyrene (Thera), Apollonia (Corinth and Kerkyra), Massalia (Phokaia), Emporion (Massalia and Phokaia) (see map 30, top). Naukratis in Egypt seems to have evolved more organically, since it was established in the seventh century in the location of a long-standing trading emporium. The expanding geography of new communities and the diversity of Greek polities establishing them signal a scalar shift in the organization and activities of early Greek societies, as well as the institutionalization of practices that began in the eighth century.

As for the political structures of communities themselves, these seem to have undergone their most fundamental transformations in the seventh, rather than the eighth, century, although we must rely mostly on historical sources for understanding these. Whitley (2020) points out that the polis was largely unknown to Hesiod, writing around 700 BCE. He is aware of larger communities than his own village at Askra (in Boeotia) but he says nothing of the monumental architecture and complex social organization that characterize later Greek poleis and other states. By 600 BCE, we can see civil strife between aristocratic factions at Athens, complex administrative offices concerning temples and ships, and political communities with codified systems of written laws on Crete. Whitley (2020, 170) further notes the extraordinary rapidity of these processes of emergence, which took place between about 700 and 640. Like colonization, the spread of such institutional practices only could have undergone such intensifying processes in the network architecture first established in the eighth century.

The Archaic period was equally transformative for the physical vestiges of increasing social complexity—most importantly in the architectural forms that would come to characterize the Greek city-state. Most noticeable are the systems of fortifications, which became widespread in the seventh century, and by the sixth century were a staple of any polis (Frederiksen 2011). Reflecting on seventh-century settlements in general, Frederiksen (2017, 192) notes: "We could not imagine such communities without neighbourhoods of private houses separated by lanes and streets, without at least one (urban) sanctuary, designated cemeteries, a harbour or landing place, a political and commercial meeting place/agora, and so on" (see also Osborne 2009; Mazarakis Ainian 2017). We could not say this about the much more varied and village-like communities of the eighth century or of any period that came before. Still further material correlates for state formation are visible in the increasing dedications at regional sanctuaries, as well as in the "hoplite revolution" that spread across much of the Greek world in the seventh century (Snodgrass [1967] 1999, 48–60; Foxhall 2013).

Writing was *the* major catalyst for lasting social organization, the formation of political institutions, and the beginning of proper history. Our knowledge of Archaic Greek political institutions is entirely dependent on the technology of writing, as was their own longevity. As with settlements overseas, there was a scalar difference in the proliferation of writing in the seventh versus the eighth centuries. There are about 20 sites with roughly 160 examples of early Greek writing in possible or definite eighth-century contexts, with most of the examples coming from Eretria, Methone, Pithekoussai, and Kommos (see map 29). For the seventh century, the number of sites and examples more than doubles (Jeffery 1990). While the adoption of the alphabet in the eighth century constituted a media revolution in and of itself, writing did not become part of a truly structural revolution until its seventh-century deployment in political contexts. The eighth century was still very much in the realm of protohistory and mythohistory. The few examples of writing we do have indicate that writing had little to do with the recording of events or societal regulations but was used rather for economic purposes or in the convivial contexts of social interaction. By the seventh century, writing had become explicitly political, as it was turned toward the state apparatus of keeping accounts, recording laws and office holders, historical events, conflicts, and alliances. While state-like modes of social organization may be possible without writing, they are difficult to see in the early Greek world until writing and history become distinctly political.

The final fundamentally transformative development of the seventh century was the invention of coinage. Invented in Lydia (Sardis) at the end of the seventh century, coinage became widespread in the Greek world in the sixth and was a hallmark of Archaic poleis that would transform economic transactions and invoke codified political institutions across the Mediterranean. Just as writing intensified social and political processes, coinage was a structuring commodity of value that had an immeasurable impact on the economic systems of an increasingly interconnected Mediterranean (Papadopoulos 2014, 188–90). While the eighth century may have set the stage for the rapid proliferation of the social, political, economic, and material changes enumerated above, it was only in the seventh that they became widespread, institutionalized, and permanent fixtures of Greek societies.

CONCLUSIONS: MOBILITY, MEDIA, AND THE POLITICAL LANDSCAPE

The developments of the Protohistoric Iron Age in central Greece had major consequences across the Mediterranean. Some of these were shared throughout the Greek world, but there were nevertheless historical circumstances that make central Greece, and several more specific areas within it, stand out. In many ways, Snodgrass's ([1971] 2000, 416) admonition still rings true—that the changes of the eighth century are difficult to put in logical order, although they certainly make more sense when viewed in terms of what came before and after.

In the first place, dramatic growth in the overall settlement pattern suggests a population increase across the Greek mainland. This pattern, however, varies widely across regions. The areas that experience the most dramatic growth—Attica and Boeotia—had also experienced the most significant decline after the collapse of the palaces (although this occurred in Attica much more gradually, and in a very different way). Growth in other regions was marginal, while Thessaly even experienced substantial decline. To me this suggests that we cannot look to things like general population pressure as a singular motivation for the founding of Greek colonies overseas—not least because the regions that would have been most affected by rising populations were not involved in the earliest establishments of *apoikiai*. We need to look rather to a combination of regionally specific societal trajectories and particular historical circumstances. The latter are rarely detectable in the archaeological record, but in the case of central Euboea there seems to be a confluence of landscape, archaeological, and mythohistorical evidence that suggests one way in which such dynamics play out across local landscapes and the Mediterranean writ large.

At the same time, we see developments in the religious landscape that reshaped the way communities interacted with one another, due in part to regional crowding and the encroachment of certain communities into the territories of others. The emergence of regional and interregional sanctuaries as hubs of mediation suggests the evolution of particular types of responses to interpolity competition. More local responses, on the order of individual landscapes and between communities, were manifest in the form of tomb cult.

Framing all of these local and regional developments is a series of long-distance interactions that led to the reappearance of writing in the early Greek world, after a hiatus of around four centuries. This happened within a set of central Euboean-Phoenician interfaces that had been in place since the Prehistoric Iron Age. These same long-term processes provided structures for the establishment of permanent settlements in Italy and the North Aegean. At the same time, the widespread regional connections of Attic and Euboean pottery networks were the avenues through which writing dispersed so quickly after its development. While this does not "solve" the question of the location and timing of the alphabet, it pulls together a variety of circumstantial evidence concerning the structure of multiscalar, multicultural interaction to suggest a plausible model rooted in central Euboea.

This chapter has examined landscape and interaction to provide explanations for historical and cultural processes on the very cusp of history. We know more or less what happened from a variety of historical and archaeological evidence, but this is not enough to explain *why* or *how* such developments took place. Network and connectivity models rooted in geographic realities and explicitly multiscalar perspectives can be used to fill these gaps in our knowledge. Moreover, a diachronic approach shows how concurrent historical processes relate to one another and intensify human interactions in ways we might not otherwise have understood. The intensification that happens in the eighth century, especially in the transition from the Middle to the Late Geometric period, shows how social phenomena such as settlement expansion, colonization, intercommunity competition, and technological and artistic innovation acted as mutually intensifying processes across space and time. While these expanded networks and the multiplier effect of simultaneous social change are well known from a descriptive standpoint, it is only by viewing them together that we can arrive at new explanations of social and material engagements. In the case of the Protohistoric Iron Age, the end results are the framework and structures that define the Archaic period, if still in somewhat primitive form. By the end of the seventh century, however, the transition was complete: out of the village societies of early Greece and into the more widely known, more widely recognizable Archaic Greek world.

Conclusions

Early Greece and the Bigger Picture(s)

The overall conclusions of this book fall into two broad categories: contributions to our understandings of the archaeology of early Greece and contributions to the broader field of the study of complex societies. In each case I reflect on the place of this book in its wider historical, comparative, and disciplinary contexts, and I follow up with some considerations for future research. The discussions here are meant to be relevant both to archaeologists and historians of Greece and to archaeologists of other complex societies. A final concern has to do with the larger question of why early Greece matters beyond the academic communities to whom the arguments in this book are primarily addressed.

GREECE IN TRANSITION

A variety of period-specific and historical conclusions can be found in each of the foregoing chapters (3, 4, 5 and 6). Rather than enumerate them here, I focus on two core themes: (1) the long-term perspective concerning the archaeology of central Greece from the Mycenaean period through the Early Iron Age—adding diversity to dominant paradigms through a multiregional approach that seeks comparisons both within Greece and beyond; and (2) the historical-geographical phenomenon of central Greece becoming central—why this transitional period was so important for this particular part of the Mediterranean world.

Diversity through Synthesis and Multiple Modes of Polity

As a study of ancient Greek social and political landscapes, this book integrates a variety of archaeological evidence across several social and spatial scales. Systematic and unsystematic surveys, long-term research projects, and rescue excavations have all contributed valuable data from some 400 archaeological sites (and, among these, thousands of individual findspots). It is only by bringing these data together that we can see how the picture of settlement varies across the different regions under study. This observation is underscored by the amount of recent work on the topic of regionalism (see, e.g., Mazarakis Ainian, Alexandridou, and Charalambidou 2017; Eder 2019; Lemos and Kotsonas 2020). Most individual studies nevertheless focus on a single area or single time period. The long-term, multiregional perspective developed here has allowed us to see the shifting mosaic of the early Greek landscape in myriad ways.

Such a lens leads us to question several long-standing paradigms. Some of these have long been the subject of scrutiny, though rarely in a systematic, diachronic way. These include the primacy of Mycenaean palaces as powerful states with extensive territories, notions of global collapse across Greece and the eastern Mediterranean, and the idea of a rebirth or a "Greek miracle" springing out of a stagnant dark age. These are all exaggerated perspectives, but they remain present in general narratives that paint a picture of early Greece with broad strokes. More sophisticated understandings of the social and historical processes surrounding these paradigms are now possible.

Mycenaean palaces have long dominated discussions of the Late Bronze Age. Their visibility in the landscape, extensive architectural remains, elaborate cemeteries, and elite material culture have inspired authors from the time of Homer onward. Linear B gives us insights into the political and economic operation of palaces that are simply not possible for other periods of the early Greek past—indeed, not until after the eighth century BCE. This wealth of evidence concerning the palaces and the places around them, however, is in fact quite limiting when we consider the Mycenaean world as a whole. The Peloponnesian paradigm suggests that palaces in Messenia and the Argolid (and most recently Laconia) developed quickly at the end of a long Early Mycenaean period in which monumentality gradually shifted from family tombs to a central administrative structure, while interaction with neighboring civilizations intensified and political authority shifted from charismatic individuals to institutions. This is a fairly standard narrative of state formation that can be observed in several parts of the world. The central Greek case, however, shows something quite different. State formation—that is, the development of palaces—seems to have happened much more quickly in central Greece, after the Peloponnese, and only in certain areas. The evidence for palaces themselves is limited to LH IIIA2 and onward, while monumental tholos tombs appear in only two places beforehand (Thorikos and Volos) and only in a handful of locations afterward (Menidi, Orchomenos, etc.)—and all of this after the heyday of tholos tomb building in the Peloponnese. In this way, we seem to have multiple cases of secondary state formation—perhaps also a sort of tertiary state formation or the agglomerative development of peer polities—in which emerging polities only incidentally come onto the scene as actual peers of previously existing palatial centers.

This process does not happen everywhere, however, and even generous estimates of palatial territory put a large amount of the landscape well outside any likely palatial remit. Our data for all the central Greek palaces is fragmentary, but we might identify regional palatial centers at Thebes, Orchomenos, Gla, and Athens, this last being based on limited and circumstantial evidence. Something different seems to have happened in Thessaly, which may have had two palatial centers—at Palaia (Kastro Volos) and at Dimini—although the relationship between them remains unclear. Other question marks include Krisa in southern Phokis and Kanakia in Salamis. In between the palatial areas of northern Boeotia and Thessaly there is a distance of some 250 kilometers by land as well as several entire regions. These should not be seen as blank spots, or as places that "lacked" a palace, failed to achieve statehood, or otherwise missed the mark. Rather, they contained complex sociopolitical systems in their own right. Significant, if not palatial, centers can be detected in numerous places: in monumental tholos tombs at Medeon (in Phokis) and Georgiko (western Thessaly), with no known palace site nearby; in the upper Kephisos valley and East Lokris; in and around Lamia; in various parts of central Euboea; and in eastern and western Attica. These areas were occupied by people living outside any apparent centralized state, and this was probably quite deliberate. The range of complexity and social organization represented in the (often ambiguous) archaeological record across these areas suggests that we are dealing with complex communities where rank and hierarchy are important but not reified through formal institutions with a high degree of archaeological visibility (see Porter 2013).

A good overall case for comparison can be found in Mississippian chiefdoms, where more and less complex social forms existed side by side and oscillated across the macroregional landscape, and where scholarship has revealed a considerable degree of organizational diversity among contemporary political communities (Blitz 2010). Interactions between Late Woodland groups and Mississippian chiefdoms shed particular light on this issue. In this case, Late Woodland groups adopted particular elements of Mississippian culture, including Cahokian potting traditions, but largely maintained pre-Mississippian modes of social organization (Bardolph 2014). We can see a parallel in this regard with Mycenaean palaces and their interactions with nonpalatial zones, which seem to have been selective in their adoption of elements of palatial material culture. What is more, we should keep in mind that living in a state—with all its labor demands for surplus agricultural production, monumental building, and so on—would have hardly been pleasant or desirable for the vast majority of its subject-inhabitants (Scott 2009).

Based on the evidence of central Greece, we might conclude that if people could live outside the reach of state authority, they would. For most people living most of the time (in early Greece as well as in other predominantly village-based societies), subsistence agriculture was the priority—and one with which states interfered. The central Greek case suggests that Mycenaean states, such as they were, did not have a particularly long reach or deep institutional history, making them quite different from their contemporaries elsewhere in the eastern Mediterranean. This also meant that they were unlikely to emerge in a strictly evolutionary course of societal development, as is reflected in the similarity of social formations witnessed before and after the Mycenaean palaces. There was, as a consequence, remarkable variety in the political systems and modes of social organization across Mycenaean central Greece.

The palatial collapse around 1200 BCE was felt most strongly—unsurprisingly—in palatial areas. It is precisely in the modeled territories of Mycenaean palaces that there was a significant drop in settlement numbers, access to prestige goods, and monumental construction, not to mention in administrative systems that only ever existed within palatial contexts. Elsewhere, decreases in site numbers were considerably less extreme (see figure 2). In fact, there seems to be a direct correlation between the level of centralization in the Palatial period and site attrition in Postpalatial times. Boeotia has the most evidence for palaces as centralizing forces, with the Linear B tablets from Thebes and the great drainage works and monumental construction in the Kopaic Basin. This region also had the most substantial drop in site numbers. Athens and Thessaly both saw more modest drops, and indeed seem to have been less centralized in palatial times. At the same time, certain areas that were beyond the apparent influence of the palaces in the Palatial period came to thrive in Postpalatial times, precisely because they did not suffer any kind of sociopolitical collapse. It seems rather that Postpalatial communities—for example, coastal ones at Lefkandi, Kynos, Porto Rafti (Perati, Raftis Island), and Pefkakia—were able to take advantage of the power vacuum left by the disappearance of the palaces. These patterns in central Greece are most apparent in the area of the Euboean Gulf, a trend that reflects a greater amount of human mobility—especially maritime—across the Mediterranean as a whole. Traveling craftspeople, migrant groups, entrepreneurs, and traders emerged out of the breakdown of formalized diplomacy and state-sponsored travel that characterized much of the Late Bronze Age eastern Mediterranean. The age of mobility that followed happened in the wake of significant social reorganization after the decline of palatial systems.

The maritime orientation of Postpalatial times has echoes in chieftaincies in Scandinavia, and in other parts of the world, in what Ling, Earle, and Kristiansen (2018) call a maritime mode of production. Shared interests in trading and raiding are reflected in iconography, the material record, and the ethnohistoric record, especially in situations in which decentralized societies operated on the margins or in the wake of more centralized political systems. While such a maritime mode of production is apparent in some parts of the Postpalatial world (e.g., along the Euboean Gulf), there is significant continuity in the complex communities of other areas (e.g., in the Spercheios and northern Kephisos valleys), which in the previous period were nonpalatial. So, while comparative cases signal dynamic societal trajectories in some cases, there remains a significant amount of resilience in others.

Regional diversity continues to characterize our evidence for settlement and society in central Greece into the Prehistoric Iron Age. While the overall number of sites in Attica reached its nadir during this period, Athens itself seems to have flourished, both in terms of its physical extent and its influential pottery industry. On the opposite end of the study area, in Thessaly, settlement expanded considerably, as can be seen especially through funerary architecture—the small tholoi characteristic of the region in the Early Iron Age—which represents a significant and widespread set of references to the Bronze Age past. Continuities from Mycenaean times are also evident in various parts of Malis and Phokis, especially in the remarkable chamber tomb cemeteries of the Spercheios valley and Elateia. It was during this period as well that central Euboea continued to develop as the prime example of Postpalatial emergence in the wake of Palatial collapse. As at Athens, pottery production played a major role, and it can now be demonstrated that the clay quarries of central Euboea were a common link to many parts of central Greece, eventually extending throughout the Aegean and beyond (Kerschner and Lemos 2014). While new scientific evidence has put emphasis on the Early Iron Age, stylistic influence was already present in the Postpalatial Bronze Age. In this case, we do seem to have a gradual, perhaps even linear, expansion in the distribution and then the influence of Euboean ceramics, operating in tandem with Athenian influence, which started later but eventually became much stronger. The Euboean Gulf was especially important as the maritime conduit through which many of these sociotechnological interactions flowed. The arrival of iron technology in central Greece, too, is evidence of significant connections to the eastern Mediterranean, most likely to Cyprus, a long-term point of connection for early Greece. The concentration of early iron artifacts in central Greece, especially in the emergent centers of Athens and Lefkandi, signal their importance as nodal points in networks of changing pyrotechnologies, which must also be related to their uncharacteristically rich records of settlement and burial wealth, as well as to apparent levels of social inequality at the time.

There was a great infilling of settlement in the eighth century, both in the landscapes of central Greece and in various other parts of the Mediterranean. The political landscape was increasingly mediated by local shrines and regional sanctuaries. Decreasing distances between settlements meant closer and more frequent interactions between them, which decreased the necessity for longer-distance excursions and concentrated greater attention on particular parts of a landscape or region. Longer-distance interactions were still maintained intermittently at interregional and eventually panhellenic sanctuaries. At the same time, growth within communities and shrinking distances between them introduced new stresses, which seem to have resulted in community fissioning, even as aspects of local and regional identity were being reified across the landscape (Small 2019). This type of fissioning is well documented in other village societies (McGuire and Saitta 1996; Blitz 1999; Bandy 2004), but the distances and maritime orientation of the Greek case is significant and would have had dramatic effects in expanding the geography of evolving Greek notions of identity and polity.

The eighth-century establishment of Greek settlements overseas followed a long history of earlier activities in Italy and in the eastern Mediterranean from the Mycenaean period onward. Greek craftspeople, at least, and probably permanent populations too, were established much earlier throughout western Anatolia and in Cyprus, as well as in Italy. The "first" Greek colonies in Italy are therefore a historical rather than an archaeological phenomenon, but one that was nonetheless significant, since *apoikiai* did spur changes in Mediterranean settlement that are also manifest in the archaeological record. The leading role of Euboeans is important, and it is coincident with a variety other activities with apparent nexuses in central Euboea, including the adaptation of the Phoenician script into the Greek alphabet and its subsequent dissemination, as well as some record of disturbance at home, perhaps in relation to a mythohistorical Lelantine war. Monocausal explanations for overseas settlement that have to do with land hunger and population growth seem not to obtain, as increases in site numbers are in fact rather marginal in places like Euboea, while Boeotia and Athens see the greatest growth and did not seem to have played a major role in overseas settlement. More complex political processes like local conflict, social fissioning, expanding long-distance trade networks, and targeted procurement of resources are perhaps more appropriate explanations. At the same time, climatic volatility and agricultural uncertainty may have contributed to the development of new settlement strategies, including territorial consolidation or the establishment of new communities elsewhere, on regional or microregional scales.

By the end of the eighth century, we have a blueprint for the Archaic Greek world. Independent polities are evident across central Greece in the form of communities that would develop into historically known poleis; other regions followed different paths of sociopolitical complexity to become federated states or *ethne*, following the pattern of regional diversity in sociopolitical organization that characterized previous periods as well (see, e.g., Morgan 2003; Hansen and Nielsen 2004; Papadopoulos 2016a). These processes would not come to fruition, however, until the seventh and sixth centuries. There does *not* seem to have been an ur-period of polis formation, at least not in the eighth century, where poleis all over the Greek world pulled themselves up by their bootstraps on roughly equal footing. Rather, there are eighth-century episodes of community florescence, not unlike the emergence of Mycenaean palaces in that they are limited to particular regions and circumstances. The difference is that the networks and structures introduced in the eighth century—including writing and regional sanctuaries—eventually led to the wider dispersal of polis institutions in the centuries that followed.

In the long term, mutual development happened in the context of regional and interregional interactions, but there was rarely, if ever, some form of even evolution across all regions of the Greek world. Oscillations in relative importance and influence characterize central Greece from the Mycenaean period through the eighth century. While a general characterization of nonlinear development obtains across the region as a whole, the most consistent factor is diversity. The emergence of poleis with stronger, codified institutions across the seventh and sixth centuries represents a significant phase transition that signals the end of early Greece, which is characterized by village societies and examples of more and less complex communities.

Central Greece Becomes Central

While the core datasets of this book are derived from the archaeological land-scapes of central Greece, much of the discussion has referred to early Greece in general, or to the place of early Greece in the wider Mediterranean world. There are two reasons for this blended approach. On the one hand, central Greece has been subject to less synthetic treatment than other regions, most notably the Peloponnese. On the other hand, the regions investigated here collectively came to play a leading role in the development of the early Greek world during precisely this period. Between Thessaly and Attica, and including Euboea, we see several social and material phenomena emerge that highlight the importance and centrality of this geographical zone.

I argued in chapter 2 that central Greece occupies a dual crossroads, with the Euboean Gulf serving as a key maritime axis linking the north and south Aegean and the Kephisos valley and Great Isthmus Corridor serving as crucial land routes between northern and southern Greece. We can see glimpses of this already in the Early and Middle Bronze Age, when Manika in central Euboea and Eutresis in southwestern Boeotia become centers of interregional pottery and obsidian consumption in spite of their geographical distance from source areas and trading partners such as the Troad and Melos (Goldman 1931; Sampson 1985, 1988). These geographical considerations are borne out in later periods as well, with Homer's designation of Aulis as the mustering point of the Achaians and Delphi serving as the notional center of the world (and of Mediterranean politics).

The Mycenaean world might be seen as the earliest demonstrably "Greek" period of history in the Aegean, based on its connection to a more literate Early Iron Age through an oral tradition, which looked back to an "age of heroes" that was important for later aspects of collective identity formation. At the same time, aspects of Greek religion are first traceable in the names of later divinities in the Linear B tablets, providing further aspects of continuity across the Bronze Age/Iron Age divide. Such continuities may extend much further, but they at any rate seem to go through an important period of crystallization in a core area that—during the period covered by this book—includes central Greece and the Peloponnese, along with many parts of the Aegean islands. So, while diversity is ubiquitous, the connective opportunities allowed by central Greece as a geographical center signal this macroregion as an important hub in the dispersal of material culture, language, and religion that would culminate in later ideas of Pan-hellenism. If one imagines, then, a network of places that can be considered "early Greek," whether for archaeological, religious, or mythological significance, central Greece becomes increasingly central from the end of the Bronze Age to the eighth century BCE.

This increasing centrality can also be observed on the wider scale of Mediterranean affairs. Interactions between Aegean societies and their neighbors are less civilizational in emphasis and scope than they are dialogues between particular centers. Networks of consumption of eastern exotica are focused first on the Minoan palaces of Crete, most notably Knossos, and then shift northward to the Mycenaean palaces, with Mycenae by far outpacing the rest and eventually Thebes arriving on the scene (Cline 1997; Burns 2010; Murray 2017). As discussed in chapters 3 and 4, this record may be somewhat skewed; but, based on the currently available evidence, the pattern is clear (compare maps 13 and 17). Palatial period centralization is followed by Postpalatial dispersal, most notably to previously nonpalatial areas; this reflects broader patterns of decentralization in eastern Mediterranean trade and consumption in the twelfth century BCE. By the Protogeometric period, import evidence, though paltry, is found primarily in central Greece (eight sites), there being comparably less such evidence in the Peloponnese (four sites) (compare maps 17 and 23). While the Peloponnese experiences some recovery in Geometric times, especially at Olympia and Sparta, greater concentrations of imports can still be found in central Greece (see map 30). These patterns track broadly with the apparent activities of different parts of central Greece in the north Aegean, in the eastern Mediterranean, and eventually in the central Mediterranean—most notably through the wide dispersal of Athenian and Euboean pottery and, eventually, through Euboean settlements. While this summary is not intended as an argument for the preeminence of one region over another, it does demonstrate the utility of examining societal development on multiple spatial scales, based on layered notions of collective identity that include social groups operating in individual communities, regions, or culture areas.

Prospects and Potential

The archaeology of early Greece is a rich and active field of scholarship. Work in central Greece is increasingly brought to the fore by a variety of recent regional conferences and companion volumes, evincing a trend that makes the sort of synthesis presented here possible (see, e.g., Mazarakis Ainian, Alexandridou, and Charalambidou 2017; Lemos and Kotsonas 2020; Middleton 2020). I hope that this book will encourage further work at levels above the individual project, site, or region. Such a study also offers the opportunity to reflect on what is missing and to speculate about exciting prospects for future work. To my mind, these prospects fall into three main categories: (1) increased deployment of new techniques in the analysis of archaeological materials; (2) the orchestration and publication of new fieldwork in a variety of contexts; and (3) participation in a wider variety of world archaeological dialogues.

A central concern of Mediterranean archaeology remains mobility and migration, especially for the Bronze Age and Early Iron Age (see, e.g., van Dommelen and Knapp 2010; Hamilakis 2016; Molloy 2016; Driessen 2018; Iacono 2019). How much were people moving around and in what capacity were they doing so? To what extent did migration occur on a large scale? How did populations intermingle in such circumstances? How do we understand the circumstances in which migration took place? These questions have been addressed primarily through the analysis of material culture in both ancient and modern contexts. Archaeogenetics and DNA studies have long presented exciting ways forward in the analysis of human, animal, and plant remains (see, e.g., Renfrew and Boyle 2000). Such approaches have proved particularly exciting in analyzing the dispersal of early farmers across Europe, having traced a more or less direct path of migration and the diffusion of agriculture from east to west that was largely maritime (Hofmanová et al. 2016). Recent examples of DNA studies concerning the Aegean Bronze Age have been somewhat overstated, however, in their capacity to address wider questions, focused as they are on the analysis of a few samples from a handful of places (Lazaridis et al. 2017). The potential of such analyses, however, lies in their application over a wide, spatially and temporally diverse dataset. The application of such analyses to human remains from a variety of excavated sites and from a systematically selected sample of contexts would provide important insights into regional and interregional patterns of genetic diversity over time and address how changes in genetic makeup corresponded (or not) with material culture change. A wide sample would provide a novel macroregional, multiscalar dataset that could be integrated into studies of long-term social change. Up until this point, the cost of sample processing has prohibited such widespread programs; but, as the analysis of ancient DNA becomes more commonplace, costs of analysis are already dropping. The design and the permissions to carry out a study of such scope remain barriers but ones that are hopefully surmountable. Fortunately, such large-scale studies are currently in the works—with a new, multidisciplinary European Research Council Grant, for example.[1]

Provenience studies have long offered insights into the movement of materials, and thereby patterns of production and consumption (see, e.g., Knapp and Cherry 1994). As with DNA studies, provenience studies in specific cases provide new insights concerning regional ceramic traditions and their dispersal on multiple scales. The most recent example relevant to this book is the application of neutron activation analysis to Euboean or Euboean-like ceramics from multiple contexts around the Mediterranean (Kerschner and Lemos 2014). On its own, however, a

---

1. The project is funded by an ERC Consolidator Grant, directed by Molloy. For more information, see The Fall 1200 BC, accessed December 8, 2020, http://www.thefall1200.eu/.

study of pottery from a single region is limited. If we apply such methods in the context of other regional ceramic traditions, in a diachronic framework, the picture may become more complex and yield new insights into regional dynamics rather than simply the interregional reach of one or a few ceramic traditions.

Another growth field is radiometric dating. Improved C-14 calibration allows for increased chronological refinement, while at the same time accelerator mass spectrometry (AMS) techniques are able to deal with smaller samples. These are dependent on excavated contexts, however, and the survey data on which much regional evidence is based remains largely confined to stylistic dating of surface ceramics. As AMS techniques improve, we might be able to see applications that are able to date artifacts directly—for example, charcoal fragments within the fabric of coarse wares or preserved in metal slags. One obvious opportunity of increased chronological resolution is the capacity to look at synchronisms, which continue to occupy a key disciplinary space when considering things like the Late Bronze Age "collapse" in the eastern Mediterranean, as well as other site destructions and events to which the archaeological record might bear witness. Related, of course, are the issues of environmental studies and ancient climate, fields witnessing constant refinement in their own right and for which higher resolution dating is essential.

The collection of new archaeological data through fieldwork and the analysis of unstudied material are the best and most obvious means of expanding, testing, or challenging the arguments and interpretations posed here. As discussed in chapter 2, the analysis of the archaeological landscape on which much of this book is based draws on data from a variety of sources. Different types of fieldwork—unsystematic and systematic surveys, research and rescue excavations—yield fundamentally different results, unevenly distributed across the landscape. Sites and communities for which we have a wealth of systematically collected data are in the minority. For the majority of sites included in the overall analysis, therefore, we have to rely on varying degrees of inference and projection. These are informed projections, to be sure, and based on careful consideration of the available evidence, but in the end inferences and interpretation can be made with much greater certainty for some sites than for others.

Ongoing fieldwork at numerous sites will continue to refine our understanding of the early Greek world, both in central Greece and beyond. Recent publications concerning Thebes, for example, shed light on this important mega-center of the Mycenaean world, even though excavations are by nature spottily interspersed across the modern city (Aravantinos and Kountouri 2014). Ongoing projects at Gla and in the Kopais have equally exciting implications, although our knowledge of Orchomenos remains comparatively paltry. The recent publication of excavations at Dimini, too, are promising (Adrimi-Sismani 2017, 2018), and will be even more significant when work from Kastro Volos and Pefkakia reaches final publication (though see Batziou-Efstathiou 2015 and Skafida et al. 2016 for recent summaries). In the Peloponnese, new discoveries concerning the elite cemetery of Pylos offer promising insights for Early Mycenaean times (Davis and Stocker

2016; Stocker and Davis 2017). At the same time, the Mycenaean palace at Aghios Vasileios, near Sparta, discovered in 2007 and under excavation since then, provides yet another example of diversity in Mycenaean palatial architecture and organization (Kardamaki 2017).

From the Postpalatial period and Early Iron Age several major sites await final publication (e.g., Kynos, Lefkandi, Mitrou). Recently published work on the Early Iron Age of Athens offers an important resource, not least in providing a frame of reference for Attic pottery found widely distributed in other contexts (Papadopoulos and Smithson 2017 Dimitriadou 2019). In-progress research and publication at all these sites will provide significant insights concerning the arguments of this book.

The greatest opportunity for growth, however, concerns fieldwork in sites and landscapes that have not heretofore been subject to systematic investigations. Most parts of the study area examined in this book are covered by gazetteers; many have been extensively surveyed; all have registers of archaeological sites with the local ephorates of the Hellenic Ministry of Culture. However, systematic regional coverage remains quite uneven (see map 3). Areas of particular importance for future regional work include those with major and secondary centers in which very little systematic survey has been conducted: northern and central Euboea; much of Phokis; southern Thessaly; and various places in the vicinity of Lamia. Numerous microenvironments in any of these regions could benefit from more detailed attention, especially around major or secondary centers that promise more complex settlement patterns. For example, in several locations, especially in Malis, a large community in the Mycenaean period can be inferred based on cemetery remains, but no settlement is as yet known. Intensive regional survey work is also likely to answer questions concerning sites that appear to be relatively isolated in the overall settlement pattern. The amount and the variety of recent and ongoing survey work in eastern Attica is particularly encouraging (see table 3).

In the wider world of early Greek settlement patterns, large-scale sites are (for the most part) reasonably well known and investigated. Yet there is a dearth of systematic excavation projects at medium-sized and small sites, as well as at some large, but less well-known sites, such as Stephanovikeio Petra in Thessaly or Aghios Ilias in Euboea. Work in Boeotia offers good models, with surveys of hinterlands and excavations at secondary centers to complement longer-term work at major sites, most notably through the work of the Boeotia Project, the Eastern Boeotia Archaeological Project at and around Eleon, and of the Archaeological Reconnaissance of Uninvestigated Remains of Agriculture (AROURA) and the Mycenaean Northeast Kopais (MYNEKO) projects in the Kopaic Basin and at the secondary centers of Aghios Ioannis and Aghia Marina Pyrgos (e.g., Bintliff, Howard, and Snodgrass 2007; Bintliff et al. 2017; Lane et al. 2016, 2020; Burke et al. 2020). While sites with known, substantial remains are natural targets for excavation, the discipline as a whole would benefit from devoting more attention to excavations at sites documented only from surface remains. A more complete understanding of early Greek settlement patterns can only be obtained through more systematic study of sites of a variety of different scales.

COMPARATIVE INSIGHTS FROM EARLY GREECE

What can comparativists do with early Greece? This question is challenging because the archaeology of early Greece comes with a good deal of disciplinary baggage. For American anthropological archaeologists it falls generally in the broader domain of classical studies, or of classical archaeology more specifically. For archaeologists of Greece, comparison is rarely an explicit aim (though see, e.g., Bajema 2017a, 2017b; Small 2017; Whitley 2020). There are several reasons for this. The first and most straightforward is that it has not historically been a disciplinary priority. The second has to do with the practicalities of research. There is a huge bibliography on the archaeology of Greece, and it exists in several different languages, including English, French, German, and Modern Greek. Italian, Albanian, Turkish, and Bulgarian may be important as well, depending on one's interests. An equally deep and dense literature exists for the various cultures with which Greece was in contact in the wider Mediterranean world. There are therefore significant challenges at the level of basic bibliography, both for the Mediterraneanist to "keep up" and for the comparativist to engage in the first place.

For the very reason that it has often been left out of comparative dialogues, the case of early Greece has much to tell us on a number of fronts. Renfrew (1980) pointed out 40 years ago that the long history of research and the comparatively rich datasets make the ancient Mediterranean a good testing ground for broader theories concerning complex societies. This potential, however, remains largely unrealized. Rather than Mediterranean archaeologists offering up our data to archaeologists working in other parts of the world, it may perhaps be better to do the work on this end and present our research in frameworks and in terms that can transfer easily into other world archaeologies. This is what I have attempted to do in this book. Indeed, the early Greek case can contribute particularly to several underrepresented fields in the study of complex societies. Interactions between state and nonstate societies, cultures comprised of several small polities, and social complexity in ranked, transegalitarian, or village societies are only a few examples (on specific comparisons of the Maya with Mycenaean Greece and Greek city states, see also Tartaron 2008, 132–34; Small 2017). I highlight two areas in which the case study presented here has something explicit to offer: (1) the nonlinear development of societies—secondary state formation, collapse and decline, societal oscillation, cyclical patterns, boom and bust cycles; and (2) archaeologies of protohistory—how archaeologists integrate rich, but highly varied, concatenations of archaeological and textual evidence to arrive at complex understandings of the human past. I then turn to some potential future directions and areas of importance for the archaeology of complex societies.

Nonlinearity and Social Complexity

The case for regionalism outlined in the foregoing chapters is also a case of nonlinear development in complex societies. While the neoevolutionary days of band-tribe-chiefdom-state narratives are now well behind us, there remains a great imbalance between the amount of literature that deals with the formation or emergence of social complexity (especially state formation) and the amount dealing with its dissolution. This is not to say that studies of disintegration among complex polities have been completely absent, and indeed the Aegean has been a leader in this regard. Several scholars have sought to address this problem, specifically in the case of the prehistoric Aegean, through discussions of cycling and oscillation (see, e.g., Bintliff 1997; Whitley 2004; Philippa-Touchais 2011). Nonlinearity is a feature of complex systems that has been applied in archaeology since the early work of Clarke (1968) and Renfrew (1972). The explication of specific examples of nonlinear dynamics is rarer.

Part of the reason early Greece is often left out of dialogues concerning complex societies is that there are few obvious cases for comparison. The poleis of the Archaic and Classical periods often feature in broader discussions of early cities or city-states (see, e.g., Morris 1997a; Morris and Knodell 2015). Yet the early Greek polis does not, in fact, compare well at all with other early city-states, especially when one considers their small scale and the unstratified, distributed nature of political power (Whitley 2020). Mycenaean palaces, too, do not have good parallels among other early states, and they feature more often in comparative discussions of collapse than in discussions of state formation or operation (see, e.g., Middleton 2017a). The architectural scale is rather small, territories are minimal, and there is no evidence for ruler iconography or for divine kingship, both of which are major features of emergent states (Kirch 2010, 5–6; Bennet 2018). Moreover, the smaller-scale societies that came before and after have even fewer clear comparisons, and they are cast most often in the loose mold of chiefdoms or caught up in trying to define leadership based on later textual references to *basileis* (see, e.g., Wright 1995, Crielaard 2011b; Pullen 2011a, 2011b; Kõiv 2016). If we change our perspective slightly, based on the diversity seen in the early Greek settlement pattern and the modes of social organization, we might find better points of comparison—or mutually interesting case studies—in the looser modes of political organization discussed throughout this book through the lens of village societies and complex communities. Early village societies (Bandy 2004; Bandy and Fox 2010), tribal societies (Parkinson 2002), intermediate societies (Arnold 1996), or chiefdoms (Earle 1997; Pauketat 2007) all offer frameworks for studying human social organization that seem to have much more in common with Late Bronze Age and Early Iron Age Greek society than do Archaic states (Feinman and Marcus 1998; Trigger 2003). One thing that the early Greek case has to offer here is a sociopolitical landscape in which different "levels" or modes of sociopolitical complexity seem to operate simultaneously. That is to say, variation in settlement hierarchy does not necessarily mean political hierarchy. More often, and as I have shown in the foregoing chapters, it probably signals different modes of community and landscape organization—most notably with respect to palatial and nonpalatial areas in the Palatial Bronze Age, on the one hand, and to the difference between certain principal sites (like Kynos, Lefkandi, and Athens) and most other places in the Postpalatial Bronze Age and Prehistoric Iron Age, on the other.

State formation is dealt with briefly in chapters 3 and 6, although the emphasis throughout this book has been on sociopolitical reformation and nonstate entities. There is nevertheless something significant here to offer to comparative considerations of *secondary* state formation, which Fried (1960, 713; 1967, 240–42) distinguished from primary state formation based on influences from other, more complex polities (see also Price 1978). Detailed case studies in secondary state formation exist for early India (Seneviratne 1981), medieval North Africa (Boone, Myers, and Redman 1990), the Levant (Knauf 1992; Joffe 2002), Nubia and Egypt (Smith 1998), early China (Schelach and Pines 2006), and the Aegean (Parkinson and Galaty 2007). Since the 1960s and 1970s, however, there has been little attempt at large-scale comparison or synthesis in secondary state formation as a topic of anthropological interest. The early Greek case offers an example of the reemergence of political complexity that is different from others in three respects: (1) Archaic Greek city-states are completely different from the Mycenaean palaces; (2) these city-states emerged out of ranked, but not highly stratified, social orders; and (3) the political communities are exceptionally small (Whitley 2020, 179). I suspect such variety is not so rare, but in a comparative sense has gone mostly unnoticed.

It should be no surprise that researchers in the Mediterranean have often expressed interest in nonlinear, nonevolutionary narratives of complexity (see, e.g., Terrenato and Haggis 2011). Studies of cultural influence, especially those that concern more "advanced" societies, are ubiquitous in the field of classics—from the study of Near Eastern influences on early Greek poetry to Horace's notion of *Graecia capta*.[2] The roles of emulation and learning from other cultural groups have always been at least implicit in studies of secondary states. The postformation trajectories of secondary states have been less frequently compared. The Aegean offers several opportunities. Elements of Mycenaean statehood can be traced to other societies (most notably Minoan Crete) but as a whole the system was not very successful, lasting only a couple of hundred years (at best). The early Greek polis, by contrast, was extremely successful, lasting—alongside and often within other political formations—well over a millennium (Hansen and Nielsen 2004). Comparison within and beyond the Aegean may offer insights into such fundamental differences in societal trajectories (Blanton and Fargher 2008; Bajema 2017b).

---

2. *Graecia capta ferum victorem cepit et artes intulit agresti Latio* (Horace, *Epistles* 2.1.156): "Greece, captured, took captive her savage victor and brought the arts to rustic Latium." On early Greek poetry, see West's *The East Face of Helicon* (1997).

Sherratt (2001) has suggested "Potemkin palaces" as a model for Mycenaean polities, a provocative framework that suggests an aspirational quality in which elements from other states were poorly grafted onto a Mycenaean political system. While "aspiration" and "grafting" may or may not be appropriate terms, the model does invite some telling scalar comparisons between Mycenaean palaces and their eastern Mediterranean neighbors. Mycenaean palatial societies were quite small-scale in comparison to the other polities of the Late Bronze Age eastern Mediterranean. It is also not clear that they were in regular, direct competition with anyone beyond each other and the Minoan groups they seem to have superseded in Crete. While Hittite texts suggest that Mycenaeans were an occasional annoyance on the western edges of the Hittite empire, these polities were operating on vastly different scales (see chapter 3, pp. 103–105). Mycenaean polities, as far as we can tell from the Linear B texts, were much more concerned with their immediate surroundings. If long-distance trading and raiding were state activities, they did not make it into the textual record. Nevertheless, Mycenaean polities were certainly aware of and involved with their more stately neighbors. They seem to have drawn on attributes of other states, observed how they functioned, and then adapted them to their own ends (in terms of writing, land management, and taxation). By contrast, emergent Greek polities of the Early Iron Age, particularly those of the eighth century BCE, may have had more in common (and at least more contact with) each other and with neighboring civilizations in a way that normalized the widespread development of state institutions in the seventh and sixth centuries BCE.

Recent research on the emergence of social complexity has opened up to look beyond top-down, evolutionary models dependent on aggrandizers, chiefs, and kings, and turned also toward the development of cooperation as a powerful social force in both state and nonstate societies (Jennings and Earle 2016; Stanish 2017). Such forces might be detected in the early Greek case as well, especially through communal feasting and intercommunity cooperation at regional sanctuaries. While these may be seen as scenes for aggrandizers to reach a wide audience, they are also venues for group formation and cooperation (and these behaviors are not mutually exclusive). In such a context, the secondary formation of very hierarchical states—like Mycenaean palaces—would be a major disruption to previous social norms, which may in part explain their short lifespan. This may also help explain the emergence of regional institutions in nonpalatial areas, perhaps in response to the growth of palaces in neighboring regions. In this way, the less centralized polities that developed into early poleis may have developed more organically and through practices associated with group and community-integrative cooperation.

Narratives of collapse have been especially prevalent in the social sciences, and increasingly so in comparative contexts. Archaeologists, of course, have much to contribute to studies of collapse and to the question of how to approach collapse from a critical perspective (see, e.g., Renfrew 1979; Tainter 1988; Yoffee and

Cowgill 1988; Schwartz and Nichols 2006; McAnany and Yoffee 2010; O'Brien 2017; Cunningham and Driessen 2017; Middleton 2017a, 2017b; Knodell 2018). The case studies of collapse at end of the Bronze Age are increasingly well documented in the cases of both Minoan Crete and Mycenaean Greece (see, e.g., Driessen 2002; Cunningham and Driessen 2017; Middleton 2017a, 2020; Murray 2017). Of particular interest in the early Greek case is a complex but explainable instance of systems collapse, whereby several factors resulted in the destruction and ultimate rejection of a prevailing political order. While such events are historically contingent, there are common trajectories that make some societies more vulnerable to such things than others. In the Mycenaean case, we have a combination of rapid sociopolitical change, accompanied by rapid growth and development that could not be sustained socially, perhaps also in terms of human ecology—what Tainter (2006) termed an archaeology of overshoot. Early Greece also offers a case study in the archaeology of resilience (Redman 2005; Papadopoulos 2017a; Vidal-Cordasco and Nuevo-López 2021). While significant changes happened at the end of the Palatial Bronze Age, demonstrable continuities can be traced into Postpalatial times and later, many of which extend back to the Early Mycenaean period (Kramer-Hajos 2016), and even beyond. Snodgrass ([1971] 2000, 186) pointed long ago the presence of certain continuities, especially in burial customs, between the Middle Helladic and Protogeometric period. This would not seem odd at all if we simply removed the Mycenaean Palatial period in the middle.

Continuity, change, resilience, and revolution all point to oscillation or cycling rather than to linear development in the societies of early Greece. Such an assertion would probably hold up to scrutiny in most parts of the world, which raises the question of why. Is there something in the fundamental nature of human societies that makes long-term stability difficult? Societal change is obviously historically contingent, but we may be able to see broader patterns in circumstances involving the introduction of rapid change to conservative systems, to relationships with peer polities, or to levels of centralization. Environmental concerns must obtain as well, and in this respect relationships between communities, polities, and land are key. Significant shifts in agricultural regimes—for example, in certain areas at the beginning of the Palatial period—may have resulted in soil depletion and unsustainability, which itself seems to have been a disruptive cycling phenomenon in several early societies (see, e.g., Shennan 2018).

Archaeologies of Protohistory

Protohistory, in the context of this study, refers to a period in which written texts of historical interest are present but there is no formal conception of writing history as a genre. This is a nonideal term, perhaps, considering the variety of ways in which it is used, often with colonial connotations to refer to people interacting with—but on the margins of—text-producing cultures (Papadopoulos 2018; see also Schmidt and Mrozowski 2013 on "the death of prehistory" and the historical baggage of this term). Here, I am more interested in the capacity of "protohistory" to articulate a certain kind of in-betweenness, both disciplinary and in terms of societal trajectories. All the periods under study in this book might be considered protohistoric in a disciplinary sense. Writing was used in and around early Greek societies, in different ways, throughout the Late Bronze Age and Early Iron Age. Even in "prehistoric" phases, Greece was on the geographical margins of text-producing societies; from a chronological perspective, later Greek texts refer to events that are meant to have happened in prehistoric times. This protohistoric character is perhaps strongest in the eighth century, making it a defining quality of the period, even if the moniker might apply to other times as well. The term is therefore meant to capture the vagueness, variety, and incomplete nature of the scattered textual and other nonmaterial records of potential relevance for the periods dealt with in this book. In the context of the archaeology of complex societies, protohistory puts a name on the middle ground between prehistory and history, which describes real interfaces between peoples with texts and without them, and which provides a framework for considering what different types of early societies do, as well as how we study them.

For two of the four periods covered in this book, Greek textual records exist but do not purport to record history as a deliberate account of past events and behaviors. Some, but not many, people in Greece used writing in the Palatial Bronze Age and in the Protohistoric Iron Age. Later texts refer to the periods in between, both directly and as conflations of societal behaviors from several centuries, as is the case in Homer. For narrative history, in the early Greek world, we begin with the "inquiry" (ἱστορία) of Herodotus in the fifth century BCE. While the state of textual evidence is certainly not ideal, it would be a mistake not to consider it alongside the archaeological evidence, or to leave one or the other out of our interpretations completely. At the same time, of course, the historical record is limited and can rarely be taken at face value. Early Greece therefore offers an important case study for disciplinary considerations of the relationship between archaeology and text, and between prehistory and history.

Such disciplinary issues are not unique to early Greece. The Classic Maya are most frequently compared with ancient Greek city states, going back to Renfrew's (1986) original formulation of peer-polity interaction (see also Sabloff 1986; Small 2017). While differences between these groups are significant—most noticeably in terms of internal political organization and how texts are used—the multipolity regional dynamics, which involve constant competition, warfare, and alliance forming, make such a comparison more valid for the poleis of the Archaic and Classical periods than those treated in this book. Can such features really be detected, however, in prehistoric (or even protohistoric) societies? The conflicts and statecraft of Classic Maya and Archaic and Classical Greek city states are known almost exclusively from the documentary record. Mayanists have had an ongoing reckoning with this disciplinary disjuncture since the decipherment of

Maya hieroglyphs drastically transformed our knowledge of Maya social, political, and territorial organization (Garrison 2018; Ek 2020). Some comparative dialogue on the challenges of moving between prehistoric, protohistoric, and historical cultures within a diachronic narrative might therefore be fruitful for Aegean archaeologists and ancient historians, as well as for Mayanists.

Nearly all historical archaeologies must address the question of interface between prehistory and history in some form or another. While this question is most explicitly addressed in North American and Mediterranean contexts, the resonance in others should be clear as well (see, e.g., Tandy 2001; Schmidt and Mrozowski 2013). The Americas prior to European contact offer one of the more obvious points of convergence between prehistoric archaeology and text-based history on either side of a chronological divide. This is of course the case in many colonial contact situations (see, e.g., van Dommelen 1998; Stein 2005; Dietler 2010). In this way, archaeologies of protohistory should also be resonant for archaeologies of colonialism—most notably in considering indigenous forms of knowledge production and cultural memory alongside modern, archaeological, ethnographic, or historical ones.

Several long-standing questions about Homeric society concern the relationship between material and text, what nonhistorical texts and oral traditions tell us about social organization, and the role of the past in the past (see, e.g., Finley 1954; Gottschall 2008; Sherratt and Bennet 2017). Looking outward, a critical approach to protohistory invites explicit considerations of cross-cultural interaction, unequal reference and representation in different textual traditions, and ways to view disparate evidence on an even plane.

Early Greek societies also offer multiple case studies in the adoption and disappearance of writing systems (Bennet 2008; Steele 2017, 2020; Boyes and Steele 2020). Like state formation, the writing in the Aegean originated multiple times, and was largely exogenous in its initial development. There were several ways in which writing systems were developed in Greece. These involved different types of regional, societal, interregional, and intersocietal interactions. The earliest Aegean writing, on Crete, has already drawn analogies to incipient scripts in other contexts—for example in Egypt (Ferrara 2015). Cretan hieroglyphs and Linear A were likely developed in the context of inspiration, if not of direct influence, from other scribal societies. Linear B is another story entirely, this script having been adapted from Minoan Linear A to record the Mycenaean (early Greek) language. The circumstances of this adaptation remain little understood, not least owing to the lack of a plausible decipherment for Linear A (as well as our lack of knowledge concerning the language behind it). Equally relevant are the contributions of Linear A and B to comparative discussions of the disappearance of writing systems, or of script obsolescence (Houston, Baines, and Cooper 2003; Baines, Bennet, and Houston 2008). The replacement of Linear A with Linear B invites a series of questions concerning script prestige, practicality, or political takeover (Bennet 2008), while the Postpalatial disappearance of Linear B signals the status of the script as a technology of state authority, which becomes obsolete following the disappearance of such an authority.

The invention of the Greek alphabet as an adaptation of the Phoenician offers yet another example of the adoption and dissemination of early Greek writing—by far the most successful. While there are many open questions concerning the appearance and disappearance of the Aegean writing systems described above, they nevertheless offer valuable cases for comparison concerning (1) the work writing does within particular societies, and (2) how its very presence affects their constitution, operation, and reproduction. Why does the Greek alphabet, for example, last some 28 centuries (and counting) while its linguistic ancestor (Linear B) and alphabetic one (Phoenician) are long extinct? One conclusion reached here is that the proliferation of the Greek alphabet can be explained by (1) the capacity of the script to encode the sound of speech directly; (2) its resulting adaptability to different languages; and (3) the historical circumstances of its appearance, which resulted in its rapid dissemination and eventual entrenchment across disparate communities and cultural groups. The Akkadian language and cuneiform script, as the lingua and scripta franca of the ancient Near East in the Bronze Age, may offer an interesting analogy. Chinese writing is a further parallel as a writing system that has lasted some three millennia and has been adapted to record a number of different Chinese languages, as well as Japanese and Korean (Robinson 2007, 199; Gnadesikan 2009, 57; on broader comparisons between ancient Greece and China, see also Lloyd and Zhao 2018).

A final aspect of protohistory with broad resonance concerns the relationship between texts and mythohistory, in which events, happenings, and information are passed down through oral traditions and eventually recorded by early historians. Questioning the relationship between history and true events is nothing new, especially when it comes to the first Greek historians, Herodotus and Thucydides, the second of whom Cornford (1907) referred to as *Thucydides Mythistoricus* (Chambers 1991; Papadopoulos 1999, 387–88; Papadopoulos 2018). Moving beyond questions of historical accuracy to cultural significance or meaning is an obvious approach, one long in the purview of literary scholars and mythographers. It is less common to seek to explicate relationships between such narratives and actual past processes, as understood through the material record. The result, even if imperfect and selective, can still provide certain types of insights into past societies and their development, especially as the members of those societies themselves viewed it. Examples are found in this book of cases where contemporary and later written sources support, contradict, or obscure past events and processes. These must be assessed on a case-by-case basis. What we should avoid, however, are broad-brush dismissals or categorical rejections of certain types or bodies of evidence. Even if we conclude that problematic sources tell us nothing about the period of the past they purport to tell us about, they still tell us something about perceptions of the past in the past, which are intrinsically valuable considerations for long-term regional history and the mechanisms that drive it. Mobility, migration, conflict, foundation, and abandonment are key themes related to identity creation (and repression) that are resonant—regardless of whether or not they have identifiable material roots. We have little trouble talking about such modes of identity construction and imagined pasts in the context of recent and contemporary societies; protohistory offers a particular framework in which to engage such themes in archaeological contexts as well. And archaeology provides a common lens through which various types and stages of protohistoric societies can be compared.

Future Directions in the Comparative Archaeology of Complex Societies

The future directions highlighted above for the archaeology of early Greece are chiefly practical. In considering the archaeology of complex societies more generally, our concerns are necessarily more theoretical. Of course, the methodological and practical aspects of how archaeology is *done*, especially above the level of the individual site, will affect comparative approaches as well, as more data is gathered, published, and available for side-by-side comparison. But the most exciting developments in this realm concern comparative research priorities and how we think about the diversity of human pasts.

Leppard and I have recently reflected on several future prospects for the study of complex societies (Leppard and Knodell 2018). On the one hand, the rapidity of development in media and other technologies for data recording and analysis will continue to affect archaeological research across a variety of scales, most notably large-scale comparative studies that seek to aggregate and analyze large bodies of data. We have also pointed toward methodological flexibility and a diversity of research questions and priorities as a boon for regional studies in particular and the study of complex societies in general. Methodological and theoretical transparency is far more important than narrowly defined comparative approaches that seek to place societies side by side and tick boxes of attributes. In this way I suspect that comparisons are likely to become less global and more focused on particular trajectories or responses to certain problems, such as natural disaster, population growth, or climate change. Serendipity also plays a role. We can predict that advances in archaeogenetics and radiometric dating will have major impacts across nearly all subfields of archaeology, but we must also acknowledge that *unlooked for* technological innovations or material discoveries have often had transformative effects in shaping archaeological research priorities and agendas. In this way we might look to under-researched areas that are not traditionally the focus of research on complex societies to provide exciting ways forward. Central Asia, Siberia, the Arctic, and sub-Saharan Africa may well have much to offer comparative understandings of social complexity, even if these areas are underrepresented in such research—at least in comparison to the Mediterranean, the

Middle East, Mesoamerica, and the American Southwest. New research in less thoroughly investigated areas may be particularly important for the study of non-state modes of sociopolitical complexity.

In 2014 several prominent archaeologists published a paper on 25 "grand challenges for archaeology," based on the results of a survey distributed by several professional organizations for archaeologists, chiefly in North America and Europe (Kintigh et al. 2014). The survey stipulated that these challenges needed to be problems that were "solvable" or at least "addressable" through the use of empirical evidence (Kintigh et al. 2014, 7). The 25 challenges all relate to issues of culture process and coupled human and natural systems. It is no coincidence that addressing these challenges is a major research priority for the US National Science Foundation. These challenges revolve around five sets of themes: (1) emergence, community, and complexity; (2) resilience, persistence, transformation, and collapse; (3) movement, mobility, and migration; (4) cognition, behavior, and identity; and (5) human-environment interactions. I have outlined above (and in the foregoing chapters) the significance of several of these, both in general and in the early Greek case. There is no doubt that all present exciting avenues for future research in a variety of disciplinary and geographical contexts. I would speculate that the most important of these for future research and growth is human-environmental interactions. While this is a long-standing area of research in nearly all subfields of archaeology, there has already been a recent surge in interest in topics like human responses to natural disasters and climate change. As archaeology continues to follow interests and issues facing contemporary society, we might expect more work specifically on large and small-scale agricultural economies—and other aspects of food production and subsistence—in response to changing environmental circumstances. Somewhat underdeveloped in this list are questions of identity formation, imagined communities, ideology, and non-rational decision-making. While these last points are certainly more difficult to study empirically, their significance in shaping collective human behavior has been made more apparent than ever in the last decade, and across the globe.

A final potential growth area is public archaeology. This concerns interfaces between archaeologists and stakeholders in the communities in which they work, as well as the capacity of archaeology to contribute to public discourse. The grand challenges of Kintigh and other scholars (2014) were largely derived from their capacity to address "real-world" problems. But what role do archaeologists really play at the level of contemporary cultural beliefs concerning the past and its role in the present? What impact does archaeology (especially academic archaeology) have in the policy decisions of modern nation states? If our goals and challenges are to address questions of broad relevance, we must also address the challenge of reaching the right audiences. Scholarly audiences are aware of the need for context and nuance in interpreting the past, as well as in the ways that the material vestiges of the past have been (mis-)appropriated in political and ideological agendas. But we must now do a better job of confronting the challenge of making scholarship based on real research and expertise *more* relevant than sensationalist accounts of the "glories of the ancients" or the more sinister or racist messages of *Ancient Aliens* and various attempts to whitewash the classical world. As a field, archaeology is increasingly aware of these concerns. Granting agencies require statements of broader significance for research and often carry a mandate for open-access publication or writing for popular audiences. In practice, however, nonacademic publication has not traditionally been a priority for academic archaeologists, not least because the professional rewards are low and the risks (or at least the investment of time) can be quite high. This has begun to change as archaeologists consider public education and outreach—both of which are chiefly carried out through blogs, websites, online journals, and public presentations in local communities—a disciplinary priority or even an obligation. We might expect these efforts to grow in future years, and in tandem with broader academic and societal interests in social justice, inequality, and the over-exploitation of natural resources. We can hope that growing interest in these matters has a positive effect, but we should also seek more active and aggressive advocacy from archaeologists with expertise in relevant fields.

WHY EARLY GREECE MATTERS

I wrote this book during a period of considerable discord in parts of the world traditionally associated with "Western" civilization. Concepts of crisis and collapse are invoked regularly in reference to global markets. People talk about clashes of civilizations in an increasingly globalized world. Political upheavals have dramatically transformed long-standing institutions. Climate change is increasingly dangerous and disruptive. A pandemic has ravaged global health, with catastrophic consequences for social and economic life as well. In the background, technological change—most of all concerning media and interconnectivity—exaggerates and perpetuates such social transformations. While I do not draw *direct* analogies between ancient and modern societies, it is no coincidence that the themes highlighted in this book are what they are. These are issues that all human societies must grapple with. The early Greek case is particularly relevant here as the frequently cited "foundation" of "Western" civilization. Whether such a characterization has merit or not, it is a long-standing cultural phenomenon that requires scrutiny and explanation.

So, what light does an archaeology of early Greece shed on the contemporary world? Studying the trajectories of past societies allows us to see patterns and processes that are not always apparent in the present. By highlighting them in scholarship, we might better recognize where we are in our own societal trajectories; or we might at least enhance our awareness of what factors influence them. In bringing this book to a close I look at a few of these patterns and their modern relevance. I also look at the differences between the past realities of early Greek societies and historical and contemporary perceptions of them. The latter, I think, have had a more powerful effect on the modern world, and not always for the good.

One pattern that seems evident in both the early Greek case and in other complex adaptive systems is that societies are most fragile when they become highly centralized (see also Yoffee 2019). By contrast, political formations are more stable, if less comparatively powerful, when they are one of many, similarly sized systems. This is evident throughout the period treated in detail in this book—most acutely in the Mycenaean palaces but also in emergent centers like Lefkandi during the Postpalatial Bronze Age and Early Iron Age. The long-term lesson seems to be that periods of preeminence in wider systems are likely to be short term and punctuated by periods of upheaval. While scholars (and nonscholars) sometimes point to ancient Egypt as a hallmark of long-lasting cultural traditions and social institutions, Egypt was in fact characterized by long periods of instability and rupture, stemming from both internal and external forces. In spite of terminological critiques or calls for more nuanced explanations for culture change, societies do "collapse"—that is to say, they undergo rapid, fundamental transformation, which affects the ways and quality of life for large populations, often for the worse. Such phenomena typically follow periods of dramatic change in the nature of social complexity and inequality. The Mycenaean palaces rose quickly, not gradually, through dramatic transformations in the centralization of political and social power. While such transformations represented rapid pathways to power, these were also socially destabilizing forces that ultimately were not sustainable.

In various parts of this book I have argued that Greece has played a relatively minor role in the modern anthropological study of complex societies. There is no question, however, of the foundational role of "ancient Greece" in contemporary understandings of "civilization" or "the West." These conceptions have their roots in understandings of ancient Greece that formed the background of early anthropology and evolutionary models of the development of ancient societies. There is a predominant view of Greece as special in the history of Europe—an ur-civilization to which "the West" owes a particular debt (Hanink 2017). In the postcolonial, global world of the twenty-first century, there is a well-established need to critique notions of "Western" primacy. There is therefore also a need to critique the roots of such a narrative, which are in the European colonial projects of the sixteenth to nineteenth centuries. Early anthropology and ideas about how human societies (both ancient and modern) should be studied and classified were major parts of these projects. There was a fundamental difference between the ways in which colonial Europeans saw themselves and the ethnographic societies on which classifications of chiefdoms and tribes were built. As European states encountered these groups, they had to describe them in terms that were categorically different from their own social formations. Europe was seen as a world of states, whereas many parts of the colonial world were not. The ancient Greeks, so the reasoning went, were the literary and cultural forebears of Rome and Europe, and so must also have been more complex, "civilized" social formations. Europeans, including cultural historians, had the dual goal of making early Greek society (1) a demonstrable forerunner to their own; and (2) on par with or superior to the ancient civilizations of contemporary colonial or "oriental" zones.

A significant legacy of Eurocentrism is that, for all the periods under examination in this book, there has been a tendency in the scholarship to overstate the relative scale of early Greek societies in comparison with their neighbors in the eastern Mediterranean. This can in part be tied to the place of Greece in the "Western" imagination, and especially to the spectacular discoveries of the late nineteenth and early twentieth centuries regarding the prehistory of the region. The ability to connect the imagined, mythological past of Greece with material remains was powerful, even if the observed remains were recognized as having little to do with the world constructed in later myths and legends. Nevertheless, the thrill of discovery surrounding "Europe's first states" in the form of Minoan and Mycenaean civilizations put these societies on a particular kind of pedestal, which has been entangled with the identities of both Greek and Western European nation states ever since (Voutsaki 2017; see also Hamilakis 2007; Hanink 2017). This inceptive Greek/European imaginary has obscured our understanding of early Greek societies among their contemporaries, as well as in comparison to other complex societies.

Likewise, in the Early Iron Age, there has been a tendency to look to the eighth century as a revolutionary moment when the spark of Hellenism spurred the democratic political formations of the early Greek polis and spread them throughout the Mediterranean. This is what Small (2015) has called the "false narrative" of early Greek political development—a teleology culminating in classical Athens, which obscures the really quite varied range of sociopolitical formations and trajectories present in early Greece, as well as their contemporary significance (see also McInerney 1999, 9; Morgan 2003). This diversity deserves attention intrinsically, but broader trends can be highlighted by a comparative perspective that examines both societies with which Greek polities were in contact and other societies that have experienced similar paths of development.

It is worth making explicit the connections between early Greece and contemporary, global culture, in which "Western" civilization is a significant identity marker and magnet for assertions of cultural eminence. Such ideological touchstones, which mean so many different things for as many different groups, should be highlighted for careful thought and critique. One aspect of this critique—at least as presented in this book—is to expose certain myths concerning the societies of early Greece: ages of heroes, Europe's first states, fonts of democracy, and the like. Such things make have been present in early Greece in some way or another— at least they were in the ancient Greek imagination—but we should not let this obscure the fact that many equally rich (and often more sophisticated) cultural and political traditions evolved in Africa, Asia, and the Americas. We should not lose sight of the fact that Hellenism (and philhellenism) grew out of pro-European colonial projects, which, incidentally, were often anti-Modern Greek (Hanink 2017). This is not meant to disparage or undervalue the importance of studying ancient Greece, but rather to underscore the fact that Greek society (and the study of it) never developed in a vacuum; moreover, the pride of place it has been given in historical thought is a historical phenomenon worthy of study in and of itself—one that is essential to consider in any attempt to understand early Greece.

As I write this, I have just finished teaching a first-year undergraduate seminar on "The Trojan Legend: Mythology, Archaeology, and Legacy." The ten-week course covers the Homeric epics, the archaeology of Troy and the Mycenaean world, the world of Homer, and—more and more significantly, to my mind—the legacies of the Trojan Legend through its depictions and retellings in literature, art, and performance from fifth-century Athens to the present day. As is our custom, the discussion topic for the final day turned to the broad question of why the Trojan Legend matters, which of course is directly related to the equally broad question of why early Greece matters (see also Vermeule 1986).

Discussions of significance necessarily involve some form of critique. In the present day it is hard not to read the *Iliad* and see its protagonists as hypermasculine, petty, squabbling narcissists. In the material record we see evidence for competitive display and social inequality, on the one hand, and village societies mostly concerned with everyday subsistence, on the other. From the cultural context of a small liberal arts college in the Midwestern United States there is not much to recommend Homeric society as a set of moral guidelines. But should we try to understand it? Of course. We see reflections of these behaviors recurrently in "Western" history, often with explicit reference to early Greek, Homeric, or classical ideals. Such unified ideals are regularly sourced to some generic Greek or classical past that almost certainly never existed. Early Greece seems rather to have been comprised of a diverse political and cultural landscape in almost constant flux. This is a pattern that obtained in the Classical period as well. While democratic Athens (when it was democratic) may have provided some building blocks for modern democracies, Greece was still a world of tyrannies and oligarchies, many of which fell under the thumb of Athens, which may have been a democratic polis but was also a brutal and hegemonic empire. This simple history matters not least because it offers the opportunity to examine singular notions of the past and the real role they play in contemporary politics.

The period covered in this book—from the Mycenaean world to the ages of Homer—witnessed the codification of notions of Greekness and, from there, "Western" identity that would last some three millennia. These notions are hardly static, and indeed have been adapted continually over the centuries. The protohistoric "moment" of early Greece is nevertheless an important cultural touchstone that is too easy to see as uniform, and it is often caught up in contemporary politics of self-definition, intentionally or not. It is therefore well worth recognizing the significance of this past and interrogating what we actually know about it through its material remains and its associated textual traditions. The early Greek past reveals a diversity of modes of social organization, political formations, and types of cross-cultural interactions. For a world that has a history of looking at "the West" in contrast to notional "others," it is important to point out this contradiction in terms. One takeaway, perhaps, is that at face value the perceived European and American heirs of classical civilization have very little in common with early Greek societies, at least in terms of social and political values and organization. It matters also that we understand why and how we have come to think and say we do. We should not hold up the past as virtuous based solely on a connection we feel to it. Rather, we should critique these connections and the elevated positions we attribute to them.

If we look to the early Greeks for our own cultural roots, we must first acknowledge that early Greece exhibited a wealth of diversity across space and time. Second, these societies were defined by much wider sets of relations between different communities and cultures, which played out over a variety of social and spatial scales. Finally, we should note that these groups manipulated and deployed their own pasts in a variety of ways, especially in terms of defining themselves and others. Such characteristics can probably be observed in nearly all complex societies. What role this knowledge of past human behavior can play in our own local and global communities remains a pressing question.

The two maps and the table below provide the numbered locations of all sites mentioned in the foregoing text and all sites used in the quantifications, spatial analyses, and representations of settlement patterns that appear in this book (maps 31 and 32; table 8). Site names are given as they appear in the present work, along with periods of occupation, type of site, and region. This will help the reader locate the site on the two finder maps, as well as on other maps where the site may appear in chapters 2, 4, 5 and 6. See chapter 2 for a more detailed discussion of the dataset.

Most sites mapped and listed here can be found in the online databases of the Mycenaean Atlas Project (for the Mycenaean/Late Helladic periods of the Palatial and Postpalatial Bronze Age) or the Aristeia Project (for the Protogeometric and Geometric periods of the Prehistoric and Protohistoric Iron Age). These databases provide further information about individual sites and their particular bibliography. In the case of the present study, sites or findspots in close proximity were often treated together as a single *site* or *community*, as explained in chapter 2 (pp. 33–42). On the rare occasion that a location listed below cannot be found in these databases, it is derived from the relevant gazetteer or regional study listed in table 3. More specific references are given in the text, as appropriate. Note also that spelling and place names may vary slightly in the databases noted above. These variations are based on the transliteration of Greek characters into the Latin alphabet and the use of different place names in the literature. In general, I have selected the spelling used most often in scholarly literature, with a preference for Greek, rather than latinized transliteration (e.g., *-os* rather than *-us* in endings; *k*

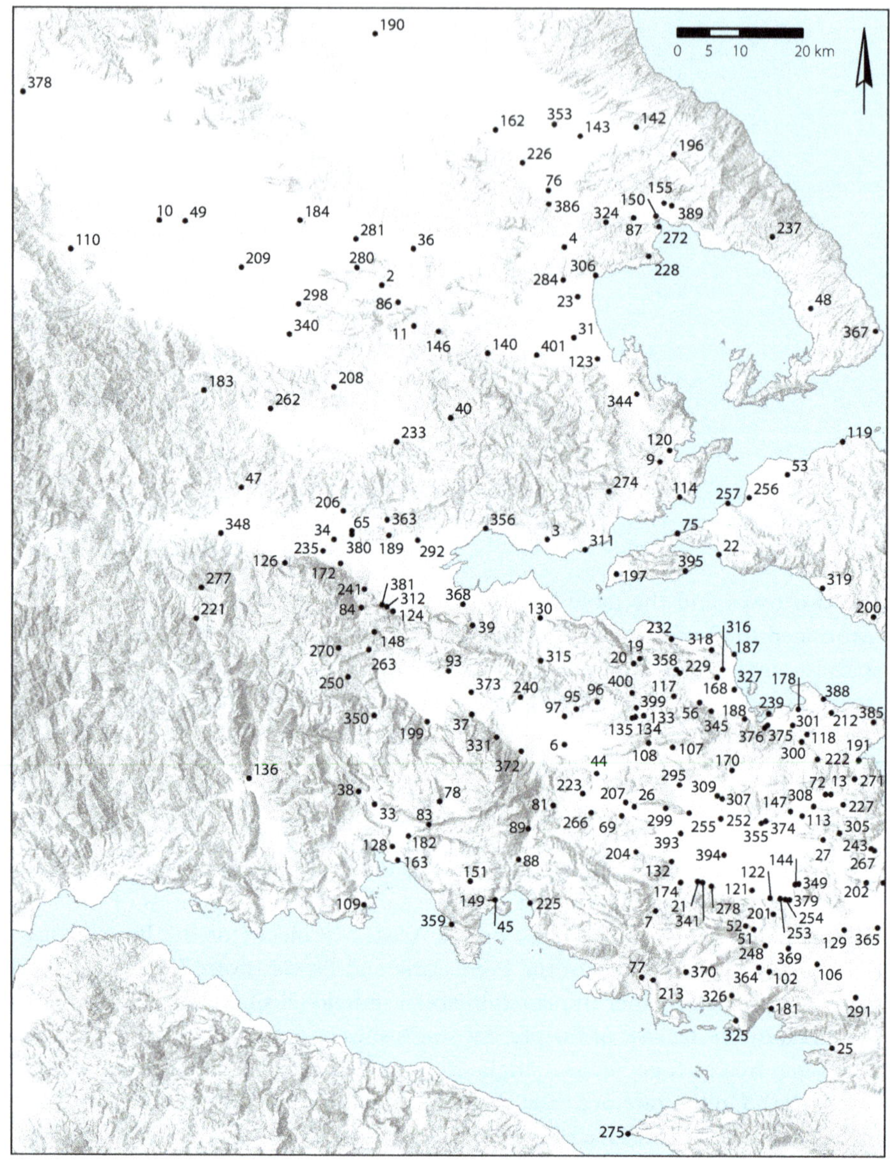

MAP 31. Sites in the western part of the study area with locations marked by number (see table 8 for further information).

rather than *c* in transliterating kappa; *d* rather than *dh* for delta; *ai* rather than *ae* in diphthongs; although these conventions are not systematically applied, since the priority here is to make site names easy to find and cross reference in the relevant databases and scholarly literature, at least as much as possible). When sites

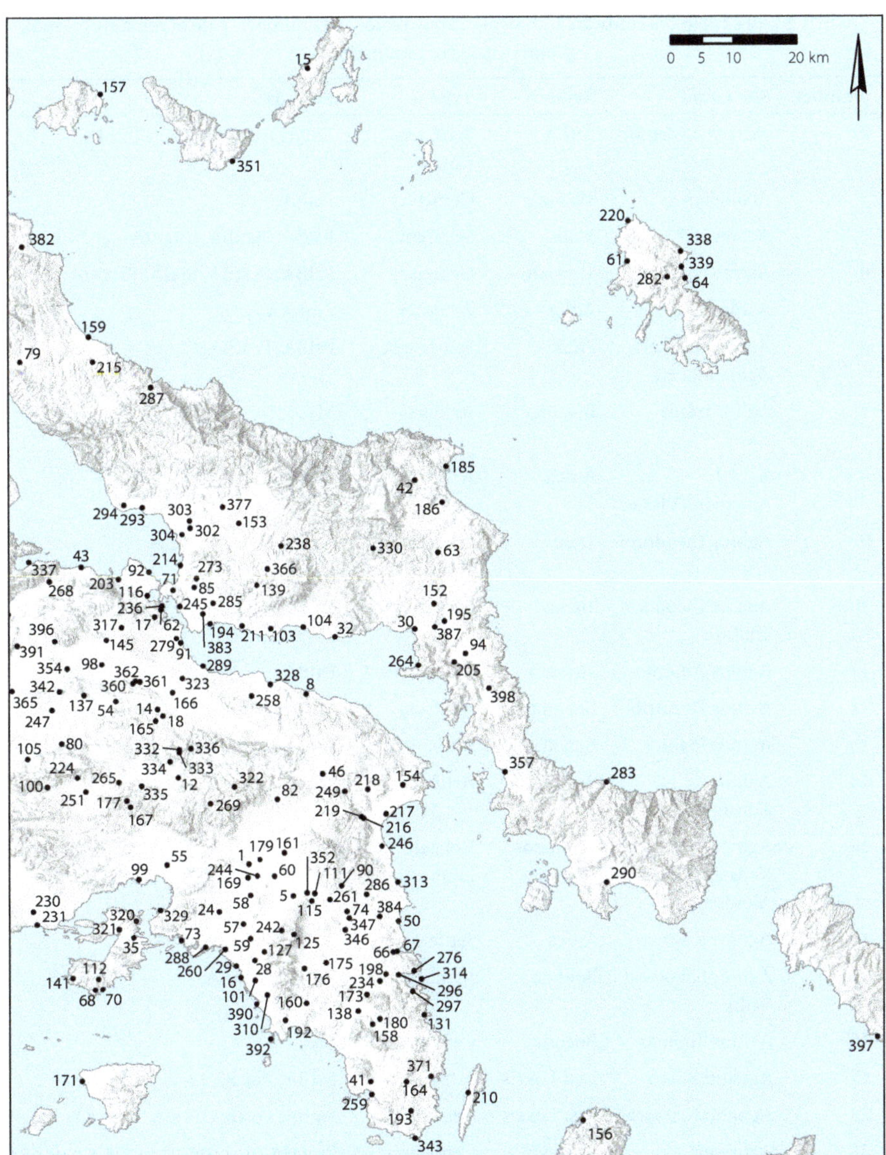

MAP 32. Sites in the eastern part of the study area with locations marked by number (see table 8 for further information).

are commonly referred to by more than one name—or, alternatively, by an ancient and a modern name—I provide both in table 8. Readers can also use the index and term searches in the open-access PDF version of this book to find relevant locations in the text and maps.

TABLE 8 All sites in the study area, showing name, region, site number, type of remains present, and periods of occupation

Number	Site name	Region	Type	Periods
1	Acharnai/Menidi	Attica	Set/Cem/Sanc	EMyc, PalBA, PreIA, ProtoIA*
2	Achilleion	Thessaly	Cemetery	PalBA
3	Achinos	Malis	Set/Cem	PalBA, PostBA, ProtoIA
4	Aerino	Thessaly	Cemetery	PalBA, PostBA, PreIA, ProtoIA
5	Aghia Paraskevi	Attica	Artifacts	ProtoIA
6	Aghia Paraskevi/ Aghia Marina	Phokis	Settlement	PalBA, PostBA
7	Aghia Triada Cave	Boeotia	Artifacts	Myc
8	Aghioi Anargyroi/Vlastos	Attica	Artifacts	PalBA, PostBA
9	Aghioi Theodoroi	Thessaly	Isolated tomb	PalBA, PostBA, PreIA
10	Aghioi Theodoroi Tholos	Thessaly	Cemetery	PreIA
11	Aghios Antonios	Thessaly	Cemetery	PalBA
12	Aghios Dimitrios	Boeotia	Artifacts	Myc
13	Aghios Ioannis	Boeotia	Settlement	EMyc, PalBA, PreIA, ProtoIA
14	Aghios Konstantinos	Boeotia	Artifacts	EMyc, PalBA, PreIA, ProtoIA
15	Aghios Konstantinos/ Alonissos	Alonissos, Sporades	Isolated tomb	PreIA
16	Aghios Kosmas	Attica	Settlement	EMyc, PalBA, PostBA
17	Aghios Nikolaos/ Vathy	Boeotia	Artifacts	PalBA, ProtoIA
18	Aghios Thomas	Boeotia	Cemetery	Myc
19	Agnanti Kastri	East Lokris	Settlement	PalBA, PostBA
20	Agnanti Kritharia	East Lokris	Cemetery	PalBA, PostBA, PreIA
21	Agoriani	Boeotia	Cemetery	ProtoIA
22	Aidepsos/ Koumbi	Euboea	Settlement	EMyc, PalBA
23	Aidhiniotiki Magoula	Thessaly	Artifacts	PalBA
24	Aigaleo	Attica	Cemetery	ProtoIA
25	Aigosthina	Attica	Artifacts	ProtoIA

TABLE 8 *(Continued)*

Number	Site name	Region	Type	Periods
26	Akontio/ Kephisos Cemetery	Boeotia	Cemetery	ProtoIA
27	Akraiphnion	Boeotia	Set/Cem	PalBA, PreIA, ProtoIA
28	Alimos	Attica	Settlement	PalBA, PostBA, ProtoIA
29	Alimos Kalamaki	Attica	Cemetery	PalBA, PostBA
30	Aliveri Magoula	Euboea	Settlement	EMyc, PalBA, PreIA PostBA
31	Almiriotiki Magoula	Thessaly	Artifacts	PalBA
32	Amarynthos	Euboea	Settlement	PalBA, PostBA, PreIA, ProtoIA
33	Amblianos Tholos	Phokis	Isolated tomb	PalBA, PostBA
34	Amouri Alabanou	Malis	Artifacts	Myc
35	Ampelakia	Salamis	Cemetery	PalBA, ProtoIA
36	Ampelia Palaiokastro	Thessaly	Cemetery	PalBA, PreIA, ProtoIA
37	Amphikleia	Phokis	Set/Cem	PalBA, PostBA, PreIA, ProtoIA
38	Amphissa	Phokis	Cemetery	ProtoIA
39	Anavra Phournos	Malis	Cemetery	ProtoIA
40	Anavra/Goura	Thessaly	Cemetery	PreIA, ProtoIA
41	Anavyssos	Attica	Set/Cem	PreIA, ProtoIA
42	Androniani	Euboea	Isolated tomb	PalBA
43	Anthedon	Boeotia	Settlement	PalBA; PostBA, ProtoIA
44	Anthochorion Levendi	Boeotia	Settlement	PalBA, PreIA?, ProtoIA?
45	Antikyra	Phokis	Settlement	EMyc, PalBA, PostBA, PreIA, ProtoIA
46	Aphidna Kotroni	Attica	Artifacts	EMyc; PalBA
47	Archani	Phokis	Cemetery	PostBA
48	Argalasti	Thessaly	Isolated tomb	PalBA, PreIA, ProtoIA
49	Arni/Pyrgos Kieriou	Thessaly	Set/Sanc	EMyc, PalBA, PostBA, PreIA, ProtoIA
50	Artemis Tauropolos	Attica	Sanctuary	EMyc, PalBA, PostBA, ProtoIA
51	Askra	Boeotia	Artifacts	PreIA, ProtoIA

Contd.

TABLE 8 *(Continued)*

Number	Site name	Region	Type	Periods
52	Askra Pyrgaki	Boeotia	Artifacts	PalBA, PreIA? ProtoIA
53	Asminion Divouni	Euboea	Artifacts	Myc, ProtoIA
54	Asopia	Boeotia	Artifacts	Myc, ProtoIA
55	Aspropyrgos	Attica	Artifacts	PreIA, ProtoIA
56	Atalanti	East Lokris	Set/Cem	Myc, PalBA?, PostBA?, PreIA, ProtoIA
57	Athens	Attica	Set/Cem	EMyc, PalBA, PostBA, PreIA, ProtoIA
58	Athens Chatzidakis	Attica	Settlement	PostBA, PreIA, ProtoIA
59	Athens Dafni Metro	Attica	Settlement	PreIA, ProtoIA
60	Athens/Olympic Stadium	Attica	Cemetery	ProtoIA
61	Atsitsa	Skyros, Sporades	Artifacts	Myc
62	Aulis	Boeotia	Settlement	PalBA, ProtoIA
63	Avlonari	Euboea	Set/Cem	EMyc, PalBA, ProtoIA
64	Basales	Skyros, Sporades	Cemetery	Myc, PreIA
65	Bikiorema/ Vikiorema	Malis	Cemetery	PalBA, PostBA, PreIA, ProtoIA
66	Brauron	Attica	Set/Cem	EMyc, PalBA, PostBA, PreIA, ProtoIA
67	Brauron/Lapoutsi	Attica	Cemetery	EMyc, PalBA, PostBA
68	Cave of Euripides	Salamis	Artifacts	PalBA, PostBA
69	Chaironeia	Boeotia	Artifacts	PalBA, ProtoIA
70	Chaliotis	Salamis	Cemetery	PalBA, PostBA
71	Chalkis	Euboea	Set/Cem	EMyc, PalBA, PostBA, PreIA, ProtoIA
72	Chantza	Boeotia	Settlement	EMyc, PalBA
73	Charavgi	Attica	Artifacts	PalBA
74	Charvati	Attica	Tomb/Sanc	PalBA, ProtoIA
75	Chersonisi	Euboea	Artifacts	ProtoIA
76	Chloi	Thessaly	Cemetery	PreIA, ProtoIA
77	Chorsiai/ Khostion	Boeotia	Artifacts	EMyc, PalBA, ProtoIA
78	Corycian Cave	Phokis	Artifacts	PalBA, ProtoIA

TABLE 8 *(Continued)*

Number	Site name	Region	Type	Periods
79	Dafni	Euboea	Artifacts	PreIA, ProtoIA
80	Dafni Plateau	Boeotia	Artifacts	Myc
81	Davleia	Phokis	Artifacts	EMyc, PalBA
82	Dekeleia	Attica	Settlement	PalBA, ProtoIA
83	Delphi	Phokis	Set/Cem	PalBA, PostBA, PreIA, ProtoIA
84	Dema	Malis	Artifacts	PalBA, PostBA
85	Dhokos	Euboea	Artifacts	Myc
86	Dilofo	Thessaly	Settlement	PalBA, PostBA, PreIA
87	Dimini	Thessaly	Set/Cem	EMyc, PalBA, PostBA, PreIA, ProtoIA
88	Distomo	Phokis	Artifacts	EMyc, PalBA, ProtoIA
89	Distomo/Schisti	Phokis	Cemetery	PalBA, PreIA, ProtoIA
90	Drafi	Attica	Cemetery	ProtoIA
91	Dramesi/Paralia Avlidos	Boeotia	Set/Cem	EMyc, PalBA, PostBA
92	Drosia Aghios Minas	Boeotia	Artifacts	ProtoIA
93	Drymaia	Phokis	Settlement	PalBA? PostBA?
94	Dystos	Euboea	Settlement	PalBA
95	Elateia Alonaki	Phokis	Cemetery	EMyc, PalBA, PostBA, PreIA, ProtoIA
96	Elateia Athena Kranaia	Phokis	Sanctuary	EMyc, PalBA, PostBA, PreIA, ProtoIA
97	Elateia Piperi/ Panagitsa	Phokis	Set/Cem	EMyc, PalBA, PostBA, PreIA, ProtoIA
98	Eleon	Boeotia	Set/Cem	EMyc, PalBA, PostBA, ProtoIA
99	Eleusis	Attica	Set/Cem	EMyc, PalBA, PostBA, PreIA, ProtoIA
100	Eleutherai	Boeotia	Set/Cem	PalBA, ProtoIA
101	Ellinikon	Attica	Artifacts	ProtoIA
102	Ellopia	Boeotia	Cemetery	PostBA, PreIA
103	Eretria	Euboea	Set/Cem/ Sanc	PalBA, PostBA, PreIA, ProtoIA
104	Eretria Magoula	Euboea	Set/Cem	EMyc, PalBA, PostBA?
105	Erythrai Pantanassa	Boeotia	Artifacts	Myc
106	Eutresis	Boeotia	Settlement	EMyc, PalBA, PostBA

Contd.

TABLE 8 *(Continued)*

Number	Site name	Region	Type	Periods
107	Exarchos	East Lokris	Cemetery	PalBA, PostBA
108	Exarchos Hyampolis	East Lokris	Settlement	PalBA, PostBA, PreIA
109	Galaxidi	Phokis	Cemetery	PalBA, PostBA, PreIA, ProtoIA
110	Georgiko Tholos	Thessaly	Isolated tomb	PalBA, PostBA
111	Gerakas Sifnos	Attica	Artifacts	ProtoIA
112	Ginani	Salamis	Settlement	PostBA, PreIA, ProtoIA
113	Gla	Boeotia	Settlement	PalBA
114	Glyfa	Malis	Cemetery	EMyc
115	Glyka Nera	Attica	Cemetery	PalBA, PostBA, ProtoIA
116	Glypha	Boeotia	Settlement	EMyc, PalBA, PostBA, ProtoIA?
117	Golemi	East Lokris	Cemetery	EMyc, PalBA, PostBA
118	Goumourades	East Lokris	Artifacts	PalBA
119	Gouvai Palaiokastro	Euboea	Artifacts	EMyc, PalBA
120	Gritsa/Pteleon	Thessaly	Set/Cem	PalBA, PostBA, PreIA
121	Haliartos	Boeotia	Settlement	EMyc, PalBA, PreIA, ProtoIA
122	Haliartos Pyrgos	Boeotia	Cemetery	ProtoIA
123	Halos Voulokalyva	Thessaly	Set/Cem	PalBA, PostBA, PreIA, ProtoIA
124	Herakleia	Malis	Artifacts	PalBA
125	Hymettos	Attica	Sanctuary	PalBA, PostBA, PreIA, ProtoIA
126	Hypati	Malis	Set/Cem	PalBA, PreIA
127	Ilioupoli/Kara	Attica	Cemetery	PalBA
128	Itea Glas	Phokis	Settlement	PalBA, PostBA, PreIA
129	Kabeirion	Boeotia	Sanctuary	PreIA, ProtoIA
130	Kainourgio	East Lokris	Cemetery	PreIA, ProtoIA
131	Kaki Thalassa	Attica	Artifacts	Myc, ProtoIA
132	Kalami	Boeotia	Artifacts	EMyc, PalBA, PostBA
133	Kalapodi	East Lokris	Set/Cem/Sanc	EMyc, PalBA, PostBA, PreIA, ProtoIA
134	Kalapodi Kokkalia	East Lokris	Cemetery	EMyc, PalBA, PostBA
135	Kalapodi Vagia	East Lokris	Cemetery	PalBA, PreIA
136	Kallion	Phokis	Set/Cem	ProtoIA
137	Kallithea Moustaphades	Boeotia	Cemetery	EMyc, PalBA

TABLE 8 *(Continued)*

Number	Site name	Region	Type	Periods
138	Kalyvia Kouvara	Attica	Cemetery	ProtoIA
139	Kamarion	Euboea	Cemetery	Myc
140	Kamila/Marmara	Thessaly	Sanctuary	ProtoIA
141	Kanakia	Salamis	Set/Cem	EMyc, PalBA, PostBA
142	Kanalia	Thessaly	Cemetery	PalBA, ProtoIA
143	Karla	Thessaly	Cemetery	PalBA, PostBA, PreIA
144	Kastraki	Boeotia	Artifacts	EMyc, PalBA
145	Kastri Lykovouno	Boeotia	Artifacts	PalBA, ProtoIA
146	Kastro Kallithea	Thessaly	Cemetery	PalBA, PreIA, ProtoIA
147	Kastro Kopais	Boeotia	Artifacts	PalBA, PreIA, ProtoIA
148	Kastro Orias	Phokis	Artifacts	PalBA
149	Kastro tou Stenou	Phokis	Set/Cem	PalBA, ProtoIA
150	Kastro Volos	Thessaly	Settlement	PalBA, PostBA, PreIA, ProtoIA
151	Kastrouli/Desfina	Phokis	Set/Cem	PalBA, PostBA, PreIA, ProtoIA
152	Katakalou	Euboea	Isolated tomb	PalBA, PostBA, ProtoIA
153	Katheni Krasas	Euboea	Artifacts	Myc, PalBA
154	Kato Souli/ Schinias	Attica	Set/Cem	PalBA, ProtoIA
155	Kazanaki Tholos	Thessaly	Isolated tomb	PalBA, PostBA
156	Kea Aghia Irini	Kea, Cyclades	Set/Cem	EMyc, PalBA, PostBA, PreIA, ProtoIA
157	Kefala	Skiathos, Sporades	Artifacts	PreIA, ProtoIA
158	Keratea	Attica	Artifacts	PalBA, PostBA, ProtoIA
159	Kerinthos	Euboea	Settlement	PalBA, PostBA, PreIA, ProtoIA
160	Kiafa Thiti/ Lamptres	Attica	Set/Cem	EMyc, PalBA, PostBA, ProtoIA
161	Kifisia	Attica	Cemetery	ProtoIA
162	Kileler Magoula	Thessaly	Cemetery	PalBA
163	Kirra	Phokis	Settlement	EMyc, PalBA, PostBA
164	Kitsos Cave	Attica	Artifacts	PalBA
165	Kleidi	Boeotia	Cemetery	EMyc, PalBA
166	Kokkali	Boeotia	Settlement	Myc
167	Kokkini	Boeotia	Artifacts	Myc

Contd.

TABLE 8 *(Continued)*

Number	Site name	Region	Type	Periods
168	Kokkinonyzes	East Lokris	Isolated tomb	EMyc, PalBA
169	Kokkinos Milos	Attica	Artifacts	ProtoIA
170	Kolaka/Kyrtoni Aghios Ioannis	Boeotia	Cemetery	PalBA
171	Kolonna	Aegina	Set/Cem/Sanc	EMyc, PalBA, PostBA, PreIA, ProtoIA
172	Kompotades	Malis	Cemetery	PalBA, PostBA, PreIA
173	Kopreza	Attica	Cemetery	PalBA, PostBA
174	Koroneia	Boeotia	Artifacts	PalBA, PreIA, ProtoIA
175	Koropi	Attica	Artifacts	PreIA, ProtoIA
176	Koropi/Kastro Tou Christou	Attica	Settlement	EMyc, PalBA
177	Korynos	Boeotia	Settlement	PostBA, PreIA
178	Kotrona Hill	East Lokris	Artifacts	Myc
179	Koukouvaounes	Attica	Artifacts	EMyc, PalBA, ProtoIA
180	Kouvaras	Attica	Cemetery	ProtoIA
181	Kreusis/Livadostro	Boeotia	Artifacts	EMyc, PalBA
182	Krisa	Phokis	Set/Cem	EMyc, PalBA
183	Ktimeni	Thessaly	Isolated tomb	PalBA, PostBA, PreIA
184	Ktouri Magoula	Thessaly	Artifacts	PalBA, PostBA, PreIA, ProtoIA
185	Kyme	Euboea	Artifacts	PalBA
186	Kyme/Viglatouri	Euboea	Set/Cem	PalBA, PostBA, PreIA, ProtoIA
187	Kynos	East Lokris	Set/Cem	EMyc, PalBA, PostBA, PreIA, ProtoIA
188	Kyparissi	East Lokris	Artifacts	PalBA, PostBA?, PreIA?, ProtoIA
189	Lamia	Malis	Cemetery	EMyc, PalBA, PostBA, PreIA, ProtoIA
190	Larissa	Thessaly	Set/Cem	PalBA, PostBA, PreIA, ProtoIA
191	Larymna	Boeotia	Settlement	PalBA, PostBA?, PreIA? ProtoIA?
192	Lathouriza/Vari	Attica	Set/Cem	EMyc, PalBA, PostBA, ProtoIA
193	Lavrio	Attica	Artifacts	ProtoIA
194	Lefkandi	Euboea	Set/Cem	EMyc, PalBA, PostBA, PreIA, ProtoIA
195	Lepoura Magoula	Euboea	Artifacts	PalBA
196	Lestiani	Thessaly	Cemetery	PreIA
197	Lichas	Euboea	Artifacts	PalBA, PreIA, ProtoIA
198	Ligori	Attica	Cemetery	PalBA, PostBA
199	Lilaia	Phokis	Artifacts	EMyc, PalBA, ProtoIA

TABLE 8 *(Continued)*

Number	Site name	Region	Type	Periods
200	Limni	Euboea	Set/Cem	PalBA, ProtoIA
201	Listi	Boeotia	Artifacts	Myc
202	Lithares	Boeotia	Cemetery	EMyc, PalBA, ProtoIA
203	Lithosoros/ Drosia	Boeotia	Settlement	EMyc, PalBA
204	Livadeia	Boeotia	Artifacts	Myc, ProtoIA
205	Loupaka	Euboea	Settlement	PalBA
206	Lygaria	Malis	Set/Cem	EMyc, PalBA
207	Magoula Balomenou	Boeotia	Settlement	EMyc, PalBA
208	Magoula Mati	Thessaly	Artifacts	PreIA
209	Magoula Theophani	Thessaly	Artifacts	PalBA
210	Makronisos/ Leondari	Attica	Artifacts	PalBA, PostBA?
211	Malakondas	Euboea	Artifacts	PreIA
212	Malesina/ Lekouna	East Lokris	Cemetery	Myc
213	Mali	Phokis	Artifacts	PostBA, PreIA, ProtoIA
214	Manika	Euboea	Set/Cem	EMyc, PalBA, PreIA, ProtoIA
215	Mantoudion	Euboea	Artifacts	ProtoIA
216	Marathon Arnos	Attica	Isolated tomb	PalBA
217	Marathon Plasi	Attica	Set/Cem/ Sanc	EMyc, PalBA, PostBA, PreIA, ProtoIA
218	Marathon Skaleza	Attica	Cemetery	ProtoIA
219	Marathon Vrana	Attica	Cemetery	EMyc, PalBA
220	Markesi	Skyros, Sporades	Artifacts	PalBA, PostBA, PreIA, ProtoIA
221	Marmara	Malis	Cemetery	PalBA, PostBA
222	Martino	East Lokris	Cemetery	Myc
223	Mavronerion	Boeotia	Artifacts	ProtoIA
224	Mazi c064	Attica	Artifacts	PalBA, PostBA
225	Medeon	Phokis	Cemetery	EMyc, PalBA, PostBA, PreIA, ProtoIA
226	Mega Monastirion Magoula	Malis	Cemetery	PalBA, PreIA

Contd.

TABLE 8 *(Continued)*

Number	Site name	Region	Type	Periods
227	Megali Katavothra	Boeotia	Settlement	PalBA, ProtoIA
228	Megali Velanidia	Thessaly	Settlement	PalBA, PostBA, PreIA, ProtoIA
229	Megaplatanos	East Lokris	Cemetery	PalBA, PostBA, PreIA
230	Megara	Attica	Set/Cem	EMyc, PalBA, PostBA, ProtoIA
231	Megara Palaiokastro	Attica	Set/Cem	PalBA, ProtoIA
232	Melidoni	East Lokris	Artifacts	PalBA, PostBA?
233	Melitaia	Malis	artifacts	PalBA
234	Merenda	Attica	Cemetery	EMyc, PalBA, PostBA, PreIA?, ProtoIA
235	Mexiates Kountsouraki	Malis	Isolated tomb	Myc
236	Mikro Vathy	Boeotia	Cemetery	EMyc, PalBA
237	Mileai	Thessaly	Cemetery	PreIA, ProtoIA
238	Mistros	Euboea	Cemetery	PalBA, PostBA
239	Mitrou	East Lokris	Settlement	EMyc, PalBA, PostBA, PreIA
240	Modi	Phokis	Cemetery	PalBA, PostBA, PreIA
241	Monasteri	Phokis	Artifacts	Myc, PreIA?, ProtoIA
242	Moni Kaisariani	Attica	Artifacts	PalBA, PostBA
243	Mouriki/ Kamelovrisi	Boeotia	Cemetery	Myc, ProtoIA
244	Nea Ionia	Attica	Cemetery	EMyc, PalBA, PreIA
245	Nea Lampsakos	Euboea	Isolated tomb	PreIA
246	Nea Makri	Attica	Cemetery	ProtoIA
247	Neochoraki	Boeotia	Cemetery	ProtoIA
248	Neochorion	Boeotia	Artifacts	ProtoIA
249	Ninoi Pan Cave	Attica	Artifacts	EMyc, PalBA
250	Oinochori	Phokis	Artifacts	Myc, PalBA
251	Oinoe	Attica	Artifacts	PalBA, PostBA
252	Old Orchomenos	Boeotia	Settlement	EMyc, PalBA?
253	Onchestos	Boeotia	Artifacts	ProtoIA
254	Onchestos Tsoumbitses/ Kazarma	Boeotia	Artifacts	EMyc, PalBA, PreIA
255	Orchomenos	Boeotia	Set/Cem	EMyc, PalBA, PostBA, PreIA, ProtoIA
256	Oreoi Kastro	Euboea	Settlement	PalBA, PostBA, PreIA, ProtoIA

TABLE 8 *(Continued)*

Number	Site name	Region	Type	Periods
257	Oreoi Nisiotissa	Euboea	Artifacts	
258	Palaios Oropos	Attica	Artifacts	EMyc, PalBA
259	Palaia Phokaia	Attica	Cemetery	ProtoIA
260	Palaio Faliro	Attica	Cemetery	PalBA, PostBA, PreIA, ProtoIA
261	Pallini	Attica	Isolated tomb	PalBA
262	Panaghia	Thessaly	Artifacts	EMyc, PalBA
263	Panaghia Aetos	Phokis	Artifacts	Myc
264	Panagitsa	Euboea	Artifacts	PreIA
265	Panakton	Boeotia	Settlement	EMyc, PostBA, PreIA
266	Panopeus	Phokis	Set/Cem	EMyc, PalBA
267	Paralimni Oungra	Boeotia	Set/Cem	EMyc, PalBA, PostBA, PreIA, ProtoIA
268	Paralimni Pyrgos (Isos)	Boeotia	Settlement	PalBA, ProtoIA
269	Parnes Pan Cave	Attica	Artifacts	PalBA, PostBA, ProtoIA
270	Pavliani	Thessaly	Cemetery	PreIA
271	Pazaraki	Boeotia	Artifacts	PalBA
272	Pefkakia	Thessaly	Settlement	EMyc, PalBA, PostBA, PreIA, ProtoIA
273	Pei	Euboea	Isolated tomb	Myc?
274	Pelasgia	Malis	Cemetery	PalBA
275	Perachora	Corinthia	Set/Sanc	ProtoIA
276	Perati	Attica	Cemetery	PalBA, PostBA
277	Perivoli	Malis	Cemetery	PreIA
278	Petra Tilphousion	Boeotia	Artifacts	PalBA, ProtoIA
279	Pharos Avlidos	Boeotia	Cemetery	PalBA
280	Pharsala	Thessaly	Set/Cem	PalBA, PostBA, PreIA, ProtoIA
281	Pharsala Mylos	Thessaly	Artifacts	PalBA
282	Pherekampos	Skyros, Sporades	Artifacts	PostBA
283	Philagra	Euboea	Settlement	Myc
284	Phthiotic Thebes	Thessaly	Settlement	PalBA, PreIA, ProtoIA
285	Phylla Vrachos	Euboea	Settlement	PreIA, ProtoIA
286	Pikermi	Attica	Cemetery	PalBA
287	Pilion	Euboea	Artifacts	Myc

Contd.

TABLE 8 *(Continued)*

Number	Site name	Region	Type	Periods
288	Piraeus	Attica	Set/Cem	EMyc, PalBA, PostBA, PreIA, ProtoIA
289	Plaka Dilesi	Boeotia	Cemetery	Myc
290	Plakari	Euboea	Set/Sanc	PreIA, ProtoIA
291	Plataia	Boeotia	Settlement	EMyc, PalBA, PostBA, PreIA, ProtoIA
292	Platania	Malis	Set/Cem	EMyc, PalBA, PostBA, PreIA, ProtoIA
293	Politika Kafkala	Euboea	Settlement	EMyc, PalBA
294	Politika Mnima	Euboea	Artifacts	PalBA
295	Polygira	Boeotia	Settlement	EMyc, PalBA, PostBA?
296	Porto Rafti	Attica	Artifacts	PalBA, PostBA, PreIA, ProtoIA
297	Porto Rafti Natso	Attica	Artifacts	PalBA, PostBA, ProtoIA
298	Proerna	Thessaly	Set/Cem	PalBA, PreIA, ProtoIA
299	Prosilio	Boeotia	Cemetery	PalBA
300	Proskynas Chiliadou	East Lokris	Artifacts	PalBA, ProtoIA
301	Proskynas Rachi	East Lokris	Settlement	Myc
302	Psachna Aghia Paraskevi	Euboea	Cemetery	Myc
303	Psachna Aghios Ilias	Euboea	Artifacts	EMyc, PalBA, PostBA, PreIA, ProtoIA
304	Psachna Glyfas	Euboea	Artifacts	PalBA, PostBA, PreIA, ProtoIA
305	Ptoion/Ptoon (Sanctuary of Apollo Ptoios/Ptoos)	Boeotia	Set/Sanc	EMyc, PalBA, ProtoIA
306	Pyrasos/Nea Anchialos	Thessaly	Artifacts	PalBA, PreIA, ProtoIA
307	Pyrgos	Boeotia	Set/Cem	PalBA
308	Pyrgos Aghia Marina	Boeotia	Set/Cem	EMyc, PalBA, ProtoIA?
309	Pyrgos Magoula	Boeotia	Settlement	EMyc, PalBA
310	Pyrnari	Attica	Artifacts	PalBA, PostBA, PreIA, ProtoIA
311	Raches Fourni	Malis	Artifacts	PalBA
312	Rachita	Malis	Artifacts	PalBA, PostBA, PreIA? ProtoIA
313	Rafina	Attica	Settlement	PalBA
314	Raftis Island	Attica	Settlement	PostBA

TABLE 8 *(Continued)*

Number	Site name	Region	Type	Periods
315	Regginio	Malis	Artifacts	PreIA, ProtoIA
316	Rema Pharmaki	East Lokris	Isolated tomb	PalBA, PostBA
317	Ritsona	Boeotia	Set/Cem	Myc, ProtoIA
318	Roustiana	East Lokris	Settlement	Myc, PalBA?
319	Rovies/Orobiai	Euboea	Artifacts	PalBA, PostBA, PreIA, ProtoIA
320	Salamis Arsenal	Salamis	Cemetery	PostBA
321	Salamis Town	Salamis	Cemetery	EMyc, PalBA, PostBA, PreIA, ProtoIA
322	Sanctuary of Zeus Parnesios	Attica	Sanctuary	PreIA, ProtoIA
323	Schimatari Profitis Ilias	Boeotia	Settlement	EMyc, PalBA, PostBA
324	Sesklo	Thessaly	Set/Cem	PalBA, PreIA, ProtoIA
325	Siphai	Boeotia	Artifacts	EMyc, PalBA
326	Siphai/ Mavrovouni	Boeotia	Set/Sanc	ProtoIA
327	Skala Atalanti	East Lokris	Artifacts	EMyc, PalBA
328	Skala Oropou/ Oropos	Attica	Settlement	EMyc, PalBA, PreIA, ProtoIA
329	Skaramanga	Attica	Cemetery	PalBA
330	Skoteini Cave	Euboea	Artifacts	PalBA, ProtoIA
331	Skoteiniani/ Aghioi Anargyroi	Phokis	Set/Cem	PalBA, PostBA, ProtoIA
332	Skourta Site B10	Boeotia	Artifacts	PreIA
333	Skourta Site B21	Boeotia	Artifacts	PalBA
334	Skourta Site B33	Boeotia	Artifacts	Myc, PreIA
335	Skourta Site C17	Boeotia	Artifacts	Myc
336	Skourta Site J2	Boeotia	Artifacts	PostBA
337	Skroponieri	Boeotia	Artifacts	PalBA
338	Skyros Kampos	Skyros, Sporades	Cemetery	PreIA, ProtoIA
339	Skyros Kastro	Skyros, Sporades	Set/Cem	EMyc, PalBA, PostBA, PreIA, ProtoIA
340	Sofiada Domokou	Thessaly	Isolated tomb	PreIA
341	Solinari	Boeotia	Cemetery	PreIA
342	Soros	Boeotia	Cemetery	EMyc, PalBA
343	Sounion	Attica	Cemetery	EMyc?, PalBA?, ProtoIA

Contd.

TABLE 8 *(Continued)*

Number	Site name	Region	Type	Periods
344	Sourpi Magoula	Thessaly	Artifacts	PalBA
345	Spartia	East Lokris	Cemetery	PalBA, PostBA
346	Spata Magoula	Attica	Cemetery	EMyc, PalBA, PostBA, ProtoIA
347	Spata Prokalisi	Attica	Artifacts	ProtoIA
348	Spercheiada	Malis	Artifacts	PreIA
349	Sphingion	Boeotia	Cemetery	Myc
350	Sta Varka/ Draghasia	Phokis	Cemetery	PostBA, PreIA, ProtoIA
351	Stafylos	Skopelos, Sporades	Isolated tomb	EMyc, PalBA
352	Stavros	Attica	Artifacts	ProtoIA
353	Stephanovikeio Petra	Thessaly	Settlement	PalBA, PostBA?
354	Stroma/Soules	Boeotia	Artifacts	PalBA
355	Stroviki/Aghios Georgios	Boeotia	Settlement	EMyc, PalBA
356	Stylida	Malis	Set/Cem	PreIA, ProtoIA
357	Styra	Euboea	Artifacts	PostBA?
358	Sventza	East Lokris	Cemetery	PalBA, PostBA
359	Sykia	Phokis	Set/Cem	PalBA, PostBA, PreIA
360	Tanagra Bratsi	Boeotia	Set/Cem	EMyc, PalBA, PostBA
361	Tanagra Dendra	Boeotia	Set/Cem	EMyc, PalBA
362	Tanagra Gephyra	Boeotia	Set/Cem	EMyc, PalBA, PostBA
363	Taratsa/Aghia Paraskevi	Malis	Cemetery	PostBA, PreIA
364	Tatiza	Boeotia	Cemetery	Myc
365	Thebes	Boeotia	Set/Cem	EMyc, PalBA, PostBA, PreIA, ProtoIA
366	Theologos	Euboea	Artifacts	ProtoIA
367	Theotokou	Thessaly	Cemetery	PreIA, ProtoIA
368	Thermopylai Alpinoi	Malis	Settlement	EMyc, PalBA
369	Thespiai	Boeotia	Artifacts	EMyc, PalBA, ProtoIA
370	Thisbe	Boeotia	Cemetery	EMyc, PalBA, PostBA, PreIA, ProtoIA
371	Thorikos	Attica	Set/Cem	EMyc, PalBA, PostBA, PreIA, ProtoIA
372	Tithorea	Phokis	Artifacts	ProtoIA

TABLE 8 *(Continued)*

Number	Site name	Region	Type	Periods
373	Tithronion	Phokis	Set/Cem	PalBA, PostBA, PreIA, ProtoIA
374	Tourlogianni	Boeotia	Settlement	PalBA
375	Tragana	East Lokris	Cemetery	PalBA, ProtoIA
376	Tragana Aghia Triada	East Lokris	Cemetery	EMyc, PalBA
377	Triada Aghia Kalliopi	Euboea	Artifacts	ProtoIA
378	Trikala	Thessaly	Set/Cem	PalBA, PostBA, PreIA, ProtoIA
379	Tsumbitses/ Aghia Panaghia	Boeotia	Artifacts	EMyc, PalBA, ProtoIA
380	Tymbanos/ Stavros	Malis	Cemetery	PalBA, PreIA, ProtoIA
381	Vardates	Malis	Isolated tomb	PalBA, PostBA
382	Vasilika Palaiokastro	Euboea	Artifacts	PalBA
383	Vasiliko	Euboea	Artifacts	PreIA
384	Velanideza	Attica	Cemetery	PalBA, PostBA
385	Velanidia	East Lokris	Artifacts	Myc
386	Velestino Pherai	Thessaly	Set/Cem	EMyc, PalBA, PostBA, PreIA, ProtoIA
387	Velousia Tholos	Euboea	Isolated tomb	PalBA
388	Vlichada	East Lokris	Artifacts	EMyc, PalBA
389	Volos Kokotsika	Thessaly	Set/Cem	PostBA, PreIA, ProtoIA
390	Voula Alyki	Attica	Cemetery	PalBA, PostBA, PreIA, ProtoIA
391	Vouliagma	Boeotia	Cemetery	PalBA
392	Vouliagmeni	Attica	Artifacts	EMyc, PalBA, ProtoIA
393	Vranesi	Boeotia	Cemetery	PreIA, ProtoIA
394	Xinos	Boeotia	Settlement	EMyc, PalBA
395	Yialtra Kasteli	Euboea	Artifacts	EMyc, PalBA, PostBA, PreIA, ProtoIA
396	Ypaton Tourleza	Boeotia	Set/Cem	PalBA, ProtoIA
397	Zagora	Andros, Cyclades	Set/Cem	ProtoIA
398	Zarakes	Euboea	Settlement	PreIA?, ProtoIA
399	Zeli Aghios Georgios	East Lokris	Cemetery	EMyc, PalBA, PostBA

Contd.

TABLE 8 *(Continued)*

Number	Site name	Region	Type	Periods
400	Zeli Kvela	East Lokris	Cemetery	PalBA?, PostBA
401	Zerelia Kastraki	Thessaly	Artifacts	EMyc, PalBA, PreIA

˙EMyc=Early Mycenaean; Myc=Mycenaean (i.e., it is unspecified whether it is Early Mycenaean, Palatial Bronze Age, or Postpalatial Bronze Age); PalBA=Palatial Bronze Age; PostBA=Postpalatial Bronze Age; PreIA=Prehistoric Iron Age; ProtoIA=Protohistoric Iron Age (see table 1 for periodization, with dates and ceramic phases); see maps 31 and 32 for numbered site locations.

Åberg, N. 1933. *Bronzezeitliche und früheisenzeitliche Chronologie.* Vol. 4, *Griechenland.* Stockholm: Kunglig Vitterhets Historie och Antikvitets Akademien.

Adrimi-Sismani, V. 2007. "Mycenaean Northern Borders Revisited: New Evidence from Thessaly." In *Rethinking Mycenaean Palaces II: Revised and Expanded Second Edition,* edited by M. L. Galaty and W. A. Parkinson, 159–77. Los Angeles: Cotsen Institute of Archaeology, University of California, Los Angeles.

———. 2016. "Dimini: An Urban Settlement of the Late Bronze Age in the Pagasitic Gulf." In *Ra-pi-ne-u: Studies on the Mycenaean World Offered to Robert Laffineur for his 70th Birthday,* edited by J. Driessen, 39–61. Louvain-la-Neuve: Presses universitaires de Louvain.

———. 2017. *Ο μυκηναϊκός οικισμός Διμηνίου: 1977–1997. 20 χρόνια ανασκαφών.* Volos: Archaeological Institute of Thessalian Studies.

———. 2018. *Ιωλκος: Η εύκτιμενη πόλη του Ομήρου. Ένα αστικό κέντρο στον μύχο του Παγασητικού Κόλπου: Το διοικητικό κέντρο, οι οικίες και το νεκροταφείο.* Volos: Archaeological Institute of Thessalian Studies.

Adrimi-Sismani, V., and S. Alexandrou. 2009. "Μυκηναϊκός θολωτός τάφος στη θέση Καζανάκι." In *Αρχαιολογικό έργο Θεσσαλίας και Στερεάς Ελλάδας 2,* edited by A. Mazarakis Ainian, 133–49. Volos: Ministry of Culture and University of Thessaly.

Adrimi-Sismani, V., and L. Godart. 2005. "Les inscriptions en Linéaire B de Dimini/Iolkos et leur contexte archéologique." *Annuario della Scuola Archeologica di Atene* 83: 47–70.

Agouridis, C. 1997. "Sea Routes and Navigation in the Third Millennium Aegean." *Oxford Journal of Archaeology* 16, no. 1 (March): 1–24.

Ahlberg-Cornell, G. 1992. *Myth and Epos in Early Greek Art: Representation and Interpretation.* Jonsered: Paul Åströms Förlag.

Alcock, S. E. 1993. *Graecia Capta: The Landscapes of Roman Greece.* Cambridge: Cambridge University Press.

BIBLIOGRAPHY

———. 1994. "Breaking up the Hellenistic World: Survey and Society." In *Classical Greece: Ancient Histories and Modern Archaeologies*, edited by I. Morris, 171–90. Cambridge: Cambridge University Press.

———. 2002. *Archaeologies of the Greek Past: Landscape, Monuments, and Memories.* Cambridge: Cambridge University Press.

Alcock S. E., and J. F. Cherry, eds. 2004. *Side-by-Side Survey: Comparative Regional Studies in the Mediterranean World.* Oxford: Oxbow Books.

———. 2006. "'No Greater Marvel': A Bronze Age Classic at Orchomenos." In *Classical Pasts: The Classical Traditions of Greece and Rome*, edited by J. I. Porter, 69–86. Princeton, NJ: Princeton University Press.

Alcock, S. E., T. N. D'Altroy, K. D. Morrison, and C. M. Sinopoli, eds. 2001. *Empires: Perspectives from Archaeology and History.* Cambridge: Cambridge University Press.

Alexandridou, A. 2017. "Some Insights into the Early Attic Society (10th–7th Centuries BC)." In *Regional Stories Towards a New Perception of the Early Greek World*, edited by A. Mazarakis Ainian, A. Alexandridou, X. Charalambidou, 155–76. Volos: University of Thessaly Press.

———. 2018. "Feasting in Early Iron Age Attika: The Evidence from the Site of the Academy." In *Feasting and Polis Institutions*, edited by F. van den Eijnde, J. H. Blok, R. Strootman, 28–59. Leiden: Brill.

———. 2020. "Athens and Attica." In *A Companion to the Archaeology of Early Greece and the Mediterranean*, edited by I. S. Lemos and A. Kotsonas, 743–62. Hoboken, NJ: John Wiley & Sons.

Alram-Stern, E. 2007. "Characteristic Small Finds of LH III C from Aigeira and Their Context." *LH III C Chronology and Synchronisms II: LH III C Middle.* S. Deger-Jalkotzy and M. Zavadil, 15–25. Vienna: Verlag der Österreichischen Akademie der Wissenschaften.

Ambraseys, N. N. 1996. "Material for the Investigation of the Seismicity of Central Greece." In *Archaeoseismology*, edited by S. Stiros, and R. E. Jones, 26–36. Athens: Institute of Geology & Mineral Exploration and the British School at Athens.

Ames, K. M. 2008. "The Archaeology of Rank." In *Handbook of Archaeological Theories*, edited by R. A. Bentley, H. D. G. Maschner, and C. Chippindale, 487–513. Lanham, MD: AltaMira Press.

Andreou, S., M. Fotiadis, and K. Kotsakis. 2001. "The Neolithic and Bronze Age of Northern Greece." In *Aegean Prehistory: A Review*, edited by T. Cullen, 259–327. Boston: Archaeological Institute of America.

Andrikou, E. 2015. "Η μυκηναϊκή περίοδος στα Μεσόγεια και τη Λαυρεωτική. Αρχαιολογία και μυθολογία." In *Πρακτικά ΙΕ´ επιστημονικής συνάντησης ΝΑ. Αττικής*, edited by A. D. Stefanis, 431–41. Kalyvia Thorikou: Εταιρεία Μελετών Νοτιοανατολικής Αττικής.

Andrikou, E., A. Dakouri-Hild, S. Davis, A. Agapiou, P. Bes, X. Charalambidou, M. Chidiroglou, et al. 2020. "The Kotroni Archaeological Survey Project (KASP) at Ancient Aphidna in Northern Attica: Results of the First Season (2019)." Paper presented at the Annual Meeting of the Archaeological Institute of America, Washington DC, January 2–5, 2020.

Antonaccio, C. 1994. "Placing the Past: The Bronze Age in the Cultic Topography of Early Greece." In *Placing the Gods: Sanctuaries and Sacred Space in Ancient Greece*, 79–104. Oxford: Clarendon Press.

———. 1995. *An Archaeology of Ancestors: Tomb Cult and Hero Cult in Early Greece*. Lanham, MD: Rowman & Littlefield.

———. 2002. "Warriors, Traders, and Ancestors: The 'Heroes' of Lefkandi." In *Images of Ancestors*, edited by J. M. Højte, 13–42. Aarhus: Aarhus University Press.

Arachoviti, P., 1994. "Θολωτός πρωτογεωμετρικός τάφος στην περιοχή των Φερών." In *Θεσσαλία: Δεκαπέντε χρόνια αρχαιολογικής έρευνας, 1975–1990. Αποτελέσματα και προοπτικές*, edited by R. Misdrachi-Kapon, 125–38. Athens: Editions Kapon.

Aravantinos, V. 2010. "Mycenaean Thebes: Old Questions, New Answers." In *Espace civil, espace religieux en Égée durant la période mycénienne: Approches épigraphique, linguistique et archéologique*, edited by I. Boehm and S. Müller-Çelka, 51–72. Lyon: Maison de l'Orient et de la Méditerranée—Jean Pouilloux.

———. 2015. "The Palatial Administration of Thebes Updated." In *Tradition and Innovation in the Mycenaean Palatial Polities*, edited by J. Weilhartner and F. Ruppenstein, 19–49. Vienna: Verlag der Österreichischen Akademie der Wissenschaften.

———. 2020. "Thebes and Boeotia." In *A Companion to the Archaeology of Early Greece and the Mediterranean*, edited by I. S. Lemos and A. Kotsonas, 763–86. Hoboken, NJ: John Wiley & Sons.

Aravantinos, V., B. Burke, B. Burns, S. Lupack, C. MacKay, and Y. Fappas. 2016a. "The Eastern Boeotia Archaeological Project 2007–2010: The Intensive Surface Survey—Eleon." *Mouseion* 13, no. 2: 293–357.

Aravantinos, V., I. Fappas, O. Kyriazi, G. Luglio, and M. Pisani. 2016b. "'No Greater Marvel' Revisited: Use and Reuse of the Mycenaean Tholos Tomb at Orchomenos." In *Αρχαιολογικό έργο Θεσσαλίας και Στερεάς Ελλάδας 4*, edited by A. Mazarakis Ainian, 929–41. Volos: Ministry of Culture, Education and Religion and University of Thessaly.

Aravantinos, V., L. Godart, and A. Sacconi, eds. 2001. *Thèbes: Fouilles de la Cadmée I: Les tablettes en Linéaire B de la Odos Pelopidou, édition et commentaire*. Rome: Istituti Editoriali e Poligrafici Internazionali.

———. 2002. *Thèbes: Fouilles de la Cadmée III: Corpus des documents d'archives en Linéaire B de Thèbes (1–433)*. Rome: Istituti Editoriali e Poligrafici Internazionali.

Aravantinos, V., and E. Kountouri. 2014. *100 χρόνια αρχαιολογικού έργου στη Θήβα. Οι πρωτεργάτες των ερευνών και οι συνεχιστές τους*. Athens: Ταμείο Αρχαιολογικών Πόρων και Απαλλοτριώσεων.

Arena, E. 2015. "Mycenaean Peripheries during the Palatial Age: The Case of Achaia." *Hesperia* 84, no. 1 (January–March): 1–46.

Arnaud, P. 2005. *Les routes de la navigation antique: Itinéraires en Méditerranée*. Paris: Editions Errance.

Arnold, B. 1995. *Celtic Chiefdom, Celtic State: The Evolution of Complex Social Systems in Prehistoric Europe*. Cambridge: Cambridge University Press.

Arnold, F., and D. Marzoli. 2009. "Toscanos, Morro de Mezquitilla una Las Chorreras im 8. Und 7. Jh. v. Chr.: Siedlungsstruktur und Wohnhaustypologie." In *Phönizisches und punisches Städtewesen*, edited by S. Helas and D. Marzoli, 437–60. Mainz: Philipp von Zabern.

Arnold, J. E., ed. 1996. *Emergent Complexity: The Evolution of Intermediate Societies*. Ann Arbor, MI: International Monographs in Prehistory.

Aro, S. 2013. "Carchemish Before and After 1200 BC." In *Luwian Identities: Culture, Language and Religion Between Anatolia and the Aegean*, edited by A. Mouton, I. Rutherford, and I. Yakubovich, 233–76. Leiden: Brill.

Arrington, N. 2016. "Talismanic Practice at Lefkandi: Trinkets, Burials and Belief in the Early Iron Age." *Cambridge Classical Journal* 62 (December): 1–30.

Arvanitopoulou, T. A. 1959. Ὄστρακα ἐκ Δεκελείας: Συλλεγέντα καὶ νῦν τὸ πρῶτον ἐκδιδόμενα τύποις ὑπὸ τῶν Α. Α. Β. Β. Πριγκιπισσῶν Σοφίας καὶ Εἰρήνης καὶ τῆς καθηγητρίας αὐτῶν Θεοφανοῦς Α. Ἀρβανιτοπούλου. Athens: Τύποις Ἀντωνίου Παπασπύρου.

Aslaksen, O. C., ed. 2016. *Local and Global Perspectives on Mobility in the Eastern Mediterranean*. Athens: Norwegian Institute at Athens.

Aubet, M. E. 2001. *The Phoenicians and the West: Politics, Colonies, and Trade*. 2nd ed. Cambridge: Cambridge University Press.

Bachhuber, C. 2006. "Aegean Interest on the Uluburun Ship." *American Journal of Archaeology* 110, no. 3 (July): 345–63.

Bächle, A. E. 2007. "Eliten in Elateia? Überlegungen ausgehend von der frühen mykenischen Keramik." In *Keimelion: Elitenbildung und elitärer Konsum von der Mykenischen Palastzeit bis zur Homerischen Epoche*, edited by E. Alram-Stern and G. Nightingale, 15–30. Vienna: Verlag der Österreichischen Akademie der Wissenschaften.

Backe-Forsberg, Y., and C. Risberg. 2002. "Archaeometallurgical Methods Applied to Remains of Iron Production from the Geometric Period at Asine." In *New Research on Old Material from Asine and Berbati in Celebration of the Fiftieth Anniversary of the Swedish Institute at Athens*, edited by B. Wells, 85–94. Stockholm: Svenska Institutet i Athen.

Baines, J., J. Bennet, and S. Houston, eds. 2008. *The Disappearance of Writing Systems: Perspectives on Literacy and Communication*. London: Equinox.

Bajema, M. J. 2017a. *Bodies of Maize, Eaters of Grain: Comparing Material Worlds, Metaphor and the Agency of Art in the Preclassic Maya and Mycenaean Early Civilisations*. Oxford: Archaeopress.

———. 2017b. "Variation on a Theme: Mycenaean Early Civilisation in a Comparative Perspective." *Journal of Greek Archaeology* 2: 81–114.

Bakhuizen, S. C. 1976. *Chalcis-in-Euboea: Iron and Chalcidians Abroad*. Leiden: Brill.

———. 1977. "Greek Steel." *World Archaeology* 9, no. 2 (October): 220–34.

———. 1985. *Studies in the Topography of Chalcis on Euboea (A Discussion of the Sources)*. Leiden: Brill.

Bandy, M. S. 2004. "Fissioning, Scalar Stress, and Social Evolution in Early Village Societies." *American Anthropologist* 106, no. 2 (June): 322–33.

Bandy, M. S., and J. R. Fox, eds. 2010. *Becoming Villagers: Comparing Early Village Societies*. Tuscon: University of Arizona Press.

Banou, E. 2008. "The Tholos Tombs of Messenia: An Overview." In *Dioskouroi: Studies Presented to W. G. Cavanagh and C. B. Mee on the Anniversary of Their 30-year Joint Contribution to Aegean Archaeology*, edited by C. Gallou, M. Georgiadis, and G. M. Muskett, 42–54. Oxford: Archaeopress.

Barabási, A.-L., and R. Albert. 1999. "Emergence of Scaling in Random Networks." *Science* 286, no. 5439 (October): 509–12.

Baran, P. 1964. "On Distributed Communications Networks." *IEEE Transactions on Communications Systems* 12, no. 1 (March): 1–9.

Bard, K. A. 2008. *Introduction to the Archaeology of Ancient Egypt*. Malden, MA: Wiley-Blackwell.

Bardolph, D. N. 2014. "Evaluating Cahokina Contact and Mississippian Identity Politics in the Late Prehistoric Central Illinois River Valley." *American Antiquity* 79, no. 1 (January): 69–89.

Barnes, J. T. 2016. "A Cultural Geography of the Southeast Aegean from the Late Helladic IIIB to the Late Protogeometric Periods." PhD diss., University of Missouri-Columbia. ProQuest (AAT 11012703).

Bass, G. F. 1967. *Cape Gelidonya: A Bronze Age Shipwreck.* Philadelphia: American Philosophical Society.

Bassiakos, Y., and T. Tselios. 2012. "On the Cessation of Local Copper Production in the Aegean in the 2nd Millennium BC." In *Eastern Mediterranean Metallurgy and Metalwork in the Second Millennium BC,* edited by V. Kassianidou and G. Papasavvas, 151–61. Oxford: Oxbow Books.

Batziou-Efstathiou, A. 1994. "Μυκηναϊκός κεραμεικός κλίβανος." In *Θεσσαλία. Δεκαπέντε χρόνια αρχαιολογικής Έρευνας, 1975–1990,* 215–24. Athens: Ministry of Culture.

———. 2015. "The Mycenaean Settlement at Pefkakia: The Harbour of Iolkos?" In *Tradition and Innovation in the Mycenaean Palatial Polities,* edited by J Weilhartner and F. Ruppenstein, 51-85. Vienna: Verlag der Österreichischen Akademie der Wissenschaften.

Beckman, G. 1996. *Hittite Diplomatic Texts.* Atlanta: Society of Biblical Literature.

Beckman, G. M., T. R. Bryce, and E. H. Cline. 2011. *The Ahhiyawa Texts.* Atlanta: Society of Biblical Literature.

Bell, C. 2009. "Continuity and Change: The Divergent Destinies of Late Bronze Age Ports in Syria and Lebanon across the LBA/Iron Age Transition." In *Forces of Transformation: The End of the Bronze Age in the Mediterranean,* edited by C. Bachhuber and R. G. Roberts, 30–38. Oxford: Oxbow Books.

Bennet, J. 1985. "The Structure of the Linear B Administration at Knossos." *American Journal of Archaeology* 85, no. 2 (April): 231–49.

———. 1995. "Space through Time: Diachronic Perspectives on the Spatial Organization of the Pylian State." In *POLITEIA: Society and State in the Aegean Bronze Age,* edited by WD. Niemeier and R. Laffineur, 587–602. Liège: Université de Liège.

———. 2008. "Now You See It; Now You Don't! The Disappearance of the Linear A Script on Crete." In *The Disappearance of Writing Systems: Perspectives on Literacy and Communication,* edited by J. Baines, J. Bennet, and S. Houston, 1–29. London: Equinox.

———. 2011. "The Geography of the Mycenaean Kingdoms." In *A Companion to Linear B: Mycenaean Greek Texts and Their World,* edited by Y. Duhoux and A. Morpurgo Davies, 137–68. Leuven: Peeters.

———. 2017. "Palaces and Their Regions: Geographical Analysis of Territorial Exploitation in Late Bronze Age Crete and Greece." *Pasiphae* 11: 151–73.

———. 2018. "Gelb and Gell in the Aegean: Thoughts on the Relations between 'Writing' and 'Art.'" In *Regional Approaches to Society and Complexity: Studies in Honor of John F. Cherry,* edited by A. R. Knodell and T. P. Leppard, 59–74. Sheffield: Equinox.

Bennet, J., and M. Galaty. 1997. "Ancient Greece: Recent Developments in Aegean Archaeology and Regional Studies." *Journal of Archaeological Research* 5, no. 1 (March): 75–120.

Bentley, R. A., and H. D. G. Maschner, eds. 2003. *Complex Systems and Archaeology: Empirical and Theoretical Applications.* Salt Lake City: University of Utah Press.

Benzi, M., and G. Graziadio. 1996. "The Last Mycenaeans in Italy? Late Helladic IIIC Pottery from Punta Meliso, Leuca." *Studi Micenei ed Egeo-Anatolici* 38: 95–138.

Béquignon, Y. 1937. *La vallée du Spercheios des origines au IVe siècle: études d'archéologie et de topographie.* Paris: E. de Boccard.

Bérard, C. 1970. *L'Hérôon à la Porte de l'Ouest.* Eretria fouilles et recherches 3. Bern: Editions Francke.

Besios, M., Y. Tzifopoulos, and A. Kotsonas. 2012. *Μεθώνη I: Επιγραφές, χαράγματα και εμπορικά σύμβολα στην υστερογεωμετρική και αρχαιολογική κεραμική από το 'Υπόγειο'.* Thessaloniki: Center for Hellenic Language.

Bevan, A. 2010. "Political Geography and Palatial Crete." *Journal of Mediterranean Archaeology* 23, no. 1 (July): 27–54.

Bevan, A., and J. Conolly. 2006. "Multiscalar Approaches to Settlement Pattern Analysis." In *Confronting Scale in Archaeology: Issues of Theory and Practice*, edited by G. Lock and B. L. Molyneaux, 217–34. New York: Springer.

Bevan, A., and A. Wilson. 2013. "Models of Settlement Hierarchy Based on Partial Evidence." *Journal of Archaeological Science* 40, no. 5 (May): 2415–27.

Bietti Sestieri, A. M. 1997. "Italy in Europe in the Early Iron Age." *Proceedings of the Prehistoric Society* 63: 371–402.

———. 2010. *L'Italia nell'età del bronzo e del ferro: Dalle palafitte a Romulo (2200–700 a.C.).* Rome: Carocci Editore.

Bintliff, J. 1977a. "The History of Archaeo-Geographic Studies of Prehistoric Greece, and Recent Fieldwork." In *Mycenaean Geography*, edited by J. L. Bintliff, 3–18. Cambridge: British Association for Mycenaean Studies.

———. 1977b. *Natural Environment and Human Settlement in Prehistoric Greece.* Oxford: British Archaeological Reports.

———. 1997. "Regional Survey, Demography, and the Rise of Complex Societies in the Ancient Aegean: Core-Periphery, Neo-Malthusian, and Other Interpretive Models." *Journal of Field Archaeology* 24, no. 1 (Spring): 1–38.

———. 1999. "Pattern and Process in the City Landscapes of Boeotia from Geometric to Late Roman Times." In *Territoire des cités grecques*, edited by M. Brunet, 15–33. Athens: École française d'Athénes.

———. 2012. *The Complete Archaeology of Greece: From Hunter-Gatherers to the 20th Century A. D.* Malden, MA: Wiley-Blackwell.

———. 2020. "Natural and Human Ecology: Geography, Climate, and Demography." In *A Companion to the Archaeology of Early Greece and the Mediterranean*, edited by I. S. Lemos and A. Kotsonas, 3–32. Hoboken, NJ: John Wiley & Sons.

Bintliff, J., E. Farinetti, B. Slapšak, and A. Snodgrass. 2017. *Boeotia Project, Volume II: The City of Thespiai. Survey at a Complex Urban Site.* Cambridge: McDonald Institute for Archaeological Research.

Bintliff, J. L., P. Howard, and A. M. Snodgrass. 2007. *Testing the Hinterland: The Work of the Boeotia Survey (1989–1991) in the Southern Approaches to the City of Thespiai.* Cambridge: McDonald Institute for Archaeological Research.

Bintliff, J., B. Noordervliet, J. van Zwienen, K. Wilkinson, B. Slapšak, V. Stissi, C. Piccoli, and A. Vionis. 2013. "The Leiden-Ljubljana Ancient Cities of Boeotia Project, 2010-2012 Seasons." *Pharos* 19, no 2: 1–34.

Bintliff, J. L., and A. M. Snodgrass. 1985. "The Cambridge/Bradford Boeotian Expedition: The First Four Years." *Journal of Field Archaeology* 12, no. 2 (Summer): 123–61.

Blackwell, N. G. 2010. "Mortuary Variability at Salamis (Cyprus): Relationships between and within the Royal Necropolis and the Cellarka Cemetery." *Journal of Mediterranean Archaeology* 23, no. 2 (January): 143–67.

———. 2018. "Contextualizing Mycenaean Hoards: Metal Control on the Greek Mainland at the End of the Bronze Age." *American Journal of Archaeology* 122, no. 4 (October): 509–39.

Blackwell, N. G., and K. O'Neill. 2014. "Metal Consumption and Production at Mitrou: Diachronic Trends from the Early Helladic Through the Protogeometric Periods." Paper read at the 2014 Annual Meeting of the Archaeological Institute of America, 2–5 January, Chicago.

Blake, E. 2008. "The Mycenaeans in Italy: A Minimalist Position." *Papers of the British School at Rome* 76: 1–34.

———. 2014. *Social Networks and Regional Identity in Bronze Age Italy*. Cambridge: Cambridge University Press.

Blandin, B. 2007. *Les pratiques funéraires d'époque géométrique à Erétrie: Espace des vivants, demeures des morts*. Gollion: Infolio Éditions.

Blanton, R. E., and L. F. Fargher. 2008. *Collective Action in the Formation of Pre-Modern States*. New York: Springer.

Blanton, R. E., S. A. Kowalewski, and G. Feinman. 1984. "The Mesoamerican World System." *American Anthropologist* 86: 673–82.

Blanton, R. E., G. M. Feinman, S. A. Kowalewski, and P. N. Peregrine. 1996. "A Dual-Processual Theory for the Evolution of Mesoamerican Civilization." *Current Anthropology* 37, no. 1 (February): 1–14.

Blegen, C. W. 1952. "Two Athenian Grave Groups of about 900 B.C." *Hesperia* 21, no. 4 (October–December): 279–94.

Blegen, C. W., and M. Lang. 1961. "The Palace of Nestor Excavations of 1960." *American Journal of Archaeology* 65, no. 2 (April): 153–63.

Blitz, J. H. 1999. "Mississippian Chiefdoms and the Fission-Fusion Process." *American Antiquity* 64, no. 4 (October): 577–92.

———. 2010. "New Perspectives in Mississippian Archaeology." *Journal of Archaeological Research* 18: 1–39.

Boardman, J. 1957. "Early Euboean Pottery and History." *Annual of the British School at Athens* 52: 1–29.

———. 1959. "Greek Potters at Al Mina?" *Anatolian Studies* 9: 163–69.

———. 1980. *The Greeks Overseas: Their Early Colonies and Trade*. 3rd ed. London: Thames and Hudson.

———. 1990. "Al Mina and History." *Oxford Journal of Archaeology* 9: 169–90.

Boffa, G., and B. Leone. 2017. "Euboean Cults and Myths Outside Euboea: Poseidon and Briareos/Aigaion." In *An Island between Two Worlds: The Archaeology of Euboea from Prehistoric to Byzantine Times*, edited by Ž. Tankosić, F. Mavridis, and M. Kosma, 381–90. Athens: Norwegian Institute at Athens.

Bohen, B. 2017. *Kratos and Krater: Reconstructing and Athenian Protohistory*. Oxford: Archaeopress.

Bondì, S. F., M. Botto, G. Garbati, and I. Oggiano. 2009. *Fenici e Cartaginesi: Una civiltà mediterranea*. Rome: Istituto Poligrafico e Zecca dello Stato.

Boone J. L., J. E. Myers, and C. L. Redman. 1990. "Archeological and Historical Approaches to Complex Societies: The Islamic States of Medieval Morocco." *American Anthropologist* 92, no. 3 (September): 630–46.

Borck, L., B. J. Mills, M. A. Peeples, and J. J. Clark. 2015. "Are Social Networks Survival Networks? An Example from the Late Pre-Hispanic US Southwest." *Journal of Archaeological Method and Theory* 22, no. 1 (March): 33–57.

Boulotis, C. 2015. "Reconstructing a Dolphin Frieze and Argonauts from the Mycenaean Citadel of Gla." In *Mycenaean Wall Painting in Context: New Discoveries, Old Finds Reconsidered*, edited by H. Brecoulaki, J. L. Davis, and S. R. Stocker, 370–403. Athens: National Hellenic Research Foundation.

Bourdieu, P. 1977. *Outline of a Theory of Practice*. Cambridge: Cambridge University Press.

Bourogiannis, G. 2020. "Between Scripts and Languages: Inscribed Intricacies from Geometric and Archaic Greek Contexts." In *Understanding Relations Between Scripts II: Early Alphabets*, edited by P. J. Boyes and P. M. Steele, 151–80. Oxford: Oxbow Books.

Boyes, P. J., and P. M. Steele, eds. 2020. *Understanding Relations Between Scripts II: Early Alphabets*. Oxford: Oxbow Books.

Bradeen, D. W. 1947. "The Lelantine War and Pheidon of Argos." *Transactions and Proceedings of the American Philological Association* 78: 223–41.

Branigan, K., ed. 2001. *Urbanism in the Aegean Bronze Age*. London: Sheffield Academic Press.

Braudel, F. 1972. *The Mediterranean and the Mediterranean World in the Age of Philip II*. New York: Harper and Row.

Brekoulaki, H., S. R. Stocker, J. L. Davis, and E. C. Egan. 2015. "An Unprecedented Naval Scene from Pylos: First Considerations." In *Mycenaean Wall Painting in Context: New Discoveries, Old Finds Reconsidered*, edited by H. Brecoulaki, J. L. Davis, and S. R. Stocker, 260–91. Athens: National Hellenic Research Foundation.

Brisart, T. 2011. *Un art Citoyen: Recherches sur l'orientalisation des artisanats en Grèce proto-archaïque*. Mémoire de la Classe des Lettres. Brussels: Académie royale de Belgique.

Brixhe, C. 2002. "Inscriptions paléo-phrygiennes: Supplément I." *Kadmos* 41: 1–102.

Brixhe, C., and M. Lejeune. 1984. *Corpus des inscriptions paléo-phrygiennes*. Paris: Editions Recherche sur les Civilisations.

Brodersen, K. 2001. "The 'Urban Myth' of Euboean Cyme: A Study in Lexicographical Tradition." *Ancient History Bulletin* 15, nos. 1–2: 25–28.

Broneer, O. 1939. "A Mycenaean Fountatin on the Athenian Acropolis." *Hesperia* 8, no. 4 (October–December): 317–443.

———. 1948. "What Happened at Athens." *American Journal of Archaeology* 52, no. 1 (January–March): 111–14.

———. 1956. "Athens in the Late Bronze Age." *Antiquity* 30, no. 117 (March): 9–18.

Broodbank, C. 2000. *An Island Archaeology of the Early Cyclades*. Cambridge: Cambridge University Press.

———. 2013. *The Making of the Middle Sea: A History of the Mediterranean from the Beginning to the Emergence of the Classical World*. London: Thames and Hudson.

Brughmans, T. 2013. "Thinking Through Networks: A Review of Formal Network Methods in Archaeology." *Journal of Archaeological Method and Theory* 20: 623–62.

Brughmans, T. A. Collar, and F. Coward, eds. 2016. *The Connected Past: Challenges to Network Studies in Archaeology and History*. Oxford: Oxford University Press.

Brughmans, T. A., and M. A. Peeples. 2020. "Spatial Networks." In *Archaeological Spatial Analysis: A Methodological Guide*, edited by M. Gillings, P. Hacıgüzeller, and G. Lock, 273–95. New York: Routledge.

Bryce, T. 2003. "Relations between Hatti and Ahhiyawa in the Last Decades of the Bronze Age." In *Hittite Studies in Honor of Harry A. Hoffner Jr. on the Occasion of His 65th Birthday*, edited by G. Beckman, R. Beal, and G. McMahon, 59–72. Winona Lake, IN: Eisenbrauns.

———. 2018. "The Kingdom of Ahhiyawa: A Hittite Perspective." Forum article with responses by E. H. Cline, J. M. Kelder, J. B. Rutter, R. Schon, M. Weeden, and A. L. D'Agata. *Studi Micenei ed Egeo-Anatolici Nuova Serie* 4: 191–230.

Brysbaert, A. 2008a. "Painted Plaster from Bronze Age Thebes, Boeotia (Greece): A Technological Study." *Journal of Archaeological Science* 35, no. 10 (October): 2761–69.

———. 2008b. *The Power of Technology in the Bronze Age Eastern Mediterranean: The Case of Painted Plaster*. London: Equinox.

———, ed. 2011. *Tracing Prehistoric Social Networks through Technology: A Diachronic Perspective on the Aegean*. New York: Routledge.

Buchner, G., and D. Ridgway. 1993. *Pithekoussai*. Rome: G. Bretschneider.

Budd, P., A. M. Pollard, B. Scaife, and R. G. Thomas. 1995. "Oxhide Ingots, Recycling and the Mediterranean Metals Trade." *Journal of Mediterranean Archaeology* 8, no. 1 (January): 1–32.

Bulle, H. 1907. *Orchomenos I: Die älteren Ansiedlungsschichten*. Munich: Verlag der Bayerischen Akademie der Wissenschaften.

Burke, B., B. E. Burns, A. Charami, T. Van Damme, N. Herrmann, and B. Lis. 2020. "Fieldwork at Ancient Eleon in Boeotia, 2011–2018." *American Journal of Archaeology* 124, no. 3 (July): 441–76.

Burke, B., B. E. Burns, and S. Lupack. 2009. "Eastern Boeotia Archaeological Project 2009." *Teiresias* 39, no. 2: 11–15.

Burn, A. R. 1929. "The So-Called 'Trade-Leagues' in Early Greek History and the Lelantine War." *Journal of Hellenic Studies* 49, part 1: 14–37.

Burns, B. E. 2010. *Mycenaean Greece, Mediterranean Commerce, and the Formation of Identity*. Cambridge: Cambridge University Press.

———. 2016. "The Rhetoric of Reciprocity in Late Bronze Age Mediterranean Exchange." *Journal of Mediterranean Archaeology* 29, no. 1 (June): 88–94.

Burrows, R. M., and P. M. Ure. 1907–8. "Excavations at Rhitsóna in Boeotia." *Annual of the British School at Athens* 14: 226–318.

Bury, J. B. 1887. "The Lombards and Venetians in Euboia. (1205–1303)." *Journal of Hellenic Studies* 7: 309–52.

Butzer, K. W., and G. H. Endfield. 2012. "Critical Perspectives on Historical Collapse." *Proceedings of the National Academy of Science* 109, no. 10 (March): 3628–31.

Caldwell, J. R. 1964. "Interaction Spheres in Prehistory." In *Hopewellian Studies*, edited by J. R. Caldwell and R. L. Hall, 133–43. Springfield: Illinois State Museum.

Callaghan, P. J., A. W. Johnston, P. M. Bikai, J. W. Hayes, and R. E. Jones. 2000. "The Iron Age Pottery from Kommos." In *Kommos IV: The Greek Sanctuary*, edited by J. W. Shaw and M. C. Shaw, 210–335. Princeton, NJ: Princeton University Press.

Cambitoglou, A., and J. K. Papadopoulos. 1993. "The Earliest Mycenaeans in Macedonia." In *Wace and Blegen: Pottery as Evidence for Trade in the Aegean Bronze Age*, edited by C. Zerner and J. Winder, 289–302. Amsterdam: J. C. Gieben.

Camp, J. McK., II. 1979. "A Drought in the Late Eighth Century B.C." *Hesperia* 48, no. 4 (October–December): 397–411.

Canuto, M. A., and J. Yaeger, eds. 2000. *The Archaeology of Communities: A New World Perspective*. New York: Routledge.

Carballo, D. M., P. Roscoe, and G. Feinman. 2014. "Cooperation and Collective Action in the Cultural Evolution of Complex Societies." *Journal of Archaeological Method and Theory* 21: 98–133.

Carstens, A. M. 2005. "To Bury a Ruler: The Meaning of the Horse in Aristocratic Burials." In *Cyprus: Religion and Society from the Late Bronze Age to the End of the Archaic Period*, edited by V. Karageorghis, H. Matthäus, and S. Rogge, 57–76. Möhnesee: Bibliopolis.

Carter, J. 1972. "The Beginning of Narrative Art in the Greek Geometric Period." *Annual of the British School at Athens* 67: 25–58.

Carter, J. B., and S. P. Morris, eds. 1995. *The Ages of Homer: A Tribute to Emily Townsend Vermeule*. Austin: University of Texas Press.

Cartledge, P., and P. Christesen, eds. Forthcoming. *The Oxford History of the Archaic Greek World*. Oxford: Oxford University Press.

Casson, S. 1921. "The Dorian Invasion Reviewed in the Light of Some New Evidence." *Antiquaries Journal* 1: 199–221.

Catling, H. W. 1964. *Cypriote Bronzework in the Mycenaean World*. Oxford: Clarendon Press.

———. 1993. "The Bronze Amphora and Burial Urn." In *Lefkandi II: The Protogeometric Building at Toumba. Part 2: The Excavation, Architecture, and Finds*, edited by M. R. Popham, P. G. Calligas, and L. H. Sackett, 81–96. London: British School at Athens.

Catling, R. W. V., and I. S. Lemos. 1990. *Lefkandi II: The Protogeometric Building at Toumba. Part 1: The Pottery*. London: British School at Athens.

Cavanagh, W., and C. Mee. 1998. *A Private Place: Death in Prehistoric Greece*. Jonsered: Paul Åströms Förlag.

Cazzella, A., and G. Recchia. 2009. "The Mycenaeans in the Central Mediterranean: A Comparison between the Adriatic and Tyrrhenian Seaways." *Pasiphae* 3: 27–40.

Chadwick, J. 1958. *The Decipherment of Linear B*. Cambridge: Cambridge University Press.

———. 1970. "Linear B Tablets from Thebes." *Minos* 10, no. 1: 115–27.

———. 1976. *The Mycenaean World*. Cambridge: Cambridge University Press.

Chamberlain, A. T. 2006. *Demography in Archaeology*. Cambridge: Cambridge University Press.

Chambers, M. 1991. "Cornford's *Thucydides Mythistoricus*." In *The Cambridge Ritualists Reconsidered*, edited by W. M. Calder III, 61–77. Atlanta: Scholars Press.

Chang, K. C. 1975. "Ancient Trade as Economics or as Ecology." In *Ancient Civilization and Trade*, edited by J. Sabloff and C. C. Lamberg-Karlovsky, 211–24. Albuquerque: University of New Mexico Press.

Chapin, A. 2010. "Frescoes." In *The Oxford Handbook of the Bronze Age Aegean*, edited by E. Cline, 223–36. Oxford: Oxford University Press.

Chapman, R. 1990. *Emerging Complexity: The Later Prehistory of South-East Spain, Iberia, and the West Mediterranean*. Cambridge: Cambridge University Press.

————. 2003. *Archaeologies of Complexity*. London: Routledge.

Charalambidou, X. 2017. "Euboea and the Euboean Gulf Region: Pottery in Context." In *Interpreting the Seventh Century BC: Tradition and Innovation*, edited by X. Charalambidou and C. Morgan, 123–49. Oxford: Archaeopress.

Charalambidou, X., and C. Morgan, eds. 2017. *Interpreting the Seventh Century BC: Tradition and Innovation*. Oxford: Archaeopress.

Cherry, J. F. 1977. "Investigating the Political Geography of an Early State by Multidimensional Scaling of Linear B Tablet Data." In *Mycenaean Geography*, edited by J. Bintliff, 76–83. Cambridge: British Association for Mycenaean Studies.

————. 1983a. "Evolution, Revolution, and the Origins of Complex Society in Minoan Crete." In *Minoan Society*, edited by O. Krzyszkowska and L. Nixon, 33–45. Bristol: Bristol Classical Press.

————. 1983b. "Frogs Round the Pond: Perspectives in Current Archaeological Survey Projects." In *Archaeological Survey in the Mediterranean Area*, edited by D. Keller and D. Rupp, 375–416. Oxford: Archaeopress.

————. 1986. "Polities and Palaces: Some Problems in Minoan State Formation." In *Peer Polity Interaction and Socio-Political Change*, edited by C. Renfrew and J. F. Cherry, 19–46. Cambridge: Cambridge University Press.

————. 2010. "Sorting Out Crete's Prepalatial Off-Island Interactions." In *Archaic State Interaction: The Eastern Mediterranean in the Bronze Age*, edited by W. A. Parkinson and M. L. Galaty, 107–40. Santa Fe, NM: School for Advanced Research Press.

————. 2017. "Middle Helladic Reflections." In *Social Change in Aegean Prehistory*, edited by C. Wiersma and S. Voutsaki, 168–84. Oxford: Oxbow Books.

Cherry, J. F., and J. L. Davis. 2001. "'Under the Sceptre of Agamemnon': The View from the Hinterlands of Mycenae." In *Urbanism in the Aegean Bronze Age*, edited by K. Branigan, 141–59. London: Sheffield Academic Press.

Cherry, J. F., D. Margomenou, and L. E. Talalay, eds. 2005. *Prehistorians Round the Pond: Reflections on Aegean Prehistory as a Discipline*. Ann Arbor, MI: Kelsey Museum of Archaeology.

Childe, V. G. 1925. *The Dawn of European Civilisation*. New York: Knopf.

————. 1936. *Man Makes Himself*. London: Watts.

————. 1942. *What Happened in History*. Harmondsworth: Penguin.

————. 1958. *The Prehistory of European Society*. Harmondsworth: Penguin.

Christodoulou, D. 2015. "Οι 'Ταφές Πολεμιστών' στο Λευκαντί." In *Αρχαιολογικές συμβολές. Τόμος Γ: Βοιωτία & Εύβοια*, edited by S. Oikonomou, 197–208. Athens: Museum of Cycladic Art.

Clarke, D. L. 1968. *Analytical Archaeology*. London: Methuen.

————, ed. 1972. *Models in Archaeology*. London: Methuen.

————. 1973. "Archaeology: The Loss of Innocence." *Antiquity* 47: 6–18.

Clay, J. S., I. Malkin, and Y. Z. Tzifopoulos, eds. 2017. *Panhellenes at Methone: Graphê in Late Geometric and Protoarchaic Methone, Macedonia (ca. 700 BCE)*. Berlin: De Gruyter.

Clay, R. 2003. "Theft and Iconoclasm: The Treatment of Catholic Objects in Eighteenth-Century France." *Oxford Art Journal* 26: 1–22.

Cline, E. H. 1994. *Sailing the Wine-Dark Sea: International Trade and the Late Bronze Age Aegean*. Oxford: Tempus Reparatum.

————. 1995. "'My Brother, My Son': Rulership and Trade between the Late Bronze Age Aegean, Egypt, and the Near East." In *The Role of the Ruler in the Prehistoric Aegean*, edited by P. Rehak, 142–50. Liège: Université de Liège.

————. 1997. "A Wrinkle in Time: Orientalia and the Mycenaean Occupation(s) of Crete." In *Egypt, the Aegean, and the Near East: Studies in Honor of Martha Rhoads Bell*. Vol. 1, edited by J. Phillips, L. Bell, and B. B. Williams, 163–67. San Antonio, TX: Van Siclen.

————. 2007. "Rethinking Mycenaean International Trade with Egypt and the Near East." In *Rethinking Mycenaean Palaces II: Revised and Expanded Second Edition*, edited by M. L. Galaty and W. A. Parkinson, 190–200. Los Angeles: Cotsen Institute of Archaeology, University of California, Los Angeles.

————, ed. 2010. *The Oxford Handbook of the Bronze Age Aegean*. Oxford: Oxford University Press.

————. 2014. *1177 B.C.: The Year Civilization Collapsed*. Princeton, NJ: Princeton University Press.

Cline, E. H., and D. O'Connor. 2003. "The Mystery of the Sea Peoples." In *Mysterious Lands*, edited by D. O'Connor, and S. Quirke, 215–37. London: UCL Press.

Cline, E. H. and S. M. Stannish. 2011. "Sailing the Great Green Sea? Amenhotep III's 'Aegean List' from Kom el-Hetan, Once More." *Journal of Ancient Egyptian Interconnections* 3, no. 2: 6–16.

Coldstream, J. N.(1968) 2008. *Greek Geometric Pottery: A Survey of Ten Local Styles and Their Chronology*. 2nd ed. Bristol: Phoenix Press.

————. (1977) 2003. *Geometric Greece: 900–700 BC*. 2nd ed. New York: Routledge.

————. 1983. "The Meaning of Regional Styles in the Eighth Century BC." In *The Greek Renaissance of the Eighth Century B.C.: Tradition and Innovation*, edited by R. Hägg, 17–25. Stockholm: Skrifter utgivna av Svenska Institutet i Athen.

————. 1995. "The Rich Lady of the Areiopagos and Her Contemporaries: A Tribute in Memory of Evelyn Lord Smithson." *Hesperia* 64, no. 4 (October–December): 391–403.

————. 2007. "Foreigners at Lefkandi?" In *Oropos and Euboea in the Early Iron Age*, edited by A. Mazarakis Ainian, 135–39. Volos: University of Thessaly.

Cole, S. G. 2000. "Landscapes of Artemis." *Classical World* 93, no. 5 (May–June): 471–81.

Coleman, J. E, K. O'Neill, M. Pomeroy, K. E. Carr, and A. Heafitz. 1992. "Excavations at Halai, 1990–1991." *Hesperia* 61, no. 3 (July–September): 265–89.

Cook, J. M. 1962. *The Greeks in Ionia and the East*. London: Thames and Hudson.

Cornford, F. M. 1907. *Thucydides Mythistoricus*, Cambridge: Cambridge University Press.

Cosmopoulos, M. 2001. *The Rural History of Ancient Greek City-States: The Oropos Survey Project*. Oxford: Archaeopress.

————. 2005. "State Formation in Mycenaean Greece: Pylos and the Iklaina Archaeological Project." *Ancient Greece at the Turn of the Millennium: Recent Work and Future Perspectives*, edited by N. M. Kennell and J. E. Tomlinson, 45–68. Athens: Canadian Institute in Greece.

————. 2006. "The Political Landscape of Mycenaean States: *A-pu*$_2$ and the Hither Province of Pylos." *American Journal of Archaeology* 110, no. 2 (April): 205–28.

————. 2014. *The Sanctuary of Demeter at Eleusis: The Bronze Age*. Athens: Archaeological Society at Athens.

————. 2015. *Bronze Age Eleusis and the Origins of the Eleusinian Mysteries*. New York: Cambridge University Press.

Coulton, J. 1993. "The Toumba Building: Description and Analysis of the Architecture." In *Lefkandi II: The Protogeometric Building at Toumba*. Part 2, *The Excavation, Architecture and Finds*, edited by M. R. Popham, P. G. Calligas, and L. H. Sackett, 33–70. London: British School at Athens.

———. 2002. "Excavations." In *The Fort at Phylla, Vrachos: Excavations at a Late Archaic Fort in Central Euboea*, edited by, J. J. Coulton, 7–46. London: British School at Athens.

Crielaard, J. P. 1996. "The Euboeans Overseas: Long-Distance Contacts and Colonization as Status Activities in Early Iron Age Greece." PhD diss., University of Amsterdam.

———. 2006. "*Basileis* at Sea: Elites and External Contacts in the Euboian Gulf Region from the End of the Bronze Age to the Beginning of the Iron Age." In *Ancient Greece: From the Mycenaean Palaces to the Age of Homer*, edited by S. Deger-Jalkotzy and I. S. Lemos, 271–97. Edinburgh: University of Edinburgh.

———. 2009. "The Ionians in the Archaic Period: Shifting Identities in the Changing World." In *Ethnic Constructs in Antiquity: The Role of Power and Tradition*, edited by T. Derks and N. Roymans, 37–84. Amsterdam: Amsterdam University Press.

———. 2011a. "Preliminary Report on the 2011 Season at Karystos-Plakari, Euboia." Unpublished Excavation Report. Amsterdam: University of Amsterdam.

———. 2011b. "The '*Wanax* to *Basileus* Model' Reconsidered: Authority and Ideology after the Collapse of the Mycenaean Palaces." In *The "Dark Ages" Revisited: An International Symposium in Memory of William D. E. Coulson*, edited by A. Mazarakis Ainian, 83–111. Volos: University of Thessaly.

Crielaard, J. P., X. Charalambidou, M. Chidirouglou, M. Kosma, and F. Songu. 2015. "The Plakari Archaeological Project: Preliminary Report on the Fourth Field Season (2013)." *Pharos* 21, no. 2: 117–33.

Crielaard, J. P., and F. Songou. 2017. "Connectivity and Insularity in 1st-Millennium Southern Euboea: The Evidence from the Sanctuary of Karystos-Plakari." In *An Island between Two Worlds: The Archaeology of Euboea from Prehistoric to Byzantine Times*, edited by Ž. Tankosić, F. Mavridis, and M. Kosma, 275–90. Athens: Norwegian Institute at Athens.

Crouwel, J. H. 1992. *Chariots and Other Wheeled Vehicles in Iron Age Greece*. Amsterdam: Allard Pierson Museum.

———. 2007. "Pictorial Pottery of LH IIIC Middle and Its Antecedents." In *LH III C Chronology and Synchronisms II, LH III C Middle*, edited by S. Deger-Jalkotzy and M. Zavadil, 73–88. Vienna: Verlag der Österreichischen Adademie der Wissenschaften

———. 2009. "Pictorial Pottery of the Latest Bronze Age and the Early Iron Age." In *LH III C Chronology and Synchronisms III: LH III C Late and the Transition to the Early Iron Age*, edited by S. Deger-Jalkotzy and A. E. Bächle, 41–60. Vienna: Verlag der Österreichischen Akademie der Wissenschaften.

Crowley, J. L. 2008. "Mycenaean Art and Architecture." In *The Cambridge Companion to the Aegean Bronze Age*, edited by C. Shelmerdine, 258–88. Cambridge: Cambridge University Press.

Crumley, C. L. 1995. "Heterarchy and the Analysis of Complex Societies." In *Heterarchy and the Analysis of Complex Societies*, edited by R. M. Ehrenreich, C. L. Crumley, and J. E. Levy, 1–5. Arlington, VA: American Anthropological Association.

Csapo, E., A. W. Johnston, and D. Geagan. 2000. "The Iron Age Inscriptions." In *Kommos IV: The Greek Sanctuary*, edited by J. W. Shaw and M. C. Shaw, 101–34. Princeton, NJ: Princeton University Press.

Cullen, T., ed. 2001. *Aegean Prehistory: A Review*. Boston: Archaeological Institute of America.

Cullen, T., L. E. Talalay, D. R. Keller, E. Karimali, and W. R. Farrand. 2013. *The Prehistory of the Paximadi Peninsula, Euboea*. Philadelphia: INSTAP Academic Press.

Cunningham, T., and J. Driessen. 2004. "Site by Site: Combining Survey and Excavation Data to Chart Patterns of Socio-political Change in Bronze Age Crete." In *Side-by-Side Survey: Comparative Regional Studies in the Mediterranean World*, edited by S. E. Alcock and J. F. Cherry, 101–13. Oxford: Oxbow Books.

———, eds. 2017. *Crisis to Collapse: The Archaeology of Social Breakdown*. Louvain-la-Neuve: Presses universitaires de Louvain.

Dakoronia, F. 1990. "War-Ships on Sherds of LH III C Kraters from Kynos." In *2nd International Symposium on Ship Construction in Antiquity, Delphi, 27, 28, 29 August 1987: Proceedings*, edited by H. E. Tzalas, 117–22. Athens: Hellenic Institute for the Preservation of Nautical Tradition.

———. 1991. "Late Helladic III, Submycenaean and Protogeometric Finds in the Spercheios Valley." In *The Great Isthmus Corridor Route. Explorations of the Phokis-Doris Expedition*, edited by E. W. Kase, G. J. Szemler, N. C. Wilkie, and P. W. Wallace, 70–73. Dubuque: Kendall-Hunt.

———. 1993. "Homeric Towns in East Lokris: Problems of Identification." *Hesperia* 62, no. 1 (January–March): 115–27.

———. 1994. "Spercheios Valley and the Adjacent Area in the Late Bronze Age and Early Iron Age." In *Θεσσαλία: Δεκαπέντε χρόνια αρχαιολογικής έρευνας, 1975–1990*, 233–42. Athens: Ministry of Culture.

———. 1999. "Representations of Sea-Battles on Mycenaean Sherds from Kynos." In *5th International Symposium on Ship Construction in Antiquity, Nauplia, 26, 27, 28 August 1993: Proceedings*, edited by H. E. Tzalas, 119–28. Athens: Hellenic Institute for the Preservation of Nautical Tradition.

———. 2003. "The Transition from Late Helladic III C to The Early Iron Age at Kynos." In *LH III C Chronology and Synchronisms*, edited by S. Deger-Jalkotzy and M. Zavadil, 37–51. Vienna: Verlag der Österreichischen Adademie der Wissenschaften.

———. 2006. "Mycenaean Pictorial Style at Kynos, East Lokris." In *Pictorial Pursuits: Figurative Painting on Mycenaean and Geometric Pottery*, edited by R. Rystedt and B. Wells, 23–29. Stockholm: Svenska Institutet i Athen.

———. 2009. "Northeast Phokis." *Archaeology: Euboea and Central Greece*, edited by A. G. Vlachopoulos, 292–301. Athens: Melissa Publishing House.

Dakoronia, F., and P. Kounouklas. 2009. "Kynos' Pace to the Early Iron Age." In *LH III C Chronology and Synchronisms III, LH III C Late and the Transition to the Early Iron Age*, edited by S. Deger-Jalkotzy and A. E. Bächle, 61–76. Vienna: Verlag der Österreichischen Adademie der Wissenschaften.

Dakouri-Hild, A. 2005. "Something Old, Something New: Current Research on the 'Old Kadmeion' of Thebes." *Bulletin of the Institute of Classical Studies of the University of London* 48: 173–86.

———. 2010a. "Boeotia." In *The Oxford Handbook of the Bronze Age Aegean*, edited by E. H. Cline, 614–30. Oxford: Oxford University Press.

———. 2010b. "Thebes." In *The Oxford Handbook of the Bronze Age Aegean*, edited by E. H. Cline, 690–711. Oxford: Oxford University Press.

Davies, J. K. 2009. "The Historiography of Archaic Greece." In *A Companion to Archaic Greece*, edited by K. A. Raaflaub and H. van Wees, 3–21. Malden, MA: Wiley-Blackwell.

Davis, J. L., and S. Stocker 2016. "The Lord of the Gold Rings: The Griffin Warrior of Pylos." *Hesperia* 85, no. 4 (October–December): 627–55.

Decourt, J.-Cl. 1990. *La vallée de l'Énipeus en Thessalie: Études de topographie et de géographie antique*. Athénes: École française d'Athénes.

Decourt, J.-Cl., T. H. Nielsen, and B. Helly. 2004. "Thessalia and Adjacent Regions." In *An Inventory of Archaic and Classical Poleis: An Investigation Conducted by the Copenhagen Polis Centre for the Danish National Research Foundation*, edited by M. H. Hansen and T. H. Nielsen, 676–731. Oxford: Oxford University Press.

Deger-Jalkotzy, S. 1998. "The Last Mycenaeans and Their Successors Updated." In *Mediterranean Peoples in Transition: Thirteenth to Early Tenth Centuries BCE, In Honor of Professor Trude Dothan*, edited by S. Gitin, A. Mazar, and E. Stern, 114–28. Jerusalem: Israel Exploration Society.

———. 2006. "Late Mycenaean Warrior Tombs." In *Ancient Greece: From the Mycenaean Palaces to the Age of Homer*, edited by S. Deger-Jalkotzy and I. S. Lemos, 151–79. Edinburgh: Edinburgh University Press.

———. 2009. "From LH IIIC Late to the Early Iron Age: The Submycenaean Period at Elateia." In *LH III C Chronology and Synchronisms III, LH III C Late and the Transition to the Early Iron Age*, edited by S. Deger Jalkotzy and A. E. Bächle, 77–116. Vienna: Verlag der Österreichischen Adademie der Wissenschaften.

Deger-Jalkotzy, S., and A. E. Bächle, eds. 2009. *LH III C Chronology and Synchronisms III, LH III C Late and the Transition to the Early Iron Age*. Vienna: Verlag der Österreichischen Adademie der Wissenschaften.

Deger-Jalkotzy, S., and I. S. Lemos, eds. 2006. *Ancient Greece: From the Mycenaean Palaces to the Ages of Homer*. Edinburgh: University of Edinburgh.

Deger-Jalkotzy, S., and O. Panagl, eds. 2006. *Die neuen Linear B-Texte aus Theben*. Vienna: Verlag der Österreichischen Akademie der Wissenschaften.

Deger-Jalkotzy, S., and M. Zavadil, eds. 2003. *LH III C Chronology and Synchronisms*. Vienna: Verlag der Österreichischen Adademie der Wissenschaften.

———. 2007. *LH III C Chronology and Synchronisms II, LH III C Middle*. Vienna: Verlag der Österreichischen Adademie der Wissenschaften.

Del Freo, M. 2009. "The Geographical Names in the Linear B Texts from Thebes." *Pasiphae* 3: 41–68.

Demakopoulou, K. 1988. "Glypha (or Vlicha), Chalkis: A Major Mycenaean Settlement on the Boeotian Shore Near Aulis." *Teiresias* 18: 1–18.

———. 2007. "Laconia and Arcadia in LH III C Middle: Pottery and Other Finds." In *LH III C Chronology and Synchronisms II: LH III C Middle*, edited by S. Deger-Jalkotzy and M. Zavadil, 161–74. Vienna: Verlag der Österreichischen Akademie der Wissenschaften.

Demand, N. H. 2011. *The Mediterranean Context of Early Greek History*. Chichester: Wiley-Blackwell.

De Marrais, E., and T. Earle. 2017. "Collective Action Theory and the Dynamics of Complex Societies." *Annual Review of Anthropology* 46: 183–201.

Demesticha, S., and A. B. Knapp, eds. 2016. *Maritime Transport Containers in the Bronze-Iron Age Aegean and Eastern Mediterranean*. Uppsala: Åströms Förlag.

de Montmollin, O., 1989. *The Archaeology of Political Structure: Settlement Analysis in a Classic Maya Polity*. Cambridge: Cambridge University Press.

de Polignac, F. 1994. "Mediation, Competition, and Sovereignty: The Evolution of Rural Sanctuaries in Geometric Greece." In *Placing the Gods: Sanctuaries and Sacred Space in Ancient Greece*, edited by S. E. Alcock and R. Osborne, 3–18. Oxford: Clarendon Press.

———. 1995. *Cults, Territory, and the Ancient Greek City-State*. Translated by J. Lloyd. Chicago: University of Chicago Press.

de Ridder, A. 1895. "Fouilles d'orchomène." *Bulletin de correspondance hellénique* 19: 137–224.

Desborough, V. R. d'A. 1952. *Protogeometric Pottery*. Oxford: Clarendon Press.

———. 1964. *The Last Mycenaeans and Their Successors: An Archaeological Survey, c. 1200–1000 B.C.* Oxford: Clarendon Press.

———. 1972. *The Greek Dark Ages*. London: Ernest Brown.

Descoeudres, J.-P. 2008. "Central Greece on the Eve of the Colonisation Movement." In *Greek Colonisation: An Account of Greek Colonies and Other Settlements Overseas*, Vol. 2, edited by G. R. Tsetskhladze, 289–382. Leiden: Brill.

Descoeudres, J.-P., and S. A. Paspalas, eds. 2015. *Zagora in Context: Settlements and Intercommunal Links in the Geometric Period (900–700 BC)*. Sydney: Mediterranean Archaeology.

de Waele, J. A. K. E. 1998. "The Layout of the Lefkandi 'Heroon.'" *Annual of the British School at Athens* 93: 379–84.

Diamant, S. 1982. "Theseus and the Unification of Attica." In *Studies in Attic Epigraphy, History and Topography Presented to Eugene Vanderpool*, 38–47. Princeton, NJ: American School of Classical Studies.

Dickinson, O. T. P. K. 1977. *The Origins of Mycenaean Civilisation*. Gothenburg: Paul Åströms Förlag.

———. 1994. *The Aegean Bronze Age*. Cambridge: Cambridge University Press.

———. 2006. *The Aegean from Bronze Age to Iron Age: Continuity and Change between the Twelfth and Eighth Centuries BC*. New York: Routledge.

———. 2010. "The Collapse at the End of the Bronze Age." In *The Oxford Handbook of the Bronze Age Aegean*, edited by E. H. Cline, 483–90. Oxford: Oxford University Press.

———. 2020. "The Irrelevance of Greek 'Tradition.'" In *Collapse and Transformation: The Late Bronze Age to Early Iron Age in the Aegean*, edited by G. D. Middleton, 153–59. Oxford: Oxbow Books.

Dietler, M. 2010. *Archaeologies of Colonialism: Consumption, Entanglement, and Violence in Ancient Mediterranean France*. Berkeley: University of California Press.

Dietler, M., and B. Hayden, eds. 2001. *Feasts: Archaeological and Ethnographic Perspectives on Food, Politics, and Power*. Washington, DC: Smithsonian Institution Press.

Dimitriadou, E. 2019. *Early Athens: Settlements and Cemeteries in the Submycenaean, Geometric, and Archaic Periods*. Los Angeles: Cotsen Institute of Archaeology Press.

Dobres, M. 2000. *Technology and Social Agency: Outlining a Practice Framework for Archaeology*. Malden, MA: Wiley-Blackwell.

Docter, R., F. Chelbi, B. Maraoui Telmini, A. Nijboer, H. van der Plicht, W. van Neer, K. Mansel, and S. Garsallah. 2008. "New Radiocarbon Dates from Carthage: Bridging the Gap Between History and Archaeology?" In *Beyond the Homeland: Markers in Phoenician Chronology*, edited by C. Sagona, 379–422. Leuven: Peeters.

Docter, R., and M. Webster. Forthcoming. *Thorikos: Reports and Studies XII*. Leuven: Peeters.

Domergue, C., ed. 2008. *Les mines antiques: la production des métaux aux époques grecque et romaine*. Paris: Éditions A. et J. Picard.

Donlan, W. 1970. "Archilochus, Strabo and the Lelantine War." *Transactions and Proceedings of the American Philological Association* 101: 131–42.

Donnellan, L. 2016. "'Greek Colonisation' and Mediterranean Networks: Patterns of Mobility and Interaction at Pithekoussai." *Journal of Greek Archaeology* 1: 109–48.

———. 2017. "The 'Euboean' Koine: Reassessing Patterns of Cross-Cultural Interaction and Exchange in the North-Western Aegean Region." In *Material Koinai in the Greek Early Iron Age and Archaic Period*, edited by S. Handberg and A. Gadolou, 43–64. Aarhus: Aarhus University Press.

———, ed. 2020. *Archaeological Networks and Social Interaction*. London: Routledge.

Donnellan, L. V. Nizzo, G.-J. Burgers, eds. 2016. *Conceptualising Early Colonisation*. Brussels: Belgisch Historisch Instituut te Rome.

Doonan, R., and A. Mazarakis Ainian. 2007. "Forging Identity in Early Iron Age Greece: Implications of the Metalworking Evidence from Oropos." In *Oropos and Euboea in the Early Iron Age*, edited by A. Mazarakis Ainian, 361–78. Volos: University of Thessaly.

Dor, L., J. Jannoray, H. Van Effenterre, and M. Van Effenterre. 1960. *Kirrha. 'Etude de préhistoire phocidienne*. Paris: E. de Boccard.

Doronzio, A. 2018. *Athen Im 7. Jahrhundert V. Chr.: Räume Und Funde Der Frühen Polis*. Berlin: de Gruyter.

Duplouy, A. 2006. *Le prestige des élites: Recherches sur le modes de reconnaissance sociale en Grèce entre les Xe et Ve siècles avant J.-C.* Paris: Les Belles Lettres.

Douzougli, A., and J. K. Papadopoulos. 2011. "Liatovouni: A Molossian Cemetery and Settlement in Epirus." *Jahrbuch des Deutschen Archäologischen Instituts* 125: 1–87.

Driessen, J. 2001. "History and Hierarchy. Preliminary Observations on the Settlement Pattern in Minoan Crete." In *Urbanism in the Aegean Bronze Age*, edited by K. Branigan, 51–71. London: Sheffield Academic Press.

———. 2002. "Towards an Archaeology of Crisis: Defining the Long-Term Impact of the Bronze Age Santorini Eruption." In *Natural Disasters and Cultural Change*, edited by R. Torrence and J. Grattan, 250–63. London: Routledge.

———. 2018. *An Archaeology of Forced Migration: Crisis-Induced Mobility and the Collapse of the 13th c. BCE Eastern Mediterranean*. Louvain: Presses universitaires de Louvain.

Earle, T. K. 1987. "Chiefdoms in Archaeological and Ethnohistorical Perspective." *Annual Review of Anthropology* 16: 279–308.

———. 1997. *How Chiefs Come to Power: The Political Economy in Prehistory*. Stanford, CA: Stanford University Press.

———. 2010. "Routes through the Landscape: A Comparative Approach." *Landscapes of Movement: Trails, Paths, and Roads in Anthropological Perspective*, edited by J. E. Snead, C. L. Erickson, and J. A. Darling, 253–69. Philadelphia: University of Pennsylvania Press.

Edel, E. 1966. *Die Ortsnamenlisten aus dem Totentempel Amenophis III*. Bonn: Hanstein.

Eder B., 2007. "Im Spiegel der Siegel: Die nördlichen und westlichen Regionen Griechenlands im Spannungsfeld der mykenischen Paläste." In *Keimelion: Elitenbildung und elitärer Konsum von der mykenischen Palastzeit bis zur Homerischen Epoche*, edited by E. Alram-Stern and G. Nightingale, 81–124. Vienna: Verlag der Österreichischen Akademie der Wissenschaften.

———. 2019. "The Role of Sanctuaries and the Formation of Greek Identities in the Late Bronze Age/Early Iron Age Transition." In *Beyond the Polis: Rituals, Rites and Cults in Early and Archaic Greece (12th–6th Centuries BC)*, edited by I. S. Lemos and A. Tsingarida, 25–52. Brussels: CReA-Patrimoine.

Eder, B., and R. Jung. 2005. "On the Character of Social Relations between Greece and Italy in the 12th/11th c. BC." In *Emporia: Aegeans in the Central and Eastern Mediterranean*, edited by R. Laffineur and E. Greco, 485–95. Liège and Austin: Université de Liège, Histoire de l'art et archéologie de la Grèce antique and University of Texas at Austin, Program in Aegean Scripts and Prehistory.

———. 2015. "'Unus pro omnibus, omnes pro uno': The Mycenaean Palace System." *Tradition and Innovation in the Mycenaean Palatial Polities*, edited by J. Weilhartner and F. Ruppenstein, 113–40. Vienna: Verlag der Österreichischen Akademie der Wissenschaften.

Eisenstadt, S. N. 1988. "Beyond Collapse." In *The Collapse of Ancient States and Civilizations*, edited by N. Yoffee and G. Cowgill, 236–43. Tuscon: University of Arizona Press.

Eiteljorg, H. 1980. "The Fast Wheel, the Multiple-Brush Compass and Athens as Home of the Protogeometric Style." *American Journal of Archaeology* 84, no. 4 (October): 445–52.

Ek, J. D. 2020. "The Inertia of Old Ideas: A Historical Overview of Theoretical and Methodological Challenges in the Study of Classic Maya Political Organization." *Journal of Archaeological Research* 28, no 2 (June): 241–87.

Elayi, J. 2018. *The History of Phoenicia*. Atlanta: Lockwood Press.

Engels, F. (1884) 1972. *The Origin of the Family, Private Property and the State*. New York: International Publishers.

Étienne. R., ed. 2010. *La Méditerranée au VIIe siècle av. J.-C. (Essais d'analyses archéologiques)*. Travaux de la Maison René-Ginouvès 7. Paris: De Boccard.

———. 2017. "Introduction: Can One Speak of the Seventh Century BC?" In *Interpreting the Seventh Century BC: Tradition and Innovation*, edited by X. Charalambidou and C. Morgan, 9–14. Oxford: Archaeopress.

Evans, A. J. 1921. *The Palace of Minos: A Comparative Account of the Successive Stages of the Early Cretan Civilization as Illustrated by the Discoveries at Knossos*. Vol. 1, *The Neolithic and Early and Middle Minoan Ages*, London: Macmillan.

Evely, D., ed. 2006. *Lefkandi IV, The Bronze Age: The Late Helladic IIIC Settlement at Xeropolis*. London: British School at Athens.

Fachard, S. 2009. "A Cyclopean Wall at Loupaka, near Dystos?" In *Αρχαιολογικό έργο Θεσσαλίας και Στερεάς Ελλάδας* 2, edited by A. Mazarakis Ainian, 907–23. Volos: Ministry of Culture and University of Thessaly.

———. 2012. *La défense du territoire: Étude de la chôra érétrienne et de ses fortifications*. Eretria fouilles et recherches 21. Gollion: Infolio Éditions.

———. 2016. "Modelling the Territories of Attic Demes: A Computational Approach." In *The Archaeology of Greece and Rome: Studies in Honour of Anthony Snodgrass*, edited by J. Bintliff and K. Rutter, 192–222. Edinburgh: Edinburgh University Press.

Fachard, S., and A. R. Knodell. 2020. "Out of Attica: Modeling Mobility in the Mycenaean Period." In *Athens and Attica in Prehistory*, edited by N. Papadimitriou, J. C. Wright, S. Fachard, and N. Polychronakou-Sgouritsa, 407–16. Oxford: Archaeopress.

Fachard, S., A. R. Knodell, and E. Banou. 2015. "The 2014 Mazi Archaeological Project (Attica)." *Antike Kunst* 58: 178–86.

Fachard, S., D. Knoepfler, K. Reber, A. Karapaschalidou, T. Krapf, T. Theurillat, P. Kalamara. 2017. "Recent Research at the Sanctuary of Artemis Amarysia in Amarynthos (Euboea)." *Archaeological Reports* 63: 167–80.

Fachard, S., and D. Pirisino. 2015. "Routes out of Attica." In *Autopsy in Athens: Recent Archaeological Research in Athens and Attica*, edited by M. Miles, 139–53. Oxford: Oxbow Books.

Fachard, S., and S. Verdan. Forthcoming. "Chalkis and Eretria." In *The Oxford History of the Archaic Greek World*, edited by P. Cartledge and P. Christesen. Oxford: Oxford University Press.

Farinetti, E. 2011. *Boeotian Landscapes: A GIS-Based Study for the Reconstruction and Interpretation of the Archaeological Datasets of Ancient Boeotia*. Oxford: Archaeopress.

Faulseit, R. K., ed., 2016. *Beyond Collapse: Archaeological Perspectives on Resilience, Revitalization, and Transformation in Complex Societies*. Carbondale: Southern Illinois University Press.

Feinman, G., and J. Marcus, eds. 1998. *Archaic States*. Santa Fe, NM: School of American Research Press.

Feldman, M. 2006. *Diplomacy by Design: Luxury Arts and an 'International Style' in the Ancient Near East, 1400-1200 BCE*. Chicago: University of Chicago Press.

———. 2014. *Communities of Style: Portable Luxury Arts, Identity and Collective Memory in the Iron Age Levant*. Chicago: University of Chicago Press.

Felsch, R. C. S. 1981. "Mykenischer Kult im Heiligtum bei Kalapodi?" In *Sanctuaries and Cults in the Aegean Bronze Age*, edited by R. Hägg and N. Marinatos, 81–89. Stockholm: Svenska Institutet i Athen.

———, ed. 1996. *Kalapodi: Ergebnisse der Ausgrabungen im Heiligtum der Artemis und des Apollon von Hyampolis in der antiken Phokis*. Vol. 2, *Die spätmykenische bis frühgeometrische Keramik; die korinthische keramik; die Graffiti auf der Keramik; the Byzantine and Later Pottery*. Mainz: Verlag Philipp von Zabern.

———, ed. 2007. *Kalapodi: Ergebnisse der Ausgrabungen im Heiligtum der Artemis und des Apollon von Hyampolis in der antiken Phokis*. Vol. 2, *Zur Stratigraphy des Heiligtums; die Bronzefunde; die Angriffswaffen*. Mainz: Verlag Philipp von Zabern.

Ferrara, S. 2015. "The Beginnings of Writing on Crete: Theory and Context." *Annual of the British School at Athens* 110, no. 1 (November): 27–49.

Feuer, B. 1983. *The Northern Mycenaean Border in Thessaly*. Oxford: British Archaeological Reports.

———. 2011. "Being Mycenaean: A View from the Periphery." *American Journal of Archaeology* 115, no. 4 (October): 505–36.

———. 2016a. *Boundaries, Borders and Frontiers in Archaeology: A Study of Spatial Relationships*. Jefferson: McFarland & Company.

———. 2016b. "Mycenaeanisation in Thessaly: A Study in Differential Acculturation." *Beyond Thalassocracies: Understanding Processes of Minoanisation and Mycenaeanisation in the Aegean*, edited by E. Gorogianni, P. Pavúk, and L. Girella, 186–201. Oxford: Oxbow Books.

Finley, M. 1954. *The World of Odysseus*. New York: The Viking Press.

Finné, M., K. Holmgren, H. S. Sundqvist, E. Weiberg, and M. Lindblom. 2011. "Climate in the Eastern Mediterranean, and Adjacent Regions, During the Past 6000 Years—A Review." *Journal of Archaeological Science* 38, no. 12 (December): 3153–73.

Fischer, P. M., and T. Bürge, eds. 2017. *"Sea Peoples" Up-to-Date: New Research on Transformations in the Eastern Mediterranean in the 13th–11th Centuries BCE*. Vienna: Verlag der Österreichischen Akademie der Wissenschaften.

Fischer, R. 2010. *Die Ahhiyawa-Frage*. Weisbaden: Harrassowitz.

Fisher, E. A. 1988. "A Comparison of Mycenaean Pottery from Apulia with Mycenaean Pottery from Western Greece." PhD diss., University of Minnesota. ProQuest (AAT 8820476).

Fitzsimons, R. D. 2006. "Monuments of Power and the Power of Monuments: The Evolution of Elite Architectural Styles at Bronze Age Mycenae." PhD diss., University of Cincinnati. ProQuest (AAT 3231145).

———. 2011. "Monumental Architecture and the Construction of the Mycenaean State." In *State Formation in Italy and Greece: Questioning the Neoevolutionist Paradigm*, edited by N. Terrenato and D. C. Haggis, 75–118. Oxford: Oxbow Books.

Flannery, K. V. 1968. "Archaeological Systems Theory and Early Mesoamerica." In *Anthropological Archaeology in the Americas*, edited by B. J. Meggers, 67–87. Washington, DC.: Anthropological Society of Washington.

———. 1976. "Empirical Determination of Site Catchments in Oaxaca and Tehuacán." In *The Early Mesoamerican Village*, edited by K. V. Flannery, 103–17. New York: Academic Press.

Fletcher, R. 2008. "Fragments of Levantine Iron Age Pottery in Chalcidice." *Mediterranean Archaeology* 21: 3–7.

Fossey, J. M. 1986. *The Ancient Topography of Eastern Phokis*. Amsterdam: J. C. Gieben.

———. 1988. *Topography and Population of Ancient Boiotia*. Chicago: Ares.

———. 1990. *The Ancient Topography of Opountian Lokris*. Amsterdam: J. C. Gieben.

Fowles, S. M. 2002. "From Social Type to Social Process: Placing 'Tribe' in a Historical Framework." In *The Archaeology of Tribal Societies*, edited by W. A. Parkinson, 13–33. Ann Arbor: International Monographs in Prehistory.

Fox, R. S. 2012. *Feasting Practices and Changes in Greek Society from the Late Bronze Age to Early Iron Age*. Oxford: Archaeopress.

Foxhall, L. 1995. "Bronze to Iron: Agricultural Systems and Political Structures in Late Bronze Age and Early Iron Age Greece." *Annual of the British School at Athens* 90: 239–50.

———. 2013. "Can We See the 'Hoplite Revolution' on the Ground? Archaeological Landscapes, Material Culture, and Social Status in Early Greece." In *Men of Bronze: Hoplite Warfare in Ancient Greece*, edited by D. Kagan and G. F. Viggiano, 194–221. Princeton, NJ: Princeton University Press.

———. 2020. "The Village beyond the Village: Communities in Rural Landscapes in Ancient Greek Countrysides." *Journal of Modern Greek Studies* 38, no. 1 (May): 1-20.

Frederiksen, R. 2011. *Greek City Walls of the Archaic Period, 900–480 BC*. Oxford: Oxford University Press.

———. 2017. "Fortifications in the Seventh Century: Where and Why?" In *Interpreting the Seventh Century BC: Tradition and Innovation*, edited by X. Charalambidou and C. Morgan, 186–92. Oxford: Archaeopress.

Fried, M. 1960. *On the Evolution of Social Stratification and the State*. Indianapolis: Bobbs-Merrill.

———. 1967. *The Evolution of Political Society: An Essay in Political Anthropology*. New York: Random House.

————. 1975. *The Notion of Tribe*. Menlo Park, CA: Cummings.

Froussou, E., ed. 1999. *Η περιφέρεια του μυκηναϊκού κόσμου*. Lamia: ΙΔ΄ Εφορεία Προϊστορικών και Κλασικών Αρχαιοτήτων.

Gailledrat, E., M. Dietler, and R. Plana-Mallart, eds. 2018. *The Emporion in the Ancient Western Mediterranean: Trade and Colonial Encounters from the Archaic to the Hellenistic Period*. Montpellier: Presses Universitaires de la Méditerranée.

Galaty, M. L. 2007. "Wealth Ceramics, Staple Ceramics: Pots and the Mycenaean Palaces." In *Rethinking Mycenaean Palaces II: Revised and Expanded Second Edition*, edited by M. L. Galaty and W. A. Parkinson, 74–86. Los Angeles: Cotsen Institute of Archaeology, University of California, Los Angeles.

————. 2018. "Prestige-Goods Economies: The Prehistoric Aegean and Modern Northern Highland Albania Compared." In *Regional Approaches to Society and Complexity: Studies in Honor of John F. Cherry*, edited by A. R. Knodell and T. P. Leppard, 75–93. Sheffield: Equinox.

Galaty, M. L., and W. A. Parkinson, eds. 2007. *Rethinking Mycenaean Palaces II: Revised and Expanded Second Edition*. Los Angeles: Cotsen Institute of Archaeology, University of California, Los Angeles.

Galaty, M. L., W. A. Parkinson, D. J. Pullen, and R. M. Seifried. 2015. "Mycenaean-scapes: Geography, Political Economy, and the Eastern Mediterranean World-System." In *PHYSIS: l'environnement naturel et la relation homme-milieu dans le monde égéen protohistorique*, edited by G. Touchai, R. Laffineur, and F. Rougemont, 449–54. Leuven: Peeters.

Gallant, T. W. 1989. "Crisis and Response: Risk-Buffering Behavior in Hellenistic Greek Communities." *Journal of Interdisciplinary History* 19, no. 3 (Winter): 393–413.

Gallis, K. I. 1992. *Άτλας των προϊστορικών θέσεων της ανατολικής Θεσσαλίας*. Larissa: Εταιρεία Ιστορικών Ερευνών Θεσσαλίας.

Garfinkel, Y. 2003. *Dancing at the Dawn of Agriculture*. Austin: University of Texas Press.

Garrison, T. G. 2018. "Embedded Heterarchies of the Maya: Political Structure and Interactions Inspired by Peer Polity Interaction." In *Regional Approaches to Society and Complexity: Studies in Honor of John F. Cherry*, edited by A. R. Knodell and T. P. Leppard, 246–67. Sheffield: Equinox.

Gauß, W. 2003. "The Late Mycenaean Pottery from the North Slope of the Athenian Acropolis." In *LH III C Chronology and Synchronism*, edited by S. Deger-Jalkotzy and M. Zavadil, 93–104. Vienna: Verlag der Österreichischen Akademie der Wissenschaften.

Gauß, W. and E. Kiriatzi. 2011. *Pottery Production and Supply at Bronze Age Kolonna, Aegina: An Integrated Archaeological and Scientific Study of a Ceramic Landscape*. Ägina-Kolonna Forschungen und Ergebnisse 5. Vienna: Verlag der Österreichischen Akademie der Wissenschaften.

Gauß, W., and A. R. Knodell. 2020. "Aeginetan Pottery in the Aegean World: Mapping Distributions around an Island Hub." In *From Past to Present: Studies in Memory of Manfred O. Korfmann*, edited by S. Blum, T. Efe, T. Kienlin, and E. Pernicka, 245–262. Bonn: Habelt.

Georganas, I. 2000. "Early Iron Age Tholos Tombs in Thessaly (*c.* 1100–700 BC)." *Mediterranean Archaeology* 13: 47–54.

————. 2002. "Constructing Identities in Early Iron Age Thessaly: The Case of the Halos Tumuli." *Oxford Journal of Archaeology* 21, no. 3 (December): 289–98.

———. 2003. "The Archaeology of Early Iron Age Thessaly (ca. 1100–700 BC)." PhD diss., University of Nottingham. ProQuest (AAT 10061255).

———. 2011. "The Transition from the Late Bronze to the Early Iron Age in Thessaly: Some Thoughts." In *The "Dark Ages" Revisited: An International Symposium in Memory of William D. E. Coulson*, edited by A. Mazarakis Ainian, 627–33. Volos: University of Thessaly.

Georgiadis, M. 2009. "The South-Eastern Aegean in the LH IIIC Period: What Do the Tombs Tell Us?" In *Forces of Transformation: The End of the Bronze Age in the Mediterranean*, edited by C. Bachhuber and R. G. Roberts, 92–99. Oxford: Oxbow Books.

Gerstel, S. E. J. 2020. "Perspectives on the Greek Village." *Journal of Modern Greek Studies* 38, no. 1 (May): vii–x.

Ghilardi, M., M. Colleu, K. Pavlopoulos, S. Fachard, D. Psomiadis, P. Rochette, F. Demory, et al. 2013. "Geoarchaeology of Ancient Aulis (Boeotia, Central Greece): Human Occupation and Holocene Landscape Changes." *Journal of Archaeological Science* 40, no. 4 (April): 2071–83.

Giddens, A. 1984. *The Constitution of Society: Outline of the Theory of Structuration.* Berkeley: University of California Press.

Gillings, M., P. Hacıgüzeller, and G. Lock, eds. 2020. *Archaeological Spatial Analysis: A Methodological Guide.* New York: Routledge.

Gilstrap, W. D., P. M. Day, and V. Kilikoglou. 2016. "Pottery Production at Two Neighbouring Centres in the Late Bronze Age Saronic Gulf: Historical Contingency and Craft Organisation." *Journal of Archaeological Science: Reports* 7: 499–509.

Gnanadesikan, A. E. 2009. *The Writing Revolution: Cuneiform to the Internet.* Malden, MA: Wiley-Blackwell.

Godart, L., and A. Sacconi. 2020. *Les archives du roi Nestor. Corpus des inscriptions en linéaire B de Pylos (2 vols.: Vol. I: Aa-Fr.; Vol II: Gn-Xn.).* Pisa: Fabrizio Serra.

Goette, H. R. 2001. *Athens, Attica and the Megarid: An Archaeological Guide.* London: Routledge.

———, ed. 2002. *Ancient Roads in Greece.* Hamburg: Kovac.

Goffman, E. 1967. *Interaction Ritual: Essays on Face-to-Face Behavior.* New York: Anchor Books.

Goldman, H. 1931. *Excavations at Eutresis in Boeotia.* Cambridge, MA: Harvard University Press.

Gottschall, J. 2008. *The Rape of Troy: Evolution, Violence, and the World of Homer.* Cambridge: Cambridge University Press.

González de Canales, F., L. Serrano, and J. Llompart. 2006. "The Pre-colonial Phoenician Emporium of Huelva ca 900–770 BC." *Bulletin Antieke Beschaving* 81: 13–29.

Gould, S. J. 2007. *Punctuated Equilibrium.* Cambridge: Belknap Press.

Graml, C. A. Doronzio, and V. Capozzoli, eds. 2019. *Rethinking Athens before the Persian Wars.* Munich: Utzverlag.

Grammenou, A. 1996. "The Mycenaean Chamber Tombs at Spata in Attica: New Research on an Excavation of 1877." *Bulletin of the Institute of Classical Studies of the University of London* 41: 140–41.

Granovetter, M. S. 1973. "The Strength of Weak Ties." *American Journal of Sociology* 78, no. 6 (May): 1360–80.

Greenhalgh, P. A. L. 1973. *Early Greek Warfare: Horsemen and Chariots in the Homeric and Archaic Ages*. Cambridge: Cambridge University Press.

Güterbock, H. G. 1983. "The Hittites and the Aegean World: Part 1, The Ahhiyawa Problem Reconsidered." *American Journal of Archaeology* 87, no. 2 (April): 133–38.

Haagsma, M. J. 2019. "The Central Achaia Phthiotis Survey (CAPS): The 2019 Pilot Year." Canadian Institute in Greece. Accessed November 2, 2020. https://www.cig-icg.gr /content/central-achaia-phthiotis-survey-caps-2019-pilot-year.

Hägg, R., ed. 1983. *The Greek Renaissance of the Eighth Century B.C.: Tradition and Innovation*. Stockholm: Svenska Institutet i Athen.

Haggis, D. 2001. "A Dark Age Settlement System in East Crete, and a Reassessment of the Definition of Refuge Settlements." In *Defensive Settlements of the Aegean and the Eastern Mediterranean after c. 1200 B.C.*, edited by V. Karageorghis and C. E. Morris, 41–59. Nicosia: Trinity College Dublin and the A. G. Leventis Foundation.

———. 2013. "Social Organization and Aggregated Settlement Structure in an Archaic Greek City on Crete (ca. 600 B.C.)" In *From Prehistoric Villages to Cities: Settlement Aggregation and Community Transformation*, edited by J. Birch, 63–86. New York: Routledge.

Hall, J. 1997. *Ethnic Identity in Greek Antiquity*. Cambridge: Cambridge University Press.

———. 2002. *Hellenicity: Between Ethnicity and Culture*. Chicago: University of Chicago Press.

———. 2007. *A History of the Archaic Greek World: ca. 1200–479 BCE*. Malden, MA: Wiley-Blackwell.

———. 2008. "Foundation Stories." In *Greek Colonisation: An Account of Greek Colonies and Other Settlements Overseas*, Vol. 2, edited by G. R. Tsetskhladze, 383–426. Leiden: Brill.

Halstead, P. 1989. "The Economy has a Normal Surplus: Economic Stability and Social Change Among Early Farming Communities of Thessaly, Greece." In *Bad Year Economics*, edited by P. Halstead and J. O'Shea, 68–80. Cambridge: Cambridge University Press.

———. 1992. "The Mycenaean Palatial Economy: Making the Most of the Gaps in the Evidence." *Proceedings of the Cambridge Philological Society* 38: 57–86.

———. 1994. "The North-South Divide: Regional Paths to Complexity in Prehistoric Greece." In *Development and Decline in the Mediterranean Bronze Age*, edited by C. Mathers and S. Stoddart, 194–219. Sheffield: John Collis Publications.

———. 2006. *What's Ours is Mine? Village and Household in Early Farming in Greece*. Amsterdam: Amsterdams Archeologisch Centrum van de Universiteit van Amsterdam.

———. 2007. "Toward a Model of Mycenaean Palatial Mobilization." In *Rethinking Mycenaean Palaces II: Revised and Expanded Second Edition*. edited by M. L. Galaty and W. A. Parkinson, 66–73. Los Angeles: Cotsen Institute of Archaeology, University of California, Los Angeles.

Hamilakis, Y. 1996. "Wine, Oil and the Dialectics of Power in Bronze Age Crete: A Review of the Evidence." *Oxford Journal of Archaeology* 15: 1–32.

———, ed. 2002. *Labyrinth Revisited. Rethinking 'Minoan' Archaeology*. Oxford: Oxbow Books.

———. 2007. *The Nation and Its Ruins: Antiquity, Archaeology, and National Imagination in Greece*. Oxford: Oxford University Press.

———. 2016. "Archaeologies of Forced and Undocumented Migration." *Journal of Contemporary Archaeology* 3, no. 2: 121–294.

Handberg, S., and A. Gadolou, eds. 2017. *Material Koinai in the Greek Early Iron Age and Archaic Period.* Aarhus: Aarhus University Press.

Hanink, J. 2017. *The Classical Debt: Greek Antiquity in an Era of Austerity.* Cambridge, MA: Harvard University Press.

Hankey, V. 1952. "Late Helladic Tombs at Khalkis." *Annual of the British School at Athens* 47: 49–95.

Hansen, M. H., ed. 2000. *A Comparative Study of Thirty City-state Cultures: An Investigation Conducted by the Copenhagen Polis Centre.* Copenhagen: Royal Danish Academy of Sciences and Letters.

Hansen, M. H., and T. H. Nielsen, eds. 2004. *An Inventory of Archaic and Classical Poleis: An Investigation Conducted by the Copenhagen Polis Centre for the Danish National Research Foundation.* Oxford: Oxford University Press.

Haskell, H. W., R. E. Jones, P. M. Day, and J. T. Killen. 2011. *Transport Stirrup Jars of the Bronze Age Aegean and Eastern Mediterranean.* Philadelphia: INSTAP Academic Press.

Havelock, E. A. 1986. *The Muse Learns to Write: Reflections on Orality and Literacy from Antiquity to the Present.* New Haven, CT: Yale University Press.

Hayden, B. 2009. "Funerals as Feasts: Why are they so Important?" *Cambridge Archaeological Journal* 19, no. 1 (February): 29–52.

Haynes, S. 2005. *Etruscan Civilization: A Cultural History.* Los Angeles: J. Paul Getty Museum.

Helly, B. 1999. "Modèle, de l'archéologie des cités à l'archéologie du paysage." In *Territoires des cités grecques,* edited by M. Brunet. 99–124. Athens: École française d'Athènes.

Heurtley, W. A. 1925. "Notes on the Harbours of S. Boeotia, and Sea-Trade between Boeotia and Corinth in Prehistoric Times." *Annual of the British School at Athens* 26: 38–45.

Hitchcock, L. A., R. Laffineur, and J. Crowley, eds. 2008. *Dais: The Aegean Feast.* Liège: Université de Liège.

Hitchcock, L. A., and A. M. Maeir. 2016. "A Pirate's Life for Me: The Maritime Culture of the Sea Peoples." *Palestine Exploration Quarterly* 148, no. 4 (December): 245–64.

Hodder, I. 2012. *Entangled: An Archaeology of the Relationships between Humans and Things.* Malden, MA: Wiley-Blackwell.

Hodos, T. 2006. *Local Responses to Colonization in the Iron Age Mediterranean.* New York: Routledge.

———. 2009. "Colonial Engagements in the Global Mediterranean Iron Age." *Cambridge Archaeological Journal* 19, no. 2 (June): 221–41.

———, ed. 2017. *The Routledge Handbook of Archaeology and Globalization.* New York: Routledge.

———. 2020. *The Archaeology of the Mediterranean Iron Age: A Globalizing World c. 1100–600 BCE.* Cambridge: Cambridge University Press.

Hofmanová, Z., S. Kreutzer, G. Hellenthal, C. Sell, Y. Diekmann, D. Díez-del-Molino, L. van Dorp, et al. 2016. "Early Farmers from Across Europe Directly Descended from Neolithic Aegeans." *Proceedings of the National Academy of Sciences* 113, no. 25 (June): 6886–91.

Hope Simpson, R. 1981. *Mycenaean Greece.* Park Ridge, NJ: Noyes Press.

———. 2014. *Mycenaean Messenia and the Kingdom of Pylos.* Philadelphia: INSTAP Academic Press.

Hope Simpson, R., and O. T. P. K. Dickinson. 1979. *A Gazetteer of Aegean Civilization in the Bronze Age*. Vol. 1, *The Mainland and the Islands*. Gothenburg: Paul Åströms Forlag.

Hope Simpson, R., and D. K. Hagel. 2006. *Mycenaean Fortifications, Highways, Dams and Canals*. Sävedalen: Paul Åströms Förlag.

Hope Simpson, R., and J. F. Lazenby. 1970. *The Catalogue of Ships in Homer's* Iliad. Oxford: Clarendon Press.

Horden, P., and N. Purcell. 2000. *The Corrupting Sea: A Study of Mediterranean History*. Malden, MA: Wiley-Blackwell.

Horrocks, G. 2010. *Greek: A History of the Language and Its Speakers*. 2nd ed. Malden, MA: Wiley-Blackwell.

Houston, S. D. 1994. "Literacy among the Pre-Columbian Maya: A Comparative Perspective." In *Writing without Words: Alternative Literacy in Mesoamerica and the Andes*, edited by E. H. Boone and W. D. Mignolo, 27–49. Durham: Duke University Press.

———. 2004. "The Archaeology of Communication Technologies." *Annual Review of Anthropology* 33: 223–50.

Houston, S. D., J. Baines, and J. Cooper. 2003. "Last Writing: Script Obsolescence in Egypt, Mesopotamia, and Mesoamerica." *Comparative Studies in Society and History* 45, no. 3 (July): 430–79.

Houston, S. D., and D. Stuart. 1992. "On Maya Hieroglyphic Literacy." *Current Anthropology* 33, no. 5 (December): 589–93.

Howey, M. C. L., 2007. "Using Multi-criteria Cost Surface Analysis to Explore Past Regional Landscapes: A Case Study of Ritual Activity and Social Interaction in Michigan, AD 1200–1600." *Journal of Archaeological Science* 34, no. 11 (November): 1830–46.

Hurst, H., and S. Owen, eds. 2005. *Ancient Colonizations: Analogy, Similarity and Difference*. London: Gerald Duckworth.

Hurwitt, J. 1999. *The Athenian Acropolis: History, Mythology, and Archaeology from the Neolithic Era to the Present*. Cambridge: Cambridge University Press.

Iakovidis, S. E. 1962. *Η μυκηναϊκή ακρόπολις της Αθήνας*. Athens: Ελευθερουδάκης.

———. 1980. *Excavations of the Necropolis at Perati*. Los Angeles: Institute of Archaeology, University of California, Los Angeles.

———. 1989. *Γλας I: Η ανασκαφή 1955–1961*. Athens: Archaeological Society at Athens.

———. 1998. *Γλας II: Η ανασκαφή 1981–1991*. Athens: Archaeological Society at Athens.

———. 2001. *Gla and the Kopais in the 13th Century B.C.* Athens: Archaeological Society at Athens.

———. 2003a. "Late Helladic IIIC at Perati." In *LH III C Chronology and Synchronisms*, edited by S. Deger-Jalkotzy and M. Zavadil, 125–30. Vienna: Verlag der Österreichischen Adademie der Wissenschaften.

———. 2003b. "Late Mycenaean Perati and the Levant." In *The Synchronisation of Civilisations in the Eastern Mediterranean in the Second Millennium B.C. II*, edited by M. Bietak and H. Hunger, 501–11. Vienna: Verlag der Österreichischen Akademie der Wissenschaften.

———. 2006. *The Mycenaean Acropolis of Athens*. Athens: Archaeological Society at Athens.

Iacono, F. 2015. "Feasting at Roca: Cross-Cultural Encounters and Society in the Southern Adriatic during the Late Bronze Age." *European Journal of Archaeology* 18, no. 2: 259–81.

———. 2016a. "From Networks to Society: Pottery Style and Hegemony in Bronze Age Southern Italy." *Cambridge Archaeological Journal* 26, no. 1 (February): 121–40.

———. 2016b. "Value, Power, and Encounter between the Eastern and Central Mediterranean during the Late Bronze Age." *Studi Micenei ed Egeo-Anatolici Nuova Serie* 2: 101–18.

———. 2019. *The Archaeology of Late Bronze Age Interaction and Mobility at the Gates of Europe: People, Things, and Networks around the Southern Adriatic Sea.* London: Bloomsbury.

Iacovou, M. 2005. "Cyprus at the Dawn of the First Millennium BCE: Cultural Homogenisation versus the Tyranny of Ethnic Identification." In *Archaeological Perspectives on the Transmission and Transformation of Culture in the Eastern Mediterranean*, edited by J. Clarke, 125–34. Oxford: Council for British Research in the Levant.

Immerwahr, S. A. 1971. *The Neolithic and Bronze Ages.* The Athenian Agora 13. Princeton, NJ: American School of Classical Studies at Athens.

Ingvarsson, A., and Y. Bäckström. 2019. "Bioarchaeological field analysis of human remains from the mass graves at Phaleron, Greece. With an introduction by Stella Chryssoulaki and an appendix by Anna Linderholm, Anna Kjellström, Vendela Kempe Lagerholm, and Maja Krzewińska." *Opuscula* 12: 7–158.

Isayev, E. 2017. *Migration, Mobility and Place in Ancient Italy.* Cambridge: Cambridge University Press.

Janes, S. 2010. "Negotiating Island Interactions: Cyprus, the Aegean and the Levant in the Late Bronze to Early Iron Ages." In *Material Connections in the Ancient Mediterranean: Mobility, Materiality and Identity*, edited by P. van Dommelen and A. B. Knapp, 127–46. New York: Routledge.

Janko, R. 2015. "From Gabii and Gordion to Eretria and Methone: The Rise of the Greek Alphabet." *Bulletin of the Institute of Classical Studies* 58: 1–32.

———. 2018. "The Greek Dialects of the Palatial and Postpalatial Late Bronze Age." In *Studies in Ancient Greek Dialects: From Central Greece to the Black Sea*, edited by G. Giannakis, E. Crespo, and P. Filos, 107–29. Berlin: De Gruyter.

Jansen, A. G. 2002. *A Study of the Remains of Mycenaean Roads and Stations of Bronze-Age Greece.* Lewiston: The Edwin Mellen Press.

Jasnow, B., C. Evans, and J. S. Clay. 2018. "Poetic and Geographical Organization in the Catalogue of Ships." *Transactions of the American Philological Association* 148, no. 1 (Spring): 1–44.

Jeffery, L. H. 1980. "The Graffiti." In *Lefkandi I: The Iron Age Settlement and Cemeteries*, edited by M. R. Popham, L. H. Sackett, and P. G. Themelis, 89–93. London: Thames and Hudson.

———. 1990. *The Local Scripts of Archaic Greece: A Study of the Origin of the Greek Alphabet and Its Development from the Eighth to the Fifth Centuries B.C.* Rev. ed., with supplement by A. W. Johnston. Oxford: Oxford University Press.

Jennings, J., and T. Earle. 2016. "Urbanization, State Formation, and Cooperation: A Reappraisal." *Current Anthropology* 57, no. 4 (August): 474–93.

Joffe, A. H. 2002. "The Rise of Secondary States in the Iron Age Levant." *Journal of the Economic and Social History of the Orient* 45, no. 4: 425–67.

Jones, R. E. 1980. "Analyses of Bronze and Other Base Metal Objects from the Cemeteries." In *Lefkandi I: The Iron Age Settlement and Cemeteries*, edited by M. R. Popham, L. H. Sackett, and P. G. Themelis, 447–59. London: British School at Athens.

Jones, R., S. T. Levi, M. Bettelli, and L. Vagnetti. 2014. *Italo-Mycenaean Pottery: The Archaeological and Archaeometric Dimensions.* Rome: CNR—Istituto di studi sul Mediterraneo antico.

Jones, S. 1997. *The Archaeology of Ethnicity: Constructing Identities in the Past and Present.* Oxford: Routledge.

Jung, R. 2015. "Imported Mycenaean Pottery in the East: Distribution, Context and Interpretation." In *Policies of Exchange: Political Systems and Modes of Interaction in the Aegean and the Near East in the 2nd Millennium B.C.E.*, edited by B. Eder and R. Pruzsinsky, 243–75. Vienna: Austrian Academy of Sciences Press.

———. 2016. "'Friede den Hütten, Krieg den Palästen!'—in the Bronze age Aegean." *In Arm und Reich—Zur Ressourcenverteilung in prähistorischen Gesellschaften*, edited by H. Meller, H. P. Hahn, R. Jung and R. Risch. Halle: Tagungen des Landesmuseums für Vorgeschichte Halle.

Jung, R., H. Mommsen, and M. Picciarelli. 2015. "From West to West: Determining Production Regions of Mycenaean Pottery of Punta di Zambrone (Calabria, Italy)." *Journal of Archaeological Science: Reports* 3 (September): 455–63.

Jusseret, S. and M. Sintubin, eds. 2017. *Minoan Earthquakes: Breaking the Myth through Interdisciplinarity.* Leuven: Leuven University Press.

Kaiser, I., L.-C. Rizzoto, and S. Strack. 2011. "Development of a Ceramic Cultic Assemblage: Analyzing Pottery from Late Helladic IIIC through Late Geometric Kalapodi." In *Early Iron Age Pottery: A Quantitative Approach*, edited by S. Verdan, T. Theurillat, and A. Kenzelmann Pfyffer, 29–44. Oxford: Archaeopress.

Kakavogianni, O., ed. 2003. *Archaeological Investigations at Merenda, Marcopoulo at the New Race-Course and Olympic Equestrian Centre.* Athens: 2nd Ephorate of Prehistoric and Classical Antiquities.

———. 2009. "Attica. Historical and Archaeological Background: Prehistoric Times." In *Archaeology: Euboea and Central Greece*, edited by A. G. Vlachopoulos, 94–103. Athens: Melissa Publishing House.

Kakavogiannis, E. 1999–2001. "Μυκηναϊκό νεκροταφείο στο λόφο Φούρεσι του δήμου των Γλυκών Νερών Αττικής." *Athens Annals of Archaeology* 32–34: 55–70.

Kalamara, P., M. Kosma, K. Boukaras, and Y. Chairetakis. 2015. *The City of Chalkis: Chalkis—Euripus, Negroponte—Egriboz.* Athens: Ministry of Culture and Sports, Ephorate of Antiquities of Euboea.

Karantzali, E. 2013. "Mycenaeans within the Spercheios Valley: The Inhabitations at Frantzis and Lygaria." In *Φιλική Συναυλία: Studies in Mediterranean Archaeology for Mario Benzi*, edited by G. Graziadio, R. Guglielmino, V. Lenuzza, and S. Vitale, 139–53. Oxford: Archaeopress.

Kardamaki, E. 2017. "The Late Helladic IIB to IIIA2 Pottery Sequence from the Mycenaean Palace at Ayios Vasileios, Laconia." *Archaeologia Austriaca* 101: 73–142.

Kardulias, P. N., and T. D. Hall. 2008. "Archaeology and World-Systems Analysis." *World Archaeology* 40, no. 4 (December): 572–83.

Karouzou, E. 2017. "Thessaly from the Protogeometric to the Early Archaic Period (1100–600 BC)." In *Regional Stories Towards a New Perception of the Early Greek World*, edited by A. Mazarakis Ainian, A. Alexandridou, X. Charalambidou, 343–81. Volos: University of Thessaly Press.

———. 2020. "Thessaly." In *A Companion to the Archaeology of Early Greece and the Mediterranean*, edited by I. S. Lemos and A. Kotsonas, 883–912. Hoboken, NJ: John Wiley & Sons.

Kase, E. W. 1970. "A Study of the Role of Krisa in the Mycenaean Era." Master's thesis, Loyola University, Chicago.

————. 1972. "A Surface Exploration in Search of Mycenean Roads in Nomos Fokidhos and Nomos Fthiatidhos." PhD diss., Loyola University, Chicago.

Kase, E. W., G. J. Szemler, N. W. Wilkie, and P. W. Wallace, eds. 1991. *The Great Isthmus Corridor Route. Explorations of the Phokis-Doris Expedition.* Dubuque, IA: Kendall-Hunt.

Kasseri, A. 2012. "Φοινικικοί εμπορικοί αμφορείς από τη Μεθώνη Πιερίας." In *Κεραμέως παῖδες: Αντίδωρο στον Καθηγητή Μιχάλη Τιβέριο από τους μαθητές του,* edited by E. Kephalidou and D. Tsiafaki, 299–308. Thessaloniki: Εταιρεία Ανδρίων Επιστημόνων.

Katakouta, S., 2009. "Τα Φάρσαλα στην Πρώιμη Εποχή του Σιδήρου." In *Αρχαιολογικό έργο Θεσσαλίας και Στερεάς Ελλάδας 2,* edited by A. Mazarakis Ainian, 241–50. Volos: Ministry of Culture and University of Thessaly.

Kauffman, S. 1993. *The Origins of Order: Self-Organization and Selection in Evolution.* New York: Oxford University Press.

Kayafa, M. 1999. "Bronze Age Metallurgy in the Peloponnese, Greece." PhD diss., University of Birmingham.

————. 2020. "The Metal Resources of Laurion during the Early Bronze Age: A Synthesis of the Archaeological and Archaeometric Data." In *Athens and Attica in Prehistory,* edited by N. Papadimitriou, J. C. Wright, S. Fachard, and N. Polychronakou-Sgouritsa, 193–202. Oxford: Archaeopress.

Kelder, J. M. 2010. *The Kingdom of Mycenae: A Great Kingdom in the Late Bronze Age Aegean.* Bethesda, MD: Capital Decisions.

————. 2012. "Horseback Riding and Cavalry in Mycenaean Greece." *Ancient West & East* 11: 1–18.

Kelekna, P. 2009. *The Horse in Human History.* Cambridge: Cambridge University Press.

Keller, D. R. 1985. "Archaeological Survey in Southern Euboea, Greece: A Reconstruction of Human Activity from Neolithic Times Through the Byzantine Period." PhD diss., Indiana University. ProQuest (AAT 8527015).

Keller, D. R., and E. Hom. 2010. "Ancient Land Routes on the Paximadi Peninsula, Karystos, Euboea." *Mediterranean Archaeology and Archaeometry* 10, no. 3: 1–9.

Kennett, D. J., and N. Marwan. 2015. "Climatic Volatility, Agricultural Uncertainty, and the Formation, Consolidation, and Breakdown of Preindustrial Agrarian States." *Philosophical Transactions of the Royal Society* 373: https://doi.org/10.1098/rsta.2014.0458.

Kerschner, M. and I. S. Lemos, eds. 2014. *Archaeometric Analyses of Euboean and Euboean Related Pottery: New Results and Their Interpretations.* Vienna: Österreichisches Archäologisches Institut.

Kenzelmann Pfyffer, A., T. Theurillat, and S. Verdan. 2005. "Graffiti d'époque géométrique provenant du sanctuaire d'Apollon Daphnéphoros à Erétrie." *Zeitschrift für Papyrologie und Epigraphik* 151: 51–86.

Khatchadourian, L. 2016. *Imperial Matter: Ancient Persia and the Archaeology of Empires.* Berkeley: University of California Press.

Killen, J. T. 1998. "The Role of the State in Wheat and Olive Production in Mycenaean Crete." *Aevum* 72: 19–23.

————. 2015. *Economy and Administration in Mycenaean Greece: Collected Papers on Linear B,* edited by M. Del Freo. Rome: CNR—Istituto di studi sul Mediterraneo antico.

Kilian, K. 1988. "The Emergence of the *Wanax* Ideology in Mycenaean Palaces." *Oxford Journal of Archaeology* 7, no. 3 (November): 291–302.

Kintigh, K. W., J. H. Altschul, M. C. Beaudry, R. D. Drennan, A. P. Kinzig, T. A. Kohler, W. F. Limp, et al. 2014. "Grand Challenges for Archaeology." *American Antiquity* 79, no. 1 (January): 5–24.

Kirch, P. V. 2010. *How Chiefs Became Kings: Divine Kingship and the Rise of Archaic States in Ancient Hawai'i*. Berkeley: University of California Press.

Kirchhoff, A. 1887. *Studien zur Geschichte des griechischen Alphabets*. Gütersloh: Bertelsmann.

Kiriatzi, E., and C. Knappett, eds. 2016. *Human Mobility and Technological Transfer in the Prehistoric Mediterranean*. Cambridge: Cambridge University Press.

Kirk, G. S. 1949. "Ships on Geometric Vases." *Annual of the British School at Athens* 44: 93–153.

Knapp, A. B. 2000. "Archaeology, Science-Based Archaeology and the Mediterranean Bronze Age Metals Trade." *European Journal of Archaeology* 3, no. 1 (April): 31–56.

———. 2008. *Prehistoric and Protohistoric Cyprus: Identity, Insularity and Connectivity*. Oxford: Oxford University Press.

———. 2012. "Metallurgical Production and Trade on Bronze Age Cyprus: Views and Variations." In *Eastern Mediterranean Metallurgy and Metalwork in the Second Millennium BC*, edited by V. Kassianidou and G. Papasavvas, 14–25. Oxford: Oxbow Books.

Knapp, A. B., and J. F. Cherry. 1994. *Provenience Studies and Bronze Age Cyprus: Production, Exchange and Politico-Economic Change*. Madison, WI: Prehistory Press.

Knapp, A. B., and S. Demesticha. 2017. *Mediterranean Connections: Maritime Transport Containers and Seaborne Trade in the Bronze and Early Iron Ages*. New York: Routledge.

Knapp, A. B., and S. W. Manning, 2016. "Crisis in Context: The End of the Late Bronze Age in the Eastern Mediterranean." *American Journal of Archaeology* 120, no. 1 (January): 99–149.

Knappett, C. 2011. *An Archaeology of Interaction: Network Perspectives on Material Culture and Society*. Oxford: Oxford University Press.

———, ed. 2013. *Network Analysis in Archaeology: New Approaches to Regional Interaction*. Oxford: Oxford University Press.

Knappett, C., and I. Schoep. 2000. "Continuity and Change in Minoan Palatial Power." *Antiquity* 74, no. 284 (June): 365–71.

Knauf, E. A. 1992. "The Cultural Impact of Secondary State Formation: The Cases of the Edomites and Moabites." In *Early Edom and Moab: The Beginning of the Iron Age in Southern Jordan*, edited by P. Bienkowski, 47–54. Sheffield: J. R. Collis.

Knauss, J. 1987. *Die Melioration des Kopaisbeckens durch die Minyer im 2. Jt. v. Chr.* Bericht Nr. 57. Munich: Institut für Wasserbau und Wassermengenwirtschaft der Technischen Universität München.

Knauss, J., B. Heinrich, and H. Kalcyk. 1984. *Die Wasserbauten der Minyer in der Kopais: Die älteste Flussregulierung Europas*. Munich: Institut für Wasserbau und Wassermengenwirtschaft der Technischen Universität München.

Knigge, U. 1991. *The Athenian Kerameikos: History, Monuments, Excavations*. Athens: Deutsches Archäologisches Institut.

Knodell, A. R. 2013. "Small-World Networks and Mediterranean Dynamics in the Euboean Gulf: An Archaeology of Complexity in Late Bronze Age and Early Iron Age Greece." PhD diss., Brown University. https://doi.org/10.7301/Z0G15KHB.

———. 2017. "A Conduit Between Two Worlds: Geography and Connectivity in the Euboean Gulf." In *An Island between Two Worlds: The Archaeology of Euboea from Prehistoric to Byzantine Times*, edited by Ž. Tankosić, F. Mavridis, and M. Kosma, 195–213. Athens: Norwegian Institute at Athens.

———. 2018. "Collapse and Failure in Complex Societies." *Cambridge Archaeological Journal* 28, no. 44 (November): 713–17.

———. Forthcoming. "Palatial and Non-Palatial Landscapes in the Mycenaean World: Territorial Models for Central Greece." In *Political Geographies of the Bronze Age Aegean*, edited by G. J. van Wijngaarden and J. Driessen. Leuven: Peeters.

Knodell, A. R., S. Fachard, and K. Papangeli. 2016. "The 2015 Mazi Archaeological Project: Regional Survey in Northwest Attica (Greece)." *Antike Kunst* 59: 132–52.

———. 2017. "The Mazi Archaeological Project 2016: Survey and Settlement Investigations in Northwest Attica (Greece)." *Antike Kunst* 60: 146–63.

Knodell, A. R., and T. P. Leppard, eds. 2018. *Regional Approaches to Society and Complexity: Studies in Honor of John F. Cherry*. Sheffield: Equinox.

Knoepfler, D. 1981. "Argoura. Un toponyme eubéen dans la Midienne de Démosthène." *Bulletin de Correspondance Hellénique* 105: 289–329.

———. 1997. "Les territoire d'Erétrie et l'organisation politique de la cité (dêmoi, chôroi, phylai)." In *The Polis as an Urban Centre and the Political Community*, edited by M. H. Hansen, 352–449. Copenhagen: Royal Danish Academy of Sciences and Letters.

Kohl, P. 1987. "The Use and Abuse of World Systems Theory: The Case of the 'Pristine' West Asian State." *Advances in Archaeological Method and Theory* 11: 1–35.

Kohler, T. A. 2012. "Complex Systems and Archaeology." In *Archaeological Theory Today*. 2nd ed., edited by I. Hodder, 93–123. Cambridge: Polity Press.

Kohring, S., and S. Wynne-Jones, eds. 2007. *Socialising Complexity: Structure, Interaction and Power in Archaeological Discourse*. Oxford: Oxbow Books.

Kõiv, M. 2016. "Communities and Rulers in Early Greece: Development of Leadership Patterns in Euboia and Argolis (12th–6th Centuries BC)." In *Kings, Gods and People: Establishing Monarchies in the Ancient World*, edited by T. R. Kämmerer, M. Kõiv, and V. Sazonov, 293–354. Münster: Ugarit-Verlag.

Kontogiannis, N. 2012. "Euripos-Negroponte-Eğriboz: Material Culture and Historic Topography of Chalcis from Byzantium to the End of Ottoman Rule." *Jahrbuch der Österreichischen Byzantinistik* 62: 29–56.

Kontorli-Papadopoulou, L. 1995. "Mycenaean Tholos Tombs: Some Thoughts on Burial Customs and Rites." In *Klados: Essays in Honour of J. N. Coldstream*, edited by C. Morris, 111–22. London: Institute of Classical Studies, University of London.

Kopanias, K. 2008. "The Late Bronze Age Near Eastern Cylinder Seals from Thebes (Greece) and Their Historical Implications." *Mitteilungen des Deutschen Archäologischen Instituts, Athenische Abteilung* 123: 39–96.

———. 2017. Mercenaries or Refugees? The Evidence from the Inscriptions of Merenptah on the 'Sea Peoples.'" *Journal of Greek Archaeology* 2: 115–30.

Korres, M., ed. 2010. *Αττικής Οδοί: Αρχαίοι Δρόμοι της Αττικής*. Athens: Melissa Publishing House.

Kosiba, S., and A. M. Bauer. 2013. "Mapping the Political Landscape: Toward a GIS Analysis of Environmental and Social Difference." *Journal of Archaeological Method and Theory* 20: 61–101.

Kosma, M. 2012. "The Lady of Lefkandi." In *Princesses of the Mediterranean in the Dawn of History*, edited by N. C. Stampolidis and M. Giannopoulou, 58–69. Athens: Museum of Cycladic Art.

———. 2015. "Η τοπογραφία της αρχαίας Χαλκίδας υπό το πρίσμα της πρόσφατης έρευνας." In *Αρχαιολογικές συμβολές. Τόμος Γ: Βοιωτία & Εύβοια*, edited by S. Oikonomou, 209–20. Athens: Museum of Cycladic Art.

Kostoglou, M. 2008. *Iron and Steel in Ancient Greece: Artefacts, Technology and Social Change in Aegean Thrace from Classical to Roman Times*. Oxford: Archaeopress.

Kotsonas, A. 2012. "Η ενεπίγραφη κεραμική του 'Υπογείου': Προέλευση, τυπολογία, χρονολόγηση και ερμηνεία." In *Μεθώνη I: Επιγραφές, χαράγματα και εμπορικά σύμβολα στην υστερογεωμετρική και αρχαιολογική κεραμική από το "Υπόγειο"* by M. Besios, Y. Tzifopoulos, and A. Kotsonas, 113–304. Thessaloniki: Center for Hellenic Language.

———. 2015. "What Makes a Euboean Colony or Trading Station? Zagora in the Cyclades, Methone in the Thermaic Gulf, and Aegean Networks in the 8th Century BC." *Mediterranean Archaeology* 25: 243–57.

———. 2016. "Politics of Periodization and the Archaeology of Early Greece." *American Journal of Archaeology* 120, no 2 (April): 239–70.

———. 2020. "History of Research." In *A Companion to the Archaeology of Early Greece and the Mediterranean*, edited by I. S. Lemos and A. Kotsonas, 75–96. Hoboken, NJ: John Wiley & Sons.

Kotsonas, A., and J. Mokrišová. 2020. "Mobility, Migration, and Colonization." In *A Companion to the Archaeology of Early Greece and the Mediterranean*, edited by I. S. Lemos and A. Kotsonas, 217–46. Hoboken, NJ: John Wiley & Sons.

Kountouri, E. 2014. "Γεωμετρική Θήβα: Τα Δεδομένα από τις Σύγχρονες Έρευνες." In *100 χρόνια αρχαιολογικού έργου στη Θήβα. Οι πρωτεργάτες των ερευνών και οι συνεχιστές τους*, edited by V. Aravantinos and E. Kountouri, 213–29. Athens: Ταμείο Αρχαιολογικών Πόρων και Απαλλοτριώσεων.

Kountouri, E., N. Petrochilos, D. Koutsoyiannis, N. Mamassis, N. Zarkadoulas, A. Vött, H. Hadler, P. Henning, and T. Willershäuser. 2012. "A New Project of Surface Survey, Geophysical and Excavation Research of the Mycenaean Drainage Works of the North Kopais: The First Study Season." In *IWA Specialized Conference on Water and Wastewater, 22–24 March 2012*, 467–76. London: IWA Publishing.

Kourou, N. 2002. "Tenos, Xombourgo: From a Refuge Place to an Extensive Fortified Settlement." In *Excavating Classical Culture: Recent Archaeological Discoveries in Greece*, edited by K. Stamatopoulou and D. Geroulanou, 258–68. Oxford: Oxford University Press.

———. 2015. "Cypriots and Levantines in the Central Aegean During the Geometric Period: The Nature of Contacts." In *Zagora in Context: Settlements and Intercommunal Links in the Geometric Period (900–700 BC)*, edited by J.-P. Descoeudres and S. A. Paspalas, 215–27. Sydney: Mediterranean Archaeology.

———. 2017. "The Archaeological Background of the Earliest Graffiti and Finds from Methone." In *Panhellenes at Methone: Graphê in Late Geometric and Protoarchaic Methone, Macedonia (ca. 700 BCE)*, edited by J. S. Clay, I. Malkin, and Y. Z. Tzifopoulos, 20–35. Berlin: De Gruyter.

Kowalzig, B. 2018. "Cults, Cabotage and Connectivity: Experimenting with Religious and Economic Netowrks in the Greco-Roman Mediterranean." In *Maritime Networks in the Ancient Mediterranean World*, edited by J. Leidwanger and C. Knappett, 93–131. Cambridge: Cambridge University Press.

Kraiker, W. 1939. *Die Nekropolen des 12. bis 10. Jahrhunderts*. Kerameikos: Ergebnisse der Ausgrabungen 1. Berlin: De Gruyter.

Kramer-Hajos, M. 2006. "A Man from Halai? Problems with a-ra-o in the Theban Linear B Tablets." *Kadmos* 45: 85–92.

———. 2008. *Beyond the Palace: Mycenaean East Lokris*. Oxford: Archaeopress.

———. 2016. *Mycenaean Greece and the Aegean World: Palace and Province in the Late Bronze Age*. Cambridge: Cambridge University Press.

Kramer-Hajos, M., and K. O'Neill. 2008. "The Bronze Age Site of Mitrou in East Lokris: Finds from the 1988–1989 Surface Survey." *Hesperia* 77, no. 2 (April–June): 163–250.

Krapf, T. 2011. "Amarynthos in der Bronzezeit: Der Wissensstand nach den Schweizer Grabungen 2006 und 2007." *Antike Kunst* 54: 144–59.

Krause, G. 1975. *Untersuchungen zu den ältesten Nekropolen am Eridanos in Athen*. Hamburg: Buske.

Kristiansen, K., and T. B. Larsson. 2005. *The Rise of Bronze Age Society: Travels, Transmissions and Transformations*. Cambridge: Cambridge University Press.

Kroll, J. H. 2008. "Early Iron Age Balance Weights at Lefkandi, Euboea." *Oxford Journal of Archaeology* 27, no. 1 (January): 37–48.

Kübler, K. 1943. *Neufunde aus der Nekropole des 11. und 10. Jahrhunderts*. Kerameikos: Ergebnisse der Ausgrabungen 4. Berlin: De Gruyter.

———. 1954. *Die Nekropole des 10. bis 8. Jahrhunderts*. Kerameikos: Ergebnisse der Ausgrabungen 5. Berlin: De Gruyter.

Laffineur, R. 2010. "Thorikos." In *The Oxford Handbook of the Bronze Age Aegean*, edited by E. H. Cline, 712–21. Oxford: Oxford University Press.

Laffineur, R., and W.-D. Niemeier, eds. 1995. *Politeia: Society and State in the Aegean Bronze Age*. Liège: Université de Liège.

Lambert, S. D. 1982. "A Thucydidean Scholium on the 'Lelantine War.'" *Journal of Hellenic Studies* 102: 216–20.

Lambrinoudakis, V., and O. Philaniotou-Hadjianastasiou. 2001. "The Town of Naxos at the End of the Late Bronze Age: The Mycenaean Fortification Wall." In *Defensive Settlements of the Aegean and the Eastern Mediterranean after c. 1200 BC*, edited by V. Karageorghis and C. E. Morris, 157–69. Nicosia: Trinity College Dublin and Anastasios G. Leventis Foundation.

Lane, M. F., T. J. Horsely, A. Charami, and W. Bittner. 2016. "Archaeological Geophysics of a Bronze Age Agricultural Landscape: The AROURA Project, Central Mainland Greece." *Journal of Field Archaeology* 41, no. 3 (June): 271–96.

Lane, M. F., V. Aravantinos, T. J. Horsley, and A. Charami. 2020. "The AROURA Project: Discoveries in Central Greece, 2010-2014." *Hesperia* 83, no. 3 (July–September): 413–74.

Lane Fox, R. 2008. *Travelling Heroes in the Epic Age of Homer*. New York: Alfred A. Knopf.

Lang, M. L. 1969. *The Palace of Nestor at Pylos in Western Messenia*. Vol. 2, *The Frescoes*. Princeton, NJ: Princeton University Press.

Langdon, M. L. 1976. *A Sanctuary of Zeus on Mount Hymettos*. Princeton, NJ: American School of Classical Studies at Athens.

Langdon, S., ed. 1993. *From Pasture to Polis: Art in the Age of Homer*. Columbia: University of Missouri Press.

————, ed. 1997. *New Light on a Dark Age: Exploring Geometric Greece*. Columbia: University of Missouri Press.

————. 2008. *Art and Identity in Dark Age Greece, 1100–700 BCE*. Cambridge: Cambridge University Press.

Latacz, J. 2004. *Troy and Homer: Towards a Solution of an Old Mystery*. Oxford: Oxford University Press.

Lazaridis, I., A. Mittnik, N. Patterson, S. Mallick, N. Rohland, S. Pfrengle, A. Furtwängler, et al. 2017. "Genetic Origins of the Minoans and Mycenaeans." *Nature* 548: 214–18.

Leake, W. M. 1821. *The Topography of Athens: With Some Remarks on Its Antiquities*. London: John Murray.

LeCount, L. J., and J. H. Blitz. 2010. "A Comment on 'Funerals as Feasts: Why Are They So Important?'" *Cambridge Archaeological Journal* 20, no. 2 (June): 263–65.

Lehner, M. 2015. "Labor and the Pyramids: The Heit el-Ghurab 'Workers Town' at Giza." In *Labor in the Ancient World*, edited by P. Steinkeller and M. Hudson, 397–522. Dresden: ISLET-Verlag.

Lemonnier, P. 1993. *Technological Choices: Transformation in Material Cultures Since the Neolithic*. London: Routledge.

Lemos, I. S. 1998. "Euboeans and Their Aegean Koine." In *Euboica: L'Eubea e la presenza euboica in Calädica e in Occidente*, edited by M. Bats and B. d'Agostino, 45–58. Naples: Centre Jean Bérard.

————. 1999. "Some Aspects of the Transition from the Late Bronze Age to the Early Iron Age in Central Greece." In *The Periphery of the Mycenaean World*, edited by N. Kyparissi-Apostolika and M. Papakonstantinou, 21–25. Lamia: 14th Ephorate of Prehistoric and Classical Antiquities.

————. 2001. "The Lefkandi Connection: Networking in the Aegean and the Eastern Mediterranean." In *Italy and Cyprus in Antiquity: 1500–450 BC*, edited by L. Bonfante and V. Karageorghis, 215–26. Nicosia: Costakis and Leto Severis Foundation.

————. 2002. *The Protogeometric Aegean: The Archaeology of the Late Eleventh and Tenth Centuries BC*. Oxford: Oxford University Press.

————. 2007. "The Migrations to the West Coast of Asia Minor: Tradition and Archaeology." In *Frühes Ionien: eine Bestandsaufnahme*, edited by J. Cobet, V. von Graeve, W.-D. Niemeier, and K. Zimmerman, 713–27. Mainz: Verlag Philipp von Zabern.

————. 2010a. "The Excavation at Lefkandi-Xeropolis (2003–2009): Summary of the Mycenaean Seminar, 12 May 2010." *Bulletin of the Institute of Classical Studies of the University of London* 53: 134–36.

————. 2010b. "Lefkandi." In *Ausgegraben! Schweizer Archäologen erforschen die griechische Stadt Eretria: Eine Ausstellung der Schweizerischen Archäologischen Schule in Griechenland in Zusammenarbeit mit dem Antikenmuseum Basel und Sammlung Ludwig*, edited by C. M. Pruvot, K. Reber, and T. Theurillat, 56–63. Basel: Verlag Schwabe.

————. 2012. "Euboea and Central Greece in the Post-Palatial and Early Greek Periods." *Archaeological Reports* 58: 19–27.

————. 2018. "A Ship Scene for Fanouria." In Πύρρα. Μελέτες για την αρχαιολογία στην Κεντρική Ελλάδα προς τιμήν της Φανουρίας Δακορώνια, edited by M.-F. Papakonstantinou, C. Kritzas, and I. P. Touratsoglou, 159–67. Athens: Sema Editions.

————. 2020. "Euboea." In *A Companion to the Archaeology of Early Greece and the Mediterranean*, edited by I. S. Lemos and A. Kotsonas, 787–814. Hoboken, NJ: John Wiley & Sons.

Lemos, I. S., and H. Hatcher. 1986. "Protogeometric Skyros and Euboea." *Oxford Journal of Archaeology* 5, no. 3 (November): 323–37.

Lemos, I. S., and A. Kotsonas, eds. 2020. *A Companion to the Archaeology of Early Greece and the Mediterranean.* Hoboken, NJ: John Wiley and Sons.

Lemos, I. S., A. Livieratou, and M. Thomatos. 2009. "Post-Palatial Urbanization: Some Lost Opportunities." In *Inside the City in the Greek World: Studies of Urbanism from the Bronze Age to the Hellenistic Period,* edited by S. Owen and L. Preston, 62–84. Oxford: Oxbow Books.

Lemos, I. S., and D. Mitchell. 2011. "Elite Burials in Early Iron Age Aegean: Some Preliminary Observations Considering the Spatial Organization of the Toumba Cemetery at Lefkandi." In *The "Dark Ages" Revisited: Acts of the International Symposium in Memory of W.D. E. Coulson,* edited by A. Mazarakis Ainian, 635–44. Volos: University of Thessaly Press.

Lemos, I. S., and A. Tsingarida, eds. 2019. *Beyond the Polis: Rituals, Rites and Cults in Early and Archaic Greece (12th–6th Centuries BC).* Brussels: CReA-Patrimoine.

Letesson, Q. and C. Knappett, eds. 2017. *Minoan Architecture and Urbanism.* Oxford: Oxford University Press.

Leppard, T. P., and A. R. Knodell. 2018. "Retrospect and Prospect in Regional Archaeology." In *Regional Approaches to Society and Complexity: Studies in Honor of John F. Cherry,* edited by A. R. Knodell and T. P. Leppard, 320–37. Sheffield: Equinox.

Leroi-Gourhan, A. 1964. *Le Geste et la Parole.* Paris: A. Michel.

Leone, B. 2015. "A Trade Route between Euboea and the Northern Aegean." In *Zagora in Context: Settlements and Intercommunal Links in the Geometric Period (900–700 BC),* edited by J.-P. Descoeudres and S. A. Paspalas, 229–41. Sydney: Mediterranean Archaeology (special issue).

Ling, J., T. Earle, and K. Kristiansen. 2018. "Maritime Mode of Production: Raiding and Trading in Seafaring Chiefdoms." *Current Anthropology* 59, no. 5 (August): 488–524.

Lis, B. 2015. "From Cooking Pots to Cuisine: Limitations and Perspectives of a Ceramic-Based Approach." In *Ceramics, Cuisine and Culture: The Archaeology and Science of Kitchen Pottery in the Ancient Mediterranean World,* edited by M. Spataro and A. Villing, 104–14. Oxford: Oxbow Books.

———. 2017. "Foodways in Early Mycenaean Greece: Innovative Cooking Sets and Social Hierarchy at Mitrou and Other Settlements on the Greek Mainland." *American Journal of Archaeology* 121, no. 2 (April): 183–217.

Lis, B., E. Kiriatzi, A. Batziou, and Š. Rückl. 2020a. "Dealing with the Crisis: Mobility of Aeginetan-Tradition Potters around 1200 B.C." *Annual of the British School at Athens,* 1–59.

Lis, B., H. Mommsen, J. Maran, and S. Prillwitz. 2020b. "Investigating Pottery Production and Consumption Patterns at the Late Mycenaean Cemetery of Perati." *Journal of Archaeological Science: Reports* 32 (August): 102453.

Lis, B. and Š. Rückl. 2011. "Our Storerooms Are Full: Impressed Pithoi from Late Bronze/Early Iron Age East Lokris and Phokis and Their Socio-economic Significance." In *Our Cups Are Full: Pottery and Society in the Aegean Bronze Age. Papers Presented to Jeremy B. Rutter on the Occasion of his 65th Birthday,* edited by W. Gauß, M. Lindblom, R. A. K. Smith, and J. C. Wright, 154–68. Oxford: Archaeopress.

Lis, B., Š. Rückl, and M. Choleva. 2015. "Mobility in the Bronze Age Aegean: The Case of Aeginetan Potters." *The Transmission of Technical Knowledge in the Production of Ancient*

Mediterranean Pottery, edited by W. Gauß, G. Klebinder-Gauß, and C. von Rüden, 63–75. Vienna: Österreichisches Archäologisches Institut.

Liston, M. A., and J. K. Papadopoulos. 2004. "The 'Rich Athenian Lady' Was Pregnant: The Anthropology of a Geometric Tomb Reconsidered." *Hesperia* 73, no. 1 (January–March): 7–38.

Liverani, M. 1987. "The Collapse of the Near Eastern Regional System at the End of the Bronze Age: The Case of Syria." In *Centre and Periphery in the Ancient World*, edited by M. Rowlands, M. Larsen, and K. Kristiansen, 66–73. Cambridge: Cambridge University Press.

Livieratou, A. 2011. "Regional Cult Systems from the Late Bronze to the Early Iron Age." In *The "Dark Ages" Revisited: Acts of the International Symposium in Memory of W. D. E. Coulson*, edited by A. Mazarakis Ainian, 147–64. Volos: University of Thessaly.

———. 2012. "Phokis and East Lokris in the Light of Interregional Contacts at the Transition from the Late Bronze to the Early Iron Age." In *Cyprus and the Aegean in the Early Iron Age: The Legacy of Nicolas Coldstream*, edited by M. Iacovou, 77–127. Nicosia: Bank of Cyprus Cultural Foundation.

———. 2015. "East Phokis Revisited: Its Development in the Transition from the Late Bronze to the Early Iron Age in the Light of the Latest Finds." In *Aegis: Essays in Mediterranean Archaeology Presented to Matti Egon by the Scholars of the Greek Archaeological Committee UK*, edited by Z. Theodoropoulou Polychroniadis and D. Evely, 93–105. Oxford: Archaeopress.

———. 2020. "East Locris and Phocis." In *A Companion to the Archaeology of Early Greece and the Mediterranean*, edited by I. S. Lemos and A. Kotsonas, 815–36. Hoboken, NJ: John Wiley & Sons.

Lloyd, G. E. R., and J. J. Zhao, eds. 2018. *Ancient Greece and China Compared*. Cambridge: Cambridge University Press.

Lo Schiavo, F. 2012. "Cyprus and Sardinia, beyond the Oxhide Ingots." In *Eastern Mediterranean Metallurgy and Metalwork in the Second Millennium BC*, edited by V. Kassianidou and G. Papasavvas, 142–50. Oxford: Oxbow Books.

Loader, N. C. 1998. *Building in Cyclopean Masonry with Special Reference to the Mycenaean Fortifications on Mainland Greece*. Jonsered: Paul Åströms Förlag.

Lock, P. 1986. "The Frankish Towers of Central Greece." *Annual of the British School at Athens* 81: 101–23.

———. 1996. "The Towers of Euboea: Lombard or Venetian, Agrarian or Strategic." In *The Archaeology of Medieval Greece*, edited by P. Lock and G. D. R. Sanders, 107–22. Oxford: Oxbow Books.

Lock, G., and B. L. Molyneaux, eds. 2006. *Confronting Scale in Archaeology: Issues of Theory and Practice*. New York: Springer.

Lohmann, H. 2002. "Ancient Roads in Attica and the Megaris." In *Ancient Roads in Greece*, edited by H. R. Goette, 73–91. Hamburg: Kovac.

———. 2005. "Prähistorischer und antiker Blei-Silberbergbau im Laurion." In *Anatolian Metal III*, edited by Ü. Yalçın, 105–36. Bochum: Deutsches Bergbau-Museum.

———. 2010. "Kiapha Thiti und der Synoikismos des Theseus." In *Attika: Archäologie einer "zentralen" Kulturlandschaft*, edited by H. Lohmnann and T. Mattern, 35–46. Wiesbaden: Harrassowitz Verlag.

Lohmann, Hans and Torsten Mattern, eds. 2010. *Attika: Archäologie einer "zentralen" Kulturlandschaft*. Wiesbaden: Harrassowitz Verlag.

Lolos, Y. G. 2001a. "Dark Age Citadels in Southern Salamis." *In Defensive Settlements of the Aegean and the Eastern Mediterranean after c. 1200 B.C.*, edited by V. Karageorghis and C. E. Morris, 115–36. Nicosia: Trinity College Dublin and the Anastasios G. Leventis Foundation.

———. 2001b. "Kaphereus and Kyme: Late Bronze Age shipwrecks off Euboea, A Summary." In *6th International Symposium on Ship Construction in Antiquity, Lamia, 28, 29, 30 August 1996: Proceedings*, edited by H. Tzalas, 399–400. Athens: Hellenic Institute for the Preservation of Nautical Tradition.

———. 2007. "Το μυκηναϊκό ἄστυ της Σαλαμίνας.", In Έπαλθον: Αρχαιολογικό συνέδριο προς τιμήν του Αδώνιδος Κ. Κύρου, Πορος, edited by In E. Konsolaki-Yiannopoulou, 221–52. Athens: Demos Porou.

———. 2012. Σαλαμίς I: Συμβολή στην αρχαιολογία του Σαρωνικού. Ioannina: Πανεπιστήμιο Ιωαννίνων.

López-Ruiz, C., and B. R. Doak, eds. 2019. *The Oxford Handbook of the Phoenician and Punic Mediterranean.* Oxford: Oxford University Press.

Lucas, J. C. A. Murray, and S. Owen, eds. 2019. *Greek Colonization in Local Contexts: Case Studies in Colonial Interactions.* Oxford: Oxbow Books.

Luke, J. 2003. *Ports of Trade, Al Mina and Geometric Greek Pottery in the Levant.* Oxford: Archaeopress.

Mac Sweeney, N. 2016. "Anatolian-Aegean Interactions in the Early Iron Age: Migration, Mobility, and the Movement of People." In *Of Odysseys and Oddities: Scales and Modes of Interaction between Prehistoric Aegean Societies and Their Neighbors*, edited by B. P. Molloy, 411–33. Oxford: Oxbow Books.

———. 2017. "Separating Fact from Fiction in the Ionian Migration." *Hesperia* 86, no. 3 (July–September): 379–421.

———. 2018. *Troy: Myth, City, Icon.* New York: Bloomsbury.

Maggidis, C. 2020. "Glas and Boeotia." In *Collapse and Transformation: The Late Bronze Age to Early Iron Age in the Aegean*, edited by G. D. Middleton, 107–20. Oxford: Oxbow Books.

Malkin, I. 1987. *Religion and Colonization in Ancient Greece.* Leiden: Brill.

———. 1998. *The Returns of Odysseus: Colonization and Ethnicity.* Berkeley: University of California Press.

———. 2011. *A Small Greek World: Networks in the Ancient Mediterranean.* Oxford: Oxford University Press.

Maner, Ç. 2012. "A Comparative Study of Hittite and Mycenaean Fortification Architecture." In *Athanasia: The Earthly, the Celestial and the Underworld in the Mediterranean from the Late Bronze Age and the Early Iron Age*, edited by N. C. Stampolidis, A. Kanta, and A. Giannikouri, 53–64. Heraklion: University of Crete.

Manning, S. W. 2010. "Chronology and Terminology." In *The Oxford Handbook of the Bronze Age Aegean*, edited by E. Cline, 11–28. Oxford: Oxford University Press.

———. 2018. "The Development of Complex Society on Crete: The Balance between Wider Context and Local Agency." In *Regional Approaches to Society and Complexity: Studies in Honor of John F. Cherry*, edited by A. R. Knodell and T. P. Leppard, 29–58. Sheffield: Equinox.

Maran, J. 1992. *Kiapha Thiti. Ergebnisse der Ausgrabungen II2 (2.Jt.v.Chr.: Keramik und Kleinfunde).* Marburg: Koch.

———. 1993. "Middle and Late Bronze Age Pottery from Kiapha Thiti (Attica): A Preliminary Report." In *Wace and Blegen: Pottery as Evidence for Trade in the Aegean Bronze Age 1939–1989*, edited by C. Zerner, P. Zerner, and J. Winder, 201–7. Amsterdam: J. C. Gieben.

———. 2001. "Political and Religious Aspects of Architectural Change on the Upper Citadel of Tiryns. The Case of Building T." In *Potnia: Deities and Religion in the Aegean Bronze Age*, edited by R. Laffineur and R. Hägg, 113–22. Liège: Université de Liège.

Maran, J., and J. C. Wright. 2020. "The Rise of the Mycenaean Culture, Palatial Administration, and Its Collapse." In *A Companion to the Archaeology of Early Greece and the Mediterranean*, edited by I. S. Lemos and A. Kotsonas, 99–132. Hoboken, NJ: John Wiley & Sons.

Marcus, J. 1998. "The Peaks and Valleys of Ancient States: An Extension of the Dynamic Model." In *Archaic States*, edited by G. M. Feinman and J. Marcus, 59–94. Santa Fe, NM: School of American Research Press.

Marcus, J., and J. A. Sabloff, eds. 2008. *The Ancient City: New Perspectives on Urbanism in the Old and New Worlds*. Santa Fe, NM: School for Advanced Research Press.

Marinatos, S. 1972. "Pre-Hellenic and Proto-Hellenic Discoveries at Marathon." In *Acta of the 2nd International Colloquium on Aegean Prehistory: The First Arrival of Indo-European Elements in Greece*, edited by E. Arditis, 184–90. Athens: Ministry of Culture and Sciences, General Directorate of Antiquities.

Mariolakos, I. V. Nikolopoulos, I. Bantekas, and N. Palyvos. 2010. "Oracles on Faults: A Probable Location of a 'Lost' Oracle of Apollo near Oroviai (Northern Euboea Island, Greece) Viewed in Its Geological and Geomorphological Context." *Bulletin of the Geological Society of Greece* 43, no. 2: 829–44.

Markoe, G. E. 1992. "In Pursuit of Metal: Phoenicians and Greeks in Italy." In *Greece Between East and West: 10th–8th Centuries BC*, edited by G. Kopcke and I. Tokumaru, 61–84. Mainz: Philipp von Zabern.

Martin, S., and N. Grube. 2008. *Chronicle of the Maya Kings and Queens: Deciphering the Dynasties of the Ancient Maya*. 2nd ed. New York: Thames and Hudson.

Martin, R., and P. Sunley. 2007. "Complexity Thinking and Evolutionary Economic Geography." *Journal of Economic Geography* 7, no. 5 (September): 573–601.

Mastrogiannopoulou, V., and A. Sampson. 2017. "Euboea During the Neolithic Period: A Review of the Evidence." In *An Island between Two Worlds: The Archaeology of Euboea from Prehistoric to Byzantine Times*, edited by Ž. Tankosić, F. Mavridis, and M. Kosma, 33–50. Athens: Norwegian Institute at Athens.

Mauss, M. 1935. "Les techniques du corps." *Journal de Psychologie* 32: 271–93.

Mazarakis Ainian, A. 1987. "Geometric Eretria." *Antike Kunst* 30, no. 1: 3–24.

———. 1997. *From Rulers' Dwellings to Temples: Architecture, Religion and Society in Early Iron Age Greece (1100–700 B.C.)*. Jonsered: Paul Åströms Förlag.

———. 2002. "Les fouilles d'Oropos et la fonction des périboles dans les agglomérations du début de l'Âge du Fer." In *Habitat et urbanisme dans le monde grec de la fin des palais mycéniens à la prise de Milet (494 av. J.-C.)*, edited by J.-M. Luce, 183–227. Toulouse: Presses Universitaires du Mirail.

———, ed. 2006. *Αρχαιολογικό έργο Θεσσαλίας και Στερεάς Ελλάδας 1*. Volos: Ministry of Culture and University of Thessaly.

———. 2007a. *Ἔνδον σκάπτε*: The Tale of an Excavation." In *Oropos and Euboea in the Early Iron Age*, edited by A. Mazarakis Ainian, 21–59. Volos: University of Thessaly.

———, ed. 2007b. *Oropos and Euboea in the Early Iron Age*. Volos: University of Thessaly Press.

———, ed. 2009. *Αρχαιολογικό έργο Θεσσαλίας και Στερεάς Ελλάδας 2*. Volos: Ministry of Culture and University of Thessaly.

———, ed. 2011. *The "Dark Ages" Revisited: Acts of an International Symposium in Memory of William D. E. Coulson*. Volos: University of Thessaly.

———. 2012a. "Des quartiers specializes d'artisans à l'époque géométrique?" In *"Quartiers" artisanaux en Gréce ancienne: Une perspective méditerranéenne*, edited by A. Esposito and G. M. Sanidas, 125–54. Lille: Septentrion Presses Universitaires.

———. 2012b. "Euboean Mobility towards the North: New Evidence from the Sporades." In *Cyprus and the Aegean in the Early Iron Age: The Legacy of Nicolas Coldstream*, edited by M. Iakovou, 53–75. Nicosia: Bank of Cyprus Cultural Foundation.

———, ed. 2012c. *Αρχαιολογικό έργο Θεσσαλίας και Στερεάς Ελλάδας 3*. Volos: Ministry of Culture and Tourism and University of Thessaly.

———, ed. 2016. *Αρχαιολογικό έργο Θεσσαλίας και Στερεάς Ελλάδας 4*. Volos: Ministry of Culture, Education and Religion and University of Thessaly.

———. 2017. "Conservativism versus Innovation: Architectural Forms in Early Archaic Greece." In *Interpreting the Seventh Century BC: Tradition and Innovation*, edited by X. Charalambidou and C. Morgan, 173–85. Oxford: Archaeopress.

———, ed. 2020. *Αρχαιολογικό έργο Θεσσαλίας και Στερεάς Ελλάδας 5*. Volos: Ministry of Culture, Education and Religion and University of Thessaly.

Mazarakis Ainian, A., and A. Alexandridou. 2011. "The 'Sacred House' of the Academy Revisited." In *The "Dark Ages" Revisited: Acts of an International Symposium in Memory of William D. E. Coulson*. Vol. 1, edited by A. Mazarakis Ainian, 165–89. Volos: University of Thessaly.

Mazarakis Ainian, A., A. Alexandridou, and X. Charalambidou, eds. 2017. *Regional Stories toward a New Perception of the Early Greek World*. Volos: University of Thessaly.

Mazarakis Ainian, A. and A. Livieratou. 2010. "The Academy of Plato in the Early Iron Age." In *Attika: Archäologie einer "zentralen" Kulturlandschaft*, edited by H. Lohmann and T. Mattern, 87–100. Wiesbaden: Harrassowitz Verlag.

Mazarakis Ainian, A., and V. Vlachou 2014. "Archaeometric Analysis of Early Iron Age Pottery Samples from Oropos: Local or Euboean Production?" In *Archaeometric Analyses of Euboean and Euboean Related Pottery: New Results and Their Interpretations*, edited by M. Kerschner and I. S. Lemos, 95–107. Vienna: Österreichisches Archäologisches Institut.

McAnany, P., and N. Yoffee, eds. 2010. *Questioning Collapse: Human Resilience, Ecological Vulnerability, and the Aftermath of Empire*. Cambridge: Cambridge University Press.

McConnell, J. R., A. I. Wilson, A. Stohl, M. M. Arienzo, N. J. Chellman, S. Eckhardt, E. M. Thompson, A.M. Pollard, and J.P. Steffensen. 2018. "Lead Pollution Recorded in Greenland Ice Indicates European Emissions Tracked Plagues, Wars, and Imperial Expansion During Antiquity." *Proceedings of the National Academy of Sciences* 115, no. 22 (May): 5726–31.

McCoy, M., and T. Ladefoged, 2009. "New Developments in the Use of Spatial Technology in Archaeology." *Journal of Archaeological Research* 17, no. 3 (September): 263–95.

McDonald, W. A., W. D. E. Coulson, and J. Rosser, eds. 1983. *Excavations at Nichoria in Southwest Greece, Vol. III: Dark Age and Byzantine Occupation*. Minneapolis: University of Minnesota Press.

McGuire, R. H., and D. J. Saitta. 1996. "Although They Have Petty Captains, They Obey Them Badly: The Dialectics of Prehispanic Western Pueblo Social Organization." *American Antiquity* 61, no. 2 (April): 197–216.

McInerney, J. 1999. *The Folds of Parnassos: Land and Ethnicity in Ancient Phokis*. Austin: University of Texas Press.

———. 2011. "Delphi and Phokis: A Network Theory Approach." *Pallas: Revue d'Etudes Antiques* 87: 95–106.

Mee, C. B., and W. G. Cavanagh. 1984. "Mycenaean Tombs as Evidence for Social and Political Organisation." *Oxford Journal of Archaeology* 3, no. 3 (November): 45–64.

Michailidou, A. 2008. "Late Bronze Age Economy: Copper/Bronze in Linear B Script and Material Evidence." In *Colloquium Romanum: atti del XII colloquio internazionale di micenologia*, edited by A. Sacconi, M. Del Freo, L. Godart, and M. Negri, 521–40. Pisa: Fabrizio Serra.

Middleton, G. D. 2017a. *Understanding Collapse: Ancient History and Modern Myths*. Cambridge: Cambridge University Press.

———. 2017b. "The Show Must Go On: Collapse, Resilience, and Transformation in 21st-Century Archaeology." *Reviews in Anthropology* 46, nos. 2–3 (August): 78–105.

———, ed. 2020. *Collapse and Transformation: The Late Bronze Age to Early Iron Age in the Aegean*. Oxford: Oxbow Books.

Milgrim, S. 1967. "The Small World Problem." *Psychology Today* 1, no. 1 (May): 60– 67.

Miller, S. G. 2016. "Hellenistic Royal Palaces." In *A Companion to Greek Architecture*, edited by M. Miles, 288–99. Malden, MA: Wiley-Blackwell.

Mills, B. 2017. "Social Network Analysis in Archaeology." *Annual Review of Anthropology* 46: 379–97.

Mills, B., M. A. Peeples, W. R. Haas Jr., L. Borck, J. J. Clark, and J. M. Roberts Jr. 2015. "Multiscalar Perspectives on Social Networks in the Late Prehispanic Southwest." *American Antiquity* 80, no. 1 (January): 3–24.

Mills, S. 1997. *Theseus, Tragedy, and the Athenian Empire*. Oxford: Clarendon.

Minetti, A. E., C. Moia, G. S. Roi, D. Susta, and G. Ferretti. 2002. "Energy Cost of Walking and Running at Extreme Uphill and Downhill Slopes." *Journal of Applied Physiology* 93: 1039–46.

Mitchell, M. 2009. *Complexity: A Guided Tour*. Oxford: Oxford University Press.

Molloy, B. 2010. "Swords and Swordsmanship in the Aegean Bronze Age." *American Journal of Archaeology* 114, no. 3 (July): 403–28.

———, ed. 2016. *Of Odysseys and Oddities: Scales and Modes of Interaction between Prehistoric Aegean Societies and Their Neighbors*. Oxford: Oxbow Books.

Mommsen, H. 2014. "Provenancing by Neutron Activation Analyses and Results of Euboean and Euboean Related Pottery." In *Archaeometric Analyses of Euboean and Euboean Related Pottery: New Results and Their Interpretations*, edited by M. Kerschner and I. S. Lemos, 13–36. Vienna: Österreichisches Archäologisches Institut.

Morgan, C. 1993. "The Origins of Pan-Hellenism." In *Greek Sanctuaries: New Approaches*, edited by N. Marinatos and R. Hägg, 18–44. London: Routledge.

———. 2001. "Ethne, Ethnicity, and Early Greek States, ca. 1200–480 B.C.: An Archaeological Perspective." In *Ancient Perceptions of Greek Ethnicity*, edited by I. Malkin, 75–112. Cambridge, MA: Center for Hellenic Studies.

———. 2003. *Early Greek States Beyond the Polis*. London: Routledge.

———. 2006. "Ethne in the Peloponnese and Central Greece." In *Ancient Greece: From the Mycenaean Palaces to the Age of Homer*, edited by S. Deger-Jalkotzy and I. S. Lemos, 233–54. Edinburgh: Edinburgh University Press.

Morpurgo-Davies, A. 1979. "Terminology of Power and Terminology of Work in Greek and Linear B." In *Colloquium Mycenaeum*, edited by E. Risch and H. Mühlestein, 87–108. Geneva: Université de Neuchâtel.

Morris, I. 1986. "The Use and Abuse of Homer." *Classical Antiquity* 5, no. 1 (April): 81–138.

———. 1987. *Burial and Ancient Society: The Rise of the Greek City-State*. Cambridge: Cambridge University Press.

———. 1989. "Circulation, Deposition and the Formation of the Greek Iron Age." *Man* 24, no. 3 (September): 502–19.

———. 1994. "Archaeologies of Greece." In *Classical Greece: Ancient Histories and Modern Archaeologies*, edited by I. Morris, 8–47. Cambridge: Cambridge University Press.

———. 1997a. "An Archaeology of Equalities? The Greek City-States." In *The Archaeology of City-States: Cross-Cultural Approaches*, edited by D. L. Nichols and T. Charlton, 91–105. Washington, DC: Smithsonian Institution Press.

———. 1997b. "Periodization and the Heroes: Inventing a Dark Age." In *Inventing an Ancient Culture: Historicism, Periodization, and the Ancient World*, edited by M. Golden and P. Toohey, 96–131. London: Routledge.

———. 2000. *Archaeology as Cultural History: Words and Things in Iron Age Greece*. Malden, MA: Wiley-Blackwell.

———. 2009. "The Eighth-Century Revolution." In *A Companion to Archaic Greece*, edited by K. A. Raaflaub and H. van Wees, 64–80. Malden, MA: Wiley-Blackwell.

Morris, I., and A. R. Knodell. 2015. "Greek Cities in the First Millennium BCE." In *The Cambridge World History, Volume 3: Early Cities in Comparative Perspective, 4000 BCE— CE 1200*, edited by N. Yoffee, 343–63. Cambridge: Cambridge University Press.

Morris, I., and B. B. Powell, eds. 1997. *A New Companion to Homer*. Leiden: Brill.

Morris, S. P. 1992. *Daidalos and the Origins of Greek Art*. Princeton, NJ: Princeton University Press.

———. 2009/2010. "Prehistoric Torone: A Bronze Age Emporion in the Northern Aegean. Preliminary Report on the Lekythos Excavations 1986 and 1988–1990." *Mediterranean Archaeology* 22/23: 1–67.

Morris, S. P., J. K. Papadopoulos, M. Bessios, A. Athanassiadou, and K. Noulas. 2020. "The Ancient Methone Archaeological Project: A Preliminary Report on Fieldwork, 2014–2017." *Hesperia* 89, no. 4 (October–December): 659–723.

Mountjoy, P. A. 1983. *Orchomenos V: Mycenaean Pottery from Orchomenos, Eutresis, and Other Boeotian Sites*. Munich: Verlag der Bayerischen Akademie der Wissenschaften.

———. 1990. "Regional Mycenaean Pottery." *Annual of the British School at Athens* 85: 245–70.

———. 1995a. *Mycenaean Athens*. Gothenburg: Paul Åströms Förlag.

———. 1995b. "Thorikos Mine No. 3: The Mycenaean Pottery." *Annual of the British School at Athens* 90: 195–228.

———. 1998. "The East Aegean-West Anatolian Interface in the Late Bronze Age: Mycenaeans and the Kingdom of Ahhiyawa." *Anatolian Studies* 48: 33–67.

———. 1999. *Regional Mycenaean Decorated Pottery*. Rahden: Verlag Marie Leidorf.

———. 2006. "Mycenaean Pictorial Pottery from Anatolia in the Transitional LH IIIB2– LH IIIC Early and the LH IIIC phases." In *Pictorial Pursuits: Figurative Painting on

Mycenaean and Geometric Pottery, edited by E. Rystedt and B. Wells, 107–21. Stockholm: Svenska Institutet i Athen.

———. 2015. "The North-East Peloponnese and the Near East: Ceramic Evidence for Contacts in LH III." In *Mycenaeans Up to Date: The Archaeology of the North-Eastern Peloponnese—Current Concepts and New Directions*, edited by A.-L. Schallin and I. Tournavitou. Stockholm: Svenska Institutet i Athen.

Muhly, J. D. 2008. "Metal Deposits in the Aegean Region." In *Anatolian Metal IV*, edited by Ü. Yalçin, 67–75. Bochum: Deutches Bergbau-Museum Bochum.

Müller, K. O. 1824. *Die Dorier*. Breslau: Josef Max.

Müller, S. 1992. "Delphes et sa région à l'époque mycénienne." *Bulletin de Correspondance Hellénique* 116: 445–96.

Müller-Çelka, S., T. Krapf, and S. Verdan. 2013. "La céramique helladique du sanctuaire d'Apollon Daphnéphoros à Érétrie (Eubée)." In *Bulletin de correspondance hellénique* 135, no. 1: 21–55.

Munn, M. H. 1989. "New Light on Panakton and the Attic-Boiotian Frontier." In *Boiotika, Vorträge vom 5. Internationalen Böotien-Kolloquium zu Ehren von Professor Dr. Siegfried*, edited by H. Beister and J. Buckler, 231–44. Munich: Lauffer.

———. 1996. "The First Excavations at Panakton on the Attic-Boiotian Frontier." In *Boeotia Antiqua VI*, edited by J. M. Fossey, 47–58. Amsterdam: J. C. Gieben.

Munn, M. H., and M. L. Z. Munn. 1989. "Studies on the Attic-Boiotian Frontier: The Stanford Skourta Plain Project, 1985." *Boeotia Antiqua I: Papers on Recent Work in Boeotian Archaeology and History*, edited by J. M. Fossey, 73–127. Amsterdam: J. C. Gieber.

———. 1990. "On the Frontiers of Attica and Boiotia: The Results of the Stanford Skourta Plain Project." In *Essays in the Topography, History and Archaeology of Boiotia*, edited by A. Schachter, 33–40. Montreal: Department of Classics, McGill University.

Murray, R. L., Jr. 1975. *The Protogeometric Style: The First Greek Style*. Gothenburg: Paul Åströms Förlag.

Murray, S. C. 2013. "Trade, Imports, and Society in Early Greece: 1300–900 B.C.E." PhD diss., Stanford University.

———. 2017. *The Collapse of the Mycenaean Economy: Imports, Trade, and Institutions 1300–700 BCE*. Cambridge: Cambridge University Press.

———. 2018a. "Imported Exotica and Mortuary Ritual at Perati in LH IIIC East Attica." *American Journal of Archaeology* 122, no. 1 (January): 33–64.

———. 2018b. "Lights and Darks: Data, Labeling, Language, and Paradigm in the History of Scholarship on Early Iron Age Greece." *Hesperia* 87, no. 1 (January–March): 17–54.

Murray, S. C., C. E. Pratt, R. P. Stephan, M. C. McHugh, and G. K. Erny. Forthcoming. "The 2019 Bays of East Attica Regional Survey (BEARS) Project." *Mouseion*.

Mylonas, G. E. 1975. *Τὸ δυτικὸν νεκροταφεῖον τῆς Ἐλευσῖνος*. Athens: Archaeological Society at Athens.

Mylonas Shear, I. 1999. "The Western Approach to the Athenian Akropolis." *Journal of Hellenic Studies* 119: 86–127.

Nagy, G. 1996. *Homeric Questions*. Austin: University of Texas Press.

Nakassis, D. 2012. "Prestige and Interest: Feasting and the King at Mycenaean Pylos." *Hesperia* 81, no. 1 (January): 1–30.

———. 2013a. *Individuals and Society in Mycenaean Pylos*. Leiden: Brill.

———. 2013b. "Structuration and the State in Mycenaean Greece." In *Agency in Ancient Writing*, edited by J. Englehardt, 231–47. Boulder: University Press of Colorado.

Nakassis, D., M. L. Galaty, and W. A. Parkinson. 2016. "Reciprocity in Aegean Palatial Societies: Gifts, Debt, and the Foundations of Economic Exchange." *Journal of Mediterranean Archaeology* 29, no. 1 (June): 61–132.

Nakassis, D., W. A. Parkinson, and M. L. Galaty. 2011. "Redistributive Economies from a Theoretical and Cross-Cultural Perspective." *American Journal of Archaeology* 115, no. 2 (April): 177–84.

Nakassis, D., K. Pluta, and J. Hruby. 2021. "The Pylos Tablets Digital Project: Aegean scripts in the 21st century," in *New Approaches to Ancient Material Culture in the Greek & Roman World*, edited by C.L. Cooper, 161–71. Leiden: Brill.

Nazou, M. 2017. "Euboean Connections with Attica and Kea: A View from Final Neolithic and Late Early Bronze Age II Pottery." In *An Island between Two Worlds: The Archaeology of Euboea from Prehistoric to Byzantine Times*, edited by Ž. Tankosić, F. Mavridis, and M. Kosma, 111–20. Athens: Norwegian Institute at Athens.

Negbi, O. 1992. "Early Phoenician Presence in the Mediterranean Islands: A Reappraisal." *American Journal of Archaeology* 96, no. 4 (October): 599–615.

Niemeier, W.-D. 1999. "Mycenaeans and Hittites in War in Western Asia Minor." In *Polemos: Le context guerrier en Égée à l'âge du Bronze*, edited by R. Laffineur, 141–55. Liège: University of Liège.

———. 2005. "The Minoans and Mycenaeans in Western Asia Minor: Settlement, Emporia, or Acculturation?" In *Emporia: Aegeans in the Central and Eastern Mediterranean*, edited by R. Laffineur and E. Greco, 199–204. Liège: University of Liège.

———. 2009. "Kalapodi. The Sanctuary of Apollo at Abai." In *Archaeology: Euboea and Central Greece*, edited by A. G. Vlachopoulos, 302–5. Athens: Melissa Publishing House.

———. 2013. "Kultkontinuität von der Bronzezeit bis zur römischen Kaiserzeit im Orakel-Heiligtum des Apollon von Abai (Kalapodi)." In *Sanktuar und Ritual: Heilige Plätze im archäologischen Befund*, edited by I. Gerlach and D. Raue, 33–42. Rahden: Verlag Marie Leidorf.

———. 2016. "Ritual in the Mycenaean Sanctuary at Abai (Kalapodi)." In *Metaphysis: Ritual, Myth and Symbolism in the Aegean Bronze Age*, edited by E. Alram-Stern, F. Blakolmer, S. Deger-Jalkotzy, R. Laffineur, and J. Weilhartner, 303–10. Leuven: Peeters.

Niemeyer, H. G. 2000. "The Early Phoenician City-States on the Mediterranean: Archaeological Elements for Their Description." In *A Comparative Study of Thirty City-State Cultures: An Investigation Conducted by the Copenhagen Polis Centre*, edited by M. H. Hansen, 89–115. Copenhagen: Royal Danish Academy of Sciences and Letters.

———. 2006. "The Phoenicians in the Mediterranean, Between Expansion and Colonisation: A Non-Greek Model of Overseas Settlement and Presence." In *Greek Colonisation: An Account of Greek Colonies and Other Settlements Overseas*. Vol. 1, edited by G. R. Tsetskhladze, 143–68. Leiden: Brill.

Nightingale, G. 2009. "Glass and Faience Beads from Perati: The End of the Mycenaean Tradition, the Beginning of the New Tradition of the Early Iron Age in Greece." In *Δῶρον: τιμητικός τόμος για τον καθηγητή Σπύρο Ιακωβίδη*, edited by D. Danielidou, 495–512. Athens: Ακαδημία Αθηνών, Κέντρον Ερεύνης της Αρχαιότητος.

Nijboer, A. J. 2008. "A Phoenician Family Tomb, Lefkandi, Huelva and the Tenth Century BC in the Mediterranean." In *Beyond the Homeland: Markers in Phoenician Chronology*, edited by C. Sagona, 365–77. Leuven: Peeters.

Nijboer, A. J., and J. van der Plicht. 2006. "An Interpretation of the Radiocarbon Determinations." of the Oldest Indigenous-Phoenician Stratum Thus Far, Excavated at Huelva, Tartessos (South-West Spain)." *Bulletin Antieke Beschaving* 81: 31–36.

Nikoloudis, S. 2008a. "Multiculturalism in the Mycenaean World." In *Anatolian Interfaces: Hittites, Greeks and Their Neighbors*, edited by B. J. Collins, M. R. Bachvarova, and I. C. Rutherford, 45–56. Oxford: Oxbow Books.

———. 2008b. "The Role of the *ra-wa-ke-ta*: Insights from PY Un 718." In *Colloquium Romanum: atti del XII colloquio internazionale di micenologia*, edited by A. Sacconi, M. Del Freo, L. Godart, and M. Negri, 587–94. Pisa: Fabrizio Serra.

Nikolopoulos, V. 2015. "Η προϊστορική εποχή της Εύβοιας." In *Αρχαιολογικές συμβολές. Τόμος Γ: Βοιωτία & Εύβοια*, edited by S. Oikonomou, 165–84. Athens: Museum of Cycladic Art.

Nosch, M.-L. 2008. "Administrative Practices in Mycenaean Palace Administration and Economy." In *Colloquium Romanum: atti del XII colloquio internazionale di micenologia*, edited by A. Sacconi, M. Del Freo, L. Godart, and M. Negri, 595–604. Pisa: Fabrizio Serra.

Nosch, M.-L., and R. Laffineur, eds. 2012. *Kosmos: Jewellery, Adornment and Textiles in the Aegean Bronze Age*. Leuven: Peeters.

Nowicki, K. 2000. *Defensible Sites in Crete, c. 1200–800 BC (LM IIIB/C through Early Geometric)*. Liège: Université de Liège.

O'Brien, S. 2017. "Boredom with the Apocalypse: Resilience, Regeneration, and Their Consequences for Archaeological Interpretation." In *Crisis to Collapse: The Archaeology of Social Breakdown*, edited by T. Cunningham and J. Driessen, 295–303. Louvain: Presses universitaires de Louvain.

Oggiano, I. 2000. "La ceramica fenicia di Sant'Imbenia (Alghero-SS)." In *La ceramica fenicia di Sardegna: Dati, problematiche, confronti*, edited by P. Bartoloni and L. Camanella, 235–58. Rome: Consiglio nazionale delle ricerche.

Oldfather, W. A. 1916. "Studies in the History and Topography of Locris I." *American Journal of Archaeology* 20, no. 1 (January–March): 32–61.

Olivier, J.-P., J. L. Melena, and C. Piteros. 1990. "Les inscriptions en linéaire B des nodules de Thèbes (1982): la fouille, les documents, les possibilités d'interprétation." *Bulletin de correspondance hellénique* 114, no 1: 101–84.

Olsen, B., M. Shanks, T. Webmore, and C. Witmore. 2012. *Archaeology: The Discipline of Things*. Berkeley: University of California Press.

Ong, W. J. 1982. *Orality and Literacy: The Technologizing of the Word*. London: Methuen.

Oren, E. D. 2000. *The Sea Peoples and Their World: A Reassessment*. Philadelphia: University Museum.

Orgeolet, R., D. Skorda, J. Zurbach, L. de Barbarin, R.-M. Bérard, B. Chevaux, J. Hubert, et al. 2017. "Kirrha 2008–2015: un bilan d'étape, 1. La fouille et les structures archéologiques." *Bulletin de correspondance hellénique* 141, no. 1: 41–116.

Osborne, R. 1985. *Demos: The Discovery of Classical Attika*. Cambridge: Cambridge University Press.

———. 1989. "A Crisis in Archaeological History? The Seventh Century B.C. in Attica." *Annual of the British School at Athens* 84: 297–322.

———. 1994. "Archaeology, the Salaminioi, and the Politics of Sacred Space in Archaic Attica." In *Placing the Gods: Sanctuaries and Sacred Space in Ancient Greece*, edited by S. E. Alcock and R. Osborne, 143–60. Oxford: Clarendon.

———. 1998. "Early Greek Colonization? The Nature of Greek Settlement in the West." In *Archaic Greece: New Approaches and New Evidence*, edited by N. Fisher and H. van Wees, 251–70. London: Gerald Duckworth.

———. 2009. *Greece in the Making, 1200–479 BC*. 2nd ed. London: Routledge.

———. 2020. "Collapse and Transformation in Athens and Attica." In *Collapse and Transformation: The Late Bronze Age to Early Iron Age in the Aegean*, edited by G. D. Middleton, 137–44. Oxford: Oxbow Books.

Owen, S., and L. Preston, eds. 2009. *Inside the City in the Greek World: Studies of Urbanism from the Bronze Age to the Hellenistic Period*. Oxford: Oxbow Books.

Padgug, R. A. 1972. "Eleusis and the Union of Attika." *Greek, Roman, and Byzantine Studies* 13, no. 2: 135–50.

Pakkanen, J., and P. Pakkanen. 2000. "The Toumba Building at Lefkandi: Some Methodological Reflections on Its Plan and Function." *Annual of the British School at Athens* 95: 239–52.

Palaima, T. G. 1995. "The Nature of the Mycenaean Wanax: Non-Indo-European Origins and Priestly Functions." In *The Role of the Ruler in the Prehistoric Aegean*, edited by P. Rehak, 119–39. Liège: Université de Liège.

———. 2006. "*Wanaks* and Related Power Terms in Mycenaean and Later Greek." In *Ancient Greece: From the Mycenaean Palaces to the Age of Homer*, edited by S. Deger-Jalkotzy and I. S. Lemos, 53–71. Edinburgh: Edinburgh University Press.

———. 2010. "Linear B." In *The Oxford Handbook of the Bronze Age Aegean*, edited by E. Cline, 356–72. Oxford. Oxford University Press.

———. 2011. "Euboea, Athens, Thebes and Kadmos: The Implications of the Linear B References." In *Euboea and Athens*, edited by D. W. Rupp and J. E. Tomlinson, 53–75. Athens: Canadian Institute in Greece.

———. 2015. "The Mycenaean Mobilization of Labor in Agriculture and Building Projects: Institutions, Individuals, Compensation, and Status in the Linear B Tablets." In *Labor in the Ancient World*, edited by P. Steinkeller and M. Hudson, 617–48. Dresden: ISLET-Verlag.

Palaiokrassa-Kopitsa, L, and E. Vivliodetis. 2015. "The Sanctuaries of Artemis Mounichia and Zeus Parnessios: Their Relation to the Religious and Social Life in the Athenian City-State until the End of the 7th Century B.C." In *Pots, Workshops and Early Iron Age Society: Function and Role of Ceramics in Early Greece*, edited by V. Vlachou, 155–80. Brussels: CReA-Patrimoine.

Palme-Koufa, A. 1996. "Die Graffiti auf der Keramik." In *Kalapodi I: Ergebnisse der Ausgrabungen im Heiligtum der Artemis und des Apollon von Hyampolis in der antiken Phokis*, edited by R. Felsch, 273–331. Mainz: Verlag Philipp von Zabern.

Palmer, R. 1992. "Wheat and Barley in Mycenaean Society." In *Mykenaïka. Actes du IXe Colloque international sur les textes mycéniens et égéens*, edited by J.-P. Olivier, 475–97. Paris: Diffusion de Boccard.

———. 1994. *Wine in the Mycenaean Palace Economy*. Liège: Université de Liège.

———. 1998–99. "Models in Linear B Landholding: An Analysis of Methodology." In *A-na-qo-ta. Studies Presented to J. T. Killen*, edited by J. Bennet and J. Driessen, 223–50. Minos, vols. 33–34. Salamanca: Ediciones Universidad de Salamanca.

———. 2001. "Bridging the Gap: The Continuity of Greek Agriculture from the Mycenaean to the Historical Period." In *Prehistory and History: Ethnicity, Class and Political Economy*, edited by D. W. Tandy, 41–84. Montréal: Black Rose Books.

————. 2008. "Wheat and Barley in Mycenaean Society 15 Years Later." In *Colloquium Romanum: atti del XII colloquio internazionale di micenologia*, edited by A. Sacconi, M. Del Freo, L. Godart, and M. Negri, 621–39. Pisa: Fabrizio Serra.

Pantou, P. A. 2010. "Mycenaean Dimini in Context: Investigating Regional Variability and Socioeconomic Complexities in Late Bronze Age Greece." *American Journal of Archaeology* 114, no. 3 (July): 381–401.

Papadimitriou, N. 2001. *Built Chamber Tombs of Middle and Late Bronze Age Date in Mainland Greece and the Islands*. Oxford: John and Erica Hedges.

————. 2017. "Συνοίκησις in Mycenaean Times? The Political and Cultural Geography of Attica in the Second Millennium BCE." *CHS Research Bulletin* 5, no. 2: http://nrs.harvard .edu/urn-3:hlnc.essay:PapadimitriouN.Synoikisis_in_Mycenaean_Times.2017.

Papadimitriou, N., and M. B. Cosmopoulos. 2020. "The Political Geography of Attica in the Middle and Late Bronze Age." In *Athens and Attica in Prehistory*, edited by N. Papadimitriou, J. C. Wright, S. Fachard, and N. Polychronakou-Sgouritsa, 373–86. Oxford: Archaeopress.

Papadimitriou, N., J. C. Wright, S. Fachard, and N. Polychronakou-Sgouritsa, eds. 2020. *Athens and Attica in Prehistory*. Oxford: Archaeopress.

Papadopoulos, J. K. 1989. "An Early Iron Age Potter's Kiln at Torone." *Mediterranean Archaeology* 2: 9–44.

————. 1993. "To Kill a Cemetery: The Athenian Kerameikos and the Early Iron Age in the Aegean." *Journal of Mediterranean Archaeology* 6, no. 2 (December): 175–206.

————. 1994. "Early Iron Age Potters' Marks in the Aegean." *Hesperia* 63, no. 4 (October–December): 437–507.

————. 1996a. "Dark Age Greece." In *The Oxford Companion to Archaeology*, edited by B. M. Fagan, 253–55. Oxford: Oxford University Press.

————. 1996b. "Euboians in Macedonia? A Closer Look." *Oxford Journal of Archaeology* 15, no. 2 (July): 151–81.

————. 1996c. "The Original Kerameikos of Athens and the Siting of the Classical Agora," *Greek, Roman and Byzantine Studies* 37: 107–28.

————. 1997. "Phantom Euboians." *Journal of Mediterranean Archaeology* 10, no. 2 (December): 191–219.

————. 1999. "Archaeology, Myth-History, and the Tyranny of the Text: Chalkidike, Torone, and Thucydides." *Oxford Journal of Archaeology* 18: 377–94.

————. 2001. "Magna Achaea: Akhaian Late Geometric and Archaic Pottery in South Italy and Sicily." *Hesperia* 70, no. 4 (October–December): 373–460.

————. 2003. *Ceramicus Redivivus: The Early Iron Age Potters' Field in the Area of the Classical Athenian Agora*. Princeton, NJ: American School of Classical Studies at Athens.

————. 2004. Review of *The Protogeometric Aegean: The Archaeology of the Late Eleventh and Tenth Centuries B.C.*, by I. S. Lemos. *Bryn Mawr Classical Review* 40 (March): https://bmcr.brynmawr.edu/2004/2004.03.40/.

————. 2005a. *The Early Iron Age Cemetery at Torone: Excavations Conducted by the Australian Archaeological Institute at Athens in Collaboration with the Athens Archaeological Society*. Los Angeles: Cotsen Institute of Archaeology, University of California, Los Angeles.

————. 2005b. "Inventing the Minoans: Archaeology, Modernity, and the Quest for European Identity." *Journal of Mediterranean Archaeology* 18, no. 1 (June): 87–149.

———. 2011. "'Phantom Euboians'—A Decade On." In *Euboea and Athens*, edited by D. W. Rupp and J. E. Tomlinson, 113–34. Athens: Canadian Institute in Greece.

———. 2012. "Money, Art, and the Construction of Value in the Ancient Mediterranean." In *The Construction of Value in the Ancient World*, edited by J. K. Papadopoulos and G. Urton, 261–87. Los Angeles: Cotsen Institute of Archaeology, University of California, Los Angeles.

———. 2014. "Greece in the Early Iron Age: Mobility, Commodities, Polities and Literacy." In *The Cambridge Prehistory of the Bronze and Iron Age Mediterranean*, edited by A. B. Knapp and P. van Dommelen, 178–95. Cambridge: Cambridge University Press.

———. 2015. "Owls to Athens: Imported Pottery in Early Iron Age Athens." In *Pots, Workshops and Early Iron Age Society: Function and Role of Ceramics in Early Greece*, edited by V. Vlachou, 201–15. Brussels: CReA-Patrimoine.

———. 2016a. "Komai, Colonies and Cities in Epirus and Southern Albania: The Failure of the Polis and the Rise of Urbanism on the Fringes of the Greek World." In *Of Odysseys and Oddities: Scales and Modes of Interaction between Prehistoric Aegean Societies and Their Neighbors*, edited by B. Molloy, 435–60. Oxford: Oxbow Books.

———. 2016b. "The Early History of the Greek Alphabet: New Evidence from Eretria and Methone." *Antiquity* 90, 353 (October): 1238–54.

———. 2017a. "Epilogue: Social and Historical Conclusions." In *The Early Iron Age: The Cemeteries*, by J. K. Papadopoulos and E. L. Smithson, 973–84. Princeton, NJ: American School of Classical Studies at Athens.

———. 2017b. "To Write and to Paint: More Early Iron Age Potters' Marks in the Aegean." In *Panhellenes at Methone: Graphê in Late Geometric and Protoarchaic Methone, Macedonia (ca. 700 BCE)*, edited by J. S. Clay, I. Malkin, and Y. Z. Tzifopoulos, 36–104. Berlin: De Gruyter.

———. 2018. "Greek Protohistories." *World Archaeology* 50, no. 5 (December): 690–705.

Papadopoulos, J. K., B. N. Damiata, and J. M. Marston. 2011. "Once More with Feeling: Jeremy Rutter's Plea for the Abandonment of the Term Submycenaean Revisited." In *Our Cups are Full: Pottery and Society in the Aegean Bronze Age*, edited by W. Gauß, M. Lindblom, R. A. K. Smith, and J. C. Wright, 187–202. Oxford: Archaeopress.

Papadopoulos, J. K., and E. L. Smithson. 2017. *The Early Iron Age: The Cemeteries*. Athenian Agora 36. Princeton, NJ: American School of Classical Studies at Athens.

Papadopoulos, J. K., J. F. Vedder, and T. Schreiber. 1998. "Drawing Circles: Experimental Archaeology and the Pivoted Multiple Brush." *American Journal of Archaeology* 102, no. 3 (July): 507–29.

Papadopoulos, T. J. 1999. "Warrior-Graves in Achaean Mycenaean Cemeteries." In *Polemos: Le contexte guerrier en Égée á l'âge du Bronze*, edited by R. Laffineur, 267–74. Liège: Université de Liège.

Papadopoulos, T. J., and L. Kontorli-Papadopoulou. 2014. *Vravron: The Mycenaean Cemetery*. Uppsala: Åströms.

Papadopoulou, Z. 2017. "The Funerary and Habitation Evidence of Central Greece: A Discussion on the Early Iron Age Social Organisation." In *Regional Stories Towards a New Perception of the Early Greek World*, edited by A. Mazarakis Ainian, A. Alexandridou, X. Charalambidou, 293–322. Volos: University of Thessaly Press.

Papageorgiou, D. 2008. "The Marine Environment and Its Influence on Seafaring and Maritime Routes in the Prehistoric Aegean." *European Journal of Archaeology* 11, nos. 2–3 (August): 199–222.

Papakonstantinou, M.-F. 2009. "The Spercheios Valley. Malis—Oitaia—Ainis." In *Archaeology: Euboea and Central Greece*, edited by A. G. Vlachopoulos, 316–25. Athens: Melissa Publishing House.

———, ed. 2015. Καθ᾽Οδόν . . . *Αρχαιότητες και δημόσια έργα στη Φθιώτιδα, 2004–2014*. Lamia: Ephorate of Antiquities of Fthiotida and Evrytania.

Papakonstantinou, M.-F., A. Penttinen, G. N. Tsokas, P. I. Tsourlos, A. Stampolidis, I. Fikos, G. Tassis, et al. 2013. "The Makrakomi Archaeological Landscapes Project (MALP): A preliminary report on investigations carried out in 2010–2012." *Opuscula* 6: 211–60.

Papakonstantinou, M.-F., T. Krapf, N. Koutsokera, A. Gkotsinas, A. Karathanou, K. Vouvalidis, and G. Syridis. 2016. "Αγία Παρασκευή Λαμίας, θέση 'Πλατάνια'. Το πολιτισμικό και φυσικό περιβάλλον ενός οικισμού στη δελταϊκή πεδιάδα του Σπερχειού κατά τη Μέση Εποχή του Χαλκού. " In *Αρχαιολογικό έργο Θεσσαλίας και Στερεάς Ελλάδας 4*, edited by A. Mazarakis Ainian, 989–98. Volos: Ministry of Culture and University of Thessaly.

Papakonstantinou, M.-F., C. Kritzas, and I. P. Touratsoglou. 2018. *Πύρρα. Μελέτες για την αρχαιολογία στην Κεντρική Ελλάδα προς τιμήν της Φανουρίας Δακορώνια*. Athens: Sema Editions.

Papalexandrou, N. 2005. *The Visual Poetics of Power: Warriors, Youths, and Tripods in Early Greece*. Lanham, MD: Lexington Books.

Papangeli, K., S. Fachard, and A. R. Knodell. 2018. "The Mazi Archaeological Project 2017: Test Excavations and Site Investigations." *Antike Kunst* 61: 153–63.

Papapostolou, I. A. 2011. "The New Excavations under the Early Archaic Temple of Thermos: Megaron A, Megaron B, and the Ash-Altar." In *The "Dark Ages" Revisited: Acts of an International Symposium in Memory of William D. E. Coulson*, edited by A. Mazarakis Ainian, 127–45. Volos: University of Thessaly Press.

Papathanasiou, A. 2009. "Το ανθρωπολογικό οστεολογικό υλικό από τον μυκηναϊκό θολωτό τάφο στη θέση Καζανάκι Βόλου." In *Αρχαιολογικό έργο Θεσσαλίας και Στερεάς Ελλάδας 2*, edited by A. Mazarakis Ainian, 151–61. Volos: Ministry of Culture and University of Thessaly.

Pappa, E. 2013. *Early Iron Age Exchange in the West. Phoenicians in the Mediterranean and the Atlantic*. Leuven: Peeters.

———. 2019. "The Poster Boys of Antiquity's 'Capitalism' Shunning Money? The Spread of the Alphabet in the Mediterranean as a Function of a Credit-Based, Maritime Trade." *Revista do Museu de Arqueologia e Etnologia* 33: 91–138.

Pappas, A. 2011. "Arts in Letters: The Aesthetics of Ancient Greek Writing." In *Visible Writings: Cultures, Forms, Readings*, edited by M. Shaw and M. Dalbello, 37–54. New Brunswick, NJ: Rutgers University Press.

———. 2017. "Form Follows Function? Toward an Aesthetics of Early Greek Inscriptions at Methone." In *Panhellenes at Methone: Graphê in Late Geometric and Protoarchaic Methone, Macedonia (ca. 700 BCE)*, edited by J. S. Clay, I. Malkin, and Y. Z. Tzifopoulos, 285–308. Berlin: De Gruyter.

Parker, V. 1997. *Untersuchungen zum Lelantischen Krieg und verwandten Problemen der frühgriechischen Geschichte*. Stuttgart: Franz Steiner Verlag.

Parkinson, W. A., ed. 2002. *The Archaeology of Tribal Societies*. Ann Arbor: International Monographs in Prehistory.

———. 2010. "Beyond the Peer: Social Interaction and Political Evolution in the Bronze Age Aegean." In *Political Economies of the Bronze Age Aegean*, edited by D. Pullen, 11–34. Oxford: Oxbow Books.

———. 2018. "Continent, Region, Microregion, Site: Settlement Nucleation in the European Neolithic." In *Regional Approaches to Society and Complexity: Studies in Honor of John F. Cherry*, edited by A. R. Knodell and T. P. Leppard, 94–108. Sheffield: Equinox.

Parkinson, W. A., and M. L. Galaty. 2007. "Secondary States in Perspective: An Integrated Approach to State Formation in the Prehistoric Aegean." *American Anthropologist* 109, no. 1 (March): 113–29.

———, eds. 2010. *Archaic State Interaction: The Eastern Mediterranean in the Bronze Age.* Santa Fe, NM: School of Advanced Research Press.

Parlama, L. 1979. "Μικρή ανασκαφική έρευνα στον προϊστορικό λόφο της Αμαρύνθου (Εύβοια)." *Athens Annals of Archaeology* 12: 2–14.

Paschalidis, C. 2007. "Euboea at the Crossroads of the Metal Trade: The Aegean and the Black Sea in the Late Bronze Age." In *Between the Aegean and Baltic Seas: Prehistory Across Borders*, edited by I. Galanaki, H. Tomas, Y. Galanakis, and R. Laffineur, 433–45. Liège: Université de Liège.

Pascual, J. 2009. "Η εφαρμογή των γεωγραφικών συστημάτων πληροφοριών στην ιστορική ανάλυση της Επικνημίδιας Λοκρίδας." In *Αρχαιολογικό έργο Θεσσαλίας και Στερεάς Ελλάδας* 2, edited by A. Mazarakis Ainian, 1207–21. Volos: Ministry of Culture and University of Thessaly.

Pascual, J. and M.-F. Papakonstantinou, eds. 2013. *Topography and History of Ancient Epicnemidian Locris.* Leiden: Brill.

Pauketat, T. R. 2007. *Chiefdoms and Other Archaeological Delusions.* Lanham, MD: AltaMira Press.

Pearce, M. 2007. *Bright Blades and Red Metal: Essays on North Italian Prehistoric Metalwork.* London: Accordia Research Institute.

Peeples, M. A. 2019. "Finding a Place for Networks in Archaeology." *Journal of Archaeological Research* 27, no. 1 (March): 451–99.

Pelon, O., 1976. *Tholoi, Tumuli et Cercles Funéraires. Recherches sur les monuments funéraires de plan circulaire dans l'Égée de l'âge du Bronze (IIIe et IIe millénaires av. J.-C.),* Athens: École française d'Athenes.

Petrakis, V. P. 2011. "Politics of the Sea in the Late Bronze Age II–III Aegean: Iconographic Preferences and Textual Perspectives." In *The Seascape in Aegean Prehistory*, edited by G. Vavouranakis, 185–234. Athens: Danish Institute at Athens.

Petrakos, V. 2014. "Θήβα." *Το Έργον της Αρχαιολογικής Εταιρείας* 61: 28–31.

Phialon, L. 2011. *L'émergence de la civilisation mycénienne en Grèce centrale.* Liège: Peeters.

Philippa-Touchais, A. 2011. "Cycles of Collapse in Greek Prehistory: Reassessing Social Change at the Beginning of the Middle Helladic and the Early Iron Age." In *The "Dark Ages" Revisited*, edited by A. Mazarakis Ainian, 31–44. Volos: University of Thessaly Press.

Philippson, A. 1951. *Die griechischen Landschaften: Der Nordosten der griechischen Halbinsel.* Band I. Frankfurt: V. Klostermann.

Photos, E., and R. F. Tylecote. 1988. "The Possibility of Smelting Nickel-Rich Lateritic Ores in the Hellenistic Settlement of Petres, N. W. Greece." In *Aspects of Ancient Mining and Metallurgy*, edited by J. E. Jones, 35–43. Bangor: Classical Association, Bangor and North Wales Branch.

Piteros, C., J.-P. Olivier, and J. L. Melena. 1990. "Les inscriptions en linéaire B des nodules de Thèbes." *Bulletin de correspondance hellénique* 144: 103–84.

Platon, N. 1968. "Τα προβλήματα χρονολογήσεως των μινωικών ανακτόρων." *Αρχαιολογική Εφημερίς:* 1–58.

Polychronakou-Sgouritsa, N., Y. Papadatos, A. Balitsari, and E. Prevedorou. 2016. "Marathon in the Middle and Late Bronze Age: New Evidence from an Old Excavation. Preliminary Results from the Excavation of the University of Athens at Plasi." In *Ra-pi-ne-u: Studies on the Mycenaean World offered to Robert Laffineur for his 70th Birthday*, edited by J. Driessen, 305–15. Louvain-la-Neuve: Presses universitaires de Louvain.

Pool, I., and M. Kochen. 1978. "Contacts and Influence." *Social Networks* 1: 1–48.

Popham, M. R. 1980. "Appendix B: The Ancient Name of the Site." In *Lefkandi I: The Iron Age Settlement and Cemeteries*, edited by M. R. Popham, L. H. Sackett, and P. G. Themelis, 423–27. London: Thames and Hudson.

———. 1983. "Euboean Exports to al Mina, Cyprus, and Crete: A Reassessment." *Annual of the British School at Athens* 78: 281–90.

———. 1993. "The Main Excavation of the Building (1981–3)." In *Lefkandi II: The Protogeometric Building at Toumba*. Part 2, *The Excavation, Architecture and Finds*, edited by M. R. Popham, P. G. Calligas, and L. H. Sackett, 7–32. London: British School at Athens.

———. 1994. "Precolonisation: Early Greek Contact with the East." In *The Archaeology of Greek Colonisation. Essays dedicated to Sir John Boardman*, edited by G. R. Tsetskhladze and F. De Angelis, 11–34. Oxford: Oxford University School of Archaeology.

———. 1995. "An Engraved Near Eastern Bronze Bowl from Lefkandi." *Oxford Journal of Archaeology* 14: 103–7.

Popham, M. R., P. G. Calligas, and L. H. Sackett. 1989. "Further Excavation of the Toumba Cemetery at Lefkandi, 1984 and 1986, A Preliminary Report." *Archaeological Reports* 35: 117–29.

———, eds. 1993. *Lefkandi II: The Protogeometric Building at Toumba*. Part 2: *The Excavation, Architecture and Finds*. London: British School at Athens.

Popham, M. R., and I. S. Lemos. 1995. "A Euboean Warrior-Trader." *Oxford Journal of Archaeology* 14: 151–57.

———. 1996. *Lefkandi III: The Toumba Cemetery (Plates)*. London: British School at Athens.

Popham, M. R., and L. H. Sackett. 1980. "Historical Conclusions." In *Lefkandi I: The Iron Age Settlement and Cemeteries*, edited by M. R. Popham, L. H. Sackett, and P. G. Themelis, 355–70. London: Thames and Hudson.

Popham, M. R., L. H. Sackett, and P. G. Themelis, eds. 1980. *Lefkandi I: The Iron Age Settlement and Cemeteries*. London: Thames and Hudson.

Popham, M. R., E. Touloupa, and L. H. Sackett. 1982. "The Hero of Lefkandi." *Antiquity* 56: 169–74.

Porada, E. 1981. "The Cylinder Seals Found at Thebes in Boeotia, with Contributions on the Inscriptions from Hans G. Güterbock and John A. Brinkman." *Archiv für Orientforschung* 28, no. 1: 1–78.

Porter, B. W. 2013. *Complex Communities: The Archaeology of Early Iron Age West-Central Jordan*. Tuscon: University of Arizona Press.

Powell, B. B. 1989. "Why Was the Greek Alphabet Invented? The Epigraphical Evidence." *Classical Antiquity* 8, no. 2 (October): 321–50.

———. 1991. *Homer and the Origin of the Greek Alphabet*. Cambridge: Cambridge University Press.

———. 1997. "From Picture to Myth, from Myth to Picture: Prolegomena to the Invention of Mythic Representation in Greek Art." In *New Light on a Dark Age: Exploring the Culture of Geometric Greece*, edited by S. Langdon, 154–93. Columbia: University of Missouri Press.

———. 2002. *Writing and the Origins of Greek Literature*. Cambridge: Cambridge University Press.

———. 2009. *Writing: Theory and History of the Technology of Civilization*. Malden, MA: Wiley-Blackwell.

Price, B. 1978. "Secondary State Formation: An Exploratory Model." In *Origins of the State: The Anthropology of Political Evolution*, edited by R. Cohen, 161–224. Philadelphia: Institute for the Study of Human Issues.

———. 1981. "Complexity in "Non-Complex" Societies." In *Archaeological Approaches to the Study of Complexity*, edited by S. E. van der Leeuw, 55–99. Amsterdam: University of Amsterdam.

Pritchett, W. K. 1980. *Studies in Ancient Greek Topography Part III (Roads)*. Berkeley: University of California Press.

———. 1982. *Studies in Ancient Greek Topography. Part IV (Passes)*. Berkeley: University of California Press.

Privitera, S. 2013. *Principi, Pelasgi e pescatori: L'Attica nella Tarda Età del Bronzo*. Athens: Scuola Archeologica Italiana di Atene.

Pulak, C. 2008. "The Uluburun Shipwreck and Late Bronze Age Trade." In *Beyond Babylon: Art Trade, and Diplomacy in the Second Millennium B.C.*, edited by J. Aruz, K. Benzel, and J. M. Evans, 288–310. New York: Metropolitan Museum of Art; New Haven, CT: Yale University Press.

Pullen, D. J. 2003. "Site Size, Territory, and Hierarchy: Measuring Levels of Integration and Social Change in Neolithic and Bronze Age Aegean Societies." *Metron: Measuring the Aegean Bronze Age*, edited by K. P. Foster and R. Laffineur, 29–36. Liège and Austin: Université de Liège, Histoire de l'art et archéologie de la Grèce antique, and University of Texas at Austin, Program in Aegean Scripts and Prehistory.

———. 2011a. "Before the Palaces: Redistribution and Chiefdoms in Mainland Greece." *American Journal of Archaeology* 115, no. 2 (April): 185–95.

———. 2011b. "Measuring Levels of Integration and Social Change in Neolithic and Bronze Age Aegean Societies: From Chiefdoms to Proto-States." In *State Formation in Italy and Greece: Questioning the Neoevolutionist Paradigm*, edited by N. Terrenato and D. C. Haggis, 18–31. Oxford: Oxbow Books.

Pullen, D. J., and T. F. Tartaron. 2007. "Where's the Palace? The Absence of State Formation in Late Bronze Age Corinthia." In *Rethinking Mycenaean Palaces II: Revised and Expanded Second Edition*, edited by M. L. Galaty and W. A. Parkinson, 146–58. Los Angeles: Cotsen Institute of Archaeology, University of California, Los Angeles.

Purcell, N. 1990. "Mobility and the Polis." In *The Greek City: From Homer to Alexander*, edited by O. Murray and S. Price, 29–59. Oxford: Clarendon Press.

Purves, A. 2010. *Space and Time in Ancient Greek Narrative*. Cambridge: Cambridge University Press.

Quinn, J. 2018. *In Search of the Phoenicians*. Princeton, NJ: Princeton University Press.

Raaflaub, K. A., and H. van Wees, eds. 2009. *A Companion to Archaic Greece*. Malden, MA: Wiley-Blackwell.

Rapp, G. 2013. "The Topography of the Pass at Thermopylae Circa 480 BC." In *Beyond the Gates of Fire: New Perspectives on the Battle of Thermopylae*, edited by C. Matthew and M. Trundle, 39–59. Barnsley: Pen & Sword.

Rapp, G., Jr., R. E. Jones, S. R. B. Cooke, and E. L. Henrickson. 1978. "Analyses of the Metal Artifacts." In *Excavations at Nichoria in Southwest Greece*. Vol. 1, *Site Environs and Techniques*, edited by G. Rapp Jr. and S. E. Aschenbrenner, 166–81. Minneapolis: University of Minnesota Press.

Reber, K., D. Knoepfler, A. Krapaschalidou, T. Krapf, T. Theurillat, G. Luisoni, G. Ackermann. 2019. "Les activités de l'École suisse d'archéologie en Grèce en 2018: L'Artémision d'Amarynthos et la Palestre Sud d'Érétrie." *Antike Kunst* 62: 144–57.

Redman, C. 2005. "Resilience Theory in Archaeology." *American Anthropologist* 107, no. 1 (March): 70–77.

Rehder, J. E. 2000. *The Mastery and Uses of Fire in Antiquity*. Montreal: McGill-Queen's University Press.

Reinders, H. R., ed. 2004. *Prehistoric sites at the Almirós and Soúrpi Plains (Thessaly, Greece)*. Assen: Koninklijke Van Gorcum.

Renfrew, C. 1969. "Trade and Culture Process in European Prehistory." *Current Anthropology* 10: 151–69.

———. 1972. *The Emergence of Civilisation: The Cyclades and the Aegean in the Third Millennium B.C.* London: Methuen.

———. 1975. "Trade as Action at a Distance: Questions of Integration and Communication." In *Ancient Civilization and Trade*, edited by J. A. Sabloff and C. C. Lamberg-Karlovsky, 3–60. Albuquerque: University of New Mexico Press.

———. 1979. "Systems Collapse as Social Transformation: Catastrophe and Anastrophe in Early State Societies." In *Transformations: Mathematical Approaches to Culture Change*, edited by C. Renfrew and K. L. Cooke, 481–506. New York: Academic Press.

———. 1986. "Introduction: Peer Polity Interaction and Socio-Political Change." In *Peer Polity Interaction and Socio-Political Change*, edited by C. Renfrew and J. F. Cherry, 1–18. Cambridge: Cambridge University Press.

Renfrew, C., and K. Boyle, eds. 2000. *Archaeogenetics: DNA and the Population Prehistory of Europe*. Cambridge: McDonald Institute for Archaeological Research.

Renfrew, C., and J. F. Cherry, eds. 1986. *Peer Polity Interaction and Socio-Political Change*. Cambridge: Cambridge University Press.

Ridgway, D. 1992. *The First Western Greeks*. Cambridge: Cambridge University Press.

Robinson, A. 2007. *Story of Writing: Alphabets, Hieroglyphs, and Pictograms*. London: Thames and Hudson.

Rolfe, J. C. 1890. "Discoveries at Anthedon in 1889." *American Journal of Archaeology and of the History of Fine Arts* 6, nos. 1–2 (March–June): 96–107.

Rop, J. 2019. "The Phocian Betrayal at Thermopylae." *Historia* 68, no. 4 (October): 413–35.

Rose, C. B. 2008. "Separating Fact from Fiction in the Aiolian Migration." *Hesperia* 77, no. 3 (July–September): 399–430.

Rose, C. B., and G. Darbyshire, eds. 2011. *The New Chronology of Iron Age Gordion*. Philadelphia: University of Pennsylvania Museum of Archaeology and Anthropology.

Routledge, B. 2014. *Archaeology and State Theory: Subjects and Objects of Power*. New York: Bloomsbury.

Routledge, B., and K. McGeough. 2009. "Just What Collapsed? A Network Perspective on 'Palatial' and 'Private' Trade at Ugarit." In *Forces of Transformation: The End of the Bronze Age in the Mediterranean*, edited by C. Bachhuber and R. G. Roberts, 22–29. Oxford: Oxbow Books.

Ruppenstein, F. 2007. *Die submykenische Nekropole: Neufunde und Neubewertung.* Kerameikos: Ergebnisse der Ausgrabungen 18. Munich: Hirmer Verlag.

———. 2012. "Gesellschaftliche Transformationen und politisch-soziale Krisen im frühen Griechenland. Überlegungen zur Entstehung der mykenischen Palaststaaten." In *Krise und Transformation*, edited by S. Deger-Jalkotzy and A. Suppan, 37–68. Vienna: Österreichische Akademie der Wissenschaften.

Ruscillo, D. 2017. "The Faunal Remains." In *The Early Iron Age: The Cemeteries*, by J. K. Papadopoulos and E. L. Smithson, 561–74. Athenian Agora 36. Princeton, NJ: American School of Classical Studies at Athens.

Russell, A. 2010. "Foreign Materials, Islander Mobility and Elite Identity in Late Bronze Age Sardinia." *Material Connections in the Ancient Mediterranean: Mobility, Materiality and Mediterranean Identities*, edited by P. van Dommelen and A. B. Knapp, 106–26. New York: Routledge.

Rutter, J. B. 1978. "A Plea for the Abandonment of the Term 'Submycenaean.'" In *Studies of New and Little Known Materials from the Aegean Bronze Age*, edited by P. Betancourt, 58–65. Philadelphia: Temple University.

———. 1993. "Review of Aegean Prehistory II: The Prepalatial Bronze Age of the Southern and Central Greek Mainland." *American Journal of Archaeology* 97, no. 4 (October): 745–97.

———. 2014a. "Reading Post-Palatial Mycenaean Iconography: Some Lessons from Lefkandi." In *Αθύρματα: Critical Essays on the Archaeology of the Eastern Mediterranean in Honour of E. Susan Sherratt*, edited by Y. Galanakis, T. Wilkinson, and J. Bennet, 197–205. Oxford: Archaeopress.

———. 2014b. "The Canaanite Transport Amphora within the Late Bronze Age Aegean: A 2013 Perspective on a Frequently Changing Picture." In *KE-RA-ME-JA: Studies Presented to Cynthia W. Shelmerdine*, edited by D. Nakassis, J. Gulizio, and S. A. James, 53–69. Philadelphia: INSTAP Academic Press.

Sabatini, S. 2016. "Revisiting Late Bronze Age Oxhide Ingots: Meanings, Questions and Perspectives." *Local and Global Perspectives on Mobility in the Eastern Mediterranean*, edited by O. C. Aslaksen, 15–62. Athens: Norwegian Institute at Athens.

Sabloff, J. A. 1986. "Interaction among Classic Maya Polities: A Preliminary Examination." In *Peer Polity Interaction and Socio-Political Change*, edited by C. Renfrew and J. F. Cherry, 109–16. Cambridge: Cambridge University Press.

Sackett, L. H., V. Hankey, R. J. Howell, T. W. Jacobsen, and M. R. Popham. 1966. "Prehistoric Euboea: Contributions toward a Survey." *Annual of the British School at Athens* 61: 33–112.

Sahlins, M. D. 1963. "Poor Man, Rich Man, Big-man, Chief: Political Types in Melanesia and Polynesia." *Comparative Studies in Society and History* 5, no. 3 (April): 285–303.

———. 1972. *Stone Age Economics.* New York: De Gruyter.

Sahlins, M. D., and E. Service. 1960. *Evolution and Culture.* Ann Arbor: University of Michigan Press.

Sakellariou, M. B. 2009. *Ethne grecs à l'âge du Bronze.* Athens: Centre de recherches de l'antiquité grecque et romaine.

Salowey, C. A. 1994. "Herakles and the Waterworks: Mycenaean Dams, Classical Fountains, Roman Aqueducts." In *Archaeology in the Peloponnese: New Excavations and Research,* edited by Kenneth A. Sheedy, 77–94. Oxford: Oxbow Books.

Saltz, D. 1978. "Greek Geometric Pottery in the East: The Chronological Implications." Ph.D. diss., Harvard University.

Sampson, A. 1985. *Μάνικα I: Μία πρωτοελλαδική πόλη στη Χαλκίδα.* Athens: Society for Euboean Studies.

———. 1988. *Μάνικα II: Ο πρωτοελλαδικός οικισμός και το νεκροταφείο.* Athens: Demos of Chalkida.

Sapouna-Sakellaraki, E. 1987. "Γλύφα ή Βλύχα Βοιωτίας. Η μυκηναϊκή Αυλίδα;" *Athens Annals of Archaeology* 20: 191–210.

———. 1989. "Έρευνα στην προϊστορική Αμάρυνθο και στη Μαγούλα Ερέτριας." *Αρχείον Ευβοϊκών Μελετών* 28: 91–104.

———. 1995. "Ανασκαφή στο Καστρί Λιχάδας Ευβοίας το 1994." *Αρχείον Ευβοϊκών Μελετών* 31: 96–195.

———. 1996. "Mycenaean Kerinthos." In *Minotaur and Centaur: Studies in the archaeology of Crete and Euboea presented to Mervyn Popham,* edited by D. Evely, I. S. Lemos, and S. Sherratt, 106–10. British Archaeological Reports International Series 638. Oxford: Tempus Reparatum.

———. 1998. "Geometric Kyme. The Excavation at Viglatouri, Kyme on Euboea." In *Euboica. L'Eubea e la presenza euboica in Calcidica e in Occidente,* edited by M. Bats and B. d'Agostino, 59–104. Naples: Centre Jean Bérard.

Sarri, K. 2010. *Orchomenos IV: Die Keramik der Mittelbronzezeit.* Munich: Verlag der Bayerischen Akademie der Wissenschaften.

Sass, B. 1990. "Arabs and Greeks in Late First Temple Jerusalem." *Palestine Exploration Quarterly* 122, no. 1: 59–61.

———. 2002. "Wenamun and His Levant." *Egypt and the Levant* 12: 247–55.

———. 2005. *The Alphabet at the Turn of the Millennium: The West Semitic Alphabet ca. 1150–850 BCE. The Antiquity of the Arabian, Greek, and Phrygian Alphabets.* Tel Aviv: Emery and Claire Yass Publications in Archaeology.

Sauvage, C. 2012. *Routes maritimes et systèmes d'échanges internationaux: Au Bronze Récent en Méditeranée orientale.* Lyon: Maison de l'Orient et de la Méditeranée.

Schelach, G., and Y. Pines. 2006. "Secondary State Formation and the Development of Local Identity: Change and Continuity in the State of Qin (770–221 B.C.)." In *The Archaeology of Asia,* edited by M. Stark, 202–30. Malden, MA: Wiley-Blackwell.

Schilardi, D. 2016. *Koukounaries, Paros: The Excavations and History of a Most Ancient Aegean Acropolis.* Athens: Paros Excavations—Center of Historical and Archaeological Studies.

Schläger, H., D. J. Blackman, and J. Schäfer. 1968. "Der Hafen von Anthedon mit Beiträgen zur Topographie und Geschichte der Stadt." *Archäologischer Anzeiger* 1: 21–102.

Schliemann, H. 1874. *Trojanische Alterthümer: Bericht über die Ausgrabungen in Troja.* Leipzig: F. A. Brockhaus.

———. 1881. *Orchomenos: Bericht über meine Ausgrabungen im böotischen Orchomenos.* Leipzig: F. A. Brockhaus.

Schmidt, P. R., and S. A. Mrozowski, eds. 2013. *The Death of Prehistory.* Oxford: Oxford University Press.

Schneider, J. 1977. "Was There a Pre-capitalist World System?" *Peasant Studies* 6: 20–29.

Schortman, E. M. 1989. "Interregional Interaction in Prehistory: The Need for a New Perspective." *American Antiquity* 54, no. 1 (January): 52–65.

Schortman, E. M., and P. A. Urban. 1987. "Modeling Interregional Interaction in Prehistory." *Advances in Archaeological Method and Theory* 11: 37–95.

———, eds. 1992. *Resources, Power, and Interregional Interaction.* New York: Plenum Press.

Schwartz, G. M., and J. J. Nichols, eds. 2006. *After Collapse: The Regeneration of Complex Societies.* Tuscon: University of Arizona Press.

Scott, J. C. 2009. *The Art of Not Being Governed: An Anarchist History of Upland Southeast Asia.* New Haven, CT: Yale University Press.

Seneviratne, S. 1981. "Kalinga and Andhra: The Process of Secondary State Formation in Early India." In *The Study of the State*, edited by H. J. M. Claessen and P. Skalnik, 317–38. The Hague: Mouton.

Sergent, B. 1994. "Les petits nodules et la grande Béotie (première partie)." *Revue des études anciennes* 96, nos. 3–4: 365–84.

———. 1997. "Les petits nodules et la grande Béotie (deuxième partie)." *Revue des études anciennes* 99, nos. 1–2: 11–32.

———. 1999. "Les petits nodules et la grande Béotie (3° partie)." *Revue des études anciennes* 101, nos. 3–4: 309–29

Seroglou, F. K. 2009. "The Dissemination of Attic Pottery During the Protogeometric and Geometric Periods." In *The Aegean and Its Cultures*, edited by G. Deligiannakis and Y. Galanakis, 27–36. Oxford: Archaeopress.

Service, E. 1962. *Primitive Social Organization: An Evolutionary Perspective.* New York: Random House.

Shelmerdine, C. 2006. "Mycenaean Palatial Administration." In *Ancient Greece: From the Mycenaean Palaces to the Age of Homer*, edited by S. Deger-Jalkotzy and I. S. Lemos, 73–86. Edinburgh: Edinburgh University Press.

———. 2008. "Background, Sources, and Methods." In *The Cambridge Companion to the Aegean Bronze Age*, edited by C. Shelmerdine, 1–18. Cambridge: Cambridge University Press.

———. 2013. "Economic Interplay Among Households and States." *American Journal of Archaeology* 117, no. 3 (July): 447–52.

Shelmerdine, C. W. and T. G. Palaima, eds. 1984. *Pylos Comes Alive: Industry and Administration in a Mycenaean Palace.* New York: Archaeological Institute of America.

Shennan, S. 2018. *The First Farmers of Europe: An Evolutionary Perspective.* Cambridge: Cambridge University Press.

Sherratt, E. S. 1980. "Regional Variation in the Pottery of the Late Helladic IIIB." *Annual of the British School at Athens* 75: 175–202.

———. 1994. "Commerce, Iron, and Ideology: Metallurgical Innovation in 12th–11th Century Cyprus." In *Cyprus in the 11th Century B.C.*, edited by V. Karageorghis, 59–106. Nicosia: A. G. Leventis Foundation.

———. 2000. "Circulation of Metals and the End of the Bronze Age in the Eastern Mediterranean." In *Metals Make the World Go Round: The Supply and Circulation of Metals in Bronze Age Europe*, edited by C. F. E. Pare, 82–98. Oxford: Oxbow Books.

———. 2001. "Potemkin Palaces and Route-Based Economies." In *Economy and Politics in the Mycenaean Palace States*, edited by S. Voutsaki and J. Killen, 214–38. Cambridge: Cambridge Philological Society.

————. 2004. "Feasting in Homeric Epic." *Hesperia* 73, no. 2 (April–June): 301–37.

————. 2006a. "LH IIIC Lefkandi: An Overview." In *Lefkandi IV, The Bronze Age: The Late Helladic IIIC Settlement at Xeropolis*, edited by D. Evely, 303–17. London: British School at Athens.

————. 2006b. "The Pottery in a Wider Context." In *Lefkandi IV, The Bronze Age: The Late Helladic IIIC Settlement at Xeropolis*, edited by D. Evely, 218–31. London: British School at Athens.

Sherratt, S., and J. Bennet, eds. 2017. *Archaeology and Homeric Epic.* Oxford: Oxbow Books.

Sherratt, S., and A. Sherratt. 1991. "From Luxuries to Commodities: The Nature of Mediterranean Bronze Age Trading Systems." In *Bronze Age Trade in the Mediterranean*, edited by N. H. Gale, 351–86. Jonsered: Paul Åströms Forlag.

————. 1993. "The Growth of the Mediterranean Economy in the Early First Millennium BC." *World Archaeology* 24, no. 3 (February): 361–78.

Shipley, G. 2010. "Pseudo-Skylax on Attica." In *Ergasteria: Works Presented to John Ellis Jones on his 80th Birthday*, edited by N. Sekunda, 99–113. Gdańsk: Institute of Archaeology, Gdańsk University.

Sideris, A. 2014. *Αντίκυρα: Ιστορία και αρχαιολογία.* Athens: Demos of Distomo.

Sideris, A., and I. Liritzis. 2018. "The Mycenaean Site of Kastrouli, Phokis, Greece: Second Excavation Season, July 2017." *Mediterranean Archaeology and Archaeometry* 18, no. 3 (November): 209–24.

Simon, P. 2002. "Nouvelles activités de prospection dans le territoire Erétrien." *Antike Kunst* 45: 125–27.

Skafida, E., A. Karnava, and J.-P. Olivier. 2012. "Two New Linear B Tablets from the Site of Kastro-Palaia in Volos." In *Études mycéniennes 2010.* Pisa: Biblioteca di Pasiphae.

Skafida, E., A. Karnava, J.-P. Olivier, T. Rehren, E. Asderaki-Tzoumerkioti, M. Vaxervavopoulos, I. Maniatis, et al. 2016. "Ο οικισμός της Ύστερης Εποχής Χαλκού στο 'Κάστρο-Παλαιά' Βόλου: Από τις ανασκαφικές έρευνες του Δ. Θεοχάρη στα νέα ευρήματα της πρόσφατης διεπιστημονικής έρευνας." In *Αρχαιολογικό έργο Θεσσαλίας και Στερεάς Ελλάδας 4*, edited by M. Mazarakis Ainian, 145–57. Volos: Ministry of Culture, Education and Religion and University of Thessaly.

Sloterdijk, P. 2006. "Mobilization of the Planet from the Spirit of Self-Intensification." *Drama Review* 50, no. 4 (Winter): 36–43.

Small, D. B. 1998. "Surviving the Collapse: The Oikos and Structural Continuity between Late Bronze Age and Later Greece." In *Mediterranean Peoples in Transition: Thirteenth to Early Tenth Centuries BCE. In Honor of Professor Trude Dothan*, edited by S. Gitin, A. Mazar, and E. Stern, 283–91. Jerusalem: Israel Exploration Society.

————. 2007. "Mycenaean Polities: States or Estates?" In *Rethinking Mycenaean Palaces II: Revised and Expanded Second Edition*, edited by M. L. Galaty and W. A. Parkinson, 47–53. Los Angeles: Cotsen Institute of Archaeology, University of California, Los Angeles.

————. 2009. "The Dual-Processual Model in Ancient Greece: Applying a Post-Neoevolutionary Model to a Data-Rich Environment." *Journal of Anthropological Archaeology* 28: 205–21.

————. 2015. "A Defective Master Narrative in Greek Archaeology." In *Classical Archaeology in Context: Theory and Practice in Excavaton in the Greek World*, edited by D. Haggis and C. M. Antonaccio, 71–86. Berlin: De Gruyter.

————. 2017. "Classical Archaeology Comes of Age: Supplying Theory to Other World Archaeologies." In *Theoretical Approaches to the Archaeology of Ancient Greece:*

Manipulating Material Culture, edited by L. Nevett, 51–68. Ann Arbor: University of Michigan Press.

———. 2019. *Ancient Greece: Social Structure and Evolution*. Cambridge: Cambridge University Press.

Smith, A. 1999. "The Making of an Urartian Landscape in Southern Transcaucasia: A Study of Political Architectonics." *American Journal of Archaeology* 103, no. 1 (January): 45–71.

———. 2003. *The Political Landscape: Constellations of Authority in Early Complex Polities*. Berkeley: University of California Press.

———. 2015. *The Political Machine: Assembling Sovereignty in the Bronze Age Caucasus*. Princeton, NJ: Princeton University Press.

Smith, J. S. 1993. "The Pylos Jn Series." *Minos* 27–28: 167–259.

———. 2009. *Art and Society in Cyprus from the Bronze Age into the Iron Age*. Cambridge: Cambridge University Press.

Smith, M. E., ed. 2011. *The Comparative Archaeology of Complex Societies*. Cambridge: Cambridge University Press.

Smith, S. T. 1998. "Nubia and Egypt: Interaction, Acculturation, and Secondary State Formation from the Third to First Millennium B.C." In *Studies in Culture Contact: Interaction, Culture Change, and Archaeology*, edited by James G. Cusick, 256–87. Carbondale: Southern Illinois University.

Smith, T. R. 1987. *Mycenaean Trade and Interaction in the West Central Mediterranean 1600–1000 B.C.* Oxford: British Archaeological Reports.

Smithson, E. L. 1968. "The Tomb of a Rich Athenian Lady, ca. 850 B.C." *Hesperia* 37, no. 1 (January–March): 77–116.

Snodgrass, A. M. (1967) 1999. *Arms and Armor of the Greeks*. Baltimore: Johns Hopkins Univerisity Press.

———. (1971) 2000. *The Dark Age of Greece: An Archaeological Survey of the Eleventh to the Eighth Centuries BC*. 2nd ed. New York: Routledge.

———. 1980a. *Archaic Greece: The Age of Experiment*. London: J. M. Dent & Sons.

———. 1980b. "Iron and Early Metallurgy in the Mediterranean." In *The Coming of the Age of Iron*, edited by T. A. Wertime and J. D. Muhly, 335–74. New Haven, CT: Yale University Press.

———. 1986. "Interaction by Design: The Greek City State." In *Peer Polity Interaction and Socio-Political Change*, edited by C. Renfrew and J. F. Cherry, 47–58. Cambridge: Cambridge University Press.

———. 1987. *An Archaeology of Greece: The Present State and Future Scope of a Discipline*. Berkeley: University of California Press.

———. 1989. "The Coming of the Iron Age in Greece: Europe's Earliest Bronze/Iron Transition." In *The Bronze Age-Iron Age Transition in Europe: Aspects of Continuity and Change in European Societies c. 1200–500 BC*, edited by M. L. Stig Sørensen and R. Thomas, 22–35. Oxford: British Archaeological Reports.

———. 1994. "The Euboeans in Macedonia: A New Precedent for Westward Expansion." In *A.I.O.N. Annali di archeologia e storia antica: Dipartimento di studi del mondo classico e del mediterraneo antico (n.s. 1), APOIKIA, I più antichi insediamenti greci in occidente: funzioni e modi dell'organizzazione politica e sociale. Scritti in onore di Giorgio Buchner*, edited by B. d'Agostino and D. Ridgway, 87–93. Naples: Instituto Universitario Orientale.

———. 1998. *Homer and the Artists: Text and Picture in Early Greek Art*. Cambridge: Cambridge University Press.

———. 2017. "Homer, the Moving Target." *Archaeology and Homeric Epic*, edited by S. Sherratt and J. Bennet, 1–9. Oxford: Oxbow Books.

Spyropoulos, T. 1971. "Αρχαία βοιωτικαί πόλεις έρχονται στο φως." *Athens Annals of Archaeology* 4, no. 3: 319–31.

———. 1974. "Το ανάκτορον του Μινύου εις βοιωτικόν Ορχομενόν." *Athens Annals of Archaeology* 7: 313–25.

———. 2015. "Wall Paintings from the Mycenaean Palace of Boiotian Orchomenos." In *Mycenaean Wall Painting in Context: New Discoveries, Old Finds Reconsidered*, edited by H. Brecoulaki, J. L. Davis, and S. R. Stocker, 354–68. Athens: National Hellenic Research Foundation.

Spyropoulos, T., and J. Chadwick. 1975. *Thebes Tablets II*. Salamanca: Ediciones Universidad de Salamanca.

Stamatopoulou, M. 2011. "Thessaly (Archaic to Roman)." *Archaeological Reports* 57: 73–84.

Stampolidis, N. C., and M. Giannopoulou, eds. 2012. *Princesses of the Mediterranean in the Dawn of History*. Athens: Museum of Cycladic Art.

Stanish, C. 2017. *The Evolution of Human Cooperation: Ritual and Social Complexity in Stateless Societies*. Cambridge: Cambridge University Press.

Stanzel, M. 1991. "Die Tierreste aus dem Artemis-/Apollon-Heiligtum bei Kalapodi in Böotien/Griechenland." PhD diss., Ludwig-Maximilians-Universität.

Steele, P. M., ed. 2017. *Understanding Relations Between Scripts: The Aegean Writing Systems*. Oxford: Oxbow Books.

———. 2020. "Script and Literacy." In *A Companion to the Archaeology of Early Greece and the Mediterranean*, edited by I. S. Lemos and A. Kotsonas, 247–69. Hoboken, NJ: John Wiley & Sons.

Stefanis, A. D., ed. 2015. *Πρακτικά ΙΕ΄ επιστημονικής συνάντησης ΝΑ. Αττικής*. Kalyvia Thorikou: Εταιρεία Μελετών Νοτιοανατολικής Αττικής.

Steidl, C. 2020. "The Dynamics of Belonging: Comparative Community Formation in the East and West Mediterranean." *Journal of Mediterranean Archaeology* 33, no. 1 (October): 79–101.

Stein, G. J. 2002. "From Passive Periphery to Active Agents: Emerging Perspectives in the Archaeology of Interregional Interaction." *American Anthropologist* 104, no. 3 (September): 903–16.

———, ed. 2005. *The Archaeology of Colonial Encounters: Comparative Perspectives*. Santa Fe, NM: School of Advanced Research Press.

Steinhilber, F., J. Beer, and C. Fröhlich. 2009. "Total Solar Irradiance During the Holocene." *Geophysical Research Letters* 36, no. 19 (October): L19704 1–5.

Steinmann, B. 2012. *Die Waffengraber der agaischen Bronzezeit: Waffenbeigaben, soziale Selbstdarstellung und Adelsethos in der minoisch-mykenischen Kultur*. Wiesbaden: Harassowitz Verlag.

Stiros, S., and R. E. Jones, eds. 1996. *Archaeoseismology*. Athens: Institute of Geology & Mineral Exploration and the British School at Athens.

Stissi, V. 2004. "Late Bronze Age." In *Prehistoric sites at the Almirós and Soúrpi Plains (Thessaly, Greece)*, edited by H. R. Reinders, 91–93. Assen: Koninklijke Van Gorcum.

Stissi, V., J. Waagen, D. Efstathiou, R. Reinders, V. Rondiri, I. Mamaloudi, and E. Stamelou. 2015. "Halos: Preliminary Report of the 2011-2013 Field Survey Campaigns." *Pharos* 21, no. 2: 63–84.

Stocker, S. R., and J. L. Davis. 2017. "The Combat Agate from the Grave of the Griffin Warrior at Pylos." *Hesperia* 86, no. 4 (October-December): 583–605.

Stos-Gale, Z. A., and N. Gale. 1982. "The Sources of Mycenaean Silver and Lead." *Journal of Field Archaeology* 9, no. 4 (Winter): 467–85.

———. 1992. "New Light on the Provenience of the Copper Oxhide Ingots Found on Sardinia." In *Sardinia in the Mediterranean: A Footprint in the Sea. Studies in Sardinian Archaeology Presented to Miriam S. Balmuth*, edited by R. H. Tykot and T. K. Andrews, 317–46. Sheffield: Sheffield Academic Press.

Stos-Gale, Z. A., and C. F. Macdonald. 1991. "Sources of Metals and Trade in the Bronze Age Aegean." In *Bronze Age Trade in the Mediterranean*, edited by N. H. Gale, 249–88. Gothenburg: Paul Åströms Förlag.

Stuart, J., and N. Revett. 1762–1816. *The Antiquities of Athens and Other Monuments of Greece*. London: Haberkorn.

Stubbings, F. H. 1947. "The Mycenaean Pottery of Attica." *Annual of the British School of Athens* 42: 1–75.

Symeonoglou, S. 1973. *Kadmeia I: Mycenaean Finds from Thebes, Greece, Excavation at 14 Oedipus St.* Gothenburg: Paul Åströms Förlag.

———. 1985. *The Topography of Thebes from the Bronze Age to Modern Times.* Princeton, NJ: Princeton University Press.

Syriopoulos, K. 1983. *Εισαγωγή εις την αρχαίαν ελληνικήν ιστορίαν: Οι μεταβατικοί χρόνοι από της μυκηναϊκής εις την αρχαϊκήν περίοδον, 1200—700 π.Χ.* Athens: Archaeological Society at Athens.

———. 1995. *Η προϊστορική κατοίκησις της Ελλάδος και η γέννεσις του ελληνικού έθνους.* Athens: Archaeological Society at Athens.

Tainter, J. A., 1988. *The Collapse of Complex Societies.* Cambridge: Cambridge University Press.

———. 2006. "Archaeology of Overshoot and Collapse." *Annual Review of Anthropology* 35: 59–74.

Tandy, D. W. 2001. *Prehistory and History; Ethnicity, Class, and Political Economy.* London: Black Rose Books.

Tanelli, G., M. Benvenuti, P. Costagliola, A. Dini, P. Lattanzi, C. Maineri, I. Mascaro, G. Ruggieri. 2001. "The Iron Mineral Deposits of Elba Island: State of the Art." *Ofioliti* 26, no. 2a (December): 239–48.

Tankosić, Ž.. 2011. "Southern Euboea-Northern Cyclades: An Integrated Analysis of Final Neolithic and Early Bronze Age Interactions." PhD diss., Indiana University. ProQuest (AAT 3488118).

Tankosić, Ž.., and M. Chidiroglou. 2010. "The Karystian Kampos Survey Project: Methods and Preliminary Results." *Mediterranean Archaeology and Archaeometry* 10, no. 3 (February): 11–17.

Tankosić, Ž.., A. Laftsidis, A. Psoma, R. M. Seifried, A. Garyfallopoulos. Forthcoming. "New Data on Southern Euboean Landscapes: Results of the Norwegian Archaeological Survey in the Karystia." *Annual of the British School at Athens.*

Tankosić, Ž., F. Mavridis, and M. Kosma. 2017. *An Island Between Two Worlds: The Archaeology of Euboea from Prehistoric to Byzantine Times*. Athens: Norwegian Institute at Athens.

Tartaron, T. F. 2008. "Aegean Prehistory as World Archaeology: Recent Trends in the Archaeology of Bronze Age Greece." *Journal of Archaeological Research* 16, no. 2 (June): 83–161.

———. 2010. "Between and Beyond: Political Economy in Non-Palatial Mycenaean Worlds." In *Political Economies of the Aegean Bronze Age*, edited by D. J. Pullen, 161–83. Oxford: Oxbow Books.

———. 2013. *Maritime Networks in the Mycenaean World*. Cambridge: Cambridge University Press.

Taylour, W. 1958. *Mycenaean Pottery in Italy and Adjacent Areas*. Cambridge: Cambridge University Press.

Terrell, J. 1977. *Human Biogeography in the Solomon Islands*. Chicago: Field Museum of Natural History.

Terrenato, N. and D. C. Haggis, eds. 2011. *State Formation in Italy and Greece: Questioning the Neoevolutionist Paradigm*. Oxford: Oxbow Books.

Thaler, U. 2015. "Movement in between, into and inside Mycenaean Palatial Megara." In *Mycenaeans up to Date: The Archaeology of the North-Eastern Peloponnese—Current Concepts and New Directions*, edited by A.-L. Schallin and I. Tournavitou, 339–60. Stockholm: Svenska Institutet i Athen.

Theocharis, D. R. 1956. "Ἀνασκαφαί εν Ἰωλκώ." *Praktika*: 119–30.

———. 1957. "Ἀνασκαφαί εν Ἰωλκώ." *Praktika*: 54–69.

———. 1960. "Ἀνασκαφαί εν Ἰωλκώ." *Praktika*: 49–59.

———. 1961. "Ἀνασκαφαί εν Ἰωλκώ." *Praktika*: 45–54.

———. 1973. *Neolithic Greece*. Translated by D. Hardy and A.-M. Lefkaditi. Athens: National Bank of Greece.

Theurillat, T. 2007. "Early Iron Age Graffiti from the Sanctuary of Apollo at Eretria." In *Oropos and Euboea in the Early Iron Age*, edited by A. Mazarakis Ainian, 331–45. Volos: University of Thessaly Press.

Tholander, E. 1971. "Evidence of the Use of Carburised Steel and Quench-Hardening in LBA Cyprus." *Opuscula Atheniensia* 10, no. 3: 15–22.

Thomas, C. G., and C. Conant. 2003. *Citadel to City-State: The Transformation of Greece, 1200–700 B.C.E.* Bloomington: Indiana University Press.

Thomas, R. 1992. *Literacy and Orality in Ancient Greece*. Cambridge: Cambridge University Press.

Thomatos, M. 2006. *The Final Revival of the Aegean Bronze Age: A Case Study of the Agolid, Corinthia, Attica, Euboea, the Cyclades and the Dodecanese during LH IIIC Middle*. Oxford: Archaeopress.

Tiverios, M. 2004. "Οι πανεπιστημιακές ανασκαφές στο Καραμπουρνάκι Θεσσαλονίκης και η παρουσία των Φοινίκων στο βόρειο Αιγαίο." In *Το Αιγαίο στην Πρώιμη Εποχή του Σιδήρου*, edited by N. Stampolidis and A. Yannikouri, 295–306. Athens: Archaeological Receipts Fund.

———. 2008. "Greek Colonisation of the Northern Aegean." In *Greek Colonisation: An Account of Greek Colonies and Other Settlements Overseas*, edited by G. Tsetskhladze, 1–154. Vol. 2. Leiden: Brill.

Tournavitou, I. 2017. *The Wall Paintings of the West House at Mycenae*. Philadelphia: INSTAP Academic Press.

Traill, J. S. 1975. *The Political Organization of Attica: A Study of the Demes, Trittyes, and Phylai and Their Representation in the Athenian Council*. Princeton, NJ: American School of Classical Studies at Athens.

Trigger, B. G. 2003. *Understanding Early Civilizations*. Cambridge: Cambridge University Press.

Tsetskhladze, G. R. 1995. "Did the Greeks Go to Colchis for Metals?" *Oxford Journal of Archaeology* 14, no. 3 (November): 307–32.

———, ed. 2006. *Greek Colonisation: An Account of Greek Colonies and other Settlements Overseas*. Vol. 1. Leiden: Brill.

———, ed. 2008. *Greek Colonisation: An Account of Greek Colonies and other Settlements Overseas*. Vol. 2. Leiden: Brill.

Tsokas, G. N., A. van de Moortel, P. I. Tsourlos, A. Stampolidis, G. Vargemezis, and E. Zahou. 2012. "Geophysical Survey as an Aid to Excavation at Mitrou: A Preliminary Report." *Hesperia* 81, no. 3 (July–September): 383–432.

Tsountas, C. 1908. *Αι προϊστορικαί ακροπόλεις Διμηνίου και Σέσκλου*. Athens: Sakellariou.

Tuan, Y-. F. 1977. *Space and Place: The Perspective of Experience*. Minneapolis: University of Minnesota Press.

Tzavella-Evjen, C. 2014. "Οι ανασκαφές Κεραμόπουλλου. Παρατηρήσεις στα ΥΕ νεκροταφεία." In *100 χρόνια αρχαιολογικού έργου στη Θήβα. Οι πρωτεργάτες των ερευνών και οι συνεχιστές τους*, edited by V. Aravantinos and E. Kountouri, 175–80. Athens: Ταμείο Αρχαιολογικών Πόρων και Απαλλοτριώσεων.

Ulf, C. 2009. "The World of Homer and Hesiod." In *A Companion to Archaic Greece*, edited by K. A. Raaflaub and H. van Wees, 81–99. Malden, MA: Wiley-Blackwell.

Ure, P. N. 1934. *Aryballoi & Figurines from Rhitsona in Boeotia: An Account of the Early Archaic Pottery and of the Figurines, Archaic and Classical, with Supplementary Lists of the Finds of Glass, Beads and Metal, from Excavations Made by R.M. Burrows and P.N. Ure in 1907, 1908, 1909 and by P.N. and A.D. Ure in 1921 and 1922*. Cambridge: Cambridge University Press.

Vaessen, R. 2014. "Ceramic Developments in Coastal Western Anatolia at the Dawn of the Early Iron Age." In *ΑΘΥΡΜΑΤΑ: Critical Essays on the Archaeology of the Eastern Mediterranean in Honour of E. Susan Sherratt*, edited by Y. Galanakis, T. Wilkinson, and J. Bennet, 223–323. Oxford: Archaeopress.

———. 2015. "The Ionian Migration and Ceramic Dynamics in Ionia at the End of the Second Millennium BC: Some Preliminary Thoughts." In *Nostoi: Indigenous Culture, Migration + Integration in the Aegean Islands + Western Anatolia During the Late Bronze Ages*, edited by N. C. Stampolidis, Ç. Maner, and K. Kopanias, 811–34. Istanbul: Koç University Press.

Vagnetti, L. 1999. "Mycenaean Pottery in the Central Mediterranean: Imports and Local Production in Their Context." In *The Complex Past of Pottery: Production, Circulation, and Consumption of Mycenaean and Greek Pottery (Sixteenth to Early Fifth Centuries B.C.)*, edited by J. P. Crielaard, V. Stissi, and G. J. van Wijngaarden, 137–61. Amsterdam: J. C. Gieben.

Van Damme, T. M. 2017a. "Euboean Connections with Eastern Boeotia: Ceramics and Synchronisms between Lefkandi and Ancient Eleon." In *An Island between Two Worlds:*

The Archaeology of Euboea from Prehistoric to Byzantine Times, edited by Ž. Tankosić, F. Mavridis, and M. Kosma, 171–82. Athens: Norwegian Institute at Athens.

———. 2017b. "Life after the Palaces: A Household Archaeology Approach to Mainland Greece during Late Helladic IIIC." PhD diss., University of California, Los Angeles. ProQuest (AAT 10619013).

———. Forthcoming. "The Mycenaean Fountain and the Transformation of Space on the Athenian Acropolis from 1200–675 B.C."

van de Moortel, A. 2009. "The Late Helladic IIIC–Protogeometric Transition at Mitrou, East Lokris." In *LH III C Chronology and Synchronisms 3: LH III C Late and the Transition to the Early Iron Age*, edited by S. Deger-Jalkotzy and A. E. Bächle, 359–72. Vienna: Verlag der Österreichischen Adademie der Wissenschaften.

van de Moortel, A., S. Vitale, B. Lis, and G. Bianco. 2019. "Honoring the Dead or Hero Cult? The Long Afterlife of a Prepalatial Elite Tomb at Mitrou." In *Mneme: Past and Memory in the Aegean Bronze Age*, edited by E. Borgna, I. Caloi, F. M. Carinci, and R. Laffineur, 277–91. Leuven: Peeters.

van de Moortel, A. and E. Zahou. 2011. "The Bronze Age-Iron Age Transition at Mitrou in East Lokris: Evidence for Continuity and Discontinuity." In *The "Dark Ages" Revisited. Acts of an International Symposium in Memory of William D. E. Coulson*, edited by A. Mazarakis Ainian, 331–47. Volos: University of Thessaly Press.

———. 2012. "Five Years of Archaeological Excavation at the Bronze Age and Early Iron Age site of Mitrou, East Lokris (2004–2008): Preliminary Results." In *Αρχαιολογικό έργο Θεσσαλίας και Στερεάς Ελλάδας 3. 2009*, edited by A. Mazarakis Ainian, 1131–46. Volos: University of Thessaly Press.

van den Eijnde, F. 2018. "Power Play at the Dinner Table: Feasting and Patronage between Palace and Polis in Attika." In *Feasting and Polis Institutions*, edited by F. van den Eijnde, J. H. Blok, and R. Strootman, 60–92. Leiden: Brill.

van der Leeuw, S., ed. 1981. *Archaeological Approaches to the Study of Complexity*. Amsterdam: University of Amsterdam.

van der Vliet, E. 2011. "The Early Greek Polis: Regime Building and the Emergence of the State." In *State Formation in Italy and Greece: Questioning the Neoevolutionist Paradigm*, edited by N. Terrenato and D. C. Haggis, 119–34. Oxford: Oxbow Books.

Vanderpool, E. 1978. "Roads and Forts in Northwestern Attica." *California Studies in Classical Antiquity* 11: 227–45.

van Dommelen, P. 1998. *On Colonial Grounds: A Comparative Study of Colonialism and Rural Settlement in First Millennium BC West Central Sardinia*. Leiden: Faculty of Archaeology, Leiden University.

———. 2005. "Colonial Interactions and Hybrid Practices: Phoenician and Carthaginian Settlement in the Ancient Mediterranean." In *The Archaeology of Colonial Encounters: Comparative Perspectives*, edited by G. J. Stein, 109–41. Santa Fe, NM: School of American Research Press.

van Dommelen, P., and A. B. Knapp, eds. 2010. *Material Connections in the Ancient Mediterranean: Mobility, Materiality and Identity*. New York: Routledge.

van Gelder, K. 1991. "The Iron-Age Hiatus in Attica and the Synoikismos of Theseus." *Mediterranean Archaeology* 4: 55–64.

van Wijngaarden, G.-J. 2002. *Use and Appreciation of Mycenaean Pottery in the Levant, Cyprus, and Italy ca. 1600–1200 BC*. Amsterdam: Amsterdam University Press.

———. 2016. "Foreign Affairs: Diplomacy, Trade, War and Migration in the Mycenaean Mediterranean (1400–1100 BC)." In *Ra-pi-ne-u: Studies on the Mycenaean World offered to Robert Laffineur for his 70th Birthday*, edited by J. Driessen, 349–63. Louvain-la-Neuve: Presses universitaires de Louvain.

Vanschoonwinkel, J. 2006. "Greek Migrations to Aegean Anatolia in the Early Dark Age." In *Greek Colonisation: An Account of Greek Colonies and other Settlements Overseas*, Vol. 1, edited by G. R. Tsetskhladze, 115–41. Leiden: Brill.

Vasilopoulou, V., and S. Katsarou-Tzeveleki, eds. 2009. *Από τα Μεσόγεια στον Αργοσαρωνικό: Β΄ Εφορεία Προϊστορικών και Κλασικών Αρχαιοτήτων. Το έργο μιας δεκαετίας, 1994–2003*. Markopoulo: Δήμος Μαρκοπούλου Μεσογαίας.

Vatin C., 1969. *Médéon de Phocide: Rapport provisoire*. Paris: École française d'Athènes, E. de Boccard.

Vavelidis, M., and S. Andreou. 2008. "Gold and Gold Working in Late Bronze Age Northern Greece." *Naturwissenschaften* 95: 361–66.

Ventris, M., and J. Chadwick. (1956) 1973. *Documents in Mycenaean Greek*. 2nd ed. Cambridge: Cambridge University Press.

Verdan, S. 2007. "Eretria: Metalworking in the Sanctuary of Apollo Daphnephoros during the Geometric Period (with an Appendix by Walter Fasnacht: Sanctuary of Apollo and West Quarter: Do Two Different Metallurgy Technologies Mean Two Different Traditions?)." In *Oropos and Euboea in the Early Iron Age*, edited by A. Mazarakis Ainian, 345–60. Volos: University of Thessaly Press.

———. 2013. *Le sanctuaire d'Apollon Daphnéphoros à l'époque géométrique*. Eretria fouilles et recherches 22. Gollion: Infolio Éditions.

Verdan, S., A. Kenzelmann Pfyffer, and C. Léderrey. 2009. *Céramique géométrique d'Érétrie*. Eretria fouilles et recherches 20. Gollion: Infolio Éditions

Vermeule, E. 1964. *Greece in the Bronze Age*. Chicago: University of Chicago Press.

———. 1986. "'Priam's Castle Blazing': A Thousand Years of Trojan Memories." In *Troy and the Trojan War*, edited by M. J. Mellink, 77–92. Bryn Mawr, PA: Bryn Mawr College.

Vianello, A. 2005. *Late Bronze Age Mycenaean and Italic Products in the West Mediterranean: A Social and Economic Analysis*. Oxford: Archaeopress.

Vidal-Cordasco, M. and A. Nuevo-López. 2021. "Resilience and Vulnerability to Climate Change in the Greek Dark Ages." *Journal of Anthropological Archaeology* 61 (March): https://doi.org/10.1016/j.jaa.2020.101239.

Visser, E. 1997. *Homers Katalog der Schiffe*. Stuttgart: B. G. Teubner.

Vita-Finzi, C., and E. S. Higgs. 1970. "Prehistoric Economy in the Mount Carmel Area: Site Catchment Analysis." *Proceedings of the Prehistoric Society* 36: 1–37.

Vitale, S. 2008. "Ritual Drinking and Eating at LH IIIA2 Early Mitrou, East Lokris: Evidence for Mycenaean Feasting Activities?" In *Dais: The Aegean Feast*, edited by L. A. Hitchcock, R. Laffineur, and J. Crowley, 229–37. Liège: Université de Liège.

———. 2011. "The Late Helladic IIIA2 Pottery from Mitrou and Its Implications for the Chronology of the Mycenaean Mainland." In *Our Cups Are Full: Pottery and Society in the Aegean Bronze Age. Papers Presented to Jeremy B. Rutter on the Occasion of his 65th Birthday*, edited by W. Gauß, M. Lindblom, R. A. K. Smith, and J. C. Wright, 331–44. Oxford: Archaeopress.

Vlachopoulos, A. 2003. "The Late Helladic IIIC 'Grotta Phase' of Naxos: Its Synchronisms in the Aegean and Its Non-Synchronisms in the Cyclades." In *LH III C Chronology and

Synchronisms, edited by S. Deger-Jalkotzy and M. Zavadil, 217–34. Vienna: Verlag der Österreichischen Akademie der Wissenschaften.

Vlachopoulos, A. and X. Charalambidou. 2020. "Naxos and the Cyclades." In *A Companion to the Archaeology of Early Greece and the Mediterranean*, edited by I. Lemos and A. Kotsonas, 1007–27. Hoboken, NJ: John Wiley & Sons.

Vlachou, V., ed. 2015. *Pots, Workshops and Early Iron Age Society: Function and Role of Ceramics in Early Greece*. Brussels: Centre de Recherches en Archéologie et Patrimoine, Université libre de Bruxelles.

Voutiras, E. 2007. "The Introduction of the Alphabet." In *A History of Ancient Greek: From the Beginnings to Late Antiquity*, edited by A.-F. Christidis, 266–76. Cambridge: Cambridge University Press.

Voutsaki, S. 1998. "Mortuary Evidence, Symbolic Meanings and Social Change: A Comparison between Messenia and the Argolid in the Mycenaean Period." In *Cemetery and Society in the Aegean Bronze Age*, edited by K. Branigan, 41–58. Sheffield: Sheffield Academic Press.

———. 2001. "Economic Control, Power and Prestige." In *Economy and Politics in the Mycenaean Palace States*, edited by S. Voutsaki and J. Killen, 195–213. Cambridge: Cambridge Philological Society.

———. 2017. "The Hellenization of the Prehistoric Past: The Search for Greek Identity in the Work of Christos Tsountas." In *Ancient Monuments and Modern Identities: A Critical History ofArchaeology in 19th and 20th Century Greece*, edited by S. Voutsaki and P. Cartledge, 130–47. London: Routledge.

Voutsaki, S. and J. Killen, eds. 2001. *Economy and Politics in the Mycenaean Palace States*. Cambridge: Cambridge Philological Society.

Voyatzis, M. E. 1990. *The Early Sanctuary of Athena Alea at Tegea and Other Archaic Sanctuaries in Arcadia*. Gothenburg: P. Åströms Förlag.

Waal, W. 2018. "On the 'Phoenician Letters': The Case for an Early Transmission of the Greek Alphabet from an Archaeological, Epigraphic, and Linguistic Perspective." *Aegean Studies* 1: 83–125.

Wace, A. J. B., and F. H. Stubbings, eds. 1962. *A Companion to Homer*. London: Macmillan.

Wace, A. J. B., and M. S. Thompson. 1912. *Prehistoric Thessaly: Being Some Account of Recent Excavations and Explorations in North-eastern Greece from Lake Kopais to the Borders of Macedonia*. Cambridge: Cambridge University Press.

Wachsmann, S. 1998. *Seagoing Ships and Seamanship in the Bronze Age Levant*. College Station: Texas A&M University Press.

Wachter, R. 2006. "Ein schwarzes Loch der Geschichte: Die Erfindung des griechischen Alphabets." In *Die Geburt des Volkalphabets aus dem Geist der Poesie: Schrift, Zahl und Ton im Medienverbund*, edited by W. Ernst and F. Kittler, 33–44. Munich: Wilhelm Fink.

Wade-Gery, H. T. 1940. "The Inscriptions on Stone." In *Perachora. The Sanctuaries of Hera Akraia and Limenia. Excavations of the British School of Archaeology at Athens, 1930–3. Architecture, Bronzes, Terracottas*, by H. Payne and others, 256–68. Oxford: Clarendon Press.

———. 1952. *The Poet of the "Iliad."* Cambridge: Cambridge University Press.

Waldbaum, J. C. 1978. *From Bronze to Iron: The Transition from the Bronze Age to the Iron Age in the Eastern Mediterranean*. Gothenburg: Paul Åströms Förlag.

———. 1999. "The Coming of Iron in the Eastern Mediterranean: Thirty Years of Archaeological and Technological Research." In *The Archaeometallurgy of the Asian Old World*, edited by V. C. Pigott, 27–57. Philadelphia: University Museum, University of Pennsylvania.

Walker, K. G. 2004. *Archaic Eretria: A Political and Social History from the Earliest Times to 490 BC*. London: Routledge.

Wallace, S. 2010. *Ancient Crete: From Successful Collapse to Democracy's Alternatives, Twelfth to Fifth Centuries BC*. Cambridge: Cambridge University Press.

———. 2011. "Formative Landscapes: Regional Experiences of the Aegean Collapse ca. 1200 BC and Their Long-Term Impact." In *The "Dark Ages" Revisited: Acts of an International Symposium in Memory of William D. E. Coulson*, edited by A. Mazarakis Ainian, 55–72. Volos: University of Thessaly Press.

———. 2018. *Travellers in Time: Imagining Movement in the Ancient Aegean World*. New York: Routledge.

Wallerstein, I. 1974. *The Modern World-System I*. New York: Academic Press.

Watts, D. J., and S. H. Strogatz. 1998. "Collective Dynamics of 'Small-World' Networks." *Nature* 393 (April): 440–42.

Webster, D. 2000. "The Not So Peaceful Civilization: A Review of Maya War." *Journal of World Prehistory* 14, no. 1 (March): 65–119.

Wecowski, M. 2017. "Wine and the Early History of the Greek Alphabet." In *Panhellenes at Methone: Graphe in Late Geometric and Proto-Archaic Methone, Macedonia (ca. 700 BCE)*, edited by J. Strauss Clay, I. Malkin, and Y. Tzifopoulos, 309–28. Berlin: De Gruyter.

Weiberg, E., A. Bevan, K. Kouli, M. Katsianis, J. Woodbridge, A. Bonnier, M. Engel, et al. 2019. "Long-Term Trends of Land Use and Demography in Greece: A Comparative Study." *Holocene* 29, no. 5 (May): 742–60.

Weniger, B., and R. Jung. 2009. "Absolute Chronology of the End of the Aegean Bronze Age." In *LH III C Chronology and Synchronisms III: LH III C Late and the Transition to the Early Iron Age*, edited by S. Deger-Jalkotzy and A. E. Bächle, 373–416. Vienna: Verlag der Österreichischen Akademie der Wissenschaften.

Wertime, T. A., and J. D. Muhly, eds. 1980. *The Coming of the Age of Iron*. New Haven, CT: Yale University Press.

West, M. L. 1997. *The East Face of Helicon: West Asiatic Elements in Greek Poetry and Myth*. Oxford: Oxford University Press.

Whitehead, D. 1986. *The Demes of Attica, 508/7–ca. 250 B.C.: A Political and Social Study*. Princeton, NJ: Princeton University Press.

Whitelaw, T. 2001. "Reading between the Tablets: Assessing Mycenaean Palatial Involvement in Ceramic Production and Consumption." In *Economy and Politics in the Mycenaean Palace States*, edited by S. Voutsaki and J. Killen, 51–79. Cambridge: Cambridge Philological Society.

———. 2004. "Alternative Pathways to Complexity in the Southern Aegean." In *The Emergence of Civilisation Revisited*, edited by J. C. Barrett and P. Halstead, 232–56. Oxford: Oxbow Books.

———. 2017. "The Development and Character of Urban Communities in Prehistoric Crete in Their Regional Context: A Preliminary Study." In *Minoan Architecture and Urbanism: New Perspectives on an Ancient Built Environment*, edited by Q. Letesson and C. Knappett, 114–80. Oxford: Oxford University Press.

———. 2018. "Recognising Polities in Prehistoric Crete." In *From the Foundation to the Legacy of Minoan Society*, edited by M. Relaki and Y. Papadatos, 210–55. Oxford: Oxbow Books.

Whitley, J. 1991. *Style and Society in Dark Age Greece: The Changing Face of a Pre-Literate Society 1100–700 BC*. Cambridge: Cambridge University Press.

———. 2002. *The Archaeology of Ancient Greece*. Cambridge: Cambridge University Press.

———. 2004. "Cycles of Collapse in Greek Prehistory: The House of the Tiles at Lerna and the 'Herôon' at Lefkandi." In *Explaining Social Change: Studies in Honour of Colin Renfrew*, edited by J. F. Cherry, C. Scarre, and S. Shennan, 193–201. Cambridge: Cambridge University Press.

———. 2017. "The Material Entanglements of Writing Things Down." In *Theoretical Approaches to the Archaeology of Ancient Greece: Manipulating Material Culture*, edited by L. Nevett, 71–103. Ann Arbor: University of Michigan Press.

———. 2020. "The Re-Emergence of Political Complexity." In *A Companion to the Archaeology of Early Greece and the Mediterranean*, edited by I. S. Lemos and A. Kotsonas, 161–86. Hoboken, NJ: John Wiley & Sons.

Wickens, J. M., S. I. Rotroff, T. Cullen, L. E. Talalay, C. Perlès, and F. W. McCoy. 2018. *Settlement and Land Use on the Periphery: The Bouros-Kastri Peninsula, Southern Euboia*. Oxford: Archaeopress.

Willey, G. R. 1953. *Prehistoric Settlement Patterns in the Viru Valley, Peru*. Washington, DC: Smithsonian Institution Press.

Witmore, C. L. 2007. "Symmetrical Archaeology: Excerpts of a Manifesto." *World Archaeology* 39, no. 4 (December): 546–62.

Woodard, R. D. 1997. *Greek Writing from Knossos to Homer: A Linguistic Interpretation of the Origin of the Greek Alphabet and the Continuity of Ancient Greek Literacy*. Oxford: Oxford University Press.

———. 2010. "*Phoinikēia Grammata*: An Alphabet for the Greek Language." In *A Companion to the Ancient Greek Language*, edited by E. J. Bakker, 25–46. Malden, MA: Wiley-Blackwell.

Wright, H. 1977. "Recent Research on the Origins of the State." *Annual Reviews of Anthropology* 6: 379–97.

Wright, J. C. 1994. "The Mycenaean Entrance System at the West End of the Akropolis of Athens." *Hesperia* 63, no. 3 (July–September): 323–60.

———. 1995. "From Chief to King in Mycenaean Society." In *The Role of the Ruler in the Prehistoric Aegean*, edited by P. Rehak, 63–80. Liège: Université de Liège.

———. 2004a. "A Survey of Evidence for Feasting in Mycenaean Society." *Hesperia* 73, no. 2 (April–June): 133–78.

———. 2004b. "Comparative Settlement Patterns During the Bronze Age in the Northeastern Peloponnesos." In *Side-by-Side Survey: Comparative Regional Studies in the Mediterranean World*, edited by S. E. Alcock and J. F. Cherry, 114–31. Oxford: Oxbow Books.

———. 2006. "The Formation of the Mycenaean Palace." In *Ancient Greece: From the Mycenaean Palaces to the Age of Homer*, edited by S. Deger-Jalkotzy and I. S. Lemos, 7–52. Edinburgh: Edinburgh University Press.

———. 2008. "Early Mycenaean Greece." In *The Cambridge Companion to the Aegean Bronze Age*, edited by C. Shelmerdine, 230–57. Cambridge: Cambridge University Press.

Yasur-Landau, A. 2010. *The Philistines and Aegean Migration at the End of the Late Bronze Age*. Cambridge: Cambridge University Press.

Yoffee, N. 1993. "Too Many Chiefs? (Or, Safe Texts for the '90s)." In *Archaeological Theory: Who Sets the Agenda?*, edited by N. Yoffee and A. Sherratt, 60–78. Cambridge: Cambridge University Press.

———. 2005. *Myths of the Archaic State: Evolution of the Earliest Cities, States, and Civilizations*. Cambridge: Cambridge University Press.

———, ed. 2015. *The Cambridge World History, Volume 3: Early Cities in Comparative Perspective, 4000 BCE—CE 1200*. Cambridge: Cambridge University Press.

———, ed. 2019. *The Evolution of Fragility: Setting the Terms*. Cambridge: McDonald Institute for Archaeological Research.

Yoffee, N., and G. L. Cowgill, eds. 1988. *The Collapse of Ancient States and Civilizations*. Tucson: University of Arizona Press.

Younger, J. 2005. "Some Similarities in Mycenaean Palace Plans." *Autochthon: Papers Presented to O. T. P. K. Dickinson on the Occasion of his Retirement*, edited by A. Dakouri-Hild and S. Sherratt, 185–90. Oxford: Archaeopress.

Zurbach, J. 2017. *Les hommes, la terre et la dette en Grèce, c. 1400–c. 500 a.C.* Bordeaux: Ausonius Éditions.

Zurbach, J., D. Skorda, R. Orgeolet, A. Lagia, I. Moutafi, T. Krapf, B. Simier, R.-M. Bérard, G. Sintès, and A. Chabrol. 2012–13. "Kirrha (Phocide)." *Bulletin de correspondance hellénique* 136–37: 569–92.

Founded in 1893,
UNIVERSITY OF CALIFORNIA PRESS
publishes bold, progressive books and journals
on topics in the arts, humanities, social sciences,
and natural sciences—with a focus on social
justice issues—that inspire thought and action
among readers worldwide.

The UC PRESS FOUNDATION
raises funds to uphold the press's vital role
as an independent, nonprofit publisher, and
receives philanthropic support from a wide
range of individuals and institutions—and from
committed readers like you. To learn more, visit
ucpress.edu/supportus.